The Trotting Season at Prospect Park Fair Grounds, Long Island—Race between "Fullerton" and "Goldsmith Maid," Monday, June 8th, 1874.

—Woodcut, The Bettmann Archive

Also by Tom Ainslie

The Compleat Horseplayer
Ainslie on Jockeys
Ainslie's Complete Guide to Thoroughbred Racing
The Handicapper's Handbook
Ainslie's Complete Hoyle

Ainslie's New Complete Guide to

HARNESS RACING
by Tom Ainslie

SIMON AND SCHUSTER | New York

Published by Simon and Schuster
A Division of Gulf & Western Corporation
Simon & Schuster Building
Rockefeller Center
1230 Avenue of the Americas
New York, New York 10020
SIMON AND SCHUSTER and colophon are trademarks of Simon & Schuster

Manufactured in the United States of America
10 9 8 7 6 5 4 3 2 1

Library of Congress Cataloging in Publication Data

Ainslie, Tom.
  Ainslie's New complete guide to harness racing.

  Published in 1970 under title: Ainslie's Complete guide to harness racing.
  Includes Rules and regulations of the United States Trotting Association.
  Bibliography: p.
  Includes index.
  1. Harness racing. 2. Horse race betting. I. United States Trotting
Association. Rules and regulations of the United States Trotting Association.
1980. II. Title. III. Title: New complete guide to harness racing.
SF333.5.A45   1980   798.4'6   80-17550

ISBN 0-671-25257-7

Contents

01187   6999

PREFACE: A GAME OF PREDICTION

SPEED EXCITES MAN. He craves it. He equates it with beauty. He prizes it above strength. He tests his own speed aground, in water and on ice and snow, envying the superior speed of others. He is an avid helmsman and eager passenger, enchanted by the speed of vehicles wheeled, winged and waterborne. As a spectator, he revels in the extreme speed of athletes, including the speed of racing animals.

Nothing could be more natural. When our subhuman ancestors resided in trees and had fingers on their feet, the ability to get from one place to another in an enormous hurry was basic to survival. Speed remained decisive during the eons in which hand-to-hand combat determined who owned what and who ruled whom. The first sporting games were war exercises, combat rehearsals from which most of the harm was subtracted. One boxed or wrestled or dueled, but not necessarily to the death. One ran as quickly as possible, but not to escape or overtake a murderous foe.

In due course, the connection between sport and war became remote. Survival no longer depends on bear hugs, parries or speed afoot. But the sporting tradition and the craving for speed are deeply ingrained. They are part of our psychological luggage. They are in our bones. They may even be instincts.

Whatever they are, they coexist in a state of sublime compatibility with another of man's profoundest inclinations, the urge to bet. It is an urge associated with the desire for material gain, but not entirely. Just as often, betting expresses a wish to test one's powers of prediction or, in some cases, a yen to question fate and get a refreshingly prompt, uncomplicated answer.

All of which accounts for the durable prosperity of horse racing. Older than history, the sport and the betting which accompanies it now flourish on an industrial scale in West and East, under flags and ideologies of all

Happy Motoring and driver Bill Popfinger win one at The Meadowlands.

hues, wherever men have leisure and spare cash to show for their toil. Continuing popularity and growth seem assured. The atmosphere has never been more favorable. The lunatic view of racing as a vice has receded from fashion in most parts of the world. Few nations any longer mistake joylessness for morality.

The earliest form of horse racing, harness racing probably came into being before the invention of the wheel the very first time a couple of prehistoric teamsters found themselves driving their sledges in the same direction. Pedestrians fortunate enough to witness the great event would have been less than Neanderthal if they had neglected to form opinions about the outcome, make bets, and have the time of their lives. Such enjoyments led inevitably to formal contests in pastures or overland and finally to the stadium spectacles which have beguiled mankind for ages.

More than thirty-five centuries ago, professional horsemen—inheritors of an already ancient tradition—were breeding, training and racing trotters for the entertainment of Near Eastern royalty. Horses large enough to be mounted by grown men would not evolve for another six or seven hundred years. But the equine midgets of history's dawn were sufficiently swift and sturdy to make the two-wheeled chariot the fastest vehicle on earth, a prime accessory for battle, hunt or sport.

At every stage of harness racing's development, betting and its proceeds have had more than a trifle to do with making the mare go. To sharpen the savor of competition and to substantiate their pride in themselves and their animals, the horsemen of old posted stakes, or side bets, and the winner took all. Nowadays the posting of stakes remains a routine precondition of the sport's most important events. For some races, staking begins before the horses are born and continues periodically until the day of competition. These side bets form a substantial proportion of the purse that ultimately is divided among the first five finishers in such a race.

The major concern of this book is, of course, the kind of betting that occurs in the game of prediction played at the pari-mutuel windows by fans, horsemen and raceway personnel. Pari-mutuel betting is central to the pleasure experienced by the customers of the industry. It is the industry's fundamental source of revenue and growth. Yet the otherwise impressive literature of harness racing is usually silent about it. Among the many works of scholarship in which enthusiasts of the sport have celebrated its past and heralded its future, not one so much as mentions the principles and techniques of handicapping—the business of trying to pick a winner—on which intelligent, fully enjoyable betting depends.

This book corrects the omission. It devotes itself entirely to the fascinations of handicapping, recognizing that fans pay their way into a track not only to watch races but to bet on them. It assumes without fear of contradiction that they would rather win than lose. Bearing this in mind, it explores the world of harness racing from tack room to board room, dwelling on the backstage activities, tendencies and trends that influence raceway performance and, therefore, affect the reader's powers of prediction.

The race that engages the fans' speculative interest is in a very real sense the result of years of activity by breeders, trainers, grooms, drivers, raceway officials and, lest we forget, horses. For some of these, the race may be the turning point or even the climax of a career. To understand the race and, more to the point, predict its outcome with any degree of confidence, one must know the industry of which the race is a product. One must even know its traditions, the molds in which its procedures are shaped. And, while knowledge of the exploits of bygone champions cannot possibly help the player to pick the winner of the fifth at Pompano Park, he is likely to be more comfortable if he understands what others are talking about when they mention certain hallowed names.

Aside from brief occasional samplings of relevant history, we shall concentrate our attention on the present, behind the scenes, where horsemen form the strategies and tactics that lead to the winner's circle and the mutuel cashier's window. Knowing that handicapping is effective only to the degree that it encompasses the actualities of the sport, we shall study those actualities in comprehensive detail. At the finish, we shall be able to pick winners. The more success-oriented among us will even be able to show a profit at it.

Horsemen Are Handicappers

As anyone must realize after overhearing the kinds of conversation that resound in raceway grandstands and clubhouses, many fans regard the racing itself as merely an incidental ceremony preceding the announcement of the winning numbers. Indeed, some players behave as if a race were the spin of a roulette wheel, with each number as likely to win as any other. But racing is not that way at all. Horses and drivers are living creatures, not numbers. Some have virtually no chance to win their races. Others are so superior to the competition that they remain attractive after the odds drop below even money.

To make dependable evaluations of that sort, one must be a good handicapper. The handicapper bases his judgments on what he knows about the sport's likelihoods. He knows about the variables of Standardbred class and fitness; the problems presented by the length and contours of the particular track; the nuances of the phenomenon called "pace"; the disparate talents of trainers and drivers; the significance of an animal's behavior during the preliminary warm-ups.

Horsemen make evaluations of the same kind. The success of any trainer or driver is largely measurable in terms of his own handicapping ability. He may never gamble (except when he posts the stakes required for entry in a major race). But he simply must be able to assess his horse and himself and their rivals in light of the opportunities and challenges presented by each new race. This is handicapping, pure and unembellished. If the horseman is not good at it, he almost surely will enter his livestock in the wrong races. And he will worsen matters by driving unintelligently, allowing better tacticians—better handicappers, if you please—to anticipate his every move and cut each race to their own cloth.

The reader may be surprised to learn that an overwhelming majority of trainers and drivers labor under the disadvantage just described, or under others even more severe. The ability to sit at home or in the stands and differentiate such horsemen from their superiors is among the most essential components of harness-race handicapping. Almost anyone with an attention span of five minutes can learn to do this with a high degree of skill. Neither are the other phases of handicapping forbiddingly difficult.

Why, then, are handicappers such rare birds? Why do so many fans persist in playing numbers instead of horses and drivers? Why do thousands haunt the mutuel booths, the washrooms, the refreshment stands and, if they can arrange it, the paddocks and barns, seeking hot tips? Is it not true that the past-performance records published in the raceway's nightly program contain far more substantial information?

Yes, it is true. Unfortunately, many racegoers are mystified by the past-performance records. Others are able to decipher the printed abbreviations and symbols, but are at a loss to interpret their significance. Doubtful of their own judgments, or unable to make judgments at all, innumerable fans look elsewhere for help. This is the main reason why raceway crowds are so easily excited by rumors and false reports. And why, in consequence, some natural 5 to 1 shots leave the starting gate at odds of 7 to 5.

The Oldest New Sport

I concede that one need not be a winning bettor to enjoy an occasional outing at the local raceway. Horse races are incomparably exciting. Moreover, these are prosperous times. Millions of men and women can afford the very minor misfortunes with which racing penalizes innocence. Unless the customer gambles insanely, his losing excursion to the track costs no more than a night on the town.

Nevertheless, it is more fun to win than to lose. Nobody with normal emotions can possibly be indifferent to the outcome of bets. Because human beings favor pastimes in which they are skilled and avoid those in which they take a thumping, one might ask why harness racing has not attempted to educate its own clientele. Why the huge omissions from the tons of literature issued by the industry and its able publicists? Has harness racing's emergence as a major "spectator" sport blinded it to the fact that most of its patrons, however enthusiastic they may be, are transients? And that, aside from a small minority of neurotically compulsive losers, persons who attend the races regularly do so because they have learned how to avoid serious financial loss?

Public ignorance of the principles of handicapping accounts for much of the profligate gambling at racetracks. By neglecting to teach people how to play the game, the tracks perpetuate gambling. Ironically, nobody benefits from this—least of all the tracks. Uninformed bettors depart the scene for good after losing more than they can afford. Tracks, horsemen and state treasuries suffer because pari-mutuel revenues are not as large as they would be if more people understood racing well enough to embrace it as a hobby. Contrary to a widespread misconception, racegoers do not bet against the track but against each other. Regardless of who wins or loses, the track and the taxing state get a fixed percentage of the wagered money. The more that is bet, the higher the revenue.

To understand why all forms of American horse racing persist in a self-defeating reluctance to educate their customers, one must realize that Puritanism is not yet extinct on this continent. Pari-mutuel betting exists by sufferance of state legislatures. The legislators welcome the tax receipts and political sinecures that derive from the betting, but they are easily unnerved by the shrill noises of which North America's vestigial, diminishing antigambling elements remain capable.

Therefore, no matter how festively cordial a legislator may be while enjoying some track operator's brandy and cigars, and no matter how readily he may vote to extend the track's season, he remains primly aloof in public. In turn, as if by treaty, the track operator attempts to conduct his business inoffensively. Which is not always possible. Should a track's advertising campaign emphasize too plainly that there are pari-mutuel machines on the premises, the piping outcries of bluenoses reverberate like thunder in the state capital. Obviously, handicapping instruction by racetracks might be regarded as the encouragement of "gambling"—a gross breach of the treaty.

Certain stirrings in Thoroughbred and Standardbred racing suggest that this ridiculous situation will end sooner rather than later. The printed programs sold to harness-racing fans at some tracks contain handicapping advice. A few tracks have been conducting useful seminars. Every little bit helps. Pending a real breakthrough, however, it would be unfair to chide harness racing for a failure to lead the way. The sport may have its roots in antiquity, but the present American form of it is scarcely out of knee britches. It is the new kid on the block. In some major cities, neither press, television nor radio give it the emphasis and promotional assistance accorded to other sports. Successful though it may be, the industry is still struggling for acceptance. Where encouragement of "gambling" is concerned, its leaders hardly can be expected to rush in where the very senior tycoons of Thoroughbred racing have long feared to tread.

Until 1940, there was no such thing as night harness racing with pari-mutuel wagering. Then came World War II. In effect, the industry as we now know it is barely thirty-five years old. It has spent virtually the entire time trying to gain popular footholds, win legislative approval and build new plants—jobs which are by no means completed as of 1980, although the sport has long since achieved major economic standing. Business now proceeds at an annual rate of at least 25 million paid admissions and wagering in the neighborhood of $2.7 billion, of which about $150 million enriches the treasuries of state governments.

Everything about harness racing is in transition, as befits a youthful, expanding industry. None of the sport's customs or procedures are held sacredly exempt from debate and change. With new raceways opening and old ones extending their seasons, an influx of young horsemen and administrators enlivens the stable areas and front offices. Many of these newcomers are ambitious, bright and competent, and their capacity for experimentation and innovation helps to intensify an atmosphere of controversy and ferment unique in major professional sport. Harness racing is an environment in which hardly anyone can afford to rest on his laurels, lest someone else whisk them out from under him.

Some of the most keenly debated issues in the sport bear substantially on the picking of winners. I shall review them now for that reason and to introduce the reader to some of the frames of reference in which he will be trying to handicap races.

For example, major tracks vary in length from one mile to five-eighths of a mile to half a mile, producing three different kinds of racing. Each type of track has its staunch supporters, disagreements among whom make the walls tremble whenever the subject arises. Meanwhile, regardless of the length of anyone's favorite raceway, the chances are that its season grows longer each year and that its racing circuit, if near a metropolitan area, operates practically the entire year round—a fundamental change from the summer entertainment of the past, and a challenge to handicappers.

With the longer season and the prudent tendency of horsemen to send better animals to the farm before the snow flies and the racing strip freezes, track managements do what they can to make the lesser winter competition as attractive as the summer. Most tinker with exactas and trifectas—forms of pie-in-the-sky betting which pay large returns to bettors lucky enough to pick two or more successful horses at a time. These lures often have the desired effect, increasing the raceway's mutuel handle. But they arouse apprehension among conservatives in the industry, who hold that the sport should stand on its own feet, unsupported by gimmicks. Behind this attitude is a wholesome dread of scandal. Hoodlums and would-be fixers gravitate like maggots to any sport on which people bet. Far from concentrating their ingenious efforts on basketball and football, they have caused many a gray hair in racing. It goes without saying that they are powerfully attracted to propositions in which odds of 1,000 to 1 are not unusual.

Whether a raceway features gimmick bets or not, its effort to improve attendance and increase the mutuel handle rests mainly on the presentation of close, exciting races. This responsibility is the racing secretary's, and he wears a furrowed brow. Horses are not created equal, yet any owner with a horse good enough to race at the particular track is entitled to a fair share of opportunities to win. To provide such opportunities without adulterating the nightly programs is quite a task. Estimating the quality of the available livestock, the racing secretary writes conditions which specify the kinds of horses eligible for entry in each race. Methods of doing this vary greatly without approaching perfection. They are in a state of rapid flux and promise to remain so for years. They differ so widely from place to place that even an experienced handicapper may find himself in deep water on his first visit to an unfamiliar raceway.

Reading the eligibility conditions printed in the evening's program, and looking at the past-performance records of the horses, he may be unable to tell whether a particular animal's latest races were against better or poorer opposition than it faces tonight.

Raceway managements fret, frown and ruminate over more than one aspect of those printed programs. Details that appeared in the program records published at your track last season may be missing this year, having been replaced with other material. Should a horse arrive at your track from a circuit where the programs employ unfamiliar notations or contain unsatisfactorily incomplete data, the record may appear in your program untranslated and unexpanded, leaving you helpless to evaluate the horse. Improvement and standardization of the past-performance records is a slow and troublesome process when each racing circuit has its own formula and the incentive of printers and track program departments is often to provide a minimum of information.

Another focus of concern is the rule book. Revised frequently to keep pace with the sport's evolving challenges, the rules are enforced with varying degrees of flexibility and competence from circuit to circuit. Some presiding judges are so knowing and so uncompromisingly firm in their administration of racing law that certain tricky drivers are afraid to perform at their tracks, having enough trouble in life without incurring more. In recent years, for example, a few top judges have been fining and suspending drivers who take the early lead and then slow the pace sufficiently to make the outcome a matter of tactics and luck rather than of Standardbred speed and fitness. These judges are even more severe with drivers who perform incompetently or, if competent, neglect to produce the best effort of which a horse seems capable. While some drivers avoid such judges, others plead to race at their tracks, hoping to prove that they can win fairly and honestly and thus live down black marks earned elsewhere. Needless to say, the standardization of racing law and its enforcement engrosses those who run the industry.

When I set forth toward the unprecedented goal of supplying harness-racing enthusiasts with a decently comprehensive book about handicapping, I found the industry cooperative. Racing secretaries, presiding judges, breeders, trainers, drivers, publicists, raceway directors, professional handicappers and national organizations were uniformly helpful. Nobody attempted to evade controversial topics. Nobody tried to sell me the Brooklyn Bridge. I was welcome to pick brains, rifle files and peek under rugs from one end of the country to the other.

The relaxed candor with which harness-racing folk discuss the prospects and problems of their sport is attributable to their utter confidence in its worth. They believe quite rightly that they are involved in something good. They foresee nothing but progress. Accordingly, they regard existing controversies as the temporary pains of growth. I praise their refreshingly mature attitudes so early in my book because I am eager to establish a positive tone. I admire the sport and its people—this book's later complaints and criticisms notwithstanding.

Not Everybody Bets

Although everyone in the harness-raceway sport is obsessed with trends in the pari-mutuel handle (from which comes the money for purses and profits), a high proportion of horsemen and executives are otherwise indifferent to betting. The industry derives from and retains much of the character of a freakish kind of horse racing in which betting, while sometimes present, has seldom been the heart of the matter.

North American harness racing was for hundreds of years an essentially rural pastime. Its participants were farmers, with a sprinkling of professional barnstormers who had forsaken the hoe in favor of full-time horsemanship, either independently or as employees of various well-funded stables owned by landed gentry.

The main locale was the country fair, where the pet that towed the family trap during the week raced to a sulky on Saturday afternoon, occasionally defeating more expensive, professionally managed livestock. Betting was largely an expression of loyalty to a particular horse, or to the family or friend or hometown that represented one's link with the animal.

During certain fairs, local billiard emporiums and taverns were sometimes the scenes of wheeling and dealing. I have been told of auction-betting pools that amounted to tens of thousands of dollars, rivaling the Calcutta pools that later troubled professional golf. And old-fashioned bookmaking was not unheard of. But at most fairs the race was the thing and gambling was hardly anyone's main reason for attending.

To this day, some of the richest and most important American harness races are conducted in that spirit. For many years, no pari-mutuel facilities existed at the Du Quoin, Ill., State Fair. Yet tens of thousands of enthusiasts flocked to that hamlet to see the nation's finest three-year-old trotters and their drivers compete in the annual Hambletonian, the prestige of which is comparable to that of the Belmont Stakes or Epsom Derby. Even after betting windows were installed, the die-hard fans were far more interested in the horses and the race than in the tote board. The Hambletonian is now being moved to The Meadowlands, where it undoubtedly will stimulate betting at record levels. But at this writing, the crucial Fox Stake for two-year-old pacers, the Horseman Stake for trotters of that age and the famous Horseman Futurities for three-year-old trotters and pacers continue to attract huge throngs to the Indianapolis

Fair Grounds, which offers no betting. The same is true of important stakes races held in Bloomsburg and Carlisle, Pa.

These classic events are by no means the only bonds between the raceway sport and the country recreation from which it so recently emerged. The racing at pari-mutuel tracks is heavily influenced by men who were breeding, training and driving Standardbreds before anyone dreamed of installing lights and mutuel machines to create a new industry. With surprisingly few exceptions, today's top raceway drivers and trainers are the sons or grandsons of harness horsemen. For many such persons, the horse comes first, the race is second and betting is irrelevant. Some bet comfortably small amounts for fun, when not working. Others get a few hundred down on their own horses when they think they have exceptionally bright chances to win.

The driver is a marked man as soon as he shows more interest in cashing a bet than in winning part of a purse. The world of the sulky driver-trainer is small. Everybody knows everybody else. In fact, everybody knows a good deal about everybody else's business, training methods and driving talents. These men not only drive against each other but frequently drive each other's horses. They sometimes even train each other's horses. They cannot fool each other. The occasional driver who tries to lose this week in hope of winning at a good mutuel price next week quickly falls from grace among his colleagues. Also, he attracts the attention of the hawkeyes in the judges' stand and the racing secretary's office. Major tracks lose no time denying stall space to a driver whose horses specialize in dramatic reversals of form.

Not that the sport is overrun with such characters. Neither is it congested with Eagle Scouts and avenging angels. But raceway operators and leading horsemen are the stewards of huge capital investments from which they and their partners extract substantial profits. They believe with good reason that their continuing prosperity depends on their ability to satisfy the public's standards of sporting rectitude. With press, prosecutors and legislators perpetually ready to make hay of athletic scandal, and with so much at stake, harness racing's severity toward wrongdoers is an expression of sheer practicality. Because the risks are so considerable, cheating is much less frequent than one might think after spending a few minutes at the raceway bar, a center of intrigue to which we shall return in a later chapter.

Is It Gambling?

By popular consent, the purchaser of common stock is entitled to call himself an investor. Depending on his choice of stock, others may refer to him as a speculator. But hardly anyone calls him a gambler. Good.

Assuming that the stock transaction results from the buyer's study of the national economy, the particular industry, the specific corporation and the stock market itself, he has committed an act of speculative investment. He has made an informed decision. He is playing a game of skill with all the skill he can muster. It is, to be sure, a game from which the element of chance is not entirely absent. But it is a game in which the informed fare better than the uninformed. It is no activity for gamblers, whom I may as well define as persons who trust to luck even when engaged in games of skill.

The only place for a gambler is a properly supervised gambling casino. Craps and roulette are games of pure chance in which the only permissible skill is knowledge of the odds. The extra penalties that befall a gambler in contests of skill are spared him in the casino. There he can entrust himself to luck, hunch and superstition. If he wins, he is lucky. If he loses, he is not, but he has had as much chance to win as any other patron of the resort.

Place that same gambler at a poker table and he is a helpless pigeon. Poker is a game of skill in which chance plays only a minimal role. Unaware of this, or unable to acknowledge it, the gambler takes his customary refuge in superstition, neurosis, guess and hope. He hasn't a prayer of success against players who know the complicated probabilities and psychological tricks of the game.

The gambler is similarly disadvantaged at a harness raceway. Here again he attempts to win by luck what seldom can be won except through skill and knowledge. The occupant of yonder box seat may be a bulwark of his community, but unless his bets derive from competent handicapping analysis, his behavior is that of a common gambler and he surely will lose more money than necessary.

I am not sure that anyone has ever emphasized this kind of thing in print before. Yet the differences between shrewd speculation and impulsive gambling are as real at the raceway as in any brokerage office or poker game. Indeed, the skills of the handicapper compare quite comfortably with those of the expert poker or bridge player and are rewarded with gratifying consistency at the counters where mutuel clerks cash winning tickets.

Why then the familiar notion that all horseplayers are nothing but gamblers? It arises partly because of a popular failure to differentiate between games of chance and games of skill: In many minds, any wager is gambling (unless, of course, the wager takes the socially exalted form of a life insurance premium, or an investment in hog futures, or the like). Also, as we have seen, many horseplayers actually *are* gamblers.

But of all contributing factors, the most important is the belief that nobody can beat the races. Though not true, this notion is so widely accepted that the friends and relatives of the racegoer may well look upon him as an eccentric (or worse) who persists in playing a game he cannot win. The logical conclusion is that he enjoys losing. Which is exactly what the Freudians have been saying about gamblers for years.

Postponing for a while our discussion of whether the reader can beat the races, I think it useful to repeat my earlier observation that normal persons do not like to lose large sums of money. They prefer to win. Ultimately, they measure their enjoyment of the harness races in terms of whether the entertainment, excitement and suspense are worth the financial cost. Handicappers of even middling competence win enough or lose so little that they can justly claim to have profited, even if they have not exactly beaten the races.

Such a person may take his wife to the track twenty times in a season and incur a total net loss of $200 after all that transportation and all those admission tickets, expensive dinners and bets. Even if he were a less capable selector and spent $300 more than he took in, the entertainment would be rather considerably cheaper than an equal number of pilgrimages to the theater or to nightclubs or, for that matter, to restaurants without pari-mutuel facilities.

In offering to explore the principles of Standardbred handicapping with my reader, I hold forth the prospect of an unparalleled hobby, one that often pays for itself. It even yields net profits, but only to persons who approach it with the studious care that marks the expert players of any great game. I believe, perhaps with more optimism than may be warranted by the facts, that these same possibilities exist for a substantial fraction of racegoers who now bet as if racing were a game of chance. It seems to me that many such persons would prefer to behave sensibly if someone would only do them the courtesy of showing them how. Which is why I am here.

For some men and women, of course, the track is a kind of pagan temple in which to commune with fate, test hunches, obey horoscopes and respond to the vibrations of lucky numbers. Whatever else such folks may be, they emote like gamblers, act like gamblers and lose like gamblers. I doubt that I can abolish their superstitions, but I can at least show them a more effective way to confront fate.

Getting Down to Cases

The earliest chapters of the book review the history and the economic realities of the harness-racing industry, the tremendously important mathematics of the pari-mutuel system—the likelihood that anyone can beat the percentages—and the nature and background of the Standardbred horse, with special attention to the mysterious subjects of breeding and conformation and their places in handicapping.

Chapter 1 describes the materials necessary or useful to the development of expert handicapping technique. It contains the most thorough analysis of past-performance programs ever published, including full directions for reading and understanding the types of program notations used on various racing circuits. Actual samples of the different programs are reproduced.

The differences among raceways, including the all-important factor of track size, are covered in Chapter 2, guaranteed to elicit howls of indignation in certain quarters. The purpose is not to stir up the natives but to arm the reader for visits to tracks of all sizes.

Succeeding chapters discuss handicapping factors such as form, class, age, sex, consistency, time, post position, pace, the racing stable, the driver and prerace warm-ups. The section devoted to trainers and drivers not only takes the measure of North America's leading conditioners and reinsmen but also offers insights into professional problems that affect the performance of horses and should, therefore, concern the handicapper.

In these chapters on the principles of handicapping, the reader will find ample guidance about the kinds of races most suitable for play; the effects of rain, wind and seasonal changes; ways to recognize an improving horse or a deteriorating one; coping with fields that include horses that frequently break stride; clocking the warm-ups; the significance of driver switches; cheating, drugging and "stiffing"; recognizing lameness and other manifestations of unreadiness to win.

The book explores the perplexing differences among conditioned, classified and claiming races, indicating the limits within which the reader may be able to appraise the relative quality of a horse entered for the first time in one type of race after having competed in either or both of the other types.

It is one of the fundamental truths of handicapping that principles are more important than procedures. Regardless of the individual's method or "system," his success depends on the fidelity with which he adheres to the established likelihoods of the sport. Nevertheless, it seems to me that orderly handicapping procedures are convenient and efficient. They are especially useful to fans who do not spend every evening at the races and must rely on the information contained in the program rather than on prior observations of their own.

With this in mind, I have included a systematic procedure (*not* a "system") which should enable the reader to handicap any playable race in not more than five minutes. Its chief virtue is the use of pencil and paper to arrive at numerical ratings for the logical contenders in the race. Many good handicappers believe that the art cannot be mechanized successfully —and are correct in that belief—but this book's numerical method does not abolish the need for judgment. It simply eliminates the mental juggling that causes fans so much difficulty and leads them into so many errors. The efficacy of the method will become apparent enough toward the end of the book, when we handicap entire programs at Hollywood Park, Sportsman's Park, Liberty Bell, The Meadowlands and Roosevelt Raceway.

Acknowledgments

It is impossible to write a book free of factual error, but I try and I usually come quite close. It also is impossible to write a completely unbiased book, and I never try. In the present case, my allegiance is to the racegoer, the consumer who pays his money and takes his choice. I am prejudiced in his behalf. I approve of anything that increases his enjoyment of the sport—especially anything that enlarges his powers of prediction. I detest and deplore the notion that he is a dunce, fit only to be misled and exploited.

If harness racing were not worth the attention of its present following and of the new fans likely to be recruited by a book of this kind, I would not have written the book at all. I am satisfied that the sport compares more than favorably with other stadium diversions. Its attitudes toward the public are more decent than most.

This does not mean that whatever is convenient or profitable for the management of a particular raceway is necessarily a boon to its customers. As one conspicuous example among several, I might cite the inadequacy of the information contained in the printed programs sold at certain tracks. To the degree that a track's program booklet fails to offer clear, comprehensive summaries of the records of horses and drivers, mystery prevails, handicapping is virtually impossible and the bettor might just as well play Bingo.

As self-appointed champion of the paying customer, I shall deal in vigorous terms with this and other matters of dissatisfaction. I shall examine various controversial issues in terms of my own consumer-oriented prejudices. Although the total effect of the book will be to promote the industry and enlarge its mutuel revenues, not everyone in the business will take kindly to every word.

For that reason, I want to make absolutely clear that the opinions expressed in this book are my own. They derive from my own experience and thought. Of the hundreds of harness-racing officials, administrators and horsemen with whom I have chatted while preparing the book, none can be justly accused of having implanted or encouraged any of these opinions. All they supplied were facts.

Among those whose generous courtesy enabled me to compile my facts with a minimum of difficulty, I am most deeply indebted to Stanley F.

Bergstein, executive vice-president of Harness Tracks of America. Although he is one of the busiest executives in all sport, he gave his time lavishly and opened numerous doors for me when I was collecting the material for the first (1970) version of this book. Among colleagues of Stan's who were particularly helpful at that time, I thank Dale Bordner, Al Buongiorne, Dick Conley, Larry Evans, Earl Flora, Walter Adamkosky, Darrell Foster, Dave Garland, Joe Goldstein, George Smallsreed and Dennis Nolan. I absolve each of responsibility for any errors or excesses which someone might otherwise blame on them.

This updated 1980 version of the book owes a great deal to the careful research and astute editorial work of Dean A. Hoffman of Columbus, Ohio, whom I thank.

I also thank the all-time great driver, trainer, breeder and good-will ambassador, Delvin C. Miller, for allowing me to poke around his barns, train the stakes-winning Tarport Birdie and absorb fundamentals of the sport that are invisible from the stands. Among racing secretaries who submitted to my inquiries with only occasional alarm or dismay, I remember Bill Connors, Phil Langley, Jim Lynch, Ed Parker and Larry Mallar.

James C. Harrison, the nation's foremost authority on the breeding of Standardbreds, has my gratitude for his attentive help. I have pilfered freely from his monumental volume, *Care and Training of the Trotter and Pacer*. The generously given ideas of Billy Haughton, Stanley Dancer, Del Miller, Ralph Baldwin, John Simpson, Sr., Frank Ervin, Joe O'Brien, Bob Farrington, Harry Pownall and Sanders Russell represent an absolute totality of existing knowledge about the training, conditioning, driving and general management of Standardbreds. I thank them for their contributions.

I thank presiding judge John Broderick and the greatest of all, Milt Taylor, for the privilege of watching many races with them and learning on the inside how rules are interpreted and enforced. I thank Philip A. Pines, director of the Hall of Fame of the Trotter at Goshen, N.Y., author of the splendid *Complete Book of Harness Racing*, for his kindness in allowing me to borrow otherwise unobtainable materials from the Hall of Fame library.

1 ARMING THE HANDICAPPER

IN THE TYPICAL NORTH AMERICAN harness race, the horses go one mile. The winning trotter or pacer usually completes its journey in slightly more than two minutes, arriving at the finish wire perhaps a fifth of a second before its closest pursuer. Often the margin is one of inches—hundredths of a second—and the officials must examine a magnified photograph to decide which horse won.

The best horse does not necessarily finish first. Its defeat often is attributed to racing luck, and properly so. Crowding and careening around sharp turns at upward of thirty miles an hour with sulkies and drivers behind is an invitation to ill fortune. Yet luck does not dominate the sport. Far from it.

What often is explained as luck is not necessarily luck at all, but the proceeds of human frailty. In the first place, the race is only in part a test of equine speed and stamina. It is mainly a competition among men. For better or worse, the unequal talents of men affect the performances of the horses. Handicapping wisdom begins with the realization that the best drivers have the best luck.

The paramount importance of the driver is literally built into the oval design of the racing strip. Every few seconds the sulkies tear around one of the semicircles that lie at either end of the oval. To take one of these turns even a few feet away from the inside rail adds yards to a horse's journey. Because the final result of the race is measured in inches and split seconds, one does not willingly waste yards. Yet the time comes when yards and the limited energies of the horse must be traded for favorable position at or near the head of the pack. The best drivers know when to attempt these rapid transactions. In carrying them off, they inflict bad luck on other drivers. By contrast, lesser drivers tend to make their bids at unfavorable times. Their attempts fail not because of bad luck but because someone else tricks them into the ill-advised action or beats them to it or hems them in or parks them out and exhausts their horses.

To the inexperienced observer, it may seem that the race actually is won in the homestretch, the final straight dash to the money. But why did the winner enter the stretch with sufficient reserve energy to retain its lead against all challenge? Or why did it have enough energy and enough racing room to overtake and pass the leader in the last yards? From the instant the race begins, every move of every horse and driver is part of a struggle for final striking position. The best drivers manage to achieve such position more often, even while conserving the stamina of their horses more efficiently.

Because he is so adept, the top reinsman wins many races in which he does not have the best horse. In fact, it is fair to say that the third most conspicuous patsy at any track is the driver who seldom wins unless he happens to have much the best horse. The second most conspicuous is the driver who seldom wins even when he *does* have much the best horse.

Lindy's Pride (center) storms between the leading Gun Runner and Dayan (left) to wrap up the $173,455 Dexter Trot at Roosevelt Raceway in 1969. Trained and driven by Howard Beissinger, the brilliant animal swept all five major stakes races for three-year-old trotters that season.

And the patsiest patsy of all is the poor soul who bets money on such people.

So much for the kind of racing (and betting) luck that has little to do with luck. Unforeseeable and unavoidable mischance does arise and does affect the outcome of races. From the outside of one rubber-tired bicycle wheel to the outside of the other, a racing sulky is more than four feet wide. It cannot go wherever the horse can go, a truth that is fundamental to the education of horses and drivers alike. Let two drivers steer toward the same opening on the rail and one must inevitably give way, very likely leaving himself and his animal in poor position. He probably has only himself to blame, and is not our concern. The problem is the domino effect of his mistake. Any driver racing directly behind a horse that swerves, slows or breaks stride is out of luck. If the resultant tumult costs him the race, he seldom is responsible for the loss. Furthermore, in trying to collect himself and his horse, he may complicate the traffic jam, leaving other horses hopelessly boxed in, and others so depleted that they have nothing left for the stretch drive. This is bad, bad luck. Yet the final winner may well be the best horse in the race. Or the fourth best horse, with the best driver.

As must now be clear, the goal of the handicapping racegoer is to find the best combination of horse and driver. Having done so, his chances of cashing a bet are as bright as possible. But he had better not make his down payment on that tropical island until the race is over. The horse's ability to trot or pace in full accordance with expectations may have been undermined minutes or hours or days before the race begins. The excellent performance last week and the splendid workout the other day may have dulled the horse's competitive edge. The attentions of a new or overzealous or negligent groom may have upset the animal. An item in the elaborate harness may be a trifle too tight or too loose or too stiff. The minor discomfort may cost a tenth of a second of speed—the difference between winning and finishing fourth by almost a half-length.

Perhaps the sulky has not been disassembled and cleaned and oiled. The accumulated debris in the wheels may act as a brake. Perhaps the horse has never taken an unsound step in its life but is thrown off tonight by new shoes that fail by the tiniest fraction of an inch or ounce to support the balanced stride on which racing success depends.

The Standardbred is a remarkably sturdy and courageous animal, frequently as docile and untemperamental as a good dog. When training and conditioning provide even half the chance to which its breeding entitles it, it will race its heart out for those who tend it. But it cannot confer with them. If they do not notice the bruise on its leg, or the heat of strained or damaged tissue; if they attribute some inconvenient change in its manner to animal perversity, and ignore or punish it; if they regard it as a racing implement, a thing, it must go to pieces sooner rather than later. The night on which it shapes up as the sharpest horse in the race may be the night of its decline.

Or something may frighten it during the race. Perhaps a discarded sandwich wrapper suddenly blows across its field of vision. Or a clod of earth kicked backward by a hoof hits its face like a projectile. Or a horse breaking stride in front of it causes it to panic at the threatened collision and break stride itself.

Or with everything in its favor and clear sailing ahead, it may skid slightly on a fault in the racing surface, thereby losing momentum and composure long enough to be passed by luckier rivals. Or a tiring horse may duck toward the rail at the instant that a second horse moves up on the outside. The best horse in the race may be boxed between such animals for four or five seconds and lose all chance.

Racing luck and human error, including his own errors of judgment, make it impossible for even the shrewdest handicapper to be right all the time. Strive as he will, no bettor is even remotely sure of coming home from the track tonight with more money than he had when he went. But a really good judge of horses and drivers who keeps his wits about him has every reason to expect more winning nights than losing ones. Reliable statistics on the performance of harness-racing handicappers do not exist. However, my own experiences at the raceways have persuaded me that four winners in every ten bets are a realistic goal for a sensible player.

Not knowing how familiar my reader is with harness racing or its galloping relative, Thoroughbred racing, I intend to compare the two as infrequently as possible. Nevertheless, I feel compelled to make one small comparison now. In more than three decades as a follower of the runners, including several recent years as a rather widely accepted authority on Thoroughbred handicapping, I can recall mighty few afternoons on which I have been able to pick as many as six winners. Indeed, I seldom find as many as six playable races on a program of nine. I go home in a mood of insufferable arrogance if I catch three or four winners in that many attempts. In Thoroughbred handicapping, to maintain a winning average in the neighborhood of 40 percent, year in and year out, requires study, application and self-control of an extremely high order.

Harness racing is more generous to the handicapper. Naturally, everything goes wrong on some nights and one's only winner pays a wretched $3.80. But the fit Standardbred is a fantastically reliable and consistent performer. When the weather is right and the quality of the horseflesh good, a sound handicapper's selections are there or thereabouts in almost every race. As subsequent illustrations will show, five or six winners are by no means impossible on a good night.

Before taking leave of mischance, the subject with which this chapter began, we had better dispose of the most bothersome and by all odds the most seriously misunderstood mischance of them all—the hated lapse from gait known as the "break."

Gaits and Breaks

The pacer is the perkiest of race horses. Its front legs move in perfect step with the hind pair. As if connected by a piston, left front and left hind stride forward in unison, and then come the right front and right hind, equally precise. The animal's weight swings from side to side in an amusing swagger, the self-important appearance of which is mightily enhanced by a bouncing, flowing mane and an impressive cargo of straps, boots, patches, poles, pads, blinkers and hobbles.

A good trotter is more elegant. Its front legs move in a marvelously symmetrical rolling motion, the sight of which has been likened to a barrel going downhill. Its hind legs are rigorously out of step with the front. Left front and right hind strike the ground almost simultaneously and then give way to right front and left hind. A good horse of this kind is all grace and power. A bad one looks from the rear like one of those horse costumes used in school plays, with a boy fore and another boy aft and feet flying all over the place at random.

It is said that both the trot and pace are artificial gaits, but I doubt it. Horses seem to have been trotting and pacing instinctively for thousands of years. What is artificial is not the gaits themselves but the rules, which require the Standardbred to maintain the trot or pace while racing as swiftly as possible. In normal circumstances, any horse asked for speed will go into a gallop. But galloping violates the rules of harness racing and fetches intermittent grief to horsemen and bettors.

When a racing trotter or pacer forgets or ignores its training and breaks into a gallop, the driver is obliged—on pain of disqualification—to restrain the animal until it recovers the proper gait. The galloping horse is forbidden to gain ground. If the driver has room, he is expected not only to take the horse back but to move it outside, away from other horses. The delay usually costs the galloper all chance in its race, although extremely sharp Standardbreds occasionally recover from a break in time to win.

As anyone could testify after merely one evening at a harness raceway, a breaking horse causes great annoyance in the stands. The ire multiplies in ratio to the amount of money that has been bet on the animal. After the race the driver is likely to be booed, as if he had encouraged the horse to break.

Awful rumors circulate. Especially among persons who do not realize that of all the many ways to try to lose a harness race the deliberate break

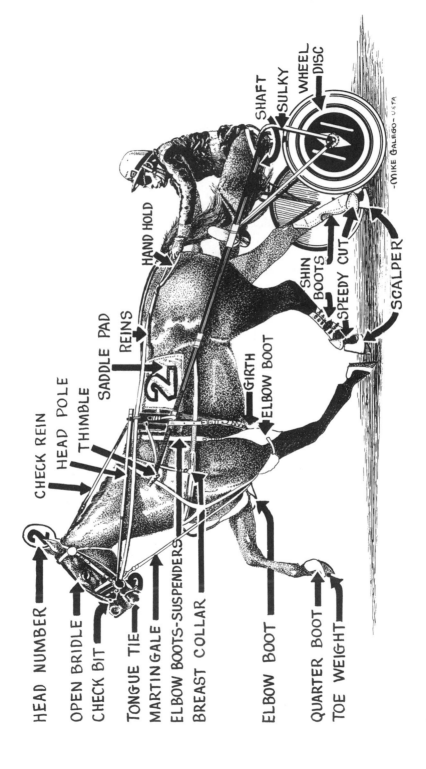

HEAD NUMBER
OPEN BRIDLE
CHECK BIT
TONGUE TIE
MARTINGALE
ELBOW BOOTS-SUSPENDERS
BREAST COLLAR
ELBOW BOOT
QUARTER BOOT
TOE WEIGHT

CHECK REIN
HEAD POLE
THIMBLE
SADDLE PAD
REINS

HAND HOLD

GIRTH
ELBOW BOOT

SHAFT
SULKY
WHEEL
DISC

SHIN BOOTS
SPEEDY CUT
SCALPER

-MIKE GALEGO- USTA

A trotter and his equipment.

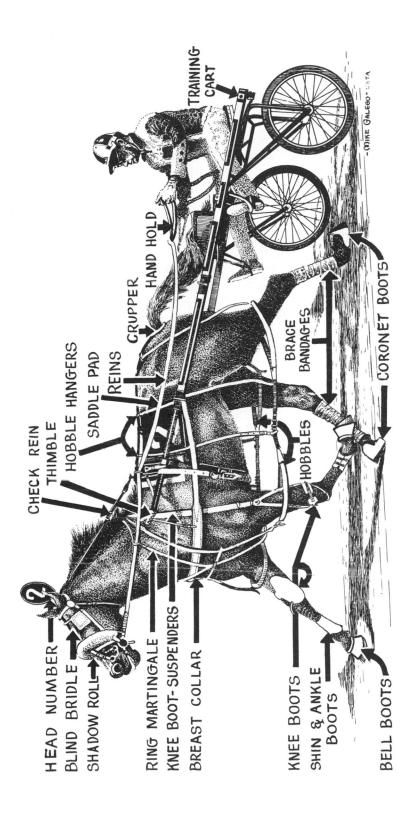

CHECK REIN
THIMBLE
HOBBLE HANGERS
SADDLE PAD
REINS
CRUPPER
HAND HOLD
TRAINING CART

HEAD NUMBER
BLIND BRIDLE
SHADOW ROLL
RING MARTINGALE
KNEE BOOT-SUSPENDERS
BREAST COLLAR

BRACE BANDAGES
HOBBLES
CORONET BOOTS

KNEE BOOTS
SHIN & ANKLE BOOTS
BELL BOOTS

— MIKE GALEGO - USTA

A pacer and his regalia.

is the least plausible. Not only does a break attract unfavorable attention; it is extremely dangerous for the horse, the driver and for others with whom they might collide. The skeletal structure of any seasoned sulky driver is a collage of healed fractures, most of them acquired in accidents caused by breaking horses. A driver suspected of encouraging horses to break stride could not survive the vengeance to which other horsemen would promptly subject him.

What explains breaks? The causes are these:

1. A horse may break while leaving the starting line if it has not yet settled into proper stride and traffic problems impel the driver to ask for more—or less—speed than the animal can manage.

2. A horse may break when too fatigued to respond in any other way to the driver's urging.

3. A horse may break under stress when other horses are breaking, or when there is a pile-up on the track.

4. A horse may break when bumped by another horse or sulky.

5. A horse may break when an unsound gait causes it to strike a leg with one of its hooves. This sometimes happens if the driver attempts to cut a turn too sharply.

6. A horse may break if deprived of racing room when eager to go, as when trapped behind a leader whose driver deliberately slows the pace, or when trapped behind and inside tiring, slowing horses.

7. A horse may break if an item of equipment fails and the driver no longer can control its gait. For example, harness straps may separate or chafe, or the bit may hurt the animal's teeth.

8. A horse may break when frightened by overzealous whipping or a wind-borne piece of paper or the splatter of mud.

As can be imagined, nobody in harness racing is fond of the break. Breeders measure their success at least in part by the increasing number of foals that prefer trotting or pacing to running. Conservative bettors refuse to bet on a horse with a history of breaking, and even avoid betting on races in which two or three such animals take part, for fear that their galloping may block the path and ruin the chances of a more reliable horse.

I don't like the break either, but I am unable to become lathered up about it. The point of harness racing, after all, is to move rapidly and bravely on the trot or pace, resisting all temptation to run. Accordingly, the breaking horse deserves to lose, and so does the unfortunate who bets on the animal. Viewed in this light, the breaking Standardbred is closely comparable to the Thoroughbred runner that gets left at the post or is disqualified for failing to run in a straight line. To contend that the rules

about breaks spoil the racing is like arguing that the dribble spoils basketball—because the most sensible way to take a basketball down court is to
tuck it under an arm and run. Or that the matador should be equipped
with a machine gun. Or that the best way to send a tennis ball across a
net is by throwing it.

Obviously, there are no pari-mutuel machines at basketball games, bull-
fights or tennis matches. But there is a certain amount of betting, and the
failure of a competitor to perform well under the limitations imposed by
rules is, often enough, the reason that his supporters lose bets.

Pacers break far less frequently than trotters do. Side-wheelers (as
pacers are called) are not more virtuous, and often are not as carefully
trained or shod. Their salvation is the help they get from hobbles, which
are leather or plastic loops, one encircling each leg. The hobble on the
right hind leg is connected by a strap to the hobble on the right front. An
identical arrangement keeps things secure on the left. Thus, when the
pacer extends a front leg, the hind leg on the same side is hauled forward.
Trotting becomes impossible and galloping also is inhibited, even if not
prevented entirely. Free-legged pacers, which race without hobbles, do
so either because they are more talented or because hobbles chafe and
discourage them.

Forced by the nature of their gait to race without the effective kind of
hobbles that keep most pacers out of trouble, trotters are the main problem in the breaking department. The bettor's protection is to read the past
performances carefully and steer clear of chronic breakers. Moreover,
extreme caution is advisable in one's approach to important races for
two- and three-year-old trotters. Being green, these young animals are
most likely to break in the heat of the stern competition they face when
racing for a large purse. The fact that a young trotter has not broken into
a gallop in any of the minor races detailed in its past-performance record
is no guarantee that it will stay flat tonight, with the $50,000 purse and the
gold cup on the line and all that speed to contend with.

The Communications Gap

We have been touching on some of the uncertainties of harness racing.
They keep the handicapping fan on the alert, where he belongs. To the
extent that he enlarges his understanding of the sport's surprises, his
expectations become more realistic and his handicapping and betting procedures become more sophisticated.

Completely accurate prediction is impossible. Intermittent disappointment is unavoidable. But the good handicapper is equipped to minimize
uncertainty. He concentrates his efforts on situations in which uncertainty is least likely to arise. Unlike the promiscuous gambler, who ri-

cochets all evening between elation and prostration, the handicapper invests no more emotion (or money) in one bet than he comfortably can afford. His view is long. His deepest pleasure lies in the knowledge that he can select a high enough percentage of winning Standardbreds to fare very well in the end. To find these truths attractive and reasonable is the first long stride toward the agreeable business of converting a casual pastime into a rewarding hobby.

As part of the process, we now consider a state of affairs which is in no way fundamental to harness racing but happens to be—at this stage in the sport's history—a frustration for the occasional racegoer. I assume that most followers of the sport are in that category. Regardless of his enthusiasms, man seldom is in complete command of his leisure time. Even when he is, he probably does not choose to spend six evenings a week at the races. If he is a good handicapper and a sensible bettor, he probably does quite nicely at major raceways, even if he visits them irregularly. But his prospects do not compare with those of the good handicapper who manages to get to the races five or six evenings a week.

The reasons for this are not good, or necessarily permanent, but they are inescapably real. In most cities, the sport is so scantily covered in the press that the fan has no hope of knowing what happens at the track unless he is there to see for himself. If the local newspaper publishes raceway results, it usually does so in a minimum of space, without information about post positions, drivers' names, fractional times, breaks and other material which might give the results more meaning.

The conscientious follower of any other major sport is able to keep fairly well abreast of developments by reading the daily press, fan magazines and trade papers. But the harness-racing enthusiast has few resources other than the past-performance program vended at the track. It would be possible to make these programs so comprehensive that the occasional racegoer who knew the sport would be able to wager on virtually an equal footing with the nightly regulars. Nobody has yet bothered to make the programs that comprehensive. The person who gets to the raceway only once in a while must therefore compensate for his lack of information by wagering with extreme caution, if winning is the name of his game.

In my conversations with professional handicappers, I have been struck by the care with which they take note of significant racing incidents. They watch every race closely, making written or mental records of happenings that reveal the improving or declining form of a horse. Much of this material could be included in the published past-performance summaries, but seldom is.

For example, a horse might rough it on the outside for the better part of a half-mile, sometimes traveling as many as three horses wide of the rail. The professional who sees this takes pains to remember it. Why?

Because the programs sold at most tracks do not show that a horse was parked three wide. Many programs might show that the horse was parked for only a quarter-mile, even though he raced on the outside much farther than that. Thousands of fans who did not see the particular race, or who made no note of what they saw, are likely to underestimate the form of such a horse when they read its published record before its next race.

For another example, a horse might encounter interference, break stride and be 20 lengths behind the leader at the half-mile call. He might then make up 15 lengths during the next three-eighths of a mile. The program's past-performance chart would show that he was five lengths behind at the stretch call, but only regular racegoers would know how well he had performed to gain that much ground—because programs do not tell how far horses lead or trail at the half-mile.

To compete on anything like even terms with the regular clients, the average handicapping fan needs to milk every available drop of significance from the available records. In the few localities where general newspapers or the *Daily Racing Form* publish detailed result charts, he is well advised to clip, save and consult those pages. Later, I shall suggest some good uses for a handicapper's notebook. For now, I think it important to become acquainted with the types of program past-performance records available at leading tracks. On the pages that follow you will find the decoding instructions published in the programs of Hollywood Park, Sportsman's Park, Liberty Bell and two big New York–area tracks, The Meadowlands and Roosevelt Raceway. I recommend that you read the instructions carefully. The rest of this book will be of small help to anyone unable to understand a past-performance record.

To substantiate my complaints about the average past-performance program and to help the reader appreciate the variety of factors that are blended in handicapping, I shall now list the major factors, showing how the programs might offer better service than they do.

FORM. A Standardbred's physical condition is the index to its readiness. The best evidence of fitness is a bravely vigorous recent performance. The little circle which means "parked out" should appear in the proper place in the record of a horse that raced on the outside through the major portion of a turn. If it raced three wide, the symbol should be doubled. If an animal's performance was not as poor as the record makes it seem, words to that effect should appear somewhere on the past-performance page. For example, "Disliked mud," or "Boxed in," or "Flushed out" (terms we shall explore later) would constitute alibis substantial enough to excuse a poor finish. On the other hand, "Sucked along," "Hung," "Passed tired ones" or "Others broke" would warn the player that the animal's performance had not been as good as it looks in the record.

CLASS. The class structure of harness racing being in a state of development and experimentation, it often is difficult to tell whether a horse is moving up in class, or down, or merely sideways. The programs should tell not only what major conditions governed eligibility for the horse's recent races but also what the purses were. Thus, when an animal goes from a conditioned or classified race to a claimer, or vice versa, the player might have some idea of the nature of the move. If a past race was for females only, or for horses in a certain age range, the past performances should show it.

IT'S EASY TO:

. . . READ THE PROGRAM

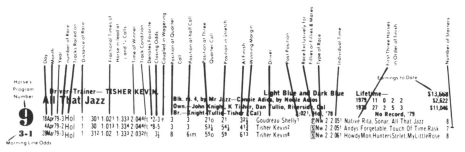

STANDARD ABBREVIATIONS AND SYMBOLS

Horse's Color	Horse's Sex	Track Conditions	Finish Information	Class of Race
b—bay	c—colt	ft—fast	no—nose	Qua—Qualifying
blk—black	f—filly	gd—good	h—head	Mat—Matinee
br—brown	g—gelding	sl—slow	nk—neck	Mdn—Maiden
ch—chestnut	h—horse	sy—sloppy	dis—distanced.	
gr—gray	m—mare	m—muddy	dnf—did not finish	
ro—roan	r—ridgeling	h—heavy	acc—accident	

RACING INFORMATION	WAGERING INFORMATION	
o—parked out	N.B.—Non-betting	c—claimed out of race
x—break	N.R.—Not reported	*--favorite
ix—interference break	e—entry	‡—free-legged
ex- -equipment break	f—field	Ⓢ--State-bred
(Cal)—Cal-bred.	♦--dead heat	im—impeded

. . . MAKE A WAGER

TO BET:
Western Harness Racing features EXPRESS BETTING, the computerized wagering system which allows you to ''DO IT ALL'' with a single visit to the window...you can place a bet and/or collect at the same time at any window. Here's how it works:
FIRST — Announce to the terminal operator the amount you want to bet. AMOUNT OF BET must be stated first.
SECOND — Announce to terminal operator the type of bet you want—win, place, show, exacta.
THIRD — Announce to terminal operator which horse you want to bet, by program number.

TO COLLECT:
When your horse wins, go to any window and collect your money. Right after each race is the best time to cash your winning tickets, but you have until 60 days after the close of this meeting to present them to Western Harness Racing offices for collection.

KINDS OF BETS:
You can bet to WIN, PLACE AND SHOW. Tickets are sold for each race in any dollar amount, $2 or more.

IF YOU BET:
TO WIN: You collect if your horse finishes first.
TO PLACE: You collect if your horse finishes first or second.
TO SHOW: You collect if your horse finishes first, second, or third.

EXACTA WAGERING:
To make an Exacta bet you select two horses, one to finish first, one to finish second. You win if they finish in that exact order. Exacta tickets are available on races as indicated in the program. Any dollar amount equaling or more than the indicated minimum may be wagered.

[From the Hollywood Park program]

HOW TO READ THE PROGRAM

In reading the top post performance line on Rambling Willie below, the information from left to right indicates the most recent start was July 26 in the 8th race at Sportsman's Park, a 5/8th mile track. Track was fast and temperature was 80 degrees. The race was a Free-For-All with a $35,000 purse, a race equal in class to his preceding race. Distance was one mile and Rambling Willie, the leader, reached the quarter mile in .28 seconds, the half mile in 57-2/5 seconds, the three-quarters in 1.28 and the mile in 1.57. Rambling Willie started from post position 8. He was first at the quarter, first at the half by one length, first by one and one-half lengths at the top of the stretch, and first by three and one-half lengths at the finish. His odds were *1·2 (-favorite) and the driver was Robert Farrington. His time for the last quarter was :29. Rambling Willie was first with Title Holder second and Keystone Smartie third.

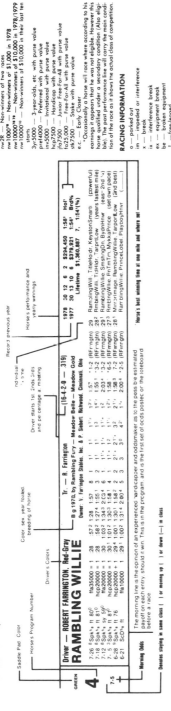

STANDARD ABBREVIATIONS AND SYMBOLS:

Track Conditions
ft — fast
gd — good
sl — slow
sy — sloppy
my — muddy
hy — heavy

Finish Information
ns — nose
hd — head
nk — neck
dis — distanced (more than 25 lengths)
dnf — did not finish
acc — accident

Horse's Color
b — bay
blk — black
br — brown
ch — chestnut
gr — gray
ro — roan

Horse's Sex
c — colt .... Male four years of age and under
f — filly .... Female four years of age and under
g — gelding ...... Any desexed male
h — horse .... Male five years of age or older
m — mare .... Female five years of age or older
r — ridgeling ... An incomplete male

HOW TO READ THE TOTE BOARD:

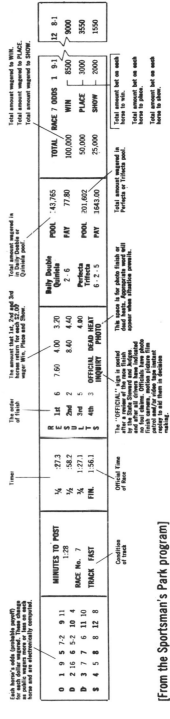

CLASS OF RACE*

Qua (Dr) — Qualifying Driver Only
Qua — Qualifying
Mat — Matinee
Mdn — Maiden
9000 — clm (actual value on horse)
nw1000 — Non-winners of $1,000 etc. lifetime
w1000 — Winners of $1,000, etc. lifetime
nw2R — Non-winners of two races
nw1000¹⁹⁷⁸ — Non-winners of $1,000 in 1978
nw10000¹⁹⁷⁸ — Non-winners of $10,000 in 1978/1979
nw10000¹⁰ — Non-winners of $10,000 in their last ten starts
3y5000 — 3-year-olds, etc with purse value
pref4000 — Preferred with purse value
inv5000 — Invitational with purse value
hcp7500 — Handicap with purse value
lfa7500 — Junior Free-For-All with purse value
stk25,000 — Stake with purse value
e.c. — Early Closer

*Occasionally a horse will race where according to his earnings it appears that he was not eligible. However this horse qualified under a secondary condition (Also eligible). The post performance line will carry the main condition of the race as it shows the actual class of competition.

RACING INFORMATION

o —parked out
im —impeded or interference
x —break
ix —interference break
ex —equipment break
be —broken equipment
l —free-legged
· —footnote
su —sulked
ck —choked down
bl —bled
A —afternoon race
(P) Provisional license — Drivers not possessing one year driving experience and 25 satisfactory starts or extended pari-mutuel meetings.

WAGERING INFORMATION

N.B. —Non-betting
N.R. —Not reported
* —favorite
e —entry
f —field
C —claimed out of that race for the amount specified.

SPEED. The ultimate measure of a Standardbred is the time it takes it to go a winning mile. But an individual track's inherent speed may vary by several seconds from one night to another. All programs should offer their customers figures that would reflect such variations. Every insider knows to within a few fifths of a second how rapidly each grade of Standardbred gets the mile under ideal conditions at the local track. It would be simple enough to determine how greatly the time of each race on an evening's program deviated from the norm for its class. The average deviation would be the track's speed variant for that night. Included with the past-performance data, the variant would put a horse's times into better perspective. Major Ontario raceway programs now include speed variants, a great leap forward for the sport in that province.

HOW TO READ THE PROGRAM

The horse's head number, saddle cloth number, program number, mutuel number and post position are the same except where there is an entry in the race. The initials following the horse's name represent color and sex, figures denote age. The names following are the horse's sire, dam, and sire of dam in that order. Under the horse's name are his lifetime earnings and lifetime record preceded by his age when record was made up to January 1 of the current year. Following the lifetime earnings is the name of the driver, his date of birth, weight and his colors. Next is the horse's best winning time on a half-mile, five-eighths, three-quarter or mile track for last year and the current racing season, followed by his starts and the number of wins, seconds, thirds in purse races and his money winnings. Beneath the horse's name are records of his six most recent races. They read from bottom to top, therefore the top line is the horse's last race.

The date of the race is followed by the name of the track. All tracks are half-mile unless followed by the figure (1) which means that it is a mile track or ($\frac{3}{4}$) which is a three-quarter mile track, etc. Then is noted the Purse, condition of the track on the day of the race, the Conditions of the race or if a Claiming Race the Claiming Price. Race distance, time of leading horse at the $\frac{1}{4}$, $\frac{1}{2}$ and $\frac{3}{4}$, follow, then comes the winner's time. The figures that follow in order show the post position of the horse, his position at the $\frac{1}{4}$, $\frac{1}{2}$, $\frac{3}{4}$, stretch with lengths behind except for the leading horse whose number denotes lengths ahead, and finish with beaten lengths. If he was a winner, it shows how far ahead of the second horse and the losers show how far they were behind the winning horse. The next figure shows the horse's actual time in that race. Whenever a small "°" appears after the calls, it denotes that the horse raced on the outside at least one-quarter of a mile. In some instances these figures won't appear because the track at which the horse raced did not have its races charted. Then follows the closing odds to the dollar, the horse's driver, and the order of finish, giving the names of the first three horses, temperature and time allowance due to cold weather.

KEY TO ABBREVIATIONS

Horses' Colors	Horses' Sex	Track Conditions	Finish Information	Wagering Information	Race Classes
b—bay	c—colt	ft—fast	P—Placing	N.B.—No Betting	Cd—Condition Race
blk—black	f—filly	gd—good	ns —nose	N.R.—Not Reported	10000 clm—Claiming price
br—brown	g—gelding	sy—sloppy	hd —head	*—favorite	Ec—Early closing event
ch—chestnut	h—horse	sl—slow	nk —neck	e—entry	FA—free for all
gr—gray	m—mare	my—muddy	dh —dead heat	f—field	JFA—Junior Free for all
ro—roan	ri—ridgling	hy—heavy	dis —distanced over 25		Hcp—Handicap Race
			lengths behind winner		Inv—Invitational Race

Racing Information
° —Raced on outside for at least $\frac{1}{4}$ mile
°° —Raced three wide
x—horse broke at this point
‡—races without hopples
†—races with trotting hopples
ix—break caused by interference
i—horse interfered with at this point
Qua (dr)—Qualifying Race for Driver
Qua (h-d)—Qualifying Race for both
            horse and driver
T.Dis—Time for race was disallowed on this horse because of a placing due to other
            than a lapped on break at finish.
(J)—Horse registered with New Jersey Breeders Association.
St.—Stable in which horse is trained

B.E.—broken equipment
ax—break caused by accident
acc—accident
ex—equipment break
dnf—did not finish
BAR—Barred in wagering
H.N.—head number

(1)—Mile Track
($\frac{5}{8}$)—$\frac{5}{8}$ Track
($\frac{3}{4}$)—$\frac{3}{4}$ Track
z—horse claimed
(c)—Conventional Sulky

Race Classes (continued):
Lc—Late Closing Event
Mdn—Maiden
Mat—Matinee (no purse)
nw—Non-Winners
nw300ps—Average Earnings
            was less than $300
            per start
Opn—Open To All
Opt Clm—Optional Claiming
Pref—Preferred
Qua—Qualifying Race
Stk—Stake Race
T—Time Trial
w—Winners - over
F-M—Fillies & Mares
NJSS—New Jersey Sires
            Stake

PROGRAM and HEAD NUMBER	Date of Race	Track Raced On	Purse	Track Condition	Type of Race	Distance of Race	Time at $\frac{1}{4}$	Time at $\frac{1}{2}$	Time at $\frac{3}{4}$	Time of Winner	Post Position	Position at $\frac{1}{4}$	Position at $\frac{1}{2}$	Position at $\frac{3}{4}$	Stretch Position and Lengths	Finish Position and Lengths Behind Winner	Horse's Actual Time	Equivalent odds to 1.00	Driver	Best Win Time of Year	Name of Winner	Name of Second Horse	Name of Third Horse	Temperature and Time Allowance

4 SENOR SKIPPER br h, 4, by Meadow Skipper—Senorita Cheetah by Adios Paul   Trainer-E. Spruce
Ernie & Marion Spruce, Rexdale, Ont.   M(1)1:53³ 1978 29 10 4 5 266,010
7-22 M(1)   25000 ft Opn mi 27² :55³1:23⁴1:53³ 3   4   3° 1   1⁶   1¹⁴   1:53³   *1.50(B.Webster)SnrSkppr,KrryGld,ShdysdTrx 89-0

[From The Meadowlands program]

PROGRAM and HEAD NUMBER, P.P. COLOR	Free Legged	Horse's Name	Lifetime Win Record / Age When Made Size of Track	Horse's Color Sex Age	Sire	Dam	Dam's Sire	Best Win Time This Year	Name of Trainer

RED 2	‡GOVERNOR SKIPPER	br h, 4, by Meadow Skipper, Adios Governess by Adios							(Tr.–B. W. Norris)
	($637,303) 3, 1:54 (1)	Ivanhoe Stables, Inc., Chicago, Ill. JOHN CHAPMAN (153)			Green-White		Lex(1) 1:54 M(1) 1:55	1979 29 17 7 3 522,148. 1978 14 7 3 3 266,102.	
	8-19 RR ft Opn hcp 35000 m 28:2 58:2 1:27 1:56:3 7 4° 1 1 1/8 1/8 1:56:3 *.60(JChp)GvmrSkpr,KrryGld,Jamboogr 76
	8-12 RR ft Opn hcp 50000 m 29:2 59:3 1:28 1:56:4 7 1 1 1 1/2‡ 1/6 1:56:4 *.50(JChap)Gov.Skpr,Jmboogr,JdePrnc 75

Date of Race	Track Raced On	Track Condition	Age, Type of Race, Purse	Distance of Race	Time at ¼	Time at ½	Time at ¾	Time of Winner	Post Position	Position at ¼	Position at ½	Position at ¾	Stretch Position and Lengths Behind Leader	Finish Position and Lengths Behind Winner	Actual Time	Odds to 1.00 Best Win Time Last Year	Driver	Name of Winner	Second Horse	Third Horse	Temperature

ABBREVIATIONS AND SYMBOLS

HORSES COLOR AND SEX

b g—bay gelding
blk c—black colt
br m—brown mare
ch h—chestnut horse
gr f—grey filly
ro—roan

TRACK SIZE

(⅝)—⅝ mile track
(¾)—¾ mile track
(1)—one mile track

TRACK CONDITIONS

ft—fast
gd—good
sy—sloppy
sl—slow
hy—heavy
my—muddy

TYPE OF RACE

Cd 2,000—Conditioned & Purse
Stk—Stake
clm 3000—$3,000 claiming race (act. value on this horse)
nw 3000 (non-winners $3,000; etc.); Opt—optional claimer
cl—classified   Opn—Open   alw—Allowance Races
ec—early closer   hcp—Handicap   Pref—Preferred
lc—late closer   Inv—Invitational
qua—qualifying   tp—Trot and Pace
mdn—maiden   amat.—amateur

RACING INFORMATION

x—Break
i—Interference
ix—Interference Break
ex—Equipment Break
°—Parked Out
••—Parked out 3 wide
pl—placed
□—Blocked in stretch
wkt—Workout

be—Broken Equipment
(P)—Provisional Driver or Trainer
‡—Free-legged Pacer
‡—Hobbled Trotter
†—Half Hopples
m—One Mile
Z—Horse Claimed
dr qua—Driver Qualifying
(NY) —N.Y. State Bred

WAGERING INFORMATION

f—mutuel field   NB—No Betting
e—entry   NR—Not Reported
°—favorite   DNF—Did Not Finish

FINISH INFORMATION

ns—nose
hd—head
nk—neck
dh—dead heat
dis—distanced
dq—Disqualified

[From the Roosevelt Raceway program]

PACE. One of the basics of Standardbred handicapping, pace is most effectively analyzed if the player knows how far behind or ahead a horse was at each stage of its race. Most programs reveal the margins only at the stretch call and finish. A few show it only at the finish. A very few show it at the ¾-mile call, stretch and finish.

TRAINER. In recent years, some good trainers have begun to concentrate on training, employing so-called "catch-drivers" to handle the reins in actual competition. Few programs tabulate the records of nondriving trainers, although such statistics are tremendously revealing. By the same token, most catch-drivers are themselves trainers. Tabulated trainer standings would disclose whether these drivers do as well with their own horses as with those from other barns.

DRIVER. Most programs include listings of the track's leading drivers, showing how many starts, victories and seconds and thirds each has had during the current meeting. After a meeting has been under way for a week or so, and active reinsmen have had a representative number of starts, these listings are helpful. Considerably more helpful are programs that summarize the record of every driver in every race, or list the records of all local drivers in a separate tabulation. Still more helpful would be a method that not only revealed the driver's record at the current meeting but also showed how he had been doing elsewhere on the circuit or—if it still be early in the season—how he fared last year.

POST POSITION. At all tracks, inside post positions are advantageous and outside ones are handicaps. Something is missing from a program that neglects to reveal how many horses have started in each post position, how many have won from each position and what the percentages have been. Statistics for recent meetings would be helpful, especially during the first weeks of a new season.

Although I consider all those deficiencies regrettable, and could mention others, I do not think that they incapacitate the player. Fortunately, the Standardbred is such a reliable beast, and some drivers are so much more dependable than others, that the information contained in most programs is sufficient for intelligent play. Knowing the kinds of facts that probably are missing from the program, the handicapper simply treads carefully if he has not been at the raceway for a while. This may not be a bad thing in itself, encouraging the prudence for which no amount of information can substitute.

Nevertheless, I think most racegoers will agree with me that it would be nice to have all relevant information in the program. It would be an encouragement and a reassurance. It would increase the handicapping fan's pleasure by permitting him greater confidence in his judgments. Which would mean more frequent visits to the raceway and more frequent bets. Nothing could be fairer than that.

Periodicals

Lean pickings await the fan who goes to the average newsstand for help with his raceway handicapping. Having developed during an era of prohibitively expensive publishing costs, harness racing lacks national periodicals comparable to baseball's *Sporting News,* Thoroughbred racing's *Daily Racing Form, The Blood-Horse* and *Thoroughbred Record,* and the flock of magazines that help to arouse and maintain informed awareness of what goes on in professional football, basketball, tennis and golf.

Significant changes in driver-trainer-owner relationships, the emergence of promising new horses and drivers, news of fines and suspensions, expertly detailed analyses of past and upcoming races—matters of this kind would be food and drink for someone interested in harness racing. Little or none is available. In the largest racing centers, the determined fan sometimes can find a newspaper sporting page on which dribs and drabs appear, but they are local in character. Out-of-town developments of the greatest importance go unreported. Horses break speed records while racing for enormous purses, and scarcely anyone outside the industry itself hears about it—perhaps not even in the city where the event occurs!

The lack of national news creates in every major racing center a weird insularity. The Yonkers fan assumes that if the feat did not take place in New York it did not take place at all. Which is why brilliant trainer-drivers such as Ron Waples and Shelly Goudreau, after setting incredible records at first-class raceways elsewhere, have been able to win at inflated mutuel prices in New York.

Among existing magazines, the following are worth attention:

Hoof Beats. Official monthly of the U.S. Trotting Association, this magazine is well edited, well written and magnificently illustrated with color photographs. Apart from short reports on matters of USTA policy, including occasional brief peeks at subjects of controversy, the magazine consists largely of personality profiles, historical reviews and technical advice on the care and training of Standardbreds. From these pieces and from various columns, the fan learns a good deal about the ideals, concerns and botherations of horsemen, and about current trends. None of this is vital to one's handicapping, but it makes the sport more enjoyable by bridging the gulf between the racing strip and the stands. The subscription rate is $12 a year from USTA, 750 Michigan Avenue, Columbus, Ohio 43215.

The Harness Horse. This weekly is one means of learning who has been winning what, and where. Not much detail, but a way of keeping up. Available at $28 a year from Box 1831, Harrisburg, Pa. 17105.

The Horseman and Fair World. Information similar to that in *The Harness Horse*, plus lists of the leading drivers at current meetings. Weekly, for $28 a year from Box 886, Lexington, Ky. 40501.

Sports Eye and *Fast Performances*. These sister tabloids blanket the New York racing scene with fact and commentary useful to handicappers at The Meadowlands, Roosevelt and Yonkers Raceways and Monticello. Of particular interest are the highly detailed race-result charts, which provide extraordinary details such as each horse's racing time for each quarter-mile, plus footnote analyses of individual performances. Past-performance tabulations also are full of pertinent data unobtainable elsewhere. Both papers are $1 on newsstands. Subscription information from 343 Great Neck Road, Great Neck, N.Y. 11021.

Daily Racing Form. The Los Angeles edition of this racing paper publishes past-performance tables and comprehensive result charts of all harness races in the area. The footnote comments and other details of the charts make Los Angeles harness handicapping an easier pastime than it is in places where such generous information is unobtainable.

Sulky. Annual handicap ratings of all active Standardbreds and leading drivers, plus a method of adjusting the figures to the particular circumstances of the race. While I doubt that an accurate handicap rating of the average horse is likely to remain accurate for a month, much less a full year, this booklet's driver ratings are fairly good. And the overall approach to handicapping a race is sound enough. The reader might enjoy trying to compare the results of his own handicapping methods with those of *Sulky*. It costs $15 a year from Sulky Publishing Co., P.O. Box 728, Newburgh, N.Y. 12550.

Books

Numerous books have been published about the handicapping of harness races. Most of them offer unproductive ideas in unreadable prose. The trouble with handicapping advice, of course, is that any charlatan can handicap a race after it is over. If he hopes to deceive the public or —as seems to be the case more often than not—if he is unable to resist deluding himself, he is perfectly free to confect unsupportable theories and generalizations. Exceptions are these:

Bettor's Guide to Harness Racing, by Steve Chaplin. This is by far the most closely reasoned and carefully detailed study of the most crucial of handicapping factors—current condition or, as the author calls it, "shape." All other relevant factors are thoroughly explored in terms of their interrelationships. The frequent racegoer will make best use of this brilliant book, but I cannot imagine any other interested reader failing to benefit from it. Published for $15 by Amerpub, 505 Eighth Avenue, New York, N.Y. 10018.

Harness Racing: Predicting the Outcome, by Hank Adams and Dr. Donald Sullivan. Adams is one of the best raceway handicappers I know. He processed his ideas through Sullivan's computer and came up with the first useful study of this game's probabilities. The resulting selection method is excellent. Sold through the mail by Stafford Publishing Company, 2 Penn Plaza, New York, N.Y. 10001.

Harness Racing Gold, by Igor Kusyshyn, Ph.D. Igor is a professor of psychology at York University, Toronto, and a great enthusiast of harness racing. Here he sets forth a simple and practical handicapping procedure based on his own statistical studies. Available through the mail from International Gaming, Inc., P.O. Box 73, Thornhill, Ontario, Canada L3T 3N1.

As I remarked much earlier, few sports have been the subject of more distinguished scholarly literature than harness racing has. Unfortunately, most of the best historical works are already out of print and seldom can be obtained from libraries without difficulty. Among these, the finest is *The American Trotter,* by John Hervey, published in 1947 by Coward-McCann. Hervey was an absolutely first-rate historian and his book is a joy, full of names, atmosphere, exploits and the glamour of the past. Of good books still available, the best are:

Care and Training of the Trotter and Pacer, by James C. Harrison. Incomparably the finest work ever published about the techniques of a sport, this enormous volume is compulsory reading for whoever wants to know harness racing. All-time great drivers and trainers join Harrison in exploring every relevant subject from shoeing to feeding to driving tactics to paying stable expenses. Handicapping and betting are beyond the scope of the book, but it surely will improve the reader's selection procedures by expanding his knowledge of the sport. Published at $7.50 in 1968 by the USTA.

The Complete Book of Harness Racing, by Philip A. Pines. The director of the Hall of Fame of the Trotter, Goshen, N.Y., is Standardbred racing's foremost living historian. His large and lively book tells the fascinating story of the breed and the game. Nothing on handicapping, but rich in the background information that every handicapper should have.

Still Hooked on Harness Racing, by Donald P. Evans. In the mid-1960s Don Evans, then a publicist at Vernon Downs, wrote *Hooked on Harness Racing,* a hilarious little volume that drew deservedly favorable attention throughout the sport. Evans later became vice-president for publicity and public relations of the USTA and executive editor of *Hoof Beats.* This sequel updates the material in the original book. Worth reading not only for its amusements but because it shows how racing gets into one's blood. Available through the USTA Book Club (see below).

USTA Book Club. Most bookstores carry little if any material on harness racing. To improve distribution of meritorious works in the field, the USTA sells many of the best titles through the mail. Nothing on handicapping when last seen, but much interesting stuff about great horses and constructive humans. For a current list, write the club at 750 Michigan Avenue, Columbus, Ohio 43215.

Inside Information

To maintain the public confidence on which prosperity rests, all sports take pains to police the conduct of competitors both on and off the field. Recurrent hullabaloo about sports personalities and hoodlums, or suspected hoodlums, is occasioned by the well-documented belief that some characters go to great lengths to bet on sure things and are not above bribing or coercing susceptible athletes.

Harness racing's main problems with the underworld have been occasioned by the energetic, even violent resourcefulness with which thugs try to cash tickets on twin doubles, twin exactas and other bonanza bets. Bullyboys have been known to make life unpleasant for fans who declined to sell "live" twin tickets (potential winning ones) at bargain prices. Drivers foolish enough to associate with hoods have been roughed up for unsatisfactory performances, such as winning key races that their chums expected them to lose.

Obviously, if shenanigans of this kind were permitted to get out of hand, the only people at raceways would be gangsters. To produce the opposite effect, the industry has been vigorous about expelling undesirables from its grandstands, clubhouses and stable areas. Horsemen, including a few talented ones, have been booted out of the business or, in lesser cases, exiled for long periods. In punishing waywardness, and preventing it, the tracks are assisted by a USTA security staff and by Harness Tracks Security, Inc., a national investigative network headed by John L. Brennan, a former FBI administrator who spent many years doing similar work in Thoroughbred racing.

In implying that the worst is over, I should be careful to emphasize that the worst was not really all that dreadful. The underworld never made connections with more than an infinitesimal number of horsemen. The bullying of customers by goons who wanted to buy up all the live twin-double tickets did not dominate the atmosphere in the stands. Anyhow, a decent human being can now pay his way into a harness track with no expectation of being jostled by thieves and with every expectation of seeing honestly competitive sport.

But the appetite for a sure thing is not entirely an underworld phenomenon. Pillars of commerce, industry and the professions are capable of extraordinary behavior when they leave the office to seek pleasure. Hundreds of otherwise sensible persons have bought Standardbred horses, incurring the heavy financial burdens of stable ownership for no reason other than their screw-loose belief that owners get hot tips.

Amusingly, some rather prominent stables are owned by folks who started as bettors and whose affection for horses, though increasing, does not yet surpass their interest in betting. Some of them wear iridescent suits, speak raucously and make a big thing of their familiarity with the famous horsemen whom they employ. The horsemen put up with this, and are even deferential to it, so long as the Johnny-come-latelies pay the bills promptly and refrain from causing embarrassment about bets.

Most horsemen are close-mouthed, even with their owners. They keep their own counsel because they were brought up that way, in the rural tradition, and because they know that hell hath no fury like that of a fool who has been steered into a few losing bets. Obviously, a competent horseman knows when his own animal has a good chance of winning, and when it does not. Alas, he also realizes that it sometimes wins when he least expects it to, and loses when he least expects it to. He knows, furthermore, that he cannot pick a higher percentage of winners than a decent handicapper can, and that he could not do so even if he were to question every other trainer before every race.

The most that anyone can get out of the typical trainer or driver about a race in which he is involved is "I think I've got a shot at it." Or "I don't think so. That other filly is real tough." Most are even less communicative than that. A few are willing to confide their frank opinions to persons whom they trust not to embarrass them. But their opinions are emphatically not more dependable than those of a good handicapper.

In disputing this perhaps disappointing fact with me recently, a race-going friend demanded, "What if the best horse in the race has gone sour in the last day or so, and only the trainer knows it? Wouldn't you want to know it, too? Wouldn't it help you to know it?"

Answer: If a horse goes seriously sour, its people scratch it from the race. If it goes only middling sour, but badly enough to endanger its chances, the change in its condition often is plainly noticeable during the prerace warm-ups and parade. Finally, it may win when sour or lose when fit. The purpose of this chapter is to arm the reader with the attitudes and insights that are basic to good handicapping. The present section of the chapter should be read and understood in that light. Inside information, or what passes for it, may sometimes help the handicapper to confirm his own judgments but should never be permitted to unhorse those judgments.

One of the most colorful bettors of modern times was active at Eastern raceways. In fact, he became an owner of horses, both as employer and partner of some of the sport's foremost trainer-drivers. What made him colorful was the enormous amounts of money he won when he was hot, and the enormous sums he lost when he was not. He was notorious for this before he owned horses, and he remained so after he began chumming around with top horsemen. He would make a small fortune, then lose it and disappear for a while until he accumulated a fresh stake. Everybody liked him. Nobody mistrusted him. If any bettor had access to inside information, it was he. It did him absolutely no good. At this writing he has been absent from the raceways for years, presumably in pursuit of a new bankroll.

A horseman I know remembers him well. The horseman is a brilliant trainer and driver who was born and brought up in the sport. A fun-loving fellow, he enjoys betting when his duties permit him to leave the paddock and frolic in the clubhouse. I have been to the races with him more than a few times, and can certify that he is a good handicapper. That is, he wins almost as many bets as he loses. In discussing the colorful bettor mentioned above, this horseman says affectionately, "A nice guy. And a pretty sharp handicapper. Did I ever tell you about the time he talked me into betting on one of my own horses and the damned thing won?"

Please note that the handicapper gave "inside information" to the horseman. And please remember that whatever inside information the handicapper got from horsemen was not dependable enough to make a long-term winner of him. He was an inconsistent selector before he ever became an owner, and inconsistent he remained.

Alleged inside information abounds at raceway bars, coffee counters and mutuel windows. Everybody is forever "giving winners" to everybody else. So-and-so says that such-and-such stable is going to bet with both hands tonight. Hot tip! The report spreads through the place and shortly is reflected in the decreasing odds on the horse. The tips are not always false. Stables do bet, and news does leak. But stables lose bets, too. And the race is not unusual in which as many as three stables bet heavily on their own horses. How hot can a tip be if other stables ignore it to bet on their own animals?

Inside information is sometimes interesting, but is almost invariably worthless. In no circumstances is it as useful to the good handicapper as his own interpretation of the facts contained in the past-performance records. To disbelieve this is to discount handicapping and commit oneself to the great fraternity of those who spend their time prospecting for tips, and lose and lose and lose.

Tip Sheets

Some excellent handicappers peddle their racing selections in the tip sheets sold at raceway entrances. So do some mediocre handicappers.

And handicappers of both kinds prepare selections for daily newspapers. The best of these public selectors develop substantial followings. Their loyal customers flock to the mutuel windows to bet as advised, and the odds drop.

A racegoer who knows nothing about the horses is undoubtedly better off with a popular tip sheet than with a hat pin. But nobody can stay ahead of the game by playing these selections, no matter how bright the tip-sheet handicapper may be.

The reason for this apparent contradiction is that the traditions of the tip-sheet trade require the handicapper to make selections in every race on every program. Moreover, to increase the number of winning selections, he often picks three or four horses per race, listing them in order of preference but claiming victory even when the second or third or fourth preference wins. Thus, to hit as many winners as the tip sheet claims for itself, the innocent customer must play three or four horses in every race, which is a recipe for disaster.

Even if he plays only the top selections, the customer courts insolvency by playing every race. Nobody can show a profit through play on every race on every program. Some races are too full of breakers to play. Others are too close for firm decision. But the tip sheets fail to make these distinctions.

All this being so, the tip sheet is of no value to a handicapper. Neither are newspaper selections. Neither, for that matter, are the track handicapper's selections published in some programs. And neither, by the way, are the "best bets" of public selectors. In naming a horse as "best bet" of the night, the tip sheet or newspaper usually singles out an animal that has a splendid chance of winning, but whose odds are too low. "Best bets" invariably lead to long-run financial loss, the percentage of winners not being high enough to overcome the skimpy mutuel prices.

The Handicapper's Notebook

On Friday evening, October 19, 1979, the ninth race at Roosevelt Raceway was a B-1/B-2 handicap pace for New York–bred horses and geldings aged three to five.

Leaving from post position 4 was this colt:

J TOWN FELLA ⓝ   b c, 3, by Most Happy Fella, Medic Beau by Thorpe Hanover   (Tr.-G. Villemure)

			G. Villemure & M. Parenti, N.Y.								M(1) 1:58:3 1979 30 5 4 5 61,635.					
($3,390) 2, 2:09:3		BEN WEBSTER (138)					Red-White-Black				Fhld 2:09:3 1978 3 1 1 1 3,390.					
10-12 YR	gd B-2 Cd	11000 m 30:1 1:02:3 1:32:2 2:03:2	5	1	3	4	3/3	4/1¼	2:03:4	6.90(NDpls)FrdmBrt,T'T'One,FllyFlyng	52
10-6 YR	ft 3yr Inv	15000 m 29:4 1:00 1:29 1:59:1	7	7	6°	7°	7/11	6/8½	2:01	15.40(Dplse)ToR'Jhny,FrdmBret,T'Chip	56
9-22 YR	sy 3yr Inv	15000 m 29:1 59:4 1:30:2 2:00:2	5	3	3	2°	2/ʰᵈ	1/ⁿᵏ	2:00:2	9.40(Dplse)JTwnFlla,ToR'Jhny,T'Thrpe	66
9-14 YR	sy 3yr Inv	15000 m 29:1 1:00:1 1:31 2:01:2	2	5	5	5°	4/3¼	2/5	2:02:2	2.70(Insko)ToRiJhny,JTwnFlla,AplloLbl	73
9-8 YR	ft 3yr Inv	15000 m 28:3 1:00 1:30:4 2:00:2	2	4	3°	1°	1/ⁿᵏ	1/¼	2:00:2	8.10(Dpls)JTwnFlla,P'T'Gme,TmlyThrp	65
8-30 YR	ft B-3 Cd	11000 m 30:1 1:01:2 1:33 2:01:4	2	5	5°	3°°3/2	4/1¼		2:02:1	*.90(Dplse)T'Chip,VkngFury,RdMcklee	74
8-23 YR	ft B-3	11000 m 30 59:3 1:29:1 1:59:1	6	4°	1°	2°	2/2½	2/4½	2:00	12.40(Insko)FuryA'hrst,JTwnFla,JSSkpr	70
8-3 M(1)	ft Cd	12000 m 29 57:2 1:26:4 1:56	5	7	7	6°	4/7	5/6¼	1:57:2	2.80(Wbstr)DellsCourt,ForKicks,Artillery	

As depicted in the raceway's past-performance program, the animal's October record was unimpressive. On October 6, he had exerted himself in the early stages of an invitational race, fighting for position outside another horse (as the small degree signs indicate) and had succeeded only in losing position. By the time the field entered the stretch, he was seventh by 11 lengths. He ended sixth by nine lengths, probably having passed horses more tired than he.

Six days later, competing against lesser company for an $11,000 pot, he did nothing to excite the student of past-performance lines. He got to the front in the beginning but quickly surrendered command and trailed the leaders the rest of the trip, finishing fourth after a final quarter in which he paced at an unremarkable :31:1 for an individual final time of 2:03:4.*

However, the October 12 performance was not as bad as implied by the program. Many of the smart handicappers in attendance on October 19 knew this very well. Some knew it because they were hawklike race watchers who kept careful notes of everything they saw on the track. Others knew it because they read the detailed result chart in *Sports Eye:*

NINTH RACE: (2429) YONKERS, FRI., OCT. 12—1 Mile Pace. B-2. 3 Year Olds. Purse $11,000.

Freedom Bret	Campbell,Jo	1	$3\frac{1}{4}$	$5\frac{1}{2}$	$5°^7$	$i5^8$	1^{hd}	30^3	32^3	30	30^1	2:03²	J.Turner	*1.00
Three Times One	Stoltzfus	2	$2\frac{1}{4}$	$1\frac{3}{4}$	$2\frac{1}{4}$	$2\frac{1}{4}$	$2\frac{3}{4}$	30^2	32^1	30	30^4	2:03²	A.Stoltzfus	7.00
Fully Flying	Filion,Her	4	$5\frac{1}{2}$	$4°^{nk}$	$3°\frac{1}{2}$	$4\frac{1}{4}$	$3\frac{3}{4}$	31^1	32	29^4	30^3	2:03³	C.Carr	3.40
J Town Fella	Dauplaise	5	$1\frac{1}{4}$	$3\frac{1}{4}$	$4\frac{1}{4}$	3^1	$4\frac{1}{4}$	30^1	32^3	30^1	30^3	2:03³	G.Villemure	6.90
Alaskan Strike	Morgan,T	3	$4\frac{1}{2}$	$2°\frac{3}{4}$	$1\frac{1}{2}$	$1\frac{1}{4}$	5^8	31	31^4	29^3	31^3	2:04	T.Morgan	4.70
My Lord Roger	Wing	6	6	6	6	6	6	31^3	31^4	31^1	31	2:05³	T.Wing	12.80

Scratched: (B) Taurus Chip-sick; (C) Viking Fury-lame.
Off: 10:46. Time: 0:30.1, 1:02.3, 1:32.2, 2:03.2. Clear-good. OTB Fin. (A-D-F).
MUTUELS: $4.00, 3.20, 2.20; $4.40, 2.60; $2.40. EXACTA (1-4) Paid $14.80. Mutuel Pool $66,306.
CONN OTB: $6.20, 3.40, 2.10; $6.40, 2.40; $2.20. EXACTA (A-D) Paid $17.20.
FREEDOM BRET left and yielded, was shuffled and pulled with cover off the third turn, was impeded on the final turn when FULLY FLYING took a bad step, lost momentum and about a length and a half, gathered together, switched into high gear turning for home and finished with a wild rush to get up under a flicking whip. THREE TIMES ONE took the lead off the first turn, yielded and regained on the second turn, yielded on the third turn, swung out at headstretch and forged to the lead but was outkicked driving. FULLY FLYING moved midway through the second turn with cover, lost cover on the third turn, made a bad step on the final turn, ducked in for the drive and finished grittily. J TOWN FELLA took the lead mid-backstretch and yielded, was shuffled back, came up the wood in the stretch but never found full clearance. ALASKAN STRIKE moved mid-second turn and rushed up, brushed into the lead on the third turn, tired in the drive. MY LORD ROGER had little.
B.c.3, by Bret Hanover, Tarport Marvis by Thorpe Hanover.

The footnote commentary strongly indicates that J. Town Fella had a persuasive excuse for his indifferent finish on October 12. He had been "shuffled back" by horses crowding in front of him along the rail. Toward the end, he tried to move up on the inside but had no room. As suggested, he could not have gone to the outside without colliding with other horses.

Now look at the result chart of the October 19 race:

---

* Readers unfamiliar with the sport's numerical notations will learn them as we go. Meanwhile, 2:03:4 means two minutes, three and four-fifths seconds. And :31:1 means thirty-one and one-fifth seconds. In some places, the same times would be presented as 2:03 4/5 and :31 1/5 or 2:03⁴ and :31¹.

NINTH RACE: (2489) ROOSEVELT, FRI., OCT. 19—1 Mile. Pace. B-1/B-2 Handicap. N.Y. Bred 3-5 Year Old Horses & Geldings. Purse $17,500.

J Town Fella	Webster	4	2^{1}_{2}	3^{1}_{2}	$1^{\circ nk}$	1^{1}_{2}	1^{nk}	30^{2}	30^{3}	29^{1}	29	1:59^{1}	G.Villemure	*1.30
Sample Fella	Campbell,Jo	5	6^{1}_{2}	$6^{\circ}\!\frac{3}{4}$	$6^{\circ 1}_{4}$	5^{nk}	22^{1}_{4}	31^{4}	29^{3}	29^{3}	28^{1}	1:59^{1}	H. Kertzner	4.80
Most Happy Diane	Marohn,J	8	1^{1}_{2}	2^{1}_{4}	3^{1}_{2}	3^{1}	3^{nk}	30^{1}	30^{2}	30	29	1:59^{3}	Jo.Grasso	33.70
Happy Play Boy	Filion,Her	2	5^{4}	4°_{2}	$4^{\circ 1}_{4}$	4^{1}	4^{1}_{2}	31	30^{1}	29^{2}	29^{1}	1:59^{4}	F.Browne	8.20
Colonel L Bar	Abbatiello,C	1	3^{1}_{2}	5^{3}_{4}	5^{1}	6^{1}_{4}	5^{nk}	30^{4}	30^{2}	29^{3}	29^{1}	2:00	M.Santa Maria	19.50
Fully Flying	Wing	3	4^{1}	1^{2}	2^{1}_{2}	2^{1}_{2}	6^{2}	30^{4}	29^{2}	30	29^{4}	2:00	C.Carr	2.30
Romeo Allegro	Insko	7	8	7^{1}_{4}	7^{1}	7^{1}_{2}	7^{4}	32^{2}	29^{1}	29^{4}	29	2:00^{2}	A.Nelson	13.00
Mike Napoleon	Patterson,J,Jr.	6	7^{1}_{4}	8°	8°	8	8	32^{1}	29^{3}	29^{4}	29^{3}	2:01^{1}	T.Ceraso,Jr.	21.00

Off: 11:15. Time: 0:30.1, 1:00.1, 1:30.1, 1:59.1. Clear-Fast. OTB Fin: (D-E-H)

MUTUELS: $4.60, 3.80, 2.40; $4.80, 4.00; $8.60. EXACTA (4-5) Paid $10.80. Mutuel pool $111,882.
$4.60, 3.00, 2.40; $4.20, 4.40; $4.60. EXACTA (D-E) Paid $28.60.

J TOWN FELLA took the lead at the ⅛ pole and yielded, pulled in the backstretch to go after the lead, took command with a rush turning for home and held with steady urging. SAMPLE FELLA followed cover approaching the half, moved three wide late on the final turn and was moving boldly in the late stages. MOST HAPPY DIANE took the lead before the quarter, yielded before the half, pulled off the wood entering the drive and squeezed between horses to come fully clear in midstretch and finished steadily. HAPPY PLAY BOY moved uncovered approaching the half, was slow moving and picked up the winner's cover in the backstretch, couldn't match the speed of the top ones in the drive. COLONEL L BAR left and yielded, came clear for the drive and lacked a strong finish under a hard whip. FULLY FLYING moved past the quarter and brushed into the lead at the 7/16 pole fought with the winner through the final quarter and tired in the lane. ROMEO ALLEGRO saved ground and was no factor. MIKE NAPOLEON followed cover but had nothing.

B.c.3, by Most Happy Fella, Medic Beau by Thorpe Hanover.

Classification: Mike Napoleon, Romeo Allegro, Most Happy Diane, Sample Fella, B-1; Colonel L-Bar, Happy Play Boy, Fully Flying, J Town Fella, B-2.

J. Town Fella won it. More to the point, he won at miserly odds of 13 to 10, despite the unimpressive top lines in his past-performance record! This means that many New York handicappers have learned to look beyond the raw facts presented in programs. When a horse has an excuse for losing, enough of them know it to drive down its odds when it turns up for another race.

Careful race watchers and chart collectors are certain to be more successful at any track than more casual fans who depend on the program alone. Having made that irrefutable statement, I must now concede that the overwhelming majority of racegoers are unwilling to spend time making notes and poring over charts. I am on their side. And I have glad tidings for them. It is possible to do very nicely at harness raceways through judicious study of past-performance programs and extrajudicious abstention from unplayable races.

Binoculars

Although one of the main virtues of half-mile tracks is good visibility from the stands, binoculars make a significant difference, even in the best seats. Whether or not you are interested in crossing every "t" and dotting every "i" to make your handicapping supremely successful, a pair of seven- or eight-power binoculars will increase your enjoyment of the sport. Seeing more, you understand more about driving tactics and the problems of the parked or boxed-in horse.

When to Handicap

Advance copies of the past-performance records are available on the day of the race at newsstands in many cities. Some tracks distribute the material a day earlier than that. Although important late developments like scratches and driver changes are not included in these advance materials, they offer the handicapper a chance to work in peace. Twenty minutes before post time is a difficult time and the track a difficult place for handicapping. The sights and sounds, the distracting remarks, the changes on the tote board and most especially the prerace performances of the horses all deserve attention, sometimes for fun and sometimes for handicapping purposes. One can't have one's nose in a program and one's eyes and ears open to other stimuli without spoiling something.

Because I enjoy the challenge of handicapping, and resent interference with that pleasure, I take pains to get most of the work done before I arrive at the track. There I quickly catch up on the late changes and adjust my figures accordingly. This leaves me free to heckle my companions, if any, while watching the warm-ups, the tote board and the races themselves.

A particularly pleasant approach is to go to the track early for dinner at a table with a good view. If alone or accompanied by someone blessed with the gift of silence, you can down the drinks and the food and do your handicapping before the action starts. As I hope to convince everyone, the handicapping itself does not take long, if done in an orderly way.

2 KNOW YOUR TRACK

MODERN TIMES BEGAN for harness racing in 1940, when George Morton Levy, a New York lawyer with tremendous political clout, obtained legislative approval for night racing with pari-mutuel betting at Roosevelt Raceway, a sometime motordrome at Westbury, Long Island.

Under less intrepid auspices, the new era might have ended almost as soon as it began. Harness racing had been mildly popular in New York at the turn of the century, but hardly anyone remembered and fewer cared. The sports fans of the metropolitan area avoided Roosevelt Raceway with great determination during its first seasons, belying the theory that they would bet on anything if given the chance.

The races were dreary. The drivers' main strategy seemed to consist of trying to gain unfair advantage by leaving the starting line ahead of everyone else, or by tricking other drivers into trying it. Repeated false starts and recalls delayed some races for more than a half-hour, leaving many horses too exhausted or unnerved to perform well. A shrewdly handled animal able to get to the first turn on the lead was a mortal cinch to finish no worse than third. Because the track was hungry for every dollar it could get at the betting windows, wagering often continued until the horses had reached that turn, a state of affairs which permitted larcenous syndicates to make last-second place and show bets on whatever nag was in front at the time.

The indomitable Levy and his faithful associates put a stop to that nonsense in 1946, when they began using the mobile starting gate, on the development of which they had invested $50,000 of their own dwindling capital. The inventor, Steve Phillips, had introduced the idea in 1937, after watching movie cameramen shoot head-on pictures of races from the back of a moving truck. His device was an automobile equipped with a barrier behind which trotters and pacers moved rapidly and fairly to the starting line, whereupon the car would speed away, leaving the animals on their own.

In 1940, a total of 59 programs of pari-mutuel harness racing had been attended by 126,000 customers in the United States. These high-rolling tourists had bet an average of less than $15 each, making the sport's total mutuel handle for that year a bit more than $1.7 million. In 1950, with the mobile gate firmly established and the sport finally becoming believable as honest competition, 1,181 programs of racing attracted almost 6.5 million customers and a handle above $245 million. And in 1980, about 25 million clients will bet upward of $3 billion. Levy and his partners were the first but by no means the last raceway operators to count their profits in the millions.

Nighttime pari-mutuels and the mobile gate were fundamental to urban acceptance of the sport. Other innovations have enhanced its popularity by heightening its excitement or, more substantially, by improving its quality and consistency. Some of these innovations, like year-round racing and multiple bets like the exacta and trifecta, have already been mentioned. Others are of quite considerable meaning to the handicapper, because they lead to the formful competition which rewards handicapping. The reader should know of these developments:

View from the clubhouse dining room at Brandywine Raceway.

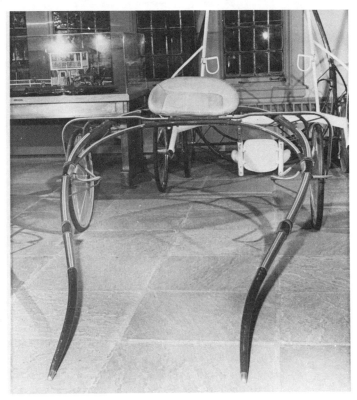

Conventional sulky.

1. *Improved equipment:* This century has seen a great deal of success-ful tinkering with the design of the racing sulky. Each change has enabled horses and drivers to reach the finish line with greater speed and safety. The old high-wheeled cart of the woodcuts gave way to a lighter model with wheels that looked almost as small and every bit as delicate as those of a bicycle. Two-minute miles promptly became more numerous. Then came wheel discs that prevented the horrible consequences of hooves becoming fouled in spokes. And in 1976, another modification brought changes as consequential as all previous ones combined.

A former aerospace engineer named Joe King redesigned the sulky so that the driver's weight was moved from its customary position over the axle. The poundage and pressure now were situated behind the wheels, exerting an upward thrust on the sulky shafts and lightening the horse's burden considerably. Overnight, handicappers learned to bet against die-hard drivers who remained loyal to the conventional vehicle. And why not? Horses pulling the new bike were pacing and trotting several seconds more rapidly than they had been able to in the past. At this writing, the so-called "modified" sulky has become dominant, and the "conven-tional" one is the exception. By the time this page reaches the reader, the

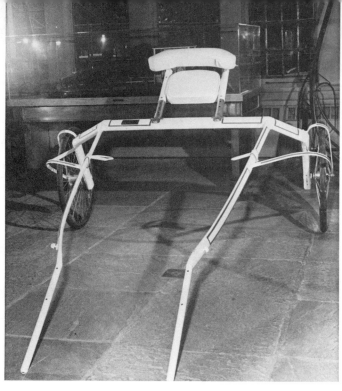

Modified sulky.

older models will be used only for the few Standardbreds whose eccentric gaits are not benefited by upward-thrusting shafts.

Other equipment changes less noticeable to the audience but significant to horse and driver include improvements in the poles and leathers that keep pacers in a straight line, and especially in the materials with which horses are shod.

Leading Harness Raceways

1⅛-Mile Track

ARLINGTON PARK, Arlington Heights, Ill.

Mile Tracks

BAY MEADOWS, San Mateo, Cal.
DU QUOIN STATE FAIR, Du Quoin, Ill.
FAIRMOUNT PARK, Collinsville, Ill.
GOLDEN BEAR RACEWAY, Sacramento, Cal.
GOLDEN GATE FIELDS, Albany, Cal.
HAWTHORNE, Cicero, Ill.
HOLLYWOOD PARK, Inglewood, Cal.
ILLINOIS STATE FAIR, Springfield, Ill.
INDIANA STATE FAIR, Indianapolis, Ind.
LATONIA RACEWAY, Florence, Ky.
THE MEADOWLANDS, East Rutherford, N.J.

NEW YORK STATE FAIR, Syracuse, N.Y.
THE RED MILE, Lexington, Ky.
WOLVERINE RACEWAY, Livonia, Mich.

¾-Mile Tracks

CAHOKIA DOWNS, East St. Louis, Ill.
SEMINOLE TURF CLUB, Casselberry, Fla.
VERNON DOWNS, Vernon, N.Y.

⅝-Mile Tracks

ATLANTIC CITY RACEWAY, Atlantic City, N.J.
BALMORAL PARK, Crete, Ill.
BLUE BONNETS, Montreal, Que
BRANDYWINE RACEWAY, Wilmington, Del.
DOVER DOWNS, Dover, Del.
FRONTENAC DOWNS, Kingston, Ont.
GREENWOOD RACEWAY, Toronto, Ont.
HAZEL PARK, Hazel Park, Mich.
KAWARTHA DOWNS, Fraserville, Ont.
LAUREL RACEWAY, Laurel, Md.
LIBERTY BELL PARK, Philadelphia, Pa.
LOS ALAMITOS, Los Alamitos, Cal.
MARQUIS DOWNS, Saskatoon, Sask.
THE MEADOWS, Meadow Lands, Pa.
MOHAWK DOWNS, Campbellville, Ont.
NEW ENGLAND HARNESS, Foxboro, Mass.
POCONO DOWNS, Wilkes-Barre, Pa.
POMPANO PARK, Pompano Beach, Fla.
QUAD CITY DOWNS, East Moline, Ill.
RACEWAY PARK, Toledo, O.
RIDEAU-CARLETON, Ottawa, Ont.
SCIOTO DOWNS, Columbus, O.
SPORTSMAN'S PARK, Cicero, Ill.
WINDSOR RACEWAY, Windsor, Ont.

Half-Mile Tracks

BANGOR RACEWAY, Bangor, Me.
BATAVIA DOWNS, Batavia, N.Y.
BLOOMSBURG FAIR, Bloomsburg, Pa.
BUFFALO RACEWAY, Hamburg, N.Y.
CARLISLE FAIR, Carlisle, Pa.
CHARLOTTETOWN, Charlottetown, P.E.I.
CONNAUGHT PARK, Lucerne, Que.
CUMBERLAND RACEWAY, Cumberland, Me.

DELAWARE FAIR, Delaware, O.
FREDERICTON, Fredericton, N.B.
FREEHOLD RACEWAY, Freehold, N.J.
GREENVILLE FAIR, Greenville, O.
HARRINGTON RACEWAY, Harrington, Del.
HINSDALE RACEWAY, Hinsdale, N.H.
HISTORIC TRACK, Goshen, N.Y.
INVERNESS, Inverness, N.S.
JACKSON RACEWAY, Jackson, Mich.
LEBANON RACEWAY, Lebanon, O.
LEWISTON RACEWAY, Lewiston, Me.
LOUISVILLE DOWNS, Louisville, Ky.
LOWER SACKVILLE, Lower Sackville, N.S.
MAYWOOD PARK, Maywood, Ill.
MIDWEST HARNESS, Henderson, Ky.
MONCTON, Moncton, N.B.
MONTICELLO RACEWAY, Monticello, N.Y.
NORTHFIELD PARK, Northfield, O.
NORTHLANDS PARK, Edmonton, Alta.
NORTHVILLE DOWNS, Northville, Mich.
OCEAN DOWNS, Ocean, Md.
OHIO STATE FAIR, Columbus, O.
RICHELIEU PARK, Montreal, Que.
ROCKINGHAM PARK, Salem, N.H.
ROOSEVELT RACEWAY, Westbury, N.Y.
ROSECROFT RACEWAY, Oxon Hill, Md.
SAINT JOHN'S, St. John's, Nfld.
SARATOGA HARNESS, Saratoga Springs, N.Y.
SCARBOROUGH DOWNS, Scarborough, Me.
SUMMERSIDE, Summerside, P.E.I.
SYDNEY, Sydney, N.S.
TRURO, Truro, N.S.
WESTERN FAIR RACEWAY, London, Ont.
WOODSTOCK, Woodstock, N.B.
YONKERS RACEWAY, Yonkers, N.Y.

2. *Improved Surfaces:* Harness raceways have pioneered in the use of synthetic racing surfaces. The Meadows and Laurel and Windsor Raceways have plastic strips. Roosevelt Raceway uses a rubber one. The artificial surfaces are uniformly fast, regardless of weather. When slightly cushioned with sand, they seem to cause less soreness and lameness than do other kinds of footing. With rare exception, modern raceways have installed advanced drainage systems and fast-drying surfaces, making for fewer reversals of form after a rain.

3. *Segregated paddocks:* Modern raceway design includes a fully enclosed paddock large enough to accommodate every horse on the program. The rules expressly bar the area to anyone not needed there, while keeping all animals in one place, safe from tamperers but visible to the audience.

4. *Prerace testing:* Simple, rapid, harmless blood tests now reveal before the race whether a horse's system contains unlawful medication. Compulsory at Ohio raceways, these tests should become standard everywhere. The conventional post-race urine test should remain in use to discourage malpractice during the interval between the prerace blood sampling and the race itself. The familiar saliva test is of little use and should be abandoned.

5. *Qualifying races:* These purseless engagements are required for horses that break stride too often or that behave badly before or during races or that fail to produce speed up to the local standard or that have been sidelined by illness or injury. At major tracks, no such horse is allowed into a betting race until demonstrating readiness in a qualifier. The "Qua," or "Q," notation in the past-performance record often causes handicapping problems—but not insoluble ones, as we shall see. The chief effect on the qualifying races (where they are properly conducted), is to assure the public that a horse permitted to start in a betting event is fit for competition.

6. *U.S. Trotting Association:* Formed in 1939 after years of chaos in which rival factions had been competing for national control of the sport, the USTA provides big-league continuity and uniformity where cannibalism once reigned. All but a very few raceways are members of the association. The non-members avail themselves of its indispensable services through contracts. The USTA licenses officials, drivers, trainers and owners, and maintains computerized records of all races and all horses. No unregistered, uncertified Standardbred can compete at any USTA track. Wherever a trotter or pacer may travel, he is accompanied by his USTA eligibility certificate, which itemizes his breeding, the names of his owners, his time and earnings records and the details of all his race performances during the current year, plus equal detail on at least six of his races during the previous year.

State regulations governing the conduct of the sport tend to conform with the USTA's own developing standards, but not in all particulars, at all times, in all places. For example, a horseman suspended at one USTA track is unlikely to find work at another, although exceptions occur.

The USTA is dictatorial neither in its powers nor preferences, but it does so well that no serious proposal has been made to decorate harness racing with the kind of "czar" resorted to by other sports. Interestingly, the USTA is the only supervisory body in major professional sport that is not fully controlled by the sport's promoters. Horsemen, owners, breeders and racing officials all are members and all, in accordance with USTA regulation, are duly represented on the board of directors. Each member has one vote, which counts as much as the vote allowed someone who owns stock in a raceway or is employed in raceway management. USTA pronouncements represent a consensus in which raceway management, while understandably influential, is far from dominant. Unlike their counterparts in professional baseball, basketball, football and flat racing, harness-raceway owners cannot cause edicts to be issued in the name of the sport.

One important feature of modern harness racing has been called an innovation, but really is not. The half-mile track has been, furthermore, a sore point among trainers and drivers since the earliest days of country-fair competition. On the other hand, it has always been a source of delight for spectators. Because the length of a track can be a problem for handicappers, the time has come for us to examine the half-miler, and then the ⅝-mile and mile tracks.

The Half-Milers

Before the pari-mutuel era, championships were decided on one-mile tracks. Horsemen acknowledged their long stretches and gradual turns as supreme tests of Standardbred speed and heart. Racing luck was a minimal factor. Wherever else trotters and pacers might have competed during the season, their moments of ultimate truth occurred in classic confrontations on mile-long ovals at Lexington, Ky.; Indianapolis, Ind.; Springfield, Ill.; and Goshen and Syracuse, N.Y.

Then as now, the title of "champion" had two meanings. For practical purposes, a harness-racing champion has always been the horse that went out and whipped the best of its age and gait, winning lots of purse money. But in the record books and other communications of the sport, "champion" also designates the animal that travels the fastest mile of the year for its age, gait and sex. A "world champion" is one that sets an all-time speed record. Moreover, seasonal and world championships are recorded for each age and sex and for trips at distances other than a mile, and for performances at various distances on half-mile, ⅝-mile and mile tracks. Literally dozens of speed champions are crowned each year, some for records set not in actual races but in time trials.

Timed speed is more than the stuff of which record books are compounded and championships confected. It is the essence of harness racing. It is the sport's fundamental measure. It is the main standard whereby horsemen identify potentially valuable breeding stock. Because the most impressive times are achieved and competition is fairest in trips that involve only two turns, the one-mile tracks retain an exalted place in the sport.

Classic trotting races like the Hambletonian and the Kentucky Futurity are still held at one-mile tracks, although competition for enormous purses at half-mile and ⅝-mile raceways invariably affects the national rankings. In pacing, the shift of championship emphasis to shorter tracks is even more noticeable, although the enormously lucrative Meadowlands Pace and Woodrow Wilson Pace are raced at the one-mile track in New Jersey.

Among the hundreds of racing strips at country fairgrounds, half-milers have always been overwhelmingly numerous. Few fair associations could afford to construct and maintain the mile tracks required for nationally significant competition. Half-milers occupied less real estate and were more practical for all but the largest fairs. Good horses often raced at those half-milers, but not usually when important issues were at stake.

The epochal success of Roosevelt Raceway demonstrated that urban audiences did not consider a half-mile track inferior. Indeed, it is suggested with vehemence that Roosevelt's success was due substantially to the pell-mell excitement of races that begin directly in front of the stands and end there after the horses have scrambled around four hairpin turns. When Yonkers Raceway was erected on the site of the old Empire City course, what had been a mile track was converted into a half-miler and became more lucrative than Roosevelt. This, plus the economics of raceway construction, encouraged most other operators to build half-milers during the sport's period of rapid expansion.

With agreement that verges on unanimity, horsemen point out that the

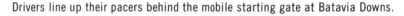

Drivers line up their pacers behind the mobile starting gate at Batavia Downs.

best horse is less likely to prevail on a half-miler than on a longer track. Where races involve four turns and the stretches are short, luck and post position play unnaturally important roles, they say. They add that powerful, long-striding Standardbreds are at serious disadvantages on the tight bends. And that horses of all kinds tend to break down under the strain. And that it's a crying shame when an animal with the great heart needed for a real stretch drive loses to nimbler horses that can skip around the turns at a half-miler and need no stretch kick because there's no stretch worth mentioning. And so on.

To all such complaints, the standard answer long has been that half-mile tracks are ideal for the spectator, who pays the bills. He can see everything. The horses pass before him three times—at the start, halfway and at the finish. And competition is keen. The short straightaways force the drivers to stay as close to the pace-setter as they can. Knowing that large amounts of lost ground seldom are recoverable in the short home-stretch, they hustle for the early lead and keep hustling for position throughout. This makes for an exciting spectacle.

What excites the spectator, however, may depress the handicapper. Horses get in each other's way more frequently at half-mile tracks. Regardless of whether the drivers use unfair tactics, the contours of the oval guarantee jams. Moreover, a horse with the slightest tendency to grab a knee with a hoof is going to do it sooner or later on one of those turns and lose a race he figured to win.

Fortunately, there is more to the question of the half-mile track than one might think after reading the foregoing review of conventional pros and cons. In harness racing, as in all other earthly pursuits, man and animal tend to adapt to the challenges of environment. A striking example of such adaptation occurred in 1950, when a 23-year-old named Stanley Dancer invaded Yonkers, won everything in sight and began what has amounted to a revolution in the racing and training of Standardbreds, not only at half-milers but everywhere else.

As implied earlier, good horses used to be educated for the competition at mile tracks. In those races, the first three-quarters of the mile were merely prelude, the all-out racing coming in the final quarter. At the start, the drivers would find positions on the rail and then would travel Indian file until the home turn, where the action began. Although these tactics were impracticable at half-mile tracks, the tendency of drivers was to modify them but slightly, reserving as much horse for the final drive as the competition would permit. And then along came Dancer.

He trained his horses to leave quickly and go as far as they could, as fast as they could. He won race after race this way, his horses often finishing on their hands and knees but with insurmountable leads. He won so often that the only recourse for other drivers was to leave with him, fight him for the lead, make him earn his way. In the process, they had to leg up their own horses for that kind of racing. The spectacle at half-mile tracks became more spectacular than ever.

Curiously, a kind of equilibrium set in. With the development and establishment of sprinting tactics especially suited to half-mile tracks, it became evident that certain horses and a small minority of drivers could sustain such tactics, whereas others could not. In light of this fact, successful handicapping became possible.

Dancer's great rival in the topmost echelon of Standardbred racing is Billy Haughton, who says, "For a horse to do any real good in New York he has to be able to rough it for five-eighths of a mile on the outside. This is a fact of life and you have to learn to live with it."

Another fact of life at half-mile tracks is that the horse may be able to rough it but may be a poor betting risk unless his driver is a certified topnotcher. The barns at Yonkers and Roosevelt are full of horses that can rough it when in shape. But relatively few drivers can be relied on to make best use of that ability in the helter-skelter of the race.

The handicapper and his onrushing competitor, the would-be handicapper, are urged to consider the following fundamental truths about half-mile tracks:

1. The short stretches and the four sharp turns enlarge the problem of racing luck. But the best drivers have the best luck.

2. Post position is important. Horses with the five inside holes enjoy pronounced advantages. If the horse marooned in position 7 or 8 is not considerably faster and fitter than any of its rivals, the handicapper prefers an animal with an inside spot.

3. Yet the talents of the driver often are more significant than the advantages of post position. As we shall see, the top driver who leaves from berth 7 or 8 is a better bet than the lesser driver who tries to navigate an equally fit horse from an inside spot in the same race.

4. If a horse has been racing at mile and ⅝-mile tracks without displaying early speed, it may be at a severe disadvantage in its first race or two at a half-miler, where slow leavers suffer.

5. A horse is seldom worth attention at a half-miler unless its record suggests readiness to rough it on the outside without perishing in the stretch. Or—and this amounts to the same thing—the horse should seem ready to produce enough early speed to stay out of trouble all the way, while reserving some wallop for the finish.

The ⅝-Milers

Recognizing the costs of constructing and maintaining a mile track, leading horsemen advocate the ⅝-miler as a fitting compromise. On a strip of this length, the traditional mile race involves only three turns, each of which is less precipitous than those at a half-mile track. Furthermore, the stretches are long enough to permit a strong horse to overtake a tiring leader in the final strides, which means that a wide range of racing tactics is possible. The driver more often can design the tactics to suit the horse and its opposition, rather than employ the sometimes unsuitable tactics dictated by the tighter contours of half-mile tracks.

As if additional elbow room and fewer problems of racing luck were not sufficient, drivers and trainers declare that horses remain sounder on ⅝-mile tracks. Also, animals with a tendency to knock knees do perfectly well on these slightly longer ovals, but encounter bad trouble on the turns at half-milers.

Although the mutuel handles and purses at Yonkers and Roosevelt are second only to those at The Meadowlands, these great half-mile operations have stiff competition for top racing stock and first-rate drivers and trainers. The top ⅝-mile track, Sportsman's Park, and the mile track at Hollywood Park offer purses that compare favorably with New York's —especially in the bread-and-butter races that predominate on any track's nightly program. It is argued, furthermore, that a fleet, reasonably sound animal of average quality can make more money on a ⅝-mile or mile track because it holds its form for longer periods.

In the mid-1950s, when Roosevelt Raceway was about to renovate, eminent horsemen tried to persuade George Morton Levy and his associates that conversion to a ⅝-mile oval would benefit one and all. Levy doubted it, but agreed to investigate. The only ⅝-mile track with a race meeting in progress at the time was Hazel Park, near Detroit. Levy and his party arrived there on a night so wet, dark and foul that it would have made the Taj Mahal look bad. And Hazel Park is not the Taj Mahal. To put it mildly, Levy was unimpressed. What really finished the idea, however, was not the weather. The death blow was the remoteness of the starting line.

At a ⅝-mile track, the traditional mile race begins on the backstretch at the five-eighths pole, three-eighths of a mile from the finish line. The horses pass directly in front of the stands only twice. Those who favor half-mile tracks regard the backstretch start as a serious drawback. They believe that fans accustomed to the excitement of seeing races start under their noses would not take kindly to the other plan. In response to the observation that most Thoroughbred races start out of sight of any customer who lacks binoculars, and that the running-horse industry is not exactly on the rocks, the adherents of half-mile tracks declare that the flats would be better off if their races began in front of the stands.

The sincerity of these views is absolutely beyond question. Managements of half-mile tracks truly believe that their patrons would dislike

⅝-mile racing, even though such racing may involve fewer upsets of form. Indeed, if the belief were not genuine, these managements might be attracted to certain other advantages of the ⅝-mile design. For one thing, Sportsman's Park can accommodate nine-horse fields, without requiring the ninth horse to start from a second tier on the rail. This extra entry means additional differences of betting opinion, helpful to the mutuel handle.

Even more helpful to trade at the windows is the fact that a horse that leaves from post position 7 at Sportsman's Park is at no great disadvantage. But at most half-milers, anything further from the rail than post 5 is in a poor situation. In fact, at certain half-milers, the four inside posts are overwhelmingly favorable. Where fields of seven and eight horses are customary, but three or four of the starters are handicapped by their post positions, competition is less keen than it might be, and betting must reflect it.

Although half-milers outnumber other pari-mutuel raceways, it is interesting to note that only two of the short ovals—the mighty Yonkers and Roosevelt—consistently offer programs of top quality. A third big-league half-miler, Brandywine, converted to a ⅝-mile strip during 1969.

If you are content with your own raceway and have no intention of traveling elsewhere to try your skill at tracks of other dimensions, these matters may not inflame your interest. But they are important to an understanding of the sport and, above all, they involve issues vital to handicapping.

At this stage of our discussion, the handicapper should keep the following facts in mind about ⅝-mile tracks:

1. Their longer stretches and fewer, more gradual turns mean winning opportunities for horses capable of stout finishes. Animals with high early speed can still win, but are less likely to back into first money than at tracks where the homestretchers are shorter.

2. As at half-milers, the driver is more important than the post position. Top drivers win more than their share of races.

3. A horse that has done well at one-mile tracks while showing good early foot is seldom at a disadvantage on a ⅝-mile track.

4. A horse that has been showing insufficient early speed but some finishing courage at half-mile tracks may improve by several lengths on a ⅝-mile track.

5. A speed horse unable to withstand challenge at half-mile tracks should be watched—but not bet on—in its first starts at a ⅝-mile track. It may lack the necessary heart and stamina. But on the other hand, the tighter turns at the half-miler may have been its only problems and it may race well on the longer oval.

The One-Milers

At a mile track, the race begins in front of the stands and ends there after the horses travel the course once. Times are fastest, interference least likely, form most reliable. There was no mystery about the overnight success of The Meadowlands, a one-miler built with state help on the New Jersey side of the Hudson River, only minutes from New York, heartland of the half-miler movement. Fans long accustomed to the tight turns of the Yonkers and Roosevelt twice-arounds had no difficulty adapting to the longer racing strip and the dependable form provided there. This helped the new track become the sport's leader in one season. Credit also is due to The Meadowlands' pleasant customer accommodations and sound promotional policies, and the management's insistence that drivers race all the way and avoid the Indian-file processions of old-fashioned mile-track racing.

The handicapper should absorb the following facts about racing at one-mile tracks:

1. Unless a horse has demonstrated its readiness to produce speed in the homestretch, it probably is not worth a bet.
2. Although these tracks surpass all others as fair tests of equine quality and fitness, with interference and luck at irreducible minimums, the top driver is still a pronounced asset. If he has the best horse, so much the better. But he need not have the best horse to outmaneuver a less resourceful driver.

The Grand Circuit

As drivers, Billy Haughton, Del Insko and George Sholty each win over $1 million in purses during an average year. As owners and trainers, they account for much more than that. To compete for every available major prize, powerful stables maintain separate divisions on two or more racing circuits at a time. Haughton commutes from New York to New Jersey to Liberty Bell or Brandywine or Chicago or California. Insko favors New York and Chicago–California. Sholty races all over the East from a base in Ohio. Herve Filion and his brothers race in New York, New Jersey, Liberty Bell–Brandywine and Canada. If the boss is driving his horses at Track "A," assistants take the reins at "B" and "C." And at the height of the season, the big stables have divisions on the Grand Circuit, the most lucrative barnstorming operation in American sport.

The Roarin' Grand, as it is called, was organized in 1873, to provide a continuous schedule of suitably rich purses for the leading stables of the time. In short order, Grand Circuit Week became the most exciting period of the year for any track able to get on the schedule. Almost a century later, interest remains high. The Hambletonian is the highlight of Grand Circuit Week at the Du Quoin, Illinois Fair. The Little Brown Jug climaxes the week at the Delaware, Ohio, Fair.

With millions of dollars in purses added to prestige beyond price, the Grand Circuit makes all the shuttling back and forth highly worthwhile for Haughton, Dancer, Insko, Joe O'Brien, Sholty, Filion, Glen Garnsey, Howard Beissinger and other handlers of first-class stock. In the bargain, these drivers and their prize animals bring to tracks like Wolverine Raceway, Saratoga, Buffalo, Blue Bonnets, The Meadows and Greenwood a quality of competition far more distinguished than can be found in those places during other phases of the season. By imparting a big-league atmosphere, the Grand Circuit heightens interest in the sport and, in a real sense, upgrades the standing of many tracks that might otherwise be written off as minor.

Just when everything is neatly in place, history can be depended on to supply unforeseen complications. The future of the Grand Circuit is by no means as secure as its record might suggest. The annual tour now has stern competition from various state and provincial programs that use government funds to fatten the purses offered in certain races. Years ago, breeding interests persuaded several legislatures to divert substantial portions of government mutuel receipts into so-called sire-stake programs for the lofty purpose of encouraging state or provincial animal husbandry. That is, the legislature actually relinquishes part of the government's share of mutuel revenues, allowing the money to inflate the purses awarded to winners of races among animals bred in the legislature's jurisdiction. Moreover, the winner's breeder collects a bonus, too. Millions of dollars are involved. Over the years, some awful horses have captured some enormous purses in these amazingly liberal government programs. And the stated purposes have been served. For example, enterprising breeders have upgraded the industry in some states, like New York, and are sure to accomplish the same in others, like New Jersey. The financial incentives are enormous.

Each week of each touring season, therefore, luminaries of the Grand Circuit must decide whether to go to the expense of shipping a horse to the tour stop for a $60,000 purse or to let it race in its own territory against softer competition for more money in a sire stake. The state and provincial programs can only get larger. During the 1980s, the Grand Circuit will surely continue to provide some of the sport's greatest moments, but the conflict with sire-stake programs will increase. Meanwhile, it is noteworthy that the richest horse race in the history of racing was a Grand Circuit event at The Meadowlands—the Woodrow Wilson Memorial Pace of 1979. Purse: $862,750.

Right Way, Wrong Way

No matter how early you arrive at the track, horses will be jogging, pacing and trotting around it, some moving counterclockwise as in a race, others going in the opposite direction. If you have done your handicapping in advance and know which animals on the program are the likeliest candidates for your support, you might want to keep an eye out for them during the warm-ups. I say "might," but I mean "should." It is possible to handicap quite well without looking at the horses, but the percentage of success increases for someone who bets on animals that behave like winners before they race.

An inexperienced racegoer can make evaluations of that kind. The techniques are explained in this book's chapter on warm-ups. But the newcomer must first become accustomed to the bewildering comings and goings on the track. The first step is to identify the horses. The second is to recognize what they are doing.

At some tracks, the color of the horse's saddle cloth identifies the number of the race in which he is entered. The number on the cloth is his program number. At other tracks, the cloth bears a large number (his program number) and a small number (the number of his race). The color of the cloth designates his post position. At still other tracks, the horses wear numbered tags on their heads. Again, color and number identify the animal and race. The printed program explains the various color and number codes, which may also be described on a board posted in the infield.

How things look as you move out of the paddock for the final warm-ups at The Meadows, in Meadowlands, Pa.

Customarily, the horses take their first warm-ups about two hours before they race, jogging a mile or two or three "the wrong way of the track" (clockwise) and then turning for a moderate workout "the right way of the track," after which they turn again and jog to the paddock to be washed, cooled and rested. An hour later they return outdoors for another jog and a stiffer workout, and then back to the paddock to cool down. After the post parade come two "scores," which are final warm-up dashes of perhaps a quarter-mile each, the right way of the track. Whether jogging, warming up or scoring, and whether moving the right or wrong way of the track, every horse is in the process of cranking up for its race. It is fun to evaluate a horse's appearance and behavior, especially when the effort is repaid at the windows.

Seats and Eats

The people least likely to know what is happening in a race are those who cluster along the rail. Everyone should do that occasionally, to hear the rattling hooves and see the flying clods and sense the competitive tension and listen to bettors berating drivers. But the place to be is high up. As high as possible, for the sharpest, clearest view of the entire track.

The clubhouse dining room is usually the best place to sit. It is high, and it is athwart the finish line. The highest of its tables are, unfortunately, the farthest removed from the track, but compromises are possible. Make advance reservations. Specify a table that is close to the finish line and from which the entire racing strip can be seen while seated. Get to the track early. If the table is not as specified, refuse to accept it. If the maître d' responds unpleasantly, offering another table that turns out to be worse, you are dealing with a bandit. Bribe him, if you feel like it, and you may get a proper table. Next time, do not make reservations in the usual way. Instead, write a letter to the president of the track (whose name will be in the program), describe your disagreeable experience with the restaurant people, name the date you want to return and ask if the track management can't arrange civilized treatment for you.

Now that track managements are annoyed and restaurant concessionaires infuriated from coast to coast, I'd like to go a step further. The truth is that I have experienced sublime courtesy and splendid meals in numerous racetrack restaurants, but seldom unless I was accompanied by the president of the track and/or the public relations director and/or the racing secretary and/or a leading horseman. I do not count the times I bought courtesy giving large tips before they had been earned. The pleasure of watching races while dining at a good table is so considerable that it is worth struggling for. I now have told you how to do it.

If you prefer to eat at home, or in some other setting less expensive than the track restaurant, you might want a reserved seat. At most tracks, unreserved seats are poorly situated and few in number. Except at extremely modern plants in which the clubhouse occupies entire upper levels of the stands on both sides of the finish line, you will notice that the best reserved seats are not in the clubhouse but in the grandstand. Clubhouses usually are located beyond the finish line, whereas grandstands tend to be right on the line, offering seats in that ideal position or a few yards to the left. Since you pay extra for reserved seats, you should investigate the possibilities and prefer a seat on the finish line or slightly to its left. The farther beyond the line you are, the poorer your view of the stretch drive and finish.

Having obtained a roost, you should forthwith determine the location of the mutuel windows and settle on the best route there and back. If you become knowledgeable about mutuel prices, as I hope, you sometimes will want to delay your betting until the final couple of minutes before the race starts. On crowded nights, you leave your seat sooner, because the ticket lines are longer. On any night, the height of foolishness is to bet too soon, yet the height of frustration is to arrive on line too late to bet. A little experience and knowledge of the traffic patterns between seat and windows will make you an expert maneuverer.

The Tote Board

Roosevelt Raceway has the finest totalizator board in the world. It stands out there behind the inside rail just like any other tote board, but it communicates more information. It shows the shifting patterns of wagering in terms of actual mutuel prices, rather than old-fashioned book-

making odds. It also gives the highest and lowest prices each horse could pay for place and show if the race were to take place immediately.

Conventional tote boards show the bookmaking odds for win, and the amounts of money bet on each horse for win, place and show, plus the totals accumulated in the win, place and show pools. Arithmeticians can calculate whether a horse listed at 3 to 1 will pay $8, $8.20, $8.40, $8.60 or $8.80. The ability to do this toward the end of the betting period is a great comfort. If the horse in question has suddenly become popular with the crowd, it might drop from 3 to 1 to 9 to 5. The chances of it doing that at the last minute are slight if the 3 to 1 actually means $8.80. Similarly, the mental wizard can tell what kind of price to expect for place if the horse and another likely contender finish 1 and 2. If everyone were an arithmetician, the Roosevelt tote board would be an ostentatious luxury. As matters stand, it is a great boon and should be imitated everywhere.

Other vital information on the tote board includes late scratches and driver changes, the condition of the racing strip, the time of day and the time at which the next race is scheduled to start. During each race, its elapsed time is displayed on the board, ticking off automatically. As each quarter-mile ends, the official clocking up to that point appears at once, enabling the handicapper to tell whether some driver is setting an unusually fast or slow pace. All these kinds of tote-board data are helpful in handicapping and make the races more fun.

Judge Hanley's Maneuver

After thousands of afternoons and evenings at racetracks of all kinds, I can recall perhaps a half-dozen occasions on which mutuel sellers yelled

Unique tote board at Roosevelt Raceway shows changing odds in terms of actual parimutuel prices, including maximum and minimum price each horse would pay for place and show.

at customers to come back and pick up forgotten change. When getting change while buying a $5 ticket with a $20 bill, I have seldom received the $10 bill before the $5 bill, and have not often been given both at once. Standard procedure is to toss the customer whatever number of small bills is due him as part of his change and, with exquisitely casual timing, withhold the large bill until it becomes evident that he plans to wait for it.

Having been bored by this glorious tradition for many a year, a friend of mine known as Judge Hanley came up with the antidote. He is not really a judge, but is called that because he is full of wisdom, as I am about to demonstrate. When the Judge buys, let us say, a $2 ticket with a $10 bill, and the seller throws him three singles at the instant the ticket emerges from the slot, Judge Hanley's Maneuver begins.

He touches neither the ticket nor the bills. He just lets them lie there. This is highly unusual. Think about it for a second. The typical bettor, full of adrenaline and hope, grabs the ticket as soon as it appears at the mouth of the slot, seizes the singles, realizes that something is absent, looks inquiringly at the seller and gets the missing five. And the untypical bettor is in such haste that he runs away with the ticket and the singles, contributing $5 to the seller.

But Judge Hanley touches nothing. This bewilders the seller.

"Whaddya want?" inquires the seller. "More tickets?"

"No," says Judge Hanley. "I want more money."

The implication enrages the seller, who could not hold a position of trust at the track if his honesty were not world-renowned. Rather than argue the point, delay the line and attract unwelcome attention, he disgorges the extra five. The next time the Judge appears at his window, the seller, having forgotten, may well go through the traditional routine again. Once more, Judge Hanley keeps his hands at his sides, touching neither the mutuel ticket nor the insufficient change. By the third race, at the latest, the seller is completely tamed. If the Judge buys a $2 ticket with a $10 bill, the ticket and three singles have scarcely hit the counter when the five arrives. Then, and not before, Judge Hanley picks up the lot, murmurs his thanks and departs.

I have tried it myself. The results are invigorating. Remember, the key to the Maneuver is to touch nothing. Let the ticket lie there. Let the singles lie there. Remain silent unless spoken to. The Maneuver is useful not only at racetracks but when purchasing tickets at theaters, stadiums and railway and bus terminals. Welcome to the club.

The Jargon

The more comfortable you are, the more you will enjoy yourself. A great aid to comfort at the raceway is to know the terminology of the sport and, rather especially, to avoid exposing oneself as a novice by employing the wrong lingo. Be advised that the unmistakable mark of harness-racing ignorance is to speak of a horse that "ran" a good or bad race. Standardbreds trot or pace. Unless they break stride, they do not run. Although harness horsemen have managed to achieve a state of profitable coexistence with the urban types who have invaded their sport, they turn a thin-lipped purple when they hear the word "run" misused. Indeed, some of them take vengeful pleasure from hornswoggling new owners who say "run" instead of "trot" or "pace." They assume that someone who does *not* say "run" may know a bit about the sport.

A comparable but less widespread offense is the use of the word "rider." Harness horsemen are drivers, not riders, although some of the loudest, most ferocious noises at Chicago, California and New York raceways issue from paying customers who bellow that "the rider run the horse too wide. If he gets a better ride, he wins."

In the final analysis, your sense of belonging increases with the frequency of your visits to the cashier's window. Pending the night when you finally hit five or six winners, and deserve to, you can feel more at home by saying "trot" or "pace" or "race" or "driver." For "front-runner" say "quick-leaver." And understand what the knowledgeable mean by terms like "brush," "score," "hung-out," "covered up," "jump" and "colt."

3 THE ARITHMETIC OF WINNING

HOW DO HUMAN BEINGS make their decisions? Among the legions of scientists who seek answers to that question, my favorites are a group of research psychologists who had the misfortune to read a book of mine called *The Compleat Horseplayer,* in which I describe a fairly cut-and-dried method of picking winners at Thoroughbred tracks. To facilitate their study of handicapping decisions, the psychologists converted the book's written advice into diagrams—thickets of circles and connecting lines in patterns which resembled giant hydrocarbon molecules. After counting all the circles and lines, the scholars advised me that the suggested handicapping procedure involved decisions five times as complex as those made by the average Wall Street securities analyst. And twelve times as complex as those of a neurosurgeon diagnosing a brain tumor.

They were impressed by the complexity. I am not. Handicapping decisions are much less complex than those made by a woman when she selects her clothing for a major social event. Neither she nor anyone else often faces quandaries more elaborate than those that arise when she stares at the contents of her closet. Yet she survives.

Putting it another way, handicapping is complicated, but not forbiddingly so. Unlike neurosurgery and the planning of investment portfolios, handicapping is a game. Its complexity is that of a good game, worth the time and effort of adults. A game (as I keep saying) much like poker, the enormous complexities of which are endlessly stimulating but in no sense burdensome.

The harness-racing handicapper uses his informed experience to find logic in the multitude of facts displayed in the printed program and on the tote board and racing strip. Some of the facts are clear, others obscure.

But each relates to all the others in ways that vary from horse to horse, driver to driver, race to race and night to night. Because the raw materials of handicapping are abundant, changeable and deceptive, the game becomes a highly personal exercise in approximation—closer to an art than to a science. Which is why the predictions and decisions of experts coincide only part of the time.

Handicapping formulas are a dime a dozen, and are no substitute for informed judgment. The best of them, in fact, are not really formulas at all, but procedures for the orderly application of judgment. No matter which method the handicapper adopts, he inevitably places his own stamp on it. Formula or not, he attempts to predict the future by interpreting past events of uncertain character and inexact significance. Yet success at the raceway demands predictions of considerable accuracy.

If certainty about the past is so limited, must not certainty about the future be terribly fragile? How can anyone profit from such confusion?

By dealing in probabilities. Likelihoods. Or, as they say at the track, by working *with* the percentages instead of against them.

Beating the Percentages

It so happens that the old saw "You can beat a race, but you can't beat the races" is quite wrong. It turns reality upside down. The truth is that nobody can be sure of beating an individual race, but lots of people win more than they lose in a season's activity at the track. There is nothing peculiar about this. In any game worth playing, the outcome of any one play is rarely a matter of absolute certainty. But someone who plays well finishes ahead in the long run.

Take poker as an example. No matter how expert the player, nothing short of a royal flush provides certainty of a winning bet. The expert is lucky if he holds one royal flush in forty years of play. In other words, he can't necessarily beat the race. But he is an expert and he makes out fine, losing a little, winning a little more. He beats the game.

Let us suppose that our poker expert competes with six of his peers in a game of jackpots. After he has been at the table with them a few times, he knows a great deal about their courage, wiles and weaknesses. He undoubtedly knows more than any handicapper can know about a field of horses. The usefulness of this knowledge varies from session to session, of course. In poker, last week's tabby is this week's tiger, his mood having modified his style for the time being. A further limitation on the expert's success is that his opponents also are experts and know a great deal about *his* style.

In the end, therefore, the poker expert's main armor against uncertainty is his knowledge of the game itself—more particularly, his knowledge of the percentages that give the game its central character. As long as he is faithful to the laws—the probabilities—embodied in those percentages, he seldom loses. And when he combines knowledge of the probabilities with accurate guesses about the tactics of his opponents, he becomes a big winner.

Allow me to pursue the matter further. By reminding the reader how the percentages are used in poker, I hope to whet his appetite for discussion of the sparser, less familiar, but equally important percentages in harness racing.

A 52-card poker deck contains slightly less than 2.6 million five-card hands. The exact probability of drawing any specific hand is a matter of established mathematical knowledge. So is the probability of improving any hand on the draw. If the expert has a chance to convert his hand into a straight by discarding one card and drawing either a nine or an ace, will he bet the money required for the gamble? It all depends.

He knows that the odds against drawing either an ace or nine are 5 to 1. He may draw the right card and lose the pot to someone who has a flush or a full house. But he will win in the long run on hands of this kind if he respects the percentages of the game. He will win in the long run if he takes the risk *only when the pot is large enough to repay him for it.* If he draws the one card on occasions when the pot pays less than a 5 to 1 gamble should, he eventually must lose. Winning one such hand in every six or seven he plays, he will take in less money than he spends on the losing hands.

Identical principles apply to horseplaying. Certain percentages are as firmly established in racing as in cards, and deserve comparable respect. They occur with astonishing uniformity year after year. They affect the handicapper's choice of horse. They affect the size and frequency of his bets.

What is more, racing is so patterned that a handicapper's own methods are sure to embody percentages of their own. If his procedures are consistent (regardless of whether they are profitable or not), they find winning horses at a rate that fluctuates hardly at all from one year to the next. Likewise, his annual rate of profit or loss on each wagered dollar varies but slightly from year to year. He may encounter long losing streaks and incredible strings of winners, but in the end his handicapping settles at its own percentage level. When he knows this percentage, and the accompanying rate of profit or loss, he is able to judge the efficiency of his methods. He remains uncertain about the outcome of an individual bet, but knows with considerable certainty that, in due course, he can expect to win a predictable minimum percentage of bets, with a predictable minimum profit or loss per invested dollar.

A life insurance company does the same kind of thing on an incomparably larger scale. It hitches its treasury to the laws of probability. It does not have the vaguest idea when you will die. But it knows, within the practical limits of earthly certainty, the percentage of people your age who will die this year, or next, or twelve years from now. It designs its premium rates accordingly. In the long run its ledgers show a predictable percentage of deaths, a predictable percentage of surviving premium-payers, and a predictable rate of profit.

Although good handicappers are faithful to the established percentages of the game, and to the percentages achieved by their own methods, handicapping is not really a mathematical pastime. Some of the best selectors use pencils only to cross out the names of horses they think will lose. Other good handicappers do simple arithmetic, but not much of it. Still others devise rather elaborate arithmetical formulas in an attempt to introduce reassuring order into the hodgepodge of information with which they deal. In harness racing, dominated by the factor of timed speed, formulas of that kind are particularly useful. They require no arithmetical skill beyond the ability to add, subtract, multiply and divide.

Even the numbers contained in this chapter need not be committed to memory. Far more important than the numbers are the conclusions they permit about the nature of the game.

At Yonkers and wherever else people bet on horses, some players get on line before they have made up their minds about the race. They continue to study the form until they find themselves eye-to-eye with the mutuel clerk, whereupon handicapping terminates and money changes hands.

The Magic Number

Anybody who bets $1,000 on horses to win races and emerges from the experience with less than $820 is doing something dreadfully wrong. A $2 bettor who selected horses with a hatpin, or by using numerology, or by consulting tea leaves, would probably lose no more than $180 in a series of 500 bets—an investment of $1,000.

It is, of course, more than theoretically possible to go broke at the track. Desperate gamblers do it every day. And victims of inefficient selection methods or wasteful betting systems also manage to run out of cash long before they should.

The shortest route to disaster is to bet too much of one's money at a time. The man with a $1,000 bankroll who plays it all on one horse has a splendid chance of losing it. The man who bets the $1,000 in five installments of $200 each also risks extinction: In any given series of five bets, no handicapper on earth can be sure of winning so much as one!

How, then, can a less-than-expert player expect to have $820 left after betting $1,000?

The magic number is 18.

Without knowing the slightest thing about horses, and betting entirely at random, the player's long-term losses should not exceed 18 percent of the total amount wagered on horses to win. To limit his losses to that extent, he need only bet in amounts small enough to assure himself of a large, representative number of bets.

It works like this. Of all money bet to win, most tracks deduct approximately 18 percent for taxes and their own revenue. The remaining 82 percent is disbursed to the holders of winning mutuel tickets.

This means that, regardless of how the individual fares with his own bet, the crowd as a whole loses 18 percent of its wagered dollar in the mutuels of every race, every night, every week, every year. A random bettor, playing horses at random, should do no worse. A selection system employing daisy petals or playing cards or dice or anything else entirely unrelated to handicapping should leave the bettor with close to 82 percent of his wagered money after a series of 500 or more bets.

Any handicapping procedure that results in annual losses as high as 18 percent of all money wagered is, therefore, no better than the hatpin method. And anyone who loses more than 18 cents of every dollar he bets in a season is—whether he realizes it or not—going far out of his way to find trouble.

Well, perhaps not so far out of the way. In recent years, money-hungry tracks and state governments have embellished the nightly race programs with gambling opportunities that increase the amounts of money wagered by the average customer. These perfectas (exactas), trifectas (triples), double perfectas and similar propositions produce mutuel payoffs much larger and therefore more attractive than those of conventional bets to win, place or show. Who would not like to collect $100 or $10,000 for a $2 bet? The fact that one must predict the first two or three horses in their exact order of finish is merely a complication. These offers inflame the gambling fever of the multitudes. And many states boost the deductions from exacta betting pools to as much as 19 percent. From trifecta pools the usual levy is a confiscatory 25 percent.

The money deducted from wagering pools by racetracks has been compared unfavorably with the smaller bites imposed by gambling casinos. A roulette player, for example, should lose only slightly more than a nickel of each dollar he bets, whereas the poor trifecta enthusiast can expect to lose not less than 25 cents from every dollar bet. But the difference is more apparent than real. It is a matter of frequency. The roulette wheel spins every few seconds, all night. The roulette fanatic makes hundreds of plays in one session. No matter how conservatively he may bet, the house "take" of 5 percent nibbles away at the original capital until none is left.

The horseplayer encounters only nine or ten races a night. If willing to wager only on horses to win, avoiding perfectas and trifectas like the hazards that they are, the player who wagers the smallest possible percentage of betting capital might play for months or years before emptying the pocket. For example, someone who allocates $500 to the entertainment of raceway betting and bets $2 on one hoped-for winner in every race should have about $413 left after 28 visits to the track. He might have much more or much less, but the track "take" *should* siphon off only $91 or so from the 252 bets he makes. If he knows absolutely nothing about horses and makes no attempt to learn, his betting to win will probably not hurt much more severely than that.

It follows that anything useful learned about racing should enable a player to begin lowering the percentage of loss. In this chapter we shall see that a mere awareness of the game's probabilities helps to reduce loss —even before the racegoer has begun to become acquainted with the ways of horses and their drivers!

Betting on Favorites

An infallible guide to the reliability or intelligence, or both, of a racing expert is his attitude toward persons who bet on favorites. All experts know that, in a representative series of harness races, about one in every three will be won by the betting favorite—the horse on which the crowd bets the most money. The conclusions various writers achieve in light of this statistic are a dead giveaway to their knowledge of probability. Anyone ignorant of probability is unable to evaluate his own chances at the track and is hopelessly unqualified to advise anyone else.

It is fashionable to sneer at "chalk players" and "bridge jumpers"— the conservative types who play nothing but favorites. Observing that favorites win approximately a third of the time, many sages proclaim, with flawless arithmetic, that the crowd is wrong two-thirds of the time. They insist that the secret of success at the track is to part company with the crowd, avoid favorites and, presumably, begin winning a lion's share of the two races in three which find the crowd wrong. Such advice is crude nonsense. Whatever truth it contains is strictly coincidental.

Any child will understand this after a few facts are presented. At major raceways, the usual race involves eight or nine horses. This means that about 80 horses perform on a representative evening. The crowd picks nine of these animals as betting favorites. Typically, about three of the nine win. Anyone who thinks it easier to find winners among 71 non-favorites than among nine favorites is thinking backward.

The fact that non-favorites win almost two-thirds of all races does not mean that non-favorites have twice as good a chance to win as favorites do. Quite the contrary. Until we handicap the entire field and see which horse is the likeliest of the lot (a task few players can perform), we know nothing about the non-favorite except that it is one of seven or eight non-favorites in its race. But we know more than that about the favorite. Without doing any handicapping, we know that the statistical expectation of victory by the favorite is one in three, which is convertible into odds of 2 to 1. But the statistical expectation of victory by a non-favorite in a nine-horse race is one in twelve—odds of 11 to 1! These figures are obtained by dividing the fraction of races that non-favorites win (⅔) by the number of non-favorites in the race (8).

We now have established that it is foolish to reject a horse simply because it is the favorite, or to stab at another horse simply because it is not. We therefore are in a better position to appreciate some interesting statistics.

During 1968, raceways sent the official result charts of 40,628 harness races to the recordkeepers at the USTA. The USTA computer told me that favorites won 36.1 percent of those races, at average odds of slightly more than 7 to 5. A flat bet on each of the favorites would have cost a player 12.3 cents per wagered dollar. That is, if someone visited twenty random raceways for as many evenings of entertainment and bet $2 on the favorite in each of 180 races, the predictable loss would have been $44.28—or $2.21 per outing.

I doubt that the picture has changed substantially during the 1970s. For one thing, trotting races are less numerous now than they were in 1968, meaning that pacing races are more numerous and, therefore, that fewer betting favorites break stride in the heat of battle. The North American percentage of winning favorites remains at 36.5 or thereabouts in an average year. Increased track and governmental deductions from mutuel pools have probably lowered the average mutuel price on winning favorites from 7 to 5 to 6 to 5. The 1980 customer who bets $2 on every favorite probably loses about $2.50 a night.

It should be apparent that someone who abandons uncritical wagering on all favorites, limiting activity to bets on especially deserving favorites, should reduce the percentage of loss. Indeed, a decent handicapper can win money at leading tracks by betting only on favored pacers, abstaining unless the individual favorite has an outstanding driver, an advantageous post position and is favored by a comfortable margin.

This last point is important for several reasons, not the least of which is the difficulty of identifying the favorites in some races until after the races are over. If you study chart books published by the program departments at leading tracks (a useful study, by the way), you will have no trouble "showing" that a flat bet on certain kinds of favorites would have made you a fortune. Beware. All too often, the favorite reported in the chart was not the favorite two or three minutes before post time. Sometimes the issue is unresolved until the final flash, when it is too late to get on line and make a bet. Where two or more horses are that closely matched, the would-be player of favorites should abstain. Not only is he likely to bet on a horse that winds up as second or third choice in the betting, but also he is likely to bet on a horse whose chances are not quite as bright as a favorite's should be. To avoid this, it is best to delay betting until the last possible moment, and to return to one's seat without a ticket if the favorite is not clearly established at that time. Considering the frequency with which insiders and other heavy bettors at leading tracks alter the odds pattern during the final seconds before the betting windows close, the average racegoer cannot be sure that a horse is the favorite unless its odds are much the lowest in the field three minutes before the race starts. To illustrate, if the animal is odds-on at 4 to 5 in an eight-horse field, nothing else should be listed at less than 8 to 5. If the horse is at even money, the second choice should be at least 9 to 5. If the horse is posted at 6 to 5, the second choice should be at least 2 to 1. And so on.

In checking result charts to see how one or another method of betting on solid favorites would have fared, the reader should be scrupulous about tossing out all races in which the odds reported for the second choice were close to those on the favorite. Chances are excellent that someone trying to apply a chalk-playing method would have put his money on that second choice often enough to throw the system entirely out of kilter. A winning 5 to 2 favorite may have dropped from 4 to 1 on the very last flash of the tote board. Obviously, the horse was favored by relatively few bettors, whose enormous late wagers more than offset the $2 and $5 contributions of the crowd at large. For a horse to drop from 4 to 1 to 5 to 2, bypassing 7 to 2 and 3 to 1, is not at all unusual in the last two or three minutes of betting at many tracks. So be guided accordingly in all your thinking about favorites.

The Tote Board and the Price

This table shows the mutuel prices represented by the figures posted on racetrack odds boards. Horses posted at 4 to 5 or higher may pay more than the minimum mutuel price, but they never pay less. The computations are revised at frequent intervals until post time.

Odds	Price	Odds	Price	Odds	Price
1–9	$2.20	2–1	$6.00	18–1	$38.00
1–8	2.20	5–2	7.00	19–1	40.00
1–7	2.20	3–1	8.00	20–1	42.00
1–6	2.20	7–2	9.00	21–1	44.00
1–5	2.40	4–1	10.00	22–1	46.00
1–4	2.40	9–2	11.00	23–1	48.00
1–3	2.60	5–1	12.00	24–1	50.00
2–5	2.80	6–1	14.00	25–1	52.00
1–2	3.00	7–1	16.00	30–1	62.00
3–5	3.20	8–1	18.00	35–1	72.00
3–4	3.40	9–1	20.00	40–1	82.00
4–5	3.60	10–1	22.00	45–1	92.00
1–1	4.00	11–1	24.00	50–1	102.00
6–5	4.40	12–1	26.00	60–1	122.00
7–5	4.80	13–1	28.00	75–1	152.00
3–2	5.00	14–1	30.00	99–1	200.00
8–5	5.20	15–1	32.00		
9–5	5.60	16–1	34.00		
		17–1	36.00		

Another aspect of betting on favorites seldom gets attention in print, except from oracles who manage to get the facts backward. I refer to the concept of ''short price.'' To say that even money is a ''short price'' and that much more profit is to be made by betting on horses at 4 to 1 is to recite gibberish. In the first place, a winning bet at even money returns the bettor a profit of 100 percent. Second, almost half of all horses that go at even money win their races. Someone who bet on all of them would lose about 4 cents per wagered dollar, year after year. But horses that go at 4 to 1 are riskier. About 14 percent of them win, yielding a net loss in the vicinity of 16 cents on the wagered dollar.

Obviously, one would not—or should not—bet on a horse just because its price is short. But if one is "looking for a good price" and is not a real handicapper, the best available price is even money or thereabouts, because the long-term losses are negligible. And stabbing at horses with higher odds is financially ruinous. The few studies that have been made of pari-mutuel patterns prove beyond doubt that horses held at low odds win higher percentages of their races than do horses that go at higher odds. In fact, horses at 2 to 1 win a higher percentage of their races than horses at 3 to 1. And horses at 6 to 1 win a higher percentage than horses at 7 to 1. And so forth. It all graphs out. The lower the odds, the higher the statistical likelihood of victory.

I sound very much like an incurable bridge jumper, but I am not. My goal at the moment is to nullify the effects of all the nonsense that is spoken and written about short-priced horses, so that the reader will approach his own handicapping with a firmer understanding of the mathematics of the game. When he becomes a good selector, he will pick favorites and non-favorites—not because of their odds but because of their records as sharp animals, fit to win in the particular circumstances that confront them.

Attainable Profits

Regardless of the individual's handicapping style, the percentages of the game govern his results. The more often he bets on longshots, the fewer tickets he cashes. And the more often he bets on low-priced horses, the more often he wins. But his rate of profit—the only meaningful index to his success—depends on whether he wins frequently enough or at odds high enough to compensate for his losses.

It has long been taken for granted in racing that a first-class handicapper can win about four bets in ten if he is extremely conservative, bets on relatively few races and inclines toward horses whose odds average about 2 to 1. Such play yields a profit of about 20 cents for every wagered dollar, increasing the handicapper's capital at a tremendous rate. For example, if he starts with $2,000 and makes an average of two $100 bets a night for 200 racing nights (spread over a period of years, perhaps), his operations return a profit of $8,000, enlarging his capital to $10,000.

Players of such accomplishment are more numerous at running tracks (where handicapping is relatively intricate) than at harness raceways (where handicapping is relatively simple). There is nothing paradoxical about this. A shrewd handicapper of Thoroughbreds can pick his spots, avoiding races in which factors like distance, weight, class and current form resist firm analysis. But the handicapper of Standardbreds often is confronted with a program of nine pacing races, each at a mile, and each with three or four logical contenders whose adequate class and superior form are clearly evident. It sometimes becomes extremely difficult, even unrealistic, to decide that one such race is more suitable for betting than another. Accordingly, the good handicapper is likely to find himself betting on six or seven races a night, a level of activity that seldom pays off at running tracks, and is no guarantee of profits at raceways, either.

If he bears in mind some of the mutuel statistics discussed earlier, the handicapper may derive some bright ideas from the following:

To earn a profit of 20 cents on the wagered dollar, a handicapper must:

1. Win half of his bets, at average odds not lower than 7 to 5, or
2. Win 40 percent of his bets, at average odds of 2 to 1, or
3. Win a third of his bets, at average odds of 13 to 5, or
4. Win 30 percent of his bets, at average odds of 3 to 1.

Anyone who hopes to do twice that well, earning profits at the rate of 40 cents on the wagered dollar, must:

1. Win half of his bets, at average odds of 9 to 5, or
2. Win 40 percent of his bets, at average odds of 5 to 2, or
3. Win a third of his bets, at average odds of more than 3 to 1, or
4. Win 30 percent of his bets, at average odds exceeding 7 to 2.

Any of the formulas on those two lists is theoretically attainable at a raceway. But the practicalities of the game, and of human self-control, suggest that the handicapper deserves a medal if he can achieve results in the neighborhood of items 2 and 3 on the first of the lists. If he does that well, he will be able to buy his own medal.

Beware the Law of Averages

Statisticians and others acquainted with the laws of probability try, wherever possible, to measure situations in precise terms. They know that averages are misleading. The classic example is a man who needs to cross a river. Being six feet tall, and having learned that the average depth of the river is only five feet, he starts to wade across. In midstream he sinks like a stone and drowns. A river with an average depth of five feet may be 12 feet deep at midstream.

Or take the following series of numbers: 1, 2, 3, 4, 5, 6, 7, 8, 9, 75. The average of those numbers is 12. But, if the numbers represent the results of something or other—like the odds paid by a series of winning bets—the average distorts reality. Nine of the ten horses ran at odds of 9 or less, yet the striker of averages struts around under the delusion that he can expect an average return of about 12 from his next series of ten winners. Unless the horse that returned 75—and threw the average out of whack—was a normal, predictable, usual selection, a statistician would prefer to say that the *median* of the series was between 5 and 6. In other words, he would look for the point that falls midway in the series. Five of the numbers in this particular series were 6 or more. The other five were 5 or less. The median is, therefore, around 5.5. Which ain't 12.

In the handicapping of Standardbreds it is essential to remember the illusory character of averages. For an extreme example, the player sometimes notices that a horse has won over $200,000 in 40 starts—an average of about $5,000 per race. To decide that the horse is the class of its race because it has the highest average earnings might be a serious mistake. It might have won most of its money last year, in so-called sire-stake competition, which offers high purses to animals bred in the particular state. The horse might never have won a race against the tougher stock it encountered in less lucrative events. Another horse in tonight's race, with average earnings of only $3,000, might have an enormous edge in class and condition.

Knowing that averages can never be more than rough yardsticks, the good handicapper looks beyond them. Above all, he pays no heed whatever to the racetrack superstition known as "the law of averages."

Example: If favorites win slightly more than one of every three races, and nine races in succession have been won by non-favorites, it is incorrect to suppose that the favorite in the tenth race has a better than ordinary chance to win. The favorite is *not* "due." Aside from what the handicapper may think of the animal's quality, which is quite another matter, its status as favorite tells only one thing about its chances. That one thing is a generality: In the long run, favorites win about one race out of three.

The long run is sometimes very long. Persons who base their play on the inevitability of victory by favorites sometimes increase the amount of their bets after every loss. They lose more than they should. In fact, if they go the route of doubling the bet after each loss, they end in ruin.

It is not unusual for ten consecutive favorites to lose. The man who bets $2 on a favorite loses it, bets $4 on the next, and $8 on the next and continues to double up in hope that the favorite is "due," will have parted with $1,022 after nine successive losses. His system will require a bet of $1,024 on the next race. If he has that much money and the courage to risk it, the bet positively will lower the odds on the favorite. If the horse wins, which is by no means inevitable, and pays as much as even money, which is problematical, the bettor emerges with a profit of $2 on an investment of $2,046.

The law of averages is equally unreliable in connection with the performances of drivers. The driver does not live who does not suffer intermittent losing streaks. Thirty or forty losses in succession are neither excessive nor unusual. A betting system based on the concept that some highly rated driver is "due" is a betting system sure to fail. Unless the player's capital and endurance are unlimited.

Similarly, the handicapper's knowledge that his selections win almost twice in every five attempts is poor grounds for an assumption that seven losses in a row will probably be followed by an immediate winner. Or that seven winners in a row make the next selection a likely loser.

Unawareness of probability causes severe harm at every raceway, every night. After a longshot wins, a disappointed player consults his program and discovers that the horse was driven and trained by its owner. No other horse in the race had been owned, driven and trained by one man. Eureka! A new system! If the horse is the only one in its race that is driven and trained by its owner, and if it has had a race in ten days, and if its last race was at this track, and if, and if, and if! The player now loses eight bets in succession on owner-driven horses.

I am trying to emphasize that one cannot determine probabilities without a large, representative series of cases. One robin does not make a spring. And, even after the probabilities have been determined, they remain nothing but probabilities. In no way do they guarantee the outcome of a single isolated event. Nor do they guarantee the outcome of a short series of events. The feeblest handicapper enjoys winning nights and winning weeks. The only inevitability in his situation is that he will end as a heavy loser if he persists in his usual methods. And the best handicapper suffers losing nights and losing weeks, but recovers the ground if he continues to play in his usual, sensible style.

As I have insisted before, and as may now seem more agreeable, you can't necessarily beat a race, but you may be able to beat the races. To do so, you will have to overcome the unfavorable percentages of the game. You will have to develop a style of play in which (1) your handicapping knowledge reveals animals with especially good chances and (2) the long-term returns on your winnings are more than sufficient to repair your long-term losses.

The House Percentage

In poker, the odds are 4 to 1 against filling a flush by drawing one card. Unless the pot contains at least four times as much money as he must pay for the one card, the good poker player drops out.

Suppose that the owner of the card table were charging the players 20 cents for every dollar in every pot, deducting that percentage before each payoff. The odds against filling a four-flush would remain 4 to 1, but the player no longer would be able to break even on such gambles unless the pot contained at least five times as much money as he paid for his fifth card.

Chances are that the player would quit the game. Or, if it were the only game in town, he would revise his methods. He would play more conservatively, incurring fewer risks. Where winning probabilities decrease, losses become more costly, more difficult to overcome.

This is exactly what has happened in horse racing. The "house"—a partnership of raceway management and the state treasury—cuts every pari-mutuel pool with a cleaver, lowering the payoff prices and making profitable handicapping much more difficult than it might be if the house percentage were lower.

The principle of pari-mutuel betting is eminently fair. The odds paid by the winning horse are—in principle—the ratio between the amount of money bet on it and the amounts bet on all the losers.

Theoretically, if members of the crowd bet $30,000 on Horse "A" and other players bet a total of $60,000 on all other horses in the race, "A" is a 2 to 1 shot (60 to 30). The mutuel price should be $6, representing the bettor's original $2 plus his $4 profit. In actuality, "A" pays nothing like $6. In states with a legal takeout of 17 percent, the horse pays only $4.80, having been cut from 2 to 1 to 7 to 5 by the house percentage.

The takeout finances track operations and provides tax revenues to the state and other governments. Tracks need funds with which to pay purses, hire employees and keep themselves spruce. Governments are undoubtedly entitled to a slice, too. It would be idle to deplore any of this. But certain trends are questionable.

I referred earlier to confiscatory takeouts such as the 25 percent deducted from most trifecta pools. Governments that do this, and tracks that cooperate in it, are engaged in the exploitation of a gullible public. A peculiar thing about such a public, however, is that it not only is gullible but transient. Gullibility is seldom a permanent condition. One day the customer realizes that the percentages are hopelessly unfavorable. Bye-bye gullibility and, alas, bye-bye customer. Whoever goes to racetracks of any kind with any frequency in this, the era of the rising takeout, can testify that the only old familiar faces to be seen (aside from those of horsefolk and track employees) belong to hard-bitten handicappers able to survive the percentages through shrewd wagering. But the noisy enthusiast who occupies the next table for weeks on end, tossing money around aimlessly, is nowhere to be found next season, having learned to refrain.

For that matter, the endurance of hard-bitten handicappers is less than infinite. States that increase the takeout on perfectas to 19 percent and trifectas to 25 are prone to boost the take on conventional wagers as well. As we shall show, the difference between a 15 percent take and one of 19 percent is quite considerable. The difference comes out of the profits paid to holders of winning tickets. The handicapper who has been able to rationalize the pastime on grounds that it cost little or nothing suddenly discovers that it is costing too much. Higher takeouts may relieve immediate financial problems for tracks and states, but create long-range problems of greater severity. For operators of arena sports, can any difficulty be more severe than a lack of customers?

At this writing (in late 1979), the takeout percentages on win-place-show betting were as follows in various harness-racing states. The figures in parentheses were the percentages in 1969:

16 percent: Illinois (15) and Maine (18).
16.5 percent: Michigan (15).
16.75 percent: California (14).
17 percent: Maryland (16), New Jersey (16), New York (16) and Pennsylvania (17).
17.5 percent: Ohio (17.5).
18 percent: Delaware (17.5) and Kentucky (17).
19 percent: Florida (17), Massachusetts (17) and New Hampshire (17).

Of all the states, only Maine had reduced its take. Whether the reduction had come in time to restore health to Maine harness racing was still undetermined.

Let us now contemplate the effects on a winning bettor's profits of small increases in the takeout.

The 14-Percent Bite

Natural Odds	Natural Mutuel Price	Actual Mutuel Price	Reduction of Profit (%)
7–1	$16.00	$13.60	17
6–1	14.00	12.00	17
5–1	12.00	10.20	18
4–1	10.00	8.60	17.5
3–1	8.00	6.80	20
2–1	6.00	5.00	25
1–1	4.00	3.40	30
4–5	3.60	3.00	37.5

The 17 Percent Bite

Natural Odds	Natural Mutuel Price	Actual Mutuel Price	Reduction of Profit (%)
7–1	$16.00	$13.20	20
6–1	14.00	11.60	20
5–1	12.00	9.80	22
4–1	10.00	8.20	22.5
3–1	8.00	6.60	23
2–1	6.00	4.80	30
1–1	4.00	3.20	40
4–5	3.60	2.80	50

The 19 Percent Bite

Natural Odds	Natural Mutuel Price	Actual Mutuel Price	Reduction of Profit (%)
7–1	$16.00	$12.80	23
6–1	14.00	11.20	23
5–1	12.00	9.60	24
4–1	10.00	8.00	25
3–1	8.00	6.40	27
2–1	6.00	4.80	30
1–1	4.00	3.20	40
4–5	3.60	2.80	50

Alert readers may have noticed some discrepancies in the tables. They are explained by the curiosity known as breakage, which we shall discuss in a moment. For now, it is useful to notice that an increase of as little as 1 percent in the takeout means a substantial loss of profit to winning bettors. A 20-cent reduction in mutuel price is a 10 percent penalty on the winning bettor's investment!

The Truth about Breakage

Let us now return to Horse "A," on which $30,000 has been bet. The natural odds against him are 2 to 1, because $60,000 has been wagered on the other horses. The win pool is $90,000.

First off, the track attends to the takeout. Assuming a 15 percent takeout, the track removes $13,500 from the mutuel pool. This leaves $76,500, including the $30,000 bet on the winning horse. The remainder of $46,500 is supposed to be the profit for the winning bettors, but is not. Look at what happens:

$$30,000 \overline{)46,500.00}$$
$$1.55$$

The $30,000 has been divided into the $46,500 to see how much money is due per dollar bet on the winning horse. Another way of saying it is that the division gives the "dollar odds" on "A."

Inasmuch as mutuel prices usually are stated in terms of a $2 bet, the next step should be to multiply 1.55 by 2. The product, 3.10, would be the profit on a $2 bet—the odds in terms of $2. To compute the actual mutuel payoff, one then would add the bettor's original $2 to the $3.10, giving a mutuel price of $5.10 on "A."

But it is not done that way.

The dollar odds of 1.55 are reduced to 1.50. If the odds had been 1.51 or anything else up to and including 1.59, they also would have been cut to 1.50. This is known as "dime breakage." Unless dollar odds turn out by themselves to end in a string of zeros, they are always cut to the next lower dime. Track and state pocket the leftover pennies—millions of dollars a year.

Back again now to Horse "A" and the poor soul who bet on it to win. Now that the dollar odds are only 1.50, the odds on the $2 bet are 3 to 2 and the mutuel price becomes $5.

The procedure lacks logic except as a pretext for inflating the takeout without seeming to. The usual practice is to divide the breakage equally between state treasury and track. This legalized pilferage from the rightful proceeds of a winning bet began years ago, when mutuel prices were computed by a slightly different method. Instead of dividing the amount bet on the *winner* into the amount bet on all the *losers*, and coming up with the basic dollar odds, the tracks worked in terms of $2 units. They divided the amount of the entire betting pool by a figure representing the number of $2 tickets sold on the winner. The answer was the winner's mutuel price. This is worth exploring further, since it shows how breakage blossomed into the larceny that it now is. Let us therefore take another look at Horse "A," this time using the old-fashioned method of calculating his mutuel price.

The $30,000 bet on him represents 15,000 mutuel tickets. The pool, after the 15 percent take, is $76,500. The arithmetic:

$$15,000 \overline{)76,500.00}$$
$$5.10$$

Under this old method, the track would have paid $5.10 to any holder of a winning $2 ticket on "A." In those days, furthermore, the track take was no higher than 10 percent, so the mutuel would have been at least $5.40. But that's another story.

Breakage arose because few mutuel prices came out in round numbers. The correct payoff on "A" might have been $5.12. Rather than bother their mutuel clerks with the chore of making chicken-feed change, the tracks adopted dime breakage, reducing the $5.12 to $5.10. As I now have shown, dime breakage under the old method was less exploitative than dime breakage as now practiced. Under the old method, the winning player collected a higher mutuel.

At some point, a procedure called "nickel breakage" came into vogue. Odds were computed at the dollar level, as they now are. If a ticket on "A" was worth 1.55 to 1.00, the mutuel remained $5.10. If the ticket was worth 1.59 to 1.00, the dollar odds were cut to 1.55 and the mutuel remained $5.10. Dollar odds that ended in anything but a zero or a 5 were always reduced to the next lower nickel.

Which paved the way for dime breakage calculated in terms of the dollar odds. A whopping increase over the old-style dime breakage. Take a horse whose dollar odds are 2.19. Under nickel breakage, the odds become 2.15 and the mutuel price is $6.30. But the new, unreasonable dime breakage reduces the dollar odds from 2.19 to 2.10. The horse pays only $6.20. Breakage that used to be 8 cents has become 18 cents.

Consider what this means to the holder of a ticket on a short-priced horse. If the dollar odds come out at .99, they are reduced to .90 and the mutuel payoff is 18 cents less than it should be. For any horse in the even-money range, breakage alone reduces the profit on a winning ticket by as much as 18 percent!

Place and Show Betting

As most racegoers—but not all—understand, the holder of a show ticket collects a profit if the horse wins or finishes second or third. A place ticket wins if the horse finishes first or second. A win ticket loses unless the horse wins.

Obviously, the best horse in the race has a better chance of finishing second or third than of winning. Some excellent handicappers try to capitalize on this truth, playing for only place or show. The profits on a successful place or show bet are low, but the players hope to compensate by winning many more bets than they lose.

Place bets pay relatively little because the money contributed to the pool by losing bettors must be divided between two groups of winners—those who hold place tickets on the winner and those who backed the horse that finished second. The profits on show bets are even lower, because the money must be divided three ways.

Consider the arithmetic:

1. To win money on horses that pay $2.20, it is necessary to cash 91 of every 100 bets.

2. To win money on horses that pay $2.40, it is necessary to cash more than 83 of every 100 bets.

3. To win money on horses that pay $2.60, it is necessary to cash more than 77 of every 100 bets.

4. To win money on horses that pay $3, it is necessary to cash more than 66 of every 100 bets.

Those are large orders.

The following statements about place and show betting can be accepted as maxims. They derive from the facts of raceway life, the patterns and percentages of the game:

1. It is harder to make money by betting for place and show than for win.

2. The number of correct predictions necessary to produce a profit in a representative series of place or show bets is unattainable except by a supremely expert, supremely patient handicapper.

3. The relatively low natural odds on place and show bets are drastically reduced by take and breakage, making the task of the place or show bettor even more difficult.

4. Anyone able to show a profit from a long series of place or show bets has the ability to make important money on straight betting—betting to win.

Calculating Place and Show Prices

The place pool consists of all the money bet on all the horses for place. Like the win pool, it is subject to take and breakage. Unlike the win pool, it is divided (after take and breakage) between two groups of bettors. Those who bet on the winning horse for place share the profits with those who bet on the runner-up for place. Here is an example:

Total amount in place pool: $48,000
Remainder after 15 percent take: $40,800
Total bet on "A" to place: $20,000
Total bet on "B" to place: $12,000

The total profit to be returned to the successful place bettors on this race is $8,800. That figure is obtained by subtracting from the net pool of $40,800 the $32,000 that was bet on "A" and "B." The remainder is what the losing bettors have lost.

The $8,800 is now divided in half, leaving $4,400 in profits for distribution to the backers of "A" and $4,400 for those who bet on "B."

Take "A" first:

$$20,000 \enspace | \enspace \underline{4,400.00}$$
$$.22$$

The correct dollar odds on "A" to place are .22. Breakage transforms this to .20, making "A" a 1 to 5 shot for place. The mutuel is $2.40.

Without take and breakage, the mutuel would be $2.80. The natural profits on "A" have been reduced by 50 percent! Cut in half!

Now for "B":

$$12,000 \enspace | \enspace \underline{4,400.00}$$
$$.36$$

Breakage reduces the odds to .30 to 1.00, making the mutuel price $2.60. But the natural price, without take and breakage, would be $3.33. The profits have been cut by 55 percent.

The difficulties of place and show betting are even more pronounced than these examples indicate. Most notably, the purchaser of a place or show ticket buys a pig in a poke. He may have reason for confidence in the horse's ability to finish second or third, but he cannot know what the ticket will be worth until the race is over—except at Roosevelt, where an unusual totalizator board displays the full possibilities. If he must share the profits with holders of place tickets on an odds-on favorite, his own ticket will be worth relatively little. If his horse wins the race and a longshot finishes second—or vice versa—the place ticket will be worth more. Thus, his position is comparable to that of a poker player with a bobtail straight who agrees to buy a card without knowing how much money is in the pot. He might as well play a slot machine.

To make this clear, let us now see what happens to the place price on the well-backed "A" if longshot "C" wins the race or finishes second. The pool remains $40,800, after deduction of the take. The crowd has bet $5,000 on "C" to place. That amount, plus the $20,000 bet on "A," is now deducted from the pool, leaving $15,800 for distribution. Holders of tickets on "A" will get $7,900. So will the supporters of "C." Compute the price on "A":

$$20,000 \enspace | \enspace \underline{7,900.00}$$
$$.39$$

The correct odds are slashed to .30 by breakage, making the mutuel price $2.60. This is more than "A" paid when the pool was shared with backers of the fairly well supported "B." But now that "B" has failed to finish first or second, the $12,000 bet on him has been lost, and the losses have increased the profits distributed to owners of cashable place tickets.

I doubt that it is necessary to work out the computations on a show pool. After the take, the amounts bet on all three horses are subtracted from the net pool. The remainder is divided into three equal parts, and the show price on each horse is then calculated in the usual way.

Place Overlays

By definition, an overlay is a horse whose chances of winning are greater than the odds indicate. A competent handicapper can tell whether a horse's chances are good, bad or indifferent. He may even have a method of describing its chances numerically, telling himself that "A" should be a 2 to 1 shot, because it can beat tonight's field 33 percent of the time, and "B" should be 10 to 1 because it hardly could be expected to win more than once in eleven tries. Needless to say, such figures are only personal estimates. Without a good computer (and years of data processing), it will not be possible to refine handicapping to the point where a horse's chances might be expressed in accurate mathematical terms.

Nevertheless, the good handicapper usually recognizes an overlay when he sees one. If he likes a horse's chances and it turns out to be a longshot, it is an overlay. If he thinks the horse should be an odds-on favorite, and its odds remain above even money, it is an overlay. If he thinks it will win in a walk and would be a good bet at 1 to 10, he considers it a big overlay at 2 to 5.

If one is capable of recognizing overlays and bets on no other kind of horse, profits are inevitable. "Any time I can get twenty to one on a natural ten to one shot, I grab it," bellows the sage of the grandstand bar. But he is not talking about overlays, even though he thinks he is. No horse is worth a bet unless it has a reasonable chance to win. I doubt that anyone can tell whether an outsider should be 10 to 1 or 20 to 1.

At smaller raceways, one frequently finds that the likeliest horse in the race is noticeably underbet for place or show. That makes the horse an overlay for place or show. If it wins, or finishes second or third, it will pay a higher mutuel price for place or show than it should.

It is easy enough to spot these opportunities. If the tote board shows that the amount of money bet on the horse to win is about a quarter of the total win pool, but that the animal accounts for only about a sixth of the place pool, it is underbet for place. Whether it is worth a place bet depends largely on what the mutuel patterns have been at the particular track. At tracks like Yonkers, Roosevelt, Hollywood, Sportsman's Park, The Meadowlands and Liberty Bell, the crowds include numerous punters who watch the board closely for discrepancies, and hasten to bet whenever a good prospect is underbet in the place or show pool. Elsewhere, the crowds often neglect such overlays, permitting shrewd operators to cash in.

In my opinion, it makes no sense to bet on horses for show, regardless of overlays. Place bets are understandable in the following circumstances:

1. When the best horse in the race is an odds-on favorite and all other likely contenders in the race are longshots. In circumstances of that kind the favorite may pay as much for place as for win.

2. When the two best horses in the race are coupled as a betting entry and the handicapper believes that they have an unusually good chance to finish first and second, a place bet may return a higher price than a win bet.

3. When the best horse in the race is a big overlay at odds of 4 to 1 or better, it often pays even money or better for place, justifying the handicapper's decision to bet for win and place.

Obviously, to make such decisions profitably, one must be capable of recognizing the best horse in the race a substantial percentage of the time.

Hedging

In connection with place bets on horses presumed to be the top contenders in their races, it is important to understand the thinking processes of players who try to minimize their losses by hedging their bets. They bet each of their selections across the board, or for win and place or win and show.

Their success depends, as usual, on handicapping ability and is limited by the effects of take and breakage. These effects, as we have seen, are most severe when the odds are short. If a player backs a horse for win and show and the animal finishes third, there is no doubt that the proceeds of the show ticket reduce the overall loss. Indeed, if the player bets six or seven times as much for show as for win, he may turn a nice profit on such a deal.

However, when the horse substantiates the player's handicapping ability by winning the race, the return on combined win and show betting is severely less than it would be if all the money were bet to win.

The inherent problem of all such maneuvering at the mutuel windows is the near impossibility of making money on place or show bets. Unless the player is able to make a profit for place or show, his hedging merely prevents him from making as much on his win bets as he otherwise might. Or, if he also is incapable of making money on win bets, the hedges will tend to reduce his overall rate of loss to some extent, while increasing his total investment. Finally, if he is good enough to break even or make a small profit on place or show bets, he almost certainly wastes time and money in the effort: He is good enough to make considerably more money than that by betting to win only!

Betting More than One Horse to Win

"I never bet against myself," declaims the sage. "Betting two horses in a race is betting against yourself."

I have been hearing that line since I was in knickerbockers and have yet to discover any logic in it. Neither is there any mathematics in it. As nearly as I can tell, the horror of "betting against yourself" derives from superstition—the idea that conflicting wishes might antagonize the gods. Or that if you bet on Horse "A" you should not weaken the potency of your wishes by also betting on Horse "B."

When it comes to the pell-mell of harness racing on half-mile tracks, however, the player can lose more money through vain wishes than through betting on two horses—each to win—in certain races. In fact, there are occasions when it is intelligent to bet on three horses, each to win. Situations of this kind arise less often at one-mile and ⅝-mile tracks, where the contention is less hectic and a horse that figures best, even if narrowly, can be counted on to arrive home first a satisfactory percentage of the time.

In a later chapter we shall discuss the kinds of races in which bets on more than one horse are the difference between profit and loss or—for a good handicapper—the difference between betting and passing the race entirely. I hardly need point out that multiple bets never are made unless each of the horses, if it wins, is likely to return a mutuel price large enough to make the total investment profitable.

Booking Percentages

In olden times, a hustler could shop among the trackside bookmakers for the best odds. Good handicappers made money that way by betting on every horse except rank outsiders, overrated favorites and other animals that figured to lose.

Booking Percentages

Odds	Percent-age	Odds	Percent-age	Odds	Percent-age
1–9	90.00	8–5	38.46	13–1	7.14
1–8	88.89	9–5	35.71	14–1	6.66
1–7	87.50	2–1	33.33	15–1	6.25
1–6	85.68	5–2	28.57	16–1	5.88
1–5	83.33	3–1	25.00	17–1	5.55
1–4	80.00	7–?	22.23	18–1	5.26
1–3	75.00	4–1	20.00	19–1	5.00
2–5	71.42	9–2	18.19	20–1	4.76
1–2	66.67	5–1	16.67	25–1	3.85
3–5	62.50	6–1	14.29	30–1	3.23
3–4	57.14	7–1	12.50	40–1	2.44
4–5	55.55	8–1	11.11	50–1	1.96
1–1	50.00	9–1	10.00	60–1	1.64
6–5	45.45	10–1	9.09	75–1	1.32
7–5	41.67	11–1	8.33	99–1	.99
3–2	40.00	12–1	7.69		

The practice was known variously as "booking against the book" and "dutching." Its basis was the bookmaker's scale of percentages, which showed how odds rose or fell in conformity with the fraction of the betting pool represented by the amount bet on each horse. For an easy example, if the player felt that an even-money choice could not win, he would operate as if half the betting pool—the proportion represented by the bets on that horse—were up for grabs. Simply by betting all other horses in the race in amounts equal or proportionate to their booking percentages, he would win. Provided that the favorite lost.

I understand that some players try the same kind of thing at the mutuel windows. However, mutuel bets are made not at the fixed odds of the bookmaking days, but at final odds. These can only be approximated when betting is in progress and are not announced until the race is over. Despite this disadvantage and the difficulties to which it leads, people persist in trying to book against the mutuel book. Knowing that the pool adds up to about 118 percent (the extra 18 being take and breakage), they try to eliminate horses whose odds represent 30 or 40 percent of the pool. They then bet on the remaining horses in proportions indicated by the table of booking percentages. If any of the horses on which they bet happens to win, they show a profit. Theoretically, that is.

Bets must be made at the last possible moment, in amounts that require lightning calculation. Enormous capital and outstanding ability as a handicapper are needed. The player cannot operate alone, because bets have to be made at more than one window. How could a solo bettor get down bets of $33, $19, $11, and $7 in the same race—and all in the final seconds before the race starts? * To bet any earlier would be to risk having the entire deal thrown awry by last-second changes in the odds.

I do not say that profitable betting of this kind is impossible. But it requires betting capital of such magnitude and handicapping talent so well developed that the rare person able to carry it off would probably do better by playing alone, betting on his own choices to win.

Progressive and System Betting

Most betting systems are mathematically unsound. They require the player to increase his bet after every losing attempt. Their theory is that the player is "due" to win at some point, and that the increased bet will return enough to make up for prior losses. We have already discussed the disaster that awaits anyone who, relying on a "law" of averages, doubles his bet after every loss on a favorite, or on a top driver. One need not double the bets, of course. Modifications of the double-up method are used by many players. But these systems only modify losses. They cannot produce profits except briefly and accidentally. Also, they require investment outlays beyond all proportion to the returns.

A pet approach of some players is called "due-column betting." The bettor decides that the raceway owes him a nightly stipend—say, $100. He therefore bets as much on each of his selections as will produce the desired return. Let us say that he likes a 4 to 1 shot in the first race. He bets $25. If the horse loses, the raceway now "owes" him $125, so he bets $63 on a 2 to 1 shot in the second race. If the horse wins, the player has about $101 in profit and goes home. Otherwise, he now needs $188 to replace his losses and supply his intended profit.

The chief shortcoming of that procedure is the supposition that anyone can make a profit at any raceway on any given night. Or in any given week. Thus, due-column betting multiplies one's losses during a losing streak, requiring bets of steadily increasing and, in time, prohibitively large size. Few players can afford such outlays.

A far more intelligent plan is to abandon due columns and double-ups

---

* Improved pari-mutuel technology now enables some tracks to accept bets of any size at any window.

and the like, allocating a *fixed percentage* of betting capital to each transaction. As capital decreases, so do the bets, enabling the player to withstand a long succession of losses. As capital increases, the bets do also, in a gratifying upward spiral.

The notion that a player should risk more when he is winning and less when he is losing is accepted as wisdom in every game that involves betting. Players who adhere to that principle make more—or lose less—than players who defy it. If two handicappers are capable of showing a 20 percent profit on flat bets, and each starts with a bankroll of $100, the one who bets 5 percent of capital on each of his selections will end the year with far more money than the one who favors due-column betting or progressive betting or other upside-down methods that violate the percentages of the game, the principles of sound investment and the tenets of common sense.

The player who bets 5 percent of capital can stay in business at a raceway for months, without winning a dime. If he goes there with $100 and loses his first twenty bets in succession, he will have $45 left. If he actually is capable of a long-term profit in the 20 percent range, he could go to the harness races for years without encountering a losing streak as awful as that, but the point is made.

The due-column or progressive bettor would be ruined by such a losing streak, even though he were just as good a handicapper as the other man. By the same token, neither the due-column bettor nor the believer in progressive betting makes as much money in a series of winning bets as the man who bets a fixed fraction of his capital.

To demonstrate, let us analyze the occasional blessing of five winners in succession. For simplicity, let us assume that each winner pays 5 to 2. The due-column bettor has a bankroll of $400 and wants to make $50 per race. He bets $20 on each of the five successive winners, netting $250 in profit and raising his bankroll to $650. He is as happy as a clam.

The adherent of progressive betting also has a $400 bankroll. He bets $20 on the first horse, planning to apply his magic formula in such a way as to bet more on the second, if the first loses. But the first wins, and so do the next four. He ends by making $250 on the winning streak. His bankroll is also $650 and he is perfectly satisfied.

The man who bets 5 percent of capital also has a $400 bankroll. His first bet nets $50, making his capital $450.

His second bet is $22, netting $55. Bankroll: $505.

His third bet is $25, netting $62.50. Bankroll: $567.50.

His fourth bet is $28, netting $70. Bankroll: $637.50.

His fifth bet is $32, netting $80. Bankroll: $717.50.

He has done better than the others. Even if his next two horses lose, he will remain in excellent condition.

He will bet $36 on the first loser, reducing his capital to $681.50.

He will bet $34 on the second loser, reducing his capital to $647.50.

The due-column bettor will lose $20 on the first unsuccessful bet and, assuming that we still are dealing with 5 to 2 shots, will drop $28 on the second. His bankroll is now down to $602.

The progressive bettor, no matter how conservative his methods, will lose at least $50 on the two bets, reducing his capital to $600 or less, with losses mounting at an unendurable rate if the unhappy streak continues.

Daily Doubles and the Like

It is hard enough to pick a winner without contracting to pick two in succession, as in the daily double. Or four in succession, as in the twin double. Or the first two finishers in exact order, as in the perfecta (exacta). Or the first two finishers in exact order in two races (double perfecta or twin exacta). Or the first two finishers, regardless of order (quinella).

The trouble with all those multiple bets, apart from the difficulty of making selections, is that the player may not have the faintest idea what the payoff will be. All too often, the return is much smaller than the risk warrants. For a typical example, a player likes a horse in the first or second race, and "wheels" it in the daily double—buying tickets that couple it with each horse in the other race. This probably costs $16 or $18. The horse wins its race at odds, let's say, of 5 to 2. The daily double pays $24. The player makes $6 or $8 on his large bet. Had he put the same amount of money on the horse he liked, it would have returned about $60, a much higher profit for a much more sensible investment.

I could carry on in this vein for pages, covering every miserable contingency, but I won't. The truth is that multiple, gimmick bets are here to stay and are becoming more numerous every season. The customers love them. But nobody beats them.

If you consider the evening incomplete on which you fail to play the daily double and all available exactas and quinellas, I cannot hope to dissuade you, but perhaps you might be willing to accept advice. Play the gimmicks without hope of making substantial money. Reserve your biggest bets for the regular windows, where you can invest in one well-handicapped selection at a time. Play the doubles for fun—pairing three horses in one race with four in another, trying to break even or almost. Never spend more than $2 for a ticket. Treat the exactas the same way. If you can narrow contention to two horses in a race, play them both ways, for $4. If you find that three horses have approximately equal chances, box them for $12, betting that each will finish first and second in tandem with the other two.

At raceways that display all possible exacta prices on television monitors during the betting period, and render the same service on daily doubles prices before the first of the two doubles races is run, an observant handicapper may sometimes notice that the odds on a combination bet are actually more favorable than on a bet to win. That is, if one's choice is going off at short odds to win, it may be possible to collect better odds on a few reasonably likely exacta combinations. The same kind of thing may occur in daily doubles. All too often, however, the extra investment goes for naught, either because the horse loses or combines in a winning combination that pays too little to justify the original outlay. As a matter of principle, nobody should buy more than one exacta or daily double combination without assurance from the odds display that the profit on each winning ticket will repay the total expense.

The Cost of the Hobby

They say that the school of experience offers no free scholarships and that one must suffer the painful lessons of loss before becoming a winner. This may be so. One does not master the principles of handicapping and betting without practice, which can be expensive.

How expensive? Transportation, admission, program and moderate refreshment are likely to cost $20 an outing. Plus the cost of mutuel tickets. In my opinion, the beginning handicapper should make no bets whatever until he has become accustomed to the tense hullabaloo of the track and until, above all, he has demonstrated through dry runs that he can pick himself some winners.

At that stage, the $2 bet becomes appropriate. Penalizing the player for his mistakes, the $2 bet is an experience quite unlike the dry run, which permits second thoughts, benefits of the doubt and other forms of self-deception. After proving that one can take in at least as much on $2 bets as one spends for the tickets, it is time to abandon the $2 window.

To be sure, $2 bets are the least expensive at the raceway.* But they offer virtually no chance to make back one's "overhead" expenses, such as transportation and admission. Assuming that the handicapper is capable of a 20 percent profit and bets on six races a night, his $12 outlay would net about $2.40. This is less than he spends to get into the place and buy his program. Now that he is a good handicapper, he might as well make real money.

During the period of education and experimentation—the period of dry runs—the player should squirrel money away in a capital fund. When finally ready to play for profit, he should have not less than $500 in his fund, and should make bets of not less than $20—but also not more than 5 percent of the fund.

* Some tracks now accept $1 bets.

Where the handicapper might net $2.40 on a typical evening of $2 bets, he carries off $24 after an equally typical evening on which he increases the bets to $20 each. His hobby has begun to pay for itself. It promises to become even more remunerative as his capital resources multiply.

How long does it take to achieve this enviable state of being? A straight answer is impossible. Some players never achieve it at all, begrudging the effort demanded for careful handicapping. At the opposite extreme, some players seem to become excellent handicappers in a few weeks—if their letters to me can be believed. On balance, I'd guess that a person who combines keen interest with moderate talent should be able to get along nicely after a couple of months of study, including at least a half-dozen betless visits to the track.

4 THE BREEDING FACTOR

THE STANDARDBRED is uniquely American, a product of the celebrated melting pot. Its emergence as a recognizable type began during the earliest years of the new republic, when matings of Thoroughbred runners with light-harness horses of uncertain origin produced some phenomenal young.

Many of these off-bred horses were more compact and docile, less leggy and fragile than the Thoroughbred, yet no less brave. Some could trot more swiftly than any horse known previously, and were gluttons for work. A few had the mysterious gift of prepotency, transmitting their high speed, deep stamina and affinity for the trot to generation after generation of their descendants.

These few were the progenitors, the founders. Their blood upgraded what had been a kind of genetic hash into what now is recognized universally as a true breed. Although official registration did not begin until 1871, the U.S. Standardbred has already made a heavy imprint on harness racing throughout the world. The breed is still new and vigorous, still evolving. Its greatest exploits lie ahead.

The name "Standardbred" arose from rules adopted in 1879 by the National Association of Trotting Horse Breeders: "In order to define what constitutes a trotting-bred horse, and to establish a breed of trotters on a more intelligent basis . . ."

The Association decreed that a horse would be acceptable as "a standard trotting-bred animal" if it went a mile in 2:30 or better, or was parent or progeny of a "standard" animal. Nowadays the standard is 2:20 for two-year-olds and 2:15 for older horses.

Some harness-race enthusiasts wish the breed had another name.

Hambletonian, from whom all Standardbreds descend.

"Standard" sounds too standard, as if the horses were not *deluxe*. "Thoroughbred," on the other hand, has an aristocratic ring to it. Nonsense. All race horses come from the same seed.

Examine pedigrees and you discover that the winner of the Hambletonian is a blood cousin of the winner of the Kentucky Derby and of every other duly registered trotter, pacer and runner on earth. The lineage of each is traceable to the late seventeenth and early eighteenth centuries, when British horsemen sought to invigorate their ancient racing stock with infusions of North African and Near Eastern blood. Three imported stallions established dominant lines—the Darley Arabian, Byerly Turk and Godolphin Barb (so called because it was thought to come from the Barbary Coast of Morocco). One of the Darley Arabian's foremost sons, Flying Childers, an undefeated runner, founded the line that led to our modern trotters and pacers, by way of the legendary Messenger and Hambletonian. A full brother to Flying Childers, called Bartlett's Childers, founded the Eclipse line, which includes most leading North American Thoroughbreds. All these descendants of the Darley Arabian are also descendants, through cross-breeding, of the Byerly Turk and Godolphin Barb.

Messenger, the spirited gray with which the whole thing is believed to have started in North America, never trotted or paced in competition. He had been an outstanding runner in England, as befitted a descendant of Flying Childers and Matchem (forebear of Man O'War). His racing career behind him, he came to Philadelphia in 1788 and went to stud, begetting not only some top runners but the line of trotters and pacers that now occupy stalls from Hollywood to Du Quoin to Hinsdale to Melbourne. The preeminence of Messenger became unmistakable as early as 1845, when his granddaughter, a twelve-year-old mare named Lady Suffolk, became the first horse in history to haul a sulky a mile in less than 2:30.

The great Hambletonian was foaled in 1849, full of Messenger blood. Like most of his era, he also was full of unidentifiable blood. His sire, Abdallah, was by a Thoroughbred out of a mare of unknown breeding. His dam was a descendant of Norfolk-Hackney road trotters. It all added up, somehow. Between 1851 and 1875, the incredible Hambletonian sired 1,331 sons and daughters whose descendants literally have obliterated every other strain of trotter and pacer in North American racing. Every single harness racer on the continent traces directly to Hambletonian, as do many of the best in other parts of the world.

On a mare descended from Diomed (winner of the first British Derby), Hambletonian got Dexter, who trotted in 2:17¼, a new world record. A Hambletonian granddaughter, Goldsmith Maid, broke that record seven times in a spectacular thirteen-year career, finally going in 2:14.

Goldsmith Maid was a remarkable horse, a national celebrity. As a gate attraction and a living advertisement for harness racing, she was a forerunner of the immortal Dan Patch, who toured the land in a private railroad car and paced in 1:55. The Maid was foaled in 1855, sired by a son of Hambletonian out of a mare of unknown lineage. She did no racing—except on roads at a gallop—until she was eight. Finally broken to harness, she made her competitive debut in a setting we now can appreciate as appropriately symbolic—the Orange County Fair at Goshen, N.Y. Before she was retired on her twentieth birthday, the mare won 119 races (332 separate heats in all), was second in 16, third in 5, fourth in 1 and unplaced only once. Her earnings of $364,200 were unequaled by any horse until 1931, when Sun Beau (a Thoroughbred descendant of Messenger) reached $376,744 on running tracks.

The awesome mare did all that in harness to lumbering sixty-pound high-wheeled sulkies over racing strips that would never pass muster today. She was a barnstormer. She traversed the continent several times, drawing huge crowds at fairs and on streets and even at railroad sidings. Her lithographed likeness adorned the walls of parlors, barns and saloons. Many historians think that she was the making of American harness racing.

After retirement, the Maid dropped only three foals, none of which

Nevele Pride at the grave of Goldsmith Maid.

contributed much to the advancement of the breed. But she had done enough. Four of her relatives—all sons of Hambletonian—attended to the improvement of the breed with such vigor that all of our leading trotters and pacers carry their blood in tail male (the male side of the pedigree). These great stallions were George Wilkes, Dictator, Happy Medium and Electioneer.

George Wilkes founded the Axworthy line, represented in recent years by the trotting sires Florican, Hickory Smoke, Dayan, Songcan, and the pacing sires Knight Dream, Duane Hanover and True Duane.

From Dictator came the Billy Direct line of pacers, represented on current sire lists by Tar Heel, Thorpe Hanover, Nansemond and Steady Star.

Happy Medium founded the greatest of trotting lines, headed by Peter the Great and his grandsons Volomite and Scotland. Those two were the lineal forebears of such trotters as Star's Pride, Speedy Crown, Super Bowl, Nevele Pride, Speedy Scot and Noble Victory as well as the pacers Bye Bye Byrd, Harold J and Keystone Ore.

The world's outstanding line of pacers was seeded by Hambletonian's son Electioneer, whose descendants include the contemporary sires Most Happy Fella, Bret Hanover, Albatross, Columbia George, Best of All, High Ideal, Strike Out, Baron Hanover, Silent Majority and the two all-time super sires, Adios and Meadow Skipper.

Adios and Meadow Skipper

Bought at auction for $21,000 by Del Miller in 1948, Adios, who had paced in 1:57½, presently became the most successful stallion of any breed in the history of horse racing. Before his death in 1965, he sired more than 600 foals. By 1969, the best of these had won over $18 million in purses—about $3 million more than the winnings credited to the get of Bull Lea, the all-time great Thoroughbred sire.

Of the first four champions that paced the mile in 1:55 or faster, three were sons of Adios: Bret Hanover (1:53:3), Adios Butler (1:54:3), and Adios Harry (1:55). No fewer than 78 of his sons and daughters took records of 2:00 or less, among them famous competitors like Bullet Hanover, Shadow Wave, Dancer Hanover, Dottie's Pick, Henry T. Adios, Countess Adios, Adios Boy, Lehigh Hanover, Meadow Ace, Adios Vic, Cold Front and the 1:55 marvels mentioned above. Adios sired the dams of 77 performers with records of 2:00 or less. His 365 yearlings that were sold at public auction fetched almost $7 million—an average of $18,512.

What Adios was to the 1950s and '60s, Meadow Skipper is to the two succeeding decades. At this writing, he stands alone and unchallenged. Over 200 of his get have taken 2:00 marks.

Adios, most successful racing sire in history.

Meadow Skipper, later to become the breed's leading stallion, warms up for the 1963 Little Brown Jug, with Earle Avery in the sulky.

The angular brown stallion had been an outstanding competitor. His 1963 duel with Overtrick at Lexington in which he took 1:55:1 mark as a three-year-old is still regarded as a classic. When he retired to Stoner Creek Stud in Paris, Ky., he promptly began siring a steady procession of champions. From his first crop came the Triple Crown winner Most Happy Fella. His second crop included the great Albatross. Subsequently he has sired Falcon Almahurst, Windshield Wiper, Nero, Jade Prince, Seatrain, Senor Skipper, Governor Skipper, Scarlet Skipper, Handle with Care and Meadow Blue Chip among dozens of other swift pacers. And he is prepotent. Most Happy Fella and Albatross, who were among his first sons to enter stud service, have already become leading sires.

Standardbred Ruggedness

Newcomers to harness racing are sometimes appalled by the demands made on the horses. Their prerace workouts are strenuous enough to leave the animals lathered in sweat, their heads down, ears drooping and tails extended, as if in utter exhaustion. In no other sport do the athletes expend so much energy in so-called warm-ups. One wonders how the trotters and pacers can have anything left for the race itself.

The fact is that many trainers now work their horses less sternly on the night of the race than they used to. Horses that race once a week for months on end seem to hold their edge longer if asked for less effort between races. But the total output of energy remains about the same as it was in the days when seasons were shorter and races fewer. Standardbreds not only are capable of fantastic exertion but require it. Their neuromuscular systems produce top speed with minimum breaks of stride only after a degree of fatigue has been established. This characteristic is comparable to that of the baseball pitcher whose control suffers if he gets more than four days of rest between starts. Asked what was wrong, he explains, "I was just too strong. Too much rest."

Associated with the Standardbred's strength is his incredible equanimity. He is as intelligent as any other racehorse, and as aware of the difference between a night of racing and a night in the barn. But he rarely gets fussed. Unless something hurts him, he stands placidly in his paddock stall, often so quietly that he seems to be dozing. A harness-race paddock, full of horses and their handlers, is quieter than the average insurance office. Some horses are more temperamental than others, but few cause real problems.

In shape, these solid equine citizens produce the same speed week after week after week. The 2:05 pacer arrives within a few ticks of that mark in every race, seldom going much faster unless sucked along behind swifter animals, and seldom going much slower unless delayed by an off track or interference or a poor drive. When the horse has an unobstructed trip and finishes it in much slower time than expected, the trainer knows that wear and tear have set in and that a vacation is indicated.

Some of the most remarkable demonstrations of Standardbred ruggedness and consistency occur on the Grand Circuit. Some of these races involve three heats on the same afternoon. Each entrant has been racing about once a week, all summer. Yet now they race two or three times in one day against the best of their age, gait and sex—and the winning time in the decisive final heat may vary by less than a second from the times recorded in the preliminary heats.

Old-timers are full of lore about the endurance of bygone trotters and pacers. The Columbian Trot of 1893 lasted nine heats (on three successive days) before Alix won it. To warm up for an exhibition at Agawam, Mass., Greyhound jogged five miles the wrong way of the track, turned and trotted six more, the last two briskly. He then was timed in 1:57.

In future decades, senior citizens of the sport will undoubtedly brag about Cardigan Bay, as sturdy a horse as ever pulled a sulky. His immortality is assured because he was the first harness horse to win more than $1 million in purses. But there was more to Cardigan Bay than that. He was a model of Standardbred courage.

When Stanley Dancer and an American syndicate bought the eight-year-old gelding for $100,000 in 1964, he was the greatest pacer in New Zealand and Australia, having won everything in sight and recording some amazing times. For example: 1:56:1 on a ⁹⁄₁₆-mile track. In 1962, a sulky wheel collapsed during a training jog, and the frightened animal had bolted to his stall, dragging the cart behind him and tearing a bone-deep hole in his right hip when he crashed into a wall. Lesser horses are put to death after such injuries, but means were found to ease this one's pain during four months of treatment which shifted Cardy's weight to his sound side. The gelding emerged barely able to walk, his right hip six inches lower than his left. But he soon was back in training.

Stanley Dancer once told Lou Effrat of *The New York Times,* "I saw Cardigan Bay win the 1964 Inter-Dominions. What actually convinced me to go ahead happened one morning while Peter Wolfenden was training him for the Final. I had the stopwatch on Old Cardy and was amazed to see him go two miles, the second in 2:02:3 and the final half in one minute flat. When I heard that Wolfenden had jogged him seventeen miles that same morning, I knew the deal had to be made."

Through much of his epochal career in the United States, the gelding was an orthopedic case. In June 1965, after winning at Roosevelt Race-

Cardigan Bay defeats Bret Hanover at Yonkers Raceway, as Stanley Dancer glances back triumphantly at Frank Ervin.

Rambling Willie and trainer-driver Bob Farrington chalk up another 2:00 mile, this time at Scioto Downs.

way, he underwent surgery for removal of a fractured splint bone. But on July 23, he was sound enough to go 1:58:3 at Roosevelt, behind Fly Fly Byrd. During the following year, when he was beating the likes of Bret Hanover, he was plagued with an ailing suspensory ligament. When Bret beat the gelding in June, Dancer blamed the injured ligament and decided that the old horse was through. But Cardigan Bay again recovered sufficiently to return to the wars. In 1968, he pushed his earnings to $1,000,671, winning in 2:01 at Freehold Raceway, and promptly was retired for keeps.

A decade after Cardigan Bay, came the equally remarkable Rambling Willie. From nondescript ancestry and as unimpressive to the eye as Cardigan Bay, Willie paced with indefatigable brilliance in the free-for-all ranks. As I write this, he has already banked over $1.5 million and is still winning races. His legs show the effects of over 58 miles in 2:00 or less, and he dwells on the brink of forced retirement while continuing to terrorize younger pacers.

Is Breeding a Science?

All great Standardbred sires of recent years have also been good race horses. But not all good race horses distinguish themselves in the boudoir. Until a stallion's offspring begin racing, nobody can be sure whether he is capable of begetting youngsters as sound and swift as he was. The suspense is enormous, and so is the cost. The breeding industry is no place for the timid, the impatient or the poor.

Our foremost authority on the breeding of trotters and pacers is James C. Harrison, who used to be general manager of the nation's premier nursery, Hanover Shoe Farms, and now is developing Lana Lobell Farm as a power in the field. He says:

> I do not know of any way in which the sire potential of a horse can be assessed positively in advance. I suppose I have probably devoted more time to this problem than any living person. I have spent hundreds of hours running up charts and laying out check lists covering the factors of speed, early speed, gait, disposition, size, general conformation, breeding, racing manners, courage, endurance, opportunity and other items of interest covering page after closely typed page. In the end, nothing came of it. I recall that on one occasion I proved conclusively that Volomite could not be a successful sire. It was then that I gave it up as a bad job and reverted to the basic philosophy of so many of the most successful breeders, "Breed the best to the best and hope for the best."

Nothing could be more reasonable. Mated with mares of high quality, Abercrombie, Green Speed, Falcon Almahurst, Sonsam, Speedy Somolli, Governor Skipper, Whata Baron, Florida Pro and other leading racers of recent seasons may beget champions. But they may not. Nobody will be competent to pass judgment on them as sires until they have sent several crops to the races for years of testing. All anyone knows is that some great racers become great sires and dams. And on this fact reposes the "hope for the best" to which Jim Harrison refers.

Most leading breeders sell their yearlings at auction, where prices naturally are highest on animals that represent matings of the best with the best. Sometimes the promise is fulfilled with minimum delay.

In 1976, for example, the highest-priced yearling sold at auction was Falcon Almahurst, who brought $150,000. After difficulties as a two-year-old, he rebounded to win almost $400,000 in his sophomore year, set several major world records and was later syndicated for $3.6 million.

The first Standardbred or Thoroughbred yearling to sell for a six-figure price was Dancer Hanover, a son of Adios, who went for $105,000 in 1958. Although he had blinding speed, the colt was bothered by a bad shoulder and never reached his full potential on the track. Retired to stud at Hanover Shoe Farms, Dancer Hanover proved his value by siring Romeo Hanover in his very first crop. Romeo won the 1966 Little Brown Jug. Dancer has sired over forty in the 2:00 category, and four of his offspring have brought at least $100,000 at auction. As Dancer Hanover demonstrates, well-bred stallions who do not earn out their purchase prices as racers can still have lucrative careers in the breeding shed. Horsefolk who pay huge sums for glamorous yearlings know this full well.

Does it seem, then, that breeding may be a precise art, even a science?

Falcon Almahurst, who fetched $150,000 as a yearling, crosses the wire with Billy Haughton in a world-record 1:55:2 to take a heat in the 1978 Little Brown Jug at Delaware, Ohio.

Not quite. If breeders and buyers were capable of uniformly accurate evaluations of bloodlines, certain winning horses would sell for many times the low prices they bring at the yearling auctions.

The champion pacer and great sire Bret Hanover cost a relatively moderate $50,000, but retired with earnings of $922,616 and earned much more than that at stud. Abercrombie cost but $9,500 and won $1 million on the track before being syndicated for $3 million. The great mare Handle with Care brought only $12,000 as a yearling, yet won $809,689 in competition and has enormous potential as a broodmare.

Fresh Yankee, by Hickory Pride, was a fantastic bargain. After being sold for $900 as a yearling, all she did was become a world champion trotting mare with a record of 1:57:1, earnings of $1,294,252, victories on both sides of the Atlantic and bright prospects as a broodmare.

It would be possible to fill hundreds of pages with rags-to-riches tales like these. They prove conclusively that the quality of a Standardbred is not always discernible in its pedigree, or even in the impressions it arouses by its physical appearance at a yearling auction. If breeding were

117

even a moderately exact science, there would be fewer surprises. Horses with the most impressive parentage not only would command the highest sales prices, as they now do, but would also win all the big races, which they do not.

Early Speed

The racegoer uses the term "early speed" to describe horses that leave quickly, reach the first turn on the lead or in competition for it, and try to cut out the pace of the race, sometimes helping and sometimes wrecking opponents that begin less rapidly. Standardbred horsemen have two other meanings for the term. One, which need not concern us here, refers to horses that seem capable of winning early in the year, while other horses are still training or racing into shape. And the third meaning, which has to do with breeding, describes horses able to perform at high speed when only two or three years old.

Now that many of the richest races are for two- and three-year-olds, and most champions retire to stud at five, it is interesting to realize that early speed is a comparatively new notion. Until an opinionated tycoon named Leland Stanford demonstrated some revolutionary breeding and training theories in the final quarter of the nineteenth century, few trotters were deemed ready for competition before age four or five.

The reasons for keeping young horses away from the races were traditional and, before Stanford, were practical as well. The original job of the road-racing harness horse, after all, had been to haul passengers and

cargo, heavy labor for which mature, full-grown animals were best suited. Secondly, while the Standardbreds of the time could almost always be taught to trot at speed, they did not usually learn rapidly. This was due partly to the uncertainties of their breeding and partly to drawn-out schooling methods which were scaled to the lowest common denominator.

Stanford considered all this idiotic. Variously president of the Union Pacific Railroad, governor of California and U.S. senator from that state, he could afford to dispute any tradition he pleased and seek proof for any upstream theory he held. It seemed to him that horses properly bred to trot would produce early speed if asked for it. So he bought Electioneer, son of Hambletonian, for $12,500, and installed the stallion with an expensive harem of trotting mares on his farm at Palo Alto, where Leland Stanford University now stands.

The foals were not subjected to heavy work, for which only mature horses were suited. All they were asked to do was abide by their heredity and trot swiftly. In the parlance of harness racing, they were "brushed" —asked for high speed over short distances. It worked. Fifteen years after the seventeen-year-old Goldsmith Maid set her world's record of 2:14, a three-year-old named Sunol, by Stanford's Electioneer, went a mile in 2:10¾. A stablemate named Arion recorded the same time at two. Stanford's trotters accumulated so many world's records for their ages that controversy ended.

Nowadays, many horsemen wish that early speed could be deemphasized, so that Standardbreds might be spared all-out effort before their bone structures mature. No doubt, animals unraced until age four might

Mares and foals in pasture at Castleton Farm, Lexington, Ky.

last longer, but the already hazardous economics of Standardbred ownership would become prohibitively risky. As matters stand, the purchaser of a yearling has some expectation of beginning to recover his investment within a year, when the animal goes to the races. To delay competition an additional two years would increase expenses greatly without necessarily increasing the possibility of profit. Indeed, illnesses and injuries suffered in training—or even in farm pastures—disable more horses than racing accidents do. The longer a horse remains unraced, the less the likelihood that he ever will race.

Another reason why the classic events for colts (the term applied to horses less than four, regardless of sex) attract so much attention is that fresh, well-bred two- and three-year-olds are the soundest, most spirited and least battleworn of racing animals. Because they are in mint condition, their performances are likely to imply much about the breeding value of their parents—to say nothing of their own potential value in that department. To this consideration must be added the psychological fact that in racing, as elsewhere in life, the young and new invariably excite more interest than the old and familiar.

Finally, as Leland Stanford demonstrated so long ago, and as has become increasingly manifest with the evolution of the breed, Standardbreds are capable of speed at ages two and three which were totally beyond the reach of their ancestors, regardless of age. Bred to race, they seem ready to prove it almost as soon as they are foaled. They now learn in weeks what could be taught to their forebears only in months or years. It's in their blood.

Trotting versus Pacing

An ironic footnote to the achievements of Leland Stanford is that the descendants of his great trotting stallion Electioneer have turned out to be the foremost pacers in the sport. Stanford detested pacers and would not have one on his premises. His purist attitude was widely shared: Good horses raced on the trot. The pace was for culls. And horses that could not pace unless strapped in hobbles were beneath notice.

Trotters remain the aristocrats of the breed. By comparison with pacers, they are hard to educate. They are more difficult to shoe. They are more difficult to maintain in winning condition. They are much more difficult to drive. They have the cherished early speed, but at two and three even the best of them are prone to break stride, causing as much agony in the barn as in the grandstand. Important stakes races for young trotters frequently turn into jumping fiascos, with horse after horse breaking stride and the race going not necessarily to the swiftest but to the luckiest. Among trotters of less talent, breaking often remains a lifelong problem.

Because many bettors hesitate to risk money on a horse that may lose because it galloped, or because another breaker got in its way, the mutuel handle suffers. As a class, trotters are not good for business and will not be until the absolutely inevitable day when the breed improves sufficiently to make breaking a rarity.

Statistics illustrate how economic realities, most especially the pressure to attract maximum mutuel handles, have affected trotters. In 1948, the USTA issued eligibility certificates for 4,563 trotters and 5,709 pacers. In 1968, there were 8,046 trotters and 22,725 pacers. In 1978, a total of 8,803 trotters represented less than 20 percent of the active Standardbred population. There were 37,042 certified pacers. During that year, harness fans watched 115,000 races of which fewer than 20,000 (about 17 percent) were for trotters.

Many of the hobbled pacers that perform at our raceways were bred to trot. For years, it has been customary in most stables to make a pacer of any animal whose development as a trotter involves more than ordinary difficulty. As one old-time horseman says with prejudiced distaste for newcomers in his field, "It takes *skill* to train a trotter. Your average used-car salesman who decides to be a trainer hasn't the know-how, the talent, the patience or the time and money it takes to gait a trotter properly and shoe it properly and hang it up properly and get it balanced so it will race flat. So he saves himself the sweat. He hangs hobbles on the horse and there he is, the trainer of a pacer."

Being truly bred to the pacing gait, descendants of Adios and Billy Direct arouse nothing but admiration among horsemen. The attitude is somewhat less favorable toward pacers with a trotting heritage. The reasoning in some quarters is that a natural-born trotter converted to pacing must have something wrong with it, ranging from physical unsoundness to inadequate early schooling. Whatever the flaw, it must ultimately take its toll, the skeptics say.

The argument may hold up in the case of a seriously unsound horse. But Skipper Walt, a stakes-winning trotter at two and three, turned pacer and took a record of 1:57:4 at age four. Eight days after that feat, trainer Roland Beaulieu sent him out for a trotting record in a time trial and he went in a world record 1:58:2. Another unusual animal, Noble Prince, paced in 1:55:2 and trotted in 2:00:4 within five days. In 1968, Reed's Waylay, a former trotter, was voted Aged Pacing Mare of the Year.

Jim Harrison and other breeding authorities are confident that indecision about whether to train Standardbreds to pace or trot will diminish in the future. With increased refinement of the breed, the progeny of trotters will trot, requiring less elaborate management to produce the gait. Indeed, the few trainers now fully expert in the development of trotters seem to agree that the trotting heritage has become stronger than it used to be. In years past, many horses could be made to trot only after being weighed down with extremely heavy shoes. Lighter ones now suffice. And all hands acknowledge that more foals than ever "hit the ground trotting" —moving on that gait at an early age, without prompting and, bless them, without ever galloping. Well, hardly ever.

And now let us get down to the meat and potatoes. Is the horse's family tree of any significance to a handicapper?

Breeding and Handicapping

I might as well be blunt. The bettor lurches headlong toward a dead end when he attempts to forecast the outcome of a race in terms of the horses' breeding.

Handicapping is a matter of assessing fitness to win a particular race on a particular evening. It is entirely a process of evaluating the competitive records of horses, drivers and trainers, plus noting the prerace appearance and deportment of the animals. The likeliest contender in the race is the horse whose record and driver seem best suited to the situation. Its record may be best because its breeding made it capable of achieving such a record, but the handicapper hardly will accept breeding as a substitute for performance.

Given knowledge of the horse's parents and of the paternal lines and maternal families combined in its pedigree, the handicapper knows only that the animal once had a certain potential. Within minutes after it was conceived in the womb of the dam, things began to happen which, for better or worse, affected that potential. The mysterious lottery of inheritance may actually have endowed it with the spirit and physique that the breeder had in mind. Or with better. Or worse. Its prenatal development may have been affected adversely by congenital illness or injury. It might flourish as a foal, bring $100,000 at a yearling auction and never win a dime at a raceway. Or, as we have seen, it might bring $900 as a yearling and turn out to be Fresh Yankee.

The only races in which breeding is even slightly useful as a handicapping factor are those involving green horses whose competitive records are too scanty for confident evaluation. If only one entrant is of outstanding parentage, and if it hails from a top barn, it may be best. But it probably is nothing to risk money on. Green horses are forever breaking stride and getting in each other's way and making life miserable for bettors.

The man with the plump tweed jacket and streamlined binoculars smiles indulgently at you when some plug pays $32.40 after staggering home first. The man implies that the outcome was inevitable because the horse is, after all, a son of So-and-so. Waste no time envying the man. He does not possess the secrets of the universe. Chances are that he's just another name dropper. Past performances are the key to handicapping. Breeding is merely interesting conversation.

You should read the following lists of leading sires, not for use in your handicapping but for the pleasure of knowing some names significant in the sport. Later in this book, when we handicap entire programs at leading raceways, you will notice that offspring of these great sires include numerous animals that can't beat cheap stock.

Leading Sires

In terms of money won by their offspring, the following stallions have been the most successful sires in each of the indicated years.

1976	1977	1978
Meadow Skipper	Meadow Skipper	Meadow Skipper
Bret Hanover	Race Time	Most Happy Fella
Overtrick	Most Happy Fella	Race Time
Most Happy Fella	Bret Hanover	Bret Hanover
Baron Hanover	Overtrick	Baron Hanover
Race Time	Baron Hanover	Adios Vic
Bye Bye Byrd	Best of All	Albatross
Adios Vic	Adios Vic	Overtrick
Tar Heel	Albatross	Columbia George
Romeo Hanover	Tar Heel	Tar Heel

Leading Maternal Grandpas

The records show that a two- or three-year-old by a top sire out of a dam by one of the following stallions has at least a potential class advantage over animals of lesser pedigree.

Tar Heel	Shadow Wave
Gene Abbe	Hoot Mon
Adios	Worthy Boy
Good Time	Speedster
Knight Dream	Bullet Hanover
Bye Bye Byrd	Duane Hanover
Star's Pride	Florican
Greentree Adios	

Leading Breeders

In 1978, Hanover-bred trotters and pacers won purses of $6,609,957, an industry record. Among Hanover stallions at that time were Albatross, Tar Heel, Super Bowl, Best of All, Columbia George, Florida Pro, Steady Star, Big Towner, Hickory Smoke, Songflori, Texas, Warm Breeze and Ayres.

The second most successful breeding operation is that of Castleton Farm, with establishments in Kentucky, Ohio and Florida. At the main farm in Lexington, Ky., are Bret Hanover, Abercrombie, Noble Gesture, Speedy Scot, Strike Out, Crash, Windshield Wiper, Bonefish and Lightning Strikes. At Wilmington, Ohio, are Lindy's Pride, Steve Lobell and Cavalcade. Arnie Almahurst and Striking Image stand at Trenton, Florida.

Walnut Hill Farm in Lexington is home for Silent Majority, Dayan, Florlis and Sampson Direct.

Lana Lobell Farm of Hanover, Pa., has branches in New York and New Jersey. At the main installation are Speedy Crown, Nero, Nansemond, ABC Freight, Entrepreneur and Salvation. Oil Burner and Speedy Somolli stand in Bedminster, N.J., and Noble Victory and Flying Bret are at Lana Lobell's place in Montgomery, N.Y.

Canada's leading stud, Armstrong Brothers Farm at Brampton, Ontario, has Dream of Glory, Armbro Jet, Jade Prince, Armbro Ranger and Horton Hanover.

Stoner Creek Stud, at Paris, Ky., is the residence of Meadow Skipper, Nevele Pride and Governor Skipper.

Almahurst Farm in Lexington has High Ideal. Blue Chip Farm, Wallkill, N.Y., stands Most Happy Fella and his son Precious Fella. At nearby Pine Hollow, the stallions are Sonsam, Green Speed, Fulla Napoleon, Hot Hitter, Songcan, Say Hello and Speedy Rodney.

Bye Bye Byrd and Hickory Pride hold court at Hempt Farms in Mechanicsburg, Pa., while Keystone Ore and Carlisle stand at the Hempt Farm in Oswego, N.Y.

5 STANDARDBRED CONFORMATION

"I DO NOT BELIEVE that we have established a definitive type of Standardbred," writes Jim Harrison. "I think that we have taken but a tiny step along the evolutionary path. . . . I cannot conceive that nature will permit the establishment of a breed of horses that are required to trot and pace and yet constantly hit their shins, cross-fire and rap their knees. I envision, instead, trotters that will never hit their shins, pacers that will never cross-fire and horses of both gaits that will never touch their knees.

"In order to establish these desirable characteristics, we must probe for a type. The type is a long-barreled trotter that will permit positive clearance between the legs on the same side. The type is a pacer that will be wider-bodied and will never cross-fire. The type is a horse, either trotter or pacer, that will pick his front foot up and lay it down again in an absolutely straight line, thus eliminating the knee-knockers."

Some Standardbreds are so well constructed that they can pace or trot at top speed without cutting or bruising their knees or legs with their own hooves or, as in so-called cross-firing, rapping one hoof with another. If they also have ample lungs and air passages and sturdy joints, tendons, ligaments and feet, they are ideal prospects. Properly schooled and equipped, these sound animals can withstand the strains of training and racing for years on end.

Such horses are a precious minority. They are the ones that, with a little bit of luck, become champions and near champions. At the opposite extreme is another, larger minority of Standardbreds shortchanged by evolution. Some are so badly made that they break down in training. Others are able to get to the races, but cannot generate high speed without hurting themselves. To avoid the pain, they develop awkward gaits, sub-

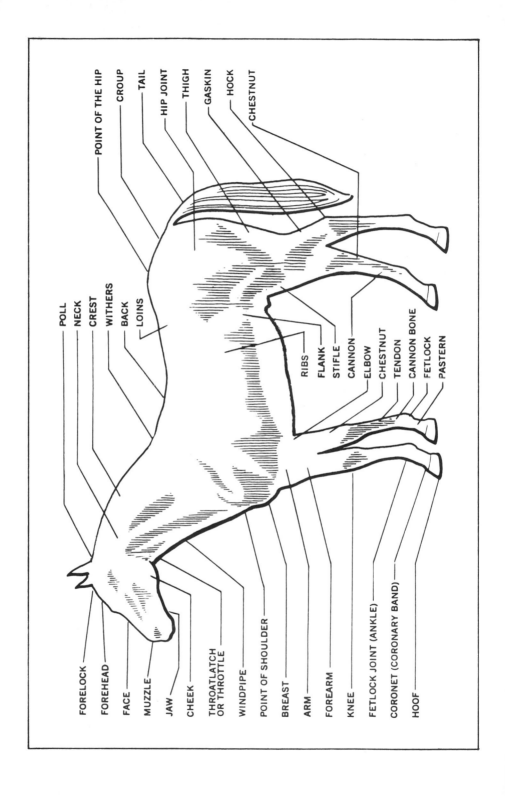

jecting their muscles and tendons to extra strain and becoming slower and less sound than ever.

A majority of Standardbreds fall between these extremes. Their physiques are flawed, but not so gravely that productive racing careers are out of the question. In the hands of genuinely expert horsemen who understand the nuances of corrective shoeing and "hanging up" (equipping), horses with noticeable physical imperfections win millions of dollars a year, holding their own in the best company, suffering no unusual aches and pains and remaining essentially sound for years. Lower on the scale, horses with unsound feet, ligaments, tendons or joints are able to qualify as "racing sound," remaining competitive enough to earn their way in claiming, conditioned and classified races at tracks of all kinds.

Pending the day when the entire breed will be free of the inherited defects which now prevent so many horses from racing long and well, horsemen are constrained to be wary when they look over the merchandise at yearling sales. In assessing the conformation of a Standardbred, they do not demand utter perfection—never having seen it except in the mind's eye. But they are quick to lose interest in a youngster whose fashionable breeding will mean a high purchase price, unless his conformation is good enough to promise relative freedom from trouble. They are far more likely to gravitate to less expensive yearlings. It is relatively easy to balance the books on a $5,000 purchase whose orthopedic problems condemn it to an undistinguished career. But when a $50,000 animal goes bad at two or three, the red ink flows.

The experts seldom disagree about horses of hopelessly poor conformation. And they drool in unison over animals that approach perfection. But disagreements arise when the boys enter the vast middle ground, the area where doubts gnaw, disappointments lurk and opportunities are missed. Billy Haughton, who has few peers as a judge of yearlings, thought that Romeo Hanover's full brother, Romulus Hanover, was the better constructed of the two. He was astounded when he was able to get Romulus for $35,000 at the 1965 Harrisburg auction.

Some mighty sharp operators did not like Romulus at all. He had a dished (slightly concave) hoof, suggesting cramped bones and possible future soreness. Also, his pasterns were longer than ideal, implying a susceptibility to tendon troubles. Haughton doubted that the foot was all that bad and was entirely unperturbed by the pasterns, which were set at a sound, strong angle. He was right. Romulus won $483,750 in three years.

Race Time, by Good Time, would have cost a fortune if the buyers had not mistrusted the shape of his knees. He went for $19,000 and paced his way to a record of 1:57 and career earnings of almost $500,000. Thorpe Hanover, another pacer with suspect knees, not only developed into a prime performer but also became a highly successful sire, his knees no longer a puzzle.

As the offspring of Most Happy Fella, two fillies named Silk Stockings and Happy Lady qualified as nobility, yet were coolly received at the yearling sales. Silk Stockings struck most buyers as too frail and spindly for hard racing and training. She went for a modest $20,000. She later won $694,894 in purses. Happy Lady came to the auction block with shin splints and sold for a mere $11,000. At two and three she earned $528,825 and set numerous track records. And then there was Jodevin, the ugly duckling that an Iowa farmer bought for $900 in 1975. In 1976, Jodevin won nineteen of twenty starts and was named national champion of his division.

Trotters are considered safer investments when they have long bodies. Yet Star's Pride, the top trotting sire, was short-barreled and begot more of the same. Evidently a trotter that picks up and puts down its feet properly can prosper despite close-coupled construction. And another animal's knees, feet or hocks may look weak without barring its access to the winner's circle. Furthermore, some horses outgrow slight deviations from acceptable conformation which drive down prices at yearling auctions. Either that, or they develop strong characteristics which compen-

The sales ring at the celebrated Tattersalls yearling auction in Lexington, Ky.

sate for the defects, as when a short-barreled trotter goes for years without rapping himself.

As already implied, good trainers often pick up where nature leaves off, keeping a relatively sound horse in shape and preventing a relatively unsound horse from going bad. On the other hand, inexpert trainers dependably fail to get the best from good horses and hasten the worst in poor ones.

Ayres, by Star's Pride out of the Hoot Mon mare Arpege, was born to win and did. John F. Simpson, Sr., president and general manager of Hanover Shoe Farms and an all-time great trainer-driver, won trotting's triple crown with this fine animal, thereby substantiating breeding theory and adding another remarkable chapter to the extraordinary history of Hanover. To do his best, Ayres required special shoes. Nothing elaborate or, strictly speaking, corrective. Shoes of the standard half-inch width were a mite too narrow. The next wider standard size, ⅝ of an inch, was a trifle too wide. So Simpson had his horseshoer make 9/16-inch shoes for Ayres. A 1/16-inch difference in width made championship performance routine for the superb animal. Under less astute management, Ayres might have gone a few ticks slower on some occasions, failing to achieve his great potential. Mind you, he had the conformation. But there is more to harness racing, obviously, than conformation.

Jimmy Cruise proves the same point every couple of years, winning important stakes races with trotters which under other auspices can barely stand, much less trot. He makes them racing sound, winning sound. Another genius, Herve Filion, makes winners of claiming racers unable to earn their hay in other stables. These are horses whose inborn defects have been magnified by the wear and tear of racing. But Filion sees something in them, claims them from cheap races and makes money with them.

Years ago, one of the nation's outstanding trainers said that he was going to claim The Rabbit, a Filion reclamation project which had been winning consistently at Liberty Bell. "Okay," said the Canadian. "But before you waste your money, take him on a trip." The other trainer wheeled the horse around the track once and returned to the paddock aghast. "You can keep him!" he exclaimed. "He's as lame as a billy goat!" Filion nodded gravely, and continued to win races with the horse, having determined the combination of special equipment, feed, care and driving technique that kept the animal in high gear, lameness notwithstanding.

I have strayed from the subject of Standardbred conformation because I want to put it in meaningful perspective for the handicapping racegoer. Clearly, conformation, like breeding, is of utmost importance to buyers at yearling sales. Equally clearly, conformation is of almost no relevance to the handicapper faced with the problem of analyzing the records of horses and drivers. Whatever is wrong with the horse is reflected in its past performances. If the records show that a particular animal has the class, current form, driver and post position to beat its field, and if it looks spry and fit during its prerace exercises, you probably have located a bet, whether you like its pasterns or not.

In a race for green two- or three-year-olds, you occasionally may spot a winner on grounds of superior physique, especially if the youngster is well bred, from a top barn, with a top driver, and behaves nicely before the race. I doubt you can make any money that way, but you may enjoy the attempt.

On a muddy track, small, nimble horses usually perform more reliably than large, long-striding ones. Players who remember this can cash tickets at excellent prices on the rare evenings when modern raceways come up muddy.

Another reason to learn a little about conformation is somewhat frivolous but is worth points in certain social situations. If a horse has been racing dismally and your companion is enchanted by its high odds, it is mighty satisfying to be able to say, "Look at his hind legs. No wonder he can't win anything. He's cow-hocked." We'll come to cow hocks shortly.

Size and Weight

Measured at the withers—the high point of the torso, directly rearward of the neck—a Standardbred usually stands between 15 and 16 hands, a hand being four inches. The term "15-1" means 15 hands plus an inch. Horses as short as 14 or as tall as 17 hands turn up once in a while. So do Standardbreds that weigh upward of half a ton, although 900 pounds is more typical.

Lou Dillon, world's champion trotter from 1903 to 1912, stood one-half inch higher than 15 hands. Nevele Pride, who became champion in 1969, was only an inch and a half taller. Greyhound, whose trotting record stood from 1937 until 1969, was unusually tall—16-1¼.

Feet and Ankles

Many horsemen inspect Standardbreds from the ground up. No foot, no horse. If the hoof is too narrow, it must absorb extra pounds of impact per square inch of its limited surface. At high speeds on hard tracks, the probability of trouble multiplies, not only in the narrow foot but also in the ankles and knees to which the concussion is transmitted.

The best forelegs are those with feet that toe straight ahead, leaving hoofprints almost exactly parallel with each other. Horses that toe in

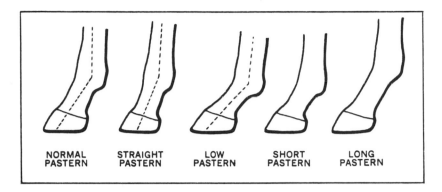

NORMAL PASTERN   STRAIGHT PASTERN   LOW PASTERN   SHORT PASTERN   LONG PASTERN

slightly are forgiven the defect, but pronounced pigeon toes can mean undue strain on ligaments and tendons—a prescription for lameness. Pigeon-toed trotters tend to rap their hind shins, a problem which sometimes can be corrected by proper shoeing.

A horse that toes out may do so because his hooves have not been trimmed correctly or, more likely, because he is badly put together. Pacer or trotter, he probably knocks his knees, the outward-pointing toe of one foreleg swinging inward and rapping the knee of the other foreleg. Really bad knee-knockers cannot race at all. Others do all right on tracks with gradual turns but come to grief at the half-milers.

As much attention is paid to pasterns as to feet. The ideal pastern slopes from fetlock to hoof at an angle of 45 degrees. If more upright than that, it is less springy than it should be. It transmits too much concussion to ankle and knee, which eventually go bad. Such a horse is said to be "up on his ankles," and his condition is regarded as more serious if the pasterns are short as well as upright. A horse whose pasterns are long or slope lower than they should is "down on his fetlocks." His pasterns are too springy, subjecting leg tendons to excessive strain.

Knee, Hock and Tendon

A horse has knees in his forelegs only. The corresponding joint in the hind legs looks like an elbow but is called a hock (horses' elbows are in the forelegs). The knee contains seven or eight bones, depending on the individual. It is so delicate and so slow to develop that good stables keep two-year-olds out of hard training until X rays show that it is fully formed.

The normal knee is situated directly below the elbow, permitting even dispersal of concussion and proper attachment of tendons. Horses whose forelegs bend backward at the knees are called "calf-kneed" or "back at the knee." They seldom last long. Unable to absorb and disperse the

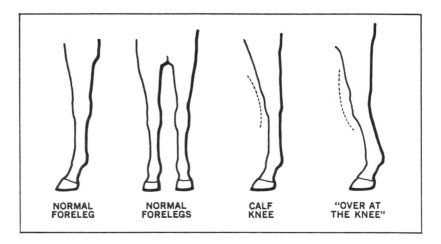

NORMAL FORELEG NORMAL FORELEGS CALF KNEE "OVER AT THE KNEE"

stress of concussion, these knees tend to chip and to develop arthritic conditions. Also, the misshapen tendons associated with them often deteriorate rapidly.

Some horses are "over at the knee" or "buck-kneed," the joint protruding forward. Such forelegs are less handsome than straight ones but are otherwise no detriment.

Horsemen prefer Standardbreds whose hind legs drop almost straight down from the hocks. If the hoof is noticeably forward of the hock, the animal is slightly downgraded for sickle hocks, which may lead to serious difficulties with tendons, but usually do not.

The worst malformation of the hocks is known as cow hock. The horse looks knock-kneed from the rear. His hind feet toe outward when walking but fly inward on the trot, virtually guaranteeing that the hoof of one leg

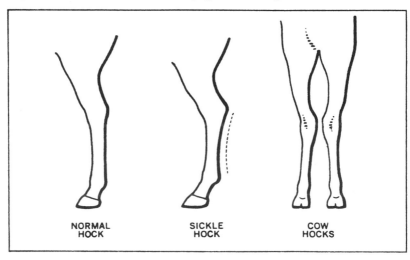

NORMAL HOCK   SICKLE HOCK   COW HOCKS

will interfere painfully with the flesh, muscle and bone of the other. Slight cow hocks are unlikely to bother a pacer, however.

Returning now to the forelegs, the judge of Standardbred conformation is especially concerned with the shape of the flexor tendon. It should stand out, firm, tight and economically straight, behind the leg, between knee and fetlock. Fat, spongy tendons are anathema. Even in an otherwise well-formed leg, they tend to rupture under strain. Such afflictions of tendon fiber or sheath are known as bows—bowed tendons—and often mean the end of a racer's usefulness.

From Chest to Hips

A narrow-chested horse not only lacks lung capacity but also suffers the handicap of forelegs that are too close to each other and too likely to interfere with each other.

A broad, deep chest keeps the legs apart and provides plenty of space for lungs. It should be accompanied by a powerful sloped shoulder for the full extension of the forelegs that produces a good long stride. Upright shoulders cramp the stride and, worse than that, absorb shock as inefficiently as the upright pasterns with which they often combine in a poorly endowed horse.

The withers should be fairly prominent, indicating the long spinal muscles of powerful stride. The muscles of the loin should also be evident. They tie the horse's rear to his front, creating the "close-coupled" appearance of well-coordinated trotters and pacers. If "light over the kidney" or "wasp-waisted"—slender-loined and slack in the coupling—a horse is less able to transmit power from rear to front.

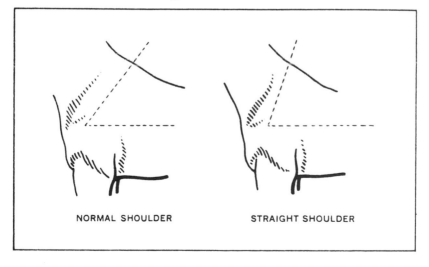

NORMAL SHOULDER   STRAIGHT SHOULDER

Head and Neck

A wide forehead suggests an adequate brain pan and, in fact, is seldom found on a stupid, unmannerly horse. Large, clear, dark eyes are another sign of kindly, manageable intelligence.

Large nostrils and a broad space between the jawbones mean ample breathing passages. Billy Haughton places four fingers under the jaws. If the fingers do not fit comfortably in the space between the bones, he rejects the animal. He says no good horse has ever flunked that test.

A long, limber neck is far preferable to a short one. Long-necked horses stride out more decisively, have better balance and more stamina.

Color and Markings

The official colors:

BAY. Brownish body and black "points" (mane, tail and lower legs). The body color ranges from a yellowish tan to a deep red mahogany or a dark brown.

DARK BAY OR BROWN. If the hairs on muzzle or flank are tan or brown, the horse is in this category.

CHESTNUT. Mane and tail are brown or flaxen, never black, although a few black hairs may be noticeable. Body color varies from a dark liver to reddish gold, copper and light yellow.

BLACK. Sometimes completely black, but as likely to look dark brown, with fine black hairs on the muzzle.

GRAY. A mixture of white and black hairs.

ROAN. A mixture of black, white and yellow hairs, or black, white and red.

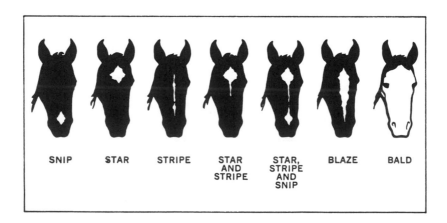

SNIP   STAR   STRIPE   STAR AND STRIPE   STAR, STRIPE AND SNIP   BLAZE   BALD

Because the patches known as "markings" are always white, they never are referred to by color.

A *snip* is a small patch of bare skin or white hairs on lip or nose.

A *star* is a small patch of white on the forehead.

A *stripe* is a narrow mark running down the face to the nose or lower.

A *blaze* is a larger patch. When it covers the entire face, the horse is called white-faced or bald-faced.

Markings also are found on the heels, the coronet of the hoof, the pasterns, ankles (half-ankle or full-ankle), and above, where they are known as socks, half-stockings or stockings. Many horsemen distrust the bone structure of horses with white legs, ankles or pasterns.

6 THE BEATABLE RACE

"THE HORSE IS ONLY a convenience. He is not a necessity," announced a wry acquaintance of mine as we watched customers stampede to the betting windows before a race so wide open that only a guru could have handicapped it.

"These people are betting on numbers, not horses," complained my friend. "They would just as soon bet on cockroaches. The day someone discovers how to make cockroach races visible in a large stadium, the horse will become obsolete."

He was joking in earnest. Some racegoers are more eager to bet than to win. They bet on every race, every double, every exacta, every trifecta in a promiscuous frenzy. The horses might as well be cockroaches. The Constitution guarantees every citizen absolute freedom to make an ass of himself, and the raceway is there to help.

In some respects, the tracks are surprisingly decent about trying to protect the player from his own worst excesses. Early in the year, races for green two- and three-year-olds are conducted without betting. This gives the youngsters a chance to get their legs under them. When they finally appear in betting races, some (but not many) have settled down a bit and have established sufficient form to deserve the attention of the handicapping fan. Another contribution to sanity is the qualifying race, a nonbetting affair in which horses show whether they have the speed and manners to compete for purses at the particular track.

Otherwise, raceway managements do their utmost to keep the customer in a state of hysterical confusion. Visualizing themselves accurately as purveyors of entertainment, they try to generate maximum excitement and suspense. From their viewpoint, the ideal race is one in which (a) contention is so close that nobody can make head or tail of it, (b) the start has to be delayed because so many customers want to make last-minute bets at the high odds which distinguish races of this kind and (c) the excitement ends with a wall of horses roaring down the stretch, nose to nose in a photo finish. The worst calamity of all, the ineradicable stain on the racing secretary's record, is the evening on which several standout horses lay over their fields and win by city blocks. That sort of thing is not considered exciting enough.

Track managements offer bookkeeping statistics to support their out-look. At most tracks, the mutuel handle seems to rise when contention is close and the races become more difficult to handicap. If the percentage of winning favorites approaches 40, as it sometimes does, and if few close finishes occur, as sometimes happens, the front office goes into deep mourning and the racing secretary develops acute digestive disturbances.

Fair competition among evenly matched athletes being the blood and bone of sport, one cannot begin to criticize the raceways for the emphasis they place on it. But one can take care not to be swept up in all the suspense and excitement, which tend to become expensive.

Sooner or later, every racegoer decides what kind of player he is going to be. Consciously or not, he decides what kind of play is the most fun. To me, and I hope to my reader, maximum fun derives from ending the season with more cash in hand than was there to begin with. The only way to scale this pinnacle of joy is to pick spots. Instead of squandering $2 or $5 or whatever on each of nine races plus a daily double and exactas and other blandishments, the spot player concentrates attention and money on races that offer a fighting chance. Races that can be handi-capped. Playable races. Beatable ones.

I do not think that you should bet less money than you now do. I think you should bet less frequently, managing the money more wisely so that you will place larger amounts on solid choices, and avoid other transac-tions altogether.

The Handicapper's View

Readers who accept the principles set forth in this book will find that harness-race handicapping is a rather straightforward process. Using the past-performance records published in the program, the handicapper compares the horses in terms of current condition, pace, class, driver and post position. Factors like career speed records, age, sex, career earnings and winning percentage are all matters of class. They vary in relevance from race to race and horse to horse. Pace, about which much is said and little is understood, often has more to do with the ability of the driver than with the character of his horse.

The primary handicapping factors are interrelated. To judge class adequately, one must study it in its relationship to current condition. And vice versa. Similarly, the driver factor is meaningless except in its relationship to class, condition and post position.

How, then, does the handicapper deal with a race in which any of these inseparable factors is obscure? Easily. He passes the race. He refuses to bet on it. Here is a useful rule:

Avoid any race in which the relative abilities of the horses are not clearly evident.

Do not expect every race to yield a selection. To the extent that temperament permits, wait in ambush until a good opportunity comes along. A good opportunity is a race in which the past-performance records permit sober judgments unpolluted by wish or guess. Here are some of the fundamentals of this approach:

1. *A race is likely to be playable if every horse in it has raced on the present track or present raceway circuit recently enough to provide a substantial indication of its current form.*

You cannot handicap a pig in a poke. Smart players bet sparingly at the beginning of the season, when some horses arrive from tracks of varying size and quality elsewhere, and others make their first efforts of the year. Until they compete on the present track, valid comparisons are difficult.

This truth practically compels abstention from betting on big stakes and invitational races at any stage of the season. If some of the glamorous contestants have been strutting their stuff elsewhere, their current form remains a matter of surmise until the race is over. One can only guess whether the recent victory of Horse "A" at the Yonkers half-miler was a more impressive display of strength than the victory of Horse "B" at the Sportsman's Park ⅝-miler, especially if neither has yet been tested at tonight's track. An added complication is the effect of shipping on equine form. Most good horses ship comfortably, barnstorming being an integral part of the sport. Yet all good horses do not ship well all the time.

2. *A race probably is playable if most of the horses have raced recently at the present track and if those without recent local starts can be regarded as losers even if they prove to be in top condition.*

If the top contenders in the stakes or invitational are racing tonight on their home grounds and have already thumped the others in races elsewhere, chances are that you needn't worry too much about the invaders. Likewise, if a horse making its local debut in a conditioned, classified or claiming race has been losing in lesser company elsewhere, you can proceed as if it were not in the race. Problems arise only when no judgment can be made about the present class and form of a horse—as when an animal returns from a long layoff to face the kind that it can beat when in shape. Lacking evidence about its present condition, one should pass the race.

3. *A race probably is not playable if the two or three top contenders seem so closely matched that no real distinction can be made among them.*

Handicapping is a process of approximation. It cannot be made precise. Therefore, occasions arise when the handicapper really cannot separate one leading contender from the other one or two. Unless the odds are generous enough to permit a bet on both contenders, or all three, the race should be passed. Bets should never be forced.

4. *The race may be playable if the leading contender is not a breaker and neither are any quick-leaving horses with post positions inside his.*

It makes little sense to bet on a horse with a tendency to break stride. If it is the best horse in the race, abstain entirely. Moreover, having found a non-breaker, it pays to make reasonably sure that the horse's own performance won't be spoiled by interference from breakers. The problem arises most often in trotting races, obviously, and is especially severe among younger ones and cheaper ones. If you insist on playing such a race, your best bet is likely to be a horse quick enough to be comfortably in front and out of trouble when the rest begin their jumping. Be particularly cautious if the jumpers seem to be early-speed types and are leaving from positions inside your choice. Their efforts to prevent him from getting the rail may be all it takes to throw them off stride. In the resulting melee, he may be piled up, backed up or hung out. Which could lose your bet for you.

5. *The race may not be playable if it is for the cheapest horses on the grounds.*

To deserve a bet, a horse should be capable of two good performances in succession. The manes and tails that appear in the cheapest races at most tracks seldom qualify in that sense. They are chronic losers, or chronic breakers, or chronic quitters, or otherwise so unsound that consistency is entirely beyond them. Their records show it. If an animal has lost fifteen consecutive races and displays improvement this week, there seldom is the slightest reason to expect additional improvement next week. Seen in light of its inconsistency, such a horse no longer shapes up as the "least bad" prospect in a bad field, and you pass the race. Unless a horse has winning qualities and has demonstrated them recently, betting is inadvisable.

6. *The race may not be playable if the leading contender has a weak or inexperienced driver.*

Beware the losing driver. He may cancel whatever advantages of class, form and post position the horse should have. Handicapping dilemmas that arise when a losing driver gets the best horse are often resolved most satisfactorily by passing the race.

Winter Racing

A handicapper's problems multiply in the freezing temperatures of a northern winter. The sport becomes a gasping, stiff-jointed parody of itself. Playable-beatable races are infrequent and immensely difficult to recognize. The fan's approach to the game under those conditions is as much a test of character as of handicapping skill.

Raceways remain open during the northern winter because it is profitable to do so and they need every dollar they can get. Many leading

Defying the elements at Roosevelt Raceway.

trainer-drivers risk their necks and jeopardize some of their less valuable livestock in winter competition for the same reason. Most of them detest every minute of it.

Good horses campaign when weather is kind and purses high, in the prime months of spring, summer and fall. Some remain active through December at Hollywood Park, safe from the hazards of winter. Sound horses with bright futures are seldom found at northern tracks between November and March.

Horses do not warm up properly in frigid air. They seem unable to absorb sufficient oxygen through their lungs. They tucker out in the stretch. Their racing times are wildly inconsistent, because the footing varies considerably from night to night and air temperature affects speed. The lower the temperature the slower the race. A horse capable of 2:09 at 40°F. is lucky to do 2:12 at 20°F. Wind, which bothers many good horses in summer, is devastating in winter.

The handicapper sits snug and warm in the glass-enclosed clubhouse, looks at his program and sees gibberish. Did Horse "A" go in 2:12 last week because of the weather or because they finally have worn him to the nub? Did his rival, Horse "B," go in 2:10:1 because of favorable footing or because of improving form or both? Considering that each animal was getting home in 2:07 only a few months ago, what is the handicapper to make of the program information?

An increasing number of raceways are trying to help. Their past-performance programs disclose the air temperature on the evening of each local race listed in a horse's record. Thus if a pacer went in 2:01 on a 40° evening and tonight's temperature is flirting with zero, the handicapper knows better than to expect another 2:01. Some raceway programs also supply a time adjustment figure or track variant, suggesting the number of fifths of a seconds of difference between normal times and the racing times on a given night. These program notations are enlightening, but scarcely overcome the realities of winter weather. Air temperature varies considerably from the beginning of a program (when the figure usually is recorded) to its end. And the effects of gusty, changeable winds make average-time adjustments little better than rough compromises.

So what can a handicapper do about winter racing? One thing to do is stay home, renew acquaintances with wife and family and spare himself some trouble. If he is determined not only to go racing in winter but to make summer-style wagers, he had better obtain special equipment, a winter survival kit. For example, he had better keep notes on the state of the racing strip, variations in air temperature and wind velocity, and the time and class of each race. These notes may supplement the program information enough to show the way to an occasional good bet. At the very least, he will be able to adjust the past-performance data to compensate for the probable effects of weather.

I doubt very much that winter handicapping can be profitable without such notes. Players unable or unwilling to compile them and equally unwilling to stay home with a good book should go to the track not to bet but to eat. Regard the place as a restaurant. Get a good table and a good meal and enjoy both. Limit bets to a minimum, risking nothing unless the horses are better than usual and the records less contradictory than usual. Spring is sure to come.

When It Rains

Innovations in the design and maintenance of raceway ovals have greatly minimized the problem of mud. In the old days, heavy rain transformed the clay surfaces into bogs. Entire programs had to be canceled because the horses were unable to pull the sulkies safely. But modern drainage systems and racing surfaces impregnated with stone dust combine to provide good footing under all but the worst conditions. Falcon Almahurst won the final heat of the 1978 Meadowlands Pace in 1:55:1 in a driving rain on a "sloppy" strip.

The description of a track as "fast," "sloppy," "good," "slow," "muddy," or "heavy" is not as precise as one might think. Even in rainless periods, varying humidity docs not libcratc thc handicappcr from the necessity of remaining hawk-eyed and prudent when trying to interpret what happened last week on an off track, or to predict what might happen tonight on another one.

Knowing the variations in speed, texture and puddled water that are encompassed by arbitrary terms like "sloppy," "good," "slow," "muddy" and "heavy," and knowing that a horse might like tonight's allegedly "sloppy" track while going frantic on next week's, the handicapper must choose between the following alternatives:

1. Make no bets when the track is anything but fast, and handicap from past performances on fast tracks only.

2. Compile and maintain long-term records showing how off tracks of various kinds have affected the form of individual horses. Confronted with a sloppy track tonight, the player uses such records to eliminate animals that have disliked slop, while upgrading others that seem to enjoy that kind of going.

Besides being easier, the first method is much less risky. The long-term records of the alternate method can produce bonanzas on occasion, but can also cause dismal disappointment. For example, the six or eight races included in a horse's program record may all have taken place on fast tracks, and may indicate that his form is improving. Lo and behold! The player's notebook reveals that the beast performed superbly in the slop six months ago, in a race not included in the program summary. The horse looks like a splendid prospect under tonight's wet conditions. The reasoning is beyond fault, the prediction sound. But the bet is less likely to pay off than if the track were fast. Here is why.

When a pacer goes at full speed on a dry, fast surface, its steel-shod feet come within a quarter-inch of its knees. A trotter's feet clear by an almost equally small margin. Let the animal slip or skid on a moist surface and it raps itself. The resultant break kills its chances and contradicts the notebook. Even if the notebook's choice remains flat, something else may flounder in the slippery going, cause interference, touch off a mass break and affect the outcome of the race. Adversely.

The footing is fast on so many evenings at the height of the season that nobody should feel compelled to bet when conditions are inferior. Sometimes, of course, the racegoer is betrayed by the Weather Bureau, finds himself in the grandstand staring at the "muddy" sign and hates to waste the evening. That is, he hates not to bet, even if he wastes a few bob in the bargain. In such circumstances, he should handicap the races as if the track were dry and fast. Having done so, he should bet on animals that (a) figure best in their races and (b) are quick types able to race in front where no mud can hit them and no breakers can obstruct them. When in doubt, favor an older horse with high career earnings that has been dying in the stretch on fast tracks, especially if a top driver is to be in the bike. The horse did not earn big money by quitting in the stretch. Chances are

Jimmy Larente after a race in the mud.

reasonable that his aches and pains have been defeating him. It is possible —although much less than a cinch—that the softer footing will help. Certainly, the top driver will do no harm. He and his peers owe some of their success to the skill with which they hold tiring or ouchy horses together in the stretch. Also, they are bravely unruffled by the very real hazards of wet tracks.

7 THE TIME FACTOR

HERE IS A REASONABLY SOUND six-year-old pacer capable of a mile in 2:05. I can buy him for $6,000. In the adjoining stall is another six-year-old pacer. I cannot buy him for $6,000. He earned more than that the other night when he won a race in 2:02. The two horses may dwell under the same roof, but they are worlds apart. The clock says so.

This is a sport in which time reigns supreme and the clock is executioner. Horsemen may approve the breeding, conformation and manners of a Standardbred, but they suspend final judgment of its quality until they see how fast it can go the mile. Its speed at the distance determines the kinds of purses for which raceway managements permit it to compete. Its earning power and market value, therefore, stand in direct proportion to its speed. Later in life, its record—the word given to the fastest official mile of its career—helps breeders to assess its potential worth as a stallion or broodmare.

With horsemen and racing secretaries dancing to the tune of the clock, it is logical that handicappers follow suit. Harness-race handicapping comes in many packages, but after all the ribbons and tissue paper are removed, you find a step-by-step procedure in which speed analysis is the main component.

Handicapping would be more complicated and speed analysis less dependable if the horses did not race at more or less weekly intervals for months on end, and if their form fluctuated sharply from race to race. Obviously, nobody could assign a meaningful speed rating to an inconsistent horse if the freshest evidence of its speed were a performance four weeks ago.

Similarly, speed analysis would become impractical, if not impossible, if the races varied in distance. As followers of Thoroughbred racing may know, the distance of the race affects each horse differently. Speeds recorded at mixed distances seldom make for useful comparison.

Fortunately, the harness-racing fan can count on several races per evening in which relatively consistent, recently active animals race at the customary distance of one mile. The fan has every reason to expect that the times of their recent races will help him to evaluate the horses' class and condition. And the fractional times—the clockings of each quarter-mile of each race—will permit him to study speed more discriminatingly, in terms of the phenomenon known as pace.

Fractional and final times are by-products of interacting elements such as class, condition, post position, driving tactics and luck. Recognizing this, many successful handicappers urge fans to go beyond raw time and examine the fundamentals from which time derives. They point out that some races are unrepresentatively fast and others are equivalently slow and that a player goes astray when he accepts such times at face value. They argue that trouble arises even when times fall within a normal range. For example, a middling horse might win a race in 2:03 on the same evening that a better horse loses another race in 2:04. But if the two engage each other next week, the better horse occasions no surprise by winning in 2:04:2, with this week's 2:03 performer finishing nowhere.

The points are unarguably valid. The good handicapper does not simply compare raw times. He tries to understand how they came about. Chances are excellent that he can predict the defeat of the 2:03 horse and the victory of the better animal when they race each other, having been able to analyze the previous races. Yet the fact remains that his handicapping is keyed to time and is most conveniently carried out in terms of

Nevele Pride blazes to the fastest mile in trotting history—1:54:4—at Indianapolis on August 31, 1969. Driver Stanley Dancer is hidden behind a galloping prompter driven by Billy Haughton.

time. And so, for that matter, are the handicapping methods of the very experts who properly warn against an uncritical emphasis on time! Time is the beginning, middle and end of handicapping.

There is no other approach. The sport is organized that way. The past-performance records are designed that way. On some race circuits, class designations in the past-performance programs are so unintelligible that equine quality can be evaluated only in terms of time. On other circuits, where programs make clearer class distinctions among past races, time tells whether an animal is likely to succeed when he tackles a relatively high-grade field, or whether his descent to a lower-grade field might mean a win. In addition, time helps the player to understand why a horse might have faded in the stretch last week and might hold together tonight. Or why the horse that led from start to finish last week might show nothing much tonight.

We shall look beyond time, but shall be careful never to let it out of our sight.

Taking a Record

In the literature of harness racing one seldom sees a Standardbred's name without a coded appendage that summarizes its quality in terms of speed. Strike Out was not just Strike Out. He was Strike Out, p, 3, 1:56:3h. That is, he was a pacer, and at age three he won a race in 1:56:3 on a half-mile track.

If he had been a trotter, the "p" would have been missing, but no "t" would have been used, it being understood that the horse is a trotter unless the letter "p" appears after its name. The age at which the career record was taken always appears next, followed by the time itself. If the mark was recorded in a time trial—a speed test against the clock rather than in an actual race—the letters "TT" precede the time figure, as in Bret Hanover, p, 4, TT, 1:53:3m. The size of the track is given as "h" for half-miler, "f" for ⅝-miler and either "m" or no letter at all for a one-miler.

Time trials are important because the sport measures its progress in fifths of a second, and the horse capable of great speed may improve the breed when he goes to stud. So the horseman takes his top animal to Springfield or Lexington or Du Quoin or Indianapolis or Syracuse, cranks him up as if for a $200,000 race and goes with him against the fence. That is, against time, under conditions likely to produce maximum speed. "Fence" signifies that the horse has the rail all the way and need waste no energy maneuvering to get there, as in a real race. To push the record-seeker to his limit, running horses serve as prompters or pace-pressers, rushing alongside (but never ahead of him) in relays and keeping his mind on his business. If the horse is in top condition and the driver's calculations pan out, the final time may be several ticks faster than anything the animal has been able to achieve in the tumult of actual competition.

The USTA accepts time trials as official Standardbred records, but only when an automatic timer is used. It seems that time-trial clockers used to suffer from a profitable affliction, "Kentucky Thumb" or "Indiana Paralysis," which caused them to start their watches after a friend's horse began its mile, rather than at the instant it crossed the starting line. Times tended to be more fast than accurate, which was rewarding for horsemen and clockers but bothered purists.

Most horses have no occasion to take time-trial records. Their career marks are taken in competition. Here again, the rules are significant. A horse may race in 1:59 without improving its career record of 2:03. How and why? Because time does not count as an individual record unless the horse wins the race.

The fastest of them all, Steady Star, whose 1:52 in a 1971 time trial astounded the harness-racing world. Notice that Steady Star was a free-legged pacer who wore no hobbles. That's Joe O'Brien in the sulky.

This is of basic importance to the racing fan. Its implications extend far beyond the taking of records, applying directly to the handicapping of ordinary races every night in the week, everywhere.

The central fact of the matter is that horses often race to better times when losing than when winning. An impartial record-keeping organization like the USTA can hardly decide that a losing effort in 1:59 was truly demonstrative of a horse's quality and that its lifetime mark should forthwith be lowered from 2:03. What would the Association then do about all other 2:03 horses whose owners argued that their own recent losses in 1:59 should also be accepted as career records? Or about the chronic 2:11 horse that finally chases other horses home in 2:09? The USTA has no choice. It must limit records to times set while winning or while competing against the stopwatch.

Handicappers are not bound by such considerations, however. They are free to differentiate among a horse's losing races, sometimes accepting and sometimes rejecting the times recorded in the past-performance chart. Before getting to this important phase of handicapping, however, it will be best to dispose of the subject of lifetime speed records.

Handicapping the Records

With regional variations which need not concern us, the past-performance programs tell the player what each horse's career record is, when it was taken, and on what kind of track. They may also show the horse's fastest winning time of the current year and its fastest winning time of the previous year. Naturally, they also show the times of the horse's most recent six or eight races.

The question before the house is whether any of these historical statistics are useful in handicapping. And if so, when and how.

A career record taken two or more years ago means only that the horse once was capable of a performance in 1:58 or 2:04 or whatever the figure is. It is of no earthly use in the handicapping of tonight's race. Too much water has trickled under the bridge. No horse, regardless of quality, is the same in 1981 as in 1979 and no 1981 race can be handicapped off 1979 figures. Needless to say, if you go to the raceway often enough you inevitably will see a longshot plod home first and will hear some clown say, "I shoulda had him. Look. He did two-oh-two in 1978. Nothing else in the race has ever done two-oh-two."

What if the career record was taken last year? And what, for that matter, if the horse's best time last year was extremely fast by comparison with any other time notations on the page?

Last year's mark bears some attention early in the season, especially in races for better horses and, most especially, when the horse in question has been out often enough and/or has performed well enough this year to suggest a resumption of last year's form. But after the doldrums of late winter and early spring are over and the weather turns fair and all six or eight races in the detailed chart are recent races, last year's record should be allowed to recede into history.

Some horses need four or five early-season efforts before achieving their best form. A few are ready to swing after a tightening race or two. If the animal is from a top stable, is racing in the kind of company suitable to a horse of its particular time credentials, and displayed an amount of lick in its race last week, you often can draw comfort and confidence from its previous year's mark. But if it is facing animals of a lower grade than might be expected from a reading of its previous year's record, and if it has been performing indifferently, it probably is a troubled horse. The prudent approach is to handicap entirely in terms of this year's form. And, as emphasized in the last chapter, pass the race if your predominant feeling is one of doubt.

What about the horse's fastest race this year? In general, your most effective handicapping will be based on the six or eight races the program summarizes in detail. Indeed, greatest emphasis should be placed on the latest race or two. So the horse's fastest race of the current year may well be irrelevant to what happens tonight. An exception might be the horse that went sour from illness, injury or overwork, turned in several poor performances after taking its record, was dropped in class, lost again and finally was given an overdue vacation. After returning to action, such a horse often recovers its form, destroying cheap fields and beginning to ascend the class ladder again. If recent efforts show steady improvement, further improvement might be predictable for tonight, especially if the animal has not yet approached the time it recorded earlier in the year.

No rule can be extracted from all this, but a principle can: A horse's most recent performances are the most eloquent forecast of what it might do tonight. However, fast time recorded earlier in the season or last year may sometimes be significant in the case of a horse that is rounding into good form after a layoff. Unless the animal has given solid evidence of improvement, its old records should be ignored.

Although few good handicappers dispute my emphasis on recent form, some of the shrewdest in the sport are careful to check the final times credited to every starter in all of its listed races. If one animal did a faster mile in one of those six or eight starts than has been credited to any of its rivals in their listed performances, these experts regard the horse as a serious threat—even though the swift performance took place a month or two or three ago. It has been argued, indeed, that a player can do very well by confining his bets to such horses, asking only that they have favorable post positions and good drivers.

I am unable to refute the theory (and its supporters are unable to sub-

The fastest female standardbred in history, Tender Loving Care, who went in 1:52:4 as a four-year-old, wins in the slop at The Meadowlands.

stantiate it), because no thorough statistical study has ever been made. There can be little doubt, however, that the horse with the best final time in the six or eight listed races is often (for additional reasons) the wisest choice in the race. Moreover, when there is nothing else on which to base a selection, this wrinkle sometimes produces a longshot winner. Casual fans interested in betting on every race may find the notion helpful.

Misleading Times

When a horse races on the front end against the rail or moves up on the outside to challenge for the lead, it must cut its own hole in the wind. In doing so, it provides a protective airfoil for any horse racing directly behind it. Sheltered behind the leader on the rail or covered up on the outside, an animal moves with less effort than usual, encountering less air resistance. In the jargon of the sport, such a horse is "sucked along." If it travels that way behind inherently faster horses for most of the journey, its final time is quite sure to be better than it could achieve without the windshields.

For this reason, smart handicappers discount the times recorded for a horse in a race that found it lollygagging behind other animals without making any real moves of its own. A racehorse should get away from the fence and bid for the lead once in a while. It should be amenable to use. If it makes no move in a race, its failure to do so may be attributable to traffic problems or a misjudged drive, but more often means poor form and should be accepted as a warning.

Horsemen and handicappers sometimes philosophize about the number of moves various kinds of horses can be induced to make in a race. Theoretically, an ordinary horse can be brushed vigorously—hard-used —only once in a race. A middling horse supposedly has two moves in it, and a really good horse can come up with three. The pell-mell sprinting style of race driving, which started at half-mile tracks and has been spreading therefrom, has tended to throw the move theory into the discard. Unless he wants to be left behind at the start, every driver makes some kind of move for early position, and one or two more to improve or hold that position, after which comes the crucial, exhausting move in the stretch.

I am bandying words, I suppose. It is true enough that a move to the outside on a turn is likely to take more out of a horse than its move to the rail at the start, or the move it may attempt on the backstretch. But it also is true that veteran horsemen have been counting three and four real moves per mile in the performances of mediocre animals at half-mile and ⅝-mile ovals. The breed is improving, racing tactics are changing and, withal, the definition of "move" probably is undergoing alterations. In any event, a horse that does nothing but ride the coattails of other horses is not making moves and is not really earning the occasionally good times in which it coasts past tired horses at the finish.

According to horsemen, some Standardbreds "don't like air." They race best behind other horses and can be trusted to win only when steered into the open in the final yards of the race, too late to balk or sulk and— hopefully but not invariably—too late to break stride. Horses of this kind often show splendid times in their past-performance charts, but their wins are few by comparison with their seconds and thirds. And the past-performance lines seldom show any attempt to reach the front end before the finish.

To demonstrate the pulled-along horse and the illusions it fosters, consider a pacer that went as the 2.10 to 1 favorite in a race at Yonkers. The animal's latest race looked, in part, like this:

29:4   1:00:3   1:33   2:03:4   1 4 5 6 6/2¼   3/1½   2:04:1

Leaving from the ordinarily advantageous rail position, the horse had been shuffled back to fourth at the quarter, and was no better than fifth after a half-mile, which the leader completed in 1:00:3. At the three-quarter call, the pacer was sixth. It was still sixth at the head of the stretch, whereupon it improved its position by less than a length, finishing third and completing its journey in 2:04:1. So far as the record showed, it had not budged from the rail throughout the trip. It apparently had taken third money by default when tired horses backed past it. If this had been its first race of the season, improvement might have been expected. But it had been competing at regular intervals. The race was simply a lackadaisical effort, a sign of unpromising form. In its next outing, as favorite, the horse endorsed that sign by finishing seventh.

The forecast would have been brighter, and so might have been the result, if the pacer's past-performance line had differed slightly. The fractional and final times would have been the same, but the racing positions would have included some signs of life:

$$1 \quad 6 \quad 5° \quad 5° \quad 5/2\frac{1}{4} \quad 3/1\frac{1}{2}$$

The two little circles would have meant that the horse got out there and roughed it for half a mile, finally battling its way to a position only 2¼ lengths behind the leader at the stretch call and gaining a bit more to place third. A wholesome race, offering promise of better.

And now let us evaluate another animal, whose last race looked better than it had been:

$$31 \quad 1:03 \quad 1:33 \quad 2:03:1 \quad 1 \quad 2 \quad 2 \quad 2 \quad 2/1\frac{1}{2} \quad 2/2 \quad 2:03:3$$

A suckalong. The program's morning line predicted that this colt would go at 6 to 1, but the crowd sent it at 4.60 to 1, probably because its final time of 2:03:3 in a recent race had been at least ⅗ second faster than the times of any of the other starters in their latest outings. This must be what some of the experts mean when they call time a booby trap.

Analyze the performance summary. The horse had settled into the second slot on the rail right at the beginning—no great feat, inasmuch as it had left from the inside post. It had remained in that same position all the way, safe and snug, doing nothing to improve its situation. The grand climax came in the stretch, where it remained second on the rail, losing half a length to the leader.

As often happens after a performance of this kind, the horse did nothing in its next start. It finished eighth and last. Its 2:03:3 clocking had been spurious. Interestingly, its career record up to that point showed victories in 2:06 and 2:07:4, offering no suggestion that it could do better than that unless pulled along behind other horses.

A more striking example of how a horse's losing times may look better than its winning ones occurred at Vernon Downs on July 28, 1979, in the $108,000 Thomas P. Gaines Memorial Pace for three-year-olds. Sonsam won the race in a blazing 1:54, erasing a track record that had survived for a quarter of a century. Finishing sixth in 1:55:2 was Genghis Khan, a good colt whose best winning time had been 1:58:1. After being reserved during the early going, Genghis Khan lost two lengths in the drive down the home stretch. His time behind Sonsam would have been quite beyond his capabilities in a situation that required him to contend for the lead without cover.

The horse that finished second to Sonsam was Hot Hitter, whose performance can be summarized:

28:1   57:3   1:25:4   1:54   2   4   4°   2°   3/1½   2¾   1:54:1

You can see that Hot Hitter was not sucked along. He was parked out in brisk contention at two calls and, after being passed by another horse at the head of the stretch, he fought back and closed to within three-quarters of a length of the winner in a final quarter timed in a remarkable 28:1. This was a performance of unmistakable quality, and no surprise. Hot Hitter had already won in 1:54:2, among other fast clockings.

In discussing the phenomenon of the sucked-along horse, we have been dealing not only with time but with current form, and what last week's performance implies for tonight's. It would be tidier to discuss each aspect of handicapping separately, covering time now and current form

Sonsam smashes the Vernon Downs record, defeating the game Hot Hitter in 1:54 during 1979. George Sholty drives.

later. But it would be artificial to do so. The elements of handicapping are inseparable. You cannot mention one without immersing yourself in another.

A sidelight on the sucked-along horse is the general belief among Standardbred horsemen that equine psychology often is as influential as wind resistance in producing performances of that kind. The herd instinct runs high in these animals. Most of them would rather trot or pace with other horses than be far in front or far behind. Thus, when the field as a whole cuts out rapid fractions, an inferior member of it may keep up quite well, losing in much better time than it has ever managed while winning.

The Perfect Trip

To horsemen, the perfect trip is one in which the horse arrives at the head of the stretch full of energy and in position for a clear, straight sail to the wire. During the early stages of such a race, everything develops as if the driver had blueprinted it. Other animals knock each other off, but the lucky one ambles along in unobstructed comfort, being used scarcely at all. It then wins as the driver pleases.

To a considerable extent, the sucked-along horse has a splendid trip, benefiting from the exertions of others without being tested severely itself. Sometimes it actually wins its race, taking a new career record and paying a land-office mutuel. With experience, handicappers learn to mistrust these sudden reversals of form, attributing them to racing luck and doubting the likelihood of repetition.

At the same time, one should not forget that every driver seeks the perfect trip for his horse, wanting to spare it all the effort he can. If it is a good horse and has been racing well, the player should not downgrade a performance in which the driver was able to save the animal, outthink other drivers and win without taxing the horse's courage and stamina.

The late, great John Chapman provided an example in August 1977, when he and Governor Skipper won the Adios, a major stake for three-year-old pacers. Until that victory, Governor Skipper had been competitive among his peers but had scarcely dominated them.

In the first heat of the Adios, Stanley Dancer's Kawartha Eagle set a scorching early pace. Chapman was able to steer Governor Skipper into comfortable shelter right behind the leader. With an eighth of a mile to go, Chapman was still behind Kawartha Eagle, but now was boxed in by Jonquil Hanover, who had taken third position on the outside. Chapman said later that he was not concerned, however, because "Governor Skipper was pacing all he could at that point."

In the stretch, Kawartha Eagle surrendered and Jonquil Hanover tired just enough to let Governor Skipper out of the pocket. Chapman reached the finish wire in a then-world-record clocking of 1:54:4f. The horse won the next heat and the trophy. Chapman was candid, saying that a "dream trip behind Kawartha Eagle" had enabled the Governor to set a world record.

Track Variants

A type of misleading time about which few racegoers can do anything is recorded on evenings when an ostensibly fast track is unusually slow, or on other evenings when the track is much faster than usual. Without the kind of daily notations mentioned earlier in this book, the player inevitably arrives at a false estimate of some horse's ability. If the problem arose frequently enough to make handicapping a waste of effort for the occasional racegoer who lacked daily notes, I would insist either that notes be kept or the races avoided. Fortunately, experience teaches the handicapper to recognize times as untypically slow or fast for the partic-

Governor Skipper sets a world record of 1:54:4f in the first heat of the 1977 Adios Stakes at The Meadows in Pennsylvania. Driver John Chapman called it a "dream trip."

ular grade of horse at a particular track. One can discount untypical times and handicap in terms of other factors.

Those who wish to keep notes, hoping to catch every possible winner and avoid every possible loser, must first form a reliable estimate of the time predictable on an ordinary evening for each grade of race. That subject is dealt with in the next chapter. After working out a schedule of normal, or par times—a laborious job—the player then goes through the results of the evening's races, noting how the time of each race differed from par. By adding these figures and dividing the total by the number of races, an average is achieved. The figure can be regarded as the track variant for the night, and the times recorded for each horse that raced that night can be adjusted accordingly.

For convenience, it is best to make the par figures unrealistically fast, so that the actual times will be slower. Thus, if $20,000 claiming races, or Class B-3 races, or conditioned races with purses of $8,000 are usually timed in about 2:05 at your track, you might set par for that class at 2:03. This probably would mean that $30,000 claiming races, or Class B-2 races, or conditioned races with purses of $8,500—whatever the next higher local class might be—would be assigned a par of 2:02:3.

On the night a $20,000 claiming race ends in 2:04:4, you note that its time is 1⅘ slower than par. Add the corresponding figures for all the races on the card and divide by the number of races to produce the average, the nightly variant. If the variant turns out to be +1⅗, you simply write it in a notebook and subtract it from the time of a horse that raced on that evening when next you encounter the horse's record in a program.

When I described the compilation of par figures as a laborious job, I understated the case. At tracks that feature conditioned racing (to be described in the next chapter), constant vigilance is necessary lest you confuse one set of conditions with another and assign the wrong par to a field of horses. The best method, indicated above, is to deal in terms of the purse values of the conditioned races, being alert to keep pace with the changing purse structure, which tends to fluctuate at various stages of a long season.

Is it necessary to do all that work? No. Persons with a more casual approach to the game can do very well without laboring over daily variant computations. Indeed, the handicapping exercises presented in later pages will not require the use of variants. But many handicapping hobbyists are remarkably studious. They seem to enjoy the toil of precision almost as much as the extra mutuel payoffs to which the effort leads. They will benefit greatly from the use of variants. Meanwhile, I hope that raceways will spend the money and energy needed to establish accurate variants as standing features of the past-performance lines in their printed programs. The enlightened Ontario Jockey Club has already done this at its harness tracks.

The 2:00 Mile

In 1897, an eight-year-old pacer named Star Pointer achieved the first 2:00 mile in the history of harness racing—1:59¼, in fact. In 1903, Lou Dillon, a five-year-old mare, trotted a flat 2:00, the first of her gait to go that fast.

For many years the 2:00 mile remained the sound barrier or timberline of this sport. It was the chief credential of a good horse. But with the introduction of the modified sulky and the emergence of The Meadowlands as North America's premier raceway, all that has changed. Not infrequently, entire racing programs at The Meadowlands consist of races timed in 2:00 or less. The ability to travel that rapidly has become commonplace.

For example, in all the recorded history of harness racing before 1969, only 992 horses had been able to go in 2:00 or better. But in the year 1978 alone, over 711 horses took 2:00 marks. And in 1979, no fewer than 915 performances in 2:00 or better were recorded at one raceway—The Meadowlands!

If the sport now has a timberline time, it may be 1:55. Before 1969, only four Standardbreds had trotted or paced that fast. By the end of 1978, the number stood at 52. Is the breed becoming swifter? Some experts believe that it surely is improving, but they also credit other factors, such as the new sulky, improved track construction and maintenance, better equine nutrition and more productive methods of training and conditioning.

Which makes Greyhound all the more extraordinary. In 1938, when the sport was barely out of its Dark Ages, he trotted a mile in 1:55¼, a record that endured without serious challenge for 31 years until Nevele Pride trotted in 1:54:4 in 1969. And as I write this, Nevele's record has survived for more than ten years.

Dan Patch's pacing mark of 1:55 lasted from 1905 to 1960, when Adios Butler went in 1:54:3. Bret Hanover lowered it to 1:54 and then to 1:53:3 in 1966, and Steady Star took it to 1:52 in 1971.

Would legendary Standardbreds like Greyhound, Dan Patch, Lou Dillon, Uhlan and Peter Manning earn millions if they could return to race for modern purses under modern conditions? It sounds plausible. But they would encounter challenges unknown in their own eras. They now would be called on to beat not two or three good horses a year but dozens. Moreover, they would be required to do it under the incorruptible eye of an electronic timing device which, untouched by human thumb, is relentlessly accurate to the last tick.

Electronics aside, hundreds of today's North American Standardbreds

The amazing Greyhound, with Sep Palin.

go the mile in times that few horses of the past could match. Continued improvement is assured in the high speed from which all-time records come. Just as human footracers finally made the 4:00 mile unremarkable, so will the evolving breed of trotters and pacers overwhelm the records of Nevele Pride and Steady Star. It is not visionary to predict records of less than 1:50. Many Standardbred fanciers consider such performances inevitable.

Lengths per Second

Just as the final time of a race is the winner's time, each of the fractional times represents the official clocking on whatever horse happened to be in the lead at the end of each quarter-mile. Thus, if a horse led all the way in one of its recent outings, the raceway program's past-performance line shows its exact time at the quarter, half, three-quarters and finish. If it was behind at any of those calls, the fractional times in its record remain the same but refer to performances by another horse or two or three— depending on how often and at what points the early lead shifted.

Putting it another way, the past-performance line shows what kind of

Fastest Trotters of All Time

Nevele Pride, 4, TT 1:55:4, Indianapolis, Ind., 1969
Florida Pro, 3, 1:55, Du Quoin, Ill., 1978
Speedy Somolli, 3, 1:55, Du Quoin, Ill., 1978
Songflori, 4, TT 1:55:1, Du Quoin, Ill., 1976
Greyhound, 6, TT 1:55¼, Lexington, Ky., 1938
Green Speed, 3, 1:55:3, Du Quoin, Ill., 1977
Noble Victory, 4, 1:55:3, Du Quoin, Ill., 1966
Dayan, 4, TT 1:55:4, Lexington, Ky., 1970
Matastar, 4, TT 1:55:4, Lexington, Ky., 1962
Count's Pride, 3, 1:56, Syracuse, N.Y., 1978

Fastest Pacers of All Time

Steady Star, 4, TT 1:52, Lexington, Ky., 1971
Falcon Almahurst, 3, TT 1:52:2, Lexington, Ky., 1978
Tender Loving Care, 4, TT 1:52:4, Lexington, Ky., 1979
Abercrombie, 4, 1:53, E. Rutherford, N.J., 1979
Warm Breeze, 4, 1:53:1, Sacramento, Cal., 1977
Sonsam, 3, 1:53:2, E. Rutherford, N.J., 1979
Wellwood Hanover, 3, TT 1:53:2, Lexington, Ky., 1978
Windshield Wiper, 3, TT 1:53:2, Lexington, Ky., 1976
Bret Hanover, 4, TT 1:53:3, Lexington, Ky., 1966
Senor Skipper, 4, 1:53:3, E. Rutherford, N.J., 1978
Whata Baron, 6, TT 1:53:3, E. Rutherford, N.J., 1978

speed was afoot in the early stages of the race but does not disclose the individual horse's own early speed. Unless, of course, it was in lead at one or more of the calls.

Final times are handled differently. The program gives the final time of the race, plus a final time for the individual horse, whether it won or not. At most raceways, a loser's final time is estimated by the program department, employing a traditional formula which equates a beaten length with ⅕ second.

Thus, if a winner is timed in 2:04, a horse that trailed by two lengths is credited with a time of 2:04:2. Margins of ½ length or less are disregarded, so that a horse that finished 3½ lengths behind the 2:04 winner would be awarded a final time of 2:04:3.

The formula is incorrect. It probably is not incorrect enough to warrant a major fuss, but it is sufficiently off the mark to justify review. The rather trivial handicapping defects to which it leads are compounded, sometimes gravely, by a tangle of related confusions:

1. Program departments disagree over what constitutes a length.

2. Unaware of the disagreement, the public mistakenly believes that the lengths recorded in one past-performance line are equivalent to those in any other.

3. Many players defeat themselves through reckless attempts to extend an already doubtful and inconsistent time-length formula into handicapping areas where it is inapplicable.

The USTA and most program departments define a length as the length of a horse—something less than eight feet. The additional length of the sulky is not included in this majority definition.

Peculiar difficulties arise. After all, horse and sulky race as an indivisible unit. For purposes of charting lengths, horse and sulky are observed most easily and accurately as a unit. When a horse races directly behind another, on the rail or elsewhere, it is both convenient and sensible to regard it as a length behind. But the prevailing wisdom insists that such a horse is 1¼ or 1½ lengths behind. Accordingly, when a typical raceway program describes a horse as having been a length behind the leader, it means that the horse was racing either inside or outside the leader—it being impossible to cram a horse and its sulky into the space of one official length.

Now consider this: No matter whether a length be that of a horse or of a horse plus its sulky, the five-lengths-per-second formula is wrong.

All self-respecting raceways have a film patrol which takes movies or television tapes of every race for scrutiny by the judges when fouls or other malpractices are suspected. These tapes show that the trotter or pacer travels across the finish line at a rate of about six lengths per second —if a length be defined in the conventional way, without regard to the presence of the sulky. That is, every beaten length represents about ⅙ second. And the horse travels about 1¼ lengths in ⅕ second. Very few programs accept 1¼ lengths as equivalent to ⅕ second. Most charge a horse more for its margin of defeat than the facts justify, adding extra fifths of seconds to the finishing times.

Having taken an overall look at the time-length rigmarole, let us now return to the question of fractional times. We already know that the program contains the fractional times of each recent race but not the fractional times of a trailing horse. Neither do most programs enable the player to calculate those times. They do not disclose the number of lengths by which a horse was racing behind the leader at the quarter, half or three-quarter calls. It therefore is impossible to apply a time-length formula to a past-performance line to estimate how rapidly a horse went the early fractions when racing behind the pace-setter.

It is impossible, but some people try. They assume that a horse was a length behind at the half if the program says it was second. It was two lengths behind if third, and so on, at the rate of one length per position. If the program shows that the horse was parked out, they assume that it was a length closer than it would have been on the rail. Thus, if the program says, "3°," the horse is thought to have been no worse than a length behind. Its time for the half is estimated at 1:03:1 instead of the 1:03 given in the program as the half-mile clocking of the race.

This is bad business, a real trap for the handicapper. While it is true that horses tend to bunch up during a race, the dimensions of the bunch are anything but uniform. Margins vary considerably. Suppose the leader at the half was in front by a nose. Where was the fifth horse? It might have been behind by half a length or half a block. Without access to detailed charts of every race, the handicapper dare not deal in matters about which the program is silent.

Similar objections apply to the widespread practice of estimating a horse's time for the final quarter in terms of the number of lengths by which it led or trailed at the stretch call and finish. There can be no doubt that the time of the individual's final quarter would be vitally useful to the handicapper. But to calculate it, he would have to know where the horse was at the three-quarter call. The information seldom is given. Where it is unavailable, the calculation should not be attempted.

To know that the horse was third at the three-quarter call is, as we have seen, to know very little. To know that it was second on the outside (2°) may be helpful, if the program actually means that the animal was on the outside *at that point*. If so, the player who assumes that the horse was a length or less behind the leader will be right more often than wrong. But the fact remains that one must have a clear idea where the horse was at the three-quarter call. To know where it was in the stretch is insufficient.

Why? In the first place, the stretch represents only a minor fraction of the final quarter-mile at most tracks. In the second place, a horse may lose or gain several lengths between the time it leaves the three-quarter pole and reaches the stretch. Yet innumerable handicappers, noticing that the horse gained two lengths in the stretch, decide that its time for the final quarter was ⅖ second faster than the official time for that decisive portion of the race.

The fact might well be that the horse's actual time was a full second faster. Perhaps it gained considerable ground between the three-quarter call and the stretch call. Or it might have lost ground at that stage while seeking position for the stretch drive, thereby making its time for the final quarter not much faster than the official clocking.

The pleasant pastime of trying to pick winners is quite difficult enough without the complications caused by wild guesses about time and lengths. Handicapping is sound only when carried on in terms of existing information. To the degree that the handicapper depends on surmise, he borrows grief. The scantiness of past-performance records may be cruel deprivation for the player, but the programs have one redeeming feature: they make elaborate handicapping procedures an unsupportable, unproductive waste of time.

I hope readers of this book will agree that handicappers cannot work with facts they do not have. I hope they also will agree that simple procedures based on known fact are easier and more dependable than some of the fanciful methods in which losers become ensnarled.

In that spirit, let's now consider a simple, factual approach to the basic factor of pace. No aspect of harness racing is misrepresented more widely and misunderstood so lamentably as pace. Yet none is more fundamental to the outcome of a race.

Simplifying Pace

If a Standardbred is broken to harness by a patient, able horseman, and is competently schooled and trained from that point onward, the chances are good that it will come to the races as a brave, cheerful, thoroughly manageable creature, devoid of serious temperamental quirks. It may never beat 2:06, but when it is in form it will produce that kind of time in race after race. Moreover, in the hands of a good driver it will put the time together in whatever style seems suitable to the circumstances of the individual race. On occasion it will leave quickly and try to hold the lead all the way. In another situation it will travel covered up, not too far off the pace, until the driver takes out for the front end. And there will be times when it will drop back to the rear, saving ground on the rail, until tiring leaders open holes through which it can make its bid.

A minority of trotters and pacers are less kindly. Sometimes through inheritance, but more often after heavy-handed treatment, they turn out to be "pullers." The harder the driver tries to restrain them, the harder they lean on the bit, frantic to go too fast too soon. Such horses cannot be rated—their energies cannot be conserved. All they can do is go until exhaustion sets in. Another unhappy type is the horse that hates air, quitting or breaking stride if asked to battle outside or in front for more than a few hundred feet. Such horses must be kept under cover, their chances of winning limited by the driver's luck in finding room for a dramatic burst of speed at the very end of the race.

And then there are horses that dislike racing against the rail. And others that hate having a horse between them and the rail. And horses that will stay neck-and-neck for the lead all day but stop as soon as they get in front. And horses that quit when whipped or not whipped.

But the majority of Standardbreds have no eccentricities that prevent a good driver from taking a fair shot at the purse. This is important. Among other things, it means that most Standardbreds have no set style of racing. They dispense their energy to the driver's order. Some are known as quick-leavers which perform well when setting the pace, but tonight's quick-leaver may come from behind next week, the driver having decided to cut the pattern that way.

Because so many of the horses are so pliable to their drivers, the handicapper cannot always look at the past performances and tell how the pace of the race is likely to develop. For example, the records might seem to make Horse "A" a cinch for the early lead. If the driver can hold "A" together at the end, it will be a wire-to-wire winner. Indeed, the race turns out that way quite often. "A" remains on top all the way or fades in the stretch and is beaten. But the handicapper has foreseen the basic pattern of the race.

I do not trust that kind of harness-race handicapping. When it works, it makes the expert look like a super-swami who can blueprint races in advance. But it does not work often enough. To see why, let us return to "A."

The quick-leaving "A" frequently does not have things all its own way in the early stages. Another horse unveils more early speed than has recently been asked of it and battles "A" from the very outset. What happens next is a matter of driving ability. If the driver of "A" is bright, he may retreat from the speed duel as soon as it starts, hoping that someone else will take out after the other horse and make life easier for him later. If this happens, the pace handicapper's forecast is wrong, whether his choice wins or not. He picked a horse to lead all the way, but it raced behind the pace, upending the predicted pattern.

When pace handicappers find more than one horse with sufficient early speed for an all-the-way victory, they usually expect the two or three pace-setting types to exhaust each other. In such a situation, they prefer to back a sharply conditioned animal that can come off the pace to beat the tiring leaders.

The theory is absolutely valid, but handicappers cannot be sure when it will apply. No good driver deliberately incurs the consequences of a speed duel unless he thinks he has enough animal to endure the duel without losing the race. By the same token, there is no great assurance that a supposed come-from-behind horse will come from behind on a given night. If the expected sprint for the early lead does not develop on schedule, because the drivers are playing possum, the pilot of the come-from-behind horse might make his move at the half and lead all the way home.

Another doctrine of the pace handicapper holds that a slow early pace favors the front horse, enabling it to save itself for the stretch. Uncountable races confirm this. The driver who wins the early lead applies the brakes in the second quarter to give his horse a long breather and retain juice for later use. Yet it is in precisely this kind of tactical situation that the biggest reversals of form occur. A horse lucky enough to have adequate racing room behind a slow pace may benefit more than the leader does and may come on at the end, as Governor Skipper did against Kawartha Eagle. And as longshot winners do every now and again at all raceways.

At this writing, a trend is developing which will inhibit the tactic of the slow early pace and will make conventional pace handicapping even less reliable than it now is. Milt Taylor of Yonkers, the foremost presiding judge in the sport, suspends the license of any driver who slows the early pace enough to place other horses at an unsporting disadvantage.

"We don't want any of those second quarters in thirty-four around here," says Taylor. "The public is paying for formful, competitive racing in which the best horse wins. If a driver is not willing to go the first half-mile in legitimate racehorse time, we tell him to go race somewhere else.

"The driver on the lead holds the stick," Taylor explains. "If he slows the pace away down and somebody tries to pass him, he can speed up just enough to keep the other man parked out. He also can cause accidents behind him when horses begin breaking because they have no place to go. It's evil. It's not competitive racing. Just suppose you are a driver. You leave from the outside and tuck in behind and then some wise guy slows the pace so that they go the first half in 1:05. Naturally, they go the second half in something like 1:01 and you have to grow wings to catch them."

Some of the very best drivers in the business conform to Taylor's rules when under his watchful eye, gleefully relapsing when they move to raceways where their tactics are supervised less stringently. The second quarter of a Yonkers race is quite likely to be slower than the first, but not by much. With drivers required to maintain racing speed at all times, they rarely try to hang each other on the outside, knowing that skirmishes of that sort can exhaust both horses. Thus, when a horse comes alongside to challenge for the early lead, the driver of the front horse usually lets him pass, giving his own animal a breather before bidding for the lead once more.

Other tracks are not yet as vigorous about discouraging slow second quarter-miles and the curious upsets that sometimes result. But it is fair to say that all leading tracks have been discouraging extreme forms of that tactic. The headlong formful racing preferred by Taylor has been attracting sober attention throughout the industry. So has its remarkable freedom from accidents, a happy by-product of what might as well be called Taylor's Law. What with one thing and another, the extremely slow second quarter is doomed.

Pending that development, the student of pace should know that a slow first half-mile usually favors the pace-setter, but sometimes does not and rarely can be foreseen. He also should know that the fast early pace usually benefits a come-from-behind horse. But beyond all else he should know that pace handicapping of the early-speed-versus-late-speed variety is an infirm basis on which to operate. With so many horses able to yield their speed in sequences improvised by the drivers, it is not possible for handicappers to foresee the surprising patterns that sometimes result from that improvisation.

Which brings us to the big question. Can a harness-racing fan use the past-performance records for pace handicapping?

The answer is yes. Vehemently. The guiding principle can be summarized:

Among horses that qualify as possible contenders because they seem to be in fit condition, the likeliest is one that recently demonstrated its ability to produce the best final time after setting or overcoming the fastest early pace.

"Best final time" and "fastest early pace" refer to comparisons of (a) the final times recorded for the possible contenders in their respective good recent races, plus (b) comparisons of the half-mile times of those races.

Note that the individual horse's racing style, if any, is not involved. The handicapper's sole concern is to find the animal, regardless of its supposed early speed, that seems able to complete the mile in comparatively good time after a race in which the half-mile clocking was relatively fast.

To oversimplify, ignoring other relevant factors, a horse that went in 2:03 last week in a race with a half-mile time of 1:01:2 would be regarded as an inherently better prospect than one that went in 2:02:3 off a half-mile time of 1:02:1.

My study of thousands of races at tracks of all sizes has satisfied me that this principle is the basis of a consistently successful approach to harness-race handicapping. When applied to the recent past performances of apparently fit and ready trotters or pacers, it turns up the horse or horses with which top drivers can get the best results, *entirely without regard to the unforeseeable developments that affect driving tactics during a race.*

Of all Standardbred handicapping concepts, this may be the most useful. Let me linger over it a bit, even at risk of repetition. The horse with sufficient form and class to get the fastest mile off the most demanding early pace is a top candidate to do just that in whatever style the driver may choose—or may have thrust on him—during the race itself.

This approach spares the player the necessity of trying to predict the pattern of a race before the drivers form that pattern themselves. It directs the player to a horse most likely to produce a vigorous stretch kick if the early pace proves unusually slow. And it directs him to the horse —the very same horse—that probably will be best able to hold together in the late stages if the early pace is unusually fast.

The key, of course, is to eliminate apparently unready horses, sucked-along horses and other probable non-contenders before analyzing pace. Then, after rating the potential pace of each probable contender, the handicapper simply adjusts the ratings in light of fundamental influences such as class, driver and post position. We shall explore those techniques in later chapters. To prepare the way, we should now agree on means of arriving at actual pace ratings.

Pace Ratings

Numbers are a useful convenience in Standardbred handicapping. The numbers used in this book's handicapping have no significance beyond convenience. We are not dealing in magical formulas, but only in simple, orderly methods of comparing the past-performance records of horses.

The pace-rating chart on the following page offers one easy way to compare the apparent pace potentialities of horses. It assigns an arbitrary point value to each official half-mile time and another point value to the final time of each horse. The assigned numbers could be larger or smaller than they are without affecting the principle. Our concern is simply to establish recognizable *differences* among recent comparable performances.

The chart is for comparison of pace figures recorded in races on dry, fast surfaces. It can be used to rate performances on good tracks, provided the handicapper is careful to do so only when all races under comparison took place on such a footing.

Pace-Rating Table

½ Mile	Points	Final Time	½ Mile	Points	Final Time
:55	150	1:53	1:10	75	2:08
:56	145	1:54	1:11	70	2:09
:57	140	1:55	1:12	65	2:10
:58	135	1:56	1:13	60	2:11
:59	130	1:57	1:14	55	2:12
1:00	125	1:58	1:15	50	2:13
1:01	120	1:59	—	45	2:14
1:02	115	2:00	—	40	2:15
1:03	110	2:01	—	35	2:16
1:04	105	2:02	—	30	2:17
1:05	100	2:03	—	25	2:18
1:06	95	2:04	—	20	2:19
1:07	90	2:05	—	15	2:20
1:08	85	2:06	—	10	2:21
1:09	80	2:07	—	5	2:22

To pace-rate a contender that went in 2:05:3 in a race timed at 1:03:1 to the half-mile, use the chart as follows:

1. Find the value for a half in 1:03—110.
2. Find the value for a mile in 2:05—90.
3. Add the numbers—110 + 90 = 200.
4. *Subtract* the fifths of seconds, if any, in the official half-mile and final times—200 − 4 = 196.

To recapitulate: *Set aside* whatever fifths of seconds appear in the half-mile and final times. Find the value for the remaining half-mile and final time figures. Add them, and then *subtract* from that total the fifths of seconds that had been set aside.

Another easy way to compute pace ratings is to compare the horses directly on a different scale, as follows:

Horse "A": 1:02:4 (20) + 2:05:3 (12) = 32
Horse "B": 1:03:1 (18) + 2:04:4 (16) = 34
Horse "C": 1:03:1 (18) + 2:04   (20) = 38

The fastest half-mile time is given a value of 20. One point is subtracted from the rating of each horse for every $\frac{1}{5}$ second of difference between the official half-mile time of its race and the fastest half-mile time. The same is done with the horses' final times—20 to the fastest and one point less for each $\frac{1}{5}$ second of difference recorded for the slower finishers. The two figures are then added. If you use the pace-rating chart for this example, you will find that it produces the same result as was achieved through direct comparison: the numbers are different, but "C" is four points better than "B" and six points better than "A."

Comparative Track Speeds

Pace handicapping or, for that matter, any other kind of handicapping is most effective when the horses have all been racing at the same track. But the temptation is great to handicap races in which some of the horses have been performing elsewhere. To encourage and assist this practice, the programs publish tables of comparative track speeds. The speed assigned each track is based on USTA figures developed from race times at the track's most recent meeting. Recent changes in footing are not likely to be encompassed in the ratings.

While I doubt that anyone can win money on races of that kind, I admit that it sometimes is fun to try. I would be more than ordinarily reluctant to tackle the problem at a half-mile track, however, unless the out-of-town shippers had also been performing at a track of that size or unless their records showed that they recently had managed well at a half-miler. At a miler or $\frac{5}{8}$-miler, I'd be reluctant to fool with a horse from a half-miler unless it had been showing some willingness to come on in the stretch.

From that point forward, the table of comparative track speeds tells the player whether to adjust the out-of-town times upward or downward, and by how much. In doing so, it is important to adjust the half-mile times as well. If tonight's raceway is rated at 2:05 and the other at 2:06, I would deduct a full second from the horse's final time and $\frac{2}{5}$ second from its half-mile time. If the first half of the race was clocked in slower figures than the second, I would deduct $\frac{3}{5}$ from the half-mile time.

If more track programs included track variants in the past-performance records, pace rating would be an even more dependable tool than it is. Nevertheless, I believe that pace rating is the safest, most profitable basis on which the occasional racegoer can build his handicapping method. Relying entirely on information contained in the program, his comparison of half-mile times and final times enables him to hold his own against handicappers who are out there every night and work with private charts. The trick, of course, is to concentrate on playable races (already discussed) and to make astute appraisals of class, form, post position and driver, adjusting the basic ratings by means we shall discuss.

Another Approach to Time and Pace

Many successful handicappers disdain pace ratings. They concentrate on the recent performances of apparently fit horses, estimating the final time of which each contender seems capable under the conditions of the upcoming race—as contrasted with the conditions under which the animals trotted or paced recently. As the reader will see, we handicap by very much the same method in these pages, but supplement the study with the factor of pace, which we regard as insurance.

An alternative approach to pace considers each contender's final times not in terms of the half-mile times of recent races but relative to the animal's own time for the final quarter-mile of the races being rated. I have already discussed the hazards of trying to calculate a horse's final-quarter time at a raceway whose program omits information about the number of lengths between a horse and the leading horse at the ¾-mile call. But in Chicago, California and at a scattering of tracks elsewhere, the programs include the desired information. Some programs even print the individual horse's final-quarter time as part of the past-performance summary line.

Statistical studies (notably the Kusyshyn and Adams-Sullivan ones mentioned on pages 48–49) indicate that a fit horse's final-quarter time in its last and/or next-to-last representative starts may bear more significantly on its final times than do the official half-mile times of the same races. I have no strong convictions in the matter, but am sure enough that a handicapper who concentrates on fit horses properly situated as to class, post position and driver and who knows how to evaluate the final times of the horse's latest representative race or two, will only strengthen the findings by noting the final-quarter times of the top contenders.

Readers who want to experiment along those lines, using the rating scale set forth on page 168, can assign a rating of 120 to a final-quarter time of :29.

8 THE CLASS FACTOR

CLASS IS QUALITY. It expresses itself as speed, soundness, stamina, gameness, stability of gait and consistency of performance. In whatever proportions these traits appear, they represent the individual Standardbred's physical and temperamental heritage, as affected by persons and events. Among environmental influences on class are nutrition, illness and injury; the variable wisdom of grooms, trainers, veterinarians and drivers; and, above all, the exertions of training and racing.

Horses of the highest class not only are faster than most other horses but also are sound enough and/or game enough to produce the speed when it counts—on the night of the race, in head-to-head confrontation with the best of their era. They are more likely than others to remain on gait even when pressed to the farthest limits of their speed and endurance. Indeed, when taxed in that way they reach into their reserves of energy for the extra yards of sustained speed that win close races and break records.

The lower the class, the smaller are these reserves of energy or the greater the disabilities that prevent the horse from drawing on them. The cheapest fields at raceways include expensively bred animals condemned to slowness at the mile by some inherited or acquired defect—a muscular, skeletal or organic flaw which limits stride or shortens breath. In the same fields are horses of former speed whose class has deteriorated with age and use.

As the lifetime speed and earnings records of horses in these cheap fields demonstrate, Standardbred class is transient. A breeder or historian evaluates a horse in light of its total achievements, including those of its distant past, but a handicapper concentrates on the present. Without present soundness and condition, class is inoperative. The glories of the past are pleasant to reminisce about but costly to bet on.

By the same criteria, if a horse of superior class has a competent driver and is in good enough shape to demonstrate its class, it is the best bet of the night, the week or the year. A slight class advantage can mean decisive victory.

Obsessed as they are with the desire for close races among evenly matched Standardbreds, raceways take great pains to prevent situations in which one horse of conspicuously superior quality lays over a soft field. Yet sometimes it happens. More often, condition-related differences in current ability make the outcome predictable in a race among animals of ostensibly equal class.

To recognize these differences when they glimmer beneath the surface of the past-performance charts, it is necessary to understand the harness-racing industry's own evolving conceptions of how horses and races should be classified, and how conditions of eligibility for entry should be determined. The class notations on the program page reflect these conceptions and the raceway's method of implementing them. To a great extent, the notations also reflect the standards whereby horsemen evaluate and manipulate their own stock.

The class patterns of harness racing have been in flux for many years. Eligibility conditions and classification methods prevalent at today's tracks differ remarkably from those of a decade ago. Each new season brings horsemen a wider and more equitable assortment of racing opportunities. Today's greater variety of races—some of which overlap or coincide in class without seeming to—challenges the knowledge and judgment of the handicapping fan. More than ever, the ability to draw fine class distinctions is crucial at the mutuel windows. The past-performance chart sometimes obscures these distinctions. The racegoer can begin to sort things out for himself when he learns how race-classification methods developed to their present state, and where they seem to be going from here.

Classified Racing

Time at the mile being the fundamental measure of a North American Standardbred's ability, racing secretaries never stray far from that statistic in deciding whether horses belong on their programs and, if so, in what kinds of races. The same criterion serves horsemen when they make their own decisions about where and when their animals should race, and in what kind of company.

The *when* is crucial. A 2:10 horse is not endlessly capable of the 2:10 mile. It is a living creature, not a robot. It cannot produce 2:10 unless fit. Minor illness, injury or plain lapses from form may affect its speed for weeks, influencing the management decisions of its trainer.

On one side, then, the racing secretary and his expert opinion of each horse's ability. On the other, the horseman and his intimate view of how the horse's *present* ability compares with its *previous* ability or, perhaps, with its *potential* ability. In the middle sits the raceway operator, whose financial outlook brightens to the degree that he can offer the public (a) exciting races and (b) races in which the results are believable because the form stands up. To achieve these goals, the industry has been tinkering for decades with the terms and conditions under which horses compete against each other.

It has not been easy. Horsemen want maximum freedom to enter each animal in the race best suited to its current abilities. Translation: the easiest race with the best purse. Raceway operators need to restrict such freedom so that fields will be as evenly matched as possible. And the public needs to understand the ground rules so that it can compare one past performance with another and assess the current class of each horse on that basis.

During the formative years of the sport, logic decreed that horses be matched on the basis of their time records. Just as a farmer with a 2:17 horse might solicit a race against a 2:20 horse, and might accept a race against some other 2:17 horse, but would avoid losing money to the owner of a 2:12 horse, the programs at country fairs and other early raceways presented fields of animals whose lifetime speed records were competitive. Horses with better records raced for better purses.

This was the logic of innocence. Horsemen quickly realized that it was more profitable to beat cheap horses in slow time than to be beaten by good horses in fast. On occasion, it was most profitable not to win at all. Listen to a veteran racing official who was there:

> The big money was for aged horses in those days. Very little was done with them at two or three. They began at four. If you had a precocious four-year-old, you wanted him to get experience. So you kept him under wraps, letting him finish second to win 25 percent of the purse, but not letting him win. In that way he got no record and could stay in easy races. Sometimes you put him into heat races and could win the first heat in fast enough time to win second money on the overall results of the three or four heats. But the horse still had no record, because he still had not been an official winner. When you finally got ready to shoot with

him, you really could make hay. Perhaps he was good enough to beat everything in the state but was still eligible to race against soft fields. You could win four, five, six races in succession, never going a tick faster than necessary.

This kind of cheating, and the crude maneuvering that caused interminable delays at the start of each race, gave the sport a reputation not greatly superior to that of the wheels of fortune and shell games with which it vied for public attention at fairs. After the war, with pari-mutuel betting and night programs offering promise of riches beyond all precedent, the USTA outlawed the so-called time bar, substituting a classification system less conducive to larceny. Without this reform, harness racing could scarcely have established itself in metropolitan areas and might even have worn out its welcome in the boondocks.

The new system divided horses into thirty classes on the basis of lifetime earnings. Class 30, the lowest, was for non-winners of $100 (the minimum was increased by USTA amendment in later years). The top class, FFA (Free-for-All), was for horses that had earned more than $50,000. Class 20 was for non-winners of $2,000; Class 11 was for non-winners of $20,000, and so forth.

The shortcomings of the class system soon became expensively apparent to horsemen. A horse was imprisoned in its class even after injury, sickness or the deterioration of age left it unable to keep up with sounder animals whose career earnings were no higher. In fact, a horse unable to win in its prescribed class often was boosted to a higher and even more impossible class after having earned a little money when it backed into a few second- or third-place finishes. Or a three-year-old would win so much against easy fields of its own age that its useful career would end at four, when it was obliged not only to face older horses but also faster ones, and no longer could win.

Despite efforts to remedy these defects by making allowances for illness or age, the class system remained unsatisfactory. By winning, horses inevitably earned their way into company too formidable for them. They then were required to lose repeatedly before qualifying for the class demotion which might enable them to resume winning. The horseman found himself in the position of racing his good animal to sure defeat during the very months when it should have been repaying him for all the time and money expended on its early training.

Class racing withered away and was replaced with classified racing, in which the racing secretary assigns the horse to whatever class he considers appropriate. The classes are designated by letter, D being the lowest. The pecking order proceeds through C to B to A to AA and then to JFA (Junior Free-for-All) and FFA. At Yonkers, Roosevelt and Monticello, where letter-classified racing is firmly entrenched, the classes are subdivided. The lowest is C-3, followed in ascending order by C-2, C-1, B-3, B-2, B-1, A-3, A-2, A-1, AA, JFA and FFA.

Acknowledging in 1955 that a racing secretary's classification of a horse was nothing but his handicapping estimate of its speed at the mile, the USTA issued a schedule of speeds by which the secretaries were required to abide. At a track where FFA pacers—the best in the country—went in about 2:03, a 2:13 pacer was assigned to D, the poorest of the ten listed classes. Each step up the scale represented about one second of improvement. Trotters were assumed to go 1⅗ seconds slower than pacers of equal class. Formulas were available for adjusting the table to the relative speed of the individual track.

The old time-bar system had pitted horsemen against an inflexible set of rules. By penalizing achievement and rewarding deceit, the time bar virtually guaranteed that trainers and drivers would be under economic compulsion to fleece each other and fool their rural public. Class racing abolished the rewards of deceit while leaving intact the penalties for achievement. Letter classification falls between its two predecessors. By its very nature it propels horsemen into a ceaseless game of truth or consequences with the racing secretary, who holds most of the trumps.

Although common sense requires the secretary to classify the horses on the basis of their speed, it also dictates that he "move up" a frequent winner, even if its speed is below normal for the higher class. By the same logic, he refuses to "back up" a losing horse to a lower class until satisfied that it cannot earn its way in the higher class. He may demote an animal after one or two losses, or may defer action for many weeks, until persuaded by additional evidence.

GARY BUXTON
Racing Secretary, Hollywood Park and Louisville Downs.

Because his decisions directly affect the revenues of racing stables, the secretary's burden is heavy. But the rules offer horsemen no incentive to lighten it. Sooner or later, each trainer finds himself sincerely convinced that one of his horses is misclassified. He knows more about the animal's current condition than the secretary does, but he cannot reasonably expect that official to demote the horse until its predicament is made visible in a few poorer races. Temptation arises to lose as abjectly as possible, in hope of hastening the secretary's decision. Similarly, the trainer with a fairly sharp horse must decide whether to win and be moved into a class where purses are higher but the horse's earning capacity may be less. The alternative is to lose and be allowed to remain for a few more races where the pickings are easier.

In self-defense, and in the interest of the all-out competition which he is paid to produce, the racing secretary watches every performance with a cold and critical eye. If he suspects that a horse's people have abandoned hope of winning and have stopped trying, he calls them onto his tear-stained carpet and says as much. To be backed up in class, a horse not only must lose but also must lose in a manner convincing to the secretary. He wants to be sure that the driver is trying.

The notion that horsemen might find it more expedient to lose than to win was rampant in raceway grandstands during the years when letter classes were the national mode. The industry found the idea intolerable. It trembled over rumors about drivers "going" or not. It feared the eventual effects on mutuel receipts of the strange last-minute odds fluctuations which accompanied some of the rumors. Furthermore, horsemen were chronically disgruntled. They wanted latitude to enter races of their own choosing.

To promote public confidence and restore tranquility backstage, the USTA has abolished classified racing in its own sphere of influence, that is, everywhere but the southern part of New York State. At Yonkers, Roosevelt and Monticello, letter classes remain in full force.

New York raceway managements cling to classified racing for the elemental reason that they consider it good for their business. They maintain that firm control of entries by an astute racing secretary assures close, exciting competition, which stimulates lively betting. Furthermore, their audiences are used to the A-B-C classes. No other method offers such simple, understandable designations. The New York fan knows that a horse moving from C-1 to B-3 is rising in class, and forms his judgments accordingly. When the New York tracks tried to operate without this system between 1963 and 1966, the financial results were branded unsatisfactory. And, finally, New York is unconvinced that chicanery waxes or wanes with changes in classification methods. Where the racing secretary and presiding judge know their business and are supported by a muscular state racing commission, cheating is no particular problem.

It is possible to muster a rebuttal for each of the foregoing arguments, and it is quite easy to rebut each rebuttal. That, in fact, is what has been going on in the industry for years. Controversy about the secessionist character of New York harness racing is deep, bitter and incessant. Although I enjoy playing the oracle, I must decline the pleasure of predicting how this debate will end. The truth is that nobody has the vaguest idea on that score. All we can do at this stage of events is see where each form of harness racing is, and where it seems to be going, and what may be implied for the handicapping enthusiast.

Conditioned Racing

At all North American raceways save the three in downstate New York, conditioned racing has supplanted classified racing. In principle, conditioned racing frees the horseman from bondage to the racing secretary. With the same blow, it liberates that functionary from responsibility for managing the careers of other people's horses. No longer required to classify them according to his assessment of their abilities, he relinquishes the power to type-cast some of them in races more difficult than their trainers and owners might consider suitable. All he does, at least in principle, is write conditions of eligibility for entry in races. The horseman is free to pick and choose among a variety of races, thus managing his animal as he sees fit.

The realities of conditioned racing do not coincide at all points with the principle, but they come quite close. Racing secretaries keep a careful

PHIL LANGLEY
Racing Secretary, Sportsman's Park.

census of the kinds of horses ready to race at their tracks, and write conditions designed to produce close contests among the available stock. The conditions are concerned mainly with earnings—lifetime, or last year, or this year, or in each horse's most recent starts. Number, frequency and recency of victories may be among the primary conditions, as may age or sex or both.

When the racing secretary is willing and able to adapt his procedures to the varying talents and credentials of the horses on his grounds, every fit animal has ample opportunities to win, or at least to cash occasional checks. And handicapping fans can tell rather accurately what grade of horse is involved in each race. Where the secretary is short on such ability, or begrudges the effort, or where the equine population is poor, the eligibility conditions tend toward the incomprehensible and so do the results of some of the races.

For example, consider an April race in which the conditions specify non-winners of $10,000 during the previous year. Some racing secretaries persist in writing such conditions, which attract wildly incompatible fields of horses. Entrants might include animals that already have won *more* than $10,000 during the *current* year, as well as animals that do not belong on the same track with them, having done little last year and less this. Similarly, a race programmed for non-winners of $4,000 during the current year might prove a soft touch for a classy animal in its second or third start of the season.

Most horsemen admire the conditions written by Phil Langley, racing secretary at Sportsman's Park. He concentrates—as trainers and handicappers must—on recent performances. Eligibility for his races is governed by the amount of money won or the number and purse values of races won in the horse's six, eight or ten most recent starts. Conditions

LARRY MALLAR
Racing Secretary, Roosevelt Raceway.

of this kind are easily understood, inspiring the confidence of horsemen and bettors alike.

Obviously, as a horse's earnings increase, so does the quality of the opposition it faces. Sooner or later it must enter conditioned races in which its chances are slim. But if it is in good physical shape, its prospects rarely are hopeless. The recent records of the other horses are, after all, similar to its own. It is astonishing to realize that here, for the first time in the history of this sport, the rules contain nothing that might be interpreted as a penalty for winning or a reward for losing.

Although the racing secretary no longer has the power to classify every horse in the park, he remains responsible for the presentation of closely contested races. The conditions he writes, however ingenious they may be, do not always accomplish this. Some horses, though eligible under the conditions, are not good enough for their races. Others are too good. The secretary negotiates for the withdrawal of such horses. Bargaining of that kind between secretaries and horsemen is most prevalent at tracks where, for one reason or another, relatively good horses and/or relatively poor ones have few opportunities to compete against stock of their own quality.

When the USTA adopted conditioned racing, it suffered no illusion that the new system would be appropriate for all kinds of horses. Its plan was double edged. On the one hand, the association sought to escape the problems attributed to classified racing. On the other, it sought to promote industry-wide acceptance of claiming races. This was a large hope. Claiming races were at odds with some cherished traditions.

Despite large obstacles, claiming races have become an integral feature of the game. More numerous every season, they are bringing about decisive changes in the arts of raceway programming, Standardbred management and handicapping. By establishing clearly delineated classes of competition for cheap horses, they help to bring order and reason to all other aspects of classified and conditioned racing. Suddenly we can see the emerging outlines of a logical gradation, or hierarchy, of Standardbred class. As the class structure becomes clearer and more rational, some of the worst perplexities of harness-race handicapping disappear.

Claiming Races

The owner of a professional baseball or football team invests millions of dollars but dares not enter his own clubhouse without an invitation. The owner of a Thoroughbred runner has a remote and cautious relationship with the animal. But the proprietor of a Standardbred really *belongs*. He has things to *do*.

Any able-bodied man, woman or adolescent can climb into a sulky and drive the average trotter or pacer. It is one of the incomparable pleasures of Standardbred ownership to get all dolled up in horseman's regalia and actually train one's animal. Proudly, and as comfortably as if he were in his easy chair, the owner jogs the horse the wrong way of the track for a couple of miles, then turns it around for a timed trip. Afterward, mud-spattered, he gives the trainer a great deal of advice about its form.

Enchanted owners develop deep attachments to their horses. So do trainers, most of whom entered the sport as the sons and grandsons of owners. The modern horse may no longer be quite the family pet that grazed in the yard between races, but it is credited with intelligence, personality and feelings. It therefore is not often treated as if it were a mere racing tool, an item of merchandise.

This warmly possessive attitude accounts for the reluctance with which harness-racing folk have accepted claiming races. Any horse entered in such a contest is automatically for sale at whatever price is stated in the eligibility conditions. A bona fide horseman can post a claim and a check before the race and lead the animal to his own stable afterward.

The main virtue of these races is fair competition among horses of equal market value, equal class. A horse entered at an unrealistically high price attracts no claims but wins no races, either. When entered at the proper level, it might win but it might also be claimed, a possibility upsetting to many owners.

What finally has tipped the balance in favor of the claiming race is that no other formula assures winning opportunities to mediocre and inferior stock. Young or old, improving or deteriorating, the average horse is best off in a claiming race against its own kind. No matter how cleverly the racing secretary drafts eligibility conditions or, in New York, classifies the horses, the average trotter or pacer is at a disadvantage. Most often, it takes a drubbing from a higher-grade animal headed for better things. If it warms out of its aches and pains enough to score an upset victory, it helps its owner and a handful of longshot fanciers, but contributes nothing to the sport's hard-earned reputation for formful competition. Its victory does not alter the fundamental truths that (a) cheap horses should race against their own kind and (b) that the only known way to assure keen competition among them is to write claiming races for them.

Claiming races were tried and abandoned fifty years ago. They were revived in 1959 at Sportsman's Park, and in 1965 the USTA began campaigning for their widespread adoption. By 1969, more than a third of all raceway events in the United States were claimers—a phenomenal growth.

At Sportsman's Park, which enjoys the third-highest mutuel handle in the country and offers purses to match, more than half of the races are claimers. To encourage this development, track management used to offer higher purses to claimers than to conditioned races of comparable speed. This sweetening of the kitty no longer is necessary. At long last, the stability of the sport's class structure rests on relatively orderly patterns. By and large, the size of the purse is an accurate index to the class of the race. All tracks do not have identical purse schedules, of course. But at the individual track, the quality of a horse is measurable in terms of the purses it has recently been able to win.

To demonstrate the equanimity with which harness horsemen have adapted to claiming races, an assortment of raceway programs from a week in February 1979 shows that Windsor Raceway offered 43 claiming races during that period, Freehold had 42, Roosevelt Raceway carded 34 and Los Alamitos and Pompano Park each had 34. At each place, the claimers constituted more than half of the week's program.

Later in this chapter I shall offer facts helpful in comparing claiming, classified and conditioned races. For now, we can agree that higher claiming prices indicate higher class at any given track, but may be misleading if two tracks are involved. The $10,000 pacer at Freehold may be precisely equivalent to $12,000 pacers at Brandywine or Yonkers. Market values and claiming prices tend to rise where purses are higher. The aged gelding that appears in the average claiming race is worth just about what it can win in a year, and its claiming price should reflect that.

By the same standard, the handicapper knows at a glance that a horse entered to be claimed for $5,000 is a horse in physical trouble if it has earned that much or more during the current year, or even during the previous year. Horsemen give nothing away for $5,000 if they can sell it for more.

The Preferred List

One kind of classified racing is accepted throughout the industry. The racing secretary posts what is known as a "preferred" list, which names the fastest horses on the grounds. These logical contenders for the meeting's richest feature races are not permitted to enter conditioned or letter-class races except in special circumstances. With similar exceptions, lesser animals are not eligible for the big features.

At most tracks, races among the listed horses are identified in the programs as "preferred." When out-of-town stars and larger purses are involved, the term usually is "invitational." At Yonkers and Roosevelt, the "preferred" designation is not used and "invitational" embraces a wider range of purses and horses.

Every season, a few mature horses of each gait prove routinely capable of 1:55 to 1:58 miles and are hailed as free-for-allers—the animals that confront the best in the world for the highest purses, with no holds barred.

Training in winter quarters at Pompano Park, Florida.

Depending on the track, their races are known as FFA (Free-for-All), open, invitational, classic, international or the like.

JFA (Junior Free-for-All) designates a race among stock too good for the average preferred field but not good enough to beat free-for-allers. A horse that races in A or AA company at Yonkers may be granted an occasional fling at a JFA purse. Moreover, if it ships to a smaller raceway, it probably competes in preferred affairs, even invitationals.

All these types of feature races are comparable with each other in terms of the purses they offer—provided that the handicapper is careful to compare races that occurred at the same track or, at least, on the same racing circuit. A $25,000 invitational almost certainly is a more severe test than a $15,000 one at the same track. But the handicapper makes unwarranted assumptions if he guesses that a $25,000 race at one track was of higher quality than a race of less value at a distant track. Purses vary with the time of year and the customs of the individual raceway. Unless the fan recognizes the names of the animals in an out-of-town race and has means of appraising the form they were in at the time, he has little to go on.

Stakes and Such

Major stakes and futurities of the type that feature Grand Circuit meetings often require nominations and entry fees while the animals still are foals. To nominate a well-bred infant to all the stakes for which it is eligible, and to maintain its eligibility until it proves as a two-year-old that it has been overrated, costs not less than $10,000. The rare creature that justifies such risks throughout its two-, three- and four-year-old form—like an Abercrombie or Green Speed—repays the enormous investments many times over. But it is sobering to realize that most Standardbreds nominated for stakes never fulfill the early hope. Some never race at all, much less compete in top company. The huge purses awarded to stake winners consist primarily of nomination fees contributed in behalf of animals that are nowhere to be seen on the day of the race.

The most promising colts actually go onto the Grand Circuit. If they withstand those severe tests as two- and three-year-olds, they become FFA and JFA competitors at four and five. They are the best. It is no trick to recognize their quality in the past-performance records, even in the unlikely event that their names are unfamiliar.

In recent years, however, it has become increasingly possible for a careless bettor to make horrible mistakes about certain young horses whose records include high earnings in stake races. Without reading those records carefully, the racegoer might assume that the animals were of Grand Circuit quality. He would be dead wrong.

The complicating factor is a type of racing subsidized by rebates from the state treasury's share of the mutuel take or breakage. Devised to encourage the home state's breeding industry and related forms of agriculture, the races are open only to the get of sires that stand in the state. The most extravagant and successful sire-stake program is the one in New York, which offers purses of $5.5 million a year and has become an instant bonanza for breeders and stable owners sharp enough to establish themselves on the ground floor.

Examples: Her Bias, a two-year-old filly, won $105,614 against weak trotters in New York sire stakes during 1978. Her best time was 2:03:3. During that same year, another trotting filly, Classical Way, won a meager $39,483 in Grand Circuit competition, posting a race mark of 2:00:2 and a time trial of 1:59:4.

Ontario's excellent sire-stake program bestowed purses of $99,322 on Dover's Surge in his two-year-old competition against animals sired in that province. The colt's best time was 2:06:3. The fastest juvenile trotter of the year was Courtly, who went in 1:59 but won less than $80,000.

With millions of dollars going practically by default to horses whose main qualifications are geographical, breeders hasten to get some of the money by using better stallions in these places—thereby upgrading the state or provincial breeding program. The effects have been salutary. Which means that the original decisions to establish these programs were correct. More and more good trotters and pacers are emerging in places that never produced decent stock before the sire stakes provided incentive. Thus, in 1977, the New York-bred Green Speed won the Hambletonian in world-record time. In 1978 another New Yorker, Happy Escort, won the Little Brown Jug.

Other stake races with which the reader should be acquainted are known as "early closers" and "late closers." Nominations and entry fees for an early closer are posted by the horseman at least six weeks—frequently many months—before the race. Subsequent changes in physical condition and improvements or deteriorations in class give these contests a sporting air akin to that of the more celebrated stake affairs. Late closers involve less financial adventure, with entries closing from four days to six weeks before the race. In attempting to estimate the probable class of such a race, when one is listed in a past-performance record, the safest criteria remain the final and fractional times.

The "Big Fives"

For three-year-old trotters, the classic tests of racing quality have long been the Hambletonian and the Kentucky Futurity. In recent decades, however, three other rich races have created a theoretical Quintuple Crown. They are the Yonkers Trot, the Dexter Cup (Roosevelt Raceway) and the Colonial (Liberty Bell).

For three-year-old pacers, the big five are the Little Brown Jug (Delaware, Ohio), the Messenger Stake (Roosevelt), the William H. Cane Pace (Yonkers), the Adios (The Meadows, Pennsylvania) and The Meadowlands Pace (New Jersey).

Class and Age

The precocious Nevele Pride set world records at age four, thereby establishing himself as a paragon of the early speed with which modern breeding and training are preoccupied. He was more horse at four than at three, however. And he almost certainly would have been even more horse at five than at four, if he had not been trundled off to make millions at stud, after going lame.

Barring accident, a Standardbred approaches its full racing powers late in its fourth year and should be at its absolute best when five and six. Nothing in the nature of the breed decrees that a trotter or pacer should go into decline at seven, but most of them do by then, if not sooner. Training and racing use them up.

Happy Escort, a belittled product of the New York sire-stake program, charges to the finish of a 1978 Little Brown Jug heat with Bill Popfinger driving. They went on to defeat Falcon Almahurst and Flight Director in the raceoff.

The rules of the sport protect young horses from ruination in races against older animals, which are known in the trade as "aged," as in "aged in the wood." Racing secretaries are forbidden to put horses less than four years of age on their preferred or invitational lists, except when (a) the younger ones have won seven races or (b) the horse's stable wants to compete against the best.

Every season, good barns make important money with young horses of less than Grand Circuit caliber by taking advantage of these rules. The newcomers to routine raceway competition are unable to beat the best of their own generation and would be destroyed by good older horses, but are much better than the stock they meet in C and B racing.

The same happens elsewhere in the country, with decent three-year-olds swamping the culls they face in races conditioned for lifetime non-winners of $3,000. A young horse that hails from a top stable and has a leading driver should always be regarded as a threat in its first few starts against undistinguished raceway stock. It may win five or more races in succession before encountering older horses with sufficient energy to put it in its place.

These young animals usually pay low odds, and lose frequently enough to keep the handicappers in extreme suspense. But they are fun to follow. They are extra-special fun when their records disclose no speed comparable to that of some of the hacks opposing them. Often enough to justify attention, they go several seconds faster in raceway company than they did in their earlier efforts. Age three is the time of life when horses are capable of the most rapid and dramatic improvement.

As a matter of handicapping principle, it is bad judgment to bet *against* a lightly raced three-year-old with a first-rate driver in a conditioned or classified field of cheap older horses. The youngster may have a pronounced class advantage. If it has not raced recently, or if its only late effort was a qualifying race in unpromisingly slow time, the safest procedure is to pass the race altogether.

Such a horse becomes a more dependable bet in its second conditioned or classified race, especially if its first was a good effort. The odds are low, but a mutuel price of $3 is, after all, a profit of 50 cents on the dollar.

In classified and conditioned races restricted to three- and four-year-olds, it pays to assume that the older animal will be strong enough to prevail over the younger, unless its own record is one of chronic slowness and repeated defeat. Putting it another way, if all else is equal (including the drivers and post positions), a 2:05 four-year-old should defeat a 2:05 three-year-old. And a 2:05 five-year-old in good form should upend both of them.

At the opposite end of the Standardbred spectrum are the relics that appear in claiming races. No horse older than 14 is allowed to compete nowadays, but steady animals of 11 and 12 win race after race. Usually geldings of former high class, they often race at claiming prices below their actual market value, because nobody dares to invest in the doubtful future of an ancient horse by claiming it. Hence, the handicapper watches for an oldster whose recent record proves it still capable of putting together successively vigorous performances against cheaper stock. If the record also shows that it has been going the mile as rapidly as any of its opponents, it probably has an edge, on grounds of its competitive honesty.

Before moving to another aspect of class, it might be well to attend to some of the technical terminology employed by Standardbred horsemen in describing age and sex. Until age four, horses of either sex are referred to in some circumstances as "colts." "Colt races" are races for young horses, usually of superior class. On the other hand, in speaking of an individual young female horse, the word "filly" is used. And a desexed male of any age is a gelding. At four, the filly becomes a mare, the colt becomes a horse and the gelding remains a gelding. Also at four, the animals are described as "aged."

Class and Sex

It is taken for granted that male Standardbreds are stronger competitors than females, but the record disproves that theory. Between 1845, when Lady Suffolk became the first trotter to go in less than 2:30, and 1969, when Nevele Pride became world champion in 1:54:4, the record had been held by ten mares, ten geldings and only two stallions, of whom Nevele Pride was the second and Cresceus (2:02¼ in 1901) was the first.

Moreover, during the very season in which he set his historic mark, Nevele Pride was defeated by Une de Mai, Fresh Yankee and Lady B. Fast, females all. Indeed, Une de Mai trounced him only one week before he broke all the watches at Indianapolis.

No fewer than eight fillies have won the Hambletonian. The mare Delmonica Hanover beat the world's best males in the International Trot not once but twice and also won France's prestigious Prix d'Amerique. And you can get an argument from many a good horseman if you try to name two male trotters of any era who would have been better than even money against Roquepine or Armbro Flight when those ladies were at their best.

What is true among championship trotters is no less true when the humble go at it for ordinary purses. Fillies and mares compete on absolutely equal terms with colts, geldings and entire horses. Some females seem to fade in the heat of summer, but so do some stallions and geldings. There may be a basis for the theory that mares are especially dependable in cold weather, but nobody has ever been able to document it. Stanley Dancer says that some are, some are not and no sweeping generalizations should be made.

It is fairly well agreed that geldings are among the least skittish members of the breed. In fact, many horsemen prefer to geld male trotters and pacers that are below top quality and lack potential breeding value. No longer subject to flights of romantic interest, geldings undoubtedly are the steadiest and most easily managed of Standardbreds. Bob Farrington says that the 2:06 gelding might have been a 2:05 stallion, but it produces the 2:06 consistently, whereas some 2:05 stallions "can throw a 2:07 at you when you least want it."

The steadiness of the gelding is worth knowing about, but I would not build a handicapping method on it. If a gelding and a sexed horse shape up as equals in terms of form, pace, class, driver and post position, the race either is too close for betting, or the fan should bet on them both. Or if the past performances of one horse reveal it as steadier than the other, and worth a bet, it matters little whether the bet is on a gelding, a mare or a stallion. What counts in handicapping is the past-performance record itself, regardless of the animal's sex.

For reasons unexplained, females are scarce among first-rate pacers. The last female able to make trouble in Free-for-All competition at that gait was Handle with Care, who won more than $800,000 between 1973 and 1976. Dottie's Pick, Phantom Lady and His Lady managed to win heats in their bids for the Little Brown Jug, but no filly has ever taken it all. With creation of the Jugette Filly Division, the pattern becomes permanent.

Despite male supremacy in the very top pacing events, the handicapper can overlook sex differences when dealing with other races at that gait. If the mare has the best record, she is a bet. A recent example was Tender Loving Care, who showed her heels to many of the best male pacers of 1979.

Class and Earnings

Racegoers love the horse of former class that suddenly reverts to type and defeats an inferior field. It is easy to identify horses of former class, but difficult to foresee the rare occasion on which one might recover its sea legs and produce something like its old speed.

Every night in the week, horses that once traveled in 2:01 are predictable losers in 2:09. Just as a Standardbred's lifetime mark seldom tells the handicapper much about its next race, its earnings record also bears small relevance to its present form and class.

Career earnings indicate bygone class. But tonight's issue is settled by tonight's class, which is evaluated in terms of the six or eight performances summarized in the program record. If these races offer no hint of ability to win in tonight's circumstances, it is a gross mistake to look for clues in the dead statistics of the past.

Every now and again, fans harvest splendiferous payoffs by betting on career earnings rather than current ability. That is not handicapping, but wishful thinking. There is no long-range profit in it. To be sure, when everything else is equal, it makes sense to go to the horse with high career earnings. But everything else seldom is equal.

Here are some ideas about the significance of earnings in various kinds of races.

CLAIMERS. If the horse drops in claiming price after a succession of poor showings and wins its race at a big mutuel, someone may be able to point out that it had the highest career earnings in the field. If you wish, you probably will be able to show that the horse had lower average annual earnings than some others did, making its career statistics meaningless. You may also be able to argue that the animal lucked into the winner's circle, as big longshots so often do. In any case, you should be calmly confident that horses win on their present ability, which if not recognizable in recent performance is not recognizable at all.

If the entire field seems to be in poor form, the race is unplayable, although I suppose one sometimes might justify a tiny bet on the one horse that is dropping in claiming price. It has been racing no more terribly than the others but at least has been doing so in relatively good company. If the driver is a big winner and the post position is adequate, the bet becomes more understandable. But career earnings remain an unreliable guide.

CLASSIFIED RACES. New York racing secretaries are mighty sharp. Horses win there when moved up in class, substantiating the secretary's judgment. They also win when backed up in class, but not often without some prior sign of imminent improvement.

Since letter classifications are assigned on the basis of current ability, without regard to historical data like career earnings, New York handicapping fans should operate accordingly. Early in the season, classified races do occur in which current ability is unclear and the racing secretary has been guided by factors not included in the printed program. Rather than handicap such races—or any races—off last year's form, including last year's earnings, I prefer to sit them out until the animals have shown what they can do this season.

CONDITIONED RACES. Here again, current ability outweighs the accomplishments of the past. This is particularly noticeable when the conditions limit the field to horses that earned less than a stated amount during the *previous* calendar year. Conditions of that kind are made to order for animals of current sharpness.

If the conditions are silent about last year's earnings but restrict eligibility to horses whose earnings during the present year are below a stated amount, a different approach may pay off. For example, one entrant may have earned a good deal of loot last year and may have performed like its old self in its latest race or two. It deserves some extra points for class.

Earnings become especially misleading when the conditions create a soft touch for a fast horse that has been racing at smaller tracks, winning relatively little money in each start. If, as is often the case, the horse is from a good barn, has been active lately and figures to perform at somewhere near its best, it could be worth a nice bet. Even recent earnings are not always a reliable index to current ability.

Class and Consistency

A sound Standardbred, properly trained, entered in the right races and driven competently, should win at least 20 percent of its starts and should be out of the money not much more than half the time. The horse has less bearing on this part of its record than its owner, trainer and driver do. By placing horses where they have fair shots at purses, Herve Filion achieves a winning consistency unapproachable by other methods. It follows that a horse may develop a good percentage of winning starts in one barn, but become inconsistent in another.

Concerned though they are with what each horse has been doing lately, good handicappers are aware that a good recent race means little unless the animal is the kind that is able to repeat its good performances or, better yet, improve them.

Consistency becomes relevant when a horse's latest effort promises winning form, the pace statistics are lively and the driver and post position are acceptable. If the horse is a chronic loser, or a habitual runner-up, little reliance can be placed on its recent good performance. The odds are extreme that it will revert to type and finish nowhere.

Exceptions occur when the horse's poor record is attributable to bad management. Perhaps it had been hopelessly outclassed for years—which happens—but began to show signs of life after entering lesser races, or shipping to a lesser track, or coming into the hands of a smarter horseman, or all three. Before betting on a chronic loser, the player should take pains to determine whether its apparent improvement might trace to new influences in its racing career. If so, the improvement can be accepted as genuine.

Consistency is not only a matter of winning or finishing close to winners a satisfactory percentage of the time. Like other manifestations of Standardbred talent, it can be clocked. When an expert handicapper decides that a horse's recent performance indicates an ability to win in good time tonight after setting or overcoming the fastest probable early pace, he has passed judgment on the horse's consistency. If its record contained no evidence that it could be *depended on* to produce winning time when fit, the record would be one of inconsistency, and the good recent performance would be dismissed as untypical.

Consistency in winning when properly placed and physically fit is a reassuring feature in the record of a Standardbred, proclaiming its reliability and the honest competence of its stable. It makes the sharpest horse in the race a better bet than it otherwise might be. But it is secondary to the fundamentals of pace, current form, driver and post position. Horses with mediocre winning averages frequently defeat horses with higher averages, and the victories often are predictable.

Class and Pace

After defining class and asserting that it is decisive, I have been trying to call attention to the vital differences between former and present class. The program record's statistical summaries tell about the previous quality of a horse. The detailed recapitulations of the animal's latest races are more useful than that. They permit inference as to whether its present ability is up to its former standard. They also show how its present ability compares with that of each of the other horses in the race.

Conventional handicappers regard the current class of a Standardbred as equivalent to the class of race in which it recently has been able to win or come close. A horse that has been winning in Class B-2 but not in B-1 is labeled, logically enough, as something less than B-1 stock. This kind of reasoning is adequate for the racing secretary's classification purposes. He keeps the horse in B-2 so long as it continues to earn occasional paychecks at that level. But a handicapping racegoer needs to make finer distinctions.

Every B-2 field is composed primarily of established B-2 horses, plus one or two from B-3 or B-1 that are being tested in a class higher or lower than usual. The player cannot assume that the refugee from B-1 outclasses the others, or that the interloper from B-3 is over its head. He might be able to single out one of the confirmed B-2 animals as a contender on grounds that it defeated the others last week, or that it has been in the money consistently, or that it has been finishing in better time. But he really does not penetrate the subject of current class until he compares the contenders in terms of pace.

Through pace analysis, the player measures contending animals with one yardstick. Above all, he assesses recent performances—the ones most likely to offer fresh clues about present abilities. We have already decided, I hope, that a fit horse of comparatively high present class can go the mile in good time after setting or overcoming a comparatively fast early pace. A fit horse of slightly lower present class might sometimes go in equally good time, but seldom after trying to cope with quite so rigorous an early pace. The probability is that it will react to the fast early pace by finishing in slower time than would be expected of a better horse. An accompanying probability is that it will be unable to match the final time of the better horse even if the early pace is slow.

Of all arguments against this approach, the most familiar emphasizes the well-known fact that horses and drivers usually go no faster than the occasion demands. The true potential of a horse remains concealed, iceberg-fashion, until the evening when it is forced to give everything it has in an effort to withstand opposition of its own quality.

The fact is well known, but does not often apply to raceway situations involving small advances or reductions in class, as from C-2 to C-3, or from a race for non-winners of $4,000 to one for non-winners of $5,000. Or from a $6,000 claimer to $6,500. Most raceway horses have long since been exposed to tests of their basic quality and have gone on from there, upward or downward. What now counts are the small fluctuations in physical condition that affect present class.

As to the improving young horse moving up through the raceway ranks, it sometimes wins in time good enough to defeat far better fields. When it wins in ordinary time, having been asked for no more exertion than necessary, it frequently does so with great authority. If its higher class is not obvious in the pace figures, it can be deduced from the margin of victory, or the strong move in the stretch, or on one or more of the turns. In the next chapter, we shall show how to modify pace figures to give credit for vigorous showings of that kind.

In suggesting that pace ratings indicate which of several fit horses is best able to cope with tonight's kind of opposition, I do not propose that class analysis be left at that. The most precise evaluations of current ability are made when the handicapper adjusts the pace ratings *to reflect the quality of the race in which the pace figures were registered.*

The reasoning here is that the opposition in a relatively cheap race is invariably less powerful than in an even slightly better race. Regardless of whether the horse's pace figures were achieved easily or with great effort, it had to contend with lesser stock on that evening than it will in tonight's better race. By the same criterion, a horse moving down in class should be given credit for having achieved its own figures in more formidable company than it faces tonight.

Therein lies a basic reason why animals on the preferred lists at minor tracks have all they can do to remain vertical in big-league competition. And why hotshot country-fair performers fail at raceways, losing to horses that would be no faster or more successful than they at the fairs. It is infinitely easier to beat one good horse than seven or eight. The cheaper the race, the less probable that more than one horse in it will be able to press a fit animal of superior quality. But as it ascends the scale of classes, that formerly superior animal must contend with more and more good horses in each race. It wins a B-1 race in 2:04, but cannot equal that speed after being rushed off its feet by the toughies in A-3. It has the courage, stamina and adaptability for the lower class but not for the higher. It has passed the limits of its present capabilities.

I therefore recommend that the handicapper make the following adjustments in his pace ratings:

1. If the pace rating is based on a race of lower class than tonight's, deduct 5 points.

2. If the pace rating is based on a race of higher class than tonight's, add 5 points.

Forgive me for repeating an earlier warning: It would be a mistake to think of these points as representing lengths or fifths of seconds. They simply are numbers that approximate the differences among horses. I shall show later that the approximations are mighty accurate, but I concede without argument that the individual handicapper may achieve bountiful results by adding or deducting three or four or seven points instead of five. Or he can do well by avoiding points altogether, preferring to act on the basis of a total impression and not wanting to get hung up with pen and paper. I suggest that the reader reserve judgment about these details until we have had a chance to cover the principles and techniques of handicapping more completely. Whoever understands those principles and adheres to them will manage nicely at his raceway, no matter what special handicapping gimmicks he devises for his own convenience.

Class, Time, Price, Purse

After noting the final times of all races at Yonkers Raceway during 1968 and 1969, I was able to compile a chart that compared Yonkers classified and claiming races in terms of purses and normal (or par) times. Believing that New York racegoers would find the tabulation helpful in rating horses that moved from claimers to classified races or vice versa, I made the mistake of publishing it in the first edition of this book. Charts of that kind are enormously helpful. They are also dependably obsolescent. Purse schedules and claiming-price patterns are sure to inflate or decrease from time to time. A chart based on last year's realities is helpful this year, but only to someone aware of the changes that have occurred. And the same chart is even more out of phase next year.

On the other hand, conscientious handicappers need charts of that kind. Without par times it is impossible to approximate the relative speed or slowness of the particular track on a given night. It therefore becomes difficult to evaluate the racing times of animals that performed on that night. To handicap without such material is to handicap at a disadvantage. And to handicap without some grasp of the class relationships among claiming and conditioned or claiming and classified races is a guarantee of defeat.

The preparation of a table of par times (and the purse values and class levels to which they apply) requires careful work. One's first table is likely to be based on last season's race times as reported in chart books or newspaper files. Confining the record to races on fast tracks, and being careful to compile a separate list of final times for each different class category, one prolongs each list until the sample is representative. That is, no fewer than eight times in each class category (if possible). One then can strike an average or, even better, a median. To get a median, you might cross out the two slowest and two fastest times on the list and then see the time around which the others cluster. Which is to say the time that separates the faster half of the list from the slower.

It occasionally is necessary to "smooth" the arithmetical results by ⅕ second one way or another, thus providing a smooth continuity in final times from the slowest and cheapest races to the fastest and most important ones. Recognizing that the final list is not Holy Scripture but simply shows the representative *differences* in racing times between any two classes of race, one is ready to make daily track variants or simply refer to the table to confirm the suspicion that the track was untypically slow or fast on a particular night and that racing times on that night need to be discounted accordingly.

On the other hand (and I hope this will not seem contradictory), a careful analyzer of raceway past-performance programs becomes able to tell whether the official times of a horse's previous race or two were approximately normal, or slow or fast. We shall demonstrate this kind of thing in our handicapping exercises toward the end of the book, using no actual variants.

Track Class

A horse that performs well in Class B-2 at Roosevelt Raceway can be expected to do equally well in invitationals at Freehold or in conditioned races with $12,000 purses at The Meadowlands.

A horse that can win one of the $800 purses at Louisville should be able to hold its own in the $4,500 claiming races for $2,300 purses at Northville Downs.

A horse that races for $5,000 purses at Buffalo will not be far out of place competing for $12,500 purses at Roosevelt.

All the statements in the preceding three paragraphs were absolutely true when written. Each is likely to be wrong by the time it appears in print. Raceways increase or lower their purses rather frequently, depending on variations in mutuel handle, in state laws and in the agreements they make with horsemen.

When Ed Parker was racing secretary at Monticello, he fortified that raceway's past-performance program with a tabulation of equivalent purses. It showed the bettors that a $900 purse at Saratoga, for example, attracted horses equal to those that competed for a $1,200 purse at Pompano Park or a $2,000 one at Roosevelt. It was a heroic effort, but the chart required constant revision. Purse structures changed so rapidly and so unevenly that new editions of the chart became obsolete as soon as they were published.

Rather than let the subject of track class go by default, I have reproduced a USTA listing of leading raceways and the average purses they dispensed during 1978. These numbers will change from year to year, but the general relationships tend to remain constant for lengthy periods. That is, the purse outlay for a race at Los Alamitos probably will remain about two-thirds of the pot awarded a comparable race at Hollywood Park.

Please note that Roosevelt Raceway's place at the top of the list is due to the generosity of New York's sire-stake program, the bonanzas of

which inflate that raceway's average-purse figure. In reality, The Meadowlands pays substantially higher purses to overnight races. By the way,
"overnight" refers to the bread-and-butter events that are the bulk of all
raceway programs. Entries remain open until two or three days (usually
three) before the races take place. That is not exactly "overnight," but
the meaning is clear.

Raceway	Average Purse
Roosevelt	$10,272
The Meadowlands	10,072
Yonkers	8,707
Sportsman's Park	6,393
Hollywood Park	5,571
Hawthorne	5,114
Maywood Park	5,009
Hazel Park	4,800
Wolverine	4,179
Mohawk	3,966
Los Alamitos	3,788
Greenwood	3,737
Arlington Park	3,503
Brandywine	3,280
Richelieu Park	3,202
Liberty Bell	3,154
Blue Bonnets	3,063
Freehold	2,671
The Meadows	2,040
Saratoga	1,958

The foregoing guidelines are useful. But no sure way exists to compare
the class of overnight races at tracks on different circuits, or accurately
to evaluate the class of an ordinary animal until it has actually raced in
your territory.

9 THE FITNESS FACTOR

CALL IT FORM, condition, fitness, sharpness. It is crucial to training, driving and handicapping. It is the readiness of a horse to perform well in a race.

The horse with a theoretical advantage in class is unable to prove it unless in adequate physical shape. Among horses of approximately equal quality, current form identifies the best prospects.

After the preliminary business of reading the top of the program page to see what kind of race it is, the handicapper's first step is to eliminate all horses whose recent records contain no signs of potential winning form. The animals that survive this process are the logical contenders, the candidates for further study. It is not compulsory to work this way, but it saves time. If the player seriously intends to handicap, rather than trust to luck, he might as well dispose immediately of horses whose current form disqualifies them.

Do off-form horses win harness races? Indeed they do. And many more races go to horses with unprepossessing recent records who turn out to be in much better form than the handicapper could possibly have guessed. But the percentages and probabilities of the sport remain overwhelmingly in favor of a handicapping method that limits play to supposedly sharp horses. For every race won by a relatively unfit lucky horse, or by a horse in unpredictably good condition, at least six or seven are won by logical contenders. By no means all of these logical contenders win at short mutuel prices.

Form and Date

Before a trotter or pacer makes its first start of the new season, the trainer puts about 120 miles of hard training under its hide. But it is not yet as sharp as it will be after a race or two or five. The typical Standardbred does not come into its own until it has been taxed the extra seconds of speed that only competition can produce.

Having achieved winning condition, or something like it, a sound animal remains chipper for months. Its percentage of victories then reflects the intelligence with which its races have been chosen and the competence with which it has been driven. Unfortunately, almost no Standardbreds are that sound, and none is impervious to illness and injury. The typical raceway horse's record therefore is one of fluctuating ability. A talented trainer capitalizes on good form and, by resting the horse or putting it in easier races, minimizes the adverse effects of declining form.

Around the barn, they usually know whether a horse is in trim or not. A sharp Standardbred eats everything in sight, has uncomplicated bowel habits, is bright-eyed, glossy of coat, eager to work, and capable of top speed without gait problems, wind problems or subsequent distress. When it goes off its feed or becomes less cheerful, something is wrong. It

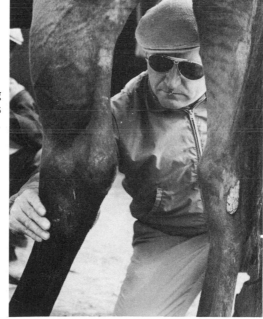

Jimmy Cruise, a genius at winning with unsound horses, examines one of his orthopedic cases.

may still be able to race, even win. But the outlook is ominous. Failure to diagnose and treat the difficulty may be the ruination of the horse. Often it needs nothing but a few weeks of rest. Good trainers provide such rest. Others do not, blaming the animal for their own failures.

Some superb specimens of Standardbred conformation have been able to win nothing in competition, even after training impressively. The only valid proof of fitness is performance on the crowded raceway—how the horse responds when asked for speed, and where it finishes and in what kinds of fractional and final times.

I doubt that many harness-racing fans are fully aware that every race is in itself a central part of the horse's training routine. When racing at intervals of a week or so, many animals only jog between engagements. The exertions of frequent racing are enough to keep them in shape. Other horses go two or three hard miles on one morning between weekly races, but not at racing speed.

Hence, tonight's form is a product of last week's form. If the horse has been in the doldrums but is beginning to round into winning condition, it usually gives notice of this improvement by performing with new vigor in a race. If it is on the ragged edge after doing its very best for two or three weeks, it gives notice by performing dully in a race. Improvement or deterioration of Standardbred form is seldom abrupt. Except among ouchy, aged animals in the lower claiming races, sudden reversals of form are quite infrequent. By analyzing the latest races of a horse and observing its behavior during the prerace warmups, a discerning player learns enough about its current condition to make sensible decisions.

The first of several key elements is the date of the horse's latest race. When the season is in full swing, an absence from competition of more than two weeks is a black mark against a run-of-the mill pacer. Trotting races being fewer, an ordinary horse of that gait may be forgiven a two-week absence on the theory that its people were unable to find a vacant spot in a suitable field during that period.

In considering date, it is a good idea to look through the records of all entered horses. How long have most of them been idle? If, as usual, most have raced within the last eight or ten days, you should be skeptical about an entrant that has not competed in more than two weeks. Unless its last race was impressive and its record includes victories after absences of such duration, you can assume that it was in drydock for repairs and will need tonight's race for exercise. Better horses usually do perfectly well after absences of two or three weeks, being able to maintain their sharpness in semiweekly training workouts.

"We don't sit around waiting for the ideal opportunity, the soft touch," says Del Miller about the training and racing of Standardbreds. "We race them. That's how we keep them in top shape. So if you see that one has been away during a week when it could have been racing, you know that there must have been a reason, and you have a right to wonder if the horse is fit.''

Excuses

Even though the horse raced recently, it does not qualify as a contender unless it raced impressively. Yet some performances seem dull because of circumstances unrelated to form. The horse may actually be in excellent condition. Before eliminating an entrant on grounds of unreadiness, the handicapper scans its latest past-performance line for indications that its poor showing was excusable. Any of the following information in the past-performance line constitutes an excuse:

1. An off track—provided that the racing strip is dry and fast tonight.
2. A break in stride or other difficulty caused by faulty equipment.
3. A break in stride caused by interference.
4. A lapse of more than two weeks between the last and next-to-last races.
5. The horse's first recent start on this racing circuit, especially if it had been racing at a track of different size.
6. A race against stock of considerably higher class than the horse could have been expected to handle—provided that it returns to its own class tonight.
7. A substitute driver with a low winning percentage—provided that a top man drives tonight.
8. An unfavorable post position, an unusually slow early pace and driving tactics that left the horse hopelessly behind when the real racing began in the final stages.
9. An unusually fast early pace, plus driving tactics that left the horse exhausted in the stretch—provided that the horse is not a habitual puller or quitter.

When an animal's most recent performance is excusable on any of the foregoing grounds—or if the performance was neither good nor bad enough for confident decision—handicappers turn their attention to the next-to-latest race. I consider it wiser to do this in doubtful cases than to eliminate the horses outright. Be especially conservative about eliminating horses that finished in the money or within three lengths of the winner in their latest starts. Unless you are quite certain that such an animal was hauled to its paycheck behind a windscreen, you should look at the previous race for positive signs.

Once in a while, good reason arises to excuse the next-to-last race. Handicappers then retreat to the third race back. But they do not often base their decisions on performances that took place more than a month earlier. Recent excuses or not, month-old form is unreliable.

Bad Signs

Where excuses are lacking, a horse should be eliminated for unsuitable current condition if:

1. Its final time was as much as three seconds slower than the final time registered by *any other starter* in a recent representative performance.

2. It failed to hustle for the lead at some point in the race, possibly on the outside. (This is especially important at half-mile tracks.)

3. It lost ground in the stretch or was badly beaten without setting or pressing a fast early pace or without roughing it on the outside.

4. It was sucked along to a spuriously good finish after having shown little in its previous race or two.

5. It broke stride and has had similar trouble in another recent race.

6. It won or lost by a narrow margin for the third time in succession and now is moving up in class.

Stated as they are, those ideas sound like rules. But they are not. They are principles, and should be applied thoughtfully. For example, it is quite true that few aged raceway horses retain their sharpness after three exhausting stretch battles in close succession. Yet some animals benefit from effort of that intensity, especially at the beginning of the season. And a really good horse might cut the mustard six or eight times in a row. Rather than eliminate a horse because of its recent exertions, it is wise to consider its overall record, its overall quality, its age, and the kind of challenge it confronts tonight.

The same kind of reasoning holds for all other items on the list. Regard them as guides, not gospel. They all derive from the one fundamental principle that informs this chapter: The horse likely to deserve a bet tonight is one that went out there and did a little something in a recent race.

The Big Decision

Having eliminated some horses for good and sufficient reason, and having excused the latest performances of others, the handicapper should review his situation.

He now must deal with the latest races of some horses, and the next-to-latest of some others. If any of these races were on out-of-town tracks, or occurred weeks ago, should he press forward, handicapping the animals by guess and by gosh?

I hope not. Handicapping is not likely to jell unless each starter can be analyzed in terms of recent action at the same track or on the same racing circuit. Balmoral Park racegoers can get by with performance lines recorded at Sportsman's Park. Brandywine and Liberty Bell are companion tracks. So are Yonkers and Roosevelt, and Greenwood and Mohawk.

But when the race is at Roosevelt and the past-performance line describes a happening at Freehold or Liberty Bell or Rosecroft, the racegoer should apply the brakes and take a few seconds for deliberation. If he is a typical fan, the kind who goes to the track at irregular intervals and relies entirely on program information, he probably should not touch a race of this sort unless:

1. The horse is a local one to begin with, has been racing steadily, and simply made the out-of-town trip for one or two starts.

2. The horse is from a topnotch stable and has a driver to match, signifying the kind of management that does not merely stumble around the country hoping to fall into a purse.

3. The player is careful to use the program's table of comparative track speeds, adjusting the half-mile and final times (as suggested on page 168) before accepting the out-of-town figures at face value.

If the horse is a young up-and-comer or is otherwise identifiable as having a touch of class, and most particularly if it has been racing well at home *and* abroad, the player may occasionally decide that its present form can be no better or worse than it was on the night of its last local race, a month or so ago. If this conclusion is a result of sober thought rather than wishful thinking, the chance may be worth taking. The better the class of the race, the less extreme the chance. But, as repeated perhaps too often in these pages, the safest course is to stick to races in which each starter's credentials are local and very recent.

Having decided to continue handicapping the race, the next step is to seek out positive signs of sharp, preferably improving form.

The Stretch Gain

In bygone years, the first half-mile was kind of an overture. The race took place in the homestretch. The time of the second half was predictably faster than that of the first half.

At mile tracks and ⅝-milers, many races still are cut that way. It also happens at half-milers, depending mainly on the battles of wits among

Winter training at Saratoga Raceway.

drivers. But modern racing emphasizes early speed. I imagine that the first half-mile is the faster in at least half of the races at half-mile tracks.

With everybody going lickety-split for early position and the stretch drive often rewarding the animal that decelerates least, handicappers have mixed attitudes toward ground gained in the stretch. "He passed tired horses. It means nothing. Look at those fast early fractions," says one handicapper about a horse that finished third after gaining four lengths on the leader.

Or: "Why shouldn't he gain ground? He did nothing until the end, got lucky, found room and picked up a few yards. But they crawled the last quarter in thirty-three."

We have already noticed that a sucked-along horse may well pick up a few lengths in the stretch, when the animals in front back up to it.

Stretch gains apparently should not be accepted uncritically. But I believe they should be viewed with respect. If the horse was in the race at all and the fractional and final times were good for the class, the stretch gain is a prime demonstration of strength.

Barring horses dragged to victory or a piece of the purse, the stretch gain therefore deserves extra credit in anyone's handicapping. On the other hand, a *loss* of ground in the stretch is an unpromising sign, unless excused by the horse's impressive exertions or bad racing luck in the earlier stages.

Under the point system I have been describing, players should add a point to the basic rating for every length gained in the stretch. If the horse led at the stretch call and won going away, it does no harm to add the full winning margin. If it led by a considerable distance at the stretch call and won eased up, losing some ground in the process, calculate the points on the basis of its lead at the stretch call.

If fractions of lengths are involved, credit each half-length or more as a point. A horse 2½ lengths behind at the stretch call is regarded as three lengths behind. If it wins by 1½ lengths, it earns five extra points for the gain of ground.

It probably goes without saying that these credits are awarded only to qualified contenders—horses whose recent efforts were good enough to warrant the pace ratings and class adjustments discussed earlier.

Roughing It

Most programs are quite conscientious about including the little degree symbol (°), which indicates that a horse traveled on the outside for a quarter-mile, including most of a turn. Generally, the program places the symbol before or after the horse's racing position, to indicate the stage of the race at which it was parked.

The symbol indicates that the animal's performance was sturdier than the other figures might suggest. It traveled extra ground, either because its driver pulled out to fight for position or because he was flushed out by another driver and was parked there for the duration of the turn.

To be parked outside one horse on a complete turn is to travel about 16 feet farther than the inside horse does. This is true regardless of the size of the track. One might suppose that a horse would lose more ground racing outside on a turn at a mile track, because the turn is a quarter-mile long. Not so. At any track, a turn is a semicircle. To rough it on the outside is to travel a semicircle of about five feet greater radius than the semicircular path traversed by an inside horse. Five feet of radius adds about 16 feet to the circumference of any semicircle.

As an emblem of extra effort, the parked-out symbol adds considerable luster to a good past-performance line. It also may transform an apparently indifferent finish into a fully acceptable one. Some excellent handicappers credit a horse with a full second of additional speed for each parked-out symbol. They reason that the animal not only traveled at least two extra lengths but spent important energy getting to the outside and fighting for headway while there.

I think the reader should consider the following approach:

1. Accept any horse as fit if its latest, most relevant past-performance line contains the symbol and the animal nevertheless managed to finish within eight lengths of the winner. Allow a larger beaten margin if the line contains more than one of the symbols.

2. At the very least, regard a parked-out symbol as an excuse for lengths lost in the stretch. Before eliminating a horse that lost ground in the stretch, see if parked-out symbols cancel the loss.

3. If apparent good form qualifies a horse as a contender, each parked-out symbol in the past-performance line is worth 5 points. The points should be added to the pace rating, as adjusted for class and stretch gain.

Example:

1:06:2   7 8 7° 8°   7/8   3/4   2:10:4

The horse obviously is in sharp condition. It not only gained four lengths in the stretch but also roughed it for a half-mile. Its final time and the half-mile time of the race earn it a pace rating of 164 according to the procedure explained on page 167. Its stretch gain of four lengths is worth an additional 4, and the two parked-out symbols are worth 10. Its rating becomes 178.

If the horse had lost ground in the stretch, the two symbols would have excused the loss. Many examples of this kind of thing will arise later, when we handicap entire programs at leading tracks.

Form and Class

Like all animals, including man, Standardbreds are creatures of habit. They learn easily but forget slowly. When they acquire bad habits, the trainer cannot discuss the problems with them. He must undertake a program of re-education. It is not always easy.

Among bad habits is the losing habit. Having been trained from birth to respond as best they can to human direction, race horses sometimes carry the whole thing beyond reasonable limits. The colt that loses its first two or three races may be impressed enough by the raceway hullabaloo to try to repeat the performance the next time it finds itself in the same kind of uproar. It refuses to pass the horse in front of it.

This kind of psychological conditioning may be at work in the phenomenon that horsemen call "confidence." A seasoned raceway animal that loses repeatedly because it repeatedly is outclassed does not automatically win when dropped into the kind of company it should beat. It often needs a race or two in the lower class before recovering its supposed confidence and turning on its true speed.

This happens often enough to be a prominent factor in handicapping. A horse moving up in class after decisive victories is usually a better bet to win at the first asking in the new class than is a horse that backs up after five or six losses. Horsemen believe that successive triumphs "brave up" a Standardbred.

Confidence—if that is what it is—might as well be regarded as synonymous with fitness. It is a problem with some dropped-down horses and not with others. The best evaluation of the dropped-down horse is made in terms of its recent form and pace, with adjustment for the change in class. If you find that your figures too often put losers on top by overestimating the prospects of dropped-down animals, you might try withholding class credit from dropdowns until they have had a race in the new, low class. I have encountered little difficulty of that kind, but it is not unimaginable.

Qualifying Races

If the player is properly devoted to the principle that breaking horses deserve no bets, and that races full of breaking horses should be avoided, the qualifying race becomes an endurable problem.

As you know, horses race in qualifiers if they have been breaking stride or misbehaving behind the gate or swerving or finishing in truck-horse time, or if they have been absent from the local scene for a while.

The past-performance record contains strong clues as to why an animal's latest race was a qualifier. The break symbols or times or dates of its previous races tell the tale.

If the horse is a breaker, it is, by definition, out of form, regardless of the fact that it got through a qualifier in adequate time without breaking. The animal may hold together tonight and win at a price, but no law decrees that a handicapper should lose money by backing another horse in the race. If anything in the breaker's record hints that it might whip tonight's field, the handicapper should abstain from the race altogether.

A slow horse that finally qualifies for evening competition is also no riddle. Being slow, it hardly figures to become fast all of a sudden. The chances are enormous that its time in the qualifier was barely good enough to earn entry in tonight's race. Others in the field will have better figures and will attract the handicapper's attention.

If the horse has been unmannerly (which can be deduced if it has been neither a breaker nor slow nor absent, but went in a qualifying race or two before being readmitted to the fold), the handicapper can be fairly confident that its personality problems have been modified by training. It therefore can be dealt with as if it were any other horse. Does its record include a race good enough and recent enough for handicapping? If so, the player is in the clear. If not, the player must decide whether the horse might nevertheless be a real threat, in which case it is advisable to avoid the race.

On occasion, the qualifying race is itself fast enough to be used for handicapping purposes. At most tracks, horses race in times just about two seconds faster than their qualifying times. At other tracks, including those in New York, qualifying standards are more severe, and racing times may be only a second faster.

An extraordinarily dependable bet at any track is the nonbreaking animal that wins a qualifying race in faster time than its opponents have been recording in their best recent performances. This kind of opportunity bobs up several times a season, and should not be overlooked. If the horse has a top driver, it is as close to a cinch as one ever finds in this sport.

Darkened Form

If a horse is in condition to win but its recent past-performance lines look like those of an unfit animal, the audience is fooled, the odds inflate and somebody cashes a nice bet. Tearing up his losing tickets, gnashing his teeth and looking at the winner's record to see if he missed something, the handicapper concludes that he missed nothing. The horse's form had been darkened.

The next morning, the animal's trainer stands uneasily before the desk of the presiding judge and explains with all the sincerity at his command that the horse just suddenly woke up. "He hasn't been liking the track and I haven't been able to do a thing with him," says the trainer, shifting his weight from foot to foot, "but last week the groom moved him into an end stall and put a puppy in with him and he began doing better. I trained him on Wednesday and he was like a wild horse. Went in ten and change and could have gone all day. Damned near pulled my arms out of the socket. Never saw anything like it."

The judge looks at the trainer with the enthusiasm of an exterminator studying a roach. "Cashed a pretty good bet, did you?"

"Bet?" says the trainer.

"Bet," says the judge. "You and that pool hustler you work for, you didn't bet?"

"Well, sure," says the trainer. "We naturally bet a little when the horse begins doing good like he did. I mean, I don't know how much anybody else bet, but I had the man bet a little for me."

"A little?" asks the judge. "The odds drop to five to one in the last flash and you only bet a little?"

"Aw, you know how it is, Judge. You can't keep secrets around here. Must have been ninety people saw the horse train on Wednesday. Everybody and his brother must have sent it in last night."

"Strike two!" says the judge. "One more miraculous reversal of form and you wind up pumping gas somewhere."

"Thanks, Judge."

A favorite way to darken the form of a horse is to keep it out of competition for weeks, legging it up at a private training track. Then, after a lackadaisical performance in a qualifying race at a track that is lenient about such things, the stable cracks down. The crowd disregards the horse because it has been out of action.

Another method, often effective at smaller raceways, is to take the horse to a few country fairs, losing in poor company and returning to raceway competition with two or three horrible past-performance lines.

Other techniques:

1. At raceways where paddock supervision is lax or inexpert, change the animal's equipment sufficiently to assure a losing race. For example, change the length of the hobbles or the weight of the shoes, or rig the nose band to hamper breathing.

2. Change the horse's feeding and watering routines, or work it too severely between races.

3. On the night of the race, warm it up in faster or slower time than is needed for a good performance.

4. Put an incompetent driver in the bike.

5. Make premature moves during the race, wasting the horse's energy.

The better the raceway, the less practical these methods become. Major-league paddock judges have complete records of every horse's normal equipment, check it carefully and demand a thorough explanation for the slightest change. Illogical driver assignments, though permitted on occasion, mark the trainer and the horse for continued scrutiny thereafter. Moreover, downright incompetent driving is punished almost as severely as fraudulent driving. Changes in training routines become subjects of gossip, which echoes sooner or later in the front office.

Although numerous trainers and owners covet the tax-free proceeds of nice bets at good odds, they do not often try to build those odds by making a horse lose a race that it might win. Shenanigans of that kind not only invite the unwelcome attention of raceway officials but also defy common sense. After all, horses are not endlessly able to win. Trainers and owners tend to want the purse when they can get it.

The darkening of form becomes more practical when the horse is unable to win and, from the stable's point of view, might as well acquire an imposingly miserable past-performance line while getting some needed exercise. Perhaps the horse is returning to form after a layoff. Perhaps it is on the downgrade after several tough efforts and needs time to recover. If the horse cannot win, is it unethical for the stable to face that fact and let it lose?

I think so. Until such time as the rules permit horses to be barred from the betting on grounds that they are out for exercise, every animal that starts in a race does so with an implied guarantee that its stable will try to win. Its slim chances are then reflected in long odds. But if no effort is made to win or, indeed, every effort is made to lose badly, the stable perpetrates fraud on whoever is seduced into betting on the horse.

None of this contradicts the fact that the driver should deal intelligently and humanely with a horse that proves itself unable to win. It is foolish, wasteful and cruel to punish an animal that has nothing left in the stretch. It is equally brutal to demand a second big move from a horse that gave what little it had in a vain bid for the early lead. The average driver is sensible enough to excuse his hopelessly beaten horse from needless effort. But first he gives the horse its opportunity to win, and he gives the audience its money's worth.

Where deliberately darkened form is concerned, the interests of the handicapper coincide, as usual, with those of the sport itself. The handicapper may have an advantage over other customers, sometimes interpreting pace figures, parked-out symbols and driver switches as evidence that a supposedly unfit horse is about to blossom. But it is not a wholesome advantage and it is not likely to be a lastingly profitable one at a track where the deliberate darkening of form is more than an occasional occurrence. If permitted to get away with such manipulation, betting horsemen are entirely capable of concealing form so well that no handicapper could find any sign of fitness in a winner's past-performance record.

When the crowd boos a surprise winner and curses the driver of the beaten favorite, it usually is wrong. But the indignant noise is a constructive influence. It keeps the judges and racing secretaries on their toes. It makes the raceway management suitably nervous. It bothers the honest horsemen, the majority, making them less tolerant than ever toward the incompetent training and driving that cause most upsets and the dishonest training and driving that cause a few.

Taking a sample for the pre-race blood test.

Incidentally, a primary objective of prerace blood testing is to develop means of identifying a fit horse through analysis of its blood. This is not as fanciful an idea as it may seem. Biochemists already have the necessary knowledge. When more tracks require the testing, formfulness will increase.

Doping

Many disabling afflictions of equine muscle, tendon, ligament and bone are painful inflammations associated with arthritic damage or plain wear and tear, or both. Certain anti-inflammatory chemicals, such as Butazolidin, relieve the painful symptoms, making potential winners of horses that might otherwise be too crippled to race. In recent years, most state racing commissions have legalized the use of these medicines.

With less than complete candor, horsemen who pressed for the legalization of Bute argued that it does not make racers go faster than they should. It is not a pep pill, they say, but is more like an aspirin, relieving discomfort sufficiently to allow a horse to perform at its normal speed.

The truth is that no law should prevent the use of anti-inflammatory agents as part of the legitimate medical care of an ouchy horse. In most cases, the medicine is an excellent supplement to more basic measures, of which the foremost is rest. But no law should allow horses to race while active doses of the chemicals are still in their systems. If the horse cannot race unless it is under the influence of Bute, the chances are that the exertions of racing will worsen the tissue damage that gave rise to inflammation in the first place.

The racegoer should remain alert. If Bute or anything like it is legal in his state, he should avoid the track until the tracks begin to supply information about which horses have been dosed and which have not.

So much for that. As for other kinds of doping, the National Association of State Racing Commissioners declares that the defense never catches up with the offense. There is a constant lag between the development of new drugs and the ability of raceway laboratories to detect them in the blood, urine or saliva of horses. Nevertheless, no present reason exists to regard doping as a serious problem.

The facts are that when the labs finally learn how to detect a new drug, they almost never find it in the blood, urine or saliva of a Standardbred. The explanation is obvious enough. Cheating horsemen do not know when the defense will catch up with the offense, and do not propose to be caught when it does. They rarely dope a sick or sore horse to make it win when it should be resting or losing. Such doping cases as are reported in the press almost invariably represent feats of daring by hoodlums, not horsemen.

Corking

A horse finishes second in its first engagement of the year, after matching strides with the winner all the way from the three-quarter pole. Its time surpasses its career record. A week later it goes again as an odds-on favorite and finishes fifth. A week later it goes at 2 to 1 and finishes sixth. By this time the owner should have shot the trainer. The horse has been asked for too much too early in the season. It was not ready to tiptoe a mile in good company. It has been corked. Gutted. It may round into winning condition in two months, but there is no certainty.

A horse forced to win or come close before achieving sharp condition suffers dreadfully. It stops eating. Its digestive apparatus knots up. It may be able to produce a second hard race before collapsing, or it may turn sour after the one prematurely hard effort.

Hence, if a horse in tonight's race has been out only twice this year and the first performance was considerably better than the second, the handicapper should beware. If it has been out three times and the first two were considerably better than the third, equal caution is indicated. The corked horse is a trap for the unwary. Far preferable is the animal that has not yet won but has been gathering strength and has begun to show it. Tonight could be the night!

Form Angles

In raceway lingo, an angle is something significant which may be overlooked by handicappers concerned with fundamental factors. One of the most familiar angles is actually basic to the selection methods of thousands of racegoers: They watch the tote board to see where the late money is going. I have already commented on that kind of play, suggesting that the reader stick with his own selections and not try to decide which horses are being backed by "smart money," or even which money is "smart."

Another angle finds players at half-mile tracks betting the favorite when it has a top driver and an inside post. This is handicapping to the extent that it conforms with the percentages of the sport—a favorite of that kind is quite likely to win. But the angle is non-handicapping to the extent that the player has no way of knowing whether the animal deserves to be favorite, not having studied its record and that of the other horses.

Yet another angle depends on the phenomenon of Standardbred "confidence." Many New Yorkers automatically play horses that lost their last races while dropping in class. The theory is that such a horse, having regained its confidence, may do better in its second or third attempt in the lower class. It's a reasonable theory but of no use to readers of this book, who will be looking at the horse's latest lines to see whether it has begun to race vigorously. This is more effective than an attempt to psychoanalyze the animal.

Of all angles, I can recommend only two. First of these is the angle of the beaten favorite. If a horse qualifies in terms of form, pace, class, driver, etc., and happens also to have been beaten as the betting favorite in its race, it deserves extra respect. Beaten favorite or not, the horse would be eliminated unless the performance had been impressive, or unless the loss was excusable. But since the horse does qualify, and since it was so highly regarded last time, it becomes more attractive tonight. One reason for this is that the crowd occasionally underbets such a horse in its next start, having been disappointed by its loss. When it wins, it may well pay a few pennies more than it should. In the numerical handicapping procedure I recommend, a qualified beaten favorite gets 5 extra points.

A second potent angle derives from the traditional selection method known as "comparison handicapping." If Horse "A" beat "B" and "B" beat "C," the comparison handicapper assumes that "A" is better than "C." This is foolishness, because it overlooks the special circumstances of pace and driving tactics that might explain why previous races ended as they did, and why tonight's race might turn out quite differently. Comparison handicappers also tend to favor "A" over "C" if "A" finished ahead of the other in their last encounter. Here again, errors are inevitable unless thorough handicapping reveals that the pattern of the previous race might repeat itself tonight.

Because few readers of this book are likely to ignore the fundamentals of handicapping when they make their future raceway selections, they will find one kind of comparison handicapping useful. The angle becomes appropriate when fewer than 5 points separate the two top contenders in the race. That is, when all fit starters have been given pace ratings, adjusted for class, stretch gains, parked-out symbols, post position, driver and the beaten-favorite angle. If these final ratings leave two horses within 4 or fewer points of each other, check to see whether each is being rated on the basis of its latest race. If one or both is being handicapped in terms of a *previous* race, see whether they have faced each other in a *subsequent* race. If so, and if one performed more powerfully than the other on that occasion, give it an extra 5 points. This angle may change one selection for you in a month of racegoing. More often than not, it will change the selection for the better.

Because I have been dispensing the numerical rating procedure piecemeal, readers may be having trouble keeping track of it. I have done this deliberately, believing that the basic principles deserve emphasis over procedure. In Chapter 13, we review the procedure completely.

10   THE POST-POSITION FACTOR

THE STARTING POSITION closest to the inside rail is a substantial advantage at half-mile tracks, where races usually begin only 200 feet from the first of four crucial turns. Leaving from that ideal position, the driver with a reasonably quick horse can be expected to enter the first turn on the lead or, at least, with nobody directly in front of him. Without losing an inch of ground on the turn, he adjusts his throttle to sap any horse that tries to overtake him. He cuts the earliest pace to his own pattern. Emerging from the turn onto the backstretch, he has the only horse that has contended for the lead without really being used. If he decides to let someone pass at that point, he remains comfortable in the second hole on the rail, awaiting developments. Having been guaranteed a pleasant trip for the hectic first quarter of the race, the pole horse need not always be best to win. Statistics prove it.

Even if the animal starts rather sluggishly, the inside position helps. Before the drivers of quicker ones can exploit their advantage, the turn arrives and the pole horse is tucked in, saving ground and getting into gear. With a middle or outside starting position, the slow-leaving horse must shuffle back to find a spot on the rail, lest it be parked for the entire first turn. In either eventuality, it enters the backstretch with problems. To a lesser extent, so does a quick horse with a middle or outside start. Unless it is clearly the best animal in the bunch, it may pay later for the exertion of capturing the lead before or during the first turn.

The advantage of the rail position and the difficulties of outside positions diminish as (a) distance increases between the starting point and the first turn and (b) distance increases between the head of the stretch and the finish line. At Sportsman's Park, a ⅝-mile track, the race begins 440

Steve Lobell, on the extreme outside, roars down the long Du Quoin stretch to take a heat in the 1976 Hambletonian. He and Billy Haughton later won the race in a fourth heat.

feet from the first turn, and the homestretch is 902 feet long. At the beginning, a fast-leaving horse can use the straightaway to reach the rail and the lead without covering more than a foot of extra ground. At the end, a fast-finishing horse can overcome earlier obstacles to catch tiring leaders.

While the rail position is always better than the extreme outside at ⅝-mile and one-mile tracks, middle ramps such as 5 and 6 often produce higher percentages of winners than does the inside spot. The chief reason for this statistic is that the footing near the rail sometimes is deeper, damper and slower than in the middle lanes, from which moisture drains more readily. The statistics are more striking at certain large tracks whose inside posts are not greatly superior when the footing is hard and fast. A slight difference in the texture of the racing strip—even when it is pronounced "fast" or "good"—means an advantage to horses in the middle of the gate. At half-milers, on the other hand, these slight differences in footing seldom compensate for the advantages of the rail positions.

The Probabilities

The evaluation of post positions is one of the few phases of handicapping for which the player can arm himself with solid, proven probabilities. If one of every five horses that leave from the pole position at Yonkers

Raceway wins its race, and if about half of all races there are won by horses from the three inside positions, the Yonkers racegoer has something substantial to work with. Because handicapping is inevitably an attempt to estimate probabilities, I would be intensely suspicious of a selection method that failed to take full advantage of what is known about the relative values of post positions.

Most racing fans seem to understand that positions 1 and 2 are advantageous and that 7 and 8 (8 and 9 or 9 and 10 at larger ovals) are bad news. The horse that performed well from an outside start is credited with extra sharpness, and attracts much play if it draws a more favorable position in its next race. A horse that accomplished little from an inside post is expected to perform even less vibrantly if shunted to the far outside for its next attempt.

Those principles are sound. Equally sound is the refusal of many good handicappers to touch a horse with an extreme outside post at a half-mile or ⅝-mile track unless they think that it is two seconds better than anything else in the field. Methods of measuring this detail vary. Some handicappers use intuition. Others use slide rules. All would be better off if they knew more precisely how each starting position affects performance at the individual raceway.

At every track in the world, the question can be answered with statistics. At a few tracks in North America, adequate statistics are available. At others, the statistics are inadequate. At some, the managements seem to keep no statistics at all. No matter which track he patronizes, the serious handicapper has some homework to do before developing a clear picture of the post-position factor.

The necessary statistics would cover a meaningful, recent series of at least 100 dry-track races. They would show how many horses started in each position and how many horses won from each position. Dividing the number of winners by the numbers of starters would produce a percentage for each position. A comparison of the percentages would disclose the probable influence of each position on a typical race.

Some tracks publish statistics which show only the number of winners from each post position, without regard to the number of animals that actually raced. The figures give a reasonably accurate general impression but are useless beyond that. Certain experts have been known to spin elaborate theories from these misleading figures—adding the number of races held during the season and then computing the percentage won from each position. The trouble with such figuring (and the reason that it would offend any bright high school mathematics student) is that it gives meaningless results. For example, the outside post at many tracks is unoccupied in at least one-third of the races, since the fields are short of horses. But the kind of statistical mess now under discussion treats every position as if the same number of horses had performed in every race.

Illustration: At Northville Downs during 1967, 1968 and 1969, 282 winners left from the extreme inside and only 93 from berth 8. The supposition might be that the inside is three times as favorable as the outside at the Michigan raceway, but a handicapper could lose money if he made his selections accordingly. The fact is that only *1,030 horses left from post 8 during those three years, whereas 1,569 left from post 1!* In short, the inside produced twice as well as the outside, which is a considerable advantage but is not three times as good.

With help from the USTA, Harness Tracks of America and a scattering of raceway managements, I once assembled post-position winning percentages for various leading tracks, which I published in the first edition of this book. In preparing the new edition, I discovered that the old percentages had been more serviceable as generalities than as specifics. That is, while the inside post at a half-mile track is superior to, let us say, post 6, the difference between them is changeable. Weather affects it. Track maintenance affects it. Renovations of racing strips and drainage systems affect it even more.

Rather than mislead with a list of track names and percentages that might give a sense of permanence unwarranted by the facts, I shall recommend that conscientious handicappers take the trouble of ascertaining from local records the number of starters and the number of winners from each post during the previous season, and update the figures during the current season. Special attention should be paid to the shifting influences of different posts when a track is wet or when it is drying out from heavy rain.

Using the Percentages

Persons unable or unwilling to spend their time logging post-position statistics can make effective use of general principles. For them, and for everyone else, the problem of post position comes in three parts:

1. Evaluating the horse's latest representative race in terms of the probable effect of the gate position from which it left.
2. Drawing conclusions about the probable effect of tonight's position.
3. Deciding whether tonight's driver compensates for a poor post position.

The best positions at some tracks are three times as good as the worst. And at other tracks the best are twice as good. At still others the differences are small.

Players who prefer to handicap mentally, without resort to numerical formulas, can probably go on from there, making mental allowances for the effects of one or another kind of starting position. I strongly believe, however, that greater ease and precision—and far better results—are obtainable with pen and paper.

The following tabulation is intended for use with the numerical handicapping procedure which we have been developing, step by step, in these pages. On it are representative point values for the post positions at one-milers, ⅝-milers and half-milers. In the likely absence of decent statistics in the past-performance program of your own raceway, and in case you do not bother to compile statistics of your own, these will be better than no statistics at all.

Post Positions

	1	2	3	4	5	6	7	8	9
Half-milers	8	7	6	5	5	4	3	3	—
⅝-milers	6	5	5	5	6	4	3	3	3
One-milers	7	6	5	5	6	5	4	4	4

Note: At some ⅝-milers, where nine-horse fields are normal, post 5 often is worth a point more than post 1. Note also that these point values are not winning percentages. They are percentages divided by a factor of 2, 3 or 4 to produce round numbers that preserve the basic proportions.

Consult the tabulation briefly, and then see how the figures are used.

1. To compensate for the effect of post position on the past performance, *deduct* the value of the post position from the pace rating.

2. To allow for the probable effect of tonight's post position, *add* its value to the rating.

Example:
Tonight's race is a C-1 pace at Yonkers. Last week the horse started in lane 8 in the same class of race. Tonight it draws position 2. Its past-performance line looks like this:

$$1:03 \quad 8 \; 6 \; 6 \; 6° \; 5/5 \; 3/2 \quad 2:06:2$$

The basic pace rating is 193 (see p. 167). No class adjustment is necessary because the horse has not been raised or lowered in class. Credits for roughing it on the outside plus gaining three lengths in the stretch increase the rating to 201 (see pp. 203 and 204). Deducting the value of last week's post position (3 points), and adding tonight's (7 points), makes the rating 205. If the horse had raced from post 2 last week and was exiled to 8 tonight, its rating would be 197—8 points less. In actual handicapping, as we shall see, these wide swings become a tremendous factor.

I recommend that readers obtain whatever local post-position statistics are available, and modify the tabulated figures accordingly. Assuming that the local statistics, if any, list total winners in each starting position, but give no clue as to the number of horses that started, the handicapper should move cautiously. To reduce the distortions embodied in statistics of that kind, it is a good idea to increase the number of winners listed for the extreme outside post by 30 percent. And increase the number given for the next-to-outside post by 20 percent. If the adjusted totals seem greatly out of phase with the figures given on page 216 for tracks of the local raceway's size, proceed cautiously, experimenting with dry-run handicapping before risking much money. The effort will reward you.

The Two-Second Rule

I remarked that some good handicappers refuse to play a horse with an outside post position unless they think it is best in its field by at least two seconds. I do not know how all of them achieve this precise evaluation. I suspect that some merely guess at it. The numerical method I am trying to propound in this book seems to take ample care of the so-called two-second rule. If a horse leaving from the outside or next-to-outside post at any raceway of any size does not have a topnotch driver plus a record of outstanding current form and speed, I throw it out as a probable non-contender.

In the next chapter we shall suggest that some drivers are such consistent winners that they are worth 10 extra points in the handicapping process. Others are worth 5. Without a 5- or 10-point driver in the sulky, and without some extra zip in its rated race (such as a good stretch gain and at least one parked-out symbol), I cannot recommend supporting a horse that leaves from the far outside unless it has a rating margin of at least 10 points. But with those extra strengths, a 3-point margin should suffice. If the horse does not sport the extras mentioned, or lacks the necessary point margin, the handicapper probably should pass the race, except when the second-highest rating goes to a horse that has some extras and will race at good odds.

11 THE DRIVER FACTOR

DURING 1978, about 10,000 drivers competed for $204 million in purses at North American raceways and fairs. Fifty of these drivers won about $60 million of the purse money. It was a normal year.

Think about it. In a representative year of harness racing, less than 1 percent of the drivers romp off with almost 30 percent of the prizes. To accomplish this, the dominant minority wins virtually all the richest stake races and captures much more than its arithmetical share of bread-and-butter dashes, six nights a week, all the year through, plus occasional afternoons.

At the typical raceway, six or seven drivers, perhaps one-tenth of the local roster, customarily take more than one-third of the races. Turnover is slow, the same men monopolizing the local winner's circle for years on end. To be a successful bettor, it is necessary to know who these local leaders are, and modify your handicapping figures accordingly. It also is necessary to know who the leading drivers are on other circuits.

To illustrate, the top drivers at The Meadowlands during 1979 were John Campbell, Jim Doherty, Ben Webster, Greg Wright and Ted Wing. At the right time and in the right race, other hot drivers were Mike Gagliardi, Cat Manzi, Lew Williams, Bob Samson and Ray Remmen. Winning racegoers remained alert to these realities and interpreted them successfully. But that was not enough. Every now and then a Ron Waples or Billy Herman would arrive in town with a good horse and catch the local audience unawares. Wherever a handicapper may be located, it is necessary that he know the names and credentials of the best drivers on other circuits—because it is nice to cash mutuel tickets on these "unknowns" when they drop in at the local raceway.

Driving Ability Defined

Before you have finished your second cup of coffee at a track kitchen, you surely will hear that certain drivers are overrated. They are not nearly as good as the public thinks. It's politics. And luck. Other drivers are much better but do not get the breaks. Take Joe Doakes. He has won only 6 percent of his starts this season and was not much more successful last year, but he actually is as sharp a horseman as you can find. He just does not have the stock. And he's not in The Clique, so he never gets a catch-drive behind somebody else's good horse. Give him a stable like Haughton's or Dancer's and he'd show them all what for.

It may be true. Perhaps we should sympathize with Doakes and root for him and form a Doakes fan club. But we had better not modify our handicapping procedures on that account. No profit comes from betting on a driver because of the feats he might achieve in a better world. Tonight's races take place in this world. Poor Doakes never seems to win unless he has much the best horse, or unless he benefits from somebody's else's bad racing luck.

In deciding who the best drivers are, the handicapper employs a cold-blooded definition of "best." For his purposes, the best drivers are those who win a high percentage of their starts—15 percent or more. Nothing else counts for much. It has been said that a hundred drivers could match Stanley Dancer's winning average (which often exceeds 30 percent) if they had access to horses like his and could afford to be as choosy as he about deciding when to drive and when to abstain. Let 'em say it. The handicapper needs only to know that Stanley Dancer gets home first with extraordinary consistency, multiplying the chances of any sharp horse he drives.

Billy Haughton believes that great drivers are born, not made. He speaks with authority and has no axe to grind. As of January 1, 1980, he had won 4,425 races and more purse money ($28,240,396) than any other driver in history except the supreme Herve Filion. He could stop driving tomorrow and continue as a power in the sport. He is a fully accomplished horseman. He does it all. He has few equals as a judge of yearlings or trainer of colts. In the delicate arts of schooling, conditioning, hanging, balancing and driving a trotter, he rates at the very top with Joe O'Brien, Del Miller, Howard Beissinger, Stanley Dancer, Billy Herman, Glen Garnsey and John Simpson, Jr. As a handler of pacers, not more than thirty men rate as his peer.

Haughton declares that while years of experience are indispensable they produce greatness only in a driver endowed with a light touch, quick reflexes, unusually wide peripheral vision and a suitable mentality.

"Light hands are the basic requirement," he says. "This has absolutely nothing to do with how big a man is. I know little men who are heavy handed and will never make it to the top for that reason. I know heavy men with light hands.

"Heavy-handed men make hard-mouthed horses. Horses with hard mouths can't respond quickly to their drivers. A driver with that kind of horse loses a fraction of a second three or four times in a race. I have run into it myself in taking over horses that had been handled by heavy-handed drivers. Their mouths are tough and hard. They just don't respond as they should to my touch. It takes quite a while before I can get them to react properly. In the meantime, I lose races I should have won."

Light hands are most effective when associated with keen, experienced intelligence and cool emotions. Great drivers are smarter than others. And more composed. Their racing tactics resemble psychological warfare. They keep their opponents in a state of chronic anxiety, upstaging them at every opportunity, playing with them like cats with mice, provoking them to move prematurely or wait too long.

If a Haughton wants the "garden spot"—the choice position on the rail directly behind the leader—he often gets it by outwitting its occupant. He flushes the man out of there by storming up on the outside as if to steal the lead. Afraid of Haughton to begin with, and incapable of weighing all the alternatives in the split second available to him, the fish bites. He becomes impetuous. He takes out to reach the lead before Haughton can. As soon as he vacates the garden spot, Haughton eases into it, saving his horse on the turn while his victim's animal, parked out, loses its sting.

It happens over and over again. And then one night, as if Haughton wanted it that way, the sucker declines to be flushed out, whereupon Haughton makes an even truer believer of him by taking the lead at once and remaining there to the finish.

If a Haughton wants to leave the rail and travel overland, he frequently finds someone to run interference. This time the pigeon may be in front or behind. It does not matter. Feinting an outward move, Haughton induces the other to try to beat him to the front. As soon as the man takes the bait, Haughton moves directly behind him, under snug cover from the wind.*

Not many drivers combine the light touch with the eyes in the back of the head, the instant reflexes, the high intelligence and the years of con-

---

* For a much more profound and comprehensive review of driving tactics than I can supply here, see Haughton's classic, "Driving the Race," in James C. Harrison's *Care and Training of the Trotter and Pacer.*

structive experience. Those who do are so obviously beneficial to fit horses that owners and trainers plead for their services.

The Catch-Drivers

The age of specialization has overtaken harness racing. Although that remarkable one-man band, the trainer-driver, remains prominent throughout the sport, his tribe diminishes. Many successful horsemen now concentrate on training, and drive scarcely at all. Some drive but leave the actual training to others. Some train and drive their best young stock, entrusting the rest to assistants. A horseman who does all his own training and driving probably has a small stable.

With horses deployed all over the map, emperors like Stanley Dancer, Billy Haughton and George Sholty do much of their training by long-distance telephone. Somebody else attends to the daily routines. The assistant who handles a local division of a big-time stable is legally accountable as its trainer and is named as such in the raceway program. Unless Haughton or Dancer or whoever heads the outfit has been driving a horse in its recent races, the inexperienced fan may have no clue that it is a Haughton or Dancer horse.

Many raceway programs clarify matters by naming the national head of the stable as well as the local trainer. The information is particularly helpful early in the season, when the probable class and readiness of a green three-year-old is more easily deduced from the name of its stable than from the names of its sire and dam. At any time of year, the fan appreciates knowing that the officially responsible trainer, Apples Thomas, is actually minding the store for Billy Haughton, or that Clint Warrington is Stanley Dancer's man, and Sandy Levy stands in for George Sholty.

Commuting from raceway to raceway in pursuit of the week's fattest prizes, and seldom roosting in one place for more than 72 hours at a time, the big operators take pains to guarantee competent drivers for their stock on nights when they are elsewhere. The various Dancers constantly fill in for each other. So do members of other raceway families such as the Farringtons, Riegles, Filions, Haughtons, Williamses, Nickellses and Popfingers. But catch-driving is more than a family convenience. It has become a source of substantial revenue for drivers who excel at it.

On the Yonkers-Roosevelt circuit, Carmine Abbatiello, Herve Filion, Lucien Fontaine and Norm Dauplaise often drive stock from top barns. At The Meadowlands, Greg Wright, John Campbell and Ben Webster are found behind the stars of many big stables. Some insiders think that Webster may be the best catch-driver in the business. Others harbor similar notions about Filion, Abbatiello, Sholty, Del Insko, Joe O'Brien, Jim Doherty and Shelly Goudreau. Also regarded highly are Jim Larente, Jack Bailey, Ted Wing, George Phalen and, beyond doubt, the driver now leading the list at your own favorite raceway.

There are dozens of genuinely good ones. Some, like Abbatiello and Fontaine, are uninterested in training horses. Others, like Sholty and O'Brien, are among the best trainers in the world. What they all have in common, aside from driving talent of the first order, is an uncanny ability to win with a strange horse. They take it on a warm-up tour and learn all they need to know.

During the past decade, dozens of trainers have been obliged to concede that expert training and expert driving are separate skills which do not necessarily coexist in the same person. So they employ catch-drivers. As they put it, "Five percent of something is better than 10 percent of nothing." The trainer's share of a purse is 5 percent, as is the driver's. A trainer-driver therefore collects 10 percent. But an Abbatiello or Webster wins the race, whereas the horse's trainer might be unable to. No longer pretending that they can drive in fast company, numerous trainers now prosper on 5 percent, where they formerly suffered for want of the 10.

With trainers and drivers playing musical chairs in the sulky, alert handicappers make hay. If a horse displayed vigor when steered by an ordinary chauffeur last week, it should fly for Webster tonight. If it won in a squeaker for Filion last week, the switch to Doakes very probably means that not much should be expected tonight.

Universal Ratings

Most raceway programs summarize drivers' recent accomplishments numerically. Adjoining each name on the list is a three-digit figure which looks like a batting average. It also looks as if it might be the driver's percentage of winning starts, but it is not. Instead, it is an average computed in accordance with the Universal Driver Rating System, an ingenious statistical procedure which assumes that a victory is 80 percent more meritorious than a second-place finish and three times as good as coming in third. It charges the driver 9 points for every start and awards him 9 for each victory, 5 for each second and 3 for each third. With 3 wins, 3 seconds and 3 thirds in 9 attempts, the driver's UDR is .630. The rating is computed by adding the win credits ($3 \times 9 = 27$), and those for finishing second ($3 \times 5 = 15$), and those for finishing third ($3 \times 3 = 9$), and dividing the sum (51) by the debits for starts ($9 \times 9 = 81$).

Anything above .300 is considered quite good for a season's action, although many leading drivers do much better. Occasionally, the system leads into strange byways. For example, a driver with 10 wins (90 points),

24 seconds (120) and 30 thirds (90) in 100 starts (900) earns a UDR of .333 —more appetizing than his miserable winning average of .100. Another driver with 20 wins (180), 18 seconds (90) and 10 thirds (30) in 100 starts (900) also rates a UDR of .333, although his winning average of .200 probably establishes him as one of the torrid drivers on the grounds and a more dependable bet than the other man.

Lacking other evidence, one surely would suppose that a driver who has been winning 20 percent of his starts has sharper horses or has been working wonders with inferior horses. The man who has been winning only 10 percent of his starts might actually be the superior driver, of course. Perhaps he gets money with impossible animals. But on whom does one bet? I should think that one bets on the man who, for whatever reason, has been winning consistently. Provided, of course, that his horse seems fit.

I recommend that handicappers be careful to note whether the decimals that accompany drivers' names are winning averages or UDR averages. If winning averages are missing, it is worthwhile to calculate them yourself.

It also is desirable to keep tabs on the leading drivers at the current local meeting so that you will have something to go on when the horses move across town to the other raceway. The raceway program supplies driver statistics only for the meeting in progress. It is silent about what happened elsewhere on the same circuit during the same season. Players who know how the reinsmen have been doing in recent months are better equipped to evaluate their chances during the first week or so of a new meeting.

The Driver's Weight

Although the so-called modified sulky (which is by way of becoming the accepted, conventional, normal one) has virtually eliminated the driver's personal weight as a factor in handicapping, the matter is worth discussion.

Even before the modification of the sulky, horsemen considered the driver's weight inconsequential on a dry track. But they agreed that when racing strips became muddy and the wheels plowed deep furrows (a rare happening at modern raceways), a lightweight driver enjoyed a big advantage.

Now that poundage in the driver's seat exerts upward leverage on the sulky shafts, some horsemen believe that heavy drivers have an advantage on any kind of footing, because they supply their horses with more "lift." If this is so, the records do not prove it. Even with the new sulky, little drivers seem to win more often and more consistently than large ones do.

Of the top money winners during 1978, the heaviest was Herve Filion at a mere 165. The others were Abbatiello (145), Ted Wing (140), John Chapman (150), Norman Dauplaise (140), Joe Marsh (125), Bill Haughton (155) and Ben Webster (135).

So far as can be ascertained, few trainers or owners make a conscious effort to employ drivers of lighter weight. Yet the lighter weights win. Pending scientific investigation, it can be assumed that lightness does more good than harm. Beyond that, it seems sensible to leave the issue in abeyance, where it was when we found it. Whether the individual be large or small, the only practical measure of driving ability is the winning percentage.

Handicapping the Drivers

The attitude of this book is that the number of wins and the total purse money accumulated by a driver during a month, a season or a career are of no particular significance in handicapping a race. What counts is the winning average, the percentage of starts that result in victory. If the racegoer bets only on seemingly fit horses, preferring those whose drivers maintain satisfactory winning averages, he is as safe as he can be. If he learns how to decide when to bet on the third-best horse in the race, because of its winning driver, he will be no safer but will have more fun.

It takes a certain amount of self-confidence to evaluate drivers in terms of their winning percentages. The list of leading money winners or race winners at every track includes at least one highly regarded reinsman with a mediocre winning percentage. There is nothing paradoxical about this. For example, consider Stan Banks, a highly competent trainer-driver who is always among the leaders on the Chicago circuit and, in fact, is usually to be found among the top 30 race winners and top 20 purse earners in North America. He always wins at least $1 million a year. Yet he rarely wins more than 13 percent of his starts and, since 1961, has never logged a UDR higher than .260. The reason for this is that Stan Banks drives more than his fair share of bad horses. At the opposite extreme are drivers such as Howard Beissinger and Billy Herman, for whom a 30 percent winning average is not unusual. In a real sense, they drive more than their fair share of good horses. And for the handicapper, the mere presence in the sulky of a high-percentage driver often means that the horse itself probably has a better than average chance in its race. But with a low-percentage driver, the horse's own record had better proclaim its superiority before we take too many chances.

In other words, drivers who win fewer than 15 percent of their starts are risky betting propositions unless their horses stand out sharply. But a driver who consistently achieves a high seasonal or annual average is worth notice, *even when he is in a slump*. And any driver, including our bedraggled Joe Doakes, should be regarded as a winner during meetings that find him in a hot streak.

To be more detailed about it, I think that good handicappers are faithful to the following ideas:

1. *Drivers do not often win with unfit horses.* Unless a horse seems sharp and well situated, the handicapper should ignore it, no matter who the driver may be. To disregard this is to bet on drivers as if horses were not involved. This is more costly than the error of betting on horses as if drivers were not involved.

2. *By winning upward of 20 percent of their annual starts and leading local and/or national standings in that department year after year, a small minority of drivers are recognizable as likely winners whenever they turn up with fit horses.* This holds true even during periods in which the raceway program shows that such a driver has been winning a low percentage of his attempts. Top drivers do not remain losers for long. Even at 60 and 70 years of age, they continue to win a large fraction of their races, although they work less frequently.

3. *At a typical raceway meeting, the dominant drivers are those who have been winning 15 percent or more of their races. If some have been achieving averages of 20, 25 or 30 percent, the handicapper should take that large difference into account.*

4. *Any driver, no matter how inconsistent his prior record, should be regarded as a potential winner if he has been getting home first with 15 percent of his horses at the current meeting, and if he goes with a sharp horse tonight.*

5. *No provisional driver is an acceptable bet unless he has been racing as frequently as others and is among the leading reinsmen at the meeting.* Provisional drivers are apprentices in the trade. Sooner or later the best of them begin winning, but consistency is not usually within their powers.

Players who do their handicapping mentally, distrusting arithmetical formulas, will get along if they confine their wagers to situations in which (a) the horse seems best and (b) the driver is either an authentic top-notcher or on a hot streak. Between two apparently equal horses, the one with the winning driver deserves support. If both drivers qualify, the player might consider making two bets—especially at half-mile tracks, where contention is so close.

This kind of handicapping requires the player to become a mental gymnast when a George Sholty or Joe O'Brien or Billy Haughton or the like turns up with a horse which, while apparently fit, is not as impressive as another horse whose driver has no special distinction. Sometimes the best horse wins. Sometimes the best driver wins. Sometimes the outcome is predictable. Certain theorists believe that the player should always take the best driver. Others think the best driver is the play at a half-miler but not on a longer oval. Still others think the race should be passed unless the best-looking horse goes with a winner in the sulky.

I have tested all these theories and have found profit in none of them. More precisely, there is profit in *all* of them, if the handicapper can determine which of them is applicable to the particular race. This puts him right back where he started, in the mental gymnasium.

I much prefer the numerical procedure that I have been piecing together at intervals throughout this book. In dealing with drivers, it awards the winning ones numerical credit for the comtribution they make to Standardbred performance. The amount of credit is uniform, as if one top driver were as good as another. This is imprecise, but it is more practical than a procedure in which the handicapper tries to decide whether O'Brien is going to catch Marsh in the stretch. Or whether O'Brien and Marsh each deserve 18 points, whereas Doakes is entitled to 4 or 7. Determinations of that kind simply cannot be made. But the probability that a driver with a high winning percentage will have a fit horse is as substantial as any probability in racing. It is on this probability that this handicapping method rests.

And it works. As the reader will see, the method sometimes indicates that a fit horse with a journeyman navigator is a better bet than another fit horse whose driver is an all-time great. In doing so, and in being right often enough to stave off the sheriff, the method eliminates the painful gyrations demanded by other approaches to handicapping.

I recommend the following:

1. *If the driver customarily is a national or local leader in terms of winning percentage (about 20 or more in most years), add 10 points to the rating of his horse.* Needless to say, the horse qualifies as a contender and has been given a pace rating, modified to take account of class, form, post position and angles.

2. *If the driver usually wins 15 percent or is doing that well at the current meeting or during the current season, add 5 points to the horse's rating.*

3. *If the horse's driver in its key race (the race that qualified it as a contender) was the kind of driver specified in items 1 or 2 above, but tonight's driver is not, deduct 5 or 10 points from the rating.*

These recommendations cover all likely situations but two. The first occurs during the first days of a meeting, when mediocre drivers may be listed among the leaders in the program's tabulation. Obviously, a record of one victory in three starts hardly makes a top man of someone who has not previously set the world ablaze. If in doubt about a driver, the best procedure is to assume that his 15 percent record means nothing unless at least ten victories are involved.

Another dilemma is that of the fan who patronizes one of our smaller raceways. What to do if a Billy Haughton turns up one night and accepts a couple of catch-drives while waiting to perform with one of his champion Standardbreds? Unless the driving colony at the track includes national leaders, the handicapper probably should add 15 points to the rating of any fit horse driven by the invader. Otherwise, 10.

The Leading Drivers

With more than 12,000 men and women licensed to drive in North American harness races, it is impossible to list all the competent ones. Instead, I offer brief profiles of some of the best and most prominent. And I renew the recommendation that all handicappers pay close attention to the driving statistics published in raceway programs.

CARMINE ABBATIELLO
Born 5/23/36, New York, N.Y.
Career earnings through 1978: $19,409,640
Career victories through 1978: 3,744

Brought to the track by his brother Tony, a capable trainer-driver, this remarkably aggressive horseman has been a fixture on the tough Roosevelt-Yonkers circuit since the early 1960s. In 1978, he led all North American drivers in purse earnings and was second only to Herve Filion in number of victories. He prefers to race on the front end, a style well suited to the New York half-milers, but adapts readily to larger tracks, as he proved by finishing among the top five in the standings at The Meadowlands. He has long been the preferred driver for the outstanding stable of Buddy Regan but is always welcome behind the livestock of other leading barns. Year in and year out, with cheap horses and free-for-allers, Abbatiello has a dependably high winning average.

STAN BANKS
Born 10/22/36, Belvidere, Ill.
Career earnings: $8,071,527
Career victories: 2,309

Banks commutes from his farm in Dwight, Ill., to vie with Daryl Busse and Walter Paisley for domination of the tough Chicago racing circuit. He attributes his success not only to competitive ability but to a special understanding of horses. He does not believe in cooping the animals in raceway stalls for months on end. Instead, he tries to give each a semi-monthly refresher on the farm. "They need freedom," he says. It works. His winning average is not high, because he drives numerous horses other than the ones from his own farm. But 200 victories and $1 million in purses are the proceeds of a routine season for him. Which means that he should never be overlooked when driving a strong contender.

HOWARD BEISSINGER
Born 5/16/23, Hamilton, Ohio
Career earnings: $5,187,887
Career victories: 1,457

This Hall of Famer has won three Hambletonians. He won in 1969 with Lindy's Pride, in 1971 with Speedy Crown and in 1978 with Speedy So-molli, a son of Speedy Crown. A master developer of trotters, he maintains a stable of high-grade Grand Circuit stock and seldom appears on ordinary raceway programs. When he does, he excels because he is a consummate tactician and keeps his animals in top shape. For example, he has been leading driver at Hollywood Park, Sportsman's Park and Maywood Park. He usually wins at least 20 percent of his starts. Bettors sometimes criticize his quiet, apparently inactive driving style, but his achievements demonstrate that there is more to this game than the flailing of arms. Besides his Hambletonian winners, other top Beissinger animals have been Widower Creed, Tarport Lib, Entrepreneur, Ahhh, South Bend and Right Time.

NORMAN "CHRIS" BORING
Born 6/17/41, Indianapolis, Ind.
Career earnings: $7,473,490
Career victories: 2,590

This son and grandson of harness horsemen prefers to remain close to his Michigan home, but nobody doubts that he could compete with the leaders at any raceway if he chose to. At 20, when most budding horsemen consider themselves lucky to drive at a county fair, Boring led all drivers at Sportsman's Park, an achievement he repeated two years later. Since 1963, his UDR has not dropped below .300, and his winning percentage is invariably around 20. He devastates the Michigan fairs with his young stock and does exceptionally well on the Grand Circuit and at Detroit raceways. His best horse has been True Duane, who upset Bret Hanover in the 1966 American Pacing Classic.

JOHN CAMPBELL
Born 4/8/55, Ailsa Craig, Ont.
Career earnings: $1,775,270
Career victories: 471

I would describe Campbell as a young man on his way to the top, if he had not already arrived. In 1979, he led all drivers in North America, with $3,308,934 in purse earnings. A fixture at the Meadowlands, he topped the list in races won at that Mecca of the sport. He first attracted attention on the Detroit-Windsor circuit, where old-timers raved about his uncanny ability to upgrade the performance of any kind of horse. Now that he has established himself among the continent's foremost catch-drivers, he hopes to develop his own stable of first-rate colts.

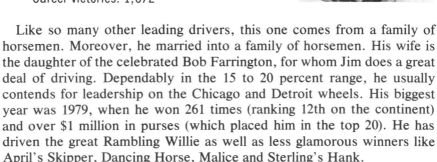

JIM CURRAN
Born 12/3/43, Jackson, Mich.
Career earnings: $6,578,023
Career victories: 1,672

Like so many other leading drivers, this one comes from a family of horsemen. Moreover, he married into a family of horsemen. His wife is the daughter of the celebrated Bob Farrington, for whom Jim does a great deal of driving. Dependably in the 15 to 20 percent range, he usually contends for leadership on the Chicago and Detroit wheels. His biggest year was 1979, when he won 261 times (ranking 12th on the continent) and over $1 million in purses (which placed him in the top 20). He has driven the great Rambling Willie as well as less glamorous winners like April's Skipper, Dancing Horse, Malice and Sterling's Hank.

DONALD DANCER
Born 10/1/55, Trenton, N.J.
Career earnings: $2,836,707
Career victories: 935

Son of the distinguished Vernon Dancer and nephew of all-time-great Stanley Dancer, young Donald has been among Standardbreds all his life. At the ripe old age of 22, he engaged the masterful Herve Filion in an incredible duel for the national driving championship. Although he finished second (with a mere 417 wins), he established himself as an outstanding driver in his own right. In the style initiated by his famous uncle, Donald prefers to get to the front promptly and stay there as long as possible. He does his best work at Liberty Bell and Brandywine. Having already become the youngest driver ever to win 300 races or $1 million in a single season, and only the second driver of any age to win as many as 400 in a year, he marked 1979 by becoming the youngest ever with a career record of 1,000 victories.

HAROLD "SONNY" DANCER, JR.
Born 10/5/35, Sharon, N.J.
Career earnings: $6,669,227
Career victories: 1,545

Son of trainer-driver Harold R. Dancer, nephew of Stanley and Vernon and cousin of Donald, this highly capable member of the imperial clan has a nice touch with colts, maintains a consistently impressive winning percentage and is in demand as a catch-driver. He has won the Fox Stake with Golden Money Maker and Ricci Reenie Time, the Betsy Ross with Ricci Reenie (dam of the aforementioned) and a Bloomsburg Fair Stake with Ricci Reenie First; and he has been driving champion at Monticello, Freehold and Roosevelt.

STANLEY DANCER
Born 7/25/27, Edinburg, N.J.
Career earnings: $20,463,446
Career victories: 3,319

This immortal has won four Little Brown Jugs, three Hambletonians and countless other stakes. He has trained and driven an unbelievable number of Standardbred superstars, among them Nevele Pride, Albatross, Super Bowl, Noble Victory, Bonefish, Keystone Ore, Henry T, Adios, Su Mac Lad, Cardigan Bay and Most Happy Fella. Although he has cut his driving schedule after some health difficulties, he continues in his tradition of going postward with nothing but live contenders. His normal winning percentage exceeds 25. He is a particular threat on the Grand Circuit and in New York sire-stake competition with the marvelous colts he develops for himself and his clients.

VERNON DANCER
Born 8/3/23, Red Valley, N.J.
Career earnings: $8,897,941
Career victories: 1,714

A dairy farmer who took up harness racing as a hobby because brother Stanley was so enthusiastic about it, Vernon Dancer drove his first winner in 1952, became an accepted topnotcher in the early 1960s and has been going at a 15–20 percent clip ever since. Like Stanley, whose farm is across the way from his own in New Egypt, N.J., he is a fully rounded horseman with a penchant for the Grand Circuit, sire stakes and the doings at The Meadowlands, Roosevelt, Yonkers and Liberty Bell. In effect this requires him to operate three different kinds of Standardbred strings. He does it well, if not on so large a scale as Stanley. A racing accident in 1977 and the meteoric rise of son Donald combined to diminish his race driving at the end of the 1970s.

NORMAN DAUPLAISE
Born 1/29/40, Drummondville, Ont.
Career earnings: $10,902,125
Career victories: 1,790

"The Master of the Measured Win" is what railbirds on the Yonkers-Roosevelt circuit call this Canadian after he gets some winner's nose in front in the final strides. What they call him when he arrives a stride too late after biding his time during the earlier going need not be repeated here. Suffice to observe that he wins about 15 percent of the time and is in great demand as a catch-driver. Among his own best horses have been Sirota Anderson, Leader's Dream, Delmonico and Mickie Rodney. He drives at least 1,000 times a year and earns over $1 million in purses, almost entirely in the New York area.

JIM DENNIS
Born 5/9/23, Rexburg, Idaho
Career earnings: $10,141,591
Career victories: 2,333

Son of Noah, nephew of Warren and brother of Ted, this Dennis drove his first professional race in 1948 at Santa Anita, and won. Inclined to wait for things to sort themselves out before making his own move, he excels in the homestretches of one-mile and ⅝-mile tracks. A fierce competitor, he has topped all drivers at several major California and Chicago meetings. His best horse has been Sir Dalrae, 1973 Horse of the Year, who won more than $678,000. He also trained and drove the great Adios Vic, who upset Bret Hanover four times.

JIM DOHERTY
Born 9/27/40, St. John, N.B.
Career earnings: $5,649,157
Career victories: 1,864

After an apprenticeship behind his father's horses at raceways in the Maritime Provinces, Doherty invaded New England and by 1972 was biggest winner in that territory. He decided to try his luck at The Meadowlands and discovered that it wasn't luck but talent, of which he had plenty. In 1977, he raced a full New Jersey season and won almost $1.3 million in purses against the world's best. With a winning percentage around 15, he has become one of the most respected catch-drivers at The Meadowlands, as witness his accomplishments behind Young Quinn, Master Nick, Fortune Moy, Stonegate Count and Persuadable.

MERRITT DOKEY
Born 5/15/39, Kalamazoo, Mich.
Career earnings: $7,899,444
Career victories: 1,503

The little Michigander started as a jockey of quarter horses but turned to the sulky under the guidance of the great Joe Marsh, Jr., and has never regretted it. After establishing himself as a star in his own state, he took some good horses to New York and caught on rapidly. In 1976, he won $1,929,967—more than any driver except Herve Filion. A solid 15-percenter who drives aggressively and wins in bunches, he deserves reverent attention during his hot streaks and should never be overlooked at other times.

BEA FARBER
Born 11/8/40, Kinde, Mich.
Career earnings: $1,465,427
Career victories: 443

Husband Chuck trains them and Bea drives them with extraordinary skill. In 1973, the former legal secretary posted a .536 UDR in winning the driving title at Northville Downs. Two years later, she topped the list at Bay Meadows with a .512. Her winning percentage is comfortably above 20, and nobody wonders any longer whether women can compete against men in raceway competition.

HENRI FILION
Born 5/22/41, Angers, Que.
Career earnings: $8,923,524
Career victories: 1,829

After ups and downs in Canada, New England and Illinois, Herve's brother arrived in New York and proved himself a first-rate driver in his own right. Trainers who can obtain his services do not hesitate to put him behind animals of the highest quality. He does well on the Grand Circuit. In 1977, he won the Hambletonian Filly Stake with Elmsford. He also has won major events with Governor Skipper, Rockwell Hanover, Bob Hilton, Royal Ascot N and Seatrain. He wins 15 percent of his starts and sometimes gets live horses in streaks, which accounts for the nickname "Hot Hands Henri."

HERVE FILION
Born 2/1/40, Angers. Que.
Career earnings: $25,810,950
Career victories: 6,705

Being mortal, Filion undoubtedly has limitations. Nobody in harness racing has been able to discover what they are. His 637 wins in 1974 were an all-time record for one driver in one year. During the following year, his total career victories reached 5,312, making him the winningest driver of all time. Part of the explanation is the man's boundless energy. When pursuing a driving title, he thinks nothing of commuting by helicopter from an afternoon of races at Freehold to an evening at The Meadowlands, Yonkers, Roosevelt, or wherever the biggest opportunities beckon. A larger part of the explanation is his supreme talent in the sulky. He is first and foremost a horseman who learns what he needs to know about an animal on extremely brief acquaintance. He wins with has-beens and never-weres, and has few peers behind a decent horse.

He started with 29 wins in 1953, at age 13, and has never looked back. The big-timers began to take him seriously when he beat Cardigan Bay with Fly Fly Byrd, Romulus Hanover with Meadow Paige and Armbro Flight with All Aflame. He can drive in any style but prefers to come from off the pace, believing that most horses race more gamely that way. In recent years, at the peak of his powers, he has won the Little Brown Jug with Nansemond and Hot Hitter. Watch for him. He will race at your track and he will win his 15 to 20 percent.

LUCIEN FONTAINE
Born 4/12/39, Pointe aux Trembles, Que.
Career earnings: $15,457,932
Career victories: 2,998

After breaking in under Keith Waples in Canada, Loosh immigrated and became the protégé of the great Clint Hodgins, for whom he drove Bye Bye Byrd, Elaine Rodney and other good ones. Primarily a catch-driver, Fontaine has some solid raceway stock in association with Steve Demas, the trainer. He has begun to try his hand on the Grand Circuit and, of course, does not overlook the New York sire-stake program, for which he invariably has a couple of good candidates. Since 1965, he has been a regular on the Roosevelt-Yonkers wheel and a fixture on the continental list of leading dash winners and money winners. Inclined to move early—a sound tactic at half-milers—Fontaine has good hands and a splendid sense of pace, and he usually ends the year at 15 percent or better.

MIKE GAGLIARDI
Born 8/25/48, Newark, N.J.
Career earnings: $4,021,104
Career victories: 1,111

Watching the energetic Gagliardi drive can be an exhausting experience. Whipping, rocking, jumping around in the sulky, he is all out to get the most he can from every horse. And he has more finesse than meets the eye. After driving important Standardbreds like Right Direction and Power Hitter, he drove the troublesome Bret's Star in 1974 for trainer

Billy Haughton and wound up winning the Matron Stake, the W. E. Miller Memorial and a heat in the Little Brown Jug. He wins about 15 percent of his starts, preferring one-mile strips like The Meadowlands and Hollywood Park.

BILL GALE
Born 10/18/48, Toronto, Ont.
Career earnings: $3,255,321
Career victories: 1,195

In 1976, this protégé of the legendary Morris McDonald went to the gate in 1,463 races and won 293 of them (20 percent), which made him the fourth leading dash winner in North America. In 1977, he won 266, which kept him in the continent's top 10. His high winning percentage and the consistency with which he lands in the money even when not winning make him one of the top catch-drivers in the Detroit area, where he has won several titles. If he decides to move to another circuit—or if he happens to stop off for a night or two at your own—he will earn instant respect.

GLEN GARNSEY
Born 1/1/33, Clayton, N.Y.
Career earnings: $4,914,762
Career victories: 1,672

Garnsey first made a name for himself on the spacious ¾-miler at Vernon, N.Y., where he shared driving honors with Jack Bailey for several seasons. In 1968, he became head trainer for K. D. Owen's private stable and a year later succeeded Ralph Baldwin in that responsibility for Castleton Farm. While training for Castleton, Garnsey developed and raced an enormous number of top-flight Standardbreds such as Colonial Charm, Alert Bret, Striking Image, Racy Goods, All Alert, Hoot Speed, Noble Florie and Berna Hanover. In 1978, he resumed operation of his own public stable. Among his charges was Horse of the Year Abercrombie, winner of $703,260. Concentrating on Grand Circuit competition, Garnsey is second to none as a driver of young horses, especially trotters. Wins 25 percent.

GILLES GENDRON
Born 1/20/45, Quebec City, Que.
Career Earnings: $5,762,730
Career victories: 2,234

The dominant figure in Quebec racing, Gendron has won more than 200 races each year since 1972. In 1978, his 306 victories placed him sixth in the North American standings. He practically owns the Blue Bonnets Raceway driving title, and in 1973 he became the first driver ever to win the dash, percentage and money crowns at Richelieu. His winning percentage invariably exceeds 15. When he makes one of his rare excursions to the U.S., it is not for fun. More than a few of his peers have compared his skills to those of Herve Filion.

SHELLY GOUDREAU
Born 5/27/48, Chatham, Ont.
Career earnings: $5,258,858
Career victories: 1,596

This Canadian has won driving titles at Hollywood Park, Los Alamitos and Windsor Raceway and is highly regarded at The Meadowlands. Well he might be. His winning average frequently surpasses 20 percent, and his fearless aggressiveness combines nicely with a kindly pair of hands. "Your desire to win has to be so strong that nothing fazes you," he once said. In 1970, his desire was so powerful that he was involved in eight driving accidents. Instead of becoming gun shy, he emerged sharper than ever. Among his charges have been the world champion Tender Loving Care, Superman, Try Scotch, Captivating Girl, Mighty Phantom and Arrochar Replica.

TOM HARMER
Born 8/21/50, Pontiac, Mich.
Career earnings: $2,457,337
Career victories: 1,139

This ambitious young driver likes to set the pace or stalk the leaders in every race he can. "I figure that the race is up front, so I like to move early," he explains. The style has served him well, particularly on the half-mile strip at Northville Downs, where he has won several driving titles. He also races successfully at Hazel Park and Wolverine. For a comparative newcomer competing in tough company, Harmer achieves impressive statistics. His annual winning percentage tops 20. And he is a horseman's driver. Veterans who have raced against him are sure that he is on his way to the top.

BILLY HAUGHTON
Born 11/2/23, Gloversville, N.Y.
Career earnings: $27,158,057
Career victories: 4,352

In 1969, Haughton became the first driver in USTA history to win 3,000 races and the first to achieve a career total of $14 million in purse winnings. He has not exactly lost his touch since then, winning from 20 to 25 percent of his annual starts and bobbing up year after year with strong divisions of Grand Circuit and raceway horses. His stable is always there or thereabouts in competition for annual age and gait championships. In 1978, for example, he had the world champion pacer, Falcon Almahurst; the titlists, Green Speed and Cold Comfort; the splendid mare Keystone Pioneer, the leading juvenile pacer, Crackers; the winner of the Kentucky Futurity, Doublemint; and Wellwood Hanover, a pacer who went in 1:53:2.

Over the years, he has set records with Handle with Care, Steve Lobell, Belle Acton, Bachelor Hanover, Armbro Omaha, Quick Chief, Duke Rodney, Vica Ranover, Charming Barbara, Laverne Hanover, Rum Customer, Carlisle, Flamboyant and Romulus Hanover, among others. To list all his outstanding horses would require the rest of this book.

Whenever Haughton chooses to remain in one place long enough to compete for a driving championship, he is a good bet to win it. Interestingly enough, he seldom pays as much money for yearlings as other bigtimers do. He is notorious for making fortunes with bargain horses. Which proves that he knows a Standardbred when he sees it and knows exactly what to do after he gets it. As to driving, everyone agrees that he is as good as they come. With years of activity ahead, he can be expected to rewrite the record books time and again.

JACQUES HEBERT
Born 8/22/42, Drummondville, Ont.
Career earnings: $4,360,724
Career victories: 1,626

Here is another in the endless succession of Canadian drivers able to compete on equal terms with the best in the world. Except for brief flings at Vernon Downs in upstate New York, Hebert has made a career in the year-round racing at Montreal. His record of nip-and-tuck finishes with Gilles Gendron and various Filions has established his prowess. It now is taken for granted among Standardbred horsemen in the U.S. that Hebert will do handsomely on any major circuit if he ever decides to leave home. Each year he drives more than 1,000 times, winning his 15 percent or more. Unlike many drivers on half- and ⅝-mile tracks, he prefers to come from behind, a style that suits a great many of the longshots that he handles.

BILLY HERMAN
Born 2/21/40, Frankfort, Ohio
Career earnings: $3,289,023
Career victories: 828

After several years as George Sholty's strong right hand, this superb trainer-driver became head man at the powerful Hanover Shoe Farms Stable, previously bossed by Hall of Famers such as Tom Berry, Henry Thomas and John Simpson, Sr. Herman soon demonstrated his fitness for the position, winning the 1977 Kentucky Futurity with Texas, and subsequently developing champions Scarlet Skipper and Hazel Hanover and major winners like Cora T, Unexpected Guest and Mostest Yankee. Herman has always been a driver with an uncanny sense of timing and conspicuous ability to win the big ones. Pinch-hitting for Sholty behind Boyden Hanover, he won the 1974 Cane Pace. In 1975, when injury made Jimmy Arthur vacate the sulky behind the difficult colt Noble Rogue after the first heat of the Kentucky Futurity, Herman took over and won the next two heats and the trophy. Herman had never driven Noble Rogue before. In 1978, Herman's extraordinary UDR of .460 ranked him third among North American drivers with fewer than 200 starts. With Hanover Shoe stock, he will continue indefinitely as a high-percentage winner.

DELMER INSKO
Born 7/10/31, Amboy, Minn.
Career earnings: $27,158,057
Career victories: 4,352

He broke in with his horseman father at Midwestern fairs in 1946 and installed himself on the annual list of leading dash winners in 1957, apparently for keeps. All these years later, he usually rates among the tops in that department and among leading money winners as well. Insko drives more than 1,000 times a year in most years and does not always achieve a 15 percent average, but is so obviously a great driver that handicappers expect the best whenever he turns up behind a fit contender. He competes on the Grand Circuit, in sire stakes and at major New York raceways. A genius at finding cover for a horse that needs it and at provoking other drivers into beating themselves, Insko conforms to no pattern other than the one calculated to suit the horse and the situation. He is so adept at giving an animal its best chance that handicappers write off any horse that gets another driver after racing poorly for Del. If it were fit, Insko would have moved it ahead a few lengths at some stage of its race. And, as this implies, if Insko got better livestock to handle, he would win more frequently than he does. Meanwhile, he has handled many great horses. Besides Overcall, he has had champions like Henry T. Adios, Speedy Rodney and Savoir. He is permanently entrenched among the great drivers in the history of the sport.

JOE MARSH, Jr.
Born 6/20/34, Curtice, Ohio
Career earnings: $9,112,033
Career victories: 2,761

Starting as a groom for his father in 1952, he began swinging on the big time in 1959, when his .316 UDR was twelfth-highest on the continent. He has topped the driver standings at Hollywood Park, Sportsman's Park, Hazel Park and numerous lesser raceways, and now spends most of his time in the New York area, where he is usually good for a winning average of at least 15 percent. Few drivers in the world are able to leave the gate more quickly than Marsh, who also is a fine judge of pace, with an almost intuitive capacity for making his final move at the right time. Planning to diminish his raceway activity a bit, Marsh has been entrusting some of the driving chores to his promising son, Ronnie.

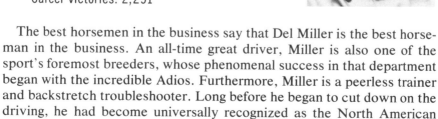

DELVIN MILLER
Born 7/5/13, Woodland, Cal.
Career earnings: $8,797,829
Career victories: 2,291

The best horsemen in the business say that Del Miller is the best horseman in the business. An all-time great driver, Miller is also one of the sport's foremost breeders, whose phenomenal success in that department began with the incredible Adios. Furthermore, Miller is a peerless trainer and backstretch troubleshooter. Long before he began to cut down on the driving, he had become universally recognized as the North American

Standardbred industry's foremost ambassador of good will, a distinction he retains. Nothing that will help harness racing is too much trouble for this remarkable man, including an occasional competitive appearance in the sulky (when he demonstrates that he can still drive with the best). Besides Adios, Miller has handled great ones like Direct Rhythm, Dale Frost, Countess Vivian, Thorpe Hanover and Dottie's Pick. He has won only one Hambletonian (Lusty Song in 1950), but could have won again in 1953 if he had not insisted that the owners permit his assistant, Harry Harvey, to drive the victorious Helicopter. He has won only one Little Brown Jug (Dudley Hanover, 1950) but could have won with his great Tar Heel in 1951. Instead, he put Del Cameron behind Tar Heel and finished second with his other horse, Solicitor. He knew Tar Heel was the better, but felt obliged to drive the other, a more difficult animal to handle.

J. P. MOREL
Born 3/30/36, St. Theodore, Que.
Career earnings: $2,741,356
Career victories: 1,820

Jean Paul seems to have permanent residence in the winner's circle at Saratoga Raceway. In 1977, when he won 242 times, 236 of those triumphs were at Saratoga, a new record for most wins at one track in one season. As one might imagine, the trainers at the raceway fall all over themselves to put him behind the best horses. And why not? He does the animals full justice, ending each season with a winning average in the 18–20 percent range.

JOE O'BRIEN
Born 6/25/17, Alberton, P.E.I.
Career earnings: $16,577,563
Career victories: 4,005

Second to none as a trainer and driver, the uncompromising O'Brien races from May through December and then withdraws to his California farm, offended by the notion that anyone would race a good horse more than 30 times a year just to pick up extra money. At Chicago and Hollywood, on the Grand Circuit and with occasional forays to The Meadowlands and New York, he does things exactly his own way. It works. He ends every year among the leaders in everything—purses and dashes won, UDR, Grand Circuit and winning average. He always wins more than 20 percent of his starts, has taken numerous driving championships and has won more than 400 races in 2:00 or less—surpassing all other drivers. Among his great horses: Armbro Flight, Sunbelle, Shadow Wave, Fresh Yankee, Scott Frost, Governor Armbro, Adios Express, Sunnie Tar, Melvin's Woe, Armbro Nesbit and Armbro Ranger. His driving style is old-fashioned; he likes to sit under cover on the rail until the stretch and then come blasting home. Despite such tactics, he has won every major event at Yonkers and Roosevelt. They call him the "Ice Man." I call him the handicapper's benefactor.

WALTER PAISLEY
Born 3/10/41, Berwyn, Ill.
Career earnings: $9,234,050
Career victories: 2,393

At 18, the precocious Paisley drove his father's Algiers Eblis in the Hambletonian and finished eleventh behind Diller Hanover. Things have improved. He now drives about 1,500 times a year, yet manages to win about 20 percent of the time with a UDR comfortably above .300. His two rivals on the Chicago circuit, Stan Banks and Daryl Busse, do not match those statistics. Paisley is much demanded as a catch-driver for invading stake horses. In that capacity, he won the 1974 American Pacing Championship with Armbro Nesbit and also won divisions of the American National stake with Tremor and Valerian.

BILL POPFINGER
Born 10/9/36, Pittsburgh, Pa.
Career earnings: $4,495,078
Career victories: 1,098

Bill and his successful older brother, Frank, have taken separate roads to the top. Bill trains a Grand Circuit stable full of blue-blooded two- and three-year-olds. Frank sticks with less glamorous raceway stock in New York. In 1978, Bill began the season with two of the top-rated three-year-old pacers. But his Spicy Charlie fell victim to a leg problem and his superstar Say Hello came up with a throat ailment. All Popfinger did was guide his third-string colt Happy Escort to victory in the Little Brown Jug, outdriving his leading rivals, Joe O'Brien and Billy Haughton. He is not driving quite as frequently as in earlier days but, as that 1978 accomplishment suggests, he yields to nobody in cleverness. Among the best horses that he has schooled, besides Happy Escort, have been Lady B. Fast, Shirley's Beau, Happy Motoring, Vanaro and Good to See You.

FRANK POPFINGER
Born 8/8/32, Pittsburgh, Pa.
Career earnings: $5,895,146
Career victories: 1,290

Horsemen like this are the backbone of the industry. Their livestock fills the bread-and-butter claiming and overnight races without which raceway programs could not be presented. After a modest start at Pennsylvania fairs, Frank was a leader at Monticello in the early 1960s and then invaded the Big Apple. He drives well either on the front end or coming from behind and takes full advantage of track geometry when he draws the inside post. Hint: He is particularly dangerous with horses making their first starts after long absences.

GEORGE SHOLTY
Born 11/2/32, Logansport, Ind.
Career earnings: $13,115,369
Career victories: 2,481

A consistent leader on the Grand Circuit and on the annual lists of money winners and dash winners, this energetic little man is in a slump when his winning average falls below 25 percent. He has won driving champions at many tracks, from Roosevelt to Hollywood. A great catch-driver, a great trainer and a great comfort to the handicapping fan, he broke into the game under an uncle and then worked for Tom Winn and Gene Sears. His own public stable includes large numbers of high-grade horses every season and he continues to cash in as a catch-driver. Among George's better stock have been Romeo Hanover, Royal Rick, Coffee Break, Bengazi Hanover, Truluck, Hammerin Hank, Sonsam, Florida Pro, Passing Glance, Songcan and Boyden Hanover. His fellow drivers rate George as second to none as a tactician and as a marvel with faint-hearted animals.

JOHN SIMPSON, Jr.
Born 6/13/43, Lumberton, N.C.
Career earnings: $4,138,224
Career victories: 848

In 1970, the 27-year-old John Simpson, Jr., became the youngest driver ever to win the Hambletonian. His horse was Timothy T. Young John came by that success honestly, having inherited his ability from the great driver who won the same race with Hickory Smoke and Ayres. The junior Simpson operates much in the manner of his father, concentrating on high-class young horses in Grand Circuit competition. He also makes frequent appearances at major raceways and likes to break in his young-sters at Vernon Downs. Among his best have been Superlou, Waymaker, Jurgy Hanover, Classical Way, Knightly Way, Exclusive Way and Hilar-ious Way. The "Way" horses all hail from Clarence F. Gaines's Gaines-way Farm. On the track, Simpson is a patient reinsman, notable for the ability to hold a wobbly trotter together long enough to save a close win. It is taken for granted that he will be a leading trainer-driver for many years to come.

RON WAPLES
Born 7/21/44, Toronto, Ont.
Career earnings: $6,305,205
Career victories: 2,015

The driving feats of Keith Waples are legendary in Canadian racing, and now comes young cousin Ron with feats of his own. In 1977, he was the first driver to win more than $1 million in a year of activity on Canadian tracks. He repeated that feat in 1978. In 1979 he was North American champion, with 443 victories. Although he competes mainly in Toronto, he is a frequent visitor to Yankee raceways, where he maintains his customary 15–20 percent pace. Seemingly a natural winner, he is among the rare navigators able to outdrive others and win with the second- or third-best horse. Among his many stake winners and FFA stars have been Dream Maker, Lime Time, Hustling Time, Fromming Hanover and Portia Lobell.

BEN WEBSTER
Born 11/8/39, Rochester, N.Y.
Career earnings: $13,337,311
Career victories: 2,405

One of the premier catch-drivers in the sport, Webster combines aggressiveness, sound judgment, superb reflexes, marvelous timing and an almost psychic ability to understand the ways of an individual horse within a few seconds of taking its reins for the first time. Although he broke in on half-milers in western New York, he seems equally at home on tracks of any size, as witness his performances at The Meadowlands.

He spends most of his time there and in New York, but he has won important races everywhere. He took the 1975 Little Brown Jug with Seatrain. He drove the mighty Oil Burner to triumphs in the American Pacing Classic, the Oliver Wendell Holmes Pace and the Monticello OTB Classic. He has also driven Walter Be Good, Nero, Flying Eagle, Andy Lobell, Keystone Model, Tarport Hap, Bestman Hanover, Jefferson Time and Bret's Champ. A dependable 15 percent performer.

BOB WILLIAMS
Born 1/14/36, Grand Rapids, Mich.
Career earnings: $6,769,504
Career victories: 1,906

Having followed brother Jack and their father into the racing business in 1954, the gifted Bob arrived at the top with a flourish in 1963, when he won more than 20 percent of his starts and led the meetings at Washington and Sportsman's Parks. He now is among the biggest money winners of every year, while maintaining a high winning percentage. Misled by his masterfully patient tactics at one-mile and ⅝-mile tracks, some critics assumed that he would be out of his element at half-milers. Bob proved otherwise when Jim Hackett, winner of the 1967 Little Brown Jug with Best of All, entrusted the horse to him. All he did was win the National Pacing Derby and the Realization at Roosevelt Raceway. Equally adept with trotters, he once catch-drove Earl Laird to a world record. Nowadays he spends most of his time on the West Coast and usually is among the leaders at Hollywood Park.

LEW WILLIAMS
Born 3/1/47, Cadiz, Ohio
Career earnings: $4,781,576
Career victories: 1,688

Horses like Whata Baron, Courageous Lady, Jilley, Plaza Bret, Real Hilarious, Mary Mel and Spare Hand have benefited greatly from the fierce determination and good hands of this aggressive driver. Although he is not particularly easy on his horses, preferring to cut out the pace in front, he frequently gets more from the animals than one might ordinarily expect. In short, he moves them up. He races primarily at The Meadowlands, where he is a fixture on the annual list of leading drivers. And in recent years he has been spending more and more time with Grand Circuit and sire-stake stock. Meanwhile, he bats at a 20 percent clip.

TED WING
Born 7/30/48, Greenville, Me.
Career earnings: $6,886,691
Career victories: 2,106

After humble beginnings at age 17 on New England tracks, Ted Wing has marched straight to the top of the profession. He seems to improve every year, boosting his earnings and his winning average. When The Meadowlands opened in 1977, Ted outdid himself, ending the year with nearly $2 million in earnings—almost four times his 1976 total. A remarkably strong finisher, he is good for a 20 percent winning average anywhere.

GREG WRIGHT
Born 1/26/46, Windsor, Ont.
Career earnings: $7,756,123
Career victories: 2,379

At age 26, and a leading driver at his hometown oval, Windsor Raceway, Greg became one of the youngest pilots ever to post a career total of 1,000 wins. In 1976, he reached 2,000. Only Herve Filion had reached that level at a younger age. Good as he was in Windsor and Detroit (in 1975 he led the list at both Hazel Park and Wolverine), he improved dramatically at The Meadowlands. During the inaugural meeting, he earned purse awards of almost $250,000 in just 24 nights. That accomplishment, plus the cool manner in which he carried it off, made him one of the hot catch-drivers at the new plant. His style is especially appropriate for racing on a one-mile strip. He takes his time, allowing his horses to lag behind in the early going, saving strength for frequently sensational stretch drives. Winning percentages above 15 are by no means unusual for him. Among his best animals have been J. R. Skipper (with whom he won five major stakes in 16 days during 1972), Napal Dew, Shealbat Rainbow, Missile Almahurst and Dreamalong Butler.

Other Leaders

MIKE ARNOLD (10/21/47): Simply outclasses most of the competition at the lesser Midwestern raceways he frequents. Wins from 20 to 25 percent of his starts and is headed for the big time.

JACK BAILEY (4/12/33): The veteran has won many dash titles, from Hollywood Park to Batavia and Vernon Downs. Remains fearless and clever, with astonishingly quick reflexes.

STAN BAYLESS (11/22/51): Joe O'Brien's stepson is an outstanding horseman in his own right, and nobody's patsy as a driver. Has frequently subbed for Joe in important races, driving in the family tradition. Competes mostly in California and Chicago. Wins 20 percent.

BERT BECKWITH (1/13/45): Enjoys training as much as driving and does both expertly enough to rank with the leaders in New England racing. Wins about 140 dashes a year and would be comfortably above 15 percent if he started fewer horses.

BILL BRESNAHAN (2/19/52): After an apprenticeship with Anthony Abbatiello, this youngster burst into prominence on the tough New York–New Jersey circuit, including its Freehold subdivision. A solid winner at least 15 percent of the time.

TIM BUTER (8/13/54): As a newcomer, the Michigander knocked 'em dead at The Meadows, winning driving championships there before returning to his home territory. A dependable driver with a high batting average, he seems to be one of the game's future stars.

WARREN CAMERON (5/29/40): Son of Hall of Famer Del Cameron, Warren races a select stable in stakes competition on the Delaware Valley circuit and at The Meadowlands. Entering relatively few races, he wins his 15 percent or more.

LEROY COPELAND (4/5/40): After capturing driving titles in New England and making a good impression during excursions elsewhere, Copeland returned to his native Michigan and continued to win consistently.

KIM CRAWFORD (10/28/54): This bold young Vermonter became successful at Saratoga during the 1970s, especially with Rebel Aaron, winner of $142,650. Will be heard from elsewhere.

JIM DOLBEE (2/1/41): A fixture on the lucrative Chicago circuit, where he trains a few horses and rakes in the loot as a catch-driver who wins between 15 and 20 percent year after year.

JERRY DUFORD (6/27/49): Started as a groom for his father, the celebrated Canadian, Wilf Duford, and is now acquiring celebrity of his own with about 100 victories a year all over the map: Toronto, Detroit, The Meadowlands.

JERRY GRAHAM (6/18/41): One of four racing sons of Herman Graham, Sr., Jerry is a 20 percent winner on the Grand Circuit, at Chicago raceways, Illinois fairs and occasional forays to the East.

DOUG HAMILTON (3/20/47): The Ontarian sports a high average in the Ohio sire-stake program and at raceways in Michigan and in the East.

FRED HASLIP (2/16/42): The trainer-driver is a powerful factor on the Buffalo-Batavia circuit of western New York.

ROSS HAYTER (10/16/40): Shares domination of Brandywine and Liberty Bell with Eddie Davis and Donald Dancer and shows little desire to branch out. Had the world champion mare Meadow Blue Chip. Wins about 15 percent.

JOHN KOPAS (2/23/54): Having accepted some of the driving chores from his talented father, Jack, this young man drove Super Clint to a 1:54 mile in upsetting Governor Skipper back in 1977. Prefers to race stake horses. Wins 15 percent.

JIM LARENTE (5/21/31): Superb catch-driver good for 20 percent average at Brandywine, Liberty Bell and The Meadowlands.

KEITH LINTON (12/5/47): Known to his Saskatchewan fans as the "Mighty Mite from Moose Jaw," this driver invariably wins about 30 percent of his starts. Won the 1978 championship at Assiniboia Downs with an incredible UDR of .501. Having outgrown his competition to that extent, he might be tempted to try larger ponds. The word is that he is good enough to win anywhere.

EDDIE LOHMEYER (10/29/43): This patient schooler of high-grade stock prefers trotters to pacers, and stake races to claimers. Is so versatile and competent that other trainers seek him for catch-drives. Wins about 20 percent against the toughest possible competition on the Eastern Seaboard.

DAVID MAGEE (12/4/53): One of the leading young catch-drivers around Chicago, this aggressive competitor loves to set or press the early pace. A comer.

MARVIN MAKER (1/17/47): A champion at Monticello, Maker is highly regarded by the big-timers who have driven against him at The Meadowlands and Liberty Bell. Wins 15 to 20 percent.

CATELLO MANZI (6/27/50): His five brothers and their father all drive in harness races. So does cousin Ed Lohmeyer. It therefore was no surprise when Cat won Monticello dash titles in his second and third years of full-fledged competition. Also does well at Pompano Park, Yonkers, Roosevelt and The Meadowlands.

SAM "CHIP" NOBLE III (12/15/53): His astounding UDR of .459 in 393 starts led North America during 1978. Won a third of those races, mainly in Ohio. Extremely selective about accepting catch-drives. With his batting average, he can afford to be picky. Headed straight to the top.

YVON PELCHAT (3/17/42): Stays home in Quebec, where he usually wins about 150 races a year, maintaining an average above 15 percent.

RAY REMMEN (5/28/47): From Saskatoon to Detroit to The Meadowlands, Remmen has excelled at every stop in his burgeoning career. Always ranks high among the local dash winners, with a percentage around 15.

BRUCE RIEGLE (4/15/54): This exciting young driver has taken the reins from his great father, Gene, who now concentrates on training their stock. Their emphasis is on high-grade colts and top raceway stock. Ohio is the home base. Bruce wins more than 20 percent.

ROBERT SAMSON (7/10/49): Splitting his time between his Quebec home and the New York circuit, this diminutive horseman is always in the running for the driving title at Blue Bonnets. In 1977, his 213 victories placed him among the top 25 dash winners in North America.

BEN STEALL (12/16/40): Respected for many years as Billy Haughton's back-up driver in the East, Steall continues to drive for that powerful stable, confining himself to the New York scene. If the horse handicaps as a strong contender, this fine driver will be right there at the finish.

TOM STRAUSS (2/11/50): Having learned the ropes from one of the greatest drivers of all time, Keith Waples, young Strauss drives over 1,000 times a year on the good Ontario circuit and wins his 15 percent.

TED TAYLOR (4/22/27): The well-versed veteran is a splendid trainer and driver of trotters as well as pacers. Races at Pompano in the winter, Detroit in summer.

GENE VALLANDINGHAM (9/14/40): An energetic, flamboyant navigator with great crowd appeal, the former Kentuckian wins well over 100 times a season, seldom straying from the major California raceways. Not a high-percentage winner but reliable with the best horse.

KEITH WAPLES (12/8/23): This Canadian legend does not drive as frequently as he used to but is still a treat for the knowing eye. As crafty as they come, and as fearless, he can still drive a sulky through the eye of a needle. If you're ever in Toronto and he is on the program, drop everything and get to the track to see something extraordinary.

BILL WELLWOOD (7/22/40): With his well-balanced stable of claimers, better raceway stock and stake colts, this sound horseman wins $500,000 a year and 15 percent of his starts in Canada and points south.

RON WRENN (2/1/52): A big winner at the Michigan fairs and Detroit raceways, this youngster won 213 times in 1977, landing himself among North America's top 25. Everyone believes that his future is extremely promising.

12 THE WARM-UPS

THE PAPER WORK IS FINISHED. Having identified the top contenders, the player has made a tentative selection in every apparently beatable race. Comes now the final phase of handicapping. Before risking transactions with mutuel clerks, the player watches the horses warm up.

With special attention to his own choices, he checks the appearance and behavior of the animals during the two workouts (sometimes one, occasionally three), which they take at intervals of about forty-five minutes. He watches them jog the wrong way of the track before and after those warm-ups. He watches them in the post parade before the race itself. If still in doubt, he watches them score (sprint past the finish line) before the starter calls them to the mobile gate.

If he keeps his mind on his business, the player makes one or more of the following discoveries about each field of horses:

1. The top contender looks like an abject loser.

2. The top contender looks neither better nor worse than its rivals.

3. The top contender looks every inch a winner by comparison with the other horses in its race.

4. A green horse, or one that has been absent for weeks, or one with poor recent races, looks more like a winner than any of the other entrants in its race.

The observations described in items 1 and 4 require the player to revise his plans. In the first example, he turns his attention to his second choice in the race, unless, as a regular racegoer, he knows that the other animal always looks miserable before winning—a rare phenomenon, but not unheard of. In the fourth example, the player either passes the race entirely or checks the odds to see whether he should bet the top contender *and* the surprisingly fit-looking sleeper. As often as not, the supposed non-contender is entered in a race previously written off as unplayable. Chances are that a more adventurous type of handicapper now changes his mind about the race and bets on the horse that caught his eye.

It can be seen that observation of the warm-ups enables a player to avoid losers and catch winners. This establishes warm-ups as important. But they are not nearly as important as the information contained in the past-performance records. A fan who knows his way through the records can register long-term profits without so much as looking at a warm-up. If he becomes interested in that final phase of handicapping, he probably can learn enough about it to spare himself one loser per week. And he may catch one winning sleeper every two or three weeks. These extra profits are not to be disdained, but they are unlikely to provide down payments for yachts.

Mountains of drivel have been published about warm-ups. Ill-informed gamblers have lost substantial fortunes by underestimating the significance of the program record and assuming that warm-ups were a source of miracles. I have seen such persons during and after their disasters. It is not a pleasant sight.

Let us agree, then, that a conscientious handicapper watches the warm-ups and helps himself by doing it. And that he helps himself most when he uses those prerace exercises as an opportunity to check on the appearance and deportment of his top choices, betting only on such of them as seem ready to race.

Looking 'Em Over

With exceptions too rare to alter the principle, a good horse looks the part. Its stride is firmly powerful, its eye boldly alert, its coat lustrous with the glow of health. Cheap horses, being less sound, seldom present so grand an appearance. Hence the fan should expect less of them. The top contender in a cheap race need not look like Bret Hanover to justify a bet. It merely should look ready to race.

Here are the major checkpoints:

MANNERS. Most Standardbreds are docile, intensively schooled creatures that know what is expected of them and are willing to produce as much of it as they can. Beware of the fractious horse that fights the bit, flails its tail, flicks its ears, tosses its head, refuses to stay on gait and otherwise challenges its driver. If it is a green animal and/or one with a previous record as a breaker, it probably has not yet learned its trade. Perhaps it is a high-strung type, frightened by the sights, sounds and tensions of the raceway. Unless it calms down thoroughly before the end of its first workout, behaves perfectly during its next, and checks out well on all other points, it is a risky bet.

A seasoned animal that behaves badly and does not warm quickly to the spirit of the occasion has very likely gone sour. Sore, ailing or just plain unstrung by overwork, it communicates reluctance in the only language it has.

EYE. When it feels well, the Standardbred is interested in its surroundings. Its bright dark eyes seem alert and ready for challenge. It scans the scene like radar. An ailing, unwilling or unready horse has a grim, uncomfortable, distracted—even tortured—look about the eye. In other cases, the eyes seem almost opaque, as if the animal had turned them off. When this unpromising sign combines with others and persists through the second workout or the post parade, it is time to revamp the handicapping figures.

COAT. If the horse is sound, fit, and well cared for, its coat looks burnished, like fine furniture. In cheaper fields, with horses that are merely racing sound, comparatively dull coats are the rule and should not be regarded as deficits. On the other hand, when a horse turns up with a healthy coat in a race of that kind and happens also to be the top contender, its prospects improve. Notice how often the green three-year-old from the good barn has the only really good-looking coat in the whole field of C-3 animals, or non-winners of two races, or the like.

Excessive foaming sweat—washiness—often accompanies nervousness, pain and other causes of unreadiness. If the horse is not particularly fractious but simply looks uncomfortable and is washy besides, see how it looks at the beginning of its next warm-up. If necessary, check its appearance during the post parade. Obviously, horses sweat profusely while jogging back to the paddock after warming up. What counts is the amount of foam discernible on the flanks and between the rear legs before the actual warm-up begins. On a hot, humid night, all the horses may seem washy. On other nights, the washy ones are conspicuous. If they get over it before the race, no harm. Otherwise, be careful.

HEAD AND EARS. An eager Standardbred may move its head jauntily from side to side, leaning on the bit, asking to go faster than the driver wants. An unruly one shakes its head and shows other signs of distress. An ouchy one tends to turn its head toward the site of pain, sometimes with a bobbing motion on that side. Occasionally, the inclination of the head to one side means that the horse is having trouble striding on the other side and is trying its best to extend the leg farther. The strenuous warm-ups give an animal ample opportunity to work out the suspected soreness. If it still seems sore during its final prerace trip, and displays other unpromising signs, save your money.

When working or racing under pressure, a fit horse pricks its ears. Drooping ears signify exhaustion, lack of interest, defeat. Flicking ears are a sign of impatience or fear and, with a swishing tail, are characteristic of unruly animals.

GAIT. A keyed-up horse can be forgiven a lapse from stride during the early stages of its first warm-up. But if the problem persists, it takes a brave sport to bet on the animal. Even while remaining flat on gait, a horse sometimes reveals problems by striding short on one side or another, as if favoring a foot or knee. Again, the horse may warm out of this. Be especially watchful as it takes the turns.

TACK. The leather should be clean. If it is not, somebody in the horse's entourage either does not know his business or does not care. Poorly cared for horses are more than likely to be poorly trained, poorly conditioned and poorly driven.

DRIVER. The racing driver does not always take the horse on its warm-up trips. Whoever does should seem to have the animal under a stout hold to keep it from wasting its pent-up energy before the race. But if the driver has to lean straight back to restrain a pulling animal, and if this accompanies other forms of struggle and unruliness, the player should be wary. Pullers are not attractive bets.

At good raceways, the trainer or the veterinarian or the presiding judge declares a noticeably unfit horse out of its race before anyone can lose money on it. At all raceways, the tendency is to let the horse race if it seems even a bit ready. The player should be on his guard, but should not attempt to practice veterinary medicine from the grandstand. He seldom should amend his handicapping figures unless (a) he spots more than one bad sign during the warm-ups and (b) the combination of problems seems to persist. If the approach of post time finds him in doubt as to the significance of what he has seen, his best course is to pass the race entirely. After missing a few winners and more than a few losers that way, he will become sufficiently familiar with Standardbred appearance and behavior to make firmer decisions.

Clocking the Warm-Ups

The horse shows unexpected signs of life during the warm-ups. The driver sends one of his cronies out of the paddock to bet. Some mutuel clerks make a small industry of such occurrences, retailing the information that So-and-so, who does the betting for Such-and-such Stable, has been shoving it in with both hands on the horse. Players haunt the windows in hope of scrounging inside tips of that kind. Nobody gets rich, but the excitement resounds in the night.

How does the horse show the unexpected signs of life? By its appearance and deportment in the paddock and on the track. By working as rapidly as usual but with less effort and no urging. Or by working much more rapidly than usual in response to no more than the usual urging. And by returning to the paddock less winded than usual. And by cooling out more rapidly and being more eager for the next trip.

Hoping to share in the spoils when one horse perks up and another turns languid, certain hard-working handicappers have equipped themselves with stopwatches. Some hang eight or nine watches on a portable board—one watch for each horse in the race. They also keep voluminous notes on the fractional and final times in which each horse customarily warms up. If a horse has been going his final preparatory mile in 2:15 with the final quarter in :32, and now goes in 2:11 with the final quarter in :31, the clocker's nose twitches. As soon as he or his betting runner has bought the tickets, the word gets out and the odds begin to plummet.

It's enough to drive a betting horseman cuckoo. To promote maximum odds on their good things, betting horsemen take pains to foil the clockers. They take the horse for a fast trip in the afternoon and merely let it amble during the prerace exercises. If that doesn't suit the animal, they mix up the fractions—asking for speed during the second and third eighths of a mile but not in the first or fourth, and certainly not in the final quarter, to which clockers are so attentive.

Not many horsemen are so preoccupied with mutuel prices. Most could not care less than they do about the activities of clockers. They merely go about their business. In the normal course of events, they vary the warm-up routines sufficiently to upend the clocker's calculations. For example, a horse has been doing poorly in its races. The trainer decides to work it faster during tonight's warm-ups. The experiment fails, and the clocker who noticed the extra speed loses his shirt. Contrarily, a trainer may decide to work the horse more slowly than usual. And the experiment may enable the horse to race more swiftly than usual, again leaving the clocker with the wrong tickets.

Stanley Dancer seldom works a horse rapidly before its race. His warm-up times are so slow that they reveal nothing about the animal's fitness. Other drivers have adopted the same approach, having begun to concede that raceway horses work hard enough in their weekly competition and suffer when overworked betweentimes.

Another deterrent to profitable clocking of warm-ups is that the race driver sometimes takes the bike in one or both of the workouts, and sometimes does not. The trainer or assistant who handles the chores has his own influence on fractional and final warm-up times. Additionally, a switch in drivers may mean an entirely new approach to the horse's warm-ups. But one cannot tell in advance whether the particular driver will choose to work the particular horse swiftly or slowly. Experimental trial and error are fundamental to horsemanship.

The main rewards to clockers in return for their all-consuming efforts are the payoffs that befall them when some cheap old horse suddenly takes leave of its arthritic discomfort and proves it with an uncommonly swift, easy workout. If the trip was genuinely easy and did not gut the animal, it usually wins. Sometimes at a long price.

Such things occur perhaps once in two weeks. To recognize the opportunity and turn it to his own advantage, the clocker must be on the scene nightly, making laboriously detailed notes about every horse and every driver in every race, plus noting the effects of weather and footing. And operating stopwatches. And conferring with his partners, who keep charts of the actual races.

I have no doubt that some of these betting syndicates catch more winners than you or I can. But what a price to pay!

13 HANDICAPPING SUMMARIZED

THE TIME HAS COME TO MOBILIZE the handicapping principles and procedures set forth in earlier chapters. We then shall be ready for a comprehensive demonstration in which we apply the techniques to programs at five major raceways.

As experienced racegoers may have noticed, and as others should be made aware, this book's approach to Standardbred handicapping is unconventional. I am convinced that traditional methods of making raceway selections are obsolete. Harness racing itself has changed radically. The handicapping ideas presented here are attuned to these changes, as well as to certain fundamental characteristics of the sport which, in my opinion, have not been properly analyzed in the past.

Our approach is unconventional in the following respects:

1. *It emphasizes current condition.*
Notwithstanding the remarkable steadiness and consistency of many Standardbreds, their physical condition fluctuates sufficiently to affect the outcome of all races. Recognition of improving or diminishing fitness is basic therefore to raceway handicapping. The prior achievements of the horse are secondary to its present class and form.

2. *It emphasizes pace, but without regard to the supposed racing styles of the animals.*
Experience shows that a good driver usually is able to modify the presumed style of a horse to suit the particular circumstances of the race.

Even when this is not possible—as in the case of a rank "puller"—the animal's chances can be estimated by the kind of pace analysis recommended in these pages.

3. *It emphasizes the role of the driver.*

For excellent reasons, experts long have deplored the tendency of some fans to bet on drivers rather than on horses. The viewpoint of this book is that the best driver does not always need the best horse, and that good handicapping evaluates horse and driver as what they are—a team.

4. *It emphasizes the relationship of class and time.*

Although a good horse may defeat an inferior one in slower time than the lesser animal registers when beating its own kind, Standardbreds of such widely contrasting quality seldom engage each other in raceway competition. Raceway horses move up and down in class, but usually in small steps. Where the class difference between tonight's race and last week's is obscure, time analysis often provides dependable answers.

5. *It assumes that few fans attend the races nightly.*

Most bettors depend entirely on information contained in the past-performance records. Although nightly observation and the compilation of personal notes are immensely useful, the printed record offers enough information for profitable play.

To understand the bases of this approach, and to appreciate that harness racing is developing in such directions as to make the approach even more valid in the future, it is necessary to read the preceding chapters.

Here is a review of handicapping principles:

THE PLAYABLE RACE. A race is most suitable for play if all starters have performed recently at the present raceway or on the present circuit.

A race is less suitable for play if the current fitness or class of any starter is obscure. If one of the entrants has an impressive record but has been on the sidelines for a month or more, or has just arrived from another circuit with which the handicapper is not familiar, prudence suggests that the race be avoided. On the other hand, if the absentee or shipper has a poor record, one can count it a loser and proceed with the handicapping.

A race is unsuitable for play if the best horse has a tendency to break stride, or if other breakers in the field threaten to cause traffic problems.

A race is seldom suitable for play unless the racing strip is pronounced "fast" or "good" and the horses' recent records include representative performances on dry tracks. All contenders should be handicapped in terms of recent races on similar footing—either fast or good. It is as impractical to compare races on good tracks with races on fast tracks as to compare races on wet tracks with races on dry tracks.

IDENTIFYING THE CONTENDERS. If a horse seems fit (see Chapter 9) and appears to enjoy a marked advantage in class or speed (see Chapter 8), it is an automatic play.

If a horse's latest outing was a qualifying race at the present track and it won in better time than its opponents have been achieving in their good recent races, it is an automatic play.

When a high-class three-year-old from a good barn faces cheap older stock, it is an automatic play—provided that it has a top driver.

In other races, the likely contenders are selected entirely on the basis of fitness displayed in recent races (see Chapter 9). Chronic losers and habitual breakers are never regarded as fit.

If a horse has been idle for more than two weeks and the rest of the field has been active during that period, the absentee usually is eliminated (see p. 198).

A horse is a contender if it raced vigorously in its latest start. When combined with a finish not more than eight lengths behind a winner, the parked-out symbol denotes vigor. So does a gain of ground in the stretch after an earlier move or after setting or overcoming a fast early pace.

A horse that lost ground in the stretch without making a substantial earlier move is eliminated as unfit.

A horse that finished close to the winner and/or in good time without making any moves is eliminated as unfit, having been pulled along by faster horses. However, if the handicapper is doubtful on this score, he checks the horse's previous race and uses it for handicapping purposes if it contains signs of fitness. As a matter of routine, it usually is wise to toss out the latest race and use the previous race of any horse that finished third or better, or that finished within three lengths of the winner in its latest—even if it seemed to do little else.

If the latest race was excusably poor, use the previous race. Excuses include wet footing, an impossibly high class of competition, interference or acciden., a poor driver or a poor post position combined with an unfavorable early pace (see pp. 199–200).

If the next-to-latest race proves unsuitable for handicapping, use the race immediately preceding. But no race that took place more than a month ago is relevant.

PACE. Among the fit horses that qualify as likely contenders, the best prospect is the animal able to finish in the fastest time after setting or overcoming the fastest early pace. All the fractional times of the horse's key race are pertinent—especially the animal's time for the final quarter-mile, which can be ascertained at some raceways but not at most. However, excellent results are attainable by evaluating the official half-mile time of the key race, plus the final time of the horse. In every case, "key race" refers to the recent race that qualified the horse as a contender.

CLASS. The horse deserves extra credit if its key race was in better company than it faces tonight. During the spring and early summer, an improving three-year-old can be granted ability to compete with better horses than it defeated in its last performance. All other horses moving up in class need superior pace figures or other advantages before being conceded the chance to do as well in the higher class as in their key races.

POST POSITION. The handicapper should estimate the effect of post position on the horse's performance in its key race, as well as the probable effect of tonight's post position (see pp. 216).

DRIVER. By consistently winning 15 percent or more of their annual starts, certain drivers have established their dependability (see pp. 224–227). During intermittent hot streaks, which may endure for an entire meeting or an entire racing season, other drivers record winning percentages of 15 or higher, qualifying as dependable so long as they maintain the high averages. If the fit horse with the most impressive key race has a dependable driver and suffers no serious disadvantages of class or post position, it is a good bet.

CLOSE DECISIONS. If no horse stands out after the kinds of analyses suggested above, contenders may be differentiated from each other by giving credit to a horse whose key performance included an impressive gain of ground in the stretch, and/or a quarter-mile or more of racing on the outside.

A horse that lost its key race but performed well and was also the betting favorite is often an excellent prospect.

If one or more of the top contenders has been evaluated in terms of its next-to-last or some other performance prior to its latest, see whether it has faced any of the other contenders in a subsequent race. If so, give extra credit to the contender that raced most vigorously on that occasion.

Although the foregoing principles are few in number and easy to understand, difficulties arise when the player attempts to weigh one factor against another. I therefore recommend that readers experiment with the numerical rating method which I have mentioned at intervals throughout this book. The method does not replace handicapping judgment, but assists it, eliminating the usual confusions and producing firm figures on which the player can base his decisions.

The method is easiest, quickest and most effective when the handicapper takes a moment to draw a simple chart, as follows:

Horse	Half-Mile	Final	Rate	Base	Cls	SG	Pk	BF	PP	Dr	Comp

Having found the fit contenders in a playable race, the handicapper lists their names in the first column.

Examining the past-performance line of each contender's key race—the race that qualified it as a contender—the handicapper writes the official half-mile time of the race in the top half of the divided box under the "Half-Mile" heading. The horse's own final time in that key race is written in the top half of the adjoining box, under the "Final" heading. The lower half of each box is for the numerical rating assigned to each time notation.

Ratings may be computed by using the tabulation on page 168. Persons willing to do simple subtraction will find an alternative pace-rating method more convenient. As described on page 169, this other method eliminates the necessity of referring to a printed tabulation.

For example:

Half-Mile		Final	
1:01:2		2:03	
	19		17
1:01:4		2:02:3	
	17		19
1:02:1		2:03:4	
	15		13
1:01:1		2:02:2	
	20		20

Note that the *half-mile time* of the top horse, 1:01:2, earns a rating of 19, being one tick slower than 1:01:1, which earns a rating of 20 as the best half-mile time on the list. By the same procedure, the *final time* of the third horse on the list, 2:03:4, earns a rating of 13, being 1⅖ seconds slower than 2:02:2, the best final time on the list.

The basic pace ratings are computed by adding the ratings in the first two boxes. Hence, the top horse's basic rating is 36, identical with that of the second horse. The third horse's rating is 28. The bottom horse's rating is 40. The figures are written in the adjoining box.

If a horse's key race was in a class higher than that of tonight's race, add 5 points to the basic rating. If the key race was in a lower class, deduct 5 points. For example:

Base	Cls
36	36
36	36
28	33
40	35

Notice that the first two horses will compete tonight in the same class of race as in their recent key efforts. The bottom horse, which had the highest pace rating, no longer is the leading contender, a rise in class having reduced his rating. The third horse, dropping in class, has improved his rating.

In the column headed "SG," the handicapper should add a point for every length gained in the stretch of the key race. Count ½ length as a full length. Thus, a horse that trailed by 1½ lengths at the stretch call but won its race by 1½ lengths would be credited with a gain of 4 lengths, worth 4 points. See pages 202–203 for the correct way to adjust the rating of a horse that led at both the stretch call and the finish.

The column headed "Pk" is for the credits earned by horses that raced on the outside in their key performances. For every parked-out symbol (°) in the past-performance line, add 5 points. In the rare event that a horse broke stride, yet raced well enough to qualify, add 5 points for the break—which usually will have been caused by interference.

If the horse was a beaten favorite in its key race, add 5 points to the rating and write the new sum in the column headed "BF."

Using the principles and point values explained in Chapter 10, adjust the rating to include the effect of post position on the key performance, plus the probable effect of tonight's post position. The adjusted rating goes in the column headed "PP."

If tonight's driver is a national or local leader (chances are that such a reinsman is listed on pages 227–257), add points as prescribed on page 226 and put the new total under "Dr."

If tonight's driver is not a top man and does not have a winning percentage of 15 or better, but if the driver in the key race was a national or local leader or had the required average, deduct 10 points.

If the numbers in the "Dr" column reveal that one horse has a rating more than 5 points higher than that of any other contender, the top-rated horse is the play.

Should a margin of 5 or fewer points separate the top-rated contenders, and if the key race of any was a race other than its most recent, check the records to see if the top-rated horses met each other in a subsequent race. If so, award 5 points to the horse that performed most vigorously on that occasion, and put the new total under "Comp."

The horse with the highest final rating is the play, provided that it looks ready during its warm-ups. If not, go to the second horse.

At half-mile tracks, where contention usually is closest and most hectic, consider playing the two contenders with the highest ratings if:

1. The ratings are 3 or fewer points apart, and
2. The animal with the *lower* rating has a leading driver, and
3. The odds on both horses are high enough to return a profit on the double bet, should either horse win.

At other tracks, consider playing the two top contenders if the ratings differ by only 1 point and the horse with the lower rating has a leading driver.

At any track, if your choice is held at odds of 4 to 1 or higher during the final three minutes of wagering, consider betting it to win and place.

We now shall handicap complete programs at each of five major raceways: Hollywood Park, Sportsman's Park, Liberty Bell, The Meadowlands and Roosevelt Raceway. We bring to that activity no special information other than the facts contained in the particular past-performance program or otherwise generally available. We invoke no expertise beyond the advice contained in this book. The results are excellent, partly because Standardbreds are dependable animals and partly because the programs took place at the height of the season in decent weather and, finally, because I rejected programs that produced unsatisfactory results. It seems to me that the way to demonstrate a handicapping procedure is to pick some winners with it. When it picks too many non-winners, the lessons lose their impact and the students learn less.

On the other hand, I did not screen many programs to come up with these. Each raceway sent me two weeks' worth of programs. I did not have to survey more than five before finding productive ones for Liberty Bell and The Meadowlands. I rejected two before landing on the one from Hollywood Park. And the first ones I touched turned out to be good examples for Sportsman's Park and Roosevelt Raceway.

As all this implies, a careful reader can expect to enjoy more than occasional success at the raceway. The trick is to pick nights when the racing strip is dry and fast and the air temperature kindly. Do your handicapping slowly. Avoid unplayable races. And bet modestly until you have gained real command of your techniques.

As to betting, you will notice that I concentrate on trying to locate a winner. I ignore quinellas, exactas (perfectas), doubles, trifectas and other exotic wagering propositions. I recommend that all casual racegoers do the same. With experience, occasional bets of the kind may be sensible, but only at raceways where television monitors or other displays inform handicappers of the probable payoffs during the prerace betting periods. At places that have no such displays, lack of odds information makes the exotic bet a pig in a poke. Or plain foolishness.

14 HOLLYWOOD PARK

September 29, 1979

THE NIGHT IS CLEAR AND BALMY, the racing strip fast. The program's list of leading drivers names few that have raced at the meeting often enough and won often enough to be judged on those local statistics alone. For example, one driver has had only 41 starts during the four weeks of the meeting, winning nine times. This sparse activity hardly makes him a fully fledged 20 percent winner, entitled to 10 extra points in our handicapping. Here is where the handicapper with access to solid statistics enjoys an advantage. Our copy of *Sulky* shows that the driver in question won at a 13 percent clip during 1977 and 1978. I would be disinclined to upgrade his rating to 15 percent—and not until he had maintained a high winning average for at least 75 drives.

The 20-percenters to whose horses we shall award 10 extra points in tonight's handicapping are Marc Aubin and Stan Bayless. The 15-percenters (5 extra points) are Rick Kuebler, Jack Parker, Jr., Brian Pelling and Ken Williams.

Hollywood Park is one of the few raceways at which proper post-position statistics are maintained. Its program publishes the number of horses that have left from each position, as well as the number that have won. No harm would come from using the rating figures provided on page 216 of this book, but the following table is somewhat more precise:

Post:	1	2	3	4	5	6	7	8	9	10
Rating:	7	6	6	6	7	7	5	4	3	3

Horseplay after dark

Western Harness Racing
1979 Official Program

$1.00 Sales Tax Included

$3 Daily Double

1 MILE PACE **PURSE $3,000**

1st Race

WELOS CLUB, Roger Harding, group rep.

CLAIMING. Purse $3,000. All ages. Claiming price $7,000. Mares allowed 20 percent.

1 — Spring Chance (5-1)

Driver—PARKER JACK JR. Trainer—Silverman Jerry. — Maroon, Blue and White

Spring Chance $7,000 — Ch. g. 8, by Majestic Chance—Indian Spring, by Quiet Water

Own.—George Bernhofen, Lancaster, Cal

Br.—J E Keenan (NZ) — No Record in U.S., '78 — No Record , '79

Lifetime— $9,351; 1979 8 0 0 0 $350; 1978 24 4 5 4 $5,696

Date Trk	Dist	¼	½	¾	fin	Odds	¼	½	¾	str	fin	Driver PP	Cond	Time	First 3 Finishers	
20Sep79-3Hol	1	:302	1:012	1:312	2:013ft	8½	2	3	53½	52¼	42¾	† Parker Jack Jr5	6000	2:021	†Pl5]O'ShnnssySlon,TobysSkppr,PrpBy	10
12Sep79-10Hol	1	:293	:59	1:293	2:004ft	17	8	8	77¾o	65	611	Rosen Robert8	8000	2:03	Piute Star, Sisco, Prudent Jim	8
5Sep79-3Hol	1	:301	1:003	1:322	2:022ft	5½	3o	3o	33½o	109½	1015	Vallandingham Gene6	8000	2:052	DncingStorm,KnightChnc,ScottshChfN.	10
29Aug79-10Hol	1	:291	:581	1:29	2:003ft	29	2	3	43¼	62¾	74¾	Vallandingham Gene9	10000	2:013	Bravado Court, K. B. King, Pacing Hi	10
24Aug79-9Hol	1	:291	:593	1:311	2:011ft	14	5	5	43½	74½	65¼	Vallandingham Gene3	14000	2:022	LehighPriest,PrettyTough,WindarraPrk	7

2 — Taverns Sam (6-1)

Driver-Trainer— PERAGINE WILLIAM. — Blue, Orange and White

Taverns Sam $7,000 — Br. h. 9, by Sampson Hanover—Willow Brook Star, by Guy KPrtctr

Own.—Bernard Woff & William Peragine, Northridge, Cal

Br.—F E Howe (NY) — 2:01, HOL, '78 — 2:033, LA , '79

Lifetime— $81,021; 1979 32 1 4 3 $7,567; 1978 39 11 3 3 $20,959

Date Trk	Dist	¼	½	¾	fin	Odds	¼	½	¾	str	fin	Driver PP	Cond	Time	First 3 Finishers	
25Sep79-5Hol	1	:312	1:012	1:312	2:012ft	14	3	3	33	34	35	Peragine William2	8000	2:022	Piute Star, Gary Golfer, Taverns Sam	10
13Sep79-3Hol	1	:29	1:001	1:291	2:003ft	56	10	10	109	96	97¾	Peragine William10	8000	2:021	KnightChnce,DncingStorm,HonestDund	10
4Sep79-7Hol	1	:303	1:021	1:33	2:03 ft	42	9	6o	33	43	73¼	Peragine William9	8000	2:034	Panawa Bay, NorthWestern,CaneCutter	9
28Aug79-5Hol	1	:292	1:00	1:303	2:01 ft	12	7	7	88	75½	79½	Peragine William8	8000	2:03	Fulla Spark, Sisco, Freddy Fender	10
19Jly79-4Sac	1	:303	1:001	1:313	2:003ft	8	7	7	63	74	32½	Peragine William4	9000	2:011	Thunderstorm A, Macali, Taverns Sam	9

3 — Swift Max N (3-1)

Driver—BAYLESS STAN. Trainer—Moore Ann. — Gold and White

Swift Max N $7,000 — B. g. 7, by Keep Away—Make Up, by Paisley Lad

Own.—Ann Moore, Del Mar,Cal

Br.—W D Ryan (NZ) — No Record in U.S., '78 — 2:03, LA , '79

Lifetime— $16,088; 1979 29 3 6 3 $10,017; 1978 8 0 1 1 $637

Date Trk	Dist	¼	½	¾	fin	Odds	¼	½	¾	str	fin	Driver PP	Cond	Time	First 3 Finishers	
20Sep79-10Hol	1	:284	:58	1:291	2:00 ft	12	10	9o	66½o	62½	65¾	Bayless Stan10	8000	2:011	Kona Coast, High Jewell, Prudent Jim	10
12Sep79-10Hol	1	:293	:59	1:293	2:004ft	4	6	5	32½o	21½	42½	Bayless Stan6	8000	2:011	Piute Star, Sisco, Prudent Jim	8
29Aug79-3Hol	1	:30	1:004	1:32	2:03 ft	*3-2	2o	1	1½	2hd	32¾	Goudreau Shelly4	c6000	2:033	TobysSkippr,HockomockDncr,SwftMxN	10
24Aug79-3Hol	1	:293	:593	1:301	2:01 ft	*6-5	7	7o	21o	25	510	Goudreau Shelly5	6000	2:03	HllzpoppinA.,HockomockDncr,BilliBFst	9
27Jly79-8Sac	1	:304	1:014	1:321	2:022ft	*2	4	4	32½	31	42	Ratchford Don3	7000	2:024	El Torento, Tru Star, Fulla Spark	8

4 — Tobys Skipper (5-2)

Driver—WILLIAMS KEN. Trainer—Smith Lester. — Red and White

Tobys Skipper $7,000 — B. g. 9, by Meadow Skipper—Cita Song, by Gay Song

Own.—Percy Lewis & Don Henley, Compton, Cal

Br.—K Katona (Mich) — No Record , '78 — 2:022, Hol, '79

Lifetime— $81,497; 1979 32 10 7 3 $14,945; 1978 0 0 0 0

Date Trk	Dist	¼	½	¾	fin	Odds	¼	½	¾	str	fin	Driver PP	Cond	Time	First 3 Finishers	
20Sep79-3Hol	1	:302	1:012	1:312	2:013ft	*3-2	5	4o	21o	2hd	22	Longo Gerald2	6000	2:02	O'ShnnesseySlon,TobysSkippr,PropBoy	10
14Sep79-1Hol	1	:293	1:01	1:314	2:013ft	5	9o	8o	95o	76	35	Williams Ken8	6000	2:023	O'ShnnssySlon,PririSunshn,TobysSkppr	10
5Sep79-4Hol	1	:302	1:02	1:322	2:022ft	*8-5	6	6o	53½o	52¼	1nk	Williams Ken7	6000	2:022	TobysSkipper,StrCheck,O'ShnnssySlon	10
29Aug79-3Hol	1	:30	1:004	1:32	2:03 ft	4	7	8	73¼o	42½	11¾	Williams Ken6	6000	2:03	TobysSkippr,HockomockDncr,SwftMxN	10
24Aug79-1Hol	1	:302	1:013	1:323	2:024ft	3½	5	5	54¼o	43½	11¾	Bayless Stan3	6000	2:024	Tobys Skipper, Four Score, First Cover	10

5 — Prairie Sunshine (12-1)

Driver—TODD JAMES II. Trainer—Olsen Jack. — Royal, Blue and Grey

Prairie Sunshine $7,000 — B. m. 7, by Irish Byrd—Senga Hope, by Adios Pick

Own.—M Garey-H Wiesenbeck-R Engelberg et al, Northridge

Br.—E W Kloeble (Can) — 2:024, LA , '78 — 2:023, SAC, '79

Lifetime— $33,117; 1979 32 2 3 2 $5,950; 1978 35 3 3 5 $9,523

Date Trk	Dist	¼	½	¾	fin	Odds	¼	½	¾	str	fin	Driver PP	Cond	Time	First 3 Finishers	
20Sep79-3Hol	1	:302	1:012	1:312	2:013ft	9¾	8	8	89	75¼x	x56¾	† Todd James II7	6000	2:03	†Pl7]O'ShnnssySlon,TobysSkppr,PrpBy	10
14Sep79-1Hol	1	:293	1:01	1:314	2:013ft	14	4	5	53	32½	23½	Todd James II1	6000	2:021	O'ShnnssySlon,PririSunshn,TobysSkppr	10
28Aug79-3Hol	1	:293	1:003	1:32	2:024ft	15	0	9	88	86¼	42¼	Todd James II6	7000	2:031	HighJewell,HopeHnoverN,DncingStorm	9
23Aug79-3Hol	1	:312	1:022	1:324	2:03 ft	34	8	8	78½o	88½	56¼	Todd James II8	7000	2:041	Fulla Spark, North Western,HighJewell	9
24Jly79-8Sac	1	:312	1:031	1:352	2:051ft	10	6	6	31¾	52¼	52¾	Olsen Jack4	7000	2:054	Andy'sMerino,CchumChief,ArmbroMgic	9

6 — Indian Victory (15-1)

Driver—RATCHFORD GUS. Trainer—Stein Roger. — Maroon, Gray and Black

Indian Victory $7,000 — Br. g. 10, by Victory Dinamic—Spring Dolly, by Adios Senator

Own.—Roger Stein, Beverly Hills, Cal

Br.—W Benner (NY) — 2:042, SCK, '78 — 2:05, SD , '79

Lifetime— $63,864; 1979 26 6 3 3 $4,713; 1978 45 7 5 7 $6,771

Date Trk	Dist	¼	½	¾	fin	Odds	¼	½	¾	str	fin	Driver PP	Cond	Time	First 3 Finishers	
19Sep79-1Hol	1	:293	:593	1:312	2:024ft	27	2o	2o	2½o	1½	25	Ratchford Gus9	5000	2:034	Chambrey, Indian Victory,Indefatigable	10
5Sep79-1Hol	1	:301	1:02	1:332	2:04 ft	44	4o	3o	21o	32½	86¾	Ratchford Gus6	5000	2:053	HockomockDncer,JmesRhythm,CrpGm	10
29Aug79-Hol	1	:303	1:013	1:322	2:021ft		6	6	66½	510	311	Ratchford Gus3	Qua	2:042	SnowJohnny,MillionMark,IndianVictory	8
4Aug79-1Sac	1	:311	1:022	1:322	2:033ft	16	7	6	79½	610	613	Ratchford Gus8	3500	2:061	Rusty Joui, Irenes King, Mike Me Boy	9
15Jun79-SD	1	:304	1:03	1:344	2:054ft	3¼	x10	10be	dnf	—	—	Walsh D5	Wo1300 L10	—	Tom And Joe, Royal Caravan, Triajo	10

7 — Bill Rader (10-1)

Driver-Trainer— SCHANKS MARTY. — Green and White

Bill Rader $7,000 — Ro. g. 6, by Frosty Rader—Penolia Oliver, by Doctor Counsel

Own.—Ira Steinberg & Marty Schanks, Arlington Hgts, Ill.

Br.—E Frazier (Ky) — 2:02, HOL, '78 — 2:014, Hol, '79

Lifetime— $21,839; 1979 24 2 0 4 $4,415; 1978 37 3 7 4 $13,162

Date Trk	Dist	¼	½	¾	fin	Odds	¼	½	¾	str	fin	Driver PP	Cond	Time	First 3 Finishers	
19Sep79-10Hol	1	:294	1:002	1:31	2:014ft	10	5	5	54¼	42½	11½	Schanks Marty2	6000	2:014	Bill Rader, Brawler, Byron Lad	10
7Sep79-1Hol	1	:30	1:004	1:311	2:004ft	14	10	10	1015	910	611	Schanks Marty9	5000	2:031	Minister, Security Chip, Waiariki	10
30Aug79-2Hol	1	:31	1:033	1:334	2:041ft	7¼	5	5	65½	75¼	44¼	Schanks Marty4	5000	2:05	SecurityChip,MrCreed,TimelyProposlN	8
25Aug79-1Hol	1	:302	1:024	1:341	2:044ft	9¼	9	10	10ex	1013	1012	Schanks Marty6	6000	2:072	EdgwoodArmt,O'ShnnssySln,EdwrdEdn	10
4Aug79-6Sac	1	:30	:593	1:313	2:022ft	10	5	5	75½	45	44¼	Schanks Marty1	6000	2:031	LordNova,HockomockDancer,MarCreed	8

8 — Senga Deano (30-1)

Driver—SUCCAROTTE WILLIAM. Trainer—Eckert Gary. — Red, White and Gold

Senga Deano $7,000 — B. g. 5, by Adios Dick—Dashing Daisy, by Adios Dream

Own.—Joel Budow & G L Eckert, Hawthorne,Cal

Br.—Bill R Curtis (Can) — No Record , '78 — 2:043, SAC, '79

Lifetime— $3,353; 1979 20 2 2 3 $3,353; 1978 0 0 0 0

Date Trk	Dist	¼	½	¾	fin	Odds	¼	½	¾	str	fin	Driver PP	Cond	Time	First 3 Finishers	
18Sep79-8Hol	1	:293	:594	1:294	2:003ft	45	5	7	108x	10dis	10dis	Succarotte William1	7000	—	Tru Star, Boehms Dandy Fella,TopRing	10
11Sep79-10Hol	1	:302	1:011	1:313	2:022ft	59	9	8o	66¾o	47	65¾	Parker Jack Jr6	7000	2:032	Classy Skipper, HopeHanoverN,TruStar	10
4Sep79-8Hol	1	:29	:594	1:302	1:591ft	89	9	9	810	811	817	Parker Jack Jr9	Nw3	2:023	TrportBlck,TheTrdMrkN,CptinKnightN	10
29Aug79-5Hol	1	:30	1:013	1:322	2:02 ft	30	7	7	76¼o	813x	711	Parker Jack Jr6	Nw3	2:043	Sychar, Classy Bye Bye, Hal Chance N	10
24Jly79-5Sac	1	:313	1:02	1:334	2:043ft	8	5	5	31½	21	11¼	SuccarotteWillim5	Nw1500 79	2:043	Senga Deano, Branigan N, Lady Orleigh	8

9 — Demons Orphan Baby (15-1)

Driver—RATCHFORD TOM. Trainer—Miskell Robert. — Gold, White and Black

Demons Orphan Baby $7,000 — B. h. 9, by Demon Vo—Lady Peg, by Scotland

Own.—Lawrence J Duffy, Long Beach, Cal

Br.—J N Smith (Ky) — 1:592, SAC, '78 — 2:013, SAC, '79

Lifetime— $126,571; 1979 32 4 4 8 $12,738; 1978 30 4 2 6 $22,327

Date Trk	Dist	¼	½	¾	fin	Odds	¼	½	¾	str	fin	Driver PP	Cond	Time	First 3 Finishers	
18Sep79-8Hol	1	:293	:594	1:294	2:003ft	9¼	4o	1	44½	920	921	Lighthill Joe9	7000	2:05	Tru Star, Boehms Dandy Fella,TopRing	10
11Sep79-10Hol	1	:302	1:011	1:313	2:022ft	*1	8	4o	12	11	98½	Bayless Stan5	7000	2:04	Classy Skipper, HopeHanoverN,TruStar	10
4Sep79-7Hol	1	:303	1:021	1:33	2:03 ft	7	2	5	88	77¼	61¼	Ratchford Tom5	8000	2:032	Panawa Bay, NorthWestern,CaneCutter	9
28Aug79-5Hol	1	:292	1:00	1:303	2:01 ft	5	5	5	32o	21½	54¾	Ratchford Tom4	8000	2:021	Fulla Spark, Sisco, Freddy Fender	10
23Aug79-5Hol	1	:293	1:012	1:313	2:021ft	3	1	2	32	33	54½	Ratchford Tom9	8000	2:031	Senga Bucyrus, Sisco, Knight For Bret	10

10 — Presence Felt (6-1)

Driver-Trainer— WASHBURN ERIC. — Green and Red

Presence Felt $7,000 — B. g. 5, by Raceaway—Bonnie Tarn, by Gay Piper

Own.—Eric Washburn, Arleta Cal

Br.—J G Allan (NZ) — 1:591, MDW, '78 — 2:012, Hol, '79

Lifetime— $24,826; 1979 10 1 3 0 $5,484; 1978 26 3 3 1 $17,961

Date Trk	Dist	¼	½	¾	fin	Odds	¼	½	¾	str	fin	Driver PP	Cond	Time	First 3 Finishers	
26Sep79-10Hol	1	:293	:592	1:30	2:012ft	15	6o	4o	43½o	41¾	1½	Washburn Eric10	7000	2:012	Presence Felt,GypsyBlue,FireForEffect	10
18Sep79-8Hol	1	:293	:594	1:294	2:003ft	6¾	9	8o	54¾o	x78	68	Washburn Eric7	7000	2:021	Tru Star, Boehms Dandy Fella,TopRing	10
5Sep79-1Hol	1	:301	1:02	1:332	2:04 ft	*8-5	8	10	108¾	97¾	98¾	Vallandingham Gene7	c5000	2:06	HockomockDncer,JmesRhythm,CrpGm	10
24Aug79-10Hol	1	:284	1:011	1:312	2:02 ft	3¼	7	7o	66¼o	53½	21¼	Vallandingham Gene4	8000	2:021	Macali, Presence Felt, Curious Note	10
17Aug79-Hol	1	:294	:594	1:302	2:012ft		6	6	65¼	54	33½	Vallandingham Gene2	Qua	2:021	Royal Waldorf, Baker Hill,PresenceFelt	7

DECLARED- J J'S PATTON and BOLD BIDDER.

Allowed prices: Prairie Sunshine, $8,400.

DELTA ALPHA PSI CHAPTER, Diane Zahn, group representative

$3 Daily Double — 2nd Race

1 MILE PACE **PURSE $4,000**

CLAIMING. Purse $4,000. All ages. Claiming price $10,000. 3-year-olds allowed 50 percent; 4-year-old mares allowed 45 percent.

1 — King Riki — 4-1

Driver-Trainer— PELLING BRIAN. Black, Red and Orange

$10,000

B. g. 11, by Pipiriki—Dianne's Own, by Our Globe

Own.—B R P Enterprises & George Aiken, Cypress, Cal

Br.—A W Absolom (Can) 1:58, HOL, '78 2:01^2, BM, '79

Lifetime— $66,623 · 1979 25 4 5 4 $22,684 · 1978 21 4 4 3 $23,108

Date Trk	Dist	¼	½	¾	fin	Odds	¼	½	¾	str	fin	Driver PP	Cond	Time	First 3 Finishers	
14Sep79-2Spk	1	$:29^4$	$1:00^3$	$1:30^4$	$2:02^1$ft	4¼	9	7o	5o	7^8	8^{12}	Wheeler Tim^6	12500	$2:04^3$	K SSoulTrain,SuburbanHanover,Garrice	9
3Sep79-10Spk	1	$:29^2$	$:59^4$	$1:31^2$	$2:01^4$ft	8½	9	9	9	7^6	$4^{2\frac{1}{2}}$	Pelling Brian^9	12500	$2:02^2$	Owl, KS Soul Train, Suburban Hanover	9
23Aug79-10Spk	1	:30	$1:00^2$	$1:31^1$	$2:01^2$ft	6	8	7o	6o	$6^{5\frac{1}{2}}$	7^{10}	Pelling Brian^7	15000	$2:03^2$	TrickyBaron,EliteHanoverA,StarFarmer	9
11Aug79-1Spk	1	$:29^1$	1:00	$1:32^1$	$2:02^4$ft	4¼	7	6o	2o	$2^{\frac{1}{2}}$	$3^{1\frac{3}{4}}$	Pelling Brian^6	15000	$2:03^1$	Burwood Sharon, Native Sue, King Riki	9
3Aug79-4Spk	1	$:29^4$	$1:01^2$	$1:32^2$	$2:02^4$ft	*2¼	8	7o	5o	4^2	3^{nk}	Pelling Brian^8	15000	$2:02^4$	WelcomeTrawler,SweetMeliss,KingRiki	9

2 — Tuatahi Ridge — 8-1

Driver—VALLANDINGHAM GENE. Trainer—Thornton Eugene. Red, White & Blue

$10,000

B. g. 5, by Nevele Holiday—Hiyaown, by Stormyway

Own.—Eugene O Thornton & Louis C Miklovik, Cypress, Cal

Br.—R D Butt (NZ) 2:02^3, HOL, '78 2:01^4, SAC, '79

Lifetime— $17,472 · 1979 33 3 4 6 $13,247 · 1978 7 2 2 0 $4,225

Date Trk	Dist	¼	½	¾	fin	Odds	¼	½	¾	str	fin	Driver PP	Cond	Time	First 3 Finishers	
22Sep79-1Hol	1	$:29^1$	$:59^1$	$1:30^1$	$2:00^2$ft	8	5	5	$3^{2\frac{1}{4}}$o	2^2	$4^{1\frac{1}{4}}$	Vallandingham Gene^1	10000	$2:00^3$	North Western, Lordling, Bronte Boy	10
18Sep79-10Hol	1	$:29^3$	1:00	1:29	1:59 ft	12	4	4	4^5	$4^{4\frac{1}{2}}$	$5^{7\frac{3}{4}}$	Vallandingham Gene^1	10000	$2:00^3$	Blakey Del, Henry's Dream N, PacingHi	9
12Sep79-8Hol	1	:29	$:59^1$	$1:29^3$	2:00 ft	11	7	7	7^{10}	$7^{7\frac{1}{2}}$	6^{11}	Vallandingham Gene^3	12000	$2:02^1$	KnghtsHonorN,HlcynHrt,BrndyAndDry	10
5Sep79-7Hol	1	$:30^1$	$1:02^3$	$1:32^1$	$2:01^3$ft	2¾	3	3	4^2	$5^{3\frac{1}{2}}$	$4^{2\frac{1}{2}}$	Vallandingham Gene^1	12000	2:02	Lisbon Lad,SengaPaula,ThunderstormA	8
29Aug79-7Hol	1	$:29^2$	$:59^3$	$1:28^4$	$1:58^3$ft	11	7	5o	$4^{4\frac{1}{2}}$o	$4^{8\frac{1}{2}}$	4^{11}	Vallandingham Gene^7	12000	$2:00^3$	HighlandChmp,RioVlet,ThunderstormA	7

3 — Gas Saver — 15-1

Driver—RATCHFORD TOM. Trainer—Ratchford Don. Gold, White and Black

$10,000

Blk. c. 3, by My Scotch Bret—Ebkey, by Peter Eblis

Own.—Angus MacPherson & D G Ratchford, Cerritos, Cal

Br.—R L Lefeld (Ohio) No Record, '78 2:03^2, SAC, '79

Lifetime— $3,470 · 1979 11 2 2 0 $3,470 · 1978 0 0 0 0

Date Trk	Dist	¼	½	¾	fin	Odds	¼	½	¾	str	fin	Driver PP	Cond	Time	First 3 Finishers	
4Sep79-8Hol	1	:29	$:59^4$	$1:30^2$	$1:59^1$ft	56	6	6	$6^{7\frac{1}{2}}$o	9^{16}	10^{22}	Ratchford Tom^4	Nw3	$2:03^3$	TrportBlck,TheTrdMrkN,CptinKnightN	10
29Aug79-5Hol	1	:30	$1:01^3$	$1:32^2$	2:02 ft	27	10	10	$10^{8\frac{3}{4}}$	7^{13}	8^{13}	Ratchford Tom^9	Nw3	$2:04^4$	Sychar, Classy Bye Bye, Hal Chance N	10
3Aug79-6Sac	1	$:29^1$	$1:02^3$	$1:32^3$	$2:02^3$ft	17	9	8	$8^{5\frac{1}{4}}$	$8^{4\frac{3}{4}}$	$7^{6\frac{1}{2}}$	Ratchford Gus^9	Nw3	2:04	FightingSon,ThTrdMrkN.,MstrSndmnN.	9
26Jly79-9Sac	1	$:33^3$	$1:03^3$	$1:34^1$	2:05 ft	*4-5	1	2	$2^{1\frac{1}{2}}$	2^2	$1^{\frac{3}{4}}$	Ratchford Don^1	Nw2	2:05	Gas Saver, High Jewell, Commodity	7
12Jly79-6Sac	1	$:30^4$	$1:01^4$	1:34	$2:03^2$ft	*3-2	2	3	3^4	3^1	2^{nk}	Ratchford Don^2	Nw2	$2:03^2$	Yankee Chine, Gas Saver, Painted Boy	9

4 — Bronte Boy — 8-5

Driver-Trainer— PERRY GARY. Maroon, White and Silver.

$10,000

B. g. 9, by Baby Boy—Nivea Peak, by Highland Laird

Own.—Alan B & Valerie A Horowitz, Yorkville, Cal

Br.—C R Hando (Aust) 2:00, HOL, '78 2:00^2, SAC, '79

Lifetime— $39,593 · 1979 20 2 4 5 $12,853 · 1978 26 1 1 3 $7,840

Date Trk	Dist	¼	½	¾	fin	Odds	¼	½	¾	str	fin	Driver PP	Cond	Time	First 3 Finishers	
22Sep79-1Hol	1	$:29^1$	$:59^1$	$1:30^1$	$2:00^2$ft	*3½	9	8	$7^{5\frac{3}{4}}$o	$4^{4\frac{1}{2}}$	3^1	Perry Gary^9	10000	$2:00^3$	North Western, Lordling, Bronte Boy	10
15Sep79-3Hol	1	$:29^4$	$1:00^4$	$1:30^1$	2:01 ft	*6-5	6	6	$6^{6\frac{1}{2}}$o	$7^{6\frac{1}{2}}$	$5^{1\frac{3}{4}}$	Perry Gary^6	10000	$2:01^2$	The Blizzard A, DayStream,SlimYankee	9
8Sep79-5Hol	1	:30	1:01	$1:30^1$	$2:00^3$ft	*3-2	1	1	$1^{1\frac{1}{2}}$	$1^{1\frac{1}{2}}$	$1^{4\frac{1}{2}}$	Perry Gary^5	10000	$2:00^3$	Bronte Boy, Yakiriki, Cachuma Chief	10
1Sep79-1Hol	1	$:29^1$	1:00	$1:30^2$	$1:59^4$ft	2¼	7	6o	$6^{4\frac{1}{4}}$o	$5^{2\frac{1}{4}}$	$3^{4\frac{1}{4}}$	Perry Gary^4	10000	$2:00^4$	Merry Time Finesse, Assure,BronteBoy	10
24Aug79-4Hol	1	:30	$1:00^1$	$1:29^4$	$1:59^4$ft	6	3	3	3^3	3^4	2^3	Perry Gary^2	12000	$2:00^2$	Butler King, Bronte Boy, Tuatahi Ridge	7

5 — Courtney — 12-1

Driver—TODD JAMES II. Trainer—Freeland Louis. Royal, Blue and Grey

$10,000

B. g. 6, by Final Adios—Little Una, by Intangible

Own.—Fritz Meinke, Sherman Oaks Cal

Br.—H J Lusa (Aust) No Record in U.S., '78 No Record in U.S., '79

Lifetime— $10,834 · 1979 14 1 0 1 $821 · 1978 15 4 2 2 $9,550

Date Trk	Dist	¼	½	¾	fin	Odds	¼	½	¾	str	fin	Driver PP	Cond	Time	First 3 Finishers	
20Sep79-10Hol	1	$:28^4$	:58	$1:29^1$	2:00 ft	21	8	10	8^8o	$7^{2\frac{3}{4}}$	$5^{5\frac{1}{2}}$	Desomer Steve^7	8000	$2:01^1$	Kona Coast, High Jewell, Prudent Jim	10
12Sep79-7Hol	1	:30	$1:00^1$	$1:31^2$	$2:01^3$ft	32	4	9	$9^{8\frac{1}{2}}$	$8^{5\frac{1}{4}}$	$7^{9\frac{1}{4}}$	Desomer Steve^6	10000	$2:03^2$	Parling, Henry's Dream N, Nechako Tar	9
5Sep79-Hol	1	$:30^4$	1:02	$1:32^2$	$2:03^1$ft		3	3	2^{nk}	2^5	$3^{5\frac{1}{4}}$	Desomer Steve^5	Qua	$2:04^1$	Trevino, Liberated Lady, Courtney	9
14Jly79-8Sac	1	$:30^3$	$1:01^1$	1:32	2:02 ft	23	5	6	2no	3^1	$4^{1\frac{1}{4}}$	Desomer Steve^3	10000	$2:02^2$	TarasGregg,HunterHnover,FlmingoMiss	9
6Jly79-10Sac	1	$:29^3$	$1:01^1$	$1:32^2$	$2:01^4$ft	11	8	7	4^3o	8^8	8^8	Desomer Steve^7	11000	$2:03^2$	Lisbon Lad, Scotch Double, DayStream	8

6 — Royal Chimes N — 15-1

Driver-Trainer— CLIFF GEORGE. Green and Gold

$10,000

B. g. 6, by Poplar Dell—Imperial Royal, by Nephew Hal

Own.—Gary & Gilda Siedelman&GeorgeCliff,RedondoBeach,Cal

Br.—M A Kay (NZ) No Record in U.S., '78 No Record in U.S., '79

Lifetime— $1,005 · 1979 3 1 0 0 $1,005 · 1978 0 0 0 0

Date Trk	Dist	¼	½	¾	fin	Odds	¼	½	¾	str	fin	Driver PP	Cond	Time	First 3 Finishers	
22Sep79-Hol	1	$:30^2$	$1:02^3$	$1:32^4$	$2:02^4$ft		5	5	4^6o	3^5	$6^{5\frac{3}{4}}$	Clift George^2	Qua	2:04	Wairala, Thurbers Boy, Always Special	8
3May79-7Sac	1	$:30^4$	$1:03^2$	$1:34^3$	2:04 ft	5	x7	7	7^4o	7^4	$7^{6\frac{1}{2}}$	Pelling Brian^6	10000	$2:05^1$	Lisbon Lad, Andys Dean,BonaparteChip	6
21Apr79-LA	1	$:30^2$	$1:01^4$	$1:33^2$	$2:04^4$ft		5	5	4	4^4	4^5	Pelling Brian^4	Qua	$2:05^4$	HalcyonHero,MisterAnders,BethanyOks	5
10Mar79 LA	1	$:29^4$	$1:00^4$	$1:32^4$	$2:03^3$ft		2	2	2	$2^{1\frac{1}{2}}$	$3^{1\frac{1}{4}}$	Longo Gerald^3	Qua	$2:03^4$	Game Too, Bay Flight, Royal Chimes N	6

17Jan79-Wel—WELLINGTON--Raced aprx 1 1/2 miles in 3:13 2/5, fin 1, M DeFilippi driv

7 — Rebecca Abbe N — 8-1

Driver-Trainer— STEMERMAN RICK. Black, Silver and Chartreuse

$10,000

B. m. 4, by Scotch Abbe—Fiery Silk, by Van Hanover

Own.—Edwin S Gray, Woodland Hills, Cal

Br.—R A & P J Kennedy (NZ) No Record in U.S., '78 No Record in U.S., '79

Lifetime— $2,635 · 1979 8 0 2 1 $1,781 · 1978 5 1 0 0 $854

Date Trk	Dist	¼	½	¾	fin	Odds	¼	½	¾	str	fin	Driver PP	Cond	Time	First 3 Finishers	
22Sep79-2Hol	1	$:28^4$	$:59^1$	$1:28^3$	$1:58^3$ft	11	5	4	$4^{3\frac{1}{4}}$	3^9	3^{15}	Stemerman Rick^1	Nw 2	$2:01^4$	AndyHenleyPeter,GuyTryx,RebeccAbbN	8
15Sep79-2Hol	1	$:29^2$	1:00	$1:28^3$	1:59 ft	19	2o	1	2^1	6^8	8^{14}	Stemerman Rick^8	Nw 2	$2:01^4$	Best Of Abbe, Guy Tryax, DrEKBuckley	10
8Sep79-3Hol	1	$:30^3$	$1:02^2$	$1:32^2$	$2:03^3$ft	5	1	1	1^{nk}	$1^{1\frac{1}{2}}$	$2^{\frac{3}{4}}$	Stemerman Rick^5	Nw2	$2:03^3$	LordMarkN,RebeccAbbeN,GrndOleOpry	9
28Aug79-10Hol	1	:30	$1:00^1$	1:31	$2:00^2$ft	12	1	2	3^2	$4^{4\frac{1}{2}}$	7^{11}	Stemerman Rick^3	Nw 2	$2:02^3$	Tarport Black, Anchor C, Best Of Abbe	10
28Jly79-Sac	1	:31	$1:02^1$	1:34	$2:02^3$ft		3	1	3	2^2	$4^{3\frac{1}{4}}$	Stemerman Rick^7	Qua	$2:03^1$	Welsh Kiwi, TarportBlack,VarietyAgain	8

8 — Yakiriki — 15-1

Driver—SHINN STEVE. Trainer—Croghan Ross. Purple and Lavender

$10,000

B. g. 9, by Pipiriki—Sukiyaki, by Bruce Hall

Own.—Stephen J Shinn, Victoria, Aust

Br.—B M Lynch (Aust) No Record in U.S., '78 2:02, SAC, '79

Lifetime— $20,454 · 1979 16 1 5 0 $3,935 · 1978 10 0 0 1 $676

Date Trk	Dist	¼	½	¾	fin	Odds	¼	½	¾	str	fin	Driver PP	Cond	Time	First 3 Finishers	
20Sep79-5Hol	1	$:29^4$	1:00	$1:30^3$	$2:00^3$ft	25	5	5	$5^{3\frac{1}{2}}$o	4^6	$5^{5\frac{1}{4}}$	Shinn Steve^8	10000	$2:01^3$	LarkMinbar,DancingStorm,WindarrPrk	10
14Sep79-9Hol	1	:29	$:59^4$	$1:30^3$	$2:01^1$ft	4¼	1	2	2^{hd}o	$2^{\frac{1}{2}}$	$7^{6\frac{1}{2}}$	Shinn Steve^7	12000	$2:02^3$	WitkiSuprem,GnrlSilvr,StormyKnightN	9
8Sep79-5Hol	1	:30	1:01	$1:30^1$	$2:00^3$ft	6¼	5	5	5^6	3^3	$2^{4\frac{1}{2}}$	Shinn Steve^3	10000	$2:01^2$	Bronte Boy, Yakiriki, Cachuma Chief	10
1Sep79-1Hol	1	$:29^1$	1:00	$1:30^2$	$1:59^4$ft	20	5	7	$8^{6\frac{1}{4}}$	$6^{4\frac{1}{4}}$	$5^{8\frac{1}{4}}$	Shinn Steve^2	10000	$2:01^2$	Merry Time Finesse, Assure,BronteBoy	10
29Aug79-Hol	1	:31	$1:02^4$	$1:33^3$	$2:03^3$ft		5	6	$7^{7\frac{1}{2}}$	$6^{6\frac{1}{2}}$	$2^{1\frac{1}{2}}$	Shinn Steve^3	Qua	2:04	Gypsy Sam, Yakiriki, Prudys Boy	8

9 — Slim Yankee — 10-1

Driver-Trainer— WILLIAMS JACK. Red and White

$10,000

B. g. 7, by Regal Yankee—Slim Jane, by Toronto Boy

Own.—Denice Fay Turner, Gold Coast, Aust

Br.—F E Newfield (NZ) No Record in U.S., '78 No Record, '79

Lifetime— $17,113 · 1979 18 0 1 3 $4,051 · 1978 25 3 3 1 $5,333

Date Trk	Dist	¼	½	¾	fin	Odds	¼	½	¾	str	fin	Driver PP	Cond	Time	First 3 Finishers	
22Sep79-1Hol	1	$:29^1$	$:59^1$	$1:30^1$	$2:00^2$ft	7¼	6	6	$5^{4\frac{1}{4}}$o	3^4	$5^{2\frac{1}{4}}$	Williams Jack^3	10000	$2:00^4$	North Western, Lordling, Bronte Boy	10
15Sep79-3Hol	1	$:29^4$	$1:00^4$	$1:30^1$	2:01 ft	47	9	9	$9^{9\frac{1}{2}}$	8^7	$3^{1\frac{1}{2}}$	Williams Ken^9	10000	$2:01^2$	The Blizzard A, DayStream,SlimYankee	9
24Aug79-4Hol	1	:30	$1:00^1$	$1:29^4$	$1:59^4$ft	31	7	7	7^7	7^{12}	6^{10}	Williams Ken^7	12000	$2:01^4$	Butler King, Bronte Boy, Tuatahi Ridge	7
1Aug79-9Sac	1	$:29^2$	$:59^4$	$1:30^4$	2:00 ft	5	5	5	$4^{5\frac{1}{2}}$	5^6	$5^{7\frac{1}{4}}$	Williams Ken^4	Nw6000	$2:01^2$	Knights Honour N,SoLongAdios,Sychar	6
27Jly79-9Sac	1	$:28^4$	$:58^4$	$1:28^3$	$1:59^2$ft	22	7	8	8^{14}	8^{10}	$5^{8\frac{1}{4}}$	Williams Ken^5	Nw1500 79	2:01	RumPirate,MajesticSkipper,MimosaPrk	8

10 — Ex Grand — 8-1

Driver-Trainer— DESOMER STEVE. Blue and White

$10,000

Br. g. 9, by Express Byrd—Grand Vision, by Plebe

Own.—Desomer Stables Inc, Elk Grove Cal

Br.—Mrs A Druitt (Aust) No Record in U.S., '78 1:59^2, HOL, '79

Lifetime— $50,757 · 1979 16 1 0 4 $6,590 · 1978 34 1 4 3 $12,512

Date Trk	Dist	¼	½	¾	fin	Odds	¼	½	¾	str	fin	Driver PP	Cond	Time	First 3 Finishers	
25Sep79-10Hol	1	$:28^2$	$1:00^2$	$1:30^4$	$2:00^4$ft	6¾	6	5o	$5^{4\frac{1}{4}}$o	$5^{2\frac{1}{2}}$	$3^{4\frac{1}{2}}$	Desomer Steve^3	10000	$2:01^3$	Sir Jim, Star Ricky, Ex Grand	10
19Sep79-6Hol	1	$:28^3$	$1:00^4$	$1:32^1$	2:01 ft	6¼e	6	5o	$4^{2\frac{1}{4}}$o	7^6	9^{10}	Knight Errol^3	14000	2:03	Midnight Choo Choo,WiseRuler,Parling	9
11Sep79-8Hol	1	$:30^1$	$:59^4$	$1:29^1$	$1:58^2$ft	21	9	9	$9^{7\frac{1}{2}}$	9^{10}	9^{17}	Longo Gerald^7	16000	$2:01^4$	Highland Champ, Charlight, Gypsy Sam	9
5Sep79-6Hol	1	$:29^2$	$1:00^1$	1:31	$2:00^2$ft	3½	5	5	$5^{3\frac{3}{4}}$	$7^{7\frac{1}{4}}$	7^{14}	Longo Gerald^4	20000	$2:03^1$	Jambo Dollar, Baker Hill, Placerville	7
28Aug79-7Hol	1	$:29^2$	$:59^2$	1:29	$1:59^2$ft	12	5	5o	4^3	$4^{2\frac{1}{2}}$	1^1	Longo Gerald^2	16000	$1:59^2$	Ex Grand, Regal Ring, Cool Gay	10

DECLARED– SIR JIM and HENRY'S DREAM N.

Allowed prices: Gas Saver, $15,000; Rebecca Abbe N, $14,500.

3rd Race

$5 Exacta
1 MILE PACE **PURSE $7,500**

CONDITIONED. Purse $7,500. All ages. Non-winners of $17,500 in 1979. Also eligible: Non-winners of $8,500 in last 6 starts.

Date	Trk Dist	1/4	1/2	3/4	fin	Odds	1/4	1/2	3/4	str	fin	Driver	PP	Cond Time	First 3 Finishers

1 — 6-1

Driver–Trainer— HUNTER CHARLES. — Green and Gold — Lifetime— $50,412
Royal Waldorf
Br. g. 6, by Mark Lobell—Derry, by Fallacy — 1979 13 1 1 5 $17,348
Own.—New Zealand Stable, Remuera, Auckland, NZ — 1978 19 0 3 3 $8,713
Br.—P Reid (NZ) — No Record in U.S., '78 — No Record in U.S., '79

22Sep79-7Hol	1 :294 1:001 1:303 1:584ft	6½	1	2	32	31	31½	Hunter Charles7	Nw 15000 79 1:59	Ripping Rick, HelloBirdie,RoyalWaldorf 7
15Sep79-9Hol	1 :293 1:003 1:283 1:582ft	9½	8	8	86	84½	73½	Hunter Charles8	Wo 10000 1:591	Native Rocket,ArmbroTawny,LittleToRi 8
23Aug79-6Hol	1 :283 :584 1:29 1:583ft	14	8	7o	44½	52½	53	Hunter Charles6	Nw50000 79 1:591	Trentonian, Hello Birdie, RomanChapel 10
17Aug79-Hol	1 :294 :594 1:302 2:012ft	2	1	11½	11½	13		Hunter Charles7	Qua 2:012	Royal Waldorf, Baker Hill,PresenceFelt 7
31Mar79-Auc—AUCKLAND—Raced aprx 1 mile in 2:01 4/5, fin 1, R Mitchell driv

2 — 15-1

Driver—ACKERMAN D R. Tr.—Ackerman Doug, Asst., Ackerman D R. — Blue and Grey — Lifetime— $33,367
Michiana Hall
B. c. 3, by Bramble Hall—Lentsch's Helen, by Diamond Hal — 1979 23 5 7 3 $24,209
Own.—Richard S Staley, Beverly Hills, Cal — 1978 20 1 4 1 $9,158
Br.—M C Ackerman (Mich) — 2:023, HOL, '78 — 2:003, DET, '79

| 22Sep79-7Hol | 1 :294 1:001 1:303 1:584ft | 10 | 7 | 7 | 64½ | 74 | 77½ | Ackerman D R5 | Nw 15000 79 2:001 | Ripping Rick, HelloBirdie,RoyalWaldorf 7 |
| 8Sep79-HP | 1 :302 1:01 1:312 2:014ft | 3 | 6 | 40 | 3½ | 2½ | | Ackerman Doug5 | Cd 2.02 | King Crickett, Michiana Hall, Salt Lick 10 |
| 3Sep79-Kal—KALAMAZOO—Raced mile in 2:04 1/5, fin 5, mile in 2:06, fin 2. |
| 26Aug79-Adr—ADRIAN—Raced mile in 2:03 2/5, fin 5; mile in 2:02 2/5, fin 4. |
| 16Aug79-Mid—MIDLAND—Raced mile in 2:01 3/5, fin 3, mile in 2:03 3/5, fin 2. |

3 — 8-1

Driver—LACOSTE LEO. Trainer—Blue Bill. — Blue and White — Lifetime— $25,405
Spangles Gold
Ch. g. 7, by Jack Chance—Spangled Hanover, by Garrison Hanover 1979 0 0 0 0
Own.—Howard M. Brown, Chicago Ill — 1978 11 4 3 0 $16,843
Br.—J W Dalgety (NZ) — 1:59, HOL, '78 — No Record, '79

26Sep79-Hol	1 :31 1:024 1:321 2:02 ft	1	1	12	14	13		Lacoste Leo4	Qua 2:02	Spangles Gold, Tacoma, Blue Tempest 7
20Dec78-May	1 :301 1:003 1:32 2:033gd*3-2	8	7	30	12	13		Alessi Carmen6	Nw 14000 2:033	Spangles Gold, Mcoscar, Tow TheMark 10
30Nov78-6Hol	1 :284 :59 1:292 1:59 ft	5	9	fog	73½	11		Pelling Brian3	30000 H 1:59	Spangles Gold, Jenlight, Idaten 7
23Nov78-7Hol	1 :301 1:00 1:313 2:003gd*8-5	3	4o	4½o	1nk	12		Pelling Brian1	30000 2:003	Spangles Gold, Cool Gay, Ellamon N 6
17Nov78-3Hol	1 :293 :584 1:291 1:582ft	2½	8	8	87½	69½	54½	Pelling Brian5	Nw5000 Last6 1:592	Bat O'Brien, Hilarious Brew,DeejayWyn 8

4 — 4-1

Driver—GATH BRIAN. Trainer—Abrams Barry. — Red and Black — Lifetime— $137,456
Apre Ski
B. g. 7, by Garrison Hanover—Ski Girl, by Johnny Globe — 1979 10 3 1 0 $15,835
Own.—Neil H Stow, Epping, Vic,. Aust — 1978 31 7 7 1 $47,554
Br.—Ross Croghan (Aust) — No Record in U.S., '78 — 1:594, MDW, '79

22Sep79-Hol—LATEST WORKOUT--Mile in :29 2/5, :59 4/5, 1:29 2/5, 1:59, track fast.

4Aug79-Mdw	1 :284 :581 1:27 1:552ft	19	6o	7o	9o	87½	78	Gath B10	Nw20000 1:57	Blazing Dave, Napal Dew, Justa Tinker 8
1Aug79-Mdw	1 :292 :581 1:28 1:571ft	*2	5	5	5o	52½	2hd	Gath B2	Nw8000 1:571	Persuadable, Apre Ski, Deity 10
28Jly79-Mdw	1 :283 :593 1:31 1:594ft	*9-5	1o	1	11½	11½	1½	Gath B7	Nw7500 1:594	Apre Ski, Columbia Brooks,PartyAhead 10
24Jly79-Mdw	1 :284 1:004 1:304 2:01 ft	5	5o	6o	35½	1nk		Shaw A G2	Q.a 2:01	Apre Ski, Tan Thor, Sargent At Arms 7

5 — 3-1

Driver—KUEBLER RICK. Trainer—Stein Roger. — Blue and Yellow — Lifetime— $24,713
Craig Del
Br. g. 5, by Armbro Del—Flying Shona, by Flying Song — 1979 20 3 6 1 $17,417
Own.—Al Ross, Los Angeles, Cal — 1978 26 4 3 2 $7,296
Br.—Mrs E E Townley (NZ) — No Record in U.S., '78 — 1:582, SAC, '79

22Sep79-9Hol	1 :292 :592 1:282 1:563ft	2e	5	31½o	1½	2nk		Kuebler Rick4	Wo 10000 1:564	Little To Ri, Craig Del, Torpids Knight 9
13Sep79-6Hol	1 :29 :583 1:284 1:574ft	*4-5e	9	9	106½o	86½x	118½	Kuebler Rick4	Sir Dalrae 1:593	CordonArgent,Trentonian,RomanChpel 12
8Sep79-9Hol	1 :283 :582 1:283 1:571ft	3½	2	3	33	2½	51½	Kuebler Rick1	Inv 1:574	Sprinkler, B. C. Count, Peter Onedin 6
1Sep79-8Hol	1 :284 :592 1:274 1:59 ft	2½	5	55	31½	13½		Kuebler Rick5	Inv 1:59	Craig Del, B. C. Count, Young Million 5
23Aug79-10Hol	1 :294 :594 1:302 2:001ft	*2-3	x8	6o	53½o	32½	2no	Kuebler Rick2	Nw7500 79 2:001	Young Million, Craig Del, Waralene 8

6 — 8-1

Driver–Trainer— PELLING BRIAN. — Black, Red and Orange — Lifetime— $37,804
Armbro Rhythm N
B. g. 5, by Armbro Del—Battle Song, by Brahman — 1979 23 4 6 4 $32,574
Own.—George E Aiken & B R P EnterprisesCorp, Cypress — 1978 35 3 2 2 $4,301
Br.—J P Ewart (NZ) — No Record in U.S., '78 — 1:591, LA , '79

15Sep79-9Spk	1 :291 :593 1:303 2:011ft	3½	6	4o	1o	11	22	Dolbee J8	Nw7500 L7 2:013	SirDnclot,ArmbroRhythmN,SuperStrike 9
1Sep79-10Spk	1 :294 :592 1:29 1:593ft	11	6	4o	4o	32½	61½	Pelling Brian8	Nw6500 L12 2:00	KensShdow,RcyThought,MjesticRenveh 9
25Aug79-7Spk	1 :29 1:01 1:291 1:593ft	6½	8	7o	6o	64½	53½	Pelling Brian6	Nw20000 2:001	RiverCircleRomo,SomrstNic,KnsShdow 9
18Aug79-6Spk	1 :30 1:001 1:304 2:002ft	3	1	1	1½	1½	Pelling Brian8	Nw6600twic79 2:002	Armbro RhythmN,SlyBrewwer,ToeTime 9
13Aug79-7Spk	1 :302 1:02 1:312 2:002ft	4½	8	5o	3	3½	36	Pelling Brian5	Nw5500may1 2:013	Wikam, Coringa Bill, Armbro RhythmN 9

7 — 12-1

Driver–Trainer→ HARDIE GEORGE. — Black and Gold — Lifetime— $47,111
Young Million
B. g. 4, by Young Charles—Merry Million, by Bachelor Hanover — 1979 15 2 3 3 $13,460
Own.—Winged Victory Stb & Henry O Mangus, Torrance, Cal. — 1978 23 4 6 3 $23,652
Br.—R L Ryan (NZ) — 1:592, HOL, '78 — 2:001, DET, '79

22Sep79-7Hol	1 :294 1:001 1:303 1:584ft	6	2	3	54	41½	43	Hardie George6	Nw 15000 79 1:592	Ripping Rick, HelloBirdie,RoyalWaldorf 7
15Sep79-10Hol	1 :293 :59 1:263 1:574ft	13	7	7	77	75½	32½	Hardie George6	Nw15000 79 1:582	Glide Time, Ripping Rick, YoungMillion 7
8Sep79-8Hol	1 :292 1:002 1:292 1:584ft	2	1	2	11	11	33½	Hardie George4	Nw10000 79 1:593	Argyll, Roman Chapel, Young Million 7
1Sep79-8Hol	1 :284 :592 1:274 1:59 ft	28	3ix	4	43½	21½	33½	Hardie George1	Inv 1:594	Craig Del, B. C. Count, Young Million 5
23Aug79-10Hol	1 :294 :594 1:302 2:001ft	4½	4	1o	11½	12	1no	Hardie George3	Nw7500 79 2:001	Young Million, Craig Del, Waralene 8

8 — 8-1

Driver—GRUNDY JAMES. Trainer—Silverman Jerry. — Grey, Blue and Red — Lifetime— $25,282
Hello Birdie
B. g. 6, by Golcourt—Star Petite, by Scottish Star — 1979 20 5 5 2 $20,901
Own.—George Bernhofen, Lancaster, Cal — 1978 16 3 1 4 $4,381
Br.—K C Burley (NZ) — No Record in U.S., '78 — 1:59, SAC, '79

22Sep79-7Hol	1 :294 1:001 1:303 1:584ft	9½	4	4	21½o	21	21½	Grundy James2	Nw 15000 79 1:592	Ripping Rick, HelloBirdie,RoyalWaldorf 7
13Sep79-6Hol	1 :29 :583 1:284 1:574ft	17	1	1	11	75½	96½	VallndinghamGene6 Sir Dalrae 1:59	CordonArgent,Trentonian,RomanChpel 12
8Sep79-7Hol	1 :292 :582 1:282 1:58 ft	9½	8	8	x819	8dis	8dis	VallandinghamGene8 Wo10000 —	Trentonian, Ripping Rick, ArmbroTawny 8
31Aug79-6Hol	1 :293 :591 1:284 1:574ft	12	4	1	11½	13	711	VllndinghmGene4	Nw100000 79 2:00	Can Can Rhythm,PeterOnedin,Sprinkler 7
23Aug79-6Hol	1 :283 :584 1:29 1:583ft	14	9	9	56	42½	21	VllndinghmGene9	Nw50000 79 1:591	Trentonian, Hello Birdie, RomanChapel 10

9 — 12-1

Driver—BAYLESS STAN. Trainer—Maier Tim. — Gold and White — Lifetime— $27,491
Direct Victory
B. g. 4, by Sampson Direct—Torchie V., by Victory — 1979 14 3 2 2 $10,163
Own.—Marc, Kenneth, Jay Carver, Los Angeles, Cal. — 1978 1 0 0 0 $272
Br.—J B Cannon (Ky) — No Record , '78 — 1:592, Hol, '79

20Sep79-4Hol	1 :293 :593 1:293 1:592ft	8½	4	43	31½	11	Bayless Stan1	Nw 7500 79 1:592	Direct Victory, Soldiers Bold, Trevino 6
13Sep79-6Hol	1 :29 :583 1:284 1:574ft	40	3o	2o	21o	1212	1218	Bayless Stan7	Sir Dalrae 1:592	CordonArgent,Trentonian,RomanChpel 12
7Sep79-9Hol	1 :304 1:01 1:304 1:592ft	6½	2	2	31½	41½	2½	Bayless Stan7	Nw5000 Last 6 1:593	IkesMarine,DirectVictory,ChiefWomble 7
1Sep79-10Hol	1 :291 1:002 1:301 1:591ft	23	9	10	109½	105½	86½	Bayless Stan9	Nw7500 79 2:003	Waralene, Almetos, Armbro Blaze N 9
25Aug79-4Hol	1 :291 1:001 1:293 2:00 ft	2	6	7	54½o	32½	1½	Bayless Stan9	Nw7500 79 2:00	DirectVictory,MiracleEddie,MasterVlue 8

10 — 6-1

Driver–Trainer— AUBIN MARC. — Blue, Red and White — Lifetime— $207,423
Proud Baron
B. h. 8, by Baron Hanover—Stunning Wick, by Gene Aobe — 1979 11 1 1 3 $11,926
Own.—William &CarolWhitlock&MarcAubin,Thousand:Oaks,Cal — 1978 34 6 5 1 $45,353
Br.—Grandview Raceway (Ohio) — 1:55, HOL, '78 — 1:591, LA , '79

21Sep79-8Hol	1 :283 :583 1:284 1:58 ft *4-5	1	1	13	12	22½	Aubin Marc4	Nw5000 Last 6 1:583	Bker'sKnight,ProudBron,HeroicHnover 8
15Sep79-Hol	1 :293 1:00 1:294 1:592ft	1	1	13	12	12	Aubin Marc6	Qua 1:592	Proud Baron, Frostword, BrilliantJackie 8
19Apr79-Mdw	1 :284 :582 1:274 1:564ft	4½	2o	2o	6	812	914	Kuebler Rick6	Nw9500 1:594	Pats Gypsy, Scott Wil, C P Dircen 9
14Apr79-Mdw	1 :293 1:004 1:311 2:001ft	25	3o	1o	3	65	79	Kuebler Rick5	80000 2:02	Besta Fella, Nautical, Sea Train 9
4Apr79-Mdw	1 :303 1:003 1:293 1:594ft	5½	2o	3	64	44½	Kuebler Rick9	Nw10500 2:003	Young Blaze, Saigon, Over Strength 9

GMAC, Sally Jensen, group representative

1 MILE PACE **PURSE $9,000**

4th Race

CLAIMING HANDICAP. Purse $9,000. All ages. Claiming prices $35,000–$40,000.

1 — 3-1

Driver–Trainer— DESOMER STEVE. Blue and White

Roman Chapel $35,000

Br. g. 9, by Chapel Chief—Mellarae, by Romelo
Own.—Desomer Stables Inc & Robert Todd, Elk Grove, Cal.
Br.—E J Schmidt (Aust) 1:572, Hol, '78

Lifetime— $79,578
1979 13 2 2 4 $18,303
1978 24 3 3 4 $21,708
2:023, BM , '79

Date Trk	Dist	¼	½	¾	fin	Odds	¼	½	¾	str	fin	Driver PP	Cond	Time	First 3 Finishers	
22Sep79-4Hol	1	:302	1:012	1:313	1:592ft	*1	2	2	21½	21½	2½	Desomer Steve1	35000 H	1:593	Nephew Bob, RomanChapel,CookieBear	5
13Sep79-6Hol	1	:29	:583	1:284	1:574ft	23	8o	8o	84½o	54¼	32½	Desomer Steve8	Sir Dalrae	1:581	CordonArgent,Trentonian,RomanChpel	12
8Sep79-8Hol	1	:292	1:002	1:292	1:584ft	*8-5	5	3	42½	31½	23	Desomer Steve5	Nw10000 79	1:592	Argyll, Roman Chapel, Young Million	7
31Aug79-6Hol	1	:293	:591	1:284	1:574ft	20	3	4	32½	33½	57½	Desomer Steve1	Nw100000 79	1:591	Can Can Rhythm,PeterOnedin,Sprinkler	7
23Aug79-6Hol	1	:283	:584	1:29	1:583ft	87	10	10	67½o	74	32	Desomer Steve10	Nw50000 79	1:59	Trentonian, Hello Birdie, RomanChapel	10
17Aug79-Hol	1	:291	:593	1:291	1:591ft		5	5	66¼	64¾	612	Desomer Steve5	Qua	2:013	Spry Sam, Waralene, Zarzuella	6

2 — 9-2

Driver–Trainer— GORDON ROBERT. Blue, Cream and Black

Armbro Blaze N $35,000

Ch. g. 6, by Armbro Hurricane—Matron Forbes, by Hi Los Forbes
Own.—O'Cal Stables Inc, Garden Grove, Cal
Br.—M Rogers (NZ) No Record in U.S., '78

Lifetime— $7,291
1979 20 3 2 1 $6,910
1978 7 0 1 1 $381
No Record in U.S., '79

Date Trk	Dist	¼	½	¾	fin	Odds	¼	½	¾	str	fin	Driver PP	Cond	Time	First 3 Finishers	
22Sep79-4Hol	1	:302	1:012	1:313	1:592ft	4	4	4	54½	32½	54¾	Gordon Robert3	35000 H	2:002	Nephew Bob, RomanChapel,CookieBear	5
14Sep79-10Hol	1	:30	:59	1:28	1:582ft	*7-5	3	4	45	44	52¼	Gordon Robert1	Nw5000 Lst 6	1:584	CookieBear,Impellere,ArmbroUltimtum	9
6Sep79-5Hol	1	:291	:591	1:293	1:583ft	2¼	5	5	53¾	42½	22¼	Gordon Robert3	Nw7500 79	1:59	Almetos, Armbro Blaze N, J R Decker	9
1Sep79-10Hol	1	:291	1:002	1:301	1:591ft	40	6	7	76¼o	64¼	31¼	Gordon Robert6	Nw7500 79	1:593	Waralene, Almetos, Armbro Blaze N	10
25Aug79-Hol	1	:302	1:01	1:321	2:022ft		7	7	5	43¼	1hd	Gordon Robert7	Qua	2:022	ArmbroBlzeN,PrideOfAll,ChitLightfoot	7

4Jun79-Wel—WELLINGTON--Raced aprx 1 1/2 miles in 3:12 4/5, fin 9, G Harris dr

3 — 6-1

Driver–Trainer— WISHARD BARRY. Gold, White and Black

Scotch Time Abbee $35,000

B. g. 8, by Scotch Time—Colleen Abbe, by Gene Abbe
Own.—L & W Ranch, Chatsworth, Cal
Br.—J Sokol (NJ) 1:582, HOL, '78

Lifetime— $119,213
1979 28 4 5 5 $26,226
1978 36 3 3 8 $36,757
1:593, SAC, '79

Date Trk	Dist	¼	½	¾	fin	Odds	¼	½	¾	str	fin	Driver PP	Cond	Time	First 3 Finishers	
22Sep79-4Hol	1	:302	1:012	1:313	1:592ft	8¾	3	3	43	53¼	43½	Wishard Barry2	35000 H	2:001	Nephew Bob, RomanChapel,CookieBear	5
14Sep79-8Hol	1	:29	:592	1:29	1:59 ft	7	8	8	89	85	52¾	Goudreau Shelly7	c25000 H	1:593	Royal Doll N., Gliding Guy, Baker Hill	8
6Sep79-6Hol	1	:303	1:023	1:333	2:014ft	8¼	1	2	31¾	31½	75¾	Goudreau Shelly9	30000	2:03	Charteris Play, Coota Frost, Emanar	9
30Aug79-6Hol	1	:294	:591	1:294	2:001ft	4½	7	7	75¾	77½	31½	Goudreau Shelly7	30000	2:003	Idaten, MisterMcJeb,ScotchTimeAbbee	7
25Aug79-3Hol	1	:29	:593	1:30	1:593ft	2½	6	6	43½	42½	31½	Goudreau Shelly5	35000	1:594	Idaten, Cookie Bear, ScotchTimeAbbee	6
4Aug79-9Sac	1	:301	1:002	1:311	2:004ft	*9-5	6	6	63	52¾	2hd	Williams Ken5	25000	2:004	MightySpry,ScotchTimeAbbe,Oki'sImg	6

4 — 4-1

Driver–Trainer— GRUNDY JAMES. Grey, Blue and Red

Cookie Bear $40,000

B. g. 5, by Scotch Abbe—Miss Armbro, by Armbro Del
Own.—D Grundy & C Fiumera, New Zealand Stab, Cerritos Ca
Br.—Mrs M P Orldwski (NZ) No Record in U.S., '78

Lifetime— $12,751
1979 16 4 2 3 $11,164
1978 19 1 2 1 $1,587
1:582, Hol, '79

Date Trk	Dist	¼	½	¾	fin	Odds	¼	½	¾	str	fin	Driver PP	Cond	Time	First 3 Finishers	
22Sep79-4Hol	1	:302	1:012	1:313	1:592ft	3	5	5	33	43	33	Grundy James4	40000 H	2:00	Nephew Bob, RomanChapel,CookieBear	5
14Sep79-10Hol	1	:30	:59	1:28	1:582ft	4	6	6	57	56	1¾	Grundy James4	Nw5000 Lst 6	1:582	CookieBear,Impellere,ArmbroUltimtum	9
6Sep79-5Hol	1	:291	:591	1:293	1:583ft	14	9	9	97½	86¾	54½	Grundy James9	Nw7500 79	1:592	Almetos, Armbro Blaze N, J R Decker	9
25Aug79-3Hol	1	:29	:593	1:30	1:593ft	10	4	4	66	63¾	2¾	Grundy James2	35000	1:594	Idaten, Cookie Bear, ScotchTimeAbbee	6
4Aug79-4Sac	1	:283	:581	1:284	1:582ft	8¾	8	8	99½	85½	610	Grundy James8	Nw6000	2:002	Craig Del, Alemtos, Cook's Creanza	9
30Jun79-9Sac	1	:322	1:023	1:313	2:011ft	3	5	5	2½o	22	84¼	Grundy James5	Pref	2:02	HelloBirdie,TreasureKey,HeroicHanover	8

5 — 7-2

Driver—GATH BRIAN. Trainer—Knight Errol. Red and Black

Nephew Bob $40,000

Br. g. 6, by High Pendant—Staten Island, by Nephew Hal
Own.—William J Cairncross, St. Johns Park, Aust
Br.—B W Hunter (Aust) No Record in U.S., '78

Lifetime— $34,430
1979 19 6 5 0 $22,450
1978 25 8 4 1 $11,017
1:591, LA , '79

Date Trk	Dist	¼	½	¾	fin	Odds	¼	½	¾	str	fin	Driver PP	Cond	Time	First 3 Finishers	
22Sep79-4Hol	1	:302	1:012	1:313	1:592ft	5½	1	1	11½	11½	1½	Gath Brian5	40000 H	1:592	Nephew Bob, RomanChapel,CookieBear	5
15Sep79-9Hol	1	:293	1:003	1:283	1:582ft	19	4	1	11	11	62¾	Knight Errol1	Wo 10000	1:59	Native Rocket,ArmbroTawny,LittleToRi	8
8Sep79-7Hol	1	:292	:582	1:282	1:58 ft	11	2	1	1nk	2nk	75½	Knight Errol1	Wo10000	1:591	Trentonian, Ripping Rick,ArmbroTawny	8
1Sep79-4Hol	1	:294	1:00	1:291	1:591ft	4	2	5	54	54	51¾	Desomer Steve2	Wo10000	1:593	J C Heel, Armbro Tawny, Graduate Boy	6
25Aug79-7Hol	1	:283	:582	1:31	1:594ft	*2-3	3	3	31	35½	27	Desomer Steve1	Wo 10000	2:011	Coota Frost, Nephew Bob, Wintario	6
22Aug79-Hol	1	:301	1:022	1:324	2:012ft		1	1	13	1½	11	Knight Errol3	Qua	2:012	Nephew Bob, Desmond, Camlar	5

6 — 5-2

Driver–Trainer— PARKER JACK JR. Maroon, Blue and White

Ripping Rick $40,000

Blk. g. 5, by Ripping Good—Cannellone, by Hillsota
Own.—First Time Stable, Florhan Park, NJ
Br.—C B & E M Houston (Del) 1:572, MDW, '78

Lifetime— $167,171
1979 29 4 7 0 $52,640
1978 38 8 6 5 $61,917
1:584, MDW, '79

Date Trk	Dist	¼	½	¾	fin	Odds	¼	½	¾	str	fin	Driver PP	Cond	Time	First 3 Finishers	
22Sep79-7Hol	1	:294	1:001	1:303	1:584ft	*1	3	1	11	11	11½	Parker Jack Jr1	Nw 15000 79	1:584	Ripping Rick, HelloBirdie,RoyalWaldorf	7
15Sep79-10Hol	1	:293	:59	1:263	1:574ft	3	3o	1	12	12½	2½	Parker Jack Jr7	Nw15000 79	1:58	Glide Time, Ripping Rick, YoungMillion	7
8Sep79-7Hol	1	:292	:582	1:282	1:58 ft	19	6	7	74	73¼	22	Todd James II6	Wo10000	1:582	Trentonian, Ripping Rick,ArmbroTawny	8
1Sep79-4Hol	1	:294	1:00	1:291	1:591ft	18	6	6	64½	65	41½	Todd James II6	Wo10000	1:593	J C Heel, Armbro Tawny, Graduate Boy	6
25Aug79-7Hol	1	:283	:582	1:31	1:594ft	6¾	4	6	53	510	411	Todd James II2	Wo 10000	2:021	Coota Frost, Nephew Bob, Wintario	6
21Jly79-Mdw	1	:292	:592	1:271	1:554ft	9	4	4	4o	78¾	616	Parker Jack Jr4	40000	1:591	JeffersonAdmirl,FlmeOfFrdom,BstBron	8

$3 Quinella
1 MILE PACE **PURSE $9,000**

5th Race

CHI ETA PHI, Zola Jones, group rep.

CONDITIONED. Purse, $9,000. All ages. Winners of over $10,000.

1 — 6-1

Driver—GATH BRIAN. Trainer—Abrams Barry. Red and Black

Dromicia — Br. g. 4, by Scotch Luck—Gentle Chamfer, by Chamfer
Own.—Oswald L Bennett, Geelong Victoria,Aust
Br.—A G Heald (Aust)

Lifetime— $20,997; 1979 14 6 1 2 $13,567; 1978 8 7 1 0 $7,430; No Record in U.S., '78; No Record in U.S., '79

22Sep79-Hol—LATEST WORKOUT--Mile in :29 4/5, 1:01, 1:30, 2:02, track fast

Date-Trk	Dist	¼	½	¾	fin	Odds	¼	½	¾	str	fin	Driver PP	Cond	Time	First 3 Finishers	
1Aug79-Mdw	1	:294	:594	1:283	1:572ft	3½	5	5	5o	45¼	37	Gath Brian4	Nw4	1:584	Mel Hanover, JefsMalpractice,Dromicia	10
19Jly79-Mdw	1	:291	:581	1:272	1:571ft	8	4o	4o	4o	54½	96¾	Gath Brian7	Nw9500	1:583	Sunro, Gay Schnell, Closest To You	10
13Jly79-Mdw	1	:283	:571	1:272	1:572ft	7½	5	5	6	74¾	45	Gath Brian1	Nw9000	1:582	Perfect Angle, Bobby B Buttler,EDBret	10
3Jly79-Mdw	1	:291	1:02	1:321	2:01 ft		4o	2o	2o	24½	24½	Gath Brian7	Qua	2:014	Boehms Hero N, Dromicia, Merlin Byrd	10

2Jun79-Moo—MOONEE VALLEY--Raced aprx 1 5/16 miles in 2:35 2/5, fin 1, B Gath dr

2 — 6-1

Driver-Trainer— HUNTER CHARLES. Green and Gold

Glide Time — B. g. 4, by Local Light—Effie Del, by Armbro Del
Own.—New Zealand Stable, B Grass,J Szilage, Aurora, Ill
Br.—R A Belcher (NZ)

Lifetime— $35,493; 1979 4 3 0 0 $9,220; 1978 1 0 1 0 $1,475; No Record , '78; 1:574, Hol, '79

Date-Trk	Dist	¼	½	¾	fin	Odds	¼	½	¾	str	fin	Driver PP	Cond	Time	First 3 Finishers	
22Sep79-9Hol	1	:292	:592	1:282	1:563ft	*2	1	4	64	52	43½	Hunter Charles1	Wo 10000	1:572	Little To Ri, Craig Del, Torpids Knight	9
15Sep79-10Hol	1	:293	:59	1:263	1:574ft	6¼	6	6	54	64	1½	Hunter Charles5	Nw15000 79	1:574	Glide Time, Ripping Rick, YoungMillion	7
8Sep79-2Hol	1	:291	:593	1:291	2:001ft	*2-5	1	3	21o	21	1¾	Hunter Charles3	Nw5000 79	2:001	GlideTime,NervesOfSteel,JamesGrattan	7
30Aug79-10Hol	1	:301	1:00	1:29	1:593ft	*3-2	1	1	21½	21½	11½	Hunter Charles5	Nw5000 79	1:593	Glide Time,IndianChief,RiskyBusinessN	10
25Aug79-Hol	1	:293	1:002	1:322	2:021ft		6	5	75¾	77¾	44	Hunter Charles4	Qua	2:03	AndysThankful,GeneralSilver,MerryOnN	7
24Nov78-10Hol	1	:30	1:011	1:302	1:581ft	5½	3	4	53¾	33½	21	Hunter Charles2	Nw15000 78	1:582	Aldan N, Glide Time, Young Million	9

3 — 8-1

Driver—KUEBLER RICK. Trainer—Stein Roger. Blue and Yellow

Graduate Boy — B. g. 8, by Pipiriki—Maree's Pal, by Walla Lawn
Own.—Al Ross, Los Angeles, Cal
Br.—B C Tangey (Aust)

Lifetime— $104,235; 1979 15 3 2 3 $24,669; 1978 14 4 0 4 $24,589; No Record in U.S., '78; 1:591, SAC, '79

Date-Trk	Dist	¼	½	¾	fin	Odds	¼	½	¾	str	fin	Driver PP	Cond	Time	First 3 Finishers	
22Sep79-9Hol	1	:292	:592	1:282	1:563ft	2e	4	1o	2hd	3½	66	Bayless Stan3	Wo 10000	1:58	Little To Ri, Craig Del, Torpids Knight	9
13Sep79-6Hol	1	:29	:583	1:284	1:574ft	*4-5e	7	7	116½	97	53¼	Goudreau Shelly11	Sir Dalrae	1:582	CordonArgent,Trentonian,RomanChpel	12
8Sep79-7Hol	1	:292	:582	1:282	1:58 ft	2½	4	2o	2nko	1nk	65½	Kuebler Rick4	Wo10000	1:591	Trentonian, Ripping Rick,ArmbroTawny	8
1Sep79-4Hol	1	:294	1:00	1:291	1:591ft	*1	5	4o	43o	43	3hd	Kuebler Rick5	Wo10000	1:592	J C Heel, Armbro Tawny, Graduate Boy	6
28Jly79-8Sac	1	:292	:584	1:301	1:591ft	*6-5	5	5	42	12	12	Ratchford Don2	Nw25000	1:591	GrduteBoy,ScotchTimeAbb,HroicHnovr	9
14Jly79-Sac	1	:303	1:03	1:34	2:03 ft		2	2	2	2hd	12½	Ratchford Gus8	Qua	2:03	GraduateBoy,TheTrdeMrket,LoclSheriff	8

4 — 12-1

Driver-Trainer— ADAMS CECIL. Turquoise and White

Argyll — Gr. h. 7, by Gamecock—Serene Yankee, by Adios Butler
Own.—Cecil Adams, Hemet, Cal.
Br.—P W Gallagher (Mass)

Lifetime— $61,757; 1979 20 4 3 3 $17,641; 1978 17 0 1 2 $4,563; No Record , '78; 1:584, Hol, '79

Date-Trk	Dist	¼	½	¾	fin	Odds	¼	½	¾	str	fin	Driver PP	Cond	Time	First 3 Finishers	
22Sep79-9Hol	1	:292	:592	1:282	1:563ft	6¼	3	3	1hdo	2½	77¼	Adams Cecil2	Wo 10000	1:581	Little To Ri, Craig Del, Torpids Knight	9
15Sep79-9Hol	1	:293	1:003	1:283	1:582ft	4¼	3	6	75	73¼	41¼	Adams Cecil5	Wo 10000	1:583	Native Rocket,ArmbroTawny,LittleToRi	8
8Sep79-8Hol	1	:292	1:002	1:292	1:584ft	8	3	4	31½	21	13	Adams Cecil2	Nw10000 79	1:584	Argyll, Roman Chapel, Young Million	7
1Sep79-4Hol	1	:294	1:00	1:291	1:591ft	11	4	2o	21o	22	63	Adams Cecil4	Wo10000	1:594	J C Heel, Armbro Tawny, Graduate Boy	6
24Aug79-7Hol	1	:302	1:013	1:313	2:01 ft	6½	3ix	3o	31¾o	32	1½	Adams Cecil1	Nw5000 Lst6	2:01	Argyll, J R Decker, Heroic Hanover	8
4Aug79-5Sac	1	:303	1:02	1:33	2:021ft	5¾	2	2	21½	21	11	Adams Cecil2	Pref	2:021	Argyll, Heroic Hanover, Placerville	4

5 — 10-1

Driver-Trainer— VOLLARO STEVE. Blue and Green

Wikam — B. g. 7, by Armbro Del—Cingalese, by Forward
Own.—Steven Vollaro & Richard Glander, Villa Park, Ill
Br.—F E Bennett (NZ)

Lifetime— $23,725; 1979 14 4 1 3 $18,068; 1978 15 0 1 0 $572; No Record in U.S., '78; 2:002, SPK, '79

Date-Trk	Dist	¼	½	¾	fin	Odds	¼	½	¾	str	fin	Driver PP	Cond	Time	First 3 Finishers	
7Sep79-8Spk	1	:284	:59	1:282	1:582ft	25	7	7	7o	68¼	66	Vollaro Steve7	Inv	1:593	BourbonStreet,SmsonChip,GerryJunior	9
31Aug79-8Spk	1	:294	:594	1:283	1:574ft	7	2	2	2	24	44½	Vollaro Steve1	Inv	1:583	Hobo Brooke, Tetarney, Chris Pick	9
22Aug79-8Spk	1	:292	1:001	1:304	2:002sy	2½	2	2	1	2hd	1¾	Vollaro Steve1	Nw20007879	2:002	Wikam, Bret Le Ru, Cross Keys	9
13Aug79-7Spk	1	:302	1:02	1:312	2:002ft	6½	6	1o	1	11½	12½	Vollaro Steve3	Nw5500may1	2:002	Wikam, Coringa Bill, Armbro RhythmN	9
1Aug79-9Spk	1	:294	1:001	1:303	2:003ft	*6-5	2o	1	1	11	34¾	Willis C4	Nw5500twic	2:013	For Land Sakes, Heldez, Wikam	9
26Jly79-Spk	1	:293	1:021	1:33	2:023ft		7	1o	1	11½	11¼	Willis C1	Qua	2:023	Wikam, Fly Bye Chief, Ed Chandler	9

6 — 5-1

Driver—SHERREN FRANK. Trainer—Sherren Jack. Green, White and Black

Torpids Knight — B. g. 3, by Torpid Vic—Armbrozene, by Armbro Del
Own.—Victoria B Perez, Hacienda Hts, Cal
Br.—Estate of L H Broom (NZ)

Lifetime— $22,781; 1979 20 8 4 2 $22,781; 1978 1 0 0 0; No Record in U.S., '78; 1:583, SAC, '79

Date-Trk	Dist	¼	½	¾	fin	Odds	¼	½	¾	str	fin	Driver PP	Cond	Time	First 3 Finishers	
22Sep79-9Hol	1	:292	:592	1:282	1:563ft	9¾	8	8	75½o	62¼	32¼	Sherren Frank7	Wo 10000	1:571	Little To Ri, Craig Del, Torpids Knight	9
19Sep79-Hol	1	:302	1:013	1:324	2:021ft		3	3	33	33½	2no	Sherren Frank6	Qua	2:021	Superman, Torpids Knight, Gentle Tag	7
28Jly79-9Sac	1	:304	1:02	1:314	2:00 ft	2	2	2	31½	22	11¼	Sherren Jack2	InvH	2:00	Torpids Knight, J C Heel, Hello Birdie	4
14Jly79-9Sac	1	:31	1:011	1:304	1:59 ft	9-5	6	6	69	54½	32¼	Sherren Jack6	InvH	1:592	HelloBirdie,HilriousBrew,TorpidsKnight	6
7Jly79-5Sac	1	:283	:584	1:30	1:59 ft	3½	4	4	54	43	1¾	Sherren Jack4	InvH	1:59	Torpids Knight, J C Heel, F T Scot	5
30Jun79-5Sac	1	:283	:584	1:291	1:571ft	2½	5	5	54	52½	4¾	Sherren Jack4	InvH	1:572	F T Scot, J C Heel, Hilarious Brew	5

7 — 7-2

Driver-Trainer— PARKER JACK JR. Maroon, Blue and White

Dells Court — B. g. 5, by Golcourt—Delecto, by Poplar Dell
Own.—Donald Alfano Jr., W. Los Angeles, Cal.
Br.—K M Brock (NZ)

Lifetime— $32,552; 1979 9 4 2 2 $29,940; 1978 4 2 0 1 $2,612; 1:592, HOL, '78; 1:56, MDW, '79

25Sep79-Hol—LATEST WORKOUT--Mile in :31 3/5, 1:02 4/5, 1:33 1/5, 2:02 1/5.

Date-Trk	Dist	¼	½	¾	fin	Odds	¼	½	¾	str	fin	Driver PP	Cond	Time	First 3 Finishers	
23Aug79-6Hol	1	:283	:584	1:29	1:583ft	*6-5	4	3	21½o	11	63	Parker Jack Jr1	Nw50000 79	1:592	Trentonian, Hello Birdie, RomanChapel	10
3Aug79-Mdw	1	:29	:572	1:264	1:56 ft	*4-5	1	1	1	13	14½	Parker Jack Jr1	Cd	1:56	Dells Court, For Kicks, Artillery	8
28Jly79-Mdw	1	:284	:59	1:272	1:554ft	13	2	2	3	31¾	3¾	Parker Jack Jr6	Opn	1:56	MtrixHnovr,BonnysColdFront,DllsCourt	8
18Jly79-Mdw	1	:291	:594	1:292	1:57 gd	*4-5	2o	1	1	12	12¾	Parker Jack Jr6	Cd	1:57	Dells Court, Richards Choice, Gordarrig	8
13Jly79-Mdw	1	:283	:58	1:271	1:562ft	7¼	2	2o	2o	12	2hd	Parker Jack Jr2	Cd	1:562	Trentonian, Dells Court, Riva	8

8 — 3-1

Driver—GOUDREAU SHELLY. Trainer—James Brian. Red and Gold

B. C. Count — Blk. g. 7, by Tar Duke—Reeds Phalla, by Reeds Knight
Own.—Charles H. Meyers, Escondido, Cal.
Br.—J&R Graham (Can)

Lifetime— $285,620; 1979 30 6 6 4 $75,360; 1978 31 8 2 6 $49,678; 1:57, GG , '78; 1:563, MDW, '79

Date-Trk	Dist	¼	½	¾	fin	Odds	¼	½	¾	str	fin	Driver PP	Cond	Time	First 3 Finishers	
15Sep79-8Hol	1	:29	:584	1:264	1:562ft	3	2	3	33	32	54¼	Lighthill Joe1	Inv	1:571	TenderLovingCre,PeterOnedin,Dsmond	5
8Sep79-9Hol	1	:283	:582	1:283	1:571ft	4¼	4	4	44½	41¾	2nk	Lighthill Joe3	Inv	1:572	Sprinkler, B. C. Count, Peter Onedin	6
1Sep79-8Hol	1	:284	:592	1:274	1:59 ft	3-2	4	3o	22o	11½	23¼	Lighthill Joe4	Inv	1:594	Craig Del, B. C. Count, Young Million	5
25Aug79-6Hol	1	:293	:584	1:273	1:572ft	*4-5	4	4	45	23	21¼	Lighthill Joe4	Inv	1:574	Silver Warrior, B. C.Count,PeterOnedin	4
28Jly79-Mdw	1	:293	:583	1:28	1:563ft	3	5	3o	1o	12½	11	Remmen Ray2	Nw20000	1:563	B CCount,StapletonPlace,BretsRichard	10
19Jly79-Mdw	1	:29	:571	1:264	1:554ft	*2½	6	6	4o	31½	2hd	Remmen Ray2	Nw15000	1:554	April Bay, B C Count, Noble Hartack	10

9 — 12-1

Driver—ACKERMAN D R. Tr.—Ackerman Doug, Asst., D R Ackerman. Blue and Grey

Archie Hanover — B. h. 5, by Best of All—Armbro Nymph, by Overtrick
Own.—Richard S. Staley, Beverly Hills, Cal.
Br.—Hanover Shoe Farms, Inc (Ill)

Lifetime— $156,238; 1979 23 3 4 5 $26,810; 1978 35 5 8 5 $67,295; 1:574, HOL, '78; 1:591, LA , '79

Date-Trk	Dist	¼	½	¾	fin	Odds	¼	½	¾	str	fin	Driver PP	Cond	Time	First 3 Finishers	
22Sep79-9Hol	1	:292	:592	1:282	1:563ft	7¾	9	9	97½	84	87¾	Ackerman D R8	Wo 10000	1:581	Little To Ri, Craig Del, Torpids Knight	9
8Sep79-HP	1	:291	1:011	1:31	2:004ft	*8-5	5	5	5o	1½	12	Ackerman Doug4	Nw5800 L6	2:004	Archie Hanover,Holland,GoodAlbatross	10
1Sep79-HP	1	:293	1:002	1:294	2:00 ft	13	2	3	4	52½	4nk	Ackerman D R5	Wo 10000	2:00	Quick Luck, Tall Oaks Jade, BlazerChip	10
25Aug79-HP	1	:284	1:003	1:294	1:592ft	6¾	7	5o	2o	43	53¾	Ackerman D R4	Wo 10000	2:001	Cedar Ridge, Caveats Egypt,THForrest	10
18Aug79-HP	1	:29	:592	1:294	2:00 gd	17	4	1	1	11	32	Ackerman D R1	Wo 10000	2:002	April Bay, Blazer Chip, Archie Hanover	10
4Aug79-HP	1	:294	1:011	1:304	1:594ft	4½	6	6	6o	65	55½	Ackerman D R6	Wo 10000	2:01	CedarRidge,HickoryCourier,BronRichrd	10

$5 Exacta
1 1/16 MILE TROT

PURSE $21,700 **6th Race**

THE SUPER BOWL STAKES. Purse, $21,700. 4-year-olds and upward. Non-winners of $50,000 in 1979.

1 — S H Song (8-1)

Driver—LIGHTHILL JOE. Trainer—Thornton Eugene. Green, White and Gold
Blk. g. 10, by Spinning Song—Hallie Cash, by William Cash
Own.—E. D. Glasco, Caruthers, Cal.
Br.—G. L. Bachert (Ill) 2:013, HOL, '78 2:021, HOL, '79

Lifetime— $75,493
1979 19 3 2 8 $28,761
1978 29 7 8 4 $41,078

Date Trk	Dist	¼	½	¾	fin	Odds	¼	½	¾	str	fin	Driver PP	Cond	Time	First 3 Finishers	
20Sep79-6Hol	1	:31	1:021	1:322	2:033ft	*1-2	5	3o	11½	12	13½	Lighthill Joe4	Nevele Pride	2:033	S H Song, FlyingSquad,PompanoPrince	5
14Sep79-2Hol	1	:311	1:014	1:301	2:012ft	18	5	5	33o	24	53¼	Lighthill Joe4	Nw 4000 1st	2:02	Compadre, Rocket Force, Lumber Joy	7
8Sep79-4Hol	1	:314	1:014	1:304	2:013ft	4¾	1	2	22	33	32	Lighthill Joe3	Nw15000 79	2:02	Mac Breton, Holy Cord, S H Song	5
1Sep79-2Hol	1	:304	1:011	1:32	2:021ft	4	4	1	11	12	11	Lighthill Joe5	Nw15000 79	2:021	S H Song, Wyn Darnley, Lumber Joy	7
22Aug79-Hol	1	:311	1:03	1:334	2:041ft		5	2o	21½o	21	3nk	Lighthill Joe2	Qua	2:041	NandinaSpecial,PompnoPrince,SHSong	6
7Jun79-5Sac	1	:31	1:033	1:343	2:034ft	3	4	4	36½	37	34	Ratchford Tom4	Cd	2:043	Dante Jay, Jeffs Pride, S H Song	5

2 — Rocket Force (5-1)

Driver—ACKERMAN D R. Tr.—Ackerman Doug, Asst., D R Ackerman. Blue and Grey
B. h. 4, by Speedy Scot—Right Away, by Bombs Away
Own.—Richard Staley, Beverly Hills, Cal
Br.—F L Vanlennep (Mich) 2:05, DET, '78 2:022, Hol, '79

Lifetime— $92,333
1979 18 4 3 1 $17,896
1978 40 8 9 8 $29,505

Date Trk	Dist	¼	½	¾	fin	Odds	¼	½	¾	str	fin	Driver PP	Cond	Time	First 3 Finishers	
21Sep79-4Hol	1	:303	1:003	1:304	2:002ft	6	5	5	42½o	32	2½	Ackerman D R5	Nw4000 1st	2:003	Compadre, Rocket Force, Mac Breton	6
14Sep79-2Hol	1	:311	1:014	1:301	2:012ft	10	7	7	77	45½	21½	Ackerman D R6	Nw 4000 1st	2:013	Compadre, Rocket Force, Lumber Joy	7
11Sep79-7Hol	1	:303	1:021	1:322	2:022ft	2	6	4o	32½o	32	11	Ackerman D R5	Nw7500 79	2:022	Rocket Force, El Vee Jay, HuntersGold	8
31Aug79-HP	1	:281	:591	1:30	2:014ft	12	7	5o	4	55½	66½	Ackerman D R5	Stk	2:031	Sunshine Barb,PortSail,ShiawayPatrich	9
23Aug79-HP	1	:30	1:012	1:32	2:032ft	2	5	4o	2	23	28	Ackerman D R6	Stk	2.05	SunshineBarb,RockertForce,OksRocket	9
18Aug79-HP	1	:30	1:011	1:323	2:042ft	6	6	6	7	63½	11	Ackerman D R4	Wo10000	2:051	RocketForce,ProspectPride,StarsBlend	9

3 — Arnies Dart (6-1)

Driver–Trainer— DENNIS TED. White and Blue
B. g. 4, by Arnie Almahurst—Picture Dart, by Dartmouth
Own.—Clyde D Genz, Boca Raton, Fla
Br.—Castleton Farm (Ky) 2:031, MEA, '78 1:584, MDW, '79

Lifetime— $49,209
1979 16 4 2 0 $22,955
1978 22 2 4 2 $8,348

Date Trk	Dist	¼	½	¾	fin	Odds	¼	½	¾	str	fin	Driver PP	Cond	Time	First 3 Finishers	
22Sep79-6Hol	1⅛	:283	:583	1:29	2:122ft	39	4	1	11½	43	610	McNeil Archie6	Amr T Clssc	2:142	JurgyHnover,KeystonePionr,CrownsStr	7
15Sep79-6Hol	1 1/16	:283	:573	1:274	2:05 ft	39	1	1	11½	2hd	811	Dennis Ted7	Amr T Clssc	2:071	JurgyHanover,ImaLul,KeystonePioneer	8
7Sep79-6Hol	1	:292	1:011	1:304	2:00 ft	24	x7	6	78¼	79¾	720	McNeil Archie2	Amr T Clssc	2:041	Jurgy Hanover, Ima Lula, Crowns Star	8
31Aug79-7Hol	1	:30	1:001	1:301	1:592ft	5¾	x8	7o	64½o	75¾	714	Dennis Ted6	Amr T Clssc	2:021	JurgyHnover,MedowDemojo,Gttysburg	8
24Aug79-6Hol	1	:29	:584	1:29	1:594ft	11	1	1	13	11½	1no	Dennis Ted6	Inv	1:594	Arnies Dart, Meadow Demojo,HolyCord	7
17Aug79-Mdw	1	:282	:581	1:284	2:024ft	2½	1	1	1	11½	21½	McNeil Archie4	Inv H	2:03	Super Marty, ArniesDart,LanceHanover	10

4 — Bettors Cup (10-1)

Driver—AUBIN MARC. Trainer—Luster George. Blue, Red and White
Br. m. 4, by Bettors Choice—Sidcup, by Sharpshooter
Own.—Edith Shaw & Irwin S Soper, Via Benton, Cal
Br.—P G Smith (NC) 2:023, LEX, '78 2:031, DET, '79

Lifetime— $46,868
1979 27 2 1 8 $23,333
1978 25 5 2 3 $22,177

Date Trk	Dist	¼	½	¾	fin	Odds	¼	½	¾	str	fin	Driver PP	Cond	Time	First 3 Finishers	
31Aug79-7Hol	1	:30	1:001	1:301	1:592ft	36	3	4	53	42½	47¼	Aubin Marc1	Amr T Clssc	2:004	JurgyHnover,MedowDemojo,Gttysburg	8
7Aug79-VD	1	:282	:592	1:294	2:002ft	14	4	4	4	43	46½	Hult A5	Nw1500	2:013	Sohys Baron, Barbo Assassin,MontStar	8
31Jly79-VD	1	:30	1:033	1:34	2:053ft	15	4	4	4	46½	35	Hult A2	Nw1500	2:063	Coaltown G B, Mont Star, Bettors Cup	8
24Jly79-VD	1	:291	1:012	1:321	2:02 ft	13	5	4	3	32	2¾	O'Brien Joe4	Nw1500	2:021	Mont Star, Bettors Cup, BarboAssassin	8
11Jly79-VD	1	:30	1:02	1:323	2:022ft	5½	4	4	5	53	56¼	Smith Preston2	Nw800	2:033	SpeedyGypsy,NncyBluechip,JubileesJog	8
6Jly79-VD	1	:291	1:003	1:304	2:003ft	48	7	7	7	79¼	714	Smith Preston7	Inv H	2:032	SpringVictory,SuperWay,BarboAssassin	8

5 — Holy Cord (6-1)

Driver—BAYLESS STAN. Trainer—McGonagle Pat. Gold and White
B. g. 8, by Holy Hal N—Cordette, by Ripcord
Own.—Arnold Zonis & Samuel Levine, Los Angeles, Cal
Br.—J D Morrison (NZ) 2:00, HOL, '78 2:012, LA, '79

Lifetime— $81,935
1979 26 4 4 4 $41,119
1978 22 4 8 3 $33,812

Date Trk	Dist	¼	½	¾	fin	Odds	¼	½	¾	str	fin	Driver PP	Cond	Time	First 3 Finishers	
21Sep79-4Hol	1	:303	1:003	1:304	2:002ft	*6-5	1	1	11	11	41	Bayless Stan1	Nw4000 1st	2:003	Compadre, Rocket Force, Mac Breton	6
14Sep79-2Hol	1	:311	1:014	1:301	2:012ft	*8-5	3	3	11o	14	42¼	VllndinghmGene1	Nw 4000 1st	2:014	Compadre, Rocket Force, Lumber Joy	7
8Sep79-4Hol	1	:314	1:014	1:304	2:013ft	*1	4	4	33½o	21	21	VllndinghmGene5	Nw15000 79	2:014	Mac Breton, Holy Cord, S H Song	5
31Aug79-7Hol	1	:30	1:001	1:301	1:592ft	9¼	7	8	75½	63¾	57¼	VllndinghmGen8	Amr T Clssc	2:004	JurgyHnover,MedowDemojo,Gttysburg	8
24Aug79-6Hol	1	:29	:584	1:29	1:594ft	4¾	6	6	47½o	44½	3¾	Vallandingham Gene5	Inv	2:00	Arnies Dart, Meadow Demojo,HolyCord	7
17Aug79-Hol	1	:314	1:04	1:34	2:04 ft		4	6	65¼	54½	4nk	Vallandingham Gene1	Qua	2:04	Royal York N, MalEspri,JohnHanoverN	7

6 — Tuteena (4-1)

Driver–Trainer— PARKER JACK JR. Maroon, Blue and White
Br. h. 7, by Tuft—Utenna, by U Scott
Own.—Jack Parker Jr & Donald Alfano, Harrington, Del
Br.—Mrs M. P. & R. C. Monk (NZ) 1:594, LA, '78 2:022, LA, '79

Lifetime— $111,884
1979 26 4 3 5 $41,049
1978 28 9 4 3 $47,636

Date Trk	Dist	¼	½	¾	fin	Odds	¼	½	¾	str	fin	Driver PP	Cond	Time	First 3 Finishers	
22Sep79-6Hol	1⅛	:283	:583	1:29	2:122ft	32	3	4	53½	64½	45	Parker Jack Jr1	Amr T Clssc	2:133	JurgyHnover,KeystonePionr,CrownsStr	7
15Sep79-6Hol	1 1/16	:283	:573	1:274	2:05 ft	40	5	5	76¼	74	56½	Parker Jack Jr4	Amr T Clssc	2:061	JurgyHanover,ImaLul,KeystonePioneer	8
31Aug79-7Hol	1	:30	1:001	1:301	1:592ft	31	4	3o	21o	53½	614	Beer Larry9	Amr T Clssc	2:021	JurgyHnover,MedowDemojo,Gttysburg	8
24Aug79-6Hol	1	:29	:584	1:29	1:594ft	5½	3	3	34½	33½	42¼	Beer Larry2	Inv	2:001	Arnies Dart, Meadow Demojo,HolyCord	7
3Aug79-7Sac	1	:311	1:013	1:322	2:023ft	3	3	4	42	31¼	23½	Beer Larry4	Inv	2:032	Dante Jay, Tuteena, Justly Joe	5
27Jly79-5Sac	1	:312	1:034	1:344	2:044ft	*6-5	1	1	11	12	2½	Beer Larry4	InvH	2:05	Dante Jay, Tuteena, Sonesta	5

7 — Pompano Prince (20-1)

Driver—TODD JAMES II. Trainer—Eckert Gary. Royal, Blue and Grey
B. g. 6, by Pompano Flash—Proud Countess, by Hickory Pride
Own.—David, Syliva & Jack Silvers, Hollywood, Cal.
Br.—R A McKenzie (NZ) No Record in U.S., '78 No Record, '79

Lifetime— $19,778
1979 12 0 1 3 $5,443
1978 29 2 6 4 $9,964

Date Trk	Dist	¼	½	¾	fin	Odds	¼	½	¾	str	fin	Driver PP	Cond	Time	First 3 Finishers	
27Sep79-4Hol	1	:301	1:013	1:321	2:024ft	6½	3	2	2hd	2½	61¾	Todd James Ii6	Nw 6000 79	2:032	Noble Victory N, El Vee Jay, Yadran	8
20Sep79-6Hol	1	:31	1:021	1:322	2:033ft	8¾	2o	4	43½	33½	34¾	Todd James II5	Nevele Pride	2:043	S H Song, FlyingSquad,PompanoPrince	5
15Sep79-Hol	1	:302	1:012	1:32	2:032ft		2	2	21	12	14	Todd James II5	Qua	2:032	Pompano Prince, Earl Dart, Speedy Sir	7
11Sep79-7Hol	1	:303	1:021	1:322	2:022ft	9¼	x8	8	89¼	812	812	Parker Jack Jr2	Nw7500 79	2:044	Rocket Force, El Vee Jay, HuntersGold	8
5Sep79-Hol	1	:30	1:02	1:323	2:043ft		1	1	12	12	1½	Parker Jack Jr4	Qua	2:043	PompanoPrince,LincolnsGale,PowerCut	8
1Sep79-2Hol	1	:304	1:011	1:32	2:021ft	22	x7x	x7x	7dis	7dis	7dis	Parker Jack Jr6	Nw15000 79	—	S H Song, Wyn Darnley, Lumber Joy	7

8 — Meadow Demojo (3-1)

Driver—GOUDREAU SHELLY. Trainer—James Brian. Red and Gold
B. h. 5, by Super Bowl—Meadow Split, by Kimberly Kid
Own.—Charles H Meyers, Escondido, Cal
Br.—D Miller (Pa) 2:014, BRD, '78 2:014, YR, '79

Lifetime— $74,654
1979 22 4 5 6 $47,580
1978 17 3 3 4 $19,947

Date Trk	Dist	¼	½	¾	fin	Odds	¼	½	¾	str	fin	Driver PP	Cond	Time	First 3 Finishers	
15Sep79-6Hol	1 1/16	:283	:573	1:274	2:05 ft	24	x7	6	43½o	63½	710	Lighthill Joe1	Amr T Clssc	2:07	JurgyHanover,ImaLul,KeystonePioneer	8
7Sep79-6Hol	1	:292	1:011	1:304	2:00 ft	6½	6	7	66¾	64¾	56¼	Lighthill Joe7	Amr T Clssc	2:012	Jurgy Hanover, Ima Lula, Crowns Star	8
31Aug79-7Hol	1	:30	1:001	1:301	1:592ft	2½	1	2	31½	21½	23½	Lighthill Joe2	Amr T Clssc	2:001	JurgyHnover,MedowDemojo,Gttysburg	8
24Aug79-6Hol	1	:29	:584	1:29	1:594ft	*9-5	2	2	23	21½	2no	Lighthill Joe1	Inv	1:594	Arnies Dart, Meadow Demojo,HolyCord	7
3Aug79-RR	1	:293	1:004	1:312	2:02 ft	3¼	6	5o	4o	x77¼	x712	Remmen Ray3	Hcp0	2:042	IdleLove,ArborScreenStr,SelneryMoors	9
26Jly79-RR	1	:31	1:031	1:354	2:06 gd	*9-5	5	3o	2o	2½	3¾	Remmen Ray4	Hcp0	2:061	WnstonHnovr,ArborScrnStr,MdowDmoj	9

9 — Compadre (6-1)

Driver—DESOMER STEVE. Trainer—McGonagle Pat. Blue and White
B. g. 7, by Jerry Adios—Solina, by Light Brigade
Own.—Our Gang Stable, Sherman Oaks Cal
Br.—C R Berkett (NZ) 2:044, LA, '78 2:002, Hol, '79

Lifetime— $29,303
1979 13 4 2 0 $18,139
1978 3 1 0 0 $3,150

Date Trk	Dist	¼	½	¾	fin	Odds	¼	½	¾	str	fin	Driver PP	Cond	Time	First 3 Finishers	
21Sep79-4Hol	1	:303	1:003	1:304	2:002ft	3	6	6	64½	53½	1½	Desomer Steve6	Nw4000 1st	2:002	Compadre, Rocket Force, Mac Breton	6
14Sep79-2Hol	1	:311	1:014	1:301	2:012ft	7¾	6	6	55o	34½	11½	Goudreau Shelly5	Nw 4000 1st	2:012	Compadre, Rocket Force, Lumber Joy	7
6Sep79-7Hol	1	:303	1:012	1:322	2:031ft	*4-5	3	1	11½	13	15	Hunter Charles6	16000 H	2:031	Compadre,DaktriHnover,SnoopyRodney	6
30Aug79-8Hol	1	:312	1:021	1:331	2:04 ft	*9-5	2	1o	12	15	2¾	Hunter Charles6	16000 H	2:041	Daktari Hanover, Compadre, Justly Joe	6
22Aug79-Hol	1	:311	1:03	1:334	2:041ft		6	6	69½o	42¼	52¼	Hunter Charles4	Qua	2:043	NandinaSpecial,PompnoPrince,SHSong	6
11May79-7Sac	1	:303	1:031	1:331	2:021ft	8	4	3o	2hdo	1½	43	Grundy James1	InvH	2:024	Staley Express, Rip Silver, S H Song	6

In accordance with CHRB Rule No 1606, Compadre and Holy Cord are uncoupled for wagering purposes only.

1 MILE PACE   PURSE $6,600   7th Race

CONDITIONED. Purse $6,600. All ages, non-winners of $10,000 in 1979. Bred in California. Also eligible: Non-winners of $3,000 1st money since September 1, 1979.

	Date	Trk	Dist	1/4	1/2	3/4	fin	Odds	1/4	1/2	3/4	str	fin	Driver PP	Cond	Time	First 3 Finishers

1   **5-2**
Driver–Trainer– ADAMS CECIL.
Trickel Charger
Turquoise and White   Lifetime— $55,653
Blk. h. 4, by Bye Bye Max—Phyllis Crest Duke, by Cedar Crst Dke   1979   22   5   2   4 $20,019
Own.—Cecil Adams, Hemet, Cal.   1978   33   6   7   2 $32,042
Br.—M Featherstone (Cal)   2:01¹, SAC, '78   1:58, SAC, '79

31Aug79-5Hol	1	:30	:58³	1:28⁴	1:58³ft	5½	5	5	21½o	23	45	Adams Cecil³	Ⓢ Wo10000 1:59³	Desmond, Howdy Mon, Bye Bye Victor	9
25Aug79-5Hol	1	:29³	1:00	1:29²	1:59 ft	7½	3	5	54o	22	1no	Adams Cecil¹	Ⓢ Wo 10000 1:59	Trickel Charger, Desmond, Howdy Mon	8
4Aug79-7Sac	1	:30	:59³	1:30²	1:59⁴ft	4³	2x	5	5dis	5dis	5dis	Adams Cecil³	Inv H	J C Heel, Spry Sam, James Mission	5
28Jly79-5Sac	1	:29¹	:59⁴	1:28²	1:58 ft	4	2	2	15	18	11¾	Adams Cecil³	Ⓢ Calbrds Stk 1:58	TrickelChrger,HowdyMon,AndysHound	5
20Jly79-5Sac	1	:31³	1:02	1:31³	2:01³ft	2½	5	5	3²	55	51¹	Adams Cecil⁴	Ⓢ InⁿH 2:02²	Placerville, Howdy Mon, Andys Hound	5

2   **7-2**
Driver–Trainer– MCGREGOR JOHN.
Bye Bye Viehover
Orange and White   Lifetime— $101,634
B. h. 5, by Bye Bye Max—Artic Wave, by Shadow Wave   1979   11   0   2   1 $5,538
Own.—J N McGregor, R Viehover & L WJarvis,LosAngeles,Cal.   1978   28   7   3   7 $37,512
Br.—J McGregor & R Viehover (Cal)   2:00¹, HOL, '78   No Record , '79

14Sep79-4Hol	1	:29²	:59⁴	1:27	1:57⁴ft	16	2	2	22	22½	47	McGregorJohn⁶	Ⓢ Nw10000 79 1:59¹	Indian Chief, Andys Hound, Placerville	9
1Sep79-3Hol	1	:29	:59²	1:30¹	2:00¹ft	5½	1	2	11	11	56½	Lighthill Joe²	Ⓢ Nw5000 79 2:01¹	WelshKiwi,SoldiersBold,ColonelButlrN	10
25Aug79-9Hol	1	:29³	1:00	1:29²	1:59 ft	25	5	6	75¾	65¾	67	Lighthill Joe²	Ⓢ Wo 10000 2:00²	Trickel Charger, Desmond, Howdy Mon	8
3Aug79-9Sac	1	:29⁴	:59¹	1:30³	2:00¹ft	2½	2	2	2½	33½	48½	Lighthill Joe³	Ⓢ Inv H 2:02	HowdyMon,RareDesign,LumberChrmer	6
24Jly79-4Sac	1	:31¹	1:03²	1:34⁴	2:03⁴ft	*3-5	1	1	12	11	22½	McGregor John³	Ⓢ InⁿH 2:04²	Rey Rico, Bye Bye Viehover,WhiskyJim	4

3   **12-1**
Driver– BAYLESS STAN. Trainer—McGonagle Pat.
Desert Beauty
Gold and White   Lifetime— $32,326
B. f. 3, by Desert Dancer—Judy Freeman, by Freeman Hanover   1979   17   4   6   0 $18,343
Own.—Arnold G. Zonis, Los Angeles, Cal.   1978   17   1   3   3 $13,983
Br.—LV&AMJohnson–JA&FJamt (Cl)   2:06, SAC, '78   2:01⁴, SAC, '79

14Sep79-4Hol	1	:29²	:59⁴	1:27	1:57⁴ft	22	7	7	77¾o	69	713	Desomer Steve⁴	Ⓢ Nw10000 79 2:00²	Indian Chief, Andys Hound, Placerville	9
1Sep79-6Hol	1	:30¹	1:01³	1:31²	2:02¹ft	3½	2	1	1½	12	617	DesomerSteve²	Ⓟ Ⓢ Red Rose 2:05⁴	Fourth Rose, Pickalady, My Little Rose	6
25Aug79-8Hol	1	:30²	1:00	1:31	2:01¹ft	3½	9	x8	9dis	9dis	9dis	VllndinghmGn⁹	Ⓢ Gold Medal	Fourth Rose, MontereyDream,ShadyDel	9
27Jly79-6Sac	1	:30¹	1:00⁴	1:31³	2:01⁴ft	4½	8	5	42	2½	11½	Desomer Steve⁸	Ⓕ Stk 2:01⁴	DesertBeauty,HillbillyFilly,SpotlightGal	9
13Jly79-5Sac	1	:29⁴	1:01³	1:32³	2:01 ft	8	7	7	31½o	42½	2¹½	Desomer Steve⁸	Ⓢ Stk 2:01⁴	FourthRose,DesertBeauty,BodyChecker	9

4   **3-1**
Driver– KUEBLER RICK. Trainer—Stein Roger.
Placerville
Blue and Yellow   Lifetime— $56,916
Br. h. 6, by Sirius—Sutters Gold, by Great Colby   1979   27   4   0   4 $11,647
Own.—My Hero Racing Stable, Northridge, Cal   1978   36   8   4   6 $30,610
Br.—B C & E Ruben (Cal)   2:00¹, GG , '78   1:58⁴, SAC, '79

21Sep79-7Hol	1	:29³	:58⁴	1:29	1:58³ft	7½	3o	1	1nk	1½	106½	Kuebler Rick⁶	22000 H 2:00	Rey Rico, Oakie's Image, Jambo Dollar	10
14Sep79-4Hol	1	:29²	:59⁴	1:27	1:57⁴ft	9	1	1	12	12½	32½	Kuebler Rick⁵	Ⓢ Nw10000 79 1:58¹	Indian Chief, Andys Hound, Placerville	9
8Sep79-6Hol	1	:29³	:59²	1:29	1:58²ft	37	1	2	3¹	32	81²	KueblerRick⁸	Ⓢ Hall Of Fame 2:00⁴	Desmond, Taijamon, Howdy Mon	8
5Sep79-6Hol	1	:29²	1:00¹	1:31	2:00²ft	9	1	2	2¹½	32½	35	Kuebler Rick⁶	20000 2:01²	Jambo Dollar, Baker Hill, Placerville	7
31Aug79-5Hol	1	:30	:58³	1:28⁴	1:58³ft	16	2	3	54½	58½	89¾	Kuebler Rick⁶	Ⓢ Wo10000 2:00³	Desmond, Howdy Mon, Bye Bye Victor	9

5   **5-1**
Driver—LONGO GERALD. Trainer—Harper Marvin.
Stud Poker
Green and Black   Lifetime— $55,098
B. g. 5, by Argo Pat—Milly Pegasus, by True Heart   1979   22   1   4   4 $12,555
Own.—Marvin M Harper, Newcastle, Cal   1978   34   11   2   4 $42,262
Br.—J D Chandler (Cal)   1:59, HOL, '78   2:03², LA , '79

14Sep79-4Hol	1	:29²	:59⁴	1:27	1:57⁴ft	12	6	6	55¾o	58x	9dis	Harper Marvin³	Ⓢ Nw10000 79	Indian Chief, Andys Hound. Placerville	9
8Sep79-6Hol	1	:29³	:59²	1:29	1:58²ft	39	4	4	85½	75½	67¾	HarperMrvin³	Ⓢ Hall Of Fame 2:00	Desmond, Taijamon, Howdy Mon	8
5Sep79-9Hol	1	:30³	1:00⁴	1:31	2:00²ft	7	7o	7	53¾o	77½	717	Harper Marvin⁵	Qua 2:03⁴	NativeRocket,BertGlenvale,SmrtPrince	9
31Aug79-5Hol	1	:30	:58³	1:28⁴	1:58³ft	7	3	2o	3²	9dis	9dis	Goudreau Shelly¹	Ⓢ Wo10000	Desmond, Howdy Mon, Bye Bye Victor	9
24Aug79-7Hol	1	:30²	1:01³	1:31³	2:01 ft	6	1	4	42¾	42½x	8dis	Harper Marvin⁴	Ⓢ Nw5000 Lst6	Argyll, J R Decker, Heroic Hanover	7

6   **10-1**
Driver—SHERREN FRANK. Trainer—Sherren Jack.
My Little Rose
Green, White and Black   Lifetime— $15,468
B. f. 3, by Hunters Star—Diamante Queen, by Junior Maplecroft   1979   33   4   6   7 $14,464
Own.—Joseph Nessim Benon, Beverly Hills,Cal.   1978   5   0   1   0 $1,004
Br.—J N Benon (Cal)   No Record , '78   2:02¹, SAC, '79

19Sep79-4Hol	1	:29⁴	1:00	1:30¹	2:00⁴ft	40	9	9	87	87½	32¾	Sherren Jack⁸	Ⓢ Nw5 2:01²	Shady Del, Andys Winner,MyLittleRose	9
13Sep79-7Hol	1	:30³	1:01	1:31³	2:01¹ft	18	7	7	75¾o	65¼	78	Sherren Jack⁷	Nw5 2:02⁴	Dellborough, Sonar, Gedar	9
5Sep79-9Hol	1	:30³	1:00⁴	1:33²	2:03¹ft	7½	5	5	55½	48	35	Sherren Jack⁵	Nw5 2:04¹	Sonar, Shady Del, My Little Rose	7
1Sep79-6Hol	1	:30¹	1:01³	1:31²	2:02²ft	20	6	6	65½	54¾	35½	Sherren Jack⁴	Ⓟ Ⓢ Red Rose 2:03³	Fourth Rose, Pickalady, My Little Rose	6
25Aug79-8Hol	1	:30²	1:00	1:31	2:01¹ft	4½	6	5	55½	713	615	Sherren Jack⁵	Ⓢ Gold Medal 2:04¹	Fourth Rose, MontereyDream,ShadyDel	9

7   **6-1**
Driver–Trainer– TISHER KEVIN.
Geometric
Light Blue and Dark Blue   Lifetime— $12,599
B. c. 3, by Scottish Design—Beauty Sampson, by Sampson Hanover   1979   6   3   0   0 $6,526
Own.—K.C.Tisher–Dan R. Tullio, Long Beach, Cal.   1978   14   1   5   2 $6,073
Br.—A E Bahouth (Cal)   2:07, SAC, '78   2:01, Hol, '79

19Sep79-4Hol	1	:29⁴	1:00	1:30¹	2:00⁴ft	*1	2	4	75½	65¼x	79	Tisher Kevin²	Ⓢ Nw5 2:01²	Shady Del, Andys Winner,MyLittleRose	9
12Sep79-9Hol	1	:30¹	1:01	1:31	2:01 ft	3e	4	6	54¼o	32½	13	Tisher Kevin³	Ⓢ Nw 2:01	Geometric, Andys Winner, Gen's Guest	9
6Sep79-4Hol	1	:31¹	1:02¹	1:33²	2:04²ft	8½	2o	2	31½	32½	12	Tisher Kevin⁸	Ⓢ Nw3 2:04²	Geometric, Fox Hound, Maxilla	8
25Aug79-8Hol	1	*:30²	1:00	1:31	2:01¹ft	24	4x	9	8dis	8dis	8dis	Tisher Kevin³	Ⓢ Gold Medal	Fourth Rose, MontereyDream,ShadyDel	9
31Jly79-9Sac	1	:29⁴	1:00⁴	1:32⁴	2:03³ft	8	7	7	66½	22	13	Tisher Kevin⁸	Ⓢ Nw2 2:03³	Geometric,TheComdyAwrd,MontryDrm	9

8   **20-1**
Driver–Trainer– DESOMER STEVE.
Gedar
Blue and White   Lifetime— $22,821
Br. g. 3, by Dutch Hill Prince—Lady B. Gay, by Gayliner   1979   9   1   0   2 $3,152
Own.—Desomer Stables, Inc., Elk Grove, Cal   1978   13   3   5   2 $19,669
Br.—H D Brahm W E Jobe (Cal)   2:02⁴, HOL, '78   2:04³, BM , '79

19Sep79-4Hol	1	:29⁴	1:00	1:30¹	2:00⁴ft	21	3o	1	21½	43½	44	Desomer Steve⁷	Ⓢ Nw5 2:01³	Shady Del, Andys Winner,MyLittleRose	9
13Sep79-7Hol	1	:30³	1:01	1:31³	2:01¹ft	46	2	3	33	33	34	Desomer Steve³	Nw5 2:02	Dellborough, Sonar, Gedar	9
5Sep79-9Hol	1	:31²	1:03¹	1:33²	2:03¹ft	11	2	2	32½	33	45½	Desomer Steve¹	Nw5 2:04¹	Sonar, Shady Del, My Little Rose	7
25Aug79-8Hol	1	:30²	1:00	1:31	2:01¹ft	13	3	2	21½	34½	715	DesomerSteve¹	Ⓢ Gold Medal 2:04¹	Fourth Rose, MontereyDream,ShadyDel	9
2Aug79-9Sac	1	:32	1:03³	1:35¹	2:04³ft	13	4	4	51⁷	54½	32	Desomer Steve⁵	Ⓢ Nw5 2:05	Body Checker, San Andreas, Gedar	9

9   **30-1**
Driver—RITCHIE ROBERT. Trainer—Slagter Ralph.
Hot Lips Rankin
Black, Gold and White   Lifetime— $26,908
B. m. 6, by J. H. Primrose—Pixie Rankin, by Newman Hanover   1979   2   0   0   0
Own.—Ralph or Harriet Slagter, Reseda, Cal   1978   37   4   5   5 $13,670
Br.—R Slagter (Cal)   2:02, HOL, '78   No Record , '79

21Sep79-1Hol	1	:29²	:59²	1:29²	2:00²ft	22	9	10	1013o	1012	1017	Ritchie Robert⁶	Ⓕ Nw 5000 L6 2:03⁴	True Gypsy, True Mission, TyroleanGirl	10
12Sep79-Hol	1	:31³	1:03³	1:33³	2:03⁴ft	3	4	33½	33	33	NewportFlowr,DoublKing,HotLipsRnkin	Ritchie Robert⁵	Qua 2:04²		8
5Sep79-Hol	1	:30⁴	1:02	1:32²	2:03¹ft	9	6²⁴	624	618	Ritchie Robert⁷	Qua 2:06⁴	Trevino, Liberated Lady, Courtney		9
3Aug79-9Sac	1	:29⁴	:59¹	1:30³	2:00¹ft	29	4	4	51²	519	6dis	Ritchie Robert¹	Ⓢ Inv H	HowdyMon,RareDesign,LumberChrmer	6
28Jly79-Sac	1	:31	1:02¹	1:34	2:03³ft	6	6	620	Ritchie Robert⁶	Qua 2:06³	Welsh Kiwi, TarportBlack,VarietyAgain		8

10   **15-1**
Driver—LACOSTE LEO. Trainer—Blue Bill.
Pickalady
Blue and White   Lifetime— $27,287
B. f. 3, by Hunters Star—Lady Abadios, by Adios Pick   1979   12   3   2   0 $13,179
Own.—F&L.Binder–J.&R.Branca, West Covina, Cal.   1978   11   2   4   1 $14,108
Br.—P Bielec (Cal)   2:02³, HOL, '78   2:01², SAC, '79

21Sep79-6Hol	1	:28³	:58¹	1:27⁴	1:57 ft	31	7	7	88½	98½	921	LaCoste Leo⁵	Ⓨ Young Miss 2:01²	Retriever, Spotlight Gal, Fourth Rose	9
1Sep79-6Hol	1	:30¹	1:01³	1:31²	2:02²ft	12	3	3²	22	22	LaCoste Leo³	Ⓟ Ⓢ Red Rose 2:03	Fourth Rose, Pickalady, My Little Rose	6
25Aug79-8Hol	1	:30²	1:00	1:31	2:01¹ft	8½	1	1	11½	11½	48½	LaCoste Leo⁵	Ⓢ Gold Medal 2:02⁴	Fourth Rose, MontereyDream,ShadyDel	9
2Aug79-6Sac	1	:32³	1:02⁴	1:33¹	2:02⁴ft	6	x6	6	61²	610	69½	LaCoste Leo⁴	Ⓕ Hc2O 2:04⁴	Consuldo,MidnightChooChoo,Skippyell	6
27Jly79-6Sac	1	:30¹	1:00⁴	1:31³	2:01⁴ft	2	1	1	1½	42½	66¾	LaCoste Leo⁴	Ⓕ Stk 2:03¹	DesertBeauty,HillbillyFilly,SpotlightGal	9

DECLARED– WHISKY JIM and ANDY'S MERINO.

ORT CENTENIAL HANDICAP
Sylvia Kline, group representative

$5 Exacta
1 MILE PACE

PURSE $12,000 # 8th Race

INVITATIONAL HANDICAP. Purse $12,000. All ages. (Post positions assigned)

1 — 6-1

Driver—ACKERMAN D R. Tr.—Ackerman Doug, Asst., Ackerman D R. Blue and Grey

Baker's Knight

B. h. 4, by Knight Time—Worthy Joy, by Worthy Boy
Own.—Gaylord & Eugenia S Vere, Adrian, Mich
Br.—G & E Vere (Mich) 1:591, DET, '78

Lifetime— $106,446
1979 25 6 4 4 $49,009
1978 29 11 3 4 $30,126
1:58, DET, '79

Date	Trk	Dist	¼	½	¾	fin	Odds	¼	½	¾	str	fin	Driver PP	Cond	Time	First 3 Finishers	
21Sep79-8Hol		1	:283	:583	1:284	1:58 ft	2¾	5	4	23o	22	12¾	Ackerman D R6	Nw5000 Lst 6	1:58	Bker'sKnight,ProudBron,HeroicHnover	6
15Sep79-9Hol		1	:293	1:003	1:283	1:582ft	12	5	3	21o	21	51¼	Ackerman D R2	Wo 10000	1:584	Native Rocket,ArmbroTawny,LittleToRi	8
8Sep79-HP		1	:294	1:001	1:294	2:001ft	16	8	9	9	98	98¼	Ackerman Doug6	Wo 10000	2:014	Boone, Dodge Acres Larry, Steady Gait	10
18Aug79-HP		1	:293	1:013	1:31	2:011ft	3	x3	4	6x	718	717	Ackerman Doug1	Wo 10000	2:043	MnnrtStndOut,AntoniusHnover,TripMt	10
11Aug79-HP		1	:284	:59	1:293	2:002ft	*2	6	6o	7o	75	63¼	Ackerman Doug3	Wo 10000	2:01	TallOksJde,GirlOMyDrem,AndysHidewy	10
4Aug79-HP		1	:29	:582	1:28	1:58 ft	2½	7	6o	4o	33	23	Ackerman Doug4	Wo 10000	1:583	BlzerChip,BkersKnight,PrinceExposure	10

2 — 9-2

Driver-Trainer— PELLING BRIAN. Black, Red and Orange

Native Rocket

B. h. 6, by Overtrick—Miss Tee, by Airliner
Own.—O.M.R. Co Inc & B.R.P. EnterprisesCorp, Beverly Hills
Br.—M Zeinfeld (Ill) 1:573, MDW, '78

Lifetime— $107,618
1979 17 8 4 1 $57,090
1978 35 8 5 3 $47,394
1:572, LA , '79

Date	Trk	Dist	¼	½	¾	fin	Odds	¼	½	¾	str	fin	Driver PP	Cond	Time	First 3 Finishers	
22Sep79-8Hol		1	:293	:59	1:29	1:564ft	9¾	4	1o	11½	2hd	56	Pelling Brian3	Inv H	1:58	SprySm,TenderLovingCre,CordonArgnt	5
15Sep79-9Hol		1	:293	1:003	1:283	1:582ft	*6-5	6	5	42½o	31½	1½	Pelling Brian3	Wo 10000	1:582	Native Rocket,ArmbroTawny,LittleToRi	8
5Sep79-Hol		1	:303	1:004	1:303	2:002ft		5	1	11½	12	19	Vallandingham Gene6	Qua	2:002	NativeRocket,BertGlenvale,SmrtPrince	9
30Jun79-Spk		1	:31	1:001	1:313	2:02 gd	*9-5	3o	2o	2	21½	63¾	Pelling Brian7	Inv	2:024	Pl4]TrportExprss,PcingRobin,RiltoRng	8
23Jun79-Spk		1	:291	:593	1:284	1:582ft	4¼	5	3o	2o	32	49½	Pelling Brian3	HcpO	2:002	Tricky Dick N, Malice, Tarport Express	8
16Jun79-8Spk		1	:284	:59	1:283	1:582ft	4¾	5	6	65¾	64¼	46½	Pelling Brian4	HcpO	1:594	Tricky Dick N, Time Shadow, Malice	9

3 — 4-1

Driver—LONGO GERALD. Trainer—Eckert Gary. Green and Black

Peter Onedin

Br. g. 3, by Young Charles—Pacific Rain, by Pacific Hanover
Own.—Gary Eckert, Hawthorne, Cal
Br.—A L Stockdale (NZ) No Record , '78

Lifetime— $70,628
1979 24 6 4 6 $70,628
1978 0 0 0 0
1:59, MDW, '79

Date	Trk	Dist	¼	½	¾	fin	Odds	¼	½	¾	str	fin	Driver PP	Cond	Time	First 3 Finishers	
22Sep79-8Hol		1	:293	:59	1:29	1:564ft	5	1	2	21½	1hd	43¼	Parker Jack Jr4	Inv H	1:572	SprySm,TenderLovingCre,CordonArgnt	5
15Sep79-8Hol		1	:29	:584	1:264	1:562ft	8¾	1	2	21½	2½	22	Parker Jack Jr3	Inv	1:564	TenderLovingCre,PeterOnedin,Dsmond	6
8Sep79-9Hol		1	:283	:582	1:283	1:571ft	4¼	1	2	21½	31½	3½	Parker Jack Jr6	Inv	1:572	Sprinkler, B. C. Count, Peter Onedin	6
31Aug79-6Hol		1	:293	:591	1:284	1:574ft	14	1	3	43o	23	22¼	Parker Jack Jr5	Nw100000 79	1:581	Can Can Rhythm,PeterOnedin,Sprinkler	7
25Aug79-6Hol		1	:293	:584	1:273	1:572ft	2½	2	2	22	33½	38¼	Vallandingham Gene1	Inv	1:591	Silver Warrior, B. C.Count,PeterOnedin	4
3Aug79-Mdw		1	:284	:571	1:264	1:551ft	7¾	3o	2o	2o	65	711	Goudreau Shelly6	Open	1:573	DirectScooter,MilesEndSteve,PtsGypsy	10

4 — 7-2

Driver-Trainer— PARKER JACK JR. Maroon, Blue and White

Little To Ri

B. g. 5, by Adios Harry—Kerry Princess, by Noble Dean
Own.—First Time Stable, Florham Park N.J.
Br.—M.C. Vinyard (Del) 1:591, MDW, '78

Lifetime— $48,791
1979 26 4 1 3 $31,225
1978 21 6 3 2 $17,566
1:563, Hol, '79

Date	Trk	Dist	¼	½	¾	fin	Odds	¼	½	¾	str	fin	Driver PP	Cond	Time	First 3 Finishers	
22Sep79-9Hol		1	:292	:592	1:282	1:563ft	8	6	6	53½o	41½	1nk	Parker Jack Jr5	Wo 10000	1:563	Little To Ri, Craig Del, Torpids Knight	9
15Sep79-9Hol		1	:293	1:003	1:283	1:582ft	15	1o	4	53	52¼	31	Parker Jack Jr6	Wo 10000	1:583	Native Rocket,ArmbroTawny,LittleToRi	8
12Sep79-Hol		1	:304	1:014	1:33	2:02 ft		8	8	77¼	57	36	Parker Jack Jr8	Qua	2:031	El Joli, Classy Fever, Little To Ri	8
23Jun79-Mdw		1	:29	1.01	1:302	1:574ft	19	7	7	6o	55½	57¼	Parker Jack Jr6	60000	1:591	StpletonPlce,FightTheFoe,FlmOfFrdom	8
14Jun79-Mdw		1	:291	:583	1:284	1:581ft	10	6	6	4o	31	13	Parker Jack Jr3	Nw12500	1:581	Little To Ri, Mr M H, Thelmas Dream	0
5Jun79-Mdw		1	:302	:592	1:294	1:582gd	7¼	9	8	6o	65½	75¾	Parker Jack Jr9	Nw11500	1:593	Great Sport, Sportsman N, Zoomer	8

5 — 3-1

Driver-Trainer— AUBIN MARC. Blue, Red and White

Spry Sam

B. g. 4, by Spry—Samaria, by Morano
Own.—Carol & WilliamWhitlock&MarcAubin,ThousandOaks,Cal
Br.—Jackson & Shaw (NZ) 1:562, HOL, '78

Lifetime— $97,316
1979 18 5 4 0 $45,640
1978 21 8 6 0 $51,676
1:564, Hol, '79

Date	Trk	Dist	¼	½	¾	fin	Odds	¼	½	¾	str	fin	Driver PP	Cond	Time	First 3 Finishers	
22Sep79-8Hol		1	:293	:59	1:29	1:564ft	5¼	2	3	33	51	12¼	Aubin Marc1	Inv H	1:564	SprySm,TenderLovingCre,CordonArgnt	5
15Sep79-8Hol		1	:29	:584	1:264	1:562ft	8½	4	1	11½	1½	43¾	Aubin Marc4	Inv	1:57	TenderLovingCre,PeterOnedin,Dsmond	5
8Sep79-9Hol		1	:283	:582	1:283	1:571ft	13	6	6	56	52¼	4½	Aubin Marc5	Inv	1:573	Sprinkler, B. C. Count, Peter Onedin	6
31Aug79-6Hol		1	:293	:591	1:284	1:574ft	13	7	7	64¾	44½	48	Aubin Marc7	Nw100000 79	1.59	Can Can Rhythm,PeterOnedin,Sprinkler	7
23Aug79-6Hol		1	:283	:584	1:29	1:583ft	2¼e	3	1	11½	21	73¼	Aubin Marc5	Nw50000 79	1:592	Trentonian, Hello Birdie, RomanChapel	10
17Aug79-Hol		1	:291	:593	1:291	1:591ft		6	6	2½o	1nk	13	Aubin Marc6	Qua	1:591	Spry Sam, Waralene, Zarzuella	6

6 — 5-2

Driver-Trainer— GOUDREAU SHELLY. Red and Gold

Sprinkler

B. h. 5, by Meadow Skipper—Sprinkle, by Henry T Adios
Own.—Irving Lieverman, Hampstead, Quebec, Can
Br.—The Village Farm (Pa) 1:553, MDW, '78

Lifetime— $167,717
1979 16 5 1 1 $61,940
1978 17 5 2 2 $59,580
1:56, MDW, '79

Date	Trk	Dist	¼	½	¾	fin	Odds	¼	½	¾	str	fin	Driver PP	Cond	Time	First 3 Finishers	
8Sep79-9Hol		1	:283	:582	1:283	1:571ft	*1	3	1	11½	1½	1nk	Goudreau Shelly2	Inv	1:571	Sprinkler, B. C. Count, Peter Onedin	6
31Aug79-6Hol		1	:293	:591	1:284	1:574ft	2	5	5	54½o	55	33½	GoudreauShelly3	Nw100000 79	1:582	Can Can Rhythm,PeterOnedin,Sprinkler	7
4Aug79-Mdw		1	:29	:584	1:264	1:56 ft	18	7	7	6	53	1½	Dauplaise N6	Open	1:56	Sprinkler,TheSaddlerGB,MatrixHanover	10
28Jly79-Mdw		1	:284	:59	1:272	1:554ft	7½	7	6o	5o	75½	84¼	Dauplaise N4	Open	1:563	MtrixHnovr,BonnysColdFront,DllsCourt	8
19Jly79-Mdw		1	:301	:574	1:262	1:552ft	6½	7	8	8	76¼	65¼	Dauplaise N3	Open	1:562	Aldan N,BonnysColdFront,TaroNPrince	10
7Jly79-Mdw		1	:29	:564	1:263	1:554ft	2¾	7	8	7o	63¼	41	Dauplaise N4	Open	1:56	Aldan N, Bonnys Cold Front,KerryGold	10

POST POSITION STATISTICS Through Sept. 26

POST	1	2	3	4	5	6	7	8	9	10
NUMBER OF STARTS	250	250	250	250	249	244	226	182	141	91
WINS	36	28	33	32	32	37	20	17	9	6
IN THE MONEY	101	89	99	92	108	99	63	54	24	23

CHECKING THE FAVORITES Through Sept. 26

	Starts	Wins	Win %	In Money	In Money %
Favorites to Date	250	87	35%	169	68%
Odds on Favorites to Date	63	34	54%	51	81%

1 MILE PACE **PURSE $5,000** # 9th Race

CONDITIONED. Purse, $5,000. 5–year–olds and under. Non–winners of $5,000 in 1979.

Date	Trk	Dist	1/4	1/2	3/4	fin	Odds	1/4	1/2	3/4	str	fin	Driver	PP	Cond	Time	First 3 Finishers

Driver–Trainer— RITCHIE ROBERT.

1 Nerves Of Steel

6-1

Black, Gold and White   Lifetime: $9,887
B. g. 5, by Caroldon Lehigh—Mighty Val, by Mighty Warrior 1979 18 2 1 1 $4,626
Own.—Harold D Gilder, Brisbane, Aust 1978 24 6 4 2 $2,839
Br.—D Kennedy (Aust) No Record in U.S., '78 2:03^2, LA , '79

22Sep79-5Hol	1	:294	:594	1:294	1:593ft	6½	x6	6	75$\frac{1}{2}$o	64½	74½	Ritchie Robert[2]	Nw 5000 79 2:002 Jersey Abbe, El Joli, Never Better N	10
20Sep79-9Hol	1	:29	:592	1:294	1:593ft	4½	5	6	63$\frac{3}{4}$o	53½	76	Ritchie Robert[2]	18000 2:004 Radiant Group, Scotch Double, GlenInn	10
8Sep79-2Hol	1	:291	:593	1:292	2:001ft	6	6	5o	42$\frac{1}{2}$o	33	23	Ritchie Robert[2]	Nw5000 79 2:002 GlideTime,NervesOfSteel,JamesGrattan	7
1Sep79-7Hol	1	:284	:584	1:301	2:01 ft	14	9	9	91$\frac{1}{2}$o	75	31½	Ritchie Robert[7]	14000 2:012 Monseigneur,Andy'sMerino,NervsOfStl	9
29Aug79-6Hol	1	:291	1:00	1:314	2:011ft	53	5	6	77½	74	41	Ritchie Robert[2]	14000 2:012 Glen Inn, Rauchen, Royal Tango	10
1Aug79-10Sac	1	:303	1:014	1:32	2:004ft	32	7	8	87½	77	76½	Ritchie Robert[6]	14000 2:021 Scotch Double, True Trick, Blakey Del	9

Driver—RATCHFORD TOM. Trainer—Ratchford Don.

2 Jersey Abbe

3-1

Gold, White and Black   Lifetime: $14,100
B. h. 4, by Abbe Gene Volo—Miss Adios Meldale, by Parad'gAdios 1979 11 3 0 0 $3,968
Own.—Angus MacPherson, Irvine, Cal 1978 22 12 5 2 $6,325
Br.—W E Reed (NJ) No Record in U.S., '78 1:593, Hol, '79

22Sep79-5Hol	1	:294	:594	1:294	1:593ft	6½	5	5	54o	31½	11½	Ratchford Tom[3]	Nw5000 79 1:593 Jersey Abbe, El Joli, Never Better N	10
15Sep79-5Hol	1	:292	:593	1:291	1:582ft	50	7o	5o	42$\frac{1}{2}$o	97½	815	Ratchford Tom[10]	Nw5000 79 2:012 SoldiersBold,MircleEddi,RiskyBusinssN	10
8Sep79-2Hol	1	:291	:593	1:291	2:001ft	.24	4	4	64½	77½	45½	Ratchford Tom[1]	Nw5000 79 2:012 GlideTime,NervesOfSteel,JamesGrattan	7
1Sep79-7Hol	1	:29	:592	1:301	2:001ft	49	5	6o	54½	54½	45	Ratchford Tom[3]	14000 2:011 WelshKiwi,SoldiersBold,ColonelButlr	9
3Aug79-8Sac	1	:30	1:01	1:322	2:023ft	8	3	3	54	44	43½	Ratchford Gus[2]	Nw1600 79 2:032 MimosaPrk,SecureDrem,RiskyBusiness	6
26Jun79-8Sac	1	:29	:591	1:30	2:002ft	14	4	4	85½	87	74	Ratchford Don[3]	Nw6000 2:011 Adios One, NeverBetterN,DirectVictory	6

Driver—BAYLESS STAN. Trainer—McGonagle Pat.

3 Master Value

10-1

Gold and White   Lifetime: $8,828
B. g. 5, by Karamea Value—Pipe Down, by Blue Prince 1979 18 0 3 1 $3,831
Own.—Merimanor Farms, Sherman Oaks Cal 1978 16 3 2 1 $3,367
Br.—A N J Hewitt (Aust) No Record in U.S., '78 No Record , '79

21Sep79-3Hol	1	:302	1:013	1:322	2:001ft	13	1	2	32	42	22½	Bayless Stan[8]	12000 2:004 DrEKBuckley,MsterVlue,RevellingSndy	8
15Sep79-3Hol	1	:294	1:004	1:301	2:01 ft	6½	8	8	88$\frac{1}{2}$o	98	95½	Croghan Ross[3]	10000 2:02 The Blizzard A, DayStream, SlimYankee	9
6Sep79-10Hol	1	:30	1:003	1:303	2:003ft	25	5	5	53$\frac{1}{2}$o	41½	2hd	Croghan Ross[3]	10000 2:003 KnightForBret, MsterVlu, MistrSndmnN	10
30Aug79-10Hol	1	:301	1:00	1:29	1:593ft	13	2	4	45	86½	911	Croghan Ross[5]	Nw5000 79 2:011 Glide Time,IndianChief,RiskyBusinssN	10
25Aug79-4Hol	1	:291	1:001	1:293	2:00 ft	54	8	5o	33$\frac{1}{2}$o	44½	34½	Croghan Ross[8]	Nw 5000 79 2:01 DirectVictory,MiracleEddie,MasterVlue	8
4Aug79-10Sac	1	:293	:593	1:302	2:003ft	16	6	6	57½	57½	55½	Croghan Ross[5]	Nw 5000 79 2:014 HighIndChmp,MerryTimeFinss,PcingHi	8

Driver—KUEBLER RICK. Trainer—Stein Roger.

4 Buck Fifty

5-1

Blue and Yellow   Lifetime: $19,071
B. g. 5, by Admiralty—Romantic Hall, by Bruce Hall 1979 9 1 0 1 $1,095
Own.—My Hero Racing Stable, Northridge, Cal 1978 15 5 1 2 $9,957
Br.—F G McPaul (Aust) No Record in U.S., '78 No Record in U.S., '79

22Sep79-5Hol	1	:294	:594	1:294	1:593ft	8	1	1	1½	2½	64	Croghan Ross[7]	Nw 5000 79 2:002 Jersey Abbe, El Joli, Never Better N	10
8Sep79-Hol	1	:32	1:03	1:332	2:031ft		1	3	44½	46	2hd	Croghan Ross[2]	Qua 2:031 WaitakiSupreme,BuckFifty,FatherDuffy	6
11Aug79-Alb—ALBION PARK—Raced aprx 1 5/16 miles in 2:45 3/5, fin 3, K Walsh driv														
8Aug79-Gol—GOLD COAST—Raced aprx 1 1/8 miles in 2:27 2/5, fin 4, K Walsh Driv														
6Mar79-Alb—ALBION PARK—Raced aprx 1 5/8 miles in 3:18 4/5, fin 6, K Walsh Driv														
9Feb79-Har—HAROLD PARK—Raced aprx 1 11/16 miles in 3:22 1/5, fin 9, McClelland dr														

Driver—LIGHTHILL JOE. Trainer—Johnson L V.

5 Halcyon Hart

20-1

Green, White and Gold   Lifetime: $33,493
B. h. 5, by Bye Bye Max—Shafter Jewel, by Freeman Hanover 1979 21 0 1 2 $4,214
Own.—E W & Earl W Durfey, Orange, Cal 1978 40 2 4 4 $15,698
Br.—E W Durfey (Cal) 2:03, LA , '78 No Record , '79

21Sep79-10Hol	1	:29	:584	1:292	1:593ft	8½	2	3	53½	1010	10dis	Longo Gerald[2]	14000 — SeminoleChif,Thundrstorm,LumbrGon	10
12Sep79-8Hol	1	:29	:591	1:293	2:00 ft	15	2	2	31½	21½	24½	Lighthill Joe[2]	12000 2:004 KnghtsHonorN,HlcynHrt,BrndyAndDry	10
5Sep79-Hol	1	:30	1:012	1:321	2:02 ft		1	2	32	21½	21½	Lighthill Joe[8]	Qua 2:022 Cross Gate, Halcyon Hart, Sunzinaries	8
24Jly79-9Sac	1	:311	1:032	1:344	2:034ft	7	x4	4	4be	x4	4dis	Lighthill Joe[2]	[S]Inv H — Rey Rico, Bye Bye Viehover, WhiskyJim	4
17Jly79-9Sac	1	:303	1:01	1:312	2:011ft	9	4	4	2½	31½	43	Ratchford Don[2]	[S]Inv H 2:014 Rey Rico, Bye ByeViehover,SanAndreas	3
11Jly79-9Sac	1	:30	1:012	1:312	2:004ft	14e	2	2	31	42½	41½	Ratchford Don[2]	[S]Inv H 2:004 TrickelChrger,HowdyMon,ByeByVihovr	9

Driver—GOUDREAU SHELLY. Trainer—Ferrante Frank.

6 Miracle Eddie

5-2

Red and Gold   Lifetime: $7,806
Blk. g. 4, by Miracle Knight—Marty's Miss, by Henry Volo 1979 5 0 3 0 $4,150
Own.—Bill & Nicole Stearns, Van Nuys, Cal 1978 8 1 0 1 $2,806
Br.—M A Runyon (Ohio) 2:03^2, LA , '78 No Record , '79

22Sep79-5Hol	1	:294	:594	1:294	1:593ft	*2	8	8	64½	53½	43½	Todd James II[5]	Nw 5000 79 2:002 Jersey Abbe, El Joli, Never Better N	10
15Sep79-5Hol	1	:292	:593	1:291	1:582ft	*8-5	8	5	74$\frac{1}{2}$o	45	24½	Goudreau Shelly[6]	Nw5000 79 1:591 SoldiersBold,MircleEddi,RiskyBusinssN	10
7Sep79-2Hol	1	:302	1:014	1:312	2:001ft	3	2	2	21½	22	x2hd	Goudreau Shelly[3]	Nw5000 79 2:001 Indian Chief,MiracleEddie,SoldiersBold	7
1Sep79-7Hol	1	:29	:592	1:301	2:001ft	6½	10	10	89o	87½	78½	Todd James II[8]	14000 2:014 WelshKiwi,SoldiersBold,ColonelButlrN	9
25Aug79-4Hol	1	:291	1:001	1:293	2:00 ft	9	7	3o	21½	2½	23	Goudreau Shelly[7]	Nw 5000 79 2:001 DirectVictory,MiracleEddie,MasterVlue	8
17Aug79-Hol	1	:302	1:021	1:332	2:024ft		3	3	33½	34½	35	Todd James II[5]	Qua 2:033 Indian Chief,SoldiersBold,MiracleEddie	6

Driver–Trainer— MUELLER JIM.

7 Gozo Star

15-1

Blue, Gold and White   Lifetime: $11,902
B. g. 4, by Clandeboye—Sweet Mimosa, by General Scott 1979 19 1 3 3 $3,878
Own.—Don Lahey & Robert Fitzpatrick, Corona Del Mar 1978 42 4 5 4 $4,444
Br.—Mr F Borg (Aust) No Record in U.S., '78 2:004, SAC, '79

22Sep79-5Hol	1	:294	:594	1:294	1:593ft	23	7	7o	87	86	54	Mueller Jim[4]	Nw 5000 79 2:002 Jersey Abbe, El Joli, Never Better N	10
13Sep79-8Hol	1	:283	1:001	1:303	1:593ft	62	7	8	96½	919	920	Mueller Jim[4]	30000 2:034 Mighty Spry, Camlar, Charteris Play	9
8Sep79-2Hol	1	:291	:593	1:291	2:001ft	6½	3o	1	11	11	610	Mueller Jim[6]	Nw5000 79 2:022 GlideTime,NervesOfSteel,JamesGrattan	7
30Aug79-10Hol	1	:301	1:00	1:29	1:593ft	3½	7	7	68o	65½	45½	Mueller Jim[4]	Nw5000 79 2:004 Glide Time,IndianChief,RiskyBusinssN	10
25Aug79-4Hol	1	:291	1:001	1:293	2:00 ft	*6-5	1	2	11½	1½	44½	Mueller Jim[5]	Nw 5000 79 2:011 DirectVictory,MiracleEddie,MasterVlue	8
3Aug79-3Sac	1	:30	1:011	1:32	2:004ft	4½	1	1	1½	11½	12½	Mueller Jim[6]	Nw1600 79 2:004 GozoStar,SummerHoliday,AndysTopper	6

Driver–Trainer— BEER LARRY.

8 Never Better N

12-1

Orange and White   Lifetime: $15,727
B. g. 5, by Nevele Romeo—Dorstan, by U Scott 1979 16 0 3 4 $4,105
Own.—Thomas G Putter, Los Angeles, Cal 1978 26 3 7 3 $11,622
Br.—W. J. Francis (NZ) 2:03, HOL, '78 No Record , '79

22Sep79-5Hol	1	:294	:594	1:294	1:593ft	43	4	32o	41½	33	Beer Larry[4]	Nw 5000 79 2:012 Jersey Abbe, El Joli, Never Better N	10
15Sep79-5Hol	1	:292	:593	1:291	1:582ft	36	4	4o	31$\frac{1}{2}$o	86½	916	Perry Randy[2]	Nw5000 79 2:012 SoldiersBold,MircleEddi,RiskyBusinssN	10
7Sep79-2Hol	1	:302	1:014	1:312	2:001ft	16 ·	5	6	75½	510	611	Beer Larry[5]	Nw5000 79 2:022 Indian Chief,MiracleEddie,SoldiersBold	7
30Aug79-10Hol	1	:301	1:00	1:29	1:593ft	32	8	8	79	55	56½	Beer Larry[1]	Nw 5000 79 2:03 Glide Time,IndianChief,RiskyBusinssN	10
25Aug79-4Hol	1	:291	1:001	1:293	2:00 ft	7	6	6	88½	611	714	Beer Larry[4]	Nw 5000 79 2:03 DirectVictory,MiracleEddie,MasterVlue	8
27Jly79-10Sac	1	:303	:582	1:29	1:593ft	2½	2o	1	2½	53½	820	Beer Larry[4]	Nw150 79 2:032 Almetos,SummerHoliday,DancingBeuxA	9

Driver–Trainer— HUNTER CHARLES. Trainer—Eckert Gary.

9 El Joli

7-2

Green and Gold   Lifetime: $6,294
B. m. 5, by Royal Commission—El Suan, by Tuft 1979 20 0 2 1 $1,933
Own.—Gary Eckert, Hawthorne, Cal 1978 14 3 1 0 $4,090
Br.—R.L. Forsyth (NZ) No Record in U.S., '78 No Record in U.S., '79

22Sep79-5Hol	1	:294	:594	1:294	1:593ft	3½	3	3	23$\frac{1}{2}$o	1½	21½	Hunter Charles[6]	Nw 5000 79 1:594 Jersey Abbe, El Joli, Never Better N	10
12Sep79-Hol	1	:304	1:014	1:33	2:02 ft	3	3	21$\frac{1}{2}$o	12	15	Hunter Charles[3]	Qua 2:02 El Joli, Classy Fever, Little To Ri	8
3Aug79-Cam—CAMBRIDGE—Raced aprx 1 mile in 2:09 2/5, fin 2, G Smith driv														
28Jly79-Auc—AUCKLAND—Raced aprx 1 3/8 miles in 2:58 3/5, fin 3, C Smith driv														
23Jun79-Mar—MARLBOROUGH—Raced aprx 1 5/16 miles in 2:45 1/5, fin 7, G O'Brien driv														
19Jun79-Nel—NELSON—Race aprx 1 1/2 miles in 3:17 2/5, fin 9, G O'Brien driv														

ALPHA CHI PI OMEGA, Avel Ford Curry, group rep.

$5 Exacta
1 MILE PACE **PURSE $6,500**

10th Race

CLAIMING. Purse, $6,500. All ages. Claiming price, $20,000. Mares allowed 20 percent; 4-year-olds allowed 25 percent.

---

1 — Father Duffy — 6-1

Driver–Trainer— ROSEN ROBERT. Blue, Gold and Black

Father Duffy $20,000

Br. g. 4, by Skipper Creek—Tiny Princess, by Briston Hanover
Own.—Mark Holden, Jack Halpern, S J Gray, HuntingtonBeach,
Br.—J A Conklin (Ohio) 1:593, HOL, '78

Lifetime— $45,446
1979 19 3 5 1 $20,457
1978 35 5 3 11 $21,915
2:004, LA, '79

Date Trk	Dist	¼	½	¾	fin	Odds	¼	½	¾	str	fin	Driver PP	Cond	Time	First 3 Finishers	
22Sep79-10Hol	1	:29	:581	1:284	1:59 ft	5¾	4	4	45	43½	21	Rosen Robert1	20000	1:591	Escudero A, Father Duffy, TimeStream	10
15Sep79-7Hol	1	:284	:593	1:283	1:592ft	12	6	7	77½	712	49½	Rosen Robert6	20000	2:01	Highland Champ, Uflex, Butler King	7
8Sep79-Hol	1	:32	1:03	1:332	2:031ft		2	4	56	56½	31	Rosen Robert3	Qua	2:032	WaitakiSupreme,BuckFifty,FatherDuffy	6
1Jun79-8Sac	1	:302	1:01	1:31	1:592ft	15	8	8o	85im	78½	58¼	Rosen Robert8	25000	2:01	F T Scot, Scotch TimeAbbee, RepusRed	8
26May79-8Sac	1	:304	1:021	1:332	2:021ft	13	7	6o	42½o	53½	54¼	Rosen Robert7	25000	2:031	F T Scot, Oakies Image, Creanza	7
19May79-6Sac	1	:30	1:002	1:302	2:00 ft	21	6	7	76½	78	712	Rosen Robert6	30000	2:022	Town Fair, Drifted In, Creanza	7

2 — Tips King — 10-1

Driver–Trainer— GRUNDY JAMES. Grey, Blue and Red

Tips King $20,000

Br. g. 6, by Lindy's Pride—Carol Hoot, by Hoot Frost
Own.—B N (Frog) Redden, Inglewood, Cal.
Br.—B N Redden (Cal) 1:591, HOL, '78

Lifetime— $24,547
1979 6 0 0 1 $1,768
1978 18 9 2 1 $22,585
No Record, '79

Date Trk	Dist	¼	½	¾	fin	Odds	¼	½	¾	str	fin	Driver PP	Cond	Time	First 3 Finishers	
22Sep79-10Hol	1	:29	:581	1:284	1:59 ft	29	7	7	79½	76½	42½	Grundy James4	20000	1:592	Escudero A, Father Duffy, TimeStream	10
15Sep79-7Hol	1	:284	:593	1:283	1:592ft	46	3	2	33	310	712	Grundy James1	20000	2:014	Highland Champ, Uflex, Butler King	7
12Sep79-Hol	1	:304	1:014	1:33	2:02 ft		6	6	43¾o	45½	67¾	Grundy James4	Qua	2:033	El Jcli, Classy Fever, Little To Ri	8
7Apr79-8LA	1	:30	1:021	1:314	2:003ft	14	3	3	33½	49½	67¾	Grundy James3	20000 H	2:02	Drifted In, Another Kiwi, Titan Irish	8
30Mar79-8LA	1	:302	1:012	1:32	2:02 ft	14	6	7m	75¾	75¾	54¼	Grundy James4	20000 H	2:024	Pl4]RdintGencrl,‡DriftcdIn,ChifDiplomt	9
2Mar79-5LA	1	:293	1:022	1:33	2:032ft	11	3	3	32	21	3¾	Grundy James1	20000 H	2:033	King Riki, Father Duffy, Tips King	8

3 — Titan Irish — 4-1

Driver—GOUDREAU SHELLY. Trainer—Ferrante Frank. Red and Gold

Titan Irish $20,000

B. g. 8, by Irish Grattan—Gladys Adios, by Champ Adios
Own.—Frank Ferrante, Redondo Beach, Cal.
Br.—L Sauteur (Aust) 1:593, Hol, '78

Lifetime— $60,516
1979 18 4 1 3 $19,194
1978 34 7 4 3 $19,344
2:001, LA, '79

Date Trk	Dist	¼	½	¾	fin	Odds	¼	½	¾	str	fin	Driver PP	Cond	Time	First 3 Finishers	
21Sep79-7Hol	1	:293	:584	1:29	1:583ft	12	1o	3	31¾	42½	53¼	Todd James II5	22000 H	1:591	Rey Rico, Oakie's Image, Jambo Dollar	10
13Sep79-8Hol	1	:283	1:001	1:303	1:593ft	7½	6o	3o	21o	21	43½	Goudreau Shelly4	30000	2:001	Mighty Spry, Camlar, Charteris Play	9
7Sep79-8Hol	1	:304	1:004	1:311	2:004ft	5¼	2	1	11½	11	11¼	Goudreau Shelly4	22000 H	2:004	Titan Irish, Mighty Spry, Lehigh Priest	8
31Aug79-9Hol	1	:293	1:003	1:312	2:004ft	6½	3	2	31½	31½	32	Goudreau Shelly4	22000 H	2:011	Charteris Play, Desert Step, Titan Irish	6
22Aug79-Hol	1	:301	1:022	1:324	2:012ft		3	3	55¾	55½	47	Todd James II2	Qua	2:024	Nephew Bob, Desmond, Camlar	5
14Apr79-2LA	1	:302	1:002	1:312	2:013ft	*8-5	1o	2	2½o	2½	52¼	Goudreau Shelly6	24000 H	2:02	YoungTennessee,TownFir,WekinGlnfrn	7

4 — Andy's Valiant — 8-1

Driver—BAYLESS STAN. Trainer—Miskell Robert. Gold and White

Andy's Valiant $20,000

Br. g. 7, by Redouble—Andys Margaret, by Worthy Mon
Own.—Adolf Scangarello, Whittier, Cal
Br.—A B Hanson (Cal) 2:021, HOL, '78

Lifetime— $37,322
1979 36 13 6 5 $26,357
1978 21 6 1 1 $5,900
1:594, SAC, '79

Date Trk	Dist	¼	½	¾	fin	Odds	¼	½	¾	str	fin	Driver PP	Cond	Time	First 3 Finishers	
21Sep79-9Hol	1	:273	:574	1:292	1:591ft	8½	5	5	54¾	52	3hd	Bayless Stan2	16000	1:591	King Jay A, LehighPriest,Andy'sValiant	8
15Sep79-4Hol	1	:314	1:024	1:313	2:003ft	5¾	2	1	1hd	32	43½	Goudreau Shelly2	Ⓢ Wo10000	2:012	Howdy Mon, Taijamon, Bye Bye Victor	6
6Sep79-9Hol	1	:294	1:002	1:314	2:004ft	2½	3	2	32	43½	11½	Goudreau Shelly1	14000	2:004	Andy'sValiant,RevellingSandy,RoylTngo	7
1Sep79-9Hol	1	:291	:584	1:293	2:003ft	5¼	8	8	78	66	33¾	Lighthill Joe7	14000	2:011	Duz Us, Pertinent, Andy's Valiant	9
25Aug79-5Hol	1	:293	1:00	1:292	1:59 ft	9½	2o	1	21	44	711	Goudreau Shelly6	Ⓢ Wo 10000	2:012	Trickel Charger, Desmond, Howdy Mon	8
17Aug79-Hol	1	:291	:593	1:291	1:591ft		2	2	31½	42¼	512	Miskell Robert1	Qua	2:013	Spry Sam, Waralene, Zarzuella	6

5 — Rauchen — 9-2

Driver—KUEBLER RICK. Trainer—Stein Roger. Blue and Yellow

Rauchen $20,000

B. g. 8, by Smokey Eric—Stellmaur, by Radiant Robert
Own.—My Hero Racing Stable, Northridge Cal
Br.—L C Post (Aust) No Record in U.S., '78

Lifetime— $29,090
1979 20 3 4 3 $17,184
1978 24 2 3 6 $6,749
1:593, Hol, '79

Date Trk	Dist	¼	½	¾	fin	Odds	¼	½	¾	str	fin	Driver PP	Cond	Time	First 3 Finishers	
25Sep79-6Hol	1	:301	1:02	1:324	2:014ft	*2	8	7	65o	52½	31¼	Kuebler Rick8	16000	2:02	Charlight, Vendor's Boy, Rauchen	8
18Sep79-5Hol	1	:291	:591	1:292	1:593ft	4¼	7	7o	75o	41	1¾	Kuebler Rick6	16000	1:593	Rauchen, DarnRomeo,BluegumSurprise	10
12Sep79-6Hol	1	:30	1:01	1:30	2:002ft	4½	1	1	11½	11	2¼	Kuebler Rick5	14000	2:002	Pertinent, Rauchen, Victor Charles	10
5Sep79-8Hol	1	:292	1:001	1:301	2:003ft	11	2	2	31½	32	52¼	Alessi Carmen3	14000	2:01	Rio Valet, Gypsy Sam, Cool Gay	9
1Sep79-7Hol	1	:284	:584	1:301	2.01 ft	9¾	1	1	2nk	64	919	Alessi Carmen9	14000	2:044	Monseigneur,Andy'sMerino,NervsOfStl	9
29Aug79-6Hol	1	:291	1:00	1:314	2:011ft	8½	2	3	33	31¼	2hd	Alessi Carmen5	14000	2:011	Glen Inn, Rauchen, Royal Tango	10

6 — Highland Champ — 8-5

Driver–Trainer— AUBIN MARC. Blue, Red and White

Highland Champ $20,000

Blk. g. 10, by Highland Laird—Virgo, by Star Chief
Own.—William & CarolWhitlock&MarcAubin,ThousandOaks,Cal
Br.—J Stranger (Aust) 2:011, HOL, '70

Lifetime— $102,087
1979 39 10 6 4 $27,664
1978 20 2 2 2 $7,045
1:582, Hol, '79

Date Trk	Dist	¼	½	¾	fin	Odds	¼	½	¾	str	fin	Driver PP	Cond	Time	First 3 Finishers	
21Sep79-7Hol	1	:293	:584	1:29	1:583ft	*4-5	10	10	106¼	83¾	63½	Aubin Marc9	25000 H	1:592	Rey Rico, Oakie's Image, Jambo Dollar	10
15Sep79-7Hol	1	:284	:593	1:283	1:592ft	*4-5	1	1	13	110	15	Aubin Marc3	20000	1:592	Highland Champ, Uflex, Butler King	7
11Sep79-8Hol	1	:301	:594	1:291	1:582ft	*1-2	4	1	11	14	15	Aubin Marc2	16000	1:582	Highland Champ, Charlight, Gypsy Sam	9
4Sep79-5Hol	1	:291	1:003	1:30	2:001ft	8-5	7	6	43o	43	11	Aubin Marc6	16000	2:001	HighlandChmp,DrnRomeo,LehighPriest	7
29Aug79-7Hol	1	:292	:593	1:284	1:583ft	*4-5	5	2o	11½	16	17	Aubin Marc4	12000	1:583	HighlandChmp,RioVlet,ThunderstormA	7
23Aug79-8Hol	1	:284	:594	1:30	2:001ft	*7-5	5	3o	2nko	13	15	Aubin Marc4	10000	2:001	Highland Champ, Parling,Baron'sJudge	9

7 — Zarzuella — 20-1

Driver—TODD JAMES II. Trainer—McGonagle Pat. Royal, Blue and Grey

Zarzuella $20,000

B. m. 6, by Scotch Abbe—Joderao, by Fallacy
Own.—William H Cotter, El Monte, Cal
Br.—M T H Baker (NZ) No Record in U.S., '78

Lifetime— $5,678
1979 9 2 1 2 $3,814
1978 11 1 2 3 $1,864
No Record in U.S., '79

Date Trk	Dist	¼	½	¾	fin	Odds	¼	½	¾	str	fin	Driver PP	Cond	Time	First 3 Finishers	
22Sep79-10Hol	1	:29	:581	1:284	1:59 ft	23	10	10	1014	1011	107¾	Vallandingham Gene7	20000	2:003	Escudero A, Father Duffy, TimeStream	10
14Sep79-7Hol	1	:284	:583	1:291	1:593ft	9¾	3o	3	43½	910	919	VllndnghmGn7	Ⓕ Nw5000 Lst6	2:032	Imminence, Senga Rosa, HeritageTootie	9
7Sep79-5Hol	1	:29	:594	1:303	2:01 ft	6½	1	2	21½	22	32½	Vallandingham Gene6	Ⓕ Cd	2:012	Pub, Senga Rosa, Zarzuella	10
1Sep79-Hol	1	:304	1:02	1:313	2:003ft		7	7	66¼	66½	63¾	Vallandingham Gene3	Qua	2:012	Rey Rico, Hilarious Brew, Derdy Lord	8
24Aug79-8Hol	1	:301	1:001	1:304	2:00 ft	6	2	3	76¾	917	9dis	Desomer Steve4	Ⓕ Inv	—	Retriever, Native Miss, Spotlight Gal	10
17Aug79-Hol	1	:291	:593	1:291	1:591ft		1	1	1½	2nk	35½	Vallandingham Gene3	Qua	2:002	Spry Sam, Waralene, Zarzuella	6

8 — Linton Son — 10-1

Driver–Trainer— DESOMER STEVE. Blue and White

Linton Son $20,000

Br. h. 8, by Goodland—Civic Delight, by U Scott
Own.—Desomer Stable Inc & Robert Todd, Elk Grove, Cal
Br.—W J Cairncross (Aust) 1:583, HOL, '78

Lifetime— $98,189
1979 14 4 0 1 $16,396
1978 35 4 10 3 $33,847
1:592, LA, '79

Date Trk	Dist	¼	½	¾	fin	Odds	¼	½	¾	str	fin	Driver PP	Cond	Time	First 3 Finishers	
21Sep79-7Hol	1	:293	:584	1:29	1:583ft	12	4	4o	42½o	52¾	74	Desomer Steve1	22000 H	1:592	Rey Rico, Oakie's Image, Jambo Dollar	10
14Sep79-8Hol	1	:29	:592	1:29	1:59 ft	6¾	1	1	11½	2½	85	Desomer Steve8	25000 H	2:00	Royal Doll N., Gliding Guy, Baker Hill	8
30Aug79-6Hol	1	:294	:591	1:294	2:001ft	13	5	4o	32o	35	42½	Desomer Steve3	30000	2:004	Idaten, MisterMcJeb,ScotchTimeAbbee	7
25Aug79-Hol	1	:29	:59	1:301	2:011ft		6	4	317	417	411	Desomer Steve5	Qua	2:032	Call Back, Sir Jim, Southern Lad	6
28Apr79-5LA	1	:301	1:004	1:301	1:594ft	*2¼e	6	6	65	67¼	68½	Desomer Steve6	Wo10000	2:013	FrnoHnovr,ArmbroRhythmN,BrightBrut	8
31Mar79-5LA	1	:29	1:002	1:302	2:001ft	*2	1	1	1½	1½	11¼	Desomer Steve5	Pref	2:001	Linton Son, China PrinceA,BrightBrute	7

9 — Dancing Beaux A — 20-1

Driver—GATH BRIAN. Trainer—Jobe Wallace. Red and Black

Dancing Beaux A $20,000

B. g. 7, by Delvin Dancer—Princess Wexford, by Ardi
Own.—Cal West Farms, Paramount Cal
Br.—W Hanson (Aust) No Record in U.S., '78

Lifetime— $22,478
1979 12 0 0 1 $872
1978 8 0 0 0
No Record in U.S., '79

Date Trk	Dist	¼	½	¾	fin	Odds	¼	½	¾	str	fin	Driver PP	Cond	Time	First 3 Finishers	
25Sep79-7Hol	1	:284	:591	1:283	1:584ft	29	5	5	55½	47½	411	Sleeth Robert6	20000 H	2:011	Regal Ring, Rajah N, Lion Brown	7
4Sep79-6Hol	1	:284	1:003	1:313	2:014ft	27	3	3	33	32	76½	LaCoste Leo3	22500	2:024	Oakie's Image, Uflex, Time Stream	7
28Aug79-6Hol	1	:301	1:001	1:302	1:594ft	9	5	5	55½	66½	67½	LaCoste Leo4	22500	2:012	Oakie's Image, Uflex, King Jay A	6
23Aug79-7Hol	1	:282	1:012	1:311	2:002ft	35	6	8	87½	88	76½	LaCoste Leo3	22500	2:013	King Jay A, Desert Step, Chief Womble	8
3Aug79-3Sac	1	:30	1:011	1:32	2:004ft	9	6	6	614	616	614	LaCoste Leo2	Nw1600 79	2:034	GozoStar,SummerHoliday,AndysTopper	6
27Jly79-10Sac	1	:293	:582	1:29	1:592ft	19	1	3	3	42½	37	LaCoste Leo2	Nw1500 79	2:004	Almetos,SummerHoliday,DancingBeauxA	9

Allowed prices: Father Duffy, $25,000; Zarzuella, $24,000.

The First Race

A claiming race for $7,000 animals. We can eliminate the following as probable non-contenders: Spring Chance, who showed very little against a cheaper field in a very slow race last time; Taverns Sam, who has won only once all year and made no effort last time; Prairie Sunshine, whose Hollywood form has been dismal and who broke stride last time; and Demons Orphan Baby, whose early efforts in his last two starts left him entirely empty in the later stages.

Let us now rate the contenders:

Swift Max N: The half-mile time of :58 and the final time of 2:01:1 produce a basic rating of 244, plus 5 for the drop in class, 10 for the two parked-out symbols, 3 for the improved post position (from the small 10 adjacent to the driver's name on the past-performance summary line to tonight's post 3), and 10 more for Stan Bayless. Final rating is 272.

Tobys Skipper: For the 1:01:2 and 2:02, a basic rating of 223, less 5 for tonight's rise in class, plus 10 for roughing it on the outside for half a mile, and 5 more as a beaten favorite, and 5 for Ken Williams, a solid 15 percent winner. Final rating: 238.

Indian Victory: A basic rating of 223 loses 5 for the substantial rise in class, gains 15 for the impressive outside effort over three-quarters of a mile, and 4 more for the improved post position. Total: 237.

Bill Rader: This one looks as if it may have been the beneficiary of an easy trip. Although it shows no real vigor in any of its starts, that winning stretch gain should be respected. The basic rating is 229, plus 5 for the stretch gain, a loss of 1 for post position and a final rating of 233. Where did the 5 come from on the stretch gain? The animal was 2½ lengths back at the stretch call. We call that 3. And it won by 1½, which we call 2. We add 3 and 2, making 5.

Senga Deano: That last race was horrible, but the genuine effort of September 11 should be rated, just in case. Nothing much comes of it. A low basic rating of 217 ends as a final rating of 225.

Presence Felt: That was a tremendous victory from post 10 last time. The basic rating of 236 increases by 3 for the stretch gain and 15 for roughing it on the outside. Final rating is 254.

With an 18-point edge on his closest rival, Swift Max N was a bargain at almost 3 to 1. He won by more than 5½ lengths, with great ease, paying $7.80. Spring Chance was second at 6 to 1, a head in front of the 6 to 1 Presence Felt. Tobys Skipper, favored at 2.40 to 1, finished fifth.

The Second Race

A somewhat better grade of claimers this time. We can eliminate King Riki on the supposition that he probably needs a race over the local strip after his trip from Sportsman's Park. Furthermore, his last two efforts in Illinois were poor enough to raise doubts about his condition. We also eliminate Gas Saver for poor form, Royal Chimes N, who lost in a qualifier last out; Rebecca Abbe N (no vigor); and Slim Yankee, winless in his last 18 starts. Of the contenders, the following three rank on top:

Tuatahi Ridge: A basic rating of 241, plus 1 for the stretch gain, 5 for the ¼-mile outside, minus 1 for the slight change in post. Final: 246.

Bronte Boy: Another basic 241, plus 5 for racing outside, 5 more as a beaten favorite and 3 for the improved post. Final: 254.

Courtney: A basic 244, less 5 for the rise in class, plus 5 for parking out, and 1 for the better post. Final: 245.

King Riki finished first at 2.40 to 1, a length and a half ahead of Bronte Boy, who had such a rough time on the final turn that the stewards posted the inquiry sign immediately. They decided that the winner had not fouled our selection, who had been favored at 3 to 2. Ex Grand was third at 7 to 1 and Courtney a good fourth at 23 to 1.

The Third Race

This is for animals that have not won $17,500 during 1979. You will notice that some have won much more than that. They are eligible for the race, however, because of their failure to win $8,500 in their most recent six starts.

The obvious non-contenders here seem to be Michiana Hall (poor form), Spangles Gold (a slow qualifier), Apre Ski (a classy shipper unraced since August), Armbro Rhythm N (another newcomer), Young Million (no effort), Hello Birdie (whose time figures do not begin to compare with others in this field) and Proud Baron, who had things all his own way against a cheaper field but faded at the end, as seems to be his habit. The rejection of Hello Birdie on grounds of comparatively poor times might just as well extend to Royal Waldorf and Direct Victory, neither of whom comes close to matching the figures earned by Craig Del. With very little experience, handicappers can save themselves considerable time and effort by looking for the contender or two or three with the best half-mile and final times and see whether any of the other contenders show plus factors that might boost lower basic ratings to a competitive level.

In this case, no arithmetic is needed to see that Craig Del begins with an enormous advantage in basic rating, and widens the margin with extra points for class, roughing it on the outside, post position and driver. He won by 3¼ lengths, handily, paying $5. Apre Ski was next at 4 to 1 and Proud Baron, second most of the way, at 6 to 1, finished third.

The Fourth Race

This is a claiming handicap for $35,000 and $40,000 animals. Here again we have an inescapable choice in terms of time and driver: Ripping Rick. Whoever objects to his last race on grounds that he seems to have paced all the way on the inside rail should note that he was pulling away in the stretch. In any case, his next-to-last effort produces even better figures than his last. He won, paying $4.20. I suggest that the reader handicap the entire field, for practice.

The Fifth Race

Let us eliminate the newcomer Dromicia and Glide Time, who showed no energy last time after three successive wins; and Wikam, another shipper; and the absentee Dells Court; and the two outside horses, who produced little steam in their latest. The contenders:

Graduate Boy: A basic rating of 263 enlarges to 272, with 5 points for roughing it on the outside, 5 more for Kuebler, and 1 off for the change in post.

Argyll: From the same race as Graduate Boy, gets a basic 262, and ends with 267 for the parked-out symbol.

Torpids Knight: A standout. Finished third, ahead of Graduate Boy and Argyll, without any advantage in post position. But tonight's post provides some advantage. Final rating is 275. He won by three-quarters of a length over the classy B. C. Count, with Dells Court a close third. Paid $7 as favorite—a generous price.

The Sixth Race

This is an interesting stake event for trotters at a mile and one-sixteenth. In my opinion, it is a race to watch but not one on which to bet. Races at odd distances are so unusual that the handicapper seldom finds one in which all the likely contenders have clearly demonstrated form at the distance. In this case, Arnies Dart, who had previously demonstrated no liking for the distance, led all the way and won, paying $15.40. Tuteena, the favorite at a lukewarm 2.70 to 1, was second. Meadow Demojo was third at 4.20 to 1.

The Seventh Race

Here is one for horses bred in California that have won less than $10,000 during 1979, or have failed to earn $3,000 as a winner since September 1. These conditions cover a multitude of possibilities. For example, Trickel Charger (whom we eliminate for absenteeism), has won over $20,000 this year and is the class of the field when in shape.

We also toss out Bye Bye Viehover for lack of energy in the stretch; Desert Beauty, who tried last time but again finished far out of it; Stud Poker, who seems unable to stand exertion; My Little Rose, a three-year-old filly whose times do not rank with those of Placerville; Geometric, a three-year-old colt who also lacks the speed; Gedar, another three year-old in a tough spot; and the two horses in the outside posts, for lack of the lick to overcome those disadvantages. This leaves us, by process of elimination, with Placerville. It happens that Trickel Charger's race of August 31 earns a higher rating than either of Placerville's latest two. But it does not pay to bet on horses that have been away so long, especially when they go off at 1.70 to 1 like Trickel Charger.

He won it. Geometric was a half-length back at 7 to 1, Bye Bye Viehover was third and Placerville was fourth after leading all the way into the stretch at odds identical with Trickel Charger's. We are not doing badly with this program of races, and cannot even dream of picking every winner.

The Eighth Race

Every starter in this invitational handicap can be accepted as a contender. The three with the most impressive basic figures are Little To Ri, Spry Sam and Sprinkler—which undoubtedly is why they were given the outside post positions. As the reader will see when working out the handicap ratings, the drivers make the difference. Shelly Goudreau, the national leader scheduled to drive Sprinkler, is not on hand. His replacement is John Bonne, which costs the horse 10 points. And Marc Aubin's 10-point standing earns Spry Sam a final edge of 3 points over Little To Ri, after adjustments have been made for stretch gains, roughing it and post positions.

Spry Sam was the odds-on favorite at .90 to 1 and finished third after a gallant effort in the stretch. The winner was Little To Ri, who led all the way and widened his margin at the end, paying $10.80. Second was Peter Onedin, who raced under cover against the fence from start to finish. Sprinkler, the crowd's second choice at an unenthusiastic 3.30 to 1, was dead last all the way.

The Ninth Race

This is conditioned for non-winners of $5,000 during 1979, aged five or less. We eliminate Master Value, who has been scratched, and Halcyon Hart, who is winless in his last 21 starts and showed no energy in his last. We might also be forgiven for eliminating Miracle Eddie, who got off to a slow start and did very little to improve matters on September 22. This becomes an example of the advantages of collecting result charts in places like Los Angeles, where the material is available. Anyone who had been at the races on September 22, or who had the charts thereof, would know that Miracle Eddie was in close quarters and had ample excuse for the apparently indifferent performance. But his effort of September 15 was excellent.

In fact, it earns Miracle Eddie the highest basic rating in the field: 246. Next come Jersey Abbe (243), El Joli (242) and Never Better N (240), but others are close behind. Nerves of Steel really put out after breaking stride on September 22, and should be awarded 10 points for roughing it (5 for overcoming the loss of ground after the break and another 5 for racing on the outside during the third quarter). After a basic rating of 239, the gelding ends with 250. Miracle Eddie gets 5 for roughing it, 5 as beaten favorite, but does not get the 10 points for Goudreau. As noted earlier, that driver is absent. With James Todd in the bike, the horse's final rating is 246.

Jersey Abbe gets 3 for the gain in the stretch, and 5 for pacing on the outside—a final rating of 251. Do the others yourself. You'll find it interesting.

Miracle Eddie won, paying a nice $9.60. Nerves of Steel, who went off at a surprising 9 to 1, was less than a length back. Buck Fifty was third at 5 to 1. Jersey Abbe, favored at 1.90 to 1, faded to fifth in the stretch. Our handicapping principles directed us to Miracle Eddie's next-to-last race, but downgraded his chances because of the driver switch. So we are wrong about the race, but the principles will serve us well in the long run.

The Tenth Race

Here is an instructive field of $20,000 claimers. What do we do with Father Duffy, who has raced along the fence in each of his local starts? As we have stated often enough, a horse should get some air up its nose before we can accept it as ready for an all-out effort. On the other hand, Father Duffy seems to have improved slightly in his last race. And his time figures for that race are by far the best in this whole field. Ordinarily, we would give the horse the benefit of the doubt after it gained those lengths in the stretch and finished second. That is, we would use its previous race. But this one's previous race is unusable. I shall eliminate him. Interestingly, he paced more vigorously in this race, and finished third at 4 to 1. The reader should find his handicap rating and notice that he would not have been our selection in any case. By eliminating him, we not only observed a principle of sound handicapping, but saved time.

We also eliminate Tips King, a type not unlike Father Duffy; Andy's Valiant, more of the same; Zarzuella, for lack of speed; and Dancing Beaux A, likewise. But on what grounds do we accept the latest race of Highland Champ? Look at the record. The old gelding has won almost 25 percent of its starts this year. On September 21, Aubin stayed on the fence, refusing to waste energy in the early stages after leaving from the next-to-outside berth. Despite the bad post, Highland Champ went as the odds-on favorite in a tougher field than this one! With a more favorable post and the remarkably consistent Aubin, he might repeat the performance of September 15. So we decide to rate the horse off that performance, its next-to-last.

The contenders:

Titan Irish gets a basic rating of 250, plus 5 for the slight drop in class, 5 more for roughing it during the first quarter and an additional point for post position. The driving switch from Todd to Goudreau is canceled. Joe Lighthill is in the bike. The final rating is 261.

Rauchen is rated off the race of September 18. The time figures for September 25 were unrepresentatively slow and the fact that the barn is sending the gelding back to the wars after only four days of rest suggests that he is at his best. We therefore use his better, next-to-last figures. The basic rating is 246, minus 5 for the rise in class, plus 2 for the stretch gain, 10 for roughing a half-mile, plus 5 for Kuebler—a final rating of 258.

Highland Champ's basic rating is 245, plus 10 for leading by that much in the stretch (see page 202), plus 4 for post position, plus 10 for Aubin. Final rating: 269.

Linton Son's basic rating is 249, plus 5 for the drop in class and 10 for roughing it. He loses 3 for post position. The final rating is 261.

Highland Champ raced on the outside for a half-mile, wore down Rauchen in the stretch and won by a head, paying $4. Rauchen led all the way to the stretch and finished more than three lengths ahead of Father Duffy. Titan Irish was fourth at 6 to 1 and Linton Son was a distant eighth at 13 to 1.

How did we do? We passed one race but made selections in the other nine. Our winners were Swift Max N ($7.80), Craig Del ($5), Ripping Rick ($4.20), Torpids Knight ($7), and Highland Champ ($4). Five winners in nine tries is better than anyone has any right to expect as a steady diet.

15 SPORTSMAN'S PARK

July 21, 1979

WEATHER CLEAR. Temperature 80 F. Track fast. And the racing here is invariably first rate. So is the printed program, whose editors try to give the racegoer maximum help. Notice the symbols under each starter's program number and morning-line odds. The + means that the animal is moving up in class. The − signifies a drop in class. And the = shows that the class of this race is the same as that of the horse's last.

Another splendid feature appears on each past-performance line, immediately to the right of the driver's name. It is the horse's own time for the final quarter-mile of the race. At most raceways, it is possible to handicap in terms of final time alone, modified by the same means as we use in modifying our own basic handicap figures. Those figures, as the reader knows, include not only the horse's final time but the official half-mile time of the particular race. That pace calculation, it seems to me, reinforces the other figures. But I have no quarrel with those who prefer to use the horse's own final-quarter-mile time rather than the official half-mile time of the race. Where the program provides the information, sparing the handicapper the bother of arithmetic and the risk of approximation, the final-quarter times seem to work admirably. To demonstrate, we shall work with them in handicapping this program.

The following drivers will earn 5 extra points for their horses, being dependable 15 percent winners: Jim Curran, Jim Dolbee, Glen Kidwell, Dave Magee, Brian Pelling, Dan Shetler and Eric Thorgren. And Stan Bayless, Robert Farrington and Walter Paisley get an extra 10 points each, as habitual winners of 20 percent of their starts.

Post positions 1 and 5 are worth 7 points. Posts 2, 3, 4, 6 and 7 get 6, with 8 worth 4 and 9 only 3. This differs only slightly from the numbers on page 216.

SPORTSMAN'S

SUMMER '79

CICERO / LARAMIE at 33rd   242-1121

ONE MILE PACE — FIRST RACE — Purse $7,250

FIRST HALF OF DAILY DOUBLE

CLAIMING. Claiming Price $15,000. 3-Year-Olds and Up.

PLEASE ASK FOR HORSE BY PROGRAM NUMBER

WARMUP COLOR—RED

RED 1 — 5-1 +

Driver—DWIGHT BANKS, White-Purple-Gold — Tr.—Les Banks (48-1-4-4—.089)

BAROMETER — B g 1973, by Baron Hanover—Okema Lee—Quick Pick. Owner: Le Ban Je Racing Stable, Batavia, Ill.

1979 24 4 2 5 $19,938 2:05 May
1978 21 2 5 2 $15,008 2:04 Haw1
Lifetime $37,752 4, 2:012 (⅝)

Date Trk Cond Temp	Class	Dist	Ldr ¼	Ldr ½	Ldr ¾	Winner's Time	PP	¼	½	¾	Str	Fin	Ind. Time	Odds	Driver	Ind ¼ Time	Order of Finish (First, Second, Third)	Comment
7-11 10Spk⅝ ft 83°	clm12500=	1	:303	1:012	1:32	2:022	3	7	84	84½	74	31¼	2:023	13-1	(DBanks)	:294	TorpedoVictory, WoodhillBen, Barometer	(big rally)
6-29 2Spk⅝ ft 61°	clm12500=	1	:30	1:023	1:343	2:041	5x	9	86	86	x814	813	2:064	4-1	(DBanks)	:31	ChrgerBy, MiteyOneTime, DynmiteRcy	(poorly)
6-21 10Spk⅝ ft 82°	clm12500=	1	:294	1:004	1:312	2:031	9	5°	11½	31½	33	31¾	2:033	24-1	(DBanks)	:314	MiracleTeddy, AliasSmith, Barometer	(big mile)
6-13 10Spk⅝ ft 69°	clm12500−	1	:294	1:013	1:332	2:032	4	5	85½	85½°	84½	62	2:034	9-1	(SBanks)	:291	SevenShot, SilverCrkBrd, HopefulOne	(closed some)
6- 1 10May ft 69°	clm13000	1	:313	1:04	1:354	2:06	3	4	74	63°	53½	54¼	2:064	5-2	(SBanks)	:302	DustyGabby, Detector, ByrdDancer	(no rally)
5-24 8May ft 55°	clm13000	1	:293	1:023	1:342	2:053	8	8	86	73½°	54	55½	2:064	9-1	(SBanks)	:313	IansSpring, Detector, MissPuff	(3- and 4-wide)

BLUE 2 — 9-2 +

Driver—DAVE WHITE, Green-White-Red-Gold — Tr.—D. White (19-0-1-1—.047)

MAJESTIC SPEED — B g 1974, by Majestic Hanover—Princess Patty—Brown Prince. Owner: James F. Reid & Harry Stout, Danville, Frankfort, Ind.

1979 7 0 1 1 $3,055 2:063 May Qua
1978 8 0 0 0 $575 2:081 BmlP⅝ Qua
Lifetime $16,683 3, 2:02 (⅝)

Date Trk Cond Temp	Class	Dist	Ldr ¼	Ldr ½	Ldr ¾	Winner's Time	PP	¼	½	¾	Str	Fin	Ind. Time	Odds	Driver	Ind ¼ Time	Order of Finish (First, Second, Third)	Comment
7-12 6Spk⅝ ft 83°	clm12500=	1	:294	1:014	1:32	2:013	5	5	11½	11	12	21¼	2:014	18-1	(DWhite)	:294	CapetownMo, MajesticSpd, SilentLeigh	(big try)
7- 7 1Spk⅝ ft 72°	clm12500=	1	:303	1:022	1:34	2:034	7	4	55¼	75	65	31¾	2:041	47-1	(DWhite)	:291	NativeSue, OvertimeVictory, MajstcSpd	(prkd early)
6-28 6Spk⅝ ft 74°	clm12500=	1	:302	1:014	1:323	2:023	1	4	21°	2½°	33½	67½	2:041	28-1	(DWhite)	:312	GrandpaLeo, StwawyTime, DustyGbby	(prkd no cver)
6-19 6Spk⅝ ft 79°	clm12500=	1	:294	1:004	1:322	2:03	1	5	77	74	65½	53¼	2:033	24-1	(DWhite)	:302	RoylSDirect, NineCarat, DoubleAllegaroo	(no excuse)
6- 7 10Spk⅝ ft 78°	clm12500+	1	:304	1:03	1:341	2:05	8im	5	55½	54	56	58½	2:064	36-1	(DWhite)	:314	SuzySue, ByrdDancer, FrostyGuyN	(off gate leaving)
5-22 6May ft 67°	nw25005	1	:311	1:033	1:34	2:04	7	7	54°	42½°	65	613	2:063	99-1	(DWhite)	:32	GalaBlueChip, ScottyFrst, MntainHdMn	(3-wide ½)

WHITE 3 — 8-1 =

Driver—DARYL BUSSE, Gray-Red — Tr.—La. Williams (202-26-30-22—.245)

BEANS TONITE — Blk h 1973, by Miracle Knight—Coffee Bean—Coffee Break. Owner: Terry & Everett Medine & Larry Williams, Kirkland, Aurora, Ill.

1979 18 1 2 2 $11,181 2:02 May
1978 43 5 3 5 $28,308 2:00 Spk⅝
Lifetime $82,873 3, 1:59 (1) T.T.

Date Trk Cond Temp	Class	Dist	Ldr ¼	Ldr ½	Ldr ¾	Winner's Time	PP	¼	½	¾	Str	Fin	Ind. Time	Odds	Driver	Ind ¼ Time	Order of Finish (First, Second, Third)	Comment
7-10 10Spk⅝ ft 82°	clm15000=	1	:29	:594	1:31	2:011	7	1°	21	21	31½	53½	2:02	7-1	(DBusse)	:304	ChargerBoy, TperChip, StarFarmer	(3-wide early)
6-23 1Spk⅝ ft 59°	clm15000−	1	:292	1:011	1:32	2:032	6	2	21¼	42¼	53	63½	2:041	*2-1	(DBusse)	:313	PellireDsty, WildwdErl, ThnkYouMm	(lacked room)
6-18 8Spk⅝ ft 60°	clm17500=	1	:294	1:01	1:311	2:023	3	2	21¼	21½	2½	5½	2:024	5-1	(DBusse)	:311	TKCnsl, BurwdSharon, EyreQuke	(led between calls)
6- 7 5Spk⅝ ft 78°	clm17500−	1	:292	1:003	1:311	2:014	3	2	32½	2hd°	3½	58¼	2:032	*9-5	(DBusse)	:321	IrishTip, NobleDee, Perryville	(batled tired)
6- 2 6May ft 69°	clm18000	1	:301	1:01	1:321	2:03	1	2	31	4¾	31	2¾	2:031	*6-5	(DBusse)	:304	StarFarmer, BeansTonite, ParsnOregn	(free too late)
5-25 8May ft 56°	clm22000	1	:30	1:012	1:314	2:03	6	3	2½°	2nk°	3¼	75¾	2:041	9-2	(DBusse)	:322	Aggravating, FrnkieLynn, AndysCoho	(prkd no-cver)

GREEN 4 — 6-1 +

Driver—REGGIE MARY, Red-Blue-White — Tr.—R. Mary (3-0-0-0—.000)

LAUDER LUMBER — Br g 1971, by Lumber Dream—Moonstorm—Stormy Way. Owner: R. T. Mary, Chicago, Ill.

1979 4 0 0 0 (——) 2:031 Spk⅝ Qua
1978 22 1 2 4 $14,460 2:003 Spk⅝
Lifetime $30,308 7, 2:003 (⅝)

Date Trk Cond Temp	Class	Dist	Ldr ¼	Ldr ½	Ldr ¾	Winner's Time	PP	¼	½	¾	Str	Fin	Ind. Time	Odds	Driver	Ind ¼ Time	Order of Finish (First, Second, Third)	Comment
7-18 Spk⅝ ft 69°	Qua	1	:292	1:001	1:313	2:031	5	1	13	18	15	14¼	2:031	NB	(RMary)		LauderLumber, WonderHorse, MrPellaire	(———)
7- 7 3Spk⅝ ft 72°	nw50004-1+	1	:293	:593	1:323	2:02	8	2°	31¾°	55°	922	9dis		44-1	(RMary)		HwthorneJoe, HidewyBill, SllyVolo	(overland route)
6-20 Spk⅝ ft 74°	Qua	1	:293	1:001	1:303	2:01	4	1	22½	25	46½	59¾	2:03	NB	(RMary)		Lovim, Owl, PrairieRock	(———)
1-23 8Spk⅝ gd 30°	nw35005	1	:303	1:02	1:342	2:05	x2	9	9dis	9dis	9dis	9dis		30-1	(RMary)		CorkysExprss, MegsFshion, GnesShw	(snowy going)
1-12 9Spk⅝ gd 23°	clm20000	1	:312	1:03	1:351	2:073	3	2	21¾	79¼	718	7dis		21-1	(RMary)		Relntless, SeaMacEddie, EvelHoosier	(snowy going)
1- 4 7Spk⅝ ft 0°	nw2000078	1	:314	1:051	1:362	2:064	5	1°	11½	42¼	711	716	2:10	8-1	(RMary)	:351	CardnlChfA, HrrcneSmpsn, McOscar	(-26 wind chill)

BLACK 5 — 6-1 —

Driver—STANLEY BANKS, White-Purple — Tr.—L. Fox (168-17-19-24—.212)

MR. PELLAIRE — B g 1974, by High Ideal—Buggy Thief—Hardy Hanover. Owner: Leroy Fox & Ellewyn Hegland, Sandwich, Ill.

1979 18 1 2 4 $11,924 2:053 May
1978 21 5 4 2 $12,921 2:043 LouD
Lifetime $19,321 3, 2:012 (⅝)

Date Trk Cond Temp	Class	Dist	Ldr ¼	Ldr ½	Ldr ¾	Winner's Time	PP	¼	½	¾	Str	Fin	Ind. Time	Odds	Driver	Ind ¼ Time	Order of Finish (First, Second, Third)	Comment
7-18 Spk⅝ ft 69°	Qua	1	:292	1:001	1:313	2:031	7	8	812°	48¼°	25	36½	2:043	NB	(SBanks)		LauderLumber, WonderHorse, MrPellaire	(———)
5-18 9May ft 67°	clm20000	1	:294	1:012	1:322	2:024	2	3	42½	63¼	53	41¾	2:031	6-1	(SBanks)	:301	FrankieLynn, AndysCoho, Agravating	(good trip)
5-12 2May ft 52°	clm18000	1	:294	1:00	1:32	2:023	1	2	31½	21	31¼	21	2:024	*2-1	(SBanks)	:303	FlyStraight, MrPellaire, StarFarmer	(free too late)
5- 5 10May ft 61°	clm18000	1	:313	1:024	1:324	2:03	7	7	84¼	63½	52¾	31¼	2:031	30-1	(SBanks)	:293	AndysCoho, StarFarmer, MrPellaire	(wide str surge)
4-27 10May gd 36°	clm16000 C	1	:30	1:004	1:324	2:054	1	1	2nk	21¼	32½	88¼	2:072	*5-2	(JCurran)	:342	DukeDancer, BretsFame, AliasSmith	(stoppd at ¾'s)
4-21 9May ft 48°	clm16000	1	:311	1:034	1:341	2:042	6	7	42¼°	41½°	64	810	2:062	5-1	(JDolbee)	:314	AndysCoho, TrooperChip, AliasSmith	(gave up ¾s)

YELLOW 6 — 8-1 —

Driver—BRIAN PELLING, Black-Red-Orange — Tr.—B. Pelling (68-11-8-8—.266)

KING RIKI — B g 1968, by Pipiriki—Dianne's Own—Our Globe. Owner: B.R.P. Enterprises & George Aiken, Cypress, Calif., Aust.

1979 19 4 4 2 $18,612 2:012 B.M1
1978 21 4 4 3 $23,108 1:58 Hol1
Lifetime $43,939 10, 1:58 (1)

Date Trk Cond Temp	Class	Dist	Ldr ¼	Ldr ½	Ldr ¾	Winner's Time	PP	¼	½	¾	Str	Fin	Ind. Time	Odds	Driver	Ind ¼ Time	Order of Finish (First, Second, Third)	Comment
6-30 3Spk⅝ gd 71°	clm22500−	1	:311	1:032	1:343	2:051	8	9	85¼	96	76¾	67	2:063	6-1	(BPelling)	:304	IrishTip, StanleyLee, FrankieLynn	(no factor)
6-15 7Spk⅝ ft 86°	clm27500=	1	:293	1:003	1:304	2:01	2	4	43¼°	41¾°	63¾	63¾	2:014	10-1	(BPelling)	:303	WeekEndSpecial, Richrdsn, BarklyLdy	(prkd w-cver)
6- 8 10Spk⅝ sy 78°	nwR60002-79+	1	:30	:594	1:322	2:032	7	8	87¾	85°	73½	54¼	2:041	10-1	(BPelling)	:304	StrredByBrt, RceTmeCarey, SocialClss	(prkd w-cver)
5-19 Sac1 ft	clm20000	1	:294	:591	1:302	2:021	8	8	8	8	53	1¾	2:021	26-1	(BPelling)		KingRiki, DukeWoollen, YoungNev	(———)
5-28 LA⅝ ft	clm22000	1	:28	:591	1:294	2:01	5	7	4°	4°	53½	88¼	2:023	7-1	(BPelling)		AnotherKiwi, ReginaldChris, CootaFrost	(———)
4-21 LA⅝ ft	clm22000	1	:294	:59	1:303	2:013	6	7	7	6°	52¾	53	2:021	5-1	(BPelling)		TownFair, CootaFrost, DukeWoollen	(———)

ORANGE 7 — 7-2 +

Driver—ERIC THORGREN, White-Black-Red — Tr.—E. Thorgren (10-1-0-2—.167)

CAPETOWN MO — B g 1971, by Witch Doctor—Countess Gem—Diamond Hal. Owner: Stonehedge Farm, Hinsdale, Ill.

1979 5 1 0 2 $5,480 2:013 Spk⅝
1978 20 0 5 3 $16,061
Lifetime $99,084 6, 2:004 (⅝)

Date Trk Cond Temp	Class	Dist	Ldr ¼	Ldr ½	Ldr ¾	Winner's Time	PP	¼	½	¾	Str	Fin	Ind. Time	Odds	Driver	Ind ¼ Time	Order of Finish (First, Second, Third)	Comment
7-12 6Spk⅝ ft 83°	clm12500−	1	:294	1:014	1:32	2:013	1	2	42½	53½	32½	11¼	2:013	9-2	(EThrgrn)	:284	CapetownMo, MajesticSpd, SilentLeigh	(flew in str.)
7- 5 7Spk⅝ ft 63°	clm15000+	1	:311	1:01	1:32	2:03	9	9	86½°	85½	96	73	2:033	35-1	(EThrgrn)	:302	HppyPcturShw, MdwWndr, EyrQuk	(some close)
6-27 10Spk⅝ ft 80°	clm12500−	1	:303	1:014	1:331	2:031	3	6	55	64	64	33	2:034	3-1	(EThrgrn)	:294	NineCart, TorpedoVictory, CpetownMo	(god last qtr)
6-19 7Spk⅝ ft 79°	clm15000=	1	:292	:592	1:304	2:01	6	6	67½	53½°	44½	43¾	2:014	10-1	(EThrgrn)	:301	CannonTurner, FrstyGuyN, TrickyBaron	(improving)
6- 7 7Spk⅝ ft 78°	clm15000+	1	:30	1:003	1:314	2:021	3	5	54½	66	56½	36¼	2:032	13-1	(EThrgrn)	:302	CombatErnie, GoodLiving, CapetownMo	(tuff winnr)
10-19 9Arl1⅛ ft 52°	clm12000	1	:301	1:012	1:311	2:021	9	9	911	99½	711	57¾	2:034	6-1	(EThrgrn)	:303	AndysCoho, SugarVallyDee, , GoRichrdGo	(dull effrt)

PURPLE 8 — 10-1 —

Driver—WALTER PAISLEY, Green-White — Tr.—R. Davino (133-26-23-18—.337)

PAKURA LAD — B g 1971, by Yankee Express—Flying Melody—Flying Song. Owner: James & Jean Errichiello, Valparaiso, Ind.

1979 15 1 1 0 $7,274 2:054 sy May
1978 7 0 0 3 $2,736 2:072 May Qua
Lifetime $24,580 6, 2:012 (⅝)

Date Trk Cond Temp	Class	Dist	Ldr ¼	Ldr ½	Ldr ¾	Winner's Time	PP	¼	½	¾	Str	Fin	Ind. Time	Odds	Driver	Ind ¼ Time	Order of Finish (First, Second, Third)	Comment
7-11 8Spk⅝ ft 83°	clm20000=	1	:294	:594	1:304	2:01	3	2	32½	2½°	1hd	76¼	2:021	20-1	(DBusse)	:311	CannonTurner, FlyStraight, TallyBoy	(parked early)
7- 3 9Spk⅝ sy 78°	clm20000+	1	:313	1:04	1:334	2:042	5	5	86½	86½	86	87¼	2:06	24-1	(DBusse)	:304	CoolLove, KeenEdge, CannonTurner	(showed little)
6-25 9Spk⅝ ft 67°	nw50008 −	1	:294	1:003	1:313	2:024	7	7	65°	53¼°	24½	46¼	2:033	8-1	(DBusse)	:312	PhinneasFinn, BrawnyBret, Lee'sBest	(parked)
6-20 7Spk⅝ ft 78°	nw800079+	1	:284	1:01	1:314	2:01	3	5	42°	33°	56	59	2:024	3-1	(DBusse)	:302	GlBlueChip, SngCycleExpress, RbbioDancr	(tuff trip)
6- 9 3Spk⅝ ft 68°	clm27500+	1	:301	1:01	1:304	2:013	7	2	31¾	32¼	33	51¾	2:02	36-1	(DBusse)	:304	Richardson, Aggravating, BarklyLady	(raced well)
5-21 8May ft 59°	nw100007879	1	:293	1:002	1:312	2:032	6	8	79½°	64¼°	52	64¾	2:042	19-1	(RMarsh)	:321	RiverCircleRomeo, BattrdBoy, HHmstr	(3-wide ⅞s)

BROWN 9 — 10-1 =

Driver—GEORGE KRAMER, Green-Gold — Tr.—G. Kramer (29-5-1-8—.284)

MY BONNIE LAD — B h 1973, by Butlers Dream—Highland Flirt—Light Brigade. Owner: John Rogers & Peter Socci, Chicago, Ill.

1979 19 1 2 3 $5,879 2:04 PPk⅝
1978 42 8 11 6 $9,542 2:02 PPk⅝
Lifetime $13,234 5, 2:02 (⅝)

Date Trk Cond Temp	Class	Dist	Ldr ¼	Ldr ½	Ldr ¾	Winner's Time	PP	¼	½	¾	Str	Fin	Ind. Time	Odds	Driver	Ind ¼ Time	Order of Finish (First, Second, Third)	Comment
7-10 10Spk⅝ ft 82°	clm15000+	1	:29	:594	1:31	2:011	6	7	77	84½	86¼	43¼	2:014	44-1	(GKramr)	:294	ChargerBoy, TperChip, StarFarmer	(mild close)
6-29 4Spk⅝ ft 61°	clm12500+	1	:304	1:004	1:313	2:024	4	2	2nk	11½	12½	42½	2:032	57-1	(GKramr)	:314	MikesRplic, EdsMrk, SbrbnHnvr	(battled on rail)
6-18 10Spk⅝ ft 60°	clm10000 C−	1	:312	1:03	1:35	2:062	4	6	86¾	75¼°	75¾	75½	2:073	34-1	(JWitwcz)	:313	MissSlo, FrostyCandy, ThereHeGoes	(never close)
6- 6 10Spk⅝ ft 78°	clm12500−	1	:301	1:021	1:342	2:042	1	3	54	74½	87	98¼	2:06	19-1	(JWitwcz)	:304	HighlandKirk, EdsMrk, MiteyOneTime	(no excuse)
5-28 9May ft 59°	nw50007879	1	:30	1:002	1:313	2:032	5	3	32¾	41½	32	53	2:04	36-1	(SBuch)	:32	AbetterCard, StarbrdBtlr, PhinneasFinn	(away fast)
5- 9 10May ft 84°	clm12000	1	:293	1:011	1:322	2:041	6	6	54½°	53	53½	62½	2:044	16-1	(JWitwcz)	:314	ChfTmmyHwk, Brmtr, HghlndKrk	(dropped a notch)

CHARLEY HORSE — 7....2....6 PARADISE — 6....3....8 MISS MAREY — 1....3....5

ONE MILE PACE — SECOND RACE — Purse $7,250

SECOND HALF OF DAILY DOUBLE & $3 QUINIELA WAGERING

CLAIMING. Claiming Price $15,000. 3-Year-Olds and up. Chief Timmy Hawk and Top Butler in for $18,750, all others $15,000.

PLEASE ASK FOR HORSE BY PROGRAM NUMBER — WARMUP COLOR—BLUE

RED 1 (6-1 =)

Driver—WALTER PAISLEY, Green-White — Tr.—R. Davino — (133-26-23-18—.337)

PELLAIRE DUSTY — B h 1972, by Brooks Hanover—Go Game—Live Dangerously
Owner: Peter Guido, Chicago, Ill.

1979	21	5	3	1	$24,541	2:03² Spk⅝
1978	41	2	3	4	$21,087	2:02⁴ Arl1¼
			Lifetime		$90,846	4, 2:01³ (⅝)

7-14 1Spk⅝ ft 73° clm15000=1 :29³ 1:01⁴ 1:31³ 2:02³ 2 4 76½ 88¼ 610 43¼ 2:03¹ 4-1 (WPaisly) 29⁴ BrmryDvne, LnclnsPldg, ChfTmmyHwk (leader tiring
7- 3¹⁰Spk⅝ sy 78° clm17500=1 :30² 1:03 1:33⁴ 2:04 9 9 9:1 64½ 55 65 2:05 12-1 (JCurran) 30² BretPower, HunnertBucks, GoodOFrisky (post hurt)
6-23 1Spk⅝ ft 59° clm15000=1 :29² 1:01¹ 1:32 2:03² 1 6 42¾⁴ 31¼⁴ 2½ 1¾ 2:03² 3-1 (JCurran) 31¹ PellireDusty, WildwdErl, ThnkYouMm (gme winner)
6-14 7Spk⅝ ft 84° clm15000+1 :29³ 1:01² 1:32¹ 2:02³ 8 8 86 86° 87 44 2:03² 10-1 (HAdams) 30 EgyptianButler, DoNotPss, AbelCain (reservsd early)
6- 5 7Spk⅝ ft 60° clm12500=1 :30³ 1:01¹ 1:33¹ 2:04¹ 7 8 75¾⁴ 11° 16 12¼ 2:04¹ 6-1 (WPaisly) 31 PllreDsty, WtsksBst, BllyGnBrks (monster move ⅜s)
5- 1¹⁰May ft 50° clm13000 1 :28⁴ 1:00³ 1:31² 2:01⁴ 6 8 8:17 816 817 718 2:05² 25-1 (DMagee) 30⁴ SilverCreekBrad, DoNotPass, LittleHrtn (dull effort)

BLUE 2 (10-1 +)

Driver—HAROLD GUERRA, Black-Gold — Tr.—H. Guerra — (11-0-0-1—.030)

HAL RIDGE — Br g 1972, by Coral Ridge—Maid Hal—Mike Hal
Owner: Estelle Walston, Palos Park, Ill.

1979	26	11	2	4	$35,367	2:02² Spk⅝
1978	11	4	2	0	$7,778	2:04² May
			Lifetime		$62,056	4, 2:00⁴ (1)

7-12 7Spk⅝ ft 83° clm12500=1 :29¹ :58³ 1:29² 2:00³ 7 1 1¹½ 22½ 55½ 76 2:01⁴ 8-1 (HGuerra) :32 MightyDream, CopperLad, Prospecting (burned up)
7- 6 1Spk⅝ ft 68° clm12500 C=1 :29⁴ 1:01¹ 1:32¹ 2:03¹ 4 1 1¾ 1½ 1½ 75½ 2:04² 5-1 (JDolbee) 32¹ TrickyBaron, JetCoe, ChiefTimmyHawk (gve wy str)
6-26¹⁰Spk⅝ ft 79° clm12500 1 :29¹ 1:00³ 1:31 2:02² 5 1 11½ 11¼ 1¹½ 1ⁿ 2:02² 7-1 (JDolbee) 31² HalRidge, FrostyCandy, BigiousDancer (all the way)
6-13¹⁰Spk⅝ ft 69° clm12500 1 :29⁴ 1:01³ 1:33² 2:03² 6 1 21 31½ 53 84¼ 2:04¹ 8-1 (DMagee) 30³ BestOfBarons, HeritageEleanor, ChrgrBoy (even try)
6- 6 6Spk⅝ ft 78° clm12500=1 :30² 1:02¹ 1:32¹ 2:03³ 4 1 21 41½ 32 42 2:04 5-1 (JDolbee) 31³ BestOfBarons, HeritageEleanor, ChrgrBoy (even try)
5-25¹⁰May ft 90° clm12500=1 :29² 1:01⁴ 1:32² 2:04² 1 1 1ⁿᵏ 1¹ 1ⁿ 1⁴ 46¼ 2:05² 9-1 (JDolbee) :33 ChiefTimmyHwk, Gllgiss, DoNotPass (gd early spot)

WHITE 3 (6-1 +)

Driver—LARRY BANKS, Green Gold — Tr.—La. Banks — (8-0-1-0—.069)

WOODHILL BEN — Ch h 1972, by Bengazi Hanover—Adios Lady Adios
Owner: Larry Banks, Elmwood Park, Ill.

1979	19	1	4	3	$8,037	2:02² PPk⅝
1978	31	7	2	5	$16,169	2:00⁴ May
			Lifetime		$57,309	6, 2:00⁴ (⅝)

7-11¹⁰Spk⅝ ft 83° clm12500=1 :30³ 1:01² 1:32 2:02² 5 2° 3¹ 3¹ 4¹½ 2° 2:02² 26-1 (LaBanks) 30¹ Torp-doVictory, WoodhillBen, Barometer (game try)
6-29 4Spk⅝ ft 61° clm12500 1 :30 1:00⁴ 1:31³ 2:02⁴ 1 4 43 64¾⁴ 69 66½ 2:04¹ 20-1 (LaBanks) 31³ MikesReplic, EdsMrk, SuburbnHnver (3-wide briefly)
6-21 7Spk⅝ ft 82° clm15000+1 :29² 1:00⁴ 1:31 2:00⁴ 1 8 81¹° 912 912 814 2:03 13-1 (LaBanks) 30² WtsekasBest, SevnSht, AvonEastwod (to much sped)
6-13¹⁰Spk⅝ ft 69° clm12500+1 :29⁴ 1:01³ 1:33² 2:03² 7 8 75° 6⁴ 63½ 42 2:03⁴ 52-1 (LaBanks) 29³ SevenShot, SilverCreekBrad, HopefulOne (tuff trip)
5-30¹⁰May ft 71° clm12000 C 1 :32 1:04¹ 1:36 2:05⁴ 1 3 21° 31° 44½ 65¾ 2:07 3-1 (DBird) 30⁴ GrndpaLeo, BllyGneBrks, HrtgeElnor (pulled, hung)
5-15 9May ft 61° clm13000 1 :30⁴ 1:03 1:33² 2:04 8 8 65 73¾ 74¼ 55¼ 2:05 11-1 (WPaisly) 30⁴ TimeBreaker, ToplineBob, Prospecting (post hurt)

GREEN 4 (8-1 =)

Driver—GEORGE KRAMER, Green-Gold — Tr.—G. Kramer — (29-5-1-8—.284)

CHIEF TIMMY HAWK — Ch g 1975, by Brooks Hanover—Sun Dell—Irmas Boy
Owner: John S. Rogers, Chicago, Ill.

1979	25	7	4	4	$24,673	2:04¹ May
1978	26	1	6	4	$5,633	2:08²
			Lifetime		$5,633	3, 2:08²

7-14 1Spk⅝ ft 73° clm15000+1 :29³ 1:01⁴ 1:31³ 2:02³ 9 7 44¼⁴ 34½° 36 3¼ 2:02⁴ 24-1 (GKramr) 30¹ BarmaryDvne, LnclnsPldge, ChfTmmyHwk (pwrfl try)
7- 6 1Spk⅝ ft 68° clm12500 C=1 :29⁴ 1:01¹ 1:32¹ 2:03¹ 7 7 74½ 74 74½ 32½ 2:03⁴ 21-1 (GKramr) 30⁴ TrickyBaron, JetCoe, ChiefTimmyHawk (late bid)
6-12 7Spk⅝ ft 63° clm14000 1 :30² 1:02¹ 1:34¹ 2:03⁴ 8 8 96¾⁴ 84½° 98¼ 9:1 2:06 9-1 (GKramr) 30⁴ BretPower, LincolnsPledge, HiHoSilvers (prkd w-cver)
6- 2 6May ft 69° clm18000 1 :30¹ 1:01¹ 1:32¹ 2:03 7 6 67½ 52¾° 84½ 86 2:04¹ 9-1 (GKramr) 31³ StarFarmer, BeansTonite, ParsonOregon (tuff foes)
5-25¹⁰May ft 56° clm14000 1 :29² 1:01⁴ 1:32² 2:04² 3 4 33 32 2ⁿ 1½ 2:04¹ *5-2 (GKramr) 31² ChiefTimmyHawk, Gllgiss, DoNotPass (in peak form)
5-17¹⁰May ft 76° clm13000 1 :30² 1:01 1:33 2:04³ 4 5 65 84° 56 11½ 2:04³ 9-1 (GKramr) 30⁴ ChiefTimmyHawk, ExtraLucky, Barometer (big rally)

BLACK 5 (9-2 =)

Driver—JIM CURRAN, Gray-Gold — Tr.—J. Wolfe — (152-23-19-18—.252)

CHARGER BOY — Br g 1970, by Tennessee Bill—Jeanie Karin—Billy Jean
Owner: P. J. Boyle, J. L. Wolfe & W. Urbanik, Ind., Ill.

1979	24	3	4	3	$18,819	2:01¹ Spk⅝
1978	46	6	7	6	$33,689	2:01⁵ Arl1¼
			Lifetime		$92,472	8, 2:01³ (1¼)

7-10¹⁰Spk⅝ ft 82° clm15000 1 :29 :59⁴ 1:31 2:01¹ 5 6 6³¼° 67¾ 1¼ 1¼ 7 2 (JCurran) 29³ ChargerBoy, TperChip, StarFarmer (well handled)
6-29 2Spk⅝ ft 61° clm12500 1 :30 1:02³ 1:34³ 2:04¹ 8 7 52½° 4¼⁴ 31 13¼ 2:04¹ 8-1 (JCurran) 29² ChargerBy, MityOneTeam, DynmiteRcy (big mile)
6-21¹⁰Spk⅝ ft 82° clm12500 C=1 :29⁴ 1:00⁴ 1:31² 2:03¹ 3 3° 21½ 63 56 84 2:04 6-1 (WMcEny) 30¹ MiracleTeddy, AliasSmith, Barometer (close up early)
6-14 6May ft 84° clm12500 C=1 :29⁴ 1:00⁴ 1:32² 2:03⁴ 7 2 31½ 31 41¼ 2:03³ 5-2 (JCurran) 30¹ NativeSue, EdsMark, SpeedyTrom (good try)
6- 6 6Spk⅝ ft 78° clm12500+1 :30² 1:02¹ 1:32¹ 2:03³ 8 8 75° 74° 54½ 3¾ 2:03⁴ 33-1 (JCurran) 30⁴ BestOfBarons, HertgeElnorChrgrBoy (big late rally)
5-30¹⁰May ft 71° clm12000 1 :32 1:04¹ 1:36 2:05⁴ 2 4 42½° 42½ 21 44¼ 2:06³ 7-1 (JCurran) 30³ GrndpaLeo, BillyGnBrks, HrtgeEinr (3 wide backsda)

YELLOW 6 (5-1 +)

Driver—DELVIN L. INSKO, White-Purple-Gold — Tr.—T. Carter — (79-8-9-12—.215)

‡TOP BUTLER — Ch c 1975, by Adios Butler—Rose Mary Dee—Harrys Dream
Owner: Tracy Carter, Aurora, Ill.

1979	13	3	2	2	$7,164	2:01¹ ScD⅝
1978	22	2	4	1	$3,939	2:03⁴ ScD⅝
			Lifetime		$8,941	3, 2:03⁴ (⅝)

7-11 5Spk⅝ ft 83° †clm10000 C=1 :30 1:03 1:32 2:02 8 3° 1¹⁴ 31½ 22 2ⁿᵏ 2:02 *3-2 (WPaisly) 29³ Reindeer, TopButler, Lisette (game effort)
6-28 5Spk⅝ ft 74° †clm10000 C=1 :30 1:01⁴ 1:31² 2:03¹ 4 7 32½° 1¹ 1½ 54¼ 2:04 *7-5 (BBilter) 32¹ FarewellPluto, BubDClmcey, TopButler (class drop)
6-18 8Spk⅝ ft 60° †clm17500+1 :29⁴ 1:01 1:31² 2:02³ 8 1 11¼ 11½ 1½ 82¼ 2:03 8-1 (BBilter) 31⁴ TKCounsel, BrwdSharon, EyreQuke (used hard early)
6- 9 ScD⅝ ft †clm10000 1 :30 1:00⁴ 1:31³ 2:01⁴ 3 5 5° 2° 3¹ 1ⁿᵏ 2:01⁴ 8-1 (BBilter) TopButler, WeHareDirector, NightTimeCnsl (———)
6- 2 ScD⅝ ft †tnw10000 1 :29² :58⁴ 1:29 2:00¹ 4 4° 2° 2° 31 79½ 2:02 7-2 (BBilter) MarttieSpinner, StarButler, SunnyArt (———)
5-26 ScD⅝ ft †tnw10000 1 :30¹ 1:01² 1:30⁴ 2:01⁴ 1 1 11¼ 34¼ 2:03 9-1 (BBilter) JudgeHanover, Chino, TopButler (———)

ORANGE 7 (7-2 +)

Driver—WAYNE TEMPLE, Red-White-Black — Tr.—W. Temple — (35-6-3-4—.257)

HASTY BROOK — Br h 1974, by Nautilus—Calypso—Brookdale
Owner: Mikes Grill, Inc., Danville, Ill.

1979	16	4	3	3	$11,935	2:01² Spk⅝
1978	30	8	3	1	$27,255	2:01² Spk⅝
			Lifetime		$45,310	4, 2:01² (⅝)

7- 9 6Spk⅝ ft 74° clm10000+1 :30¹ 1:01² 1:32 2:01² 5 1 13½ 13 13 15¼ 2:01² 4 1 (HKrnngr) 29² HastyBrook, JJsLuke, HpefulOne (never looked back)
6-24 QCD⅝ ft 80° clm8000 1 :28⁴ :59⁴ 1:31³ 2:02 6 1 1¹ 1¹ 14 110 2:02 *8-5 (HKrnngr) 30² HastyBrook, SenatorLee, SalesmanSam (———)
6-17 QCD⅝ ft 83° clm8000 1 :29³ 1:00² 1:32¹ 2:03³ 3 1 11 1½ 21¼ 2:03³ 7-2 (HKrnngr) 31² HastyBrook, DemonRandolph, LuckyTrnst (———)
6-10 QCD⅝ gd 65° clm8000 1 :30 1:01¹ 1:33² 2:05³ 3 3 63° 65½° 63½ 62⅝ 2:09 *5-2 (HKrnngr) 30⁴ AbsKnox, Cachet, PhantomAlmahurst (———)
5-30 4May ft 71° clm8000 1 :30 1:01¹ 1:32² 2:04³ 1 2 32¼ im34⁴ 45½ 47¾ 2:06¹ 3-1 (WTmple) :33 BeautySam, SundanceJulie, WstrnsEvelyn (rd trbla)
4-17 1May ft 50° clm8000 1 :30¹ 1:01² 1:32⁴ 2:04¹ 2 3 31½ 21½ 2½ 2:04² 4 1 (WTmple) 31¹ YardysSal, HastyBrook, RacewayThundr (no excusa)

PURPLE 8 (12-1 +)

Driver—MAHLON MARSHALL, Red-White — Tr.—M. Marshall — (1-0-0-0—.000)

LARGO RANGER — Br g 1974, by Nansemond—Range Line—Amscot
Owner: Trotter Range & Mahlon C. Marshall, Carmel, Wilkinson, Ind.

1979	2	0	0	0	—	(———)
1978	18	3	1	2	$12,203	2:00⁴ Spk⅝
			Lifetime		$23,240	4, 2:00⁴ (⅝)

7- 7 3Spk⅝ ft 72° nw50004-1=1 :29³ :59² 1:32³ 2:02 7 8° 9¼ 88½ 716 617 2:05² 69-1 (MMrshll) :31 Hwthornejoe, HidewyBill, SllyVolo (lacked pace)
6-27 QCD⅝ ft 76° Qua 1 :30³ 1:02² 1:34 2:04¹ 4 4 46 56° 55½ 56⅝ 2:05³ NB (MMrshll) SonCycle, FlamingH, SouthbrookSolarGB (———)
1- 6 6Spk⅝A ft 10° nw13500078 1 :32² 1:05³ 1:36² 2:07³ 4 3° 74½° 99½ 816 ? 2:08 99-1 (MMrshll) 32¹ PaleFaceYnkee, MiniShtA, MrPilre (in middle of trk)
12-30 9May gd 24° nw800078 1 :31 1:04 1:35⁴ 2:07⁴ 1 2 21¼ 31½ 42¼ 2:08² 5-1 (MMrshll) 32¹ MrPellaire, ChiefYoung, HurricaneSampsn (gd trip)
12-23 9May ft 37° nw800078 1 :31¹ 1:03¹ 1:34¹ 2:06¹ 1 1 1½ 31 52 2:05³ 8-1 (MMrshll) 31² Simpsonic, EdChandler, Uplander (battled, tired)
12-16 9MayA ft 37° nw800078 1 :31 1:02³ 1:33 2:04⁴ 6 3 42½ 33½ 58 2:06² 27-1 (MMrshll) 31³ CardinalChfA, SuperTrip, BrilliantExchge (away fast)

BROWN 9 (8-1 —)

Driver—JIM DOLBEE, Green-White-Red — Tr.—W. McLurg — (69-11-7-4—.235)

HI HO SILVERS — B g 1973, by Hickory Smoke—Janelle Hanover—Star's Pride
Owner: Howard Brown & Michael Slavin, Chicago, Ill.

1979	22	3	2	3	$15,178	2:00⁴ Spk⅝
1978	43	2	6	8	$24,456	2:04² Haw1
			Lifetime		$36,644	4, 2:02² (1)

7-11 5Spk⅝ ft 83° c¹m17500+1 :30¹ 1:02 1:29⁴ 2:00² 8 3° 21 35 43¾ 2:01¹ 3-1 (JDolbee) 30⁴ BlwShadow, SamBlack, HighlandKirk (early foot)
7- 3 2Spk⅝ ft 78° clm15000=1 :29³ :59² 1:30³ 2:00⁴ 5 1° 33 31½ 11½ 2:00⁴ 7-1 (JDolbee) 29³ Hi HoSilvers, DJTrick, RapidCanny (big rally)
6-23 3Spk⅝ ft 78° clm17500+1 :30¹ 1:02¹ 1:32 2:01 3 3 32 21° 31 79½ 2:06¹ 7-1 (JDolbee) Hi HoSilvers, RapidCanny, WildwoodWill (tuff trip)
6-12 7Spk⅝ ft 63° clm15000 C=1 :30⁴ 1:02¹ 1:34¹ 2:03⁴ 4 4 45° 32½ 32¼ 2:04¹ 4-1 (DMagee) 29⁴ BretPower, LincolnsPledge, HiHoSilvers (tuff trip)
6- 4 4Spk⅝ ft 53° clm15000+1 :30¹ 1:01¹ 1:31⁴ 2:01³ 6 6 67° 67° 44¾ 2:02 16-1 (JCurran) 30⁴ CoolLove, HiHoSilvers, WantawinChris (tuff trip)
5-18 7May ft 67° clm16000 1 :30³ 1:01² 1:32 2:02 8 8 85½ 74¾° 87x be, dnf 46-1 (DBusse) WnsmeFox, GdOFrisky, PiefceYnkee (equip problem)

CHARLEY HORSE — 5....9....7   PARADISE — 5....9....7 Best Bet   MISS MAREY — 6....5....4

ONE MILE PACE — # THIRD RACE — **Purse $7,500**

"TAMMETTES"

CONDITIONED. 3-Year-Olds and Up. Non-winners of 3 races or $7,500 in lifetime. (Races for $1,000 or less not considered.)

PLEASE ASK FOR HORSE BY PROGRAM NUMBER

WARMUP COLOR—WHITE

Date Trk Cond Temp | Class | Dist | Leader's Time ¼ ½ ¾ | Winner's Time | PP | ¼ | ½ | ¾ | Str | Fin | Ind. Time | Odds | Driver | Ind ¼ Time | ORDER OF FINISH First Second Third | Comment

---

RED **1** 5-1 =

Driver—DARYL BUSSE, Gray-Red — Tr.—La. Williams (202-26-30-22—.245)

1979 5 2 0 0 $7,164 2:01³ Spk⅝
1978 7 2 1 0 $892 2:03³ Lat¹
Lifetime $1,411 3, 2:03³ (1)

RADIANT OMAHA

B c 1975, by King Omaha—Amy's Radiant—Amscot
Owner: Rex D. Brock, John R. Neal, Keith F. Macy, Cicero, Noblesville, Ind.

7-13 7Spk⅝ ft 80° nw3R—1 :29² :59⁴ 1:29² 1:59³ 5 5 5⁵½ x9²³ 8¹⁸ 8¹⁷ 2:03 3-1 (DBusse) :29 CrossKeys, FreedomTime, FreedomSpirit (elim. self)
7- 7 5Spk⅝ ft 72° nw9000⁷⁹+1 :29 1:00³ 1:30¹ 1:59³ 4 2 2² 2³½° 2⁷ 4⁶¾ 2:01 3-1 (WTmple) :30 ChrisPick, RivrCircIRme, DcShrmn (pulled, hung)
6-25 5Spk⅝ ft 67° 3-5yrnw2R=1 :30 1:00 1:31³ 2:01³ 7 1° 1¹½ 1¹½ 1³½ 1⁸½ 2:01³ 2-1 (DBusse) :30 RdintOmh, HustlinRuss, JzzMstr (powerful mile)
6-15 1Spk⅝ ft 86° 3-5yrnw2R=1 :29 1:01 1:31⁴ 2:04 6 7 8⁶° 5³½° 2ⁿᵏ 2ⁿᵏ p1 2:04 3-1 (DBusse) :31² RadiantOmaha, IrishHeel, WildwdJulep (game mile)
6- 2 Lat¹ ft nw2R 1 :30¹ 1:00³ 1:32² 2:01 3 6 6 5° 4⁴¾ 4⁸½ 2:02³ 9-2 (RPaul) ColdKnight, DeeDeesDuffy, RyansButler (———)
5-23 Lat¹ gd Qua 1 :30³ 1:01 1:34² 2:05 1 1 1 1 1² 1⁶ 2:05 NB (RWaggnr) RadiantOmaha, HopeToWin, WeePluckEm (———)

BLUE **2** 9-2 +

Driver—BRIAN PELLING, Black-Red-Orange — Tr.—B. Pelling (68-11-8-8—.266)

1979 6 3 1 0 $5,872 2:00¹ Sac¹
1978 2 0 0 0 $95
Lifetime $95 None in U.S.A.

DIRECT GOLD N

B g 1975, by Caliburn—Robin Direct—Scottish Star
Owner: B.R.P. Enterprises Corp., Cypress, Calif.

6- 4 7Spk⅝ ft 3-4yrnwR4500-2L+1 :30 1:00 1:31² 2:02² 5 1 1² 1¹½ 1¹½ 1⁴¼ 2:02² *3-5 (BPelling) :31 DirectGldN, TrpedoVictry, BretTheBrat (pulld away)
5- 8 Sac¹ ft nw2R 1 :28² :59¹ 1:30² 2:00¹ 3 1 1 1 1¹¼ 1¾ 2:00¹ 3-1 (BPelling) DirectGoldN, RoyalBirdieN, SengaPayne (———)
5- 2 Sac¹ ft nw2R 1 :30² 1:02² 1:34 2:04⁴ 2 2 2 3 3¹½ 2¾ 2:05 5-2 (BPelling) CooksCreanza, DirectGoldN, ChineseApple (———)
4-25 LA⅝ ft nw2R 1 :31 1:02¹ 1:33² 2:03³ 7 2 3 6 6⁷½ 5⁵¼ 2:04³ 8-5 (BPelling) NativeLeader, SengaPayne, HarborPilot (———)
4-17 LA⅝ ft Mdn 1 :29² 1:01⁴ 1:33² 2:04 6 1 1 1 1½ 1½ 2:04 *6-5 (BPelling) DirectGoldN, RoyalBirdieN, SpanishByrd (———)
4- 4 LA⅝ ft Qua 1 :30⁴ 1:01⁴ 1:33¹ 2:04 5 5 5 5 5⁶ 4³ 2:04³ NB (JRWllms) DerbyLord, BoundToBeN, RoyalGrenadier (———)

WHITE **3** 10-1 +

Driver—STERLING BUCH, White-Red-Black — Tr.—J. Weeks (46-13-5-4—.372)

1979 0 0 0 0 (——)
1978 6 1 0 0 $1,499 2:01² Mea⅝
Lifetime $7,414 4, 2:01² (⅝)

DUKE DRUMMER

Br h 1974, by Chuckeen—Alabama Dale—Pinehaven Jet
Owner: H. A. Wahl, J. L. & Irma R. Weeks, Meadowlands, Pa., Holly Hill, Fla.

7-11 Spk⅝ ft 79° Qua 1 :31 1:04¹ 1:34⁴ 2:05¹ 7 5 5⁵½ 4¹½° 4⁴ 4² 2:05³ NB (SBuch) Bindy, BradleyBeetle, PatchenGirl (———)
12-25⁷⁸PPk⅝ ft nw7500⁷⁸ 1 :29² 1:00¹ 1:31¹ 2:02² 1 5 5 6 7⁴ 7²⁰¼ 2:06² 10-1 (MMcNchl) ColumbiasGem, SterlingFshion, GollyBum (———)
11-25⁷⁸Mea⅝ ft cond2200 1 :31¹ 1:04 1:34⁴ 2:04³ 6 6 6 5° 6⁶ 7¹⁰¼ 2:06³ 12-1 (LKeith) KeyCreed, ButlersBrewer, KaboomMinbar (———)
11-21⁷⁸Mea⅝ ft Qua 1 :31 1:02¹ 1:33³ 2:05⁴ 4 5 5 4° 4⁶½ 3⁷ 2:07¹ NB (RStillings) MayStar, ByeByesApril, DukeDrummer (———)
11-18⁷⁸Mea⅝ ft cond3500 1 :30 1:02 1:31¹ 2:00² 1x 5 5 5 5¹¹ 5ᵈⁱˢ 38-1 (LHawk) LCKnight, TheConsiglieri, SlickGuy (———)
10-20⁷⁸Mea⅝ ft Qua 1 :30⁴ 1:02² 1:34¹ 2:05 8 6 6 6 6⁷ 3¹²¼ 2:07² NB (CSells) AndreaVic, CindySal, DukeDrummer (———)

GREEN **4** 8-1 =

Driver—WILLIAM LAMBERTUS, Gold-White-Black — Tr.—F. Bettis (40-2-7-6—.197)

1979 8 1 1 2 $8,194 2:02 Mea⅝
1978 9 1 5 1 $2,677 2:03² Mea⅝
Lifetime $2,677 2, 2:03² (⅝)

‡WILDWOOD SWINGER

Ch c 1976, by Steady Star—Trix Hanover—Bullet Hanover
Owner: Wildwood Ga. Farms, Wildwood, Ga.

7-13 7Spk⅝ ft 80° ‡nw3R—1 :29² :59⁴ 1:29² 1:59³ 6 6 6⁶½ 5⁷ 4¹¹ 4⁸¾ 2:01² 18-1 (WLmbrts) :30³ CrossKeys, FreedomTime, FreedomSpirit (no rally)
6-29 5Spk⅝ ft61° ‡3yrstk53750+1 :30 1:01 1:31² 2:00¹ 4 5 6⁶½im5⁷½ 4¹² 4¹³ 2:02⁴ 34-1 (WLmbrts) :29⁴ Penner, EscapeArtist, JudgeHanover (bothered)
6-22 4Spk⅝ ft 63° ‡nw3R+1 :30² 1:01⁴ 1:32² 2:03¹ 7 6 6⁵½ 6⁴¼° 5⁴ 4¹¾ 2:03³ 6-1 (WLmbrts) :30² MarJimHarvey, RoadFive, ViciousVic (finished well)
6-12 9Spk⅝ ft 63° ‡3-5yrnw2R—1 :31³ 1:02¹ 1:32⁴ 2:03² 8 9 8⁸¾ 7¹¹° 6¹² 3⁵¾ 2:04³ 9-2 (WLmbrts) :29³ CrossKeys, Ghetto, WildwoodSwinger (flew in str)
6- 2 Mea⅝ ft ‡cond2700 1 :30 1:01³ 1:31² 2:02 3 1 1 1 1²½ 2ⁿᵏ 2:02 *2-1 (WLmbrts) BelovedSkiper, WildwoodSwngr, Bonus (———)
5-26 Mea⅝ sy ‡cond2700 1 :30¹ 1:01¹ 1:31 2:02³ 6 2 3 2° 2½ 5¹¾ 2:03 *9-5 (WLmbrts) SunlordHanover, BelovedSkippr, SndFight (———)

BLACK **5** 10-1 =

Driver—STANLEY BANKS, White-Purple — Tr.—H. Brown (168-17-19-24—.212)

1979 8 0 3 1 $5,581
1978 17 2 3 2 $10,324 2:00¹ Spk⅝
Lifetime $13,614 3, 2:00¹ (⅝)

RARE PEARL

Br c 1975, by Race Time—Paul's Pearl—Tar Heel
Owner: Donner Packing Company, Inc., Milwaukee, Wis.

7-13 7Spk⅝ ft 80° nw3R=1 :29² :59⁴ 1:29² 1:59³ 4 1 1¹¼ 2¹½x 9ᵈⁱˢ 9ᵈⁱˢ 33-1 (JCurran) CrossKeys, FreedomTime, FreedomSpirit (elim. self)
7- 6 5Spk⅝ ft 68° nw3R=1 :29³ 1:01 1:32 2:02² 5 3 2¹ 2¹½° 2¹¼ 9¹⁴ 2:05¹ 13-1 (DWlmsll) :32⁴ CorkysABomb, FreedomTime, HastySoot (early foot)
6-22 4Spk⅝ ft 63° nw3R=1 :30² 1:01⁴ 1:32² 2:03¹ 4 ix4° 9ᵈⁱˢ 9ᵈⁱˢ pulled up, dnf 8-1 (DBusse) MarJimHarvey, RoadFive, ViciousVic (bothered)
6- 8 5Spk⅝ sy 78° nw3R=1 :31¹ 1:03 1:34 2:04² 6 1 1²½ 1¹ 1½ 2²¼ 2:04⁴ 4-1 (DBusse) :30⁴ MarkOne, RarePearl, LittleHenryHill (prkd to ⅛th)
5-23 8May ft 50° nw3R 1 :30 1:01 1:32¹ 2:04⁴ 3 1 1¹ 2ʰᵈ 1ʰᵈ 4²¾ 2:05² *9-5 (SBanks) :33¹ TrpdoVctry, JyCntySu, TwoOnTheAisle (bttld inside)
5-14 9May sy 53° nw3R 1 :32³ 1:05⁴ 1:37 2:08³ 1 1 1¹ 1¾ 1¹¼ 2¹¾ 2:09 *3-5 (SBanks) :32 FreewayFlyer, RarePearl, JHICash (outpaced str.)

YELLOW **6** 6-1 =

Driver—DAVE MAGEE, Red-Black-White — Tr.—W. Mountjoy (166-23-19-17—.236)

1979 11 1 4 1 $9,905 2:05⁴ May
1978 11 0 1 4 $4,307
Lifetime $7,557 5, 2:04 (⅝)

PARKER B DIRECT

B g 1972, by Direct Way—Clara Parker—Parker Byrd
Owner: W. C. Mountjoy, W. Chicago, Ill.

7- 6 5Spk⅝ ft 68° nw3R+1 :29³ 1:01 1:32 2:02² 4 6 5⁴¼ 5³¼ 5³ 4³¼ 2:03 27-1 (DMagee) :30² CorkysABomb, FreedomTime, HastySoot (good trip)
6-28 7Spk⅝ ft 74° nwR5500²L—1 :29³ 1:01 1:32² 2:01⁴ 1 3 3²½ 6⁴½ 8¹⁰ 8⁹¾ 2:03⁴ 14-1 (DMagee) :30² ChiefsFinale, BaronessFshn, PeterBrmac (some spd)
6-15 2Spk⅝ ft 86° nw3R=1 :29⁴ 1:01⁴ 1:32² 2:02¹ 1 2 3¹¼im2²° 3⁹ 5¹⁰ 2:04¹ *5-2 (DMagee) :31⁴ VgbndHill, ByeByeShdy, HmeChnce (hooked wheels)
6- 2 9May ft 69° nw3R 1 :31 1:02⁴ 1:33³ 2:03³ 3 1 1¹½ 1ⁿᵏ 2¾ 2½ 2:03⁴ 10-1 (DMagee) :30¹ BaronssFshn, PrkrBDrct, EvningsChce (battled hard)
5-22 4May ft 67° nw3R 1 :31⁴ 1:05¹ 1:35⁴ 2:06² 8 3 6³½ 6³¾ 5³ 3¹ 2:06³ 5-1 (DMagee) :30 SunnyDream, JetSetTime, ParkerBDirect (gd finish)
5-12 3May ft 52° nw3R 1 :30² 1:01 1:32⁴ 2:04³ 7 2° 1¹ 1¾ 1ⁿᵏ 2ⁿᵏ 2:04³ 7-1 (DMagee) :31⁴ GrayGamecock, ParkerBDirect, RdFve (3-wide early)

ORANGE **7** 3-1 =

Driver—WALTER PAISLEY, Green-White — Tr.—W. Paisley (133-26-23-18—.337)

1979 8 3 4 1 $11,695 2:01³ Lex¹
1978 15 4 2 2 $1,674 2:07 Lewbg
Lifetime $1,674 2, 2:07

FREEDOM TIME

B c 1976, by Race Time—Mona Lobell—Solicitor
Owner: Paisley Enterprises, Inc. & John Ceren, Plainfield, Downers Grove, Il

7-13 7Spk⅝ ft 80° nw3R=1 :29² :59⁴ 1:29² 1:59³ 3 4 4⁴ 3²½°im2⁸ 2⁵¼ 2:00³ 5-2 (WPaisly) :30³ CrossKeys, FreedomTme, FrdmSprt (hooked wheels)
7- 6 5Spk⅝ ft 68° nw3R+1 :29³ 1:01 1:32 2:02² 9 9 8⁵½° 8⁵½° 6³¼ 2¾ 2:02³ *2-1 (WPaisly) :29² CorkysABomb, FreedomTime, HastySoot (late charge)
6-29 3Spk⅝ ft 61° 3-5yrnw2R+1 :30 1:01¹ 1:31³ 2:02⁴ 7 4 2¹½ 4⁴¼° 2⁴ 1ⁿᵏ 2:02⁴ *6-5 (WPaisly) :30² FreedomTime, SpeakOut, HiFisKing (super drive)
6-18 3Spk⅝ ft 60° 2-4yrnw1R=1 :32 1:02⁴ 1:36 2:05³ 3 1 1¹½ 1¹¼ 1⁴ 1⁵¼ 2:05³ *1-5 (WPaisly) :29³ FreedomTime, PresentValue, FoxCamp (easy pace)
6- 4 1Spk⅝ ft 82° 2-4yrnw1R=1 :30¹ 1:02¹ 1:32³ 2:01⁴ 7 3° 1¹¼ 2² 2² 2¹¼ 2:02 2-1 (WPaisly) :29 CrossKeys, FreedomTime, MertsCoxie (2nd best)
5-18 Lex¹ ft nw3R 1 :31¹ 1:01¹ 1:32 2:01³ x2x 7 5 4° 3² 1¹ 2:01³ *4-5 (JMartin) FreedomTime, Roanoke, SkipperKnox (———)

PURPLE **8** 12-1 =

Driver—DWAYNE PLETCHER, White-Black — Tr.—L. Pletcher (38-2-4-7—.173)

1979 19 2 2 2 $9,392 2:05² May
1978 7 0 0 0 $1,068
Lifetime $1,068

ROAD FIVE

Ch g 1976, by Shady Counsel—Flo Wind—Florlis
Owner: Donald D. & Beverly L. Pletcher, Shipshewana, Ind.

7-13 7Spk⅝ ft 80° nw3R=1 :29² :59⁴ 1:29² 1:59³ 9 8 8⁹ 6⁹ 7¹⁴ 7¹⁵ 2:02³ 99-1 (DwPlchr) :31² CrossKeys, FreedomTime, FreedomSpirit (post hurt)
6-30 9Spk⅝ gd 71° nw3R=1 :29¹ 1:00³ 1:32² 2:03³ 1 5 4⁴¼ 7⁴ 8⁶½ 9⁷¾ 2:05¹ 10-1 (DwPlchr) :32 GreenwoodJC, CrossKeys, SteadyAirdale (weakened)
6-22 4Spk⅝ ft 63° nw3R—1 :30² 1:01⁴ 1:32² 2:03¹ 8 8 7⁷ 7⁵¼°im6⁴½3¹¾p2 2:03³ 95-1 (DwPlchr) :30¹ MarJimHarvey, RoadFive, ViciousVic (road trouble)
6- 8 6Spk⅝ sy 78° nw3R=1 :31¹ 1:01³ 1:32⁴ 2:02² 7 8 8¹¹° 6⁶½ 6⁷½ 5¹³ 2:05 70-1 (DwPlchr) :30⁴ SeaHawk, NapaOne, SteadyAirdale (lost ground)
5-23 8May ft 50° nw3R 1 :30 1:01 1:32¹ 2:04⁴ 8 8 8¹⁵ 8¹⁵ 8¹⁸ 8²¹ 2:09 41-1 (DwPlchr) :33⁴ TorpedoVictory, JayCntySu, TwoOnTheAisle (dull)
5-12 3May ft 52° nw3R 1 :30² 1:01 1:32⁴ 2:04³ 1 4 5⁴½ 3²½° 3²½ 3⁴ 2:05² 9-1 (DwPlchr) :32 GrayGamecock, ParkerBDirect, RdFve (outpaced str)

BROWN **9** 6-1 =

Driver—DELVIN L. INSKO, White-Purple-Gold — Tr.—J. Mohr (79-8-9-12—.215)

1979 3 2 0 0 $6,000 2:03 Spk⅝
1978 4 0 0 0 (——)
Lifetime (——)

ELITE HANOVER A

Br g 1975, by Michael Hanover—Sunhappy—Light Brigade
Owner: J. Mohr, R. Ver Sluis & E. Welling, Mich.

7-13 7Spk⅝ ft 80° nw3R+1 :29² :59⁴ 1:29² 1:59³ 8x 9 9¹⁶ 8¹³ 6¹⁴ 6¹³ 2:02¹ 8-1 (DLInsko) :30¹ CrossKeys, FreedomTime, FreedomSpirit (elim. self)
7- 5 9Spk⅝ ft 63° 3-5yrnw2R+1 :31 1:03¹ 1:34 2:03² 1 1 1² 1² 1² 1¹½ 2:03² *4-5 (DBusse) :29² EliteHnverA, MistyCilette, MyLstTime (crushd foes)
6-25 3Spk⅝ ft 67° 2-4yrnw1R+1 :30⁴ 1:01 1:32² 2:03 1 3 1¹½ 1¹½ 1² 1²¼ 2:03 7-2 (DBusse) :30³ ElitHnverA, MdeAKing, CordovDick (shrp qtr move)
6- 6 Spk⅝ ft 71° Qua 1 :31³ 1:04⁴ 1:36 2:07² 4 2 2¹½ 1¹ 1³ 1⁴¾ 2:07² NB (DBusse) EliteHanoverA, AlbaJoy, RobbieRob (———)
8-19⁷⁸Northam Raced approx. 1⅜ miles in NR, Fin. 9 (RSangalli) Assist, ChiefKamahle, RisingPlain (———)
8- 2⁷⁸York Raced approx. 1½ miles in NR, Fin. 9 (RSangalli) TopsyTurvy, JuniorCourt, BlackRanger (———)

CHARLEY HORSE — 7....2....1 PARADISE — 7....2....1 MISS MAREY — 2....9....6

ONE MILE PACE

FOURTH RACE
$3 QUINIELA WAGERING ON THIS RACE
"THE PONTIAC" (1st Division)

Purse $7,500

STAKE. 3, 4- and 5-Year-Olds. THE MIDWEST SERIES.

PLEASE ASK FOR HORSE BY PROGRAM NUMBER

WARMUP COLOR—GREEN

RED 1 6-1 =
Driver—DENNIS TRIPP, Blue-White-Red   Tr.—R. Tripp   (10-1-0-0—.100)
COLUMBIA TRIP   Blk c 1976, by Columbia George—Melanie—Worthy Boy
Owner: Raymond G. Tripp, Poplar Grove, Ill.
1979	5	0	0	0	$1,535
1978	0	0	0	0	
Lifetime					
7-13 ³Spk⅝ ft 80° 3-5yrstk7500+1 :29² 1:00³ 1:32² 2:02² 3 1 2¹ 31½ 32¼ 42½ 2:03 17-1 (WPaisly) :30² MagioMotion, LeatheBoy, AmbroTempo (good try)
7- 5 ⁹Spk⅝ ft 63° 3-5yrnw2R+1 :31 1:03¹ 1:34 2:03² 7 8 9⁹° 66½ 59 51³ 2:06 99-1 (DTripp) :30³ EliteHnvrA., MistyCillette, MyLstTime (foes too tuff)
6-18 ³Spk⅝ ft 60° 2-4yrnw1R+1 :32 1:02⁴ 1:36 2:05³ 8 8 7¹⁶ 85¼° 78 69¼ 2:07² 20-1 (DTripp) :30¹ FreedomTime, PresentValue, FoxCam:p (tuff winner)
6- 4 ¹Spk⅝ ft 82° 2-4yrnw1R=1 :30¹ 1:02¹ 1:32³ 2:01⁴ 8 8 78¾° 69¼° 414 422 2:06¹ 21-1 (DTripp) :31⁴ CrossKeys, FreedomTime, MertsCoxie (post hurt)
5-22 Det¹ ft Mdn 1 :29³ 1:01¹ 1:32² 2:01³ 8 10 9° 8° 62½ 511½ 2:03⁴ 17-1 (DTripp) ConsiderateJoe, SaltLich, JustIdeal (—)
5-11 Det¹ ft Qua 1 :31² 1:02² 1:32⁴ 2:04 2 6 6 6 6⁶ 21½ 2:04¹ NB (DTripp) GreenHeʃTarri, ColumbiaTrip, AteMark (—)

BLUE 2 12-1 =
Driver—KELTON NOBLE, Black-Blue   Tr.—K. Noble   (28-1-1-3—.091)
LITTLE HENRY HILL   B c 1975, by Henry T Adios—Hills Verna—Hillsota
Owner: Donald Clay Forney, Huntington, Ind.
1979	9	1	1	3	$7,639	2:07 sy May
1978	2	1	0	1	$3,000	2:02³ Spk⅝
Lifetime					$3,000	3, 2:02³ (⅝)
7-13 ⁵Spk⅝ ft 80° 3-5yrstk7500=1 :31 1:00¹ 1:31¹ 2:00³ 2 4 44½ 43° 35¼ 51³ 2:03¹ 10-1 (KNoble) :31² RayCharles, RaceOnCarey, NobleMjrty (tuff winner)
7- 6 ⁵Spk⅝ ft 68° nw3R—1 :29³ 1:01 1:32 2:02² 2 4 32¼ 31¾ 31½ 53¼ 2:03¹ 7-1 (KNoble) :30⁴ CorkysABomb, FreedomTime, JetSetTime (on wood)
6-23 ⁵Spk⅝ ft 59° nw4R=1 :30¹ 1:01⁴ 1:31⁴ 2:02 1 2 31½ 52½ 52¾ 33½ 2:02⁴ 16-1 (KNoble) :30² TwoOnTheAisle, MgicMtion, LittleHenry Hill (gd trip)
6-16 ¹Spk⅝ ft 85° nw4R+1 :29 :59² 1:30² 2:00⁴ 2 3 43¾ 85 65¼ 55¼ 2:02 9-1 (KNoble) :30³ Sea Hwk, Mrngo Td, Two On The Aisle (shuffled back)
6- 8 ⁵Spk⅝ sy 78° nw3R=1 :31¹ 1:03 1:34 2:04² 4 2 22½ 32 31½ 32¾ 2:05 *2-1 (KNoble) :30³ MarkOne, RarePearl, LittleHenryHill (prkd to ⅛th)
5-22 ⁴May1 ft 67° Qua 1 :31⁴ 1:05¹ 1:35⁴ 2:06² 7 8 32 31¼° 41½ 52¾ 2:07 *1-1 (KNoble) :31 SunnyDrm, JetSetTime, PrkrBDrct (3-wide last turn)

WHITE 3 9-2 =
Driver—CLEN KIDWELL, Blue-Gold   Tr.—G. Kidwell   (26-1-7-3—.226)
RACE ON CAREY   Br c 1976, by Race Time—Thrifty Way—King's Counsel
Owner: Wayne W. Carey, Mineral Point, Wis.
1979	4	1	1	1	$5,405	2:05⁴ May Qua
1978	3	0	1	1	$190	2, 2:06² (1⅛) Qua
Lifetime					$190	2, 2:06² (1⅛) Qua
7-13 ⁵Spk⅝ ft 80° 3-5yrstk7500+1 :31 1:00¹ 1:31¹ 2:00³ 3 1° 21¼ 21¾ :22½ 23½ 2:01² 7-1 (GKidwell) :29⁴ RayCharles, RaceOnCarey, NobleMajority (game try)
7- 2 ³Spk⅝ ft 68° 2-4yrnw1R=1 :31² 1:03³ 1:35² 2:06¹ 8 7im42° 31½° 2½ 1½ 2:06¹ *2-1 (GKidwell) :29 RcOnCry, YchtsmnCky, GdMissSkppr (bothered still)
6-15 ⁴Spk⅝ ft 86° nwR5500L+1 :29¹ 1:01¹ 1:32² 2:03¹ 4 3 33 32 31 31¼ 2:03² 14-1 (GKidwell) :30³ NativeRita, ArmbroTempo, RaceOnCarey (good trip)
5-31 ⁸May gd 70° 2-5yrnw1R 1 :32¹ 1:04¹ 1:35 2:05 6 1° 11½ 21½° 34½ 624 2:09⁴ *4-5 (GKidwell) :34³ RustyStrikes, HiFisKing, JeffFrisco (costly bkn)
5-16 ⁴May ft 64° Qua 1 :32² 1:03³ 1:34⁴ 2:05⁴ 8 1° 1¹ 11½ 11½ 11¼ 2:05⁴ NB (GKidwell) RaceOnCarey, BriansBoy, MaudsBest (—)
10-18 ²Arl1¼ ft 48° 2-4yrnw1R 1 :30³ 1:00³ 1:33³ 2:04² 9 9 88½° 63½° 56½ 53¼ 2:05 *9-5 (GKidwell) :30³ DutchAtom, JohnDirect, LittleOChuckles (post hurt)

GREEN 4 3-1 =
Driver—STAN BAYLESS, Gold-White   Tr.—J. O'Brien   (35-5-5-5—.270)
MEL'S TASSEL   B f 1976, by Melvins Woe—Tassel—Butlet Hanover
Owner: Thurman Downing, Cleveland, Ohio
1979	6	3	0	0	$12,275	2:01² Spk⅝
1979	0	0	0	0		2, 2:03⁴ (1) T.T.
Lifetime						2, 2:03⁴ (1) T.T.
7-11 ⁸Nhd gd F3yrstk11600 1 :29² 1:01³ 1:32² 2:02² 7 6 5 4° 32¼ 2½ 2:02³ 6-1 (SBayless) ImHappy, MelsTassel, SilverSoulette (—)
6-26 ⁸Spk⅝ ft79° FMnwR57002L+1 :29⁴ 1:02¹ 1:31 2:01² 6 6 53½° 42¼° 33 11¼ 2:01² 3-1 (SBayless) :30 Mel'sTassel, GlamoursPat, JetSetTime (strng in str)
6-18 ⁵Spk⅝ ft 80° 2-5yrnw2R=1 :32³ 1:05¹ 1:36¹ 2:06³ 4 5 65¼ 55¼° 32 12¼ 2:06³ 3-1 (SBayless) :30 MelsTassel, SengaPayne, HastySoot (drawing away)
6- 8 ²³pk⅝ sy70° FM3-5yrnw=R 1 :32 1:04³ 1:37¹ 2:07¹ 1 4 4³½ 31½° 2ⁿᵈ× 21¼ 2:07² *4-5 (SBayless) :29⁴ MrgiesMldy, MelsTssl, MnightTrly (brk, caught fast)
5-17 Sac¹ ft Qua 1 :29⁴ :59² 1:32 2:01³ 4 6 5° 3° 21 2¾ 2:014 8-5 (SBayless) BakerHill, MelsTassel, LighAngel (—)
5-11 Sac¹ ft 2-5yrnw1R 1 :29⁴ :59¹ 1:31³ 2:02¹ 4 6 8¹¹ 55° 43 1¹ 2:02¹ *4-1 (SBayless) :29³ MelsTassel, TimeForTraci, BraniganN (flew in str)

BLACK 5 25-1 +
Driver—WALTER PAISLEY, Green-White   Tr.—H. Askew   (133-26-23-18—.337)
NORDEL NUSHIE   B c 1976, by Henry T Adios—Rose Mary Comet—Dominionmite
Owner: Herman L. Askew, Rockford, Ill.
1979	6	1	0	1	$1,271	2:05³ QCD⅝
1978	2	0	0	0		
Lifetime						
7- 7 ³Spk⅝ ft 72° nw5000⁴-1=1 :29³ :59³ 1:32² 2:02² 5 8 8³¹½ ×76¼° 8¹⁹ 8⁴¹¹ 54-1 (TWheeh) HwthorneJoe, IlidewyDill, GllyVolo (wide mile)
6-29 ³Spk⅝ ft 61° nw3R=1 :30 1:01¹ 1:31³ 2:02⁴ 8 6 8⁵¹½ 714 51⁶ 51⁴ 2:05³ 99-1 (TWheelr) :31⁴ FreedomTime, SpeakOut, H²FisKing (elim self)
6-15 ¹Spk⅝ ft 86° 3-5yrnw2R=1 :29 1:01 1:31⁴ 2:04 1 3 22° 21° 54½ 67¼ 2:05³ 7-1 (TWheelr) :33³ RadiantOmaha, IrishHeel, WildwdJulep (prkd, tired)
6- 3 QCD⅝ ft 80° nw3R 1 :29⁴ 1:00² 1:31 2:01³ 5 5 34½ 46 511½ 315 2:04³ 7-1 (RJacobs) :32² PrairieBadger, WindyWinter, NordelNshie (—)
5-31 QCD⅝ ft 68° nw1R 1 :32³ 1:03⁴ 1:36² 2:05¹ 1x 8° 34 2½° 43½ 44½ 2:10¹ *4-5 (RJacobs) :32¹ Knucklehead, IsolaDike, JayRaider (—)
5-25 QCD⅝ ft 68° nw1R 1 :29³ 1:01¹ 1:32² 2:05³ 6 1 1 1³ 11½ 11½ 2:05³ 2-1 (RJacobs) :33¹ NordelNushie, ClassyAct, DonReed (—)

YELLOW 6 25-1 =
Driver—MERLE MYERS, Blue-Green-Peach   Tr.—M. Myers   (11-0-1-0—.051)
WORTHY SCHOLAR   Br c 1976, by Winning Worthy—Majestic Nola—Majestic Hanover
Owner: Robert E. Gangloff, Logansport, Ind.
1979	6	0	0	0	$536	
1978	20	1	3	5	$4,222	2:09 gd And
Lifetime					$4,222	2:09 gd
7-13 ³Spk⅝ ft 80° 3-5yrstk7500+1 :29² 1:00³ 1:32² 2:02² 2 5 53¾° 9²½ 78 7:04 79-1 (MMyers) :31³ MgicMtion, LeatheBoy, ArmbroTmpo (3-wide briefly)
7- 5 And ft 3yrstk411 Dash in 2:07², Fin. 5 Dash in 2:06², Fin. 4 NB (MMyers) KarawayPrince, GhostRanger, Gojeffy (—)
6-25 ³Spk⅝ ft 67° 2-4yrnw1R=1 :30⁴ 1:01 1:32² 2:03 6 5 59° 59 51³ 2:05³ 3-1 (MMyers) :32 ElitHnverA., MdeAKing, CordovDick (no factor)
6- 1 ³May ft 69° 2-5yrnw1R 1 :30 1:03² 1:35 2:05⁴ 1 3 53 74¼° 64¾ 54¾ 2:06¹ 5-1 (MMyers) :30⁴ Ghetto, GoingSteadN, ShortCutHon (no close)
9-27 ²Arl1¼ ft 55° 2-4yrnw1R 1 :30 1:03¼ 1:34 2:03 9 9 912 9⁷ 916 923 2:07³ 19-1 (MMyers) :32² Donson, LittleOChuckles, TorpedoForbes (—)
9-13 ³Spk⅝ ft 82° 2-4yrnw1R+1 :30 1:00² 1:30 2:02³ 7 7 77½° 74½° 77 79½ 2:04³ 6-1 (MMyers) :33³ MnlightLve, TorpedoForbes, FireballMrk (shwd little)

ORANGE 7 10-1 =
Driver—LAWRENCE CHRISTNER, White-Green-Gold   Tr.—L. Christner   (14-0-1-3—.111)
HASTY SOOT   B c 1975, by Nautilus—Nancy B. Good—Avalon Doc
Owner: Marjory M. Silkworth, Ft. Wayne, Ind.
1979	5	0	0	3	$2,755	
1978	18	4	0	5	$3,811	2:03⁴ R.P⅝
Lifetime					$3,856	3, 2:03⁴ (⅝)
7-13 ⁹Spk⅝ ft 80° 3-5yrstk7500=1 :30 1:00¹ 1:30¹ 2:00 5 5 44¼ 45¼×58½ 2:02² 31-1 (LChrstn) :30¹ JudgeHanover, BroadwayTune, MarkOne (elim. self)
7- 6 ⁵Spk⅝ ft 68° nw3R=1 :29³ 1:01 1:32 2:02² 3 5 42¾ 42¾ 4¹ 33 2:03 72-1 (LChrstnr) :30² CorkysABomb, FreedomTime, HastySoot (raced well)
6-29 ¹Spk⅝ ft 61° 3-5yrnw2R=1 :31⁴ 1:02² 1:34² 2:05³ 6 8 9¹⁶ 86½° 6⁵ 44 2:06² 12-1 (LChrstnr) :30¹ NewYersRcer, Bulldozer, WinningPost (from far bck)
6-18 ⁵Spk⅝ ft 80° 3-5yrnw2R=1 :32³ 1:05¹ 1:36¹ 2:06³ 2 7 21¾ 31¾ 42½° 32¼ 2:07 13-1 (LChrstnr) :30² MelsTassel, SengaPayne, HastySoot (good trip)
5-26 R.P⅝ gd nw4250 1 :29¹ 1:01³ 1:34 2:06² 7 6 6⁴¾ 6⁴¾ 2:05⁴ 11-1 (LChrstnr) HopsTime, MountainMusic, HastySoot (—)
12- 8 ⁹MayAft15° 3-5yrnw600⁰⁷⁸ 1 :32 1:04³ 1:35⁴ 2:06¹ 8 8 8¹⁸ 816 820 8¹⁸ 2:09² 8-1 (LHosttlr) :30⁴ PrkwayChuck, ScotSt, BrndywineJet-WelcmeTravkⁿ (—)

PURPLE 8 10-1 =
Driver—DELVIN L. INSKO, White-Purple-Gold   Tr.—T. Carter   (79-8-9-12—.215)
MARK ONE   Br h 1974, by Henry T Adios—Carla Counsel—Scotch Prince
Owner: Robert L. & Dorothy Wooldridge, Sharpsville, Ind.
1979	6	1	1	1	$6,680	2:04² sy Spk⅝
1978	10	2	0	2	$4,524	2:04⁴ BmP⅝
Lifetime					$4,524	4, 2:04⁴ (⅝)
7-13 ⁹Spk⅝ ft 80° 3-5yrstk7500=1 :30 1:00¹ 1:31² 2:00³ 3 3 32½ 2¾° 21½ 34 2:01² 16-1 (DLInsko) :29⁴ JudgeHanover, BroadwayTune, MarkOne (good try)
6-23 ⁵Spk⅝ ft 59° nw4R=1 :30¹ 1:01⁴ 1:31⁴ 2:02 7 6 74 63° 44½ 66½ 2:03² 19-1 (SBanks) :30³ TwoOnTheAisl, MgicMtion, LittHnry Hill (mild bid)
6-16 ¹Spk⅝ ft 85° nw4R+1 :29 :59² 1:30² 2:00⁴ 6 6 65 32° 32¼ 43¾ 2:01³ 8-1 (SBanks) :30⁴ Sea Hwk, Mrngo Td, Two On The Aisle (raced well)
6-16 ⁷Spk⅝ ft 85° 2-5yrnw2R=1 :32 1:03¹ 1:34 2:04² 2 4 44½° 2½° 2½ 12¼ 2:04² 5-2 (DLInsko) :30⁴ MarkOne, RarePearl, LittleHenryHill (big mile)
5-30 ⁸May ft 71° nw3R 1 :31 1:02² 1:34 2:02² 4 1 1¹ 1½ 2½ 2:03⁴ 3-1 (DBusse) :30² TwoOnTheAisle, MrkOne, FreewayFlyr (held on well)
5-22 ⁴May ft 67° nw3R 1 :31⁴ 1:05¹ 1:35⁴ 2:06² 5 7 53¾° 42° 64 64 2:07¹ 8-1 (DLInsko) :31 SunnyDream, JetSetTime, PrkrBDrct (prkd w-cover)

FOURTH RACE CONTINUED ON NEXT PAGE

FOURTH RACE

CONTINUED FROM PRECEDING PAGE

PLEASE ASK FOR HORSE BY PROGRAM NUMBER

BROWN — 9 — 12-1 +

Driver—JIM CURRAN, Gray-Gold Tr.—R. Spadafore (152-23-19-18—.252)

1979 14 2 3 0 $7,875 $2:01^2$ Det¹
1978 0 0 0 0 (——)
Lifetime (——)

BIG RALPH

B c 1976, by Race Time—Powder Ranger—Ranger Hanover
Owner: Ralph and Paul Spadafore, Pontiac, Mich.

Date	Trk Cond Temp	Class	Dist	Leader's Time ¼	½	¾	Winner's Time	PP	¼	½	¾	Str	Fin	Ind.Time	Odds	Driver		Order of Finish (First, Second, Third)	Comment
7-16	HP⅝ gd	nw2R	1	$:31^1$	$1:02^3$	$1:33^4$	$2:04^4$	1x	7	1^{1}°	1^2	2^{hd}	$2^{3½}$	$2:05^3$	5-2	(LSattlbrg)		SaltLick, BigRalph, ShadowGraph	(———)
7-12	Det¹ ft	nw2R	1	$:28^3$	$:59^1$	$1:27^3$	1:57	1	5	5	3°	3^4	10^{24}	$2:01^4$	9-2	(LSattlbrg)		ImaDew, Denali, TVSonsplendor	(———)
7-6	Det¹ ft	$nw1500^6$	1	$:29^1$	$1:00^1$	$1:29^4$	$2:00^2$	2	5	5	1°	1^2	2½	$2:00^2$	•6-5	(LSattlbrg)		MightyTwist, BigRalph, FleetwoodFanny	(———)
6-29	Det¹ gd	$nw1500^6$	1	:31	$1:02^1$	$1:31^4$	$2:01^1$	9	9	7	6°	6^4	$6^{2¼}$	$2:01^3$	7-1	(LSattlbrg)		GoodSanta, RoyalChristmas, HijackerN	(———)
6-22	Det¹ ft	3yrstk	1	$:29^3$	$:58^1$	$1:28^1$	$1:57^1$	3	x10	10	10	10^{dis}	10^{dis}		107-1	(MOMara)		Composite, BlackAce, Crackers	(———)
6-15	Det¹ ft	C3yr	1	$:31^2$	$1:01^1$	1:30	$1:58^4$	4	4	5	5	$5^{2½}$	$8^{15½}$	$2:01^4$	12-1	(MOMara)		Penner, MichianaHall, FeistyPatch	(———)

LT. BLUE — 10 — 15-1 =

Driver—KATHY RAYMOND, Green-Gold-White Tr.—K. Raymond (4-1-0-0—.250)

1979 2 1 0 0 $3,250 $2:04^2$ Spk⅝
1978 19 7 2 0 $4,428 $2:04^4$ F.P¹
Lifetime $4,428 3, $2:04^4$ (1)

COCKATOO

B g 1975, by Gamecock—Sarah Hanover—Titan Hanover
Owner: Leon & Larry Elliston, Hinsdale, Ill.

Date	Trk Cond Temp	Class	Dist	Leader's Time ¼	½	¾	Winner's Time	PP	¼	½	¾	Str	Fin	Ind.Time	Odds	Driver		Order of Finish (First, Second, Third)	Comment
7-13	³Spk⅝ ft 80°	3-5yrstk7500=	1	$:29^2$	$1:00^3$	$1:32^1$	$2:02^2$	8	3°	3^2°	8^{11}°	9^{dis}	9^{dis}		13-1	(KRymnd)		MagicMotion, LthaBoy, ArmbroTmpo	(overland rte)
7-5	Spk⅝ ft 61°	Qua	1	:30	$1:01^3$	$1:32^3$	$2:03^4$	8	1	1^3	1^1	1½	2^{nk}	$2:03^4$	NB	(KRymnd)		GreySovereign, Cockatoo, Donson	(———)
6-22	³Spk⅝ ft 63°	$nw6000^8$+	1	$:29^4$	$1:00^4$	$1:31^3$	$2:02^1$	refused gate, stewards scratch, all wagers refunded								(KRymnd)		RvrCrclRmo, MgsFshn, TrooperChip	(caused tw rclls)
6-13	⁵Spk⅝ ft 69°	3-5yrnw2R−	1	$:29^1$	$:59^4$	$1:32^1$	$2:04^2$	4	1	1^{10}	1^6	1^8	$1^{3½}$	$2:04^2$	7-2	(KRymnd)	$:32^1$	Cockatto, ShawneeHal, SnowDncr	(came bck ready)
12-29⁷⁸	F.P¹ sy	3yr3000	1	$:31^4$	$1:05^3$	$1:39^1$	$2:10^4$	6	2	2	3	$3^{1½}$	$6^{6¾}$	$2:12^1$	12-1	(GLiles)		MindMaker, GoCount, ClassyBRaider	(———)
12-22⁷⁸	F.P¹ ft	nw4R	1	$:32^1$	$1:02^1$	$1:33^2$	$2:04^4$	5	1	2	1	1½	$4^{4¾}$	$2:05^4$	7-2	(GLiles)		QueenToBe, JKRader, MindMaker	(———)

WHITE & RED — 11 — 5-1 =

Driver—DAVE MAGEE, Red-Black-White Tr.—D. Magee (166-23-19-17—.236)

1979 19 3 2 2 $12,050 2:04 May
1978 8 1 2 1 $1,938 $2:07^4$ sy Nfld
Lifetime $1,938 3, $2:07^4$ sy

‡ARMBRO TEMPO

B g 1975, by Steady Star—Armbro Mary—Bye Bye Byrd
Owner: Dave & Deann Magee & E. A. Rice, Downers Grove, Milan, Ill.

Date	Trk Cond Temp	Class	Dist	Leader's Time ¼	½	¾	Winner's Time	PP	¼	½	¾	Str	Fin	Ind.Time	Odds	Driver		Order of Finish (First, Second, Third)	Comment
7-13	³Spk⅝ ft 80°	‡3-5yrstk7500=	1	$:29^2$	$1:00^3$	$1:32^1$	$2:02^2$	4	2°	1^1	1½	1½	$3^{2¼}$	$2:02^4$	6-1	(DMagee)	$:30^3$	MagicMotion, LeathaBoy, ArmbroTempo	(good try)
7-6	³Spk⅝ ft 68°	‡$nw6500^8$−	1	$:29^1$	1:01	$1:31^3$	$2:01^4$	5	6	4^3°	$4^{2½}$°	$3^{1½}$	$6^{4½}$	$2:02^4$	8-1	(DMagee)	$:30^3$	LttlDlghtful, PhnnsFnn, BrwnyBret	(parked tired)
6-29	⁶Spk⅝ ft 61°	‡$nw1R^6$+	1	$:30^1$	$1:01^1$	$1:31^2$	$2:01^1$	5	7	$7^{8¾}$	$6^{5¼}$°	$5^{6½}$	5^7	$2:02^3$	30-1	(DMagee)	$:30^1$	SpdyDlivery, Ken'sShdw, BrightBrute	(evenly)
6-22	⁵Spk⅝ ft 63°	‡3-5nwR5500L=	1	$:29^2$	1:00	$1:30^4$	$2:01^4$	5	5	$3^{2½}$°	$x9^{dis}$	9^{dis}	9^{dis}		9-1	(DMagee)		KeenEdge, GreenwoodJC, ThearleOver	(elim self)
6-15	⁴Spk⅝ ft 86°	‡nwR5500L+	1	$:29^1$	$1:01^1$	$1:32^2$	$2:03^1$	6	1	$1^{1½}$	1½	1^{nk}	$2^{1¼}$	$2:03^2$	10-1	(DMagee)	:31	NtiveRita, ArmbroTmpo, RceOnCarey	(hung on wire)
6-4	⁷Spk⅝ ft	‡3-4yrnwR4500-2L−	1	:30	1:00	$1:31^2$	$2:02^2$	1	2x	6^{dis}	6^{dis}	6^{dis}	6^{dis}		5-2	(DMagee)		DirectGldN, TorpedoVictory, BretTheBrat	(on ld, brk)

BLUE & WHITE — 12 — 20-1 =

Driver—ROY KEETON, Gold-Green-White Tr.—R. Keeton (3-0-1-0—.185)

1979 8 2 1 1 $3,219 $2:06^3$ LouD
1978 0 0 0 0 (——)
Lifetime (——)

SHAWNEE HAL

Br g 1975, by Masquerader—Purdue Pride E.—Purdue Hal
Owner: Lewis G. Allen, Golconda, Ill.

Date	Trk Cond Temp	Class	Dist	Leader's Time ¼	½	¾	Winner's Time	PP	¼	½	¾	Str	Fin	Ind.Time	Odds	Driver		Order of Finish (First, Second, Third)	Comment
7-18	Spk⅝ ft 69°	Qua	1	$:30^2$	$1:02^1$	$1:33^4$	2:05	3	4	3^2°	1^2	2^2	2^7	$2:06^2$	NB	(RKeeton)		SlyChick, ShawneeHal, ChanceyBecca	(———)
7-13	⁹Spk⅝ ft 80°	3-5yrstk7500+	1	:30	1:01	$1:31^2$	$2:00^3$	2	4	$4^{3½}$	$7^{9¼}$x	8^{dis}	8^{dis}		76-1	(RKeeton)		JudgeHanover, BrdwyTune, MarkOne	(makes brks)
6-25	⁵Spk⅝ ft 67°	3-5yrnw2R=	1	:30	1:00	$1:31^3$	$2:01^3$	8	4°	$4^{4½}$	6^7x	7^{dis}	8^{dis}		9-2	(RKeeton)		RdintOmh, HustlinRuss, JzzMstr	(speed it flat)
6-13	⁵Spk⅝ ft 69°	3-5yrnw2R−	1	$:29^1$	$:59^4$	$1:32^1$	$2:04^2$	2	3	3^{11}x	3^7	2^8	$2^{3½}$	$2:05^1$	3-1	(RKeeton)	$:31^2$	Cockatoo, ShawneeHal, SnowDancer	(game effort)
6-2	³May ft 69°	3-5yr6500	1	$:32^1$	$1:03^2$	$1:33^4$	$2:06^4$	4	7	$7^{5½}$ix	8^{20}	8^{20}	8^{20}p7	$2:10^4$	•2-1	(RKeeton)	:33	HawthrneRght, RoylEgyptn, GaleMahone	(bothered)
5-17	²May ft 76°	2-5yrnw2R	1	$:31^2$	$1:01^3$	$1:33^3$	$2:05^2$	4	2°	1^1°	$x6^{dis}$	6^{dis}	6^{dis}		3-1	(RKeeton)		PatchySong, MrTarB, WinterGames	(costly break)

CHARLEY HORSE — 4....3....2 **PARADISE — 4....3....8** **MISS MAREY — 3....4....9**

ONE MILE PACE

"T-JAY'S CLUB"

Purse $7,000

CONDITIONED. 3-Year-Old, and Up. Non-winners of a race for a purse of $5,500 or more twice in lifetime.

PLEASE ASK FOR HORSE BY PROGRAM NUMBER

WARMUP COLOR—BLACK

RED 1 (6-1 =)

Driver—BRIAN PELLING, Black-Red-Orange — Tr.—B. Pelling (68-11-8-8—.266)
BLACK BANNER N
Br g 1976, by Lumber Dream—Black Abbess—Light Brigade
Owner: B.R.P. Enterprises Corp., Cypress, Calif.
1979 4 1 2 0 $4,075 2:04¹ Spk⅝
1978 0 0 0 0 (——)
Lifetime (——)

7-13	2Spk⅝ ft 80°	CGnw2R+1	:30¹ 1:02² 1:33⁴ 2:03⁴	8	1°	2¹	3¹	3¹½ 58	2:05² 7-2 (BPelling)	:31³ Ghetto, JoesGrandSlam, Bulldozer (3-wide 1st turn)
6-11	6Spk⅝ ft 72°	2-4yrnw1R=1	:30² 1:03¹ 1:33⁴ 2:04¹	8	3	3²	14	16	1¾	2:04¹ 3-1 (BPelling)	:30² BtkBnnrN, CordovaDick, NewYrsRacr (mvd just rite)
5-9	Sac¹ ft	nw1R	:29³ 1:03¹ 1:32² 2:03	7	1°	11	11½	11¼ 23	2:03³ 9-5 (BPelling)	:31 HilbiHlyFilly, BlackBannerN, DrEKBuckley (——)
5-2	Sac¹ ft	2-5yrnw1R	:29³ 1:00² 1:31² 2:01⁴	2	2	11	13½	11¼ 22½	2:02² 7-2 (BPelling)	:31 BakerHill, BlackBannerN, AndysWnnr (strong brush)
4-25	LA⅝ ft		Qua	1:32 1:05¹ 1:36 2:05⁴	2	1	1	12	2½	2:06 NB (JRWilms)	BakerHill, BlackBannerN, LadyChristy (——)
3-21	LA⅝ my		Qua	1:31 1:04¹ 1:34¹ 2:05³	4	7	7	6¹¹½ 6¹²	2:08 NB (BPelling)	SoLongAdios, TrueMission, MontereyDeb (——)

BLUE 2 (6-1 +)

Driver—WILLIAM LAMBERTUS, Gold-White-Black — Tr.—D. Hamilton (40-2-7-6—.197)
MY CHICKADEE
B m 1974, by Bye Bye Andy—Miss Adios—Adios
Owner: Charles E. Metro, Middleburg Hts, Ohio
1979 6 2 0 0 $4,851 2:01³ Spk⅝
1978 22 1 4 6 $5,071 2:07² Nfld
Lifetime $7,639 3, 2:06¹

7-12	5Spk⅝ ft 83°	FMnw40007−1	:30² 1:00⁴ 1:31³ 2:01³	8	1°	2½	14¾	14¾	2:01¹ 7-1 (DHmltn)	:29¹ MyChickadee, HiTami, Cachet (easy winner)
7-6	4Spk⅝ ft 68°	FM8500=1	:30 1:00³ 1:31⁴ 2:01²	1	4	53	74¼½ im98	97½	2:01³ 53-1 (DHmltn)	:30² AmityWellmnr, PririeBeuty, JosiesChoice (bothered)
6-29	9Spk⅝ gd 61°	FM8500+1	:30¹ 1:02¹ 1:33² 2:04²	3	5	55½	52½	74	53¾	2:05¹ 30-1 (DHmltn)	:31¹ DizzieFizzie, JsiesChice, FlyingFicn (tuff winner)
6-23	Nfld ft		nw3500	1	:30³ 1:02⁴ 1:33² 2:04¹	9	5	5	4²	14	2:04¹ 4-9-5 (DlrvineJr)	MyChickadee, YoYoRainbow, WoeFonz (——)
6-16	Nfld ft		nw3500	1	:30⁴ 1:01¹ 1:32 2:03¹	5	1	7	7°	74½ 63¼	2:03⁴ 9-1 (JRossJr)	JayAgain, CareysYaycount, MissBettyKay (——)
6-8	Nfld ft		FM260ps	1	:30⁴ 1:02³ 1:33³ 2:05²	7	7	8	77	41	2:05³ 22-1 (LMrrimn)	ElizabethA, MissBretsBrat, FoolingAround (——)

WHITE 3 (10-1 −)

Driver—DON BROOKS, Green-Gold-White — Tr.—D. Brooks (62-7-8-10—.238)
EDS MARK
Br c 1975, by Mighty Edward—Linde Pence—Flying Pence
Owner: Don Brooks, Cicero, Ill.
1979 22 3 5 1 $11,533 2:02³ PPk⅝
1978 29 4 4 3 $6,058 2:04² Stga
Lifetime $6,058 2:04² Stga

7-11	6Spk⅝ ft 83°	c1m17500+1	:30¹ 1:00² 1:29⁴ 2:00²	7	9	9¹¹½	9ᵈ¹½	9ᵈ¹¹ 9ᵈ¹⁰	14-1 (DBrooks)	HighShadow, SamBlack, HighlandKirk (elim. self)
6-29	4Spk⅝ ft 61°	clm12500−1	:30⁴ 1:00⁴ 1:31³ 2:02⁴	8	3°	31½°	21½°	32¾ 22½	2:03¹ 5-1 (WPaisly)	:30² MikesRplic, EdsMrk, SbrbnHnvr (never saw rail)
6-21	7Spk⅝ ft 82°	clm15000+1	:29² 1:00⁴ 1:30 2:00¹	3	7	710	710°	810	610	2:02¹ 22-1 (LHosttlr)	:30¹ WatsekasBest, SevenShot, AvonEastwod (no rally)
6-14	6Spk⅝ ft 84°	clm12500+1	:29⁴ 1:00⁴ 1:32 2:02⁴	6	9	84¾°	4²°	1¼ 2¾	2:03² 5-1 (LHosttlr)	:31 NativeSue, EdsMark, SpedyTrom (moved 3-wide)
6-6	10Spk⅝ ft 78°	clm12500+1	:30¹ 1:02¹ 1:34² 2:04²	3	6	43°	2½°	1¼ 2½	2:04³ 13-1 (LHosttir)	:30¹ HighlandKirk, EdsMark, MilteyOneTime (big effort)
5-30	10May ft 71°	clm12000	1	:32 1:04¹ 1:36 2:05⁴	4	6	86	62¾° 87	88½	2:07³ 18-1 (LHosttir)	:31 GrndpaLeo, BillyGnBrks, HrtgeElnr (3-wide backsde)

GREEN 4 (3-1 =)

Driver—WALTER PAISLEY, Green-White — Tr.—W. Paisley (133-26-23-18—.337)
INCA GOLD
B g 1974, by Deluxe Hanover—Whatshername—Right Time
Owner: Oak Mar Stable, Bedford, Hts., Ohio
1979 9 4 0 1 $7,987 2:00¹ Spk⅝
1978 32 4 6 3 $12,116 2:01¹ Nfld
Lifetime $20,955 4, 2:01¹

7-3	1Spk⅝ ft 78°	nwR55002L=1	:29⁴ :59³ 1:30² 2:00¹	1	3	1¹	11	13	13½	2:00½ •1-2 (DHmltn)	:29¹ IncaGold, ParkwayChuck, Jurist (easy winner)
6-16	Nfld ft		nw5000	1	:30¹ 1:01² 1:31⁴ 2:01¹	5	6	4	2°	11¼ 11½	2:01¹ 2-1 (DlrvineJr)	IncaGold, BaronChuck, GypsyScamp (——)
6-9	Nfld ft		nw5000	1	:30¹ 1:01² 1:31³ 2:01¹	4	4	4	4	11½ 14½	2:01¹ 4-1 (DHmltn)	IncaGold, JPTime, CricketAdios (——)
6-2	Nfld ft		nw3500	1	:29³ 1:00¹ 1:31¹ 2:03	8	1	1	1°	13	2:03 6-1 (DHmltn)	IncaGold, SwiftDynamic, DobleyDoMcShu (——)
5-26	Nfld ft		nw3500	1	:30¹ 1:04 1:35³ 2:06³	7	7	7	4°	42¼ 44½	2:07² 7-2 (DlrvineJr)	WandasGoldPlate, GameGolda, SkipprChw (——)
5-18	Nfld ft		Qua	1	:30 1:02 1:34⁴ 2:08	5	6	6	66½ 12	2:08 NB (DlrvineJr)	IncaGold, Baracuda, SwiftScandal (——)

BLACK 5 (9-2 +)

Driver—STEVE SPRIGGS, Gold-Silver — Tr.—R. Gordon (14-1-2-2—.198)
NEVERGIVEUP
B c 1976, by Thorpe Hanover—Pretty Pence—Scottish Pence
Owner: O'Cal Stable, Inc., Garden Grove, Calif.
1979 8 3 1 0 $9,789 2:03¹ Lex¹
1978 18 1 7 2 $4,810 2:08 Mayfd
Lifetime $4,810 2, 2:08

7-9	3Spk⅝ ft 74°	2-4yrnw1R−1	:29² 1:04 1:33 2:03⁴	9	9	63¾°im53½°	2ⁿᵈ	11½ 2:03⁴	•9-5 (SSpriggs)	:30 Nevergiveup, RomeoAtlarge, AlbaJoy (the best)
6-8	Aud ft		3yrstk19339	1	:31³ 1:02⁴ 1:33³ 2:03⁴	1	3	3	3²	2²	2:04¹ 30-1 (SSpriggs)	Truth, Nevergiveup, Doubletake (——)
6-2	ScD⅝ ft		nw1000	1	:29² :58⁴ 1:29 2:00¹	8	7	7	8°	73¼ 56	2:01² 34-1 (RGarden)	MarttieSpinner, StarButler, SunnyArt (——)
5-25	Lat¹ sy		3yrstk20000	1	:30² 1:02⁴ 1:35 2:04⁴	4	1	4	5	66¼ 712¼	2:07¹ 20-1 (JFergsn)	SeaHawk, EscapeArtist, MarJimBretster (——)
5-21	Lat¹ ft		nw5000	1	:28³ :58⁴ 1:30¹ 2:01	6	6	6	6°	41½ 59½	2:02⁴ 10-1 (JFergsn)	SureShow, Chino, SunnyArt (——)
5-11	Lex¹ ft		3yrstk19400	1	:29⁴ :58³ 1:28⁴ 1:58²	5	1	5	5	54	4¹¼	1:59⁴ 13-1 (MZeile)	SeaHawk, EscapeArtist, SocialQuicksand (——)

YELLOW 6 (12-1 =)

Driver—JOHN FALKNER, Blue-Gold-White — Tr.—J. Falkner (3-0-0-2—.222)
HELDEZ
Ch g 1973, by Royal Scotchman—Light Rendez—Light Brigade
Owner: Harnic Stables, Calumet City, Ill.
1979 5 0 0 0 2:03⁴ LA⅝ Qua
1978 19 2 5 2 $6,135 None in U.S.A.
Lifetime $10,457 None in U.S.A.

7-18	Spk ft 69°		Qua	1	:29² 1:01¹ 1:31³ 2:02¹	5	3	32½	33°	45	2:03 NB (JFalkner)	FlamingByrd, TorridN, SomersetLad (——)
6-15	3Spk⅝ ft 86°	nwR5500L+1	:29¹ 1:00³ 1:31³ 2:01³	2	5	53¾°	21°	32½x824	2:06² 3-1 (JCurran)	:34³ NightMessngr, BetterBangaroo, ExpressJet (elim. self)
6-8	Spk⅝ ft 72°		Qua	1	:30² 1:00³ 1:30¹ 2:01¹	7	5	5¹¹	46°	41¼ 46	2:02⁴ NB (JFalkner)	LousGecures, BlyeAndSell (——)
5-22	6May ft 67°	nw25005	1	:31¹ 1:03³ 1:34 2:04	5	3	2°	2½°	2ⁿᵏx714	2:06⁴ 5-2 (WPaisly)	GalaBlueChip, ScottyFrst, MntainHldMn (costly brk)
5-15	6May ft 61°	nw25005	1	:29³ 1:00 1:30³ 2:03	3	6ix711	54°	53ix 74¹¹	•8-5 (WPaisly)	GenesShow, ScottysFrost, TallyBoy (costly brk)
5-9	May ft 79°		Qua	1	:31⁴ 1:04 1:35² 2:06¹	2	1	12	12½	14½ 16¼	2:06¹ NB (WPaisly)	Heldez, SuddenDepression, CoffeeChamp (——)

ORANGE 7 (8-1 =)

Driver—DAVE APTILON, Blue-White-Black — Tr.—D. Aptilon (6-0-4-0—.370)
SAM PETERSON
B g 1973, by Lumber Dream—Sally Peterson—U. Scott
Owner: C. Willis & R. Weinstein, Willow Springs, Chicago, Ill.
1979 17 3 2 2 $14,916 2:00³ PPk⅝
1978 19 4 1 4 $8,715 2:01⁴ Arl1⅝
Lifetime $6,715 5, 2:01⁴ (1⅛)

7-14	2Spk⅝ ft 73°	nwR5500L−1	:29 :58³ 1:29¹ 2:00¹	4	2	21	2¹	14¾ 73°	2:00³ 4-2 (DAptilon)	:31² ParkwayChuck, SamPtrsn, MpleLnesSctt (2nd best)
6-30	4Spk⅝ gd71°	nwR60002/79=1	:30¹ 1:00⁴ 1:31⁴ 2:04¹	3	74¼	75	75½¹53¼p4 2:05	6-1 (DAptilon)	:32¹ QunToBe, RmbingRchl, Wstrn'sWilm (shuffed back)
6-23	5Spk⅝ ft 59°	nwR65005+1	:30 1:01 1:31² 2:02	3	6	76½	66	74¾ 41	2:03² 10-1 (DAptilon)	:30⁴ Lusty TrHal, Trysmile, WildwdDuane (shuffled bck)
5-19	9May ft 64°	nw35005	1	:30 1:01¹ 1:31² 2:01⁴	8	87	84¼	73¾ 73¼	2:02³ 8-1 (DAptilon)	:30² Lovim, Richardson, SocialClass (post hurt)
4-21	6May ft 48°	nw2000078/79	1	:30³ 1:01² 1:33¹ 2:01⁴	6	6	66¾ 63½	52¼ 73¾	2:03¹ 3-1 (DAptilon)	:30² TrysSmile, FrostyPence, SamPeterson (good in str.)
4-7	PPk⅝ ft		w10001	1	:27⁴ :57 1:36¹ 1:56⁴	3	6	5	54¼ 510¼¼ 1:58⁴	31-1 (DAptilon)	WizardAtmahurst, DbleSpinder, GaySchnll (——)

PURPLE 8 (5-1 −)

Driver—HAM ADAMS, Maroon-Gray — Tr.—H. Adams (69-11-7-4—.235)
MIGHTY T S
B g 1975, by Tar Mite—Shiaway Vancy—Adios Cleo
Owner: M. F. Riviello, D. Handler, N. M. Dolgin, Dayton, Toledo, Ohio
1979 10 1 2 4 $4,965 2:00⁴ Spk⅝
1978 29 11 6 3 $12,262 2:02⁴ (¾)
Lifetime $17,900 3, 2:02⁴ (¾)

7-14	2Spk⅝ ft 73°	nwR10000/2+1	:29⁴ 1:00¹ 1:29⁴ 2:00¹	4	32½°	21°	31¼ 73¾	2:01 7-1 (RJBrown)	:31¹ LittleDelightful, Emanar, OzziesChrgr (prkd no cvr)
7-6	7Spk⅝ ft 68°	nwR50004−15=1	:31 :59⁴ 1:29⁴ 2:00⁴	3	7	76½°	33°	21½ 1⁴	2:00⁴ 51-1 (RJBrown)	:29² MightyTS, MarengoTed, MajestcRnvaeh (big upset)
6-23	Lat¹ ft		w5001	1	:30 1:01² 1:32¹ 2:02	1	5	5	5	24½ 2°	2:02 2-1 (RJBrown)	:29 ValleyRunner, MightyTS, BGCounsel (——)
6-19	ScD⅝ ft		w5001	1	:30¹ 1:00² 1:30⁴ 2:01³	6	7	8	3°	1ⁿᵈ 14¼	2:04² NB (JPotter)	MightyTS, Turnpike, FeatherMind (——)
6-16	Lat¹ ft		w5001	1	:30⁴ 1:00² 1:30⁴ 2:03³	8	6	6	6	x54½ 55½	2:04² 8-1 (RJBrown)	WonderBuck, WinterSunday, ValleyRunner (——)
6-9	Lat¹ ft		w5001	1	:29¹ 1:01¹ 1:32¹ 2:01	5	6	6	6	x43½¹x57½ 2:02²	2-1 (RJBrown)	BretterBest, Wonder, ValleyRunner (——)

BROWN 9 (12-1 −)

Driver—STANLEY BANKS, White-Purple — Tr.—R. Perry (168-17-19-24—.212)
KNIGHT CHRIS
Ch c 1976, by Chris Time—Cindy Knight—Miracle Knight
Owner: Messenger Stable, Golf, Ill.
1979 11 1 1 1 $4,097 2:06² Leb
1978 12 1 2 1 $8,374 2:03 ScD⅝
Lifetime $8,374 3, 2:03⁴ (⅞)

7-13	7Spk⅝ ft 80°	nw3R+1	:29² :59⁴ 1:29² 1:59³	7	7	712°im512	59¼ 2:01²	21-1 (DBrooks)	:29³ CrossKeys, FreedomTime, FreedomSpirit (rd trble)
7-6	3Spk⅝ ft		nwR6500B−1	:29¹ 1:01 1:31³ 2:01⁴	8	9	98¾	74¾	74¼ 43½	2:02³ 79-1 (ATrinkle)	:31³ LtltDlghtful, PhnnaFnn, BrwnyBret (lets move)
6-30	9Spk⅝ gd 71°	nw3R=1	:30¹ 1:00³ 1:32 2:03³	3	4	32¾	52½	64	54	2:04² 18-1 (ATrinkle)	:31² GreenwoodJC, CrossKeys, StdyAirdale (prkd leaving)
6-9	4Spk⅝ ft 63°	nw3R+1	:30¹ 1:01 1:32² 2:03¹	9	9	810	86	59½ 74½	2:04⁴ 18-1 (ATrinkle)	:30³ MarHimHarvey, RoadFive, ViciousVic (post hurt)
6-9	ScD⅝ ft		3yrstk5250	1	:30¹ 1:02⁴ 1:34 2:04	2	x6	4	6	58¼ 57½	2:04¹ 7-1 (ATrinkle)	SuccessfulStar, DoublePar, AndyLove (——)
6-4	ScD⅝ ft		nw3R−1	:30¹ 1:02⁴ 1:34 2:04	2 x6	6	54	21¼ 2:04¹	6-1 (ATrinkle)	Connoisseur, KnightChris, MargineChip (——)

CHARLEY HORSE — 4....5....2   **PARADISE — 4....2....5**   **MISS MAREY — 1....4....8 Best Bet**

ONE MILE PACE

SIXTH RACE

Purse $7,500

$3 PERFECTA WAGERING ON THIS RACE

"THE PONTIAC" (2nd Division)

STAKE. 3, 4- and 5-Year-Olds. THE MIDWEST SERIES.

PLEASE ASK FOR HORSE BY PROGRAM NUMBER

WARMUP COLOR—YELLOW

P.P. 1 — RED — 1 — 7-2 =

Driver—JIM DOLBEE, Green-White-Red   Tr.—H. Adams   (69-11-7-4—.235)

RAY CHARLES

B c 1975, by Meadow Skipper—Fanny Mite—Mighty Sun
Owner: William E. & Darlene M. Longo, Berkley, Mich.

1979 25 5 6 3 $56,934 2:00 Det^1
1978 5 2 1 1 $4,182 2:02^2 Det^1
Lifetime $4,182 3, 2:02^2 (1)

Date	Trk Cond Temp	Class	Dist	Leader's Time ¼	½	¾	Winner's Time	PP	¼	½	¾	Str	Fin	Ind. Time	Odds	Driver	Ind ¼ Time	Order of Finish First, Second, Third	Comment
7-13	^{5}Spk⅝ ft 80°	3-5yrstk7500=	1	:31	1:00^1	1:31^1	2:00^3	5	3°	1^{1¼}	1^{1¾}	1^{2½}	1^{3½}	2:00^3	*2-5	(JDolbee)	:29^2	RayCharles, RaceOnCarey, NobleMjrty	(classy colt)
7-3	Det^1 ft	4yrstk66700	1	:29^2	1:00^3	1:31^2	1:59^4	8	4°	3°	3°	2^1	2^{1½}	2:00	24-1	(RPutnam)		KnoxTime, RayCharles, BakersKnight	(———)
6-26	Det^1 ft	4yrstk	1	:29^4	:59^2	1:29^2	1:59^4	5	6	6	5°	3^2	3^2	2:00^1	*6-5	(RPutnam)		ShiawayPippin, Girl'O'MyDreams, RayChrls	(———)
6-23	Det^1 ft	w10000	1	:30	1:00^2	1:30^3	1:59^3	3	3	1°	1	1^{½}	4^{2¾}	2:00^1	17-1	(RPutnam)		TimelyDean, ArchieHanover, GdAlbatross	(———)
6-16	ScD⅝ ft	stk	1	:29^1	:58^4	1:28^1	1:58^2	3	3	4	5	6^{2½}	4^{4¼}	1:59^1	18-1	(JAdmsky)		Grandslammer, BretsColors, NobleFella	(———)
6-9	Det^1 ft	10001	1	:28^3	:57^4	1:28^1	1:58	9	1	2	3	3^1	5^{2¾}	1:58^3	39-1	(RPutnam)		BakersKnight, Cambeau, SoloSteve	(———)

P.P. 2 — BLUE — 2 — 5-1 =

Driver—JERRY GRAHAM, Green-Orange   Tr.—J. Fick   (63-17-14-14—.467)

MAGIC MOTION

B f 1976, by Strike Out—Chippy Time—Good Time
Owner: Marion Stable, Orland Park, Ill.

1979 8 3 4 0 $17,020 2:02^2 Spk⅝
1978 2 1 0 0 $300 2:00^4 Spk⅝
Lifetime $300 2, 2:00^3 (1) T.T.

Date	Trk Cond Temp	Class	Dist	Leader's Time ¼	½	¾	Winner's Time	PP	¼	½	¾	Str	Fin	Ind. Time	Odds	Driver	Ind ¼ Time	Order of Finish First, Second, Third	Comment
7-13	^{3}Spk⅝ ft 80°	3-5yrstk7500=	1	:29^2	1:00^3	1:32^1	2:02^2	9	6	6^{4¼}	4^{1¾}°	2^{½}	1^1	2:02^2	*3-5	(JGrahm)	:29^4	MagicMotion, LeathaBoy, ArmbroTempo	(the best)
7-3	^{5}Spk⅝ ft 78°	FMnw3R–	1	:29^3	1:00	1:30^4	1:59^4	9	1°	1^1	1^{½}	1^{1½}	2^{1¼}	2:00	*1-1	(JGrahm)	:29^1	StrikeHerRich, MgicMtin, JetSetTime	(game effort)
6-28	^{8}Spk⅝ ft 74°	FMnw14000^{79}–	1	:29	:58^4	1:29^4	1:59^3	4	6	5^{4½}	5^{2½}°	3^1	2^{¾}	1:59^4	7-1	(JGrahm)	:29^2	ChinChin, MagicMotion, MrsChancey	(strong try)
6-23	^{5}Spk⅝ ft 59°	nw4R+	1	:30^1	1:01^4	1:31^4	2:02	8	8	6^{2¾}°	4^2°	2^{½}	2^{1½}	2:02^2	5-1	(JGrahm)	:30^1	TwOnTheAisl, MgicMtin, LittlHnry Hill	(ld btwn clls)
6-14	^{4}Spk⅝ ft 84°	FMnw2R+	1	:30^4	1:03^4	1:34^4	2:04^1	4	3	3^3	1^{½}	1^{1½}	1^{1¼}	2:04^1	*1-2	(JGrahm)	:29^3	MagicMotion, FireOpal, Wndmeadw	(big burst spd)
6-5	^{2}Spk⅝ ft 60°	FMnw1R–	1	:32^1	1:03^4	1:35^3	2:06	5	2°	1^{1½}	1^{1¼}	1^{2½}	1^{2½}	2:06	*2-5	(JGrahm)	:30^2	MagicMotion, FireOpal, VicsJamie	(much the best)

P.P. 3 — WHITE — 3 — 8-1 =

Driver—STAN BAYLESS, Gold-White   Tr.—J. O'Brien   (35-5-5-5—.270)

BROADWAY TUNE

B f 1976, by Bret Hanover—Besta Time—Good Time
Owner: Thurman Downing, Cleveland, Ohio

1979 6 0 2 0 $3,938
1978 5 1 1 0 $1,344 2:04^3 ScD⅝
Lifetime $1,344 2, 2:02^3 (1) T.T.

Date	Trk Cond Temp	Class	Dist	Leader's Time ¼	½	¾	Winner's Time	PP	¼	½	¾	Str	Fin	Ind. Time	Odds	Driver	Ind ¼ Time	Order of Finish First, Second, Third	Comment
7-13	^{9}Spk⅝ ft 80°	3-5yrstk7500=	1	:30	1:01	1:31^2	2:00^3	7	8	6^{6¼}°	5^{6¼}	im5^6	2^{3½}	2:01^2	9-1	(SBayless)	:28^4	JudgeHanover, BroadwayTne, MrkOne	(blocked str)
6-30	Lat^1 ft	3yrstk13900	1	:30^3	1:02^4	1:32	2:00^1	2	3	3	3	x3^{2}xx	3^{3¼}p4	2:00^4	35-1	(SBayless)		DanieleAlmahurst, YesYesYes, SilentKathy	(———)
6-20	^{6}Spk⅝ ft 78°	FMnw2R=	1	:30	1:00^1	1:30^4	2:00^3	2	5	x9^{15}	9^{18}	9^{dis}	9^{dis}		7-2	(SBayless)		StrikeHerRich, CffeeSkiper, MistyCllette	(no chance)
6-9	^{1}Spk⅝ ft 68°	2-5yrnw2R=	1	:31	1:01^4	1:33	2:04^2	1	3	3^{1¾}	4^{1½}	4^{2¼}im	5^{1¾}	2:04^4	5-2	(SBayless)	:31^4	WintrByeBye, GrnwdJC, MnlghtLve	(trappd the mi.)
5-15	Sac^1 ft	2-5yrnw2R	1	:31^4	1:03^1	1:34^3	2:04^2	1	2	2	3	3^{1½}	2^{½}	2:04^3	9-1	(SBayless)		HillbillyFilly, BroadwayTune, RoylBirdieN	(———)
5-8	Sac^1 ft	nw2R	1	:28^2	:59^1	1:30^2	2:00^1	4	5	5^{5½}	6^7	5^9	4^{10}	2:02^1	8-1	(SBayless)	:30^2	DirectGoldN, RoyalBirdieN, SengaPayne	(wnnr tuff)

P.P. 4 — GREEN — 4 — 15-1 =

Driver—CLAUDE LORANCE, JR., Gold-Blue   Tr.—C. Lorance, Sr.   (17-0-2-4—.144)

VICIOUS VIC

B c 1976, by Adios Vic—Jan Byrd—Addio Byrd
Owner: Myrle J. & Claude R. Lorance, Sr., Laura, Ill.

1979 7 2 2 1 $7,675 2:04 May
1978 4 0 1 1 $1,664 2:07^1 QCD⅝ Qua
Lifetime $1,664 2, 2:07^1 (⅝) Qua

Date	Trk Cond Temp	Class	Dist	Leader's Time ¼	½	¾	Winner's Time	PP	¼	½	¾	Str	Fin	Ind. Time	Odds	Driver	Ind ¼ Time	Order of Finish First, Second, Third	Comment
7-13	^{5}Spk⅝ ft 80°	3-5yrstk7500=	1	:31	1:00^1	1:31^1	2:00^3	6	7	7^9	7^{5½}im	5^{7½}	4^{7½}	2:02^1	15-1	(CLrnceJr)	:29^4	RayCharles, RaceOnCarey, NobleMajrty	(rd trouble)
6-22	^{4}Spk⅝ ft 63°	nw3R=	1	:30^2	1:01^4	1:32^2	2:03^1	6	1°	2^{1½}	2^{1¼}	2^{1¼}	2^{1½}p3	2:03^3	19-1	(CLrnceJr)	:31	MarJimHarvey, RoadFive, ViciousVic	(good try)
6-8	^{6}Spk⅝ sy 78°	nw3R+	1	:30^1	1:01^3	1:32^4	2:02^2	3	3	3^{2½}	4^3	4^3	4^{8½}	2:04^1	5-1	(CLrnceJr)	:30^4	SeaHawk, NapaOne, SteadyAirdale	(away well)
6-1	^{2}May ft 69°	nw2R	1	:30^4	1:03	1:35	2:06^1	4	1	1^2	1^{¾}	1^3	1^{12}	2:06^1	*1-5	(CLrnceJr)	:31^1	ViciousVic, HallsHallie, MissStateLine	(crushd foes)
5-21	^{4}May ft 59°	nw2R	1	:31	1:02^1	1:33	2:04	1	1	1^2	1^{4½}	1^{2½}	1^3	2:04	8-5	(CLrnceSr)	:31	ViciousVic, NapaOne, Bulldozer	(wire to wire)
5-8	^{3}May ft 83°	2-5yrnw1R	1	:31	1:01^3	1:33^1	2:04^1	3	1	1^{¾}	1^{½}	1^{hd}	2^{nk}	2:04^1	5-2	(CLrnceJr)	:31	NapaOne, ViciousVic, CVKiev	(held on well)

P.P. 5 — BLACK — 5 — 10-1 =

Driver—DELVIN L. INSKO, White-Purple-Gold   Tr.—B. Cotton   (79-8-9-12—.215)

NOBLE MAJORITY

B c 1976, by Silent Majority—Reef Miss—Tar Mite
Owner: Bill F. & Philip F. Cotton, Fairfield, Ill.

1979 1 0 0 1 $900 2:04^1 Lex^1 Qua
1978 13 3 2 4 $3,076 2:07^3 Lex^1 Qua
Lifetime $3,076 2, 2:00^2 (1) T.T.

Date	Trk Cond Temp	Class	Dist	Leader's Time ¼	½	¾	Winner's Time	PP	¼	½	¾	Str	Fin	Ind. Time	Odds	Driver	Ind ¼ Time	Order of Finish First, Second, Third	Comment
7-13	^{5}Spk⅝ ft 80°	3-5yrstk7500–	1	:31	1:00^1	1:31^1	2:00^3	1	2	3^3	3^{1¾}°	4^6	3^7	2:02	8-1	(DLInsko)	:30^2	RayCharles, RaceOnCarey, NobleMajrty	(raced well)
6-27	Lex^1 ft	Qua	1	:31^1	1:02^1	1:33^1	2:04^1	3	1	1	1	1^5	1^1	2:04^1	NB	(PCotton)		NobleMajority, ArmbroValnt, SprngcrkChrs	(———)
8-25^{78}	Ind^1 ft	2yrstk	1	:28^4	:57^4	1:27^3	1:58	5	2	5	7°	11^8	12^{12}	2:00^2	NB	(PCotton)		MostestYankee, ShankHanover, Crozier	(———)
8-17^{78}	Spr^1 gd	2yrec2948	1	:29^2	1:00^1	1:31^1	2:01^3	6	2	2	2°	2^{1¾}	3^3	2:02^1	NB	(PCotton)		MarengoTed, PTGypsy, NobleMajority	(———)
8-17^{78}	Spr^1 gd	2yropn2211	1	:30^4	1:02^1	1:31	2:03^1	4	1	2	2	2^2	3^{½}	2:03^2	NB	(PCotton)		MarengoTed, PTGypsy, NobleMajority	(———)
7-31^{78}	Char gd	2yrec1250	1	:32^4	1:08	1:39	2:11^3	2	1	1	2	2^4	2^2	2:12	NB	(PCotton)		SusanDiane, NobleMajority, FreedomTime	(———)

P.P. 6 — YELLOW — 6 — 10-1 =

Driver—STEVE PLETCHER, White-Black-Red   Tr.—S. Pletcher   (73-4-6-5—.123)

BEST VICKIE

B f 1976, by Best Of All—Teffe—Tar Heel
Owner: Areta & Dwayne Pletcher, Shipshewana, Ind.

1979 6 1 1 1 $5,477 2:04^3 Spk⅝
1978 0 0 0 0 (——)
Lifetime (——)

Date	Trk Cond Temp	Class	Dist	Leader's Time ¼	½	¾	Winner's Time	PP	¼	½	¾	Str	Fin	Ind. Time	Odds	Driver	Ind ¼ Time	Order of Finish First, Second, Third	Comment
7-13	^{5}Spk⅝ ft 80°	3-5yrstk7500+	1	:31	1:00^1	1:31^1	2:00^3	4	5	5^6	5^{3½}	x7^{dis}	7^{dis}		7-1	(SPletchr)		RayCharles, RaceOnCarey, NobleMajorty	(elim. self)
7-4	^{5}Spk⅝ ft 65°	FMnw2R+	1	:31^2	1:03^1	1:34^3	2:05	9	9	8^{13}	7^{7¾}°	4^6	3^1	2:05^1	2-1	(SPletchr)	:29	PrincssDnut, Byrd'sMldy, BestVickie	(strong finish)
6-26	^{1}Spk⅝ ft 79°	Fnw1R=	1	:30^3	1:04	1:34^3	2:04^3	2	4	4^{2½}°	2^1°	2^{1½}	1^{hd}	2:04^3	2-1	(SPletchr)	:29^4	BestVickie, Vic'sJamie, AlbaJoy	(big mile)
6-12	^{1}Spk⅝ ft 63°	Fnw1R–	1	:31^3	1:03^1	1:35^1	2:05^2	7	9	9^{10}°	6^{6½}°	4^{6½}	2^{5¼}	2:06^2	11-1	(SPletchr)	:29^4	StrikeHerRich, BstVckie, YchtsmnCKy	(closed well)
5-26	^{2}May ft 61°	FMnw2R	1	:31^4	1:04	1:35^3	2:06^2	5	6	7^6	8^7	7^{8½}	5^9	2:08^1	8-1	(SPletchr)	:31^1	SpecialKiss, WdlandMrrie, AdioGnna	(wnnr too tuff)
5-18	^{3}May ft 67°	FMnw2R	1	:31^1	1:02^3	1:32^4	2:04	5	6	6^{12}	6^{12}	5^{15}	4^{9¾}	2:06	5-1	(SPletchr)	:30^4	MissCourageous, SpecialKiss, AdioGnna	(no threat)

P.P. 7 — ORANGE — 7 — 12-1 +

Driver—DALE HITEMAN, Blue-White-Gold   Tr.—D. Hiteman   (40-4-3-7—.200)

COFFEE SKIPPER

B f 1976, by Skipper Creek—Coffee Bean—Coffee Break
Owner: J. Abruzzo, R. Simon, J. Braun & D. Marzec, Chicago, Ill.

1979 9 2 1 1 $5,381 2:08 gd BmlP⅝
1978 0 0 0 0 (——)
Lifetime (——)

Date	Trk Cond Temp	Class	Dist	Leader's Time ¼	½	¾	Winner's Time	PP	¼	½	¾	Str	Fin	Ind. Time	Odds	Driver	Ind ¼ Time	Order of Finish First, Second, Third	Comment
7-10	^{6}Spk⅝ ft	3-4yrnwR4500^{2}L=	1	:29^1	:59^2	1:30^1	2:00^4	9	9	7^{11}°	5^{4½}	x8^{24}	8^{dis}		7-2	(DHitemn)		NtiveRit, SpcilKiss, SmethingGing	(elim self)
6-29	^{3}Spk⅝ ft 61°	3-5yrnw2R=	1	:30	1:01^1	1:31^3	2:02^4	1	2x	1^{1½}°x	3^{3¼}	4^{11}x	4^{11}	2:05	7-5	(DHitemn)	:33^2	FreedomTime, SpeakOut, HiFisKing	(several breaks)
6-20	^{6}Spk⅝ ft 78°	FMnw2R=	1	:30	1:00^1	1:30^4	2:00^3	5	3	3^2	2^{1½}°	2^1	2^{ns}	2:00^3	12-1	(DHitemn)	:29^2	StrikeHerRich, CffeeSkiper, MistyCllette	(just missed)
6-14	^{4}Spk⅝ ft 84°	FMnw2R–	1	:30^4	1:03^4	1:34^4	2:04^1	5	6	8^{8¼}	9^{14}	8^{17}	6^{18}	2:07^4	13-1	(DHitemn)	:30^2	MagicMotion, FireOpal, Wndmeadow	(too much spd)
4-7	^{3}BmlP⅝ ft 37°	nw3R	1	:32^3	1:04^4	1:35^1	2:07^1	1	3	ix4^{3½}°	x6^{12}°	5^{14}	5^{8¾}	2:09	*3-2	(DHitemn)	:31^2	Swoop, KaysCarry, JoJoWidower	(bothered then brk)
3-30	^{4}BmlP⅝ gd 57°	FMnw2R	1	:31^4	1:05^1	1:36^2	2:08	9	1	1^1	2^{1¼}	1^{½}	1^{3¼}	2:08	*3-2	(DHitemn)	:31^2	CoffeeSkippr, RsedleNlie, PlreSpdy	(prkd 1st turn)

P.P. 8 — PURPLE — 8 — 10-1 =

Driver—WALTER PAISLEY, Green-White   Tr.—D. Lyons   (133-26-23-18—.337)

CHIEF'S FINALE

Br c 1975, by Chief Strong—Our Luck—Torpedo Hanover
Owner: Dean B. & Ruby D. Lyons, Pontiac, Ill.

1979 7 3 0 0 $8,485 2:01^4 Spk⅝
1978 7 1 1 1 $2,881 2:02^4 Spk⅝
Lifetime $2,881 3, 2:02^4 (⅝)

Date	Trk Cond Temp	Class	Dist	Leader's Time ¼	½	¾	Winner's Time	PP	¼	½	¾	Str	Fin	Ind. Time	Odds	Driver	Ind ¼ Time	Order of Finish First, Second, Third	Comment
7-13	^{9}Spk⅝ ft 80°	3-5yrstk7500–	1	:30	1:01	1:31^2	2:00^3	5	1°	1^{1½}	3^{1¾}	3^3	4^{5¼}	2:01^3	3-1	(WPaisly)	:29^4	JudgeHanover, BroadwayTune, MarkOne	(early try)
7-7	^{5}Spk⅝ ft 72°	nw9000^{79}+	1	:29	1:00^3	1:30^1	1:59^3	6	7	6^{5¾}°	4^{4¾}°	4^{7½}	6^9	2:01^2	3-1	(WPaisly)	:30^1	ChrisPick, RivrCirclRme, DcShrmn	(too much speed)
6-28	^{7}Spk⅝ ft 74°	nwR5500^{2}L=	1	:29^3	1:01	1:32^2	2:01^4	3	5	4^{2½}°	1^1	1^2	1^{1½}	2:01^4	*7-5	(WPaisly)	:29^2	ChfsFinale, BrnssFshn, PtrBrmac	(drvr-4th straight)
6-19	^{9}Spk⅝ ft	3-5yrnwR5500^{2}L=	1	:30	1:01	1:32^3	2:02^2	5	1°	1^{1¼}	1^1	1^{3½}	1^{4¼}	2:02^2	*1-1	(WPaisly)	:29^4	Chief'sFinale, Queeny'sFlame, Keith'sPal	(big mile)
6-9	^{1}Spk⅝ ft 68°	2-5yrnw2R=	1	:31	1:01^4	1:33	2:04^2	7	6°	5^3°	2^1°	3^{1¼}	4^1	2:04^3	6-1	(DLyons)	:31^3	WinterByeBye, GrnwdJC, MnlghtLove	(3-wide ¾s)
5-28	QCD⅝ ft 76°	nw2R	1	:29^4	1:01^1	1:34	2:05^3	3ix	7	7^{5½}	5^2°	3^3	1^{nk}	2:05^3	*4-5	(DLyons)	:31^1	ChiefsFinale, BobThorpe, RRMont	(———)

SIXTH RACE CONTINUED ON NEXT PAGE

SIXTH RACE
CONTINUED FROM PRECEDING PAGE

PLEASE ASK FOR HORSE BY PROGRAM NUMBER

	Date Trk Cond Temp	Class	Leader's Time Dist ¼ ½	Winner's ¾ Time	PP ¼ ½	¾	Str	Fin Ind. Time	Ind ¼ Odds Driver	ORDER OF FINISH First	Second	Third	Comment

P.P. 10 — BROWN 9 — 8-1

Driver—RAY PARKER, Gray-Orange   Tr.—R. Parker   (2-0-1-0—.278)

LEATHA BOY   B g 1974, by Zooms Painter—Leatha Adios—Greentree Adios
Owner: Ray Dixon Parker, Corydon, Ind.

		1979	8 6 2 0	$12,525	2:01² QCD⅝
		1978	2 2 0 0	$1,250	2:06¹ F.P¹
		Lifetime		$1,250	4, 2:06¹ (1)

7-13	3Spk⅝ ft 80°	3-5yrstk7500—1	:29² 1:00³ 1:32¹ 2:02²	6im7	76¼	62¾°	42¾	2¹	2:02³	2-1 (RParker)	:29⁴ MagicMotion, LeathaBoy, ArmbroTempo	(big mile)
7- 1	QCD⅝ ft 85°	opnhcp3000	1 :27⁴ :59² 1:30² 2:01²	8	7	53½°	42°	2¹	2:01²	*2-1 (RParker)	:30³ LeathaBoy, BlackIris, AdiosFling	(——)
6-28	QCD⅝ ft 76°	Qua	1 :30² 1:02 1:34² 2:06	9	5°	2¹	21½	2ʰᵈ	2:06	NB (RParker)	LeathaBoy, ShalomTime, ActiveBen	(——)
3-31	F.P¹ ft	pref6000	1 :30 :59³ 1:30¹ 2:00³	5	5	5	4°	3¾	2:00³	7-1 (RParker)	TripleShot, LeathaBoy, GoCount	(——)
2-24	F.P¹ sl	opnprf4400	1 :31¹ 1:02¹ 1:33 2:03²	6	6	2°	1	1²	2:03²	*1-5 (RParker)	LeathaBoy, HonestSkipper, BrassyBret	(——)
2-17	F.P¹ gd	opnpref4000	1 :30² 1:01 1:31 2:01³	6	4°	1	1	1³	2:01³	*3-5 (RParker)	LeathaBoy, RibitByrd, TripleShot	(——)

P.P. 11 — LT. BLUE 10 — 9-2 =

Driver—JIM DENNIS, Green-White   Tr.—J. Dennis   (97-18-18-11—.326)

JUDGE HANOVER   B c 1976, by Albatross—Jo Hanover—Tar Heel
Owner: Odd Lots, Inc., Macomb, Ill.

		1979	8 6 0 2	$19,550	1:59¹ ScD⅝
		1978	0 0 0 0	(——)	
		Lifetime			(——)

7-13	9Spk⅝ ft 80°	3-5yrstk7500—1	:30 1:01 1:31² 2:00³	4	2°	2¹½	1¾	1¹¹	1³½	2:00³	*1-5 (JDennis)	:29¹ JudgeHanover, BroadwayTune, MrkOne	(as pleased)
7- 7	4Spk⅝ ft72°	nwR6500 2-3/1—1	:29⁴ 1:00 1:31² 2:01	7	65¾	64°	43¾	11¼	2:01	*2-5 (JDennis)	:28⁴ JudgHnvr, Mg'sFshin, TrtwdPrde	(flew thru str)
6-29	5Spk⅝ ft 61°	3yrstk53750+1	:30 1:01 1:31² 2:00¹	6	6	77½	45½	36	33¼	2:00⁴	5-2 (GSholty)	:28¹ Penner, EscapeArtist, JudgeHanover	(fast last qtr)
6-16	ScD⅝ ft	nw10000 7879	1 :28³ 1:00¹ 1:29² 1:59¹	1	3	5	6	32	1¾	1:59¹	*1-5 (Tivins)	JudgeHanover, Chino, LemTar	(——)
6- 2	ScD⅝ ft	3yrcond	1 :29² 1:01 1:29³ 1:59²	6	6	6	6	55½	32	1:59⁴	*9-5 (Tivins)	MidGrand, SureShow, JudgeHanover	(——)
5-26	ScD⅝ ft	nw10000	1 :30² 1:01² 1:30⁴ 2:01⁴	3	4	4°	2°	21¼	13½	2:01⁴	3-2 (Tivins)	JudgeHanover, Chino, TopButler	(——)

P.P. 12 — WHITE & RED 11 — 20-1

Driver—DESMOND O'DONOHOE, Green-White-Gold   Tr.—D. O'Donohoe   (9-0-0-0—.000)

DIRECT THOUGHT   B g 1975, by Sampson Direct—Late Idea—Overtrick
Owner: Desmond O'Donohoe, Momence, Ill.

		1979	14 3 1 3	$12,845	2:04² May
		1978	6 2 1 0	$2,459	2:06³ gd Nfld
		Lifetime		$2,459	3, 2:06³

7-13	5Spk⅝ ft 80°	3-5yrstk7500—1	:29² 1:00³ 1:32¹ 2:02²	1	4	42¼	52¾	64¼	65¾	2:03⁹	20-1 (DODhoe)	:30⁴ MagicMotion, LeathaBoy, ArmbroTempo	(no close)
6-23	6Spk⅝ ft 59°	nwR6500 5+1	:30 1:01 1:31² 2:02	1	5	65½	54¾	58½	89¾	2:03⁴	30-1 (DODhoe)	:31² Lusty TrHel, Trysmile, WildwdDuane	(pr position)
6- 8	R10Spk⅝ sy78°	nwR6500 2-79+1	:30 :59⁴ 1:32² 2:03²	5	6	65½	74¾	84	75	2:04²	30-1 (DODhoe)	:32⁴ StarredByBret, RaceTmeCarev, SoclalCiss	(tuff foes)
5-21	9May ft 59°	nw10000 7879	1 :29³ 1:00² 1:31² 2:03²	7	1°	11	11	1½	44	2:04¹	9-2 (DODhoe)	:32⁴ RiverCircleRomeo, BttrdBoy, Hllmstr	(used for lead)
5-11	9May ft 56°	nw16500 7879	1 :29³ 1:00¹ 1:31³ 2:02⁴	4	3	2ᵒᵒ°	53½°	8¹³	8⁴¹°	9-2 (DODhoe)	:30² WnnngSmk, BrllntExchng, StdyDndy	(prkd 1st turn)
5- 2	5May sy 64°	nw10000	1 :30¹ 1:02⁴ 1:34 2:04	8	3	21½°	2°	33¼	2:04³	20-1 (DODhoe)	:30² BeGoodTime, CharbosButler, DirectThght	(big try)

CHARLEY HORSE — 1...10...7   **PARADISE — 10...1...2**   **MISS MAREY — 1...2...8**

Scratched: OUR NARDIN

SEVENTH RACE

ONE MILE PACE — "S.L.B.B.C. PRODUCTIONS" — **Purse $8,500**

CONDITIONED. 3-Year-Olds and Up. Non-winners of a race for a purse of $6,500 or more twice since April 15, 1979. (Illinois Conceived and Foaled races not considered.)

PLEASE ASK FOR HORSE BY PROGRAM NUMBER

WARMUP COLOR—ORANGE

RED 1 — 8-1 +

Driver—DAN SHETLER, Purple-Gold-White — Tr.—D. Shetler (53-6-10-9—.266)

ROBBIE DANCER

B g 1973, by Nevele Dancer—Active Ruth—Walter McKlyo
Owner: Orville A. Rursch, Taylor Ridge, Ill.

1979 7 1 1 1 $7,540 2:06³ gd Spk⅝
1978 33 8 8 5 $85,633 1:58 Spr¹
Lifetime $144,570 5, 1:58 (1)

Date	Trk Cond Temp	Class	Dist	¼	½	¾	Winner's Time	PP	¼	½	¾	Str	Fin	Ind. Time	Odds	Driver	Ind ¼ Time	Order of Finish (First, Second, Third)	Comment
7-14	5Spk⅝ ft 73°	nw75003-25	1	:29⁴	1:01³	1:31¹	2:01²	6	7	53½°	42¼°	41½	43¾	2:02¹	7-1	(DShetler)	:30³	EdenGuy, GreySovereign, OleRed	(big try)
6-29	8Spk⅝ gd 61°	w10000787⁹+1		:30²	1:00⁴	1:32	2:01⁴	9	9	98½	85¾°	76½	811	2:04	10-1	(DShetler)	:30⁴	BttleshJohn, RedyBy, Crky'sExprss	(never in it)
6-20	7Spk⅝ ft 78°	nw800079	1	:28⁴	1:01	1:31⁴	2:01	1	4	21°	21	22	33½	2:01⁴	*6-5	(DShetler)	:29⁴	GlBlueChip, SngCycleExpress, RbbleDncr	(no rally)
6- 9	4Spk⅝ ft 68°	nwR60002/10	1	:30	1:03¹	1:33⁴	2:04	1	3	42½	53¼	32	51½	2:04²	*2-1	(DShetler)	:30	Tank, WesternsWHiam, TllyBoy	(locked in backside)
1-29	8Spk⅝ ft 12°	w10000787⁹	1	:29⁴	1:01¹	1:31²	2:02	4	6	44°	22¼°	54	83¼	2:02³	*3-2	(DShetler)	:30⁴	IonesFolly, PrairieStone, Tank	(fast fractions)
1-20	9Spk⅝gd34°	w10000787⁹	1	:31²	1:02³	1:35²	2:06³	1	3	11	11	1ⁿᵏ	1ⁿᵏ	2:06³	*4-5	(DShetler)	:31¹	RobbieDancer, PrairieStone, JamySun	(easy last ½)

BLUE 2 — 6-1 =

Driver—WALTER PAISLEY, Green-White — Tr.—L. Emke (133-26-23-18—.337)

FLAMING H.

Ch c 1975, by Flaming Bret—Honey Rader—Masquerader
Owner: Erlene & James Wilson, Riverside, Ill.

1979 16 3 4 2 $30,537 2:03 May
1978 21 6 1 5 $44,093 2:02 Haw¹
Lifetime $87,386 2, 2:00⁴ (⅝)

Date	Trk Cond Temp	Class	Dist	¼	½	¾	Winner's Time	PP	¼	½	¾	Str	Fin	Ind. Time	Odds	Driver	Ind ¼ Time	Order of Finish (First, Second, Third)	Comment
7-10	8Spk⅝ ft 82°	nwR60006	1	:29²	1:00²	1:29³	1:59³	5	1	52½	52¼°	78¾	78¾	2:01²	17-1	(CWillis)	:31¹	PacingBoy, Pharo, SlyBrewer	(fast mile)
6-27	Spk⅝ ft 76°	Qua	1	:30³	1:02²	1:34	2:04¹	6	3°	12½	12	2½	2ⁿᵏ	2:04¹	NB	(CWillis)		SonCycle, FlamingH, SouthbrookSolarGB	(———)
4-20	8May ft 62°	4yrup10000	1	:30¹	1:01²	1:33¹	2:03	3	2	1¹	1ⁿᵏ	1ⁿᵏ	1ʰᵈ	2:03	*6-5	(WPaisley)	:29⁴	FlamingH, IonesFlly, BarmryByrd	(headed cme bck)
4-13	8May ft 53°	4yrup10000	1	:30⁴	1:03	1:33¹	2:03	4	1	1½	1½	1¹	1²½	2:03	*5-2	(WPaisley)	:29⁴	FlamingH, WesternsWilliam, IonesFolly	(good drive)
4- 6	8Mayft 33°	4yrup10000	1	:30¹	1:01³	1:32⁴	2:02⁴	4	1	1¾	1½	11¼	21¼	2:03	8-1	(SBanks)	:30¹	PrairieRock, FlamingH, WesternsWilliam	(game try)
3-30	8May ft 52°	4yrupstk20000	1	:29²	1:01	1:32⁴	2:03⁴	2x10	10¹⁰	10⁷ix	acc., dnf				19-1	(JDolbee)		JamySun, RiaitoRanger, HawthorneJoe	(out of it)

WHITE 3 — 5-1 =

Driver—DARYL BUSSE, Gray-Red — Tr.—E. Cosoli (202-26-30-22—.245)

MANSERVANT

B g 1974, by Butler Byrd—Pacework—U. Scott
Owner: ZJC Building & Machine Corp., Chicago, Ill.

1979 25 3 7 2 $32,503 2:00³ May
1978 26 5 7 2 $22,795 2:02² Arl1⅛
Lifetime $23,759 4, 2:02² (1⅛)

Date	Trk Cond Temp	Class	Dist	¼	½	¾	Winner's Time	PP	¼	½	¾	Str	Fin	Ind. Time	Odds	Driver	Ind ¼ Time	Order of Finish (First, Second, Third)	Comment
7-14	4Spk⅝ ft	nwR65002-5/15	1	:27⁴	1:01³	1:32	2:01²	3	2	31½	79	79½	711	2:03³	*2-1	(DBusse)	:29⁴	LustyTarHeel, DriftedIn, FrostyPence	(pushed back)
6-30	M¹ ft	clm40000	1	:30¹	:58⁴	1:26⁴	1:57¹	6	1	2	2	22¼	41¼	1:57²	28-1	(SGdreau)		AndysTiger, TotalFreight, Boone	(———)
6-22	M¹ gd	clm50000	1	:30³	1:00	1:30	1:59³	1	3	5	7	64¾	68¾	2:01²	29-1	(CAlessi)		BstaBaron, JffrsnAdmirl, HrnThrp	(———)
6-16	M¹ ft	nw17500	1	:28²	:57⁴	1:27	1:56²	5	7	7	7	86¾	916¼	1:59³	45-1	(CAlessi)		BrtsRchrd, Kolak, HappyPlayBoy	(———)
6- 8	M¹ ft	clm90000	1	:28³	:57¹	1:26²	1:55³	6	4	4	6	1013½	10ᵈⁱˢ	2:01³	31-1	(CAlessi)		TaurusRomeo, NeveleLdr, Saigon	(———)
5-26	5May ft 61°	w10000787⁹	1	:29³	:59²	1:30²	2:00³	5	6	63¾	31¼°	31½	1ⁿᵏ	2:00³	4-1	(DBusse)	:30	Manservnt, CourageousBrian, SrDnclt	(sharp drive)

GREEN 4 — 6-1 =

Driver—HARRY SPRUNGER, Blue-Gold-White — Tr.—H. Sprunger (24-1-0-3—.083)

CORKY'S EXPRESS

Blk g 1974, by Caravelle—Flora Express—Express Colby
Owner: Ed Holdeman & Harry Sprunger, Wakarusa, Ligonier, Ind.

1979 21 4 2 5 $23,233 2:01⁴ Spk⅝
1978 29 6 2 5 $26,280 2:00¹ Spk⅝
Lifetime $28,640 4, 2:00¹ (⅝)

Date	Trk Cond Temp	Class	Dist	¼	½	¾	Winner's Time	PP	¼	½	¾	Str	Fin	Ind. Time	Odds	Driver	Ind ¼ Time	Order of Finish (First, Second, Third)	Comment
7-10	8Spk⅝	nwR60006	1	:29²	1:00²	1:29³	1:59³	2	5	74	74¾		52¼	2:00	18-1	(HSprngr)	:29²	PacingBoy, Pharo, SlyBrewer	(closed some)
6-29	8Spk⅝ 1°	w10000787⁹+1		:30²	1:00⁴	1:32	2:01⁴	2	5	53½°	21°	34¾	24¼	2:02⁴	6-1	(HSprngr)	:30³	BttleshJohn, RedyBy, Crky'sExprss	(hung out)
6-23	2Spk⅝ ..9°	nwR65006	1	:30⁴	1:01¹	1:31²	2:01⁴	5	2	34	22½		15	2:01⁴	5-1	(HSprngr)	:29⁴	Corky'sExprss, HwthorneP, TllyBoy	(romped)
6- 9	4Spk⅝ ft 68°	nwR60002/10	1	:30	1:03¹	1:33⁴	2:04	9	9	96¾	85¼	74¼	61¾	2:04²	58-1	(HSprngr)	:29²	Tank, WesternsWilliam, TallyBoy	(some close)
5-11	6May ft 56°	4yrup10000	1	:30³	1:04³	1:35⁴	2:05⁴	1	3	2ⁿᵏ°	2ʰᵈ°	21	32	2:06¹	13-1	(HSprngr)	:30²	DocSherman, WestrnsWilliam, CrkysExprss	(big try)
5- 3	4May ft 50°	nw5000787⁹	1	:31	1:02¹	1:33²	2:04²	3	2	1ʰᵈ	1¹°	11	1¾	2:04²	*6-5	(HSprngr)	:31	CorkysExprss, MoneyMiss, MdwSean	(battled hard)

BLACK 5 — 3-1 =

Driver—STEVE SPRIGGS, Gold-Silver — Tr.—E. Heigl (14-1-2-2—.198)

PHARO

B h 1973, by Steady Star—Lilac Time—Good Time
Owner: Stuart A. Niems, Los Angeles, Calif.

1979 5 0 2 1 $6,345
1978 30 5 3 9 $37,082 1:56² Hol¹
Lifetime $54,784 5, 1:56² (1)

Date	Trk Cond Temp	Class	Dist	¼	½	¾	Winner's Time	PP	¼	½	¾	Str	Fin	Ind. Time	Odds	Driver	Ind ¼ Time	Order of Finish (First, Second, Third)	Comment
7-10	8Spk⅝ ft 82°	nwR60006+1		:29²	1:00²	1:29³	1:59³	8ix	8	86	85¾	55¼	2ⁿᵏ	1:59³	5-2	(SGdreau)	:28⁴	PacingBoy, Pharo, SlyBrewer	(strong aft lm)
7- 6	7Spk⅝ ft 68°	nwR50004-15	1	:30	:59⁴	1:30⁴	2:00⁴	4	8	98½	86°	56	4ⁿᵏ	2:00⁴	*8-5	(DMagee)	:28⁴	MightyTS, MarengoTed, MajstcRnvaeh	(shffld back)
6-30	6Spk⅝ gd71°	nw10000⁵⁻¹⁰	1	:29⁴	1:03²	1:36	2:05²	7	9	75¾°	74°	42¾	32¼	2:05⁴	*9-5	(DMagee)	:29	MountlnHedMn, BretsMjesty, Phro	(reserved early)
6-21	8Spk⅝ ft 82°	w10000787⁹	1	:28³	:58	1:28³	1:59²	8	8	75°	64°	2ʰᵈ	2¾	1:59³	5-1	(DMagee)	:30¹	FrostyPence, Pharo, SlyBrewer	(big effort)
6-16	5Spk⅝ ft 85°	w10000787⁹	1	:29¹	1:00⁴	1:30⁴	1:59³	1	4	44½	44½	45	54½	2:00³	7-2	(DMagee)	:28⁴	Tarport Express, Bright Brute, Kens Shadow	(evenly)
11- 3	78Hol¹ ft	ffa21850	1¹⁄₁₆	:29⁴	1:01	1:30⁴	2:05¹	6	6	6	6°	78	710¾	2:07¹	20-1	(TRtchfrd)		JBLucas, CanCanRhythm, ArrocharReplica	(———)

YELLOW 6 — 12-1 +

Driver—WILLIAM McENERY, Red-Black-Gold — Tr.—W. McEnery (18-1-1-0—.082)

BARON THE BRUT

B g 1973, by Baron Hanover—Pretty Miss Jobe—Gene Abbe
Owner: Bell Valley Farm, Inc., Frankfort, Ill.

1979 17 1 2 1 $7,731 2:04¹ May
1978 32 4 2 10 $38,635 1:59³ Spk⅝
Lifetime $121,219 4, 1:59³ (⅝)

Date	Trk Cond Temp	Class	Dist	¼	½	¾	Winner's Time	PP	¼	½	¾	Str	Fin	Ind. Time	Odds	Driver	Ind ¼ Time	Order of Finish (First, Second, Third)	Comment
7-14	3Spk⅝ ft 73°	nw10000²/15	1	:29⁴	1:00¹	1:29⁴	2:00³	7	9	99½	96½	95	62¼	2:01	34-1	(WMcEny)	:29⁴	LittleDelightful, Emanar, OzziesChargr	(some close)
6-23	4Spk⅝ ft 59°	nw1250079	1	:29⁴	:59⁴	1:29⁴	2:00²	4	7	75½	97	67	68¾	2:02¹	51-1	(WMcEny)	:31	BrtsMjsty, MrngTd, ChrisTimPick	(shuffled back)
6-16	3Spk⅝ ft 85°	nw1000079	1	:30	1:00	1:30²	2:02	1	4	42¾	32¼°	76	89	2:03⁴	10-1	(WMcEny)	:33	Major Spike, Social Class, Peter Bromac	(tired)
6- 8	4Spk⅝ sy 78°	nw60003-15	1	:30³	1:01¹	1:33	2:05³	1	2	32½	2½°	2½	21¼	2:05⁴	5-1	(WMcEny)	:32³	Emanar, BaronTheBrut, ParamountHnvr	(game try)
5-26	9May ft 61°	nw35005	1	:30	1:01³	1:32⁴	2:03³	2	4	43½	74	85	64	2:04²	9-1	(WMcEny)	:30⁴	Richardson, TryaSmile, JohnDirect	(shuffled back)
5-19	9May ft 64°	nw35005	1	:30	1:01¹	1:31¹	2:01⁴	5	6	64½	52½	52	41½	2:02¹	11-1	(WMcEny)	:30²	Lovim, Richardson, SocialClass	(raced well)

ORANGE 7 — 10-1 =

Driver—STANLEY BANKS, White-Purple — Tr.—R. Perry (168-17-19-24—.212)

‡CHRIS TIME PICK

Br h 1973, by Chris Time—Miss Bye Bye—Bye Bye Byrd
Owner: Messenger Stable, Golf, Ill.

1979 18 2 1 2 $11,776 2:01⁴ May
1978 32 4 5 3 $36,298 1:58 Spk⅝
Lifetime $137,043 5, 1:58 (⅝)

Date	Trk Cond Temp	Class	Dist	¼	½	¾	Winner's Time	PP	¼	½	¾	Str	Fin	Ind. Time	Odds	Driver	Ind ¼ Time	Order of Finish (First, Second, Third)	Comment
7-14	6Spk⅝ ft	‡nwR65002-5/15	1	:29¹	1:01	1:30⁴	2:00³	7	2	21½	43	53½	66	2:01⁴	10-1	(SBanks)	:30²	BattleshoeJhn, MgsFshn, MjstcRnvh	(3-wide leaving)
6-30	4Spk⅝ gd	‡nwR60002/79+1		:30¹	1:00⁴	1:31⁴	2:04¹	4	1	52½x	922	916	88¼	2:05⁴	5-2	(SBanks)	:29³	QunToBe, Rmbing Rchl, Wstrn'sWllm	(strng aft brk)
6-23	4Spk⅝ ft 59°	‡nw1250079	1	:29⁴	:59⁴	1:29⁴	2:00²	2	2	31	33	32	32¾	2:01	*2-1	(SBanks)	:30³	BrtsMjsty, MrngTd, ChrisTimPick	(good trip)
6- 9	7Spk⅝ ft68°	‡w10000787⁹	1	:30	1:00³	1:31⁴	2:01²	7	1	21	31¼	51¾	62¼	2:01⁴	7-1	(SBanks)	:29⁴	DriftedIn, MountainHdMn, CoringaBill	(early try)
6- 2	8May ft 69°	‡w150007879	1	:30⁴	1:02³	1:33	2:02²	3	4	43°	41½°	31	42	2:02⁴	13-1	(SBanks)	:29²	SirDancalot, FlyFlySolly, QuickTip	(fast last qtr.)
5-23	5May ft 50°	‡nw35005	1	:29⁴	:59⁴	1:30²	2:01⁴	2	3	31½	31	2½	1ⁿᵏ	2:01⁴	*6-5	(SBanks)	:31¹	ChrisTimePick, TarprtExprss, MgsFshn	(sat perfect)

PURPLE 8 — 9-2 =

Driver—JIM DENNIS, Green-White — Tr.—J. Dennis (97-18-18-11—.326)

MAJESTIC RENVAEH

Br c 1975, by Race Time—Cynthias Majesty—Bullet Hanover
Own: W. Foerstner, Ru. Gurrola & D. Miller, Bridgeview, Ill.

1979 15 1 5 3 $14,425 1:57⁴ Sac¹
1978 21 6 2 4 $26,717 1:59² Spk⅝
Lifetime $28,102 3, 1:59² (⅝)

Date	Trk Cond Temp	Class	Dist	¼	½	¾	Winner's Time	PP	¼	½	¾	Str	Fin	Ind. Time	Odds	Driver	Ind ¼ Time	Order of Finish (First, Second, Third)	Comment
7-14	6Spk⅝ ft	nwR65002-5/15+1		:29¹	1:01	1:30⁴	2:00³	2	4	43°	1½	11½	34	2:01²	9-5	(JDennis)	:30³	BattleshoeJohn, MgsFshn, MjstcRnvh	(gd ⅝ move)
7- 6	7Spk⅝ ft 68°	nwR50004-15	1	:30	:59⁴	1:30	2:00⁴	2	4	43¾	11½	11½	3ʰᵈ	2:00⁴	7-2	(JDennis)	:30	MightyTS, MarngoTed, MjstcRnvaeh	(4-on-the-wire)
6-16	6Spk⅝ ft 85°	w10000787⁹	1	:28³	1:00³	1:3	01	7	1°	2ʰᵈ	31	32	55½	2:02¹	3-1	(JDennis)	:31¹	StarredByBret, QuickTip, FrostyPence	(used early)
6- 9	5Spk⅝ ft 68°	4yrstk101250+1		:28²	:58²	1.2	1:58¹	9	9	66½	74¼°	88	87¾	1:59⁴	11-1	(TWheelr)	:31	Abercrombie, RacyThght, RceToWin	(wnnr too tuff)
6- 5	8Spk⅝ ft 60°	inv14000+1		:31¹	1:01²	1:32³	2:02	6	6	66½	42¼°	53	63	2:02³	3-1	(JDennis)	:29³	TimeShadow, MystclHnvr, MstyRquel	(outpaced str)
5-10	Sac¹ ft	nw1100079	1	:30²	1:01	1:28⁴	1:57⁴	2	3	3	1	13	13½	1:57⁴	*1-1	(JDennis)		MajesticRenvaeh, NephewBob, Argyll	(———)

BROWN 9 — 10-1 =

Driver—BRIAN PELLING, Black-Red-Orange — Tr.—B. Pelling (68-11-8-8—.266)

ARMBRO RHYTHM N.

B g 1974, by Armbro Del—Battle Song—Brahman
Own: G. E. Aiken & B.R.P. Enterprises, Corp., Aust., Cypress, Calif.

1979 15 3 5 2 $24,699 1:59¹ LA⅝
1978 35 3 2 2 $4,301 None in U.S.A.
Lifetime $5,230 None in U.S.A.

Date	Trk Cond Temp	Class	Dist	¼	½	¾	Winner's Time	PP	¼	½	¾	Str	Fin	Ind. Time	Odds	Driver	Ind ¼ Time	Order of Finish (First, Second, Third)	Comment
7-12	8Spk⅝ ft 83°	nw1R6	1	:29	:59³	1:30²	2:00²	2	5	64	74	86½	62¾	2:01	*8-5	(BPelling)	:29⁴	WinterWiz, SuperStrike, KensShadow	(blocked str.)
5-28	Sac¹ ft	stk30000	1	:27²	:59²	1:30²	1:59³	5	1°	1	1	2½	23	2:00¹	5-2	(BPelling)		PeterOnedin, ArmbroRhythmN, MghtySpry	(———)
5-16	Sac¹ ft 78°	stk6000	1	:29⁴	:59²	1:30	1:58³	4	1	21	41¼	33½	34	1:59²	*7-5	(BPelling)	:29¹	TrpdsKnht, PtrOndn, ArmbroRythmN	(fast final qtr)
5- 9	Sac¹ ft 68°	stk6000	1	:27⁴	:58	1:28²	1:57³	8	1°	11	1½	12im	31½p2	1:58	2-1	(BPelling)		PetrOndin, ArmbroRhythmN, TrpdeKnght	(bothered)
5- 2	Sac¹ ft 73°	stk6000	1	:30³	1:00¹	1:30³	1:59⁴	7	3	31½°	2¾°	1¹	32½	2:00²	*4-5	(BPelling)	:29³	AndysHnd, TrpdosKnght, ArmbroRhythmN	(tuff trip)
4-28	LA⅝ ft 62°	w10000	1	:30¹	1:00⁴	1:30¹	1:59⁴	1	2	2	3	31½	21¾	2:00	e2-1	(BPelling)		FarnoHanvr, ArmbroRhythmN, BrghtBrute	(———)

CHARLEY HORSE — 3...5...8 Best Bet   PARADISE — 5...3...9   MISS MAREY — 1...2...7

ONE MILE PACE

EIGHTH RACE
"THE OVERCALL"

Purse $25,000

HANDICAP. 3-Year-Olds and Up.

PLEASE ASK FOR HORSE BY PROGRAM NUMBER

	Date	Trk Cond Temp	Class	Dist	Leader's Time ¼ ½ ¾	Winner's Time	PP	¼	½	¾	Str	Fin	Ind. Time	Odds	Driver	Ind ¼ Time	ORDER OF FINISH First Second Third	Comment

RED 1 — 10-1 +
Driver—BRIAN PELLING, Black-Red-Orange Tr.—B. Pelling (68-11-8-8—.266)
YOUNG TENNESSEE B g 1970, by Young Charles—Masquerade—Fallacy
Owner: B.R.P. Enterprises Corp., Cypress, Calif.
1979 17 7 1 1 $37,900 1:59 Sac1
1978 17 2 0 3 $10,565 1:584 Hol1
Lifetime $37,433 8, 1:584 (1)

7-14	8Spk⅝ ft 73°	jffa20000=1	:292 1:01 1:304 1:593	4 4 4¼ 53½ 53	51½	2:00	11-1	(BPelling)	:282	KayMichael, StarCeltic, TarportExpress	(on wood)
7- 7	9Spk⅝ ft 72°	hcp25000+1	:291 :591 1:294 1:574	2 3 33¼ 42½	43½ 35½	1:59	14-1	(BPelling)	:283	TrckyDckN., TrprtExprss, YungTnnss	(good mile)
6-30	8Spk⅝ gd 71°	inv17500=1	:294 1:022 1:33 2:021	7 7 31½ 2½°	2½ 74½	2:031	5-1	(BPelling)	:30	Malice, MistyRaquel, TimeShadow	(parked tired)
6-22	8Spk⅝ ft 63°	inv16000=1	:30 :591 1:294 1:593	5 5° 11½ 11¼	13 1hd	1:593	*3-2	(BPelling)	:294	YoungTnnsse, MystclHnvr, PacingRbn	(well driven)
6-16	7Spk⅝ ft 85°	inv16000=1	:301 1:002 1:312 2:002	3 2°xx525 5dis	5dis 5dis		*3-5	(BPelling)		CrgeousBrn, FlyFlySlly, PcingRbn	(brk thru 2nd ¼)
6- 9	8Spk⅝ ft 68°	inv16000=1	:301 1:002 1:294 1:593	1 1 11¼ 11¼	12	1:593	5-2	(BPelling)	:294	YngTnnssee, TmeShdw, MstyRquel	(confident drive)

BLUE 2 — 8-1 +
Driver—STAN BAYLESS, Gold-White Tr.—J. O'Brien (35-5-5-5—.270)
CAN CAN RHYTHM B h 1974, by Dancer Hanover—Wine Maid—Bye Bye Byrd
Owner: Frank A. Lucich, Delano, Calif.
1979 17 3 1 4 $60,370 1:562 M1
1978 25 13 3 4 $96,240 1:554 Hol1
Lifetime $98,442 4, 1:554 (1)

7-14	Det1 ft	prefinv20000	:291 1:00 1:284 1:582	5 6 8 84	64½	1:591	*2-1	(RWlmsSr)		FullaStrikes, RoanBaron, BulletBluecrest	(——)
7- 7	Det1 ft	w10001	:302 1:01 1:31 1:583	2 4 5 5	4¾ 12	1:583	*4-5	(RWlmsSr)		CanCanRhythm, Buzzeo, BaronRichard	(——)
6-30	Det1 gd	prefinv	:29 :591 1:28 1:583	1 4 4 3°	11 61½	1:584	*2-1	(RWlmsSr)		RoanBaron-BulletBluecrestdh, SctshSkppr	(——)
6-23	M1 ft	inv	:272 :562 1:27 1:544	2 4 4 4	43½ 34½	1:553	8-1	(BWebstr)		NewLew, BonnysColdFront, CanCnRhythm	(——)
6-16	M1 ft	invhcp	:282 :571 1:261 1:551	3 5 5 3°	41¾ 43	1:554	10-1	(SLevy)		TryScotch, NewLew, NpalDew	(——)
6- 8	M1 ft	inv	:281 :564 1:252 1:543	5 7 7	53½ 53¼	1:551	30-1	(SLevy)		NewLew, LeBaronRouge, BattlingBrad	(——)

WHITE 3 — 5-1 +
Driver—STERLING BUCH, White-Black-Red Tr.—C. Willis (46-13-5-4—.372)
RIALTO RANGER B c 1975, by A La Carte—Sharon Maid—Nevin Hanover
Owner: Joseph Gentile & Connel Willis, Berkeley, Willow Springs, Ill.
1979 13 5 3 3 $40,718 1:573 Spk⅝
1978 22 12 2 0 $18,719 9, 2:01 (1¼)
Lifetime $19,719 9, 2:01 (1¼)

7-13	8Spk⅝ ft 80°	inv16000=1	:29 :583 1:283 1:573	4 1 12¼ 11¾	13½ 11¾	1:573	3-1	(SBuch)	:29	RialtoRngr, ReadyBoy, MountnHdMn	(meets fastest)
6-30	7Spk⅝ gd 71°	inv15000+1	:31 1:001 1:313 2:02	8 2° 11 11¼	11½ 2:023	14-1	(CWillis)	:31	TrprtExprss, PcingRbin, RiltoRnger	(battled for led)
6-23	7Spk⅝ ft 59°	w10000 7879—1	:30 1:003 1:30 2:00	3 2 21¾ 32	2nk 12	2:00	3 1	(SBuch)	:293	RialtoRngr, BrightBru, PcingRny	(peak form)
6-11	8Spk⅝ ft 72°	w10000 7879=1	:30 1:01 1:31 2:003	2 2 11½ 12½	13½ 15½	2:001	e8-5	(SBuch)	:29	RialtoRangr, IonesFolly, RoughByrd	(sharp ½ mve)
6- 4	8Spk⅝ ft 82°	3-4yr8500=1	:301 1:01 1:31 2:003	4 5 44½° 21°	1½ 31¾	2:004	2-1	(SBuch)	:293	JohnDirect, AlexeiWellmann, RialtoRangr	(game try)
5-18	8May ft 67°	4yrup10000	:30 1:004 1:302 2:003	1 3 1ns 11	11	2:003	7-2	(SBuch)	:30	RialtoRangr, RustyslronFelt, IonesFolly	(big mile)

GREEN 4 — 6-1 +
Driver—DICK RICHARDSON, JR., Green-White-Blue Tr.—D. Richardson, Jr. (1-0-1-0—.556)
STAR CELTIC B g 1973, by Sugar Tree—Southern Manner
Owner: Rorty Stable, Pinehurst, N.C.
1979 11 1 3 3 $19,620 1:593 ScD⅝
1978 27 7 4 7 $104,132 5, 1:552 (⅝)
Lifetime $124,115 5, 1:552 (⅝)

7-14	8Spk⅝ ft 73°	jffa20000=1	:292 1:01 1:304 1:593	3 2 21½ 31¼	41¾ 2hd	1:593	9-1	(DRchnJr)	:282	KayMichael, StrCeltic, TarprtExprss	(needed rm str)
7- 7	ScD⅝ ft	inv12500	:293 1:012 1:304 1:594	3 2x 4° 5	41¾ 63½	2:002	5-2	(DRhrdsnJr)		MostLuck, NewDeal, TravalonTom	(——)
6-30	ScD⅝ sy	inv8000	:303 1:03 1:324 2:03	2 2 4 5	52¾ 21¼	2:032	2-1	(DRhrdsnJr)		NobleFella, StarCeltic, TravalonTom	(——)
6-23	ScD⅝ ft	invhcp	:283 :581 1:283 1:573	2 3 3 3	2¾ 33½	1:582	2-1	(DRhrdsnJr)		NobleFella, MostLuck, StarCeltic	(——)
6-16	ScD⅝ ft	invhcp	:291 :594 1:293 1:581	4 5 5 5°	42¼ 31¾	1:583	*1-1	(DRhrdsnJr)		CincyEd, MostLuck, StarCeltic	(——)
6- 9	ScD⅝ ft	invhcp	:284 :574 1:272 1:562	4 4 4 1°	11¾ 21½	1:564	2-1	(DRhrdsnJr)		CincyEd, StarCeltic, MostLuck	(——)

BLACK 5 — 7-2 +
Driver—AUBREY PETTY, Maroon-Black Tr.—A. Petty (17-3-1-2—.248)
KAY MICHAEL B h 1973, by Sampson Direct—Cunny's Adios Dell—Greentree Adios
Owner: Petty Stable, Inc., Mason, Tenn.
1979 3 1 1 0 $17,000 1:593 Spk⅝
1978 18 7 3 2 $97,125 1:562 (⅝)
Lifetime $235,278 5, 1:562 (⅝)

7-14	8Spk⅝ ft 73°	jffa20000=1	:292 1:01 1:304 1:593	1 3 32¾ 1ns	1hd 1hd	1:593	*6-5	(APetty)	:283	KayMichael, StarCeltic, TarprtExprss	(class showed)
7- 7	9Spk⅝ ft 72°	hcp25000=1	:291 :591 1:294 1:574	3 4 45	32¼° 32½ 46½	1:59	3-1	(APetty)	:284	TrckyDckN., TrprtExprss, YungTnnss	(off 3 months)
4-14	8May ft 51°	invhcp20000	:283 :582 1:283 2:011	3 5 45	43 32	2:012	7-2	(APetty)	:303	TimelysBestMan, KayMichael, PrettyDrct	(game try)
8-25	78Spk⅝ ft 73°	hcp25000=1	:291 :584 1:273 1:562	5 5 55¾	53¼° 54	1:562	7-2	(APetty)	:281	KayMichael, TrckyDckN, TrySctch	(new lifetime mrk)
8-11	78Spk⅝ ft 77°	hcp25000=1	:284 :581 1:271 1:553	6 7 79½	76¼° 65	44¾	1:563	2-1	(APetty)	:28	TrySctch, TrickyDickN, ThorpeMssngr	(wrld rcrd mi)
8- 5	78Spk⅝ ft 77°	hcp20000=1	:282 :583 1:282 1:572	6 6 43¾° 2hd°	1hd 23	1:58	*6-5	(APetty)	:293	TrckyDckN, KayMichl, TaurusBmbr	(big mve bckside)

YELLOW 6 — 1-1 =
Driver—WALTER PAISLEY, Green-White Tr.—W. Paisley (133-26-23-18—.337)
TRICKY DICK N B h 1972, by Lordship—Iris Hanover—Garrison Hanover
Owner: Ben L. Grass & John Szilage, Aurora, Batavia, Ill.
1979 10 7 2 0 $100,200 1:574 Spk⅝
1978 33 5 7 9 $108,756 1:57 Spk⅝
Lifetime $266,674 5, 1:564 (1)

7- 7	9Spk⅝ ft 72°	hcp25000=1	:291 :591 1:294 1:574	5 1° 11¼ 11¼	12 14¼	1:574	*1-5	(WPaisly)	:28	TrckyDckN., TrprtExprss, YungTnnss	(meets fastest)
6-23	8Spk⅝ ft 59°	hcp25000=1	:291 :593 1:284 1:582	6 3° 11¼ 1½	11 13½	1:582	*2-5	(WPaisly)	:293	TrickyDickN, Malice, TarportExpress	(strong mile)
6-10	9Spk⅝ ft 85°	hcp25000=1	:284 :60 1:283 1:582	6 2° 11¼ 11¼	11 11½	1:582	7-2	(WPaisly)	:292	TrickyDickN, TimeShadow, Malice	(pulling away)
3-24	5May ft 22°	invhcp17500	:284 1:001 1:312 2:01	4 1° 11¼ 11¼	1½ 11½	2:01	*1-2	(WPaisly)	:293	TrickyDickN, PrettyDirect, PacingRobin	(peak form)
3-17	5May ft 43°	invhcp17500	:283 :592 1:294 1:593	4 1 11¼ 11¼	11 11¾	1:593	*1-5	(WPaisly)	:293	TrickyDickN, PrettyCindy, PacingRobn	(tuff winner)
3- 3	5May sy 43°	inv17500	:30 1:02 1:331 2:032	2 ix5 521	522 523 525p4	2:082	*3-5	(WPaisly)	:304	PrettyDirect, SpdyDlvry, SheutbtRnbw	(behind brkr)

CHARLEY HORSE — 6....3....5   **PARADISE — 6....2....3**   **MISS MAREY — 3....1....2**

NINTH RACE

ONE MILE PACE — **Purse $8,500**

"B'NAI B'RITH WOMENS COUNCIL OF GREATER CHICAGO"

CONDITIONED. 3-Year-Olds and Up. Non-winners of a race for a purse of $6,500 or more twice since April 15, 1979. (Illinois Conceived and Foaled races not considered.)

PLEASE ASK FOR HORSE BY PROGRAM NUMBER

WARMUP COLOR—BROWN

RED 1 — 6-1 +

Driver—ROBERT FARRINGTON, Red-Gray — Tr.—R. Gordon (7-2-1-2—.460)

EDEN GUY

B h 1974, by Young Charles—Eden Star—Hal Tryax
Owner. Nick Matranga, Torrance, Calif.

1979 15 3 2 3 $9,330 2:012 Spk⅝
1978 18 1 2 1 $2,736 None in U.S.A.
Lifetime $3,752 None in U.S.A.

Date	Trk Cond Temp	Class	Dist	¼	½	¾	Winner's Time	PP	¼	½	¾	Str	Fin	Ind. Time	Odds	Driver	Ind ¼ Time	Order of Finish	Comment
7-14	5Spk⅝ ft 73°	nw75003-25+1	1	:294	1:013	1:311	2:012	8	8	74½°	53½°	31	11¼	2:012	28-1	(RFrrngtn)	:292	EdenGuy, GreySovereign, OleRed	(well driven)
7-7	Sac1 ft	nw400079	1	:293	:582	1:282	1:591	1	4	2°	2°	710	718	2:024	5-1	(JLighthll)		JamesMission, NeverBetterN, Camlar	(———)
6-30	Sac1 ft	pref5500	1	:322	1:023	1:313	2:011	8	8	8	7	86	53	2:014	34-1	(JLighthll)		HelloBridie-TreasureKeydh, HeroicHanover	(———)
6-14	Sac1 ft	nw250079	1	:301	:584	1:292	2:001	5	8	7	6	78½	811	2:022	3-1	(RGordon)		Uflex, KnightHanoverN, RepusRed	(———)
6-7	Sac1 ft	nw800079	1	:283	:582	1:294	1:592	4	6	7	6	33	33	2:00	7-1	(RGordon)		TreasureKey, Argyll, EdenGuy	(———)
6-2	Sac1 gd	nw4R	1	:301	1:013	1:332	2:04	5	6	5	2°	32	3¾	2:041	3-1	(GVldghm)		CookieBear, Hakatoa, EdenGuy	(———)

BLUE 2 — 8-1 =

Driver—GLEN KIDWELL, Blue-Gold — Tr.—G. Kidwell (26-1-7-3—.226)

RACE TIME CAREY

B h 1974, by Race Time—Thrifty Way—Kings Counsel
Owner: Wayne W. Carey, Mineral Point, Wis.

1979 17 1 6 0 $19,359 2:013 May
1978 17 1 4 3 $15,457 2:02 Spk⅝ Qua
Lifetime $32,797 3, 1:584 (1) T.T.

Date	Trk Cond Temp	Class	Dist	¼	½	¾	Winner's Time	PP	¼	½	¾	Str	Fin	Ind. Time	Odds	Driver	Ind ¼ Time	Order of Finish	Comment
7-12	8Spk⅝ ft 83°	nw1R6=1	1	:29	:593	1:302	2:002	4	6	53½°	41½°	1½	51½	2:004	11-1	(GKidwll)	:30	WinterWiz, SuperStrike, KensShadow	(short lead str)
7-7	4Spk⅝ft72°	nwR65002-3/1—1	1	:294	1:00	1:312	2:01	8	6	76¼	85¼°	67	47	2:022	26-1	(GKidwll)	:30	JudgHnvr, Mg'sFshin, TrtwdPrde	(no rally)
6-21	8Spk⅝ ft 82°	w100007879+1	1	:283	:58	1:283	1:592	1	3	42½	53	75	69¾	2:012	10-1	(GKidwll)	:321	FrostyPence, Pharo, SlyBrewer	(blistering pace)
6-8	10Spk⅝ sy78°	nwR60002-79—1	1	:30	:594	1:322	2:032	1	1	1hd	1¾	1½	22	2:034	•2-1	(GKdwell)	:312	StarredByBret, RceTmeCarey, SocKClss	(brisk pace)
5-26	5May ft 61°	w100007879	1	:293	:592	1:302	2:003	2	3	31¼	42¼	53½	63	2:011	6-1	(GKdwell)	:302	Manservant, CrageousBrian, SirDancalot	(blocked)
5-18	5May ft 67°	w250007879	1	:294	1:012	1:304	2:01	5	2	41½	31	31½	21¼	2:011	23-1	(GKidwell)	:301	TimeShadow, RaceTimeCarey, SrDancalot	(gd trip)

WHITE 3 — 6-1 +

Driver—TIM WHEELER, Green-White — Tr.—N. Trimble (75-12-8-3—.233)

SAMSON CHIP

Br h 1972, by Most Happy Fella—Swing Down—Tar Heel
Owner: Richard Gurrola, LaPorte, Ind.

1979 11 1 2 2 $10,070 2:022 gd May
1978 29 3 7 10 $26,435 2:012 gd V.D¾
Lifetime $62,860 5, 1:592 (¾)

Date	Trk Cond Temp	Class	Dist	¼	½	¾	Winner's Time	PP	¼	½	¾	Str	Fin	Ind. Time	Odds	Driver	Ind ¼ Time	Order of Finish	Comment
7-11	Spk⅝ ft 79°	Qua	1	:304	1:021	1:324	2:024	6	4	44	43°	31¾	1¾	2:024	NB	(RWinters)		SmsonChip, SomersetNlc, BelairPark	(———)
4-27	9May gd 36°	nw35005	1	:311	1:041	1:353	2:062	4	5	53½°	31°	2nk	32¼	2:064	6-1	(SBanks)	:31	CrageousBrian, SteadyDandy, SamsonChp	(tuff trip)
4-19	8May ft 58°	nw35005	1	:292	1:002	1:313	2:014	6	7	76½	63°	42	52¼	2:021	7-1	(SBanks)	:30	ToeTime, RaceTimeCarey, CharbosButler	(no rally)
4-8	8BmlP⅝A sy 43°	pref8000	1	:314	1:021	1:323	2:031	6	5	42½°	21¼°	42½	46¼	2:042	6-1	(SBanks)	:313	NobleFella, Manservnt, CourageousBrian	(1st to pull)
3-28	8May gd58°	nw30005	1	:301	1:011	1:321	2:022	2	4	32°	11½	11	11¾	2:022	9-2	(JDolbee)	:301	SamsnChip, RceTimeCarey, FrstyPnce	(monstr mile)
3-21	8May ft 34°	nw38505	1	:31	1:012	1:311	2:021	6	6	44½°	43½°	42½	52¾	2:024	11-1	(DBusse)	:304	MnlightSaint, DirectMagicN, WintrsBest	(tough trip)

GREEN 4 — 7-2 =

Driver—GEORGE CONLEY, Green-Red — Tr.—G. Conley (28-4-4-4—.270)

BARNEY FAHRNER

B g 1972, by Adios Cleo—Roya G—Express Colby
Owner: Geo. Conley, Robt. Peterson, E. J. Pawlak, Capron, Chicago, Ill.

1979 8 0 1 1 $9,670 2:012 M1 Qua
1978 30 6 7 2 $80,958 1:552 M1
Lifetime $136,598 6, 1:552 (1)

Date	Trk Cond Temp	Class	Dist	¼	½	¾	Winner's Time	PP	¼	½	¾	Str	Fin	Ind. Time	Odds	Driver	Ind ¼ Time	Order of Finish	Comment
7-10	8Spk⅝ ft 82°	nwR60006—1	1	:292	1:002	1:293	1:593	3x	6	42°	x63¾°	89¾	89	2:012	•6-5	(GConley)	:31	PacingBoy, Pharo, SlyBrewer	(several breaks)
7-3	7Spk⅝ sy 78°	w100007879+1	1	:284	1:014	1:314	2:022	2	4	54	52½	64im	21¼	2:023	•2-1	(GConley)	:302	SpdyDlvry, BrnyFhrnr, SlyBrwr	(out too late)
6-23	Nfld ft	opn4000	1	:30	1:014	1:324	2:042	7	7	7	7	73½	41¼	2:043	•5-2	(JNash)		VanCan, NeveleNapoleon, SilentOshorne	(———)
6-16	M1 ft	clm60000	1	:301	1:001	1:283	1:572	2	5	3°	2°	22½	54	1:581	5-1	(JNash)		FightTheFoe, TheBattler, FlameOfFreedom	(———)
6-9	M1 ft	clm60000	1	:282	:572	1:274	1:58	1	1	3	4	43¼	4¾	1:581	5-1	(JNash)		MasterNick, JeffersonAdmiral, MrPockets	(———)
6-2	M1 ft	clm70000	1	:282	:57	1:262	1:56	7	8	8	7°	66¾	68½	1:573	9-2	(JNash)		MasterNick, NeatTrick, MrPockets	(———)

BLACK 5 — 9-2 +

Driver—BRIAN PELLING, Black-Red-Orange — Tr.—B. Pelling (68-11-8-8—.266)

EMANAR

B h 1974, by Jack Chance—Port Maid—Newport Chief
Owner: B.R.P. Enterprises Corp. & O.M.R. Co., Inc., Cypress, Calif.

1979 7 3 2 1 $10,465 2:014 LA⅝
1978 31 1 0 3 $6,592 None in U.S.A.
Lifetime $8,381 None in U.S.A.

Date	Trk Cond Temp	Class	Dist	¼	½	¾	Winner's Time	PP	¼	½	¾	Str	Fin	Ind. Time	Odds	Driver	Ind ¼ Time	Order of Finish	Comment
7-14	3Spk⅝ ft 73°	nw100002/15+1	1	:294	1:001	1:294	2:003	4	6	65	63½°	52½	2¼	2:004	10-1	(BPelling)	:301	LittleDelightful, Emanar, OzziesChrgr	(finished well)
6-8	4Spk⅝ sy 78°	nw60003-15+1	1	:303	1:011	1:33	2:053	4	3	11½	1½	1½	11¼	2:053	•7-5	(BPelling)	:323	Emanar, BaronTheBrut, ParamntHnvr	(driving hard)
5-9	Sac1 ft	nw600079	1	:311	1:024	1:344	2:024	2	1	1	1	11	11½	2:024	2-1	(BPelling)		Emanar, SongCycleExpress, GlidingGuy	(———)
5-3	Sac1 ft	nw800079	1	:314	1:02	1:311	2:004	6	6	43½	31½°	2½	31	2:01	2-1	(BPelling)	:292	RepusRed, NephewBob, Emanar	(prkd w-cover)
4-28	LA⅝ ft	nw125007879	1	:293	1:002	1:304	2:003	2	1	1	1	12	21¼	2:004	•8-5	(BPelling)		NephewBob, Emanar, SongCycleExpress	(———)
4-20	LA⅝ ft	nw4R	1	:294	1:021	1:331	2:014	4	1	1	1	12	11¾	2:014	•7-5	(BPelling)		Emanar, KiwiJade, PeterOnedin	(———)

YELLOW 6 — 12-1 =

Driver—WILLIAM McENERY, Red-Black-Gold — Tr.—W. McEnery (18-1-1-0—.082)

GALA BLUE CHIP

B c 1975, by Overcall—Genes Good Girl—Gene Abbe
Owner: William McEnery, Frankfort, Ill.

1979 16 3 0 0 $10,991 2:003 PPk⅝
1978 28 9 2 6 $22,376 1:581 Lex1
Lifetime $25,507 3, 1:581 (1)

Date	Trk Cond Temp	Class	Dist	¼	½	¾	Winner's Time	PP	¼	½	¾	Str	Fin	Ind. Time	Odds	Driver	Ind ¼ Time	Order of Finish	Comment
7-14	6Spk⅝ ft	nwR65002-5/15=1	1	:291	1:01	1:304	2:003	8	8	88½	75¼°	75	76	2:014	29-1	(WMcEny)	:30	BattleshoeJohn, MegsFashion, MjstoRnvh	(no close)
7-7	6Spk⅝ft72°	nwR65002-3/1=1	1	:301	1:00	1:294	1:59	6	7	78½	76¾	77¼	57½	2:003	28-1	(WMcEny)	:292	RedyBy, BttleshJhn, TwoOnTheAisle	(too much spd)
6-30	6Spk⅝ gd71°	nw100005-10+1	1	:294	1:032	1:36	2:052	9	1°	11½	11¼	98½	912	2:074	34-1	(WMcEny)	:314	MountinHedMn, BretsMjesty, Phro	(4-wide leving)
6-20	7Spk⅝ ft 78°	nw800079—1	1	:284	1:01	1:314	2:01	7	1	11	11	12	13½	2:01	8-1	(WMcEny)	:291	GlBluChip, SngCycleExprs, RbbieDncr	(monster mi.)
6-9	6Spk⅝ ft 68°	nw1000079—1	1	:31	1:022	1:323	2:03	6	7	31°	41½°	53½	54½	2:04	8-1	(WMcEny)	:31	Uplander, DalestarN, PeterBromac	(tuff trip)
5-31	5May gd 70°	nw35005	1	:30	1:011	1:312	2:021	7	7	75°	74°	85½	63¼	2:024	32-1	(WMcEny)	:303	SkipperDale, ElHeel, Uplander	(tough trip)

ORANGE 7 — 8-1 =

Driver—WALTER PAISLEY, Green-White — Tr.—C. Willis (133-26-23-18—.337)

HAWTHORNE JOE

B g 1975, by Mighty Bret—Right Gay—Right Time
Owner: Connel Willis, Willow Springs, Ill.

1979 18 5 0 4 $35,690 2:02 Spk⅝
1978 35 8 8 8 $58,231 2:003 F.P1
Lifetime $109,436 3, 2:003 (1)

Date	Trk Cond Temp	Class	Dist	¼	½	¾	Winner's Time	PP	¼	½	¾	Str	Fin	Ind. Time	Odds	Driver	Ind ¼ Time	Order of Finish	Comment
7-14	4Spk⅝ ft	nwR65002-5/15+1	1	:274	1:013	1:32	2:012	2	4	75	55	53½	51	2:013	9-1	(WPaisly)	:283	LustyTarHeel, DriftedIn, FrostyPence	(fast last qtr.)
7-7	3Spk⅝ ft 72°	nw50004-1—1	1	:293	:593	1:323	2:02	2	4	42¾	32½	31½	1hd	2:02	3-1	(WPaisly)	:284	HwthorneJoe, HidewyBill, SllyVolo	(well handled)
6-29	6Spk⅝ ft 61°	nw1R6—1	1	:301	1:011	1:312	2:011	4	5	56½	76¼	79¾	712	2:033	37-1	(RStine)	:31	SpdyDlivery, Ken'sShdw, BrightBrute	(never close)
6-20	8Spk⅝ ft 78°	w100007879=1	1	:301	1:014	1:332	2:013	1	5	55	43½°	77½	79¾	2:033	e7-1	(CWillis)	:292	Rusty'sIronJet, BattleshoeJohn, RedyBoy	(no excuse)
4-20	8May ft 62°	4yrup10000	1	:301	1:012	1:331	2:03	1	3	52¼	52¼	53	4nk	2:03	4-1	(SBanks)	:292	FlamingH, IonesFolly, BarmaryByrd	(blocked)
4-13	8May ft 53°	4yrup10000	1	:304	1:03	1:331	2:03	5	5	54½	52¼°	63	55½	2:041	5-2	(CWillis)	:302	FlamingH, WesternsWilliam, IonesFolly	(no excuse)

PURPLE 8 — 12-1 +

Driver—STEVE SPRIGGS, Gold-Silver — Tr.—E. Heigl (14-1-2-2—.198)

MAJOR SPIKE

B h 1973, by Major Goose—Megs Gold—Knox Hanover
Owner: Stuart A. Niems, Los Angeles, Calif.

1979 5 1 0 0 $4,125 2:02 Spk⅝
1978 26 4 8 5 $21,015 2:011 Mld
Lifetime $54,547 4, 2:002

Date	Trk Cond Temp	Class	Dist	¼	½	¾	Winner's Time	PP	¼	½	¾	Str	Fin	Ind. Time	Odds	Driver	Ind ¼ Time	Order of Finish	Comment
7-14	5Spk⅝ ft 73°	nw75003-25—1	1	:294	1:013	1:311	2:012	5	6	32¼°	21°	2½x	8dis		5-1	(TWheelr)		EdenGuy, GreySovereign, OleRed	(elim. self)
7-7	4Spk⅝ft72°	nwR65002-3/1—1	1	:294	1:00	1:312	2:01	2	3	33°	21½°	23½	68¼	2:023	6-1	(DMagee)	:304	JudgHnvr, Mg'sFshin, TrtwdPrde	(prked no cover)
7-3	7Spk⅝ sy 78°	w100007879+1	1	:284	1:014	1:314	2:022	1	3	2½°	21°	ix78	7dis		11-1	(DHmltn)		SpdyDlvry, BrnyFhrnr, SlyBrwr	(interference stretch)
6-23	4Spk⅝ ft 59°	nw1250079=1	1	:294	:594	1:294	2:002	6	1	11	22	21x	57½	2:02	5-1	(DMagee)	:314	BrtsMjsty, MrngTd, ChrisTimPick	(costly break)
6-16	3Spk⅝ ft 85°	nw1000079—1	1	:30	1:00	1:302	2:02	2	5	54¼	53½°	22½	1¾	2:02	7-1	(DMagee)	:304	Major Spike, Social Class, Peter Bromac	(best in str)
9-29	78Hol1 ft	cond6300	1	:293	1:004	1:304	1:591	7	5	6	6	76¾	77¾	2:003	12-1	(TRtchfrd)		Tacoma, NevilleJamesN-BakersKnightdh	(———)

BROWN 9 — 5-1 =

Driver—DARYL BUSSE, Gray-Red — Tr.—R. Knudsen (202-26-30-22—.245)

MEG'S FASHION

B g 1972, by Fashion Tip—Meg's Song—Bomber Down
Owner: Robert & Maralyn Knudsen, Sherwood, Mich.

1979 24 2 6 7 $25,004 2:003 Spk⅝
1978 36 6 5 3 $17,686 2:002 Spk⅝
Lifetime $47,941 6, 2:002 (⅝)

Date	Trk Cond Temp	Class	Dist	¼	½	¾	Winner's Time	PP	¼	½	¾	Str	Fin	Ind. Time	Odds	Driver	Ind ¼ Time	Order of Finish	Comment
7-14	6Spk⅝ ft	nwR65002-5/15=1	1	:291	1:01	1:304	2:003	4	1	11½	21½	21½	23¼	2:011	7-2	(DBusse)	:30	BattleshoeJhn, MgsFshn, MjstcRnvh	(close thru out)
7-7	4Spk⅝ft72°	nwR65002-3/1=1	1	:294	1:00	1:312	2:01	6	1	12½	11½	13½	21¼	2:011	4-1	(DBusse)	:294	JudgHnvr, Mg'sFshin, TrtwdPrde	(big try)
6-27	7Spk⅝ ft 80°	nwR8+1	1	:292	1:003	1:311	2:003	1	1	11	1½	11	13½	2:003	•2-1	(DBusse)	:292	Meg'sFshn, SngCyclExprss, Scil Class	(drwing awy)
6-22	3Spk⅝ ft 63°	nw60008—1	1	:294	1:004	1:313	2:021	8	1	11¼	1¾	11½	21¼	2:022	15-1	(DBusse)	:304	RvrCrclRmo, MgsFshn, TrooperChip	(flew from gate)
6-9	7Spk⅝ ft 68°	w100007879+1	1	:30	1:003	1:314	2:012	5	6	68½	64	75¾	76½	2:024	23-1	(DBusse)	:301	DriftedIn, MountainHdMn, CoringaBill	(tuff foes)
5-31	5May gd 70°	nw35005	1	:30	1:011	1:312	2:021	6	1°	31½	41½	42½	42¾	2:024	9-1	(DBusse)	:31	SkipperDale, ElHeel, Uplander	(evenly)

CHARLEY HORSE — 5....4....7 PARADISE — 1....5....8 MISS MAREY — 9....5....7

ONE MILE PACE

TENTH RACE

$3 TRIFECTA WAGERING

Purse $8,000

TRIFECTA WINDOWS CLOSE 3 MINUTES BEFORE RACE TIME

CLAIMING. Claiming Prices $17,500. 3-Year-Olds and Up. Star Farmer, Silent Leigh and Good O Frisky $21,875, all others $17,500.

PLEASE ASK FOR HORSE BY PROGRAM NUMBER

WARMUP COLOR—LIGHT BLUE

RED 1 — 3-1 +

Driver—DAVE MAGEE, Red-Black-White — Tr.—J. Morrissey (166-23-19-17—.236) — 1979 18 4 1 3 $13,440 2:003 Spk⅝ — 1978 31 3 2 5 $18,718 2:043 Haw1

MIGHTY DREAM

B g 1970, by Butlers Dream—Mitzi Star—Wilmingtons Star — Lifetime $114,124 7, 2:00 (⅝)

Owner: Genevieve Buscarini, Chicago, Ill.

Date	Trk Cond Temp	Class	Dist	Leader's Time ¼	½	¾	Winner's Time	PP	¼	½	¾	Str	Fin	Ind. Time	Odds	Driver	Ind ¼ Time	Order of Finish: First, Second, Third	Comment
7-12	7Spk⅝ ft 83°	clm12500	+1	:291	:583	1:292	2:003	5	7	79½	44°	21½	11¾	2:003	*2-1	(DMagee)	:302	MightyDrm, CopperLad, Prospecting	(exploded str)
7- 2	10Spk⅝ ft 68°	clm10000	+1	:294	1:003	1:313	2:031	9	9	98½	65½°	52¾	1¾	2:031	*2-1	(JCurran)	:302	MightyDrm, ThereHeGoes, EastrnBrtn	(driving hard)
6-20	2Spk⅝ ft 78°	clm8000	−1	:294	1:003	1:313	2:02	3	5	56	33	1½	15¼	2:02	4-1	(JCurran)	:294	MightyDrem, SengaPern, TheImpchr	(drawing away)
6- 7	2Spk⅝ ft 78°	clm9000	=1	:302	1:022	1:322	2:04	4	6	65½°	64½°	74½	62¼	2:042	23-1	(JMorrssy)	:311	JJsLuke, CopperLad, FarmerJones	(no excuse)
5-29	7May ft 65°	clm9000	1	:302	1:021	1:332	2:051	4	7	77½	75½	66½	48½	2:07	15-1	(JMrrssy)	:322	DJTrick, PrinceRobro, MountainBob	(on wood)
5-19	1May ft 64°	clm8000	1	:314	1:033	1:34	2:053	5	6	66	74¼	63½	55½	2:064	18-1	(JMrrssy)	:32	TrulySahbra, TheImpeacher, MrBlackKy	(mild close)

BLUE 2 — 6-1 =

Driver—JIM CURRAN, Gray-Gold — Tr.—R. Stasak (152-23-19-18—.252) — 1979 24 3 3 3 $17,052 2:042 Spk⅝ — 1978 26 4 3 1 $21,458 2:012 Spk⅝

HIGHLAND KIRK

B g 1972, by Newport Duke—Rebel Land Chick—Rebel Land — Lifetime $47,730 4, 2:011 (1)

Owner: L. & L. R. Muniz, M. Mandich & R. Stasak, Ind., Ill.

Date	Trk Cond Temp	Class	Dist	Leader's Time ¼	½	¾	Winner's Time	PP	¼	½	¾	Str	Fin	Ind. Time	Odds	Driver	Ind ¼ Time	Order of Finish: First, Second, Third	Comment
7-11	6Spk⅝ ft 83°	clm17500	+1	:301	1:002	1:294	2:002	2	4	65	75½	58½	33¾	2:011	8-1	(JCurran)	:301	HighShadow, SamBlack, HighlandKirk	(mild close)
6-30	1Spk⅝ gd 71°	clm15000	+1	:304	1:021	1:341	2:051	3	3	32½	53°	2½	1½	2:051	17-1	(GMills)	:302	HighIndKirk, TimeBreker, GrdnLyn	(well handled)
6-21	10Spk⅝ ft 82°	clm12500	C−1	:294	1:004	1:312	2:031	8	9	85¼°	52½°	88	73½	2:04	7-1	(TWheelr)	:32	MiracleTeddy, AliasSmith, Barometer	(prkd w-cver)
6-14	7Spk⅝ ft 84°	clm15000	+1	:293	1:012	1:321	2:023	2	3	31½	21°	66½	99½	2:043	2-1	(TWheelr)	:321	EgyptianButler, DoNotPass, AbelCain	(tired badly)
6- 6	10Spk⅝ ft 78°	clm12500	−1	:301	1:021	1:342	2:042	7	8	86°	63½°	41	11¼	2:042	8-1	(TWheelr)	:291	HighlandKirk, EdsMark, MiteyOneTime	(big win)
5-25	10May ft 56°	clm14000	1	:292	1:014	1:322	2:041	1	2	2nk	21°	55½	815	2:071	7-2	(BCrone)	:343	ChiefTmmyHawk, Gallglss, DoNotPass	(bttld, tired)

WHITE 3 — 5-1 =

Driver—WILLIAM LAMBERTUS, Gold-White-Black — Tr.—D. Hamilton (40-2-7-6—.197) — 1979 20 3 2 4 $18,719 2:034 Spk⅝ — 1978 41 6 9 3 $42,622 2:014 Spk⅝

BRET POWER

B h 1973, by Bret Hanover—Wayfield—King's Counsel — Lifetime $74,870 4, 2:004 (1)

Owner: M. J. Gliozzo & D. Hamilton, Ohio

Date	Trk Cond Temp	Class	Dist	Leader's Time ¼	½	¾	Winner's Time	PP	¼	½	¾	Str	Fin	Ind. Time	Odds	Driver	Ind ¼ Time	Order of Finish: First, Second, Third	Comment
7- 3	10Spk⅝ sy 78°	clm17500	=1	:302	1:012	1:334	2:04	1	1	14	43	21	1½	2:04	7-2	(DHmltn)	:293	BretPower, HunnertBucks, GoodOFrisky	(perf. trip)
6-23	3Spk⅝ ft 59°	clm17500	+1	:311	1:023	1:34	2:041	6	6	65½	63¼°	53½x	3¾p4	2:042	6-1	(DHmltn)	:293	HunnrtBcks, RpidCanny, WildwdWill	(gametry)
6-12	7Spk⅝ ft 63°	clm15000	C−1	:304	1:021	1:341	2:034	2	2	21½	31¼	21½	1nk	2:034	13-1	(MSch'fr)	:292	BretPower, LincolnsPledge, HiHoSilvers	(gd trip)
6- 5	6Spk⅝ ft 60°	clm17500	=1	:293	1:00	1:314	2:031	9	9	88	74¼	75	74¾	2:041	16-1	(MSchlfr)	:313	Sailfleet, KeenEdge, DukeDancer	(no late kick)
5-25	9May ft 56°	nw25005	1	:294	1:02	1:314	2:024	7	7	65¾	64¾	54¾	23¼	2:032	52-1	(MSchlfr)	:303	ElHeel, BretPower, TrooperChip	(late rush)
4-21	7BmlP⅝ ft 66°	clm14000	1	:301	1:02	1:33	2:041	5	6	64	73½	54½	42	2:043	7-1	(MSchlfr)	:304	VBilly, AvonEastwood, LawnMorr	(raced well)

GREEN 4 — 8-1 +

Driver—VINCE TAMBORELLO, Red-White-Green — Tr.—V. Tamborello (31-2-10-2—.265) — 1979 21 8 2 5 $34,599 2:03 May — 1978 21 4 3 4 $11,167 2:034 Arl1⅛

STAR FARMER

B g 1975, by Steady Star—Maggie Stone—Keystoner — Lifetime $11,175 3, 2:034 (1⅛)

Owner: Agostino Siciliano, Mt. Prospect, Ill.

Date	Trk Cond Temp	Class	Dist	Leader's Time ¼	½	¾	Winner's Time	PP	¼	½	¾	Str	Fin	Ind. Time	Odds	Driver	Ind ¼ Time	Order of Finish: First, Second, Third	Comment
7-10	10Spk⅝ ft 82°	clm15000	−1	:29	:594	1:31	2:011	1	4	43½	31°	21½	32	2:013	5-2	(VTmbllo)	:302	ChargerBoy, TperChip, StarFarmer	(set face pace)
6-29	10Spk⅝ gd 61°	clm17500	−1	:301	1:004	1:32	2:022	8	9	99	87½	813	721	2:063	7-2	(VTmbllo)	:33	PrmountHnover, ScottyFrost, Hssel	(never close)
6-22	10Spk⅝ ft 63°	clm22500	+1	:294	1:01	1:32	2:02	8	8	89¼	85¾°	84¾	67	2:032	11-1	(VTmbllo)	:301	PepperShaker, BreezinHenry, AndysCoho	(evenly)
6- 8	9Spk⅝ sy 78°	clm20000	+1	:324	1:042	1:354	2:053	2	2	21¼	21½	21	1¾	2:053	5-1	(VTmbllo)	:292	StarFarmer, KellyCombat, StanleyLee	(sharp close)
6- 2	6May ft 69°	clm18000	1	:301	1:01	1:321	2:03	3	4	41½°	3½°	2hd	1¾	2:03	4-1	(VTmbllo)	:303	StarFarmer, BeansTonite, ParsnOregn	(sharp drive)
5-21	9May ft 59°	clm16000	1	:301	1:021	1:333	2:042	1	3	21°	2hd°	2hd	11¼	2:042	2-1	(VTmbllo)	:304	StarFarmer, ParsonOregon, EasyWin	(clever drive)

BLACK 5 — 6-1 —

Driver—BRIAN PELLING, Black-Red-Orange — Tr.—B. Pelling (68-11-8-8—.266) — 1979 10 2 0 0 $7,425 2:004 Sac1 — 1978 14 2 3 2 $5,187 None in U.S.A.

RADIANT NELSON

Br g 1972, by Gary Craig—Oro Nelson—Frosty Nelson — Lifetime $8,974 None in U.S.A.

Owner: Edward C. Abbott, Gwelup, Australia

Date	Trk Cond Temp	Class	Dist	Leader's Time ¼	½	¾	Winner's Time	PP	¼	½	¾	Str	Fin	Ind. Time	Odds	Driver	Ind ¼ Time	Order of Finish: First, Second, Third	Comment
6- 8	9Spk⅝ sy 78°	clm20000	+1	:324	1:042	1:354	2:053	1	1	11¼	11½	11	52¼	2:06	4-1	(BPelling)	:301	StarFarmer, KellyCombat, StanleyLee	(cut mile)
5-17	Sac1 ft	clm16000	1	:302	1:012	1:304	2:004	5	5	5	5°	32½	1¾	2:004	5-1	(BPelling)		RadiantNelson, YoungNev, SouthernLad	(———)
5-11	Sac1 ft	clm20000	1	:30	1:004	1:30	1:593	3	2	21¼	21	21½	54½	2:003	7-2	(BPelling)	:302	Creanza, DukeWoollen, Golane	(outpaced str)
5- 5	Sac1 ft	clm25000	1	:291	:584	1:294	1:594	3	3	42½	32	3¾	42	2:001	14-1	(BPelling)	:30	ScotchTimeAbbee, TownFair, Golane	(blocked)
4-28	LA⅝ ft	w10000	1	:301	1:004	1:301	1:594	7	7	7	7°	88¾	813¼	2:022	e2-1	(JSherren)		FarnoHanovr, ArmbroRhythmN, BrghtBrte	(———)
4-18	LA⅝ ft	Qua	1	:30	1:02	1:341	2:051	1	3	3	3	32½	31	2:052	NB	(BPelling)		GypsyBlue, Yakiriki, RadiantNelson	(———)

YELLOW 6 — 4-1 —

Driver—DAN SHETLER, Purple-Gold-White — Tr.—D. Shetler (53-6-10-9—.266) — 1979 12 3 3 1 $16,063 2:044 gd Spk⅝ — 1978 0 0 0 0 (——)

DALESTAR N

B g 1969, by Garrison Hanover—Kinsella—U Scott — Lifetime $13,027 7, 2:012 (1)

Owner: Streamwoods North Forty, Cicero, Ill.

Date	Trk Cond Temp	Class	Dist	Leader's Time ¼	½	¾	Winner's Time	PP	¼	½	¾	Str	Fin	Ind. Time	Odds	Driver	Ind ¼ Time	Order of Finish: First, Second, Third	Comment
7-11	8Spk⅝ ft 83°	clm20000	=1	:294	:594	1:304	2:01	2	5	53½°	32°	3½	51¾	2:012	6-1	(DShetler)	:301	CannonTurner, FlyStraight, TallyBoy	(road trouble)
6-30	10Spk⅝ gd 71°	clm20000	−1	:30	1:03	1:341	2:044	3	3	32	42½	53½	1nk	2:044	8-1	(DShetler)	:30	DalestarN, FlyStrght, BrllntExclnge	(found rn rail)
6-22	10Spk⅝ ft 63°	clm22500	+1	:294	1:01	1:32	2:02	3	4	43¾	21¾°	2nk	54½	2:03	7-1	(DShetler)	:303	PepperShkr, BreezinHnry, AndysCoho	(gd ¾ move)
6- 9	6Spk⅝ ft 68°	nw100079	=1	:31	1:022	1:323	2:03	5	5	52¼°	31¼	31½	2ns	2:03	5-1	(DShetler)	:301	Uplander, DalestarN, PeterBromac	(flew on rail)
4-11	7May sy 43°	nw100007879	1	:31	1:023	1:343	2:06	7	5	44	21°	2½	2nk	2:06	8-1	(DShetler)	:311	JackieMite, DalestarN, ParamountHanovr	(big effort)
3-30	9May ft 52°	nw100007879	1	:31	1:033	1:344	2:064	8	8	63½°	63½°	74	2¾	2:07	9-1	(DShetler)	:312	AmysLeader, DalestarN, ParamountHnvr	(late rush)

ORANGE 7 — 12-1 =

Driver—TIM WHEELER, Green-White — Tr.—L. Lettau (75-12-8-3—.233) — 1979 12 1 1 1 $6,316 2:06 Spk⅝ — 1978 29 5 6 3 $35,375 1:582 Spk⅝

BILLY JOE BEARCAT

B h 1973, by Calcaneus—Linda's Choice—Hodgen — Lifetime $95,291 5, 1:582 (⅝)

Owner: Cadet Stable, Elmwood Park, Ill.

Date	Trk Cond Temp	Class	Dist	Leader's Time ¼	½	¾	Winner's Time	PP	¼	½	¾	Str	Fin	Ind. Time	Odds	Driver	Ind ¼ Time	Order of Finish: First, Second, Third	Comment
7-14	10Spk⅝ ft 73°	clm17500	=1	:293	1:012	1:314	2:02	9	9	85¼°	96¼°	87¼	87¾	2:033	23-1	(JGrahm)	:303	HunnertBucks, BurwoodSharon, DJTrick	(post hurt)
7- 3	10Spk⅝ sy 78°	clm17500	+1	:302	1:013	1:334	2:04	8	1°	32½	32°	912	915	2.07	18-1	(DBusse)	:324	BretPower, HunnrtBucks, GoodOFrisky	(showed spd)
6-23	6Spk⅝ ft 59°	nwR65005	−1	:30	1.01	1:312	2:02	6	3	43	919	9dis	9dis		15-1	(DBusse)		Lusty TrHel, Trysmile, WildwdDuane	(off form
6-14	8Spk⅝ ft 84°	clm22500	+1	:301	1:03	1:324	2:022	5	5	43°	43½°	67	66	2:033	16-1	(DBusse)	:301	AndysCoho, IrishTip, WintersBest	(tough trip)
3-24	10May ft 22°	clm20000	1	:303	1:034	1:353	2:053	7	7	74	63°	65½	68	2:071	8-1	(JDolbee)	:31	HunnrtBucks, LittleHorton, ChiefYoung	(3-wide ⅝'s)
3-17	9May ft 43°	clm20000	1	:312	1:024	1:33	2:041	6	7	75½	64	53¼	41½	2:043	7-2	(DMagee)	:304	SomersetNic, ChiefYoung, OnasLuck	(no excuse)

PURPLE 8 — 12-1 +

Driver—LAVERN HOSTETLER, Purple-White — Tr.—M. Rogulic (75-10-9-12—.253) — 1979 11 1 0 2 $5,178 2:043 May — 1978 19 2 0 2 $6,267 2:043 QCD⅝

SILENT LEIGH

B g 1975, by Silent Majority—Cunny's Pet—Poplar Byrd — Lifetime $6,267 3, 2:043 (⅝)

Owner: Mark Rogulic, McHenry, Ill.

Date	Trk Cond Temp	Class	Dist	Leader's Time ¼	½	¾	Winner's Time	PP	¼	½	¾	Str	Fin	Ind. Time	Odds	Driver	Ind ¼ Time	Order of Finish: First, Second, Third	Comment
7-12	6Spk⅝ ft 83°	clm12500	−1	:294	1:014	1:32	2:013	7	7	77½	76	64	33	2:021	15-1	(LHosttlr)	:29	CapetownMo, MjsticSpd, SlntLeigh	(closed too late)
7- 6	10Spk⅝ ft 68°	clm17500	+1	:293	1:004	1:313	2:014	7	7	76	76½	76½	87½	2:032	31-1	(WDiBlla)	:302	NobleDee, Hassel, ScottyFrost	(evenly)
6-25	9Spk⅝ ft 67°	nw50008	−1	:294	1:003	1:313	2:022	2	3	32¼	21½°	56½	77½	2:04	17-1	(WDiBlla)	:32	PhinneasFinn, BrawnyBret, Lee'sBest	(pulled, hung)
6-18	8Spk⅝ ft 60°	clm17500	=1	:294	1:01	1:311	2:023	6	9	97½	98	85	72	2:03	20-1	(KNoble)	:301	TKCounsel, BurwoodSharon, EyreQuake	(late bid)
5-29	8May ft 65°	nw100007879	1	:304	1:013	1:322	2:05	3	5	43°im	1nk°	11	32¼	2:052	4-1	(LHosttln)	:33	Hallmaster, MiniSky, SilentLeigh	(bothered)
5-19	10May ft 64°	clm11000	1	:304	1:023	1:331	2:043	7	8	86½	52½°	2nk	11½	2:043	16-1	(LHosttlr)	:304	SilentLeigh, EdsMark, GoodMonty	(well handled)

BROWN 9 — 10-1 =

Driver—STANLEY BANKS, White-Purple — Tr.—L. Fox (168-17-19-24—.212) — 1979 25 2 10 4 $28,020 2:042 May — 1978 43 4 6 8 $17,126 2:03 Arl1⅛

GOOD O FRISKY

B g 1975, by Arrivederci Byrd—Dollette—Chucks Widower — Lifetime $17,976 3, 2:03 (1⅛)

Owner: Ellewyn Hegland & Leroy Fox, Sandwich, Ill.

Date	Trk Cond Temp	Class	Dist	Leader's Time ¼	½	¾	Winner's Time	PP	¼	½	¾	Str	Fin	Ind. Time	Odds	Driver	Ind ¼ Time	Order of Finish: First, Second, Third	Comment
7-14	10Spk⅝ ft 73°	clm17500	=1	:293	1:012	1:314	2:02	2	3	53¼	52¾	43½	51	2:021	5-1	(SBanks)	:294	HunnertBucks, BurwoodSharon, DJTrick	(raced well)
7- 3	10Spk⅝ sy 78°	clm17500	+1	:302	1:013	1:334	2:04	3	6	66	75½	44	34¼	2:044	9-1	(SBanks)	:30	BretPwr, HnnrtBcks, GdOFrsky	(lacked strong rally)
6-26	7Spk⅝ ft 79°	clm15000	=1	:291	:591	1:302	2:023	3	5	74¾	62¾	31½	2¾	2:024	9-1	(SBanks)	:314	IrishImage, GoodOFrisky, D.J.Trick	(shuffled back)
6-19	7Spk⅝ ft 79°	clm15000	−1	:292	:592	1:304	2:01	9	9	911	98¼	88	56¾	2:022	15-1	(SBanks)	:30	CannonTurner, FrstyGuyN., TrickyBaron	(no factor)
6- 7	5Spk⅝ ft 78°	clm17500	+1	:292	1:003	1:311	2:014	2	4	43½	52¼	63	46	2:03	5-1	(SBanks)	:312	IrishTip, NobleDee, Perryville	(no rally)
5-29	9May ft 65°	clm16000	1	:301	1:014	1:331	2:04	5	2	21¼	31½	31½	21¼	2:041	7-2	(DBusse)	:304	TKCounsel, GoodOFrisky, MeadowWonder	(gd trip)

CHARLEY HORSE — 5....6....1....9 PARADISE — 6....4....5....1 MISS MAREY — 9....4....5....6

The First Race

The very best last-quarter and final times in this field of $15,000 claimers belong to Capetown Mo, who now steps up a bit in class after the powerful stretch drive that won for him nine nights ago. Possibly some other starter with less impressive figures will overtake Capetown Mo when we do the actual ratings, but the practiced eye would doubt it.

Eliminations: Barometer (unable to beat lesser); Majestic Speed (likewise); Lauder Lumber (just qualified); Mr. Pellaire (another qualifier); King Riki (absentee); My Bonnie Lad (showed not nearly enough for this bad post).

We shall rate the contenders without using the rating scale on page 268. Instead we award 20 points to the fastest time in the category, and give each slower time 1 point less for each $\frac{1}{5}$ second of difference.

Beans Tonite	:30:4 (10)	2:02 (18) = 28
Capetown Mo	:28:4 (20)	2:01:3 (20) = 40
Pakura Lad	:31:1 (8)	2:02:1 (17) = 25

Having done only this much, a practiced handicapper can tell that Capetown Mo will be the selection. He loses 5 for moving up in class, but regains 4 for the stretch gain, loses another for the change from post 1 to post 7, and picks up 5 for Thorgren. The final rating is 43.

Beans Tonite adds 5 for the vigorous first quarter on July 10, and has a final rating of 33.

Pakura Lad adds 5 for dropping in class, and 5 more for being parked out, but loses 2 for the poor post and ends with 33.

Capetown Mo won easily, paying a remarkable $12.20. King Riki finished second at 3 to 1, and the favored Beans Tonite was third at 5 to 2.

The Second Race

Here are some $15,000 claimers. We can eliminate Pellaire Dusty, who showed little vigor and indifferent speed; Hal Ridge, a puller who invariably perishes in the stretch; and Largo Ranger, who has shown nothing.

Woodhill Ben	:30:1 (16)	2:02:2 (14) = 30
Chief Timmy Hawk	:30:1 (16)	2:02:4 (12) = 28
Charger Boy	:29:3 (19)	2:01:1 (20) = 39
Top Butler	:29:3 (19)	2:02 (16) = 35
Hasty Brook	:29:2 (20)	2:01:2 (19) = 39
Hi Ho Silvers	:30:4 (13)	2:01:1 (20) = 33

Woodhill Ben loses 5 for rising in class and 1 for post position, but picks up 2 for the stretch gain and 5 for roughing it. Final: 31.

Chief Timmy Hawk earns 4 for the stretch gain, 10 for roughing it and 3 for the better post. Ends with 46.

Charger Boy gets 4 for the stretch effort, 5 for pacing on the outside and 5 for Jim Curran, emerging with 53.

Top Butler loses 5 for moving up in class, but picks up 2 for the stretch gain, 5 for being parked, 5 more as a beaten favorite and 2 more for the post position. The driver switch from Walter Paisley to young Delvin Insko is costly, however. Let's charge him 5 for a net of 39.

Hasty Brook drops 5 for moving up in class, picks up 2 for the stretch gain, and loses 1 for post position. Final is 35.

Hi Ho Silvers gets 5 for dropping in class, 1 for gaining in the stretch and 5 for roughing it. Loses a point for the post but gains 5 for Jim Dolbee. Final is 47.

Charger Boy was a deserving favorite, overcoming early interference to win at $5.80. Chief Timmy Hawk went at 6 to 1 and finished second but was disqualified for interfering with Hi Ho Silvers. Second money went to Top Butler (8 to 1).

The Third Race

This is for pacers that have not won three races or $7,500 during their careers. Conditions of this kind sometimes provide opportunities for classy young horses to destroy older ones, which is essentially what happens here.

We can eliminate Radiant Omaha (scratched); Duke Drummer (a slow qualifier); Wildwood Swinger (no energy); Rare Pearl (never there at the end); Parker B Direct (no real effort); and Road Five (seems to need the inside).

Direct Gold N	:31 (12)	2:02:2 (20)	= 32
Freedom Time	:29:2 (20)	2:02:3 (19)	= 39
Elite Hanover A	:29:2 (20)	2:03:2 (10)	= 30

Direct Gold N loses 5 for moving up in class, gets 2 for the stretch gain and adds 5 for Brian Pelling, ending with 33.

I suppose I could have used Freedom Time's latest race, in which he emerged from a traffic accident with excellent final time. In general, I prefer to bypass a fracas of that kind if the next-to-last is more representative of normal competition. In this case, it probably makes no difference. The reader may enjoy rating the last race, in which the horse should get 5 for the interference as well as 5 for the park-out. In any event, the July 6 outing gets Freedom Time 2 for the stretch gain, 10 for roughing it and 5 as a beaten favorite. He gets an extra 10 for Paisley, ending with 66. At which point, it makes no sense even to bother rating Elite Hanover A, whose slower time of July 5 cannot possibly overcome the post position and other advantages enjoyed by Freedom Time.

Freedom Time, the 4 to 5 favorite, overtook Direct Gold N in the final yards, paying $3.60. Direct Gold N, the logical second choice at 2 to 1, held second. Wildwood Swinger (9 to 1) was third, and Elite Hanover A finished a distant last.

Note that with the scratch of Radiant Omaha, all the horses moved inward by one post position.

The Fourth Race

This is part of the interesting Midwest Pacing Series for younger horses. One entrant simply lays over the rest of the field and will be recognized without difficulty by moderately experienced handicappers. Others will have no difficulty learning how it is done.

The animal in question is Joe O'Brien's filly Mel's Tassel, who returns to home base after an excursion to Northfield Park. Her local effort of June 16 was a smasher. She does not earn quite as high a basic rating as Race on Carey or Mark One; but the stretch gain, the half-mile on the outside and the extraordinary Stan Bayless make the difference. By my lights, she, Race on Carey and Mark One are the only real contenders in the bunch. If you do the ratings, you will see that she develops an enormous edge over the other two.

She was favored and won from Mark One by four and a half lengths, paying $3.80. Mark One went off at 7 to 1. The second favorite, Race on Carey (3 to 1), was third.

The Fifth Race

Conditioned for horses that have never captured the winner's end of two $5,500 purses, this event handicaps as easily as the fourth, and for the same kind of reason. Inca Gold earns a higher figure than the only other real contender, My Chickadee, due mainly to the presence of Walter Paisley, plus My Chickadee's rise in class. The mediocre times and other lackluster characteristics of the others rule them out. To be sure, Knight Chris raced vigorously on July 13, before running into traffic problems, but the colt has not yet delivered at this raceway, and hardly looks the type to do so against Inca Gold from the outside post position.

Inca Gold caught Sam Peterson in the stretch and won by more than five lengths, paying $3.20. Knight Chris (7 to 1) paced a gallant final quarter to finish third. My Chickadee was a distant fifth.

The Sixth Race

Here is another installment of the Midwest Series. In the fourth race, a high-class three-year-old filly was unmistakably the pacer to beat. But here we find three-year-old fillies of less talent. Magic Motion, Broadway Tune, Best Vickie and Coffee Skipper are simply not up to some of the males in this field. For that matter, neither are Vicious Vic, Noble Majority, Chief's Finale, Leatha Boy and Direct Thought. I shall not give them handicap ratings, because I can tell that they do not figure in contention. To satisfy yourself on that score, you can rate them if you like. But before doing it, just notice the times on which the ratings will be based, and notice that even with the good drivers that some of them have, these pacers will not match the final ratings of Ray Charles or Judge Hanover.

Note that Judge Hanover and Direct Thought start the race in a second tier, directly behind Ray Charles and Magic Motion on the inside. For a sharp horse and driver, second-tier posts are no handicap.

Ray Charles	:29:2 (19)	2:00:3 (20) = 39
Judge Hanover	:29:1 (20)	2:00:3 (20) = 40

Ray Charles picks up a point for the gain in the stretch, 5 more for roughing it and 5 more for Jim Dolbee. Final: 50.

Judge Hanover gets 2 for the stretch, 5 for roughing it and 10 for Jim Dennis. I am disinclined to penalize him for the second tier. Final: 57.

Judge Hanover went as odds-on favorite and beat Ray Charles (9 to 5) by a narrowing three-quarter length, paying $3.80. Leatha Boy (19 to 1) was third and Broadway Tune (12 to 1) fourth.

The Seventh Race

Whether one rates his race of July 10 or goes back to the one of July 6, Pharo is the only possible selection in this field. In his last race he paced the final quarter in a blistering :28:4 after being forced into a break by interference shortly after the start. In the previous appearance he also had trouble, being shuffled back early but roughing his way into striking distance on the turn for home, gaining six lengths in the stretch and doing the final quarter in :28:4, an impressive habit.

This time, he went at a surprisingly plump 6 to 5 and won by two and a half lengths, paying $4.60. The second favorite was Manservant at 3 to 1, with Armbro Rhythm N third choice at 9 to 2. They finished fourth and ninth, respectively. Second place went to Robbie Dancer (19 to 1), with Corky's Express next at 20 to 1.

The Eighth Race

Last time, Tricky Dick N blazed the final quarter in :28 flat, completing the mile in 1:57:4, the fastest time of the young meeting. He now has won three successive $25,000 handicaps. Everything else in tonight's field is moving up in class somewhat. In June at The Meadowlands, Can Can Rhythm had raced to times superior to Tricky Dick's, but his figures at Detroit were not nearly so good.

So Tricky Dick N is the favorite and loses. Can Can Rhythm beats Star Celtic (12 to 1) by slightly more than two lengths in a shattering 1:55:4! This probably means that he paced indifferently at Detroit because he did not like the strip there. Or something. Everything considered, Can Can Rhythm's mutuel price of $17.20 was not overgenerous. Some of the sharper minds in the neighborhood must have known that his Detroit performances were untypical and that he would race in something more like his New Jersey form. How right they were.

The Ninth Race

Emanar and Major Spike are scratched from this race conditioned for horses that have not finished first twice when competing for purses of $6,500 or more since April 15. We can eliminate these: Samson Chip, an absentee that has just won a leisurely qualifier; Barney Fahrner, who has had bad luck here but may do well if he recovers his Meadowlands form; and Meg's Fashion, whose preference for pacing in front will do her no good from tonight's post position.

Eden Guy	:29:2 (16)	2:01:2 (17)	= 33
Race Time Carey	:30 (13)	2:00:4 (20)	= 33
Gala Blue Chip	:30 (13)	2:01:4 (15)	= 28
Hawthorne Joe	:28:3 (20)	2:01:3 (16)	= 36

Eden Guy loses 5 for moving up in class but gains 2 for the stretch gain, 10 for the half-mile of roughing, 3 for the better post and 10 more for Bob Farrington. Final rating is 53.

Race Time Carey gets 10 for racing outside and 5 for Glen Kidwell, ending with 48.

Gala Blue Chip earns 5 for parking out and 3 for the post, for a total of 36.

Hawthorne Joe gets 3 for the stretch gain and 10 for Paisley, for a final rating of 49.

Samson Chip was ready to win, and did so by a neck over the understandably favored Barney Fahrner (9 to 5), paying $21.40. I say "understandably" because Barney's last race demonstrated heart, even though he was breaking stride a lot. Furthermore, his previous race in the slop was gallant and his New Jersey form was very good. Our selection, Eden Guy, finished fourth at 5 to 2. Third went to Gala Blue Chip at 19 to 1.

The Tenth Race

We can make several eliminations from this claiming field. Highland Kirk goes, even though he gained a few lengths last time. Trouble is that he lost too many lengths in the beginning, never got off the fence and would not earn enough points for tonight's purposes. Bret Power has been away a bit too long and so has Radiant Nelson. Billy Joe Bearcat has tried repeatedly in the early stages, winding up with nothing later on. Silent Leigh has failed twice in succession from post 7 and now draws post 8. Good O Frisky has not shown the kind of energy needed for the extreme outside.

Mighty Dream	:30:2 (19)	2:00:3 (20)	= 39
Star Farmer	:30:2 (19)	2:01:3 (15)	= 34
Dalestar N	:30:1 (20)	2:01:2 (16)	— 36

Ordinarily when a claiming horse wins as authoritatively as Mighty Dream did, one can allow it to move up a notch in claiming price without penalizing it for the step. But here is a leap from $12,500 to $17,500, and we should dock Mighty Dream 5 on that account. Add 4 for the stretch gain, 5 for the roughing and 5 for Dave Magee. Final rating: 48.

Star Farmer loses 5 for moving up, gets it back for racing outside, but loses a point on post position, ending with 33.

Dalestar N adds 5 for dropping in class, 10 for the vigorous outside work and 5 for Dan Shetler. Final rating: 56.

Shetler threaded his way through traffic after being locked in, and won with a great rush in the final furlong, paying a nice $9.20. Star Farmer was fourth at 9 to 2 and Mighty Dream, favored at 2 to 1, finished fifth. Bret Power was second at 9 to 1, with Highland Kirk third at 5 to 1.

A nice evening. All ten races were playable and we came up with Capetown Mo ($12.20), Charger Boy ($5.80), Freedom Time ($3.60), Mel's Tassel ($3.80), Inca Gold ($3.20), Judge Hanover ($3.80), Pharo ($4.60) and Dalestar N ($9.20). A large number of short-priced favorites that topped our handicap figures and lived up to expectations. Otherwise, we could scarcely have picked seven winners in succession. On the other hand, Capetown Mo and Dalestar N paid nice prices. As I said, a nice evening.

16 LIBERTY BELL PARK

September 29, 1979

THE TEMPERATURE IS AN IDEAL 70 F. and the strip is fast. We shall encounter only one driver who wins 20 percent of his starts, Joe Scorsone. The 15-percenters are Sam Belote, Donald Dancer, Eddie Davis, Jim Doherty, Mark Lancaster, Marvin Maker, Cat Manzi and Jim Shafer.

We could use the average post-position scale for ⅝-mile tracks as set forth on page 216. But statistics published in the Liberty Bell program suggest a slight modification:

Post:	1	2	3	4	5	6	7	8
Rating:	7	5	6	6	6	5	4	3

TOMORROW NIGHT
Texas Tea Seeks 11th Straight
In $12,000 Invitational Pace

$1.00
Price 94¢
Pa. Sales Tax 6¢

LIBERTY BELL PARK

PHILADELPHIA, PENNSYLVANIA

OFFICIAL PAST PERFORMANCE PROGRAM

WILLIAM PENN

RACING ASSOCIATION

Track Now Open 6 Nights A Week
(Closed Monday)

FIFTY-SEVENTH NIGHT
SATURDAY, SEPTEMBER 29, 1979

(1) **PACE—1 MILE**

Warming-Up Saddle Cloth YELLOW

PURSE $2,700

ASK FOR HORSE BY PROGRAM NUMBER

1st HALF OF NITELY DOUBLE

CLAIMING ALLOWANCE
Five-Year-Olds & Older To Be Claimed For $10,000, Four-Year-Olds To Be Claimed For $12,500, Three-Year-Olds To Be Claimed For $16,000. (Fillies & Mares Allowed 20%)

6-1 **1** 12500 Red

WIMBLETON b h, 4, by Columbia George—Lovely Scott by Philip Scott — Trainer-J. G. Smith
Benjamin & Gertrude Schaffer, Kings Point, N.Y. — MR2:041 1979 24 2 1 3 6,366
$7,470 — 3, 2:074 Driver-JOE GREENE, 7-3-36 (169) WHITE-GREEN-BLACK — YR2:074 1978 23 0 2 3 7,470

9-20 LB⅝ 2700 ft 12500 clm cd mi 2921:0111:3142:03 6 5° 4° 3° 54½ 711½ 2:051 10.80 (J.G.Smith) MonaLee,Tarleton,EtcheBoy 60-0
9- 6 LB⅝ 3000 ft 12500 clm cd mi 283 :5841:2932:023 5 7 7 7 77½ 31½ 2:024 47.20 (J.G.Smith) ShoreBlack,Beanda,Winbleton 76-0
8-30 LB⅝ 3000 ft 12500 clm cd mi 3111:02 1:3312:034 2 3 3 3 4x18dis 2:101 24.60 (J.G.Smith) PrttyPtrck,ShrBlck,CaptLake 77-0
8-20 MR 2300 ft 10000 clm cd mi 3011:0211:3312:034 2 3 3° 2° 33 46 2:05 10.30 (J.G.Smith) VonlRum,SteveMilam,Punctl 68-0
8-13 MR 2300 ft 10000 clm cd mi 29 :5941:32 2:04 1 3 3 2° 1½ 32½ 2:042 21.20 (J.G.Smith) HattieBTar,VansHrtg,Wmblt 62-0
8- 7 MR 2800 ft 12500 clm cd mi 2911:0011:3232:033 1 4 3 7 58½ 410 2:053 18.50 (J.G.Smith) TruMTmp,ImBack,DavidN. 68-0
7-27 MR 2300 ft 10000 clm cd mi 3121:0241:3322:041 3 1 1 1 11 1½ 2:041 14.10 (J.G.Smith) Wimbltn,BrgtTygr,RckvWlco 70-0

10-1 **2** 15000 Blue

SALEMS MISTY b m, 4, by Parson Hanover—Tyrolean April by Ricky Hanover — Trainer-M. Schwartz
Emanuel Greenbaum, Wenonah, N.J. — LB(⅝)2:032 1979 19 1 3 4 7,310
$7,507 — 3, 2:04 (⅝) Driver-MARK SCHWARTZ, 2-10-53 (155) BLUE-WHITE-GOLD — Brd(⅝)2:04 1978 17 1 2 1 3,703

9-25 LB⅝ ft Qua mi 30 1:01 1:33 2:02 4 3 3 3 34 313½ 2:043 N.B. (M.Schwartz) MnaGrnle,FrstHlly,SalmMsty 58-0
8- 6 LB⅝ 3000 ft 15000 clm cd mi 291 :5911:3032:013 5 7 7 7 613½621½ 2:054 14.20 (M.Schwartz) NwWa'r EvrgPrby JdyGrttnN 73-0
7-30 LB⅝ 3000 ft 15000 clm cd mi 2921:0041:3242:032 5 4 4 2° 21 43½ 2:04 3.00 (M.Schwartz) JdyGratN,BlueBrk,ToddO'Sct 77-0
7-14 LB⅝ 3000 gd 15000 clm cd mi 2921:00 1:3042:03 3 5 5 5 54 3nk 2:03 2.90 (M.Schwartz) StphnTms ToddO'Sct SlmMst 72-0
7- 7 LB⅝ 3000 ft 15000 clm cd mi 293 :5911:2932:014 5 4° 3° 2 21½ 55½ 2:024 2.80 (M.Schwartz) Neopolitan,KahluaAds,Power 73-0
6-30 LB⅝ 3600 ft 18000 clm cd mi 2931:0111:3142:014 6 8 8 8° 86½ 56¾ 2:031 5.40 (M.Schwartz) Pinker on Advc'rHn GameYnk 70-0
6-22 LB⅝ 3600 sy 18000 clm cd mi 2941:0141:32 2:032 4 4 4 4 53½ 41 2:033 2.00 (M.Schwartz) TyphnTm,OverEasy,Advct'Hn 63-0

3-1 **3** 10000 White

THE VERY BEST b g, 7, by Speedy Rodney—Sparkling Molly by Stars Pride — Trainer-M. Maker
Jo Ann Maker & Paul Straub, Monticello, N.Y. — Q-LB(⅝)2:024 1979 13 1 3 2 5,262
$36,309 — 5, 2:012 (⅝) Driver-MARVIN MAKER, 1-17-47 (120) RED-WHITE-BLACK — M(1)2:012 1978 35 5 1 7 18,581

9-25 LB⅝ 2700 ft 10000 clm cd mi 2921:0031:3132:034 4 8 5° 3°°31½ 2hd 2:034 *1.80 (M.Maker) LitHassa,TheVBst,CrwnHope 64-0
9-14 LB⅝ 3000 gd 10000 clm cd mi 3011:01 1:32 2:033 6 7 6° 5° 52½ 2ns 2:033 11.90 (M.Maker) TrvsLbl,ThVryBst,B'mntShdw 68-0
9- 5 LB⅝ 3000 sy 10000 clm cd mi 2921:0141:33 2:052 3 6 6° 4°°43½ 53½ 2:06 *2.40 (M.Maker) LitHassa,SirWillim,TodaroHn 75-0
8-27 LB⅝ 3000 sy 10000 clm cd mi 3121:0441:35 2:061 6 6 4° 3° 32 32 2:063 5.90 (M.Maker) Artland,SchiffliJim,TheVBest 75-0
8-20 LB⅝ 3000 ft 10000 clm cd mi 30 1:0141:3212:023 1 4 4 5 42¾ 33½ 2:031 2.40 (M.Maker) BlmtShdw,KlytkMlsa,TVyBst 69-0
8-10 LB⅝ 3000 ft 10000 clm cd mi 3041:0221:3232:033 8 8 8 8 83 66 2:044 3.00 (M.Maker) TarDDuke,CptnLake,FrmShnn 75-0
7-30 LB⅝ ft Qua mi 3041:0121:3142:024 1 2 2 1° 15 16½ 2:024 N.B. (M.Maker) TheVBst,GeneLFrnd,Atabrat 79-0

6-1 **4** 15000 Green

JAMES MYRON b g, 3, by Adios Vic—My T. Fine by Steward Lad — Trainer-S. Milam
Bernard S. & James M. Hofler, Sunbury, N.C. — Brd(⅝)2:062 1979 12 1 0 3 2,461
$00 — Driver-STEVE MILAM, 8-26-56 (150) GREEN-WHITE — 1978 0 0 0 0

9-21 LB⅝ 2700 sy15000 clm cd mi 30 1:0231:3342:052 3 5 4° 2°°2nk 63½ 2:06 19.50 (S.Milam) BlmntShdw,MbdErn,ShrBlck 67-0
9-12 LB⅝ 2200 ft nw2 cd mi 2941:0231:3142:02 5 7 8° 8° 87½ 815½ 2:05 41.90 (S.Milam) FinianHn,OpenBid,HppyMolly 67-0
9- 3 Brd⅝ 3500 ft nw2500 Lt cd mi 3031:0131:3232:023 7 3° 2° 2° 52¾ 814½ 2:052 9.80 (S.Milam) UncleFord,ShdwMiss,JJsGino 80-0
8-25 Brd⅝ 2900gdnw2500 Lt cd mi 3041:0111:30 2:013 4 2 3 3 33¾ 33½ 2:021 10.80 (S.Milam) EgyptnCrwn,TtmHn,JmMyrn 76-0
8-17 Brd⅝ 2500 ftnw2000 L5 cd mi 2831:01 1:3212:023 4 5 4 2° 2½ 55 2:033 23.50 (S.Milam) EricJ,KanUsVic Mys ryCprGB 74-0
7-27 Brd⅝ 2400 ft nw2500 Lt cd mi 2911:00 1:3042:02 5 8 8 7 66½ 47¾ 2:033 13.10 (K.Higham) VlntnBoy,LkyBCrd,NvjoTmhk 80-0
7-18 Brd⅝ 2400 ft nw2500 Lt cd mi 29 :5911:3012:033 5 7 7 7 75½ 42½ 2:04 24.40 (S.Milam) KjmKathy,LckyBCrd,VlntBoy 78-0

12-1 **5** 10000 Black

NEVELE PRIZE b h, 8, by Nevele Pride—Egyptian Princess by Victory Song — Trainer-P. Klein
Wm. Baker, Philip Klein & Richard & Thelma Teller, N.Y. — 1979 1 0 0 0
$103,954 — 5, 2:022 Driver-PHILIP KLEIN, 4-23-50 (170) TAN-BLACK-WHITE — 1978 11 0 0 1 870

9-20 LB⅝ 2700 ft 10000 clm cd mi 2921:0111:3142:03 5 8 8 8 87¾ 814¾ 2:06 54.40 (P.Klein) MonaLee,Tarleton,EtcheBoy 60-0
9-11 LB⅝ ft Qua mi 2941:0111:34 2:061 7 7 7 6° 65 34 2:07 N.B. (P.Klein) SteveRyan,ApliBill,NvelePrz 73-0
10- 5-78 Fhld 2500 ft 8000 clm mi 2931:02 1:3312:044 8 8 8 8 813½819 2:083 62.10 (N.Balducci) PetitePalma,Padway,HappyZ 70-0
9-19-78 Fhld 3000 ft 10000 clm mi 30 1:0211:34 2:051 4 5 5 6° 75 77¾ 2:064 26.20 (N.Balducci) RylAppeal,AdoraStrN,Shaney 65-0
8-29-78 Fhld 3000 ft 10000 clm mi 2921:0121:3222:031 5 7 8 8° 810¼711¾ 2:053 137.70 (N.Balducci) DandyRhy,LTAcres,TrprtStar 85-0
8-21-78 Fhld 3000 ft 10000 clm mi 3041:0141:3242:04 7 8 6° 7° 713¼719½ 2:074 15.40 (N.Balducci) CapHousr,LTAcres,MssHnryT 84-0
8-12-78 Fhld 3000 ft 10000 clm mi 3031:02 1:3242:051 1 5 5 8° 78½ 52¾ 2:054 29.80 (N.Balducci) MdwLpnere,TrprtMrm,Fashnr 82-0

7-2 **6** 10000 Yellow

BEANDA ch g, 7, by Carloader—Saucy Look by Farvel — Trainer-C. Endicott, Jr.
Sylvanus King, Jr., Marvin Lachant & Martin Cornick, Pa. — LB(⅝)2:023 1979 15 2 1 0 4,190
$43,240 — 6, 2:004 (⅝) Driver-CHARLES ENDICOTT, JR., 1-24-41 (160) GOLD-WHITE-BLUE — PcD(⅝)2:004 1978 21 3 1 1 4,007

9-21 LB⅝ 3000 sy 12500 clm cd mi 29 1:01 1:3222:034 4 1 1 1 21½ 812¼ 2:061 *2.20 (C.EndicottJr) StrRflct,ElMgnfcA,PrjRddy 65-0
9-13 LB⅝ 3000 ft 10000 clm cd mi 29 :5921:3042:023 7 2 2 2° 1½ 1½ 2:023 3.60 (C.EndicottJr) Beanda,SnyKngt,OzzieBlgrss 66-0
9- 6 LB⅝ 3000 ft 10000 clm cd mi 283 :5841:2932:023 6 1 1 1 14½ 2¾ 2:024 7.10 (C.EndicottJr) ShoreBlack,Beanda,Winbleton 76-0
8-30 LB⅝ 2400 ft 6000 clm cd mi 283 :5831:30 2:024 8 1 1 1 115 19 2:024 40.50 (C.EndicottJr) Beanda,CarolBeau,LadyJan 80-0
8-16 LB⅝ 2400 ft 6000 clm cd mi 3011:0141:33 2:053 6 1 1 2 2¾ 44½ 2:062 16.70 (C.EndicottJr) TVKght,MrryChrs,JcksnsTrck 70-0
8- 3 LB⅝ 2400 sy 6000 clm cd mi 2921:0031:32 2:042 5 1 1 2 2nk 46¾ 2:054 17.90 (C.EndicottJr) MryChris,TVKnight,LmbrDeal 75-0
7-26 LB⅝ ft Qua mi 2931:0031:3042:021 3 3 3 3 38 314½ 2:05 N.B. (C.EndicottJr) Bartho'mw,GrtDvdeA,Beanda 82-0

4-1 **7** 10000 Pink

TRAVIS LOBELL b h, 6, by Overtrick—Tarella by Tar Heel — Trainer-C. Hauser, Jr.
Kathleen Ross, Holmdel, N.J. — Brd(⅝)2:004 1979 26 2 0 3 8,291
$56,999 — 5, 1:584 (⅝) Driver-WALTER LAUDIEN, 12-9-45 (155) BLACK-GOLD — Brd(⅝)1:584 1978 30 6 8 2 43,481

9-22 Fhld 3600 ft 10000 clm cd mi 3021:0141:3222:033 2 3 3 3° 34½ 32 2:04 *2.50 (W.Laudien) BobbyO,BrwngtGlbrt,TrvsLb 70-0
9-14 LB⅝ 3000 gd 10000 clm cd mi 3011:01 1:32 2:033 1 4 4° 3° 2¾ 1ns 2:033 9.80 (W.Laudien) TrvsLbl,ThVryBst,BlmntShdw 68-0
9- 7 LB⅝ 3600 ft 15000 clm cd mi 30 1:00 1:2942:00 8 7 7 8 813¾823¾ 2:044 33.20 (W.Laudien) GameYnk,MgtySmth,JdyGrtN 74-0
9- 3 LB⅝ 3000 ft 79nw6000 cd mi 2911:0041:31 2:004 3 6 6 5 54 46½ 2:02 18.20 (W.Laudien) HckSprte,Drumbeat,Tutatut 78-0
8-27 LB⅝ 3600 sy 15000 clm cd mi 29 1:0011:3122:032 3 6 6° 6° 7x418¾ 2:071 11.90 (W.Laudien) RmnChf,FlyBlcke,Spencerian 74-0
8-20 LB⅝ 3600 ft 15000 clm cd mi 2921:0031:3142:023 3 5 6° 7° 75¾ 66 P5 2:034 5.20 (W.Laudien) Urok,FlyngBlcke,TntrnAbbyN 75-0
8-12 LB⅝ 4000 sy 17500 clm cd mi 3041:0131:3312:032 3 5 6 7 64¾ 67½ 2:044 3.90 (W.Laudien) Trckstr,JCntryBmpkn,Togntti 56-1

5-1 **8** 10000 Black-Yellow

OZZIE BLUEGRASS b g, 6, by Main Rival—Ozark Direct by Sampson Direct — Trainer-W. Weadley
J. Cisarik, W. Weadley, R. Barr & E. Harrison, Pa. — Brd(⅝)2:023 1979 27 5 7 5 12,776
$22,573 — 4, 2:022 (⅝) Driver-EDDIE DAVIS, 11-17-43 (167) RED-WHITE — Lau(⅝)2:032 1978 33 3 3 6 5,911

9-21 LB⅝ 2700 sy10000 clm cd mi 30 1:0231:3342:052 5 1 1 1 1nk 52 2:054 4.50 (G.Cameron) BlmntShdw,MbdErn,ShrBlck 67-0
9-13 LB⅝ 3000 ft 10000 clm cd mi 29 :5921:3042:023 8 1° 1 1 2½ 35½ 2:033 11.00 (M.Maker) Beanda,SnyKngt,OzzieBlgrss 66-0
9- 6 Brd⅝ 2800 ft 8000 clm cd mi 292 :5941:3112:023 4 1 1 1 1½ 1½ 2:023 *1.90 (P.Battis) OzzBlgrss,BradSong,Pope 80-0
8-31 Brd⅝ 2800 ft 8000 clm cd mi 30 1:0041:3212:031 7 4° 2° 2° 31 42 2:033 3.80 (D.Wade) BluSue,DalveanStar,Bul'Run 80-0
8-21 Brd⅝ 2500 ft 7500 clm cd mi 2941:0221:3232:04 7 2 2 2 2½ 3½ 2:04 8.80 (S.KingJr) LglEys,LTAcres,OzzieBlugrs 74-0
8-15 Brd⅝ 3300 ft 8000 clm cd mi 2821:0121:32 2:032 9 2 2 2° 2nk 32¾ 2:04 5.00 (R.Hayter) JWFlsh,YnkBgn,OzzieBlugrss 68-0
8- 7 Brd⅝ 2500 ft 7500z clm cd mi 3021:0121:3142:041 7 1 3 4° 43 64½ 2:05 6.10 (R.McCarthy) DnmkChief,LglEyes,JrsySugr 80-0

TRACKMAN: 3—6—7

(2)

PACE—1 MILE
Warming-Up Saddle Cloth GRAY

PURSE $2,600

ASK FOR HORSE BY PROGRAM NUMBER

2nd HALF OF NITELY DOUBLE
EXACTA WAGERING THIS RACE
CLUB TWO

TWO, THREE & FOUR-YEAR-OLDS NON-WINNERS OF 3 PARI-MUTUEL RACES OR $5,000 LIFETIME.

5-1 **1** Red

‡SING SOFTLY b f, 3, by Don Baker—Peaceful World by Best Of All
Helen E. Smith, Allentown, N.J. Trainer-C. Smith, Jr.
$505 — Driver-CHARLES SMITH, JR., 10-31-37 (226) RED-WHITE
LB(⅝)2:06 1979 8 2 1 1 2,932
1978 3 0 0 1 505

9-21 LB⅝‡ 2000 sy nw2 cd mi 30¹1:01⁴1:33³2:06 2 3 3 3 3² 1½ 2:06 22.10 (C.SmithJr) SngSftly,FourCrnrs,HppyMlly 65-0
9-11 LB⅝‡ 2200 ft 3-4yr nw2 cd mi 30⁴1:01⁴1:33²2:05 6 5 4° 4° 54½ 65½ 2:06 9.50 (C.SmithJr) Supreme,GrndpaEd,CmdVivR 70-0
9- 3 LB⅝‡ 2000 ft nw1 cd mi 29²1:03¹1:33⁴2:06⁴ 1 4 4 4° 4² 1² 2:06⁴ 5.40 (C.SmithJr) SingSftl,ThrpPrd,MstWFella 78-0
8-23 LB⅝‡ ft Qua mi 29³1:01²1:32¹2:04 7 8° 8 6°°78½ 69 2:05⁴ N.B. (C.SmithJr) FlowStar,Dansemond,LadyJan 75-0
8-16 LB⅝ 2000 ft nw1 cd mi 30⁴1:03³1:35 2:05³ 7 5 7 7° 64½ 59½ 2:07³ 11.80 (C.SmithJr) GmblrDlght,AgstDin RmnPrnc 70-0
8- 2 LB⅝ 2000 sy nw1 cd mi 31²1:03¹1:34⁴2:06² 2 2 2 2° 2½ 2²½ 2:07 *2.00 (C.SmithJr) Wynskip,SingSoftly,OurJackie 75-0
7-26 LB⅝ ft Qua mi 29⁴1:01⁴1:32¹2:04¹ 3 3° 4 4° 37½ 45 2:05¹ N.B. (C.SmithJr) AmerYnk,DouglasHn,Audubon 82-0

3-1 **2** Blue

GEORGIA TECH b c, 3, by Columbia George—Sugar Hill Melody by Adios Harry
Benjamin & Gertrude Schaffer, Kingspoint, N.Y. Trainer-J. G. Smith
$2,660 — 2, 2:06 Qua Driver-JOE GREENE, 7-3-36 (169) WHITE-GREEN-BLACK
MR2:03⁴ 1979 22 2 0 3 7,402
Q-RR2:06 1978 8 0 0 1 2,660

9-20 LB⅝ 2600 ft nw3 cd mi 29¹1:00⁴1:30²2:01⁴ 2 x6 8 7 71¾15¹¼ 2:04 6.70 (J.G.Smith) GmblrDlght,DglHn,TThlyThvg 60-0
9-13 LB⅝ 3000 ft nw3 cd mi 30 1:03 1:33³2:03 2 3 3 3 3½ 3½ 2:03¹ 9.70 (J.G.Smith) EvrgSnd,GmblDlght,GeoTech 68-0
9- 6 LB⅝ 3000 ft nw3 cd mi 29²1:01²1:31³2:01² 1 4 4° 3° 3¼ 3¼ 2:01³ 7.20 (J.G.Smith) AlbaTime,GmblDlght,GeoTech 78-0
8-30 LB⅝ ft Qua mi 30²1:02¹1:34 2:04² 5 3 3 3° 2½ 1³ 2:04² N.B. (J.G.Smith) GeorgTch,RgnaHnN,FrlndHan 84-0
8-20 MR 1600 ft C2-C3 hcp mi 29⁴1:01¹1:32⁴2:03⁴ 7 6° 7° 6x acc dnf *1.30 (J.G.Smith) MikeMOke,DrHck,GzllPrncss 68-0
8-13 MR 1300 ft C3 mi 30 1:01¹1:33⁴2:03⁴ 8 6 5° 2°°2nk 1¹ 2:03⁴ 9.80 (J.G.Smith) GeoTch,CrgHbby,LouiseSctN 62-0
8- 7 MR 1300 ft C3 mi 29³1:00¹1:32³2:03² 6 7 7 7 77½ 6¹⁷ 2:06⁴ 5.00 (J.G.Smith) VlntInny,PPClns,CrgHobby 68-0

5-2 **3** White

TROJAN LOBELL b g, 3, by Airliner—Terka Heel by Tar Heel
R. O. Fournier, Que. & L. & R. Turcotte, Freehold, N.J. Trainer-R. Turcotte
$2,088 — Driver-RONALD TURCOTTE, 12-17-33 (195) BLUE-ORANGE
Fhld2:04² 1979 23 3 4 1 15,496
1978 14 0 1 2 2,088

9-21 LB⅝ 3800 sy 79nw12000 cd mi 29³1:03 1:33 2:03² 4 3 4 4 43½ 65½ 2:04² 18.80 (R.Turcotte) MrkFrrstr,DwyrLb,FtthMchl 67-0
9- 7 Brd⅝ 3500 ft nw5000 Lt cd mi 29² :59³1:29²2:00⁴ 3 2 3 3° 3½ 2nk 2:00⁴ 15.20 (R.Turcotte) FettahMchl,TrjnLbll,HnrBrn 78-0
9- 3 Tinfl 3150 gd 3yr Stk mi 30²1:03 1:36 2:06² 2 3 3 5 49 47½ 2:07⁴ N.B. (R.Turcotte) KittyCicero,TdlwHTod,StnJazz
8-26 Pisc 3150 gd 3yr C Stk mi 30⁴1:02⁴1:34 2:03¹ 5 1° 3 4 5x4¹6dis N.B. (R.Turcotte) KttyCcro,TdlHTod,KngBmbr
8-18 Fhld 14160 ft 3yr Stk mi 29²1:01²1:31⁴2:01¹ 7 5 7 7 56 54½ 2:02¹ 51.70 (R.Turcotte) DrmyIsle,KittysCicero,JllyJdg 65-0
8-10 Cwtwn 6000 gd 3yr Stk mi 30¹1:02¹1:33 2:04 6 6 7x 7 7dis 7dis N.B. (R.Turcotte) HHBattle,StonegateJazz,BlueEgl
8- 4 Fhld 14160 sy 3yr Stk mi 31¹1:00⁴1:31²2:02⁴ 4l 6 5 5 51³¼510½ 2:04⁴ 12.70 (R.Turcotte) HHBattle,Visor,GaelicRum 80-0

8-1 **4** Green

GROUP LEADER b h, 4, by Best Of All—Rescued by Direct Rhythm
Robert & Karen Zeitzer & Pink Lady Farms, Pa. & N.J. Trainer-C. Vahlsing-Oswald
$00 — 3, 2:05¹ (⅝) Qua Driver-DONALD DANCER, 10-1-55 (125) BLUE-GOLD
Brd(⅝)2:03² 1979 14 2 1 1 3,488
Q-LB(⅝)2:05¹ 1978 4 0 0 0

9-20 LB⅝ 2600 ft nw3 cd mi 29¹1:00⁴1:30²2:01⁴ 6 i5 6 6 61¹¼61⁴½ 2:04⁴ 30.10 (J.Greene) GmblrDlght,DglHn,TThlyThvg 60-0
9- 7 Brd⅝ 3500 ft nw5000 Lt cd mi 29² :59³1:29²2:00⁴ 7 5 5x 8 81²¼82²½ 2:05¹ 20.70 (P.MooreJr) FettahMchl,TrjnLbll,HnrBrn 78-0
9- 1 Brd⅝ 4000 ft nw5000 Lt cd mi 30 1:01 1:32²2:02³ 7 6 5° 2° 3½ 5²½ 2:03¹ 14.60 (P.Battis) RumTiger,CharlusCCo,Chasm 80-0
8-22 Brd⅝ 2900 ft nw2500 Lt cd mi 30 1:01³1:32¹2:03² 8 5 2° 1 1² 1½ 2:03² *1.50 (P.Battis) GroupLdr,MaidsIsle,BlzFrwd 76-0
8-15 Brd⅝ 2400 ft nw2500 Lt cd mi 30 1:01¹1:31⁴2:02⁴ 3 5 3° 3 3²½ 3² 2:03¹ *1.70 (P.Battis) VlcBoy,FourCorners,GrpLeadr 68-0
8- 5 Brd⅝ 2900 ft nw2500 Lt cd mi 30¹1:01¹1:30³2:02¹ 6 4 i5 4° 4²½ 6¹½ 2:02² 51.90 (P.Battis) ValntBoy,CharlCoCo,TmAFlee 86-0
7-28 Brd⅝ 2900 ft nw2500 Lt cd mi 31¹1:02 1:33²2:02² 4 5 5 i7 68½ 616½ 2:05³ 7.70 (P.Battis) HailCaesar,HrdyExp,StrpExp 82-0

8-1 **5** Black

ILLUSIVE b g, 4, by Stephan Smith—Easy's Lady by Adios Harry
Fay W. Williams & Walter H. Ross, Salem, N.H. Trainer-W. Ross
$2,386 — 3, 2:03² (⅝) Qua Driver-BASIL SAPIENZA, 11-15-42 (145) BLACK-TAN
Q-Brd(⅝)2:03³ 1979 27 2 4 3 6,092
Q-Brd(⅝)2:03² 1978 15 0 2 2 1,736

9-19 LB⅝ 3000 ft 79nw6000 cd mi 30 1:02 1:32³2:02⁴ 5 2° 2 2° 2² 3⁵½ 2:04 10.50 (W.Ross) AdieuHan,WbheLmbr,Illusive 54-0
9- 7 Brd⅝ 2900 ft nw2500 Lt cd mi 29³1:01⁴1:32³2:04¹ 2 i5 6° 4° 5ix3¹⁄₄68 2:05⁴ *1.60 (W.Ross) MaidIsle,BntnBob,GldcrkExp 78-0
8-31 Brd⅝ 2400 ft nw2500 Lt cd mi 31³1:03 1:32⁴2:03⁴ 7ix1 1 1 1⁵ 16½ 2:03⁴ 2.90 (W.Ross) Illusive,RumbaRebel,Maid Isle 80-0
8-25 Brd⅝ 2900 gd nw2500 Lt cd mi 30⁴1:01¹1:30 2:01³ 1 x5 4 4 46½ 44½ 2:02³ 3.60 (B.Sapienza) EgyptnCrwn,TtmHn,JmMyrn 76-0
8-18 Brd⅝ 2000 sy nw2000 L5 cd mi 30³1:02²1:33²2:04⁴ 5 1 1 1 1½ 4¹ 2:05 6.80 (W.Ross) MrJM,Egyp nCwn MstHThlm 66-0
8- 8 Brd⅝ 2000 ft nw2000 L5 cd mi 30²1:02¹1:31³2:04 7 7 8 8 8⁵ 3½ 2:04¹ 6.00 (W.Ross) BeauWest,OnceArnd,Illusive 86-0
8- 1 Brd⅝ 2400 ft nw2500 Lt cd mi 30¹1:03²1:34⁴2:04³ 5 3°ix8 7° 8⁴ 58½ 2:06¹ 3.30 (W.Ross) LadyVixen,Chasm,BlazeFrwrd 86-0

4-1 **6** Yellow

HAPPY MOLLY gr f, 3, by Bye Bye Byrd—Circle Jane by Thorpe Hanover
Bill J. Daniels, Jr., Suffolk, Va. Trainer-E. Davis
$54 — Driver-EDDIE DAVIS, 11-17-43 (167) RED-WHITE
LB(⅝)2:04 1979 6 2 0 2 2,080
1978 5 0 0 0 54

9-21 LB⅝ 2000 sy nw2 cd mi 30¹1:01⁴1:33³2:06 3 2° 1 2 1nk 3²½ 2:06² *1.30 (E.Davis) SngSftly,FourCrnrs,HppyMlly 65-0
9-12 LB⅝ 2200 ft nw2 cd mi 29⁴1:02³1:31⁴2:02 4 3 2° 1 1½ 3¼ 2:02¹ 5.80 (E.Davis) FinianHn,OpenBid,HppyMolly 67-0
9- 5 LB⅝ 2000 ft nw1 cd mi 31³1:02²1:33⁴2:04 1 2 1 1 1²½ 1⁸ 2:04 *1.30 (E.Davis) HppyMolly,Remy,AugstDalline 77-0
8-25 OD 800 ft nw2 Lt cd mi 31 1:03 1:34 2:05³ 2 3 2° 1 1²½ 1⁶ 2:05³ 3.10 (E.Davis) HpyMolly,Nantckt,CrlnaJean 78-0
8- 9 LB⅝ ft Qua mi 29 :57⁴1:28¹2:00¹ 7 6 6 5° 4dis 4dis 2:07 N.B. (E.Davis) SlamDunk,FlwStar,GsslsFsy 80-0
7-19 LB⅝ ft Qua mi 31²1:02 1:34²2:05⁴ 2 3 3x pulled up dnf N.B. (E.Davis) MitFrrstr,MissClbrn,FrlndHn 70-0
7- 5 LB⅝ ft T-P Qua mi 31⁴1:03³1:35³2:07 4 4 4 3° 2¹½ 4⁹ 2:08⁴ N.B. (E.Davis) Foreseen,FrmVctry,TrmpsHn 65-0

6-1 **7** Pink

STORM KIT b f, 3, by Airliner—Swift Kitty by Overtrick
John E. & Lucille E. Costello, Charleroi, Pa. Trainer-M. Harding
$3,728 — 2, 2:05 (⅝) Driver-MIKE HARDING, 5-20-46 (188) WHITE-GOLD-BLACK
PcD(⅝)2:02³ 1979 22 2 1 2 10,609
Mea(⅝)2:05 1978 11 1 3 1 3,728

9-21 Fhld 7768 ft 3yr Fut mi 31 1:03 1:33⁴2:03³ 1 3 4 6 57½ 47½ 2:05 N.B. (M.Harding) Fermata,HHKtn IsleBDrmin 66-0
9-10 Fhld 2280 ft nw1500 cd mi 30 1:01 1:32²2:03 1 3 3 2° 5⁴ 5⁴½ 2:04 9.30 (M.Harding) BlueEagle,TJsJimbo,Diego 70-0
9- 1 Tinfl 3075 gd 3yr F NJSS mi 31²1:02⁴1:34³2:06 3 3 1 2 3² 5⁶ 2:07¹ N.B. (M.Harding) SessyDLee,IsleO'Rain,CindyBindy
8-24 Pisc 3300 gd 3yr F NJSS mi 32²1:04⁴1:36 2:07 6 4 4° 3° 2¼ 3²½ 2:07² N.B. (M.Harding) SessyDLee,JMHussel,StormKit
8-10 Mea⅝ 2600 gd cd mi 30 1:01 1:30¹1:59² 6 6 6 6 71²½71⁹½ 2:03¹ 32.80 (M.Harding) SilentOpera,EmbEffrt,JLAds 70-0
8- 2 Fhld 13500 ft 3yr F NJSS mi 30¹1:00²1:31²2:01³ 1 3 4 7 5²½ 5⁶½ 2:03 30.80 (M.Harding) JllyAnniRev,HHK tn Technicl r 85-0
7-26 EA 2400 sy 3yr F NJSS mi 31¹1:02¹1:34¹2:05¹ 4 5 3° 3° 47½ 5¹⁶ 2:08² N.B. (M.Harding) JMHssl,Technicolor,RvlMollie

No. 6—APOLLO MAGGIE—Scratched

TRACKMAN: 3—2—6

HOLD ALL TICKETS UNTIL RESULT IS DECLARED OFFICIAL

(3) **PACE—1 MILE**
Warming-Up Saddle Cloth
WHITE

PURSE $3,200

ASK FOR HORSE BY PROGRAM NUMBER

TRIFECTA WAGERING THIS RACE

THE BOOSTER CLUB

CLAIMING ALLOWANCE
Five-Year-Olds & Older To Be Claimed For $15,000, Four-Year-Olds To Be Claimed For $17,500, Three-Year-Olds To Be Claimed For $21,000. (Fillies & Mares Allowed 20%)

10-1 **1** 15000 Red

ERIC TIME b g, 5, by Lyss Hanover—Lori Time by Betting Time
James Groff, Strasburg, Pa.
Trainer-J. Groff
Brd(⅝)2:01² 1979 20 2 1 1 8,052
LB(⅝)2:01⁴ 1978 35 2 4 3 15,646
$32,069 — 3, 1:59⁴ (⅝) Driver-MARK SCHWARTZ, 2-10-53 (155) BLUE-WHITE-GOLD
8-27 LB⅝ 3600 sy 15000 clm cd mi 29 1:00¹1:31²2:03² 7 8 8 8 8⁵¼ 4⁹ 2:05¹ 20.00 (J.Groff) RmnChf,FlyBlcke,Spencerian 74-0
8-20 LB⅝ 3600 ft 15000 clm cd mi 29²1:00³1:31⁴2:02³ 8 8 8 8 6⁵¼ 4³ 2:03¹ 60.00 (J.Groff) Urok,FlyngBlcke,TntrnAbbyN 75-0
8-12 Brd⅝ 2000 sy nw1500 L5 cd mi 29¹ :59⁴1:29¹2:01² x5x 8 8 8 8dis 8dis 11.70 (J.Groff) GoldTwnk,ArmRavn,DncrLady 58-0
8- 4 Brd⅝ 5000ft15000 clm hcp mi 29³ :59²1:29²2:00² 3 5 5 7° 7⁶ 7⁵ 2:01² 14.80 (J.Groff) CraNvlle,HghDonA,dhLsaMay 84-0
7-25 Brd⅝ 2500 ft nw2000 L4 cd mi 31¹1:01⁴1:32²2:02¹ 8 2° 3° 5° 6²¾ 5⁷¾ 2:03³ 6.00 (J.Groff) HrryLee,SnnyBnny,AftnHelm 82-0
7-15 Brd⅝ 4500ft15000zclm hcp mi 29 :59¹1:29¹2:01 1 3 3 3 3²½ 2² 2:01² 3.00 (R.Hayter) EdQFrwd,EricTm,LittleAlbie 76-0
7- 8 Brd⅝ 4700 ft 17500 clm hcp mi 30 1:00³1:30³2:00⁴ 9 1 2 4 4⁴¼ 6⁸¼ 2:02² 7.70 (R.Hayter) JesseSam,Skutlbg,LittleAlbie 80-0

6-1 **2** 21000 Blue

ROSSI COLLINS br c, 3, by Lieutenant Gray—Good Sailing by Good Time
Robert T. Lamont & Royal Shade Stable, Inc., Nutley, N.J.
Trainer-A. Nunziata
LB(⅝)2:01⁴ 1979 14 1 1 1 5,598
MR2:03³ 1978 11 3 1 2 20,214
$20 214 — 2, 2:03³ Driver-SAL SPARACINO, 5-10-35 (170) GREEN-RED-WHITE
8-27 LB⅝ 3000 sy 79nw6000 cd mi 29²1:01²1:32¹2:03² 2 1 3 5 5²¾ 5³¼ 2:04 5.50 (S.Sparacino) Nuzio,Tutatut,DouglasHanvr 75-0
8-18 LB⅝ 3000 sy 79nw6000 cd mi 30 1:03²1:33²2:04 6 2 3 3 3³ 7¹²¼ 2:06² 3.60 (S.Sparacino) VlntLeader,JoeNick,HoltLbell 64-0
8-10 LB⅝ 3000 ft 79nw6000 cd mi 29³1:01²1:31¹2:02 8 8 7 8° 8⁴¾ 8²¾ 2:02³ 10.20 (S.Sparacino) SpkdBoots,HoltLbl,ACsBrucie 75-0
8- 2 LB⅝ 3300 sy 79nw6000 cd mi 29 1:00³1:30¹2:01⁴ 4 3 3° 2° 2nk 1¾ 2:01⁴ 6.60 (S.Sparacino) RossiCollins,BigReturn,Avrum 75-0
7-23 LB⅝ 3400 ft 18000 clm cd mi 28⁴ :59¹1:29²2:00² 4 4 4 4 5³¼ 3²¾ 2:01 13.70 (S.Sparacino) BillyAstn,PotHntr,RossiCllns 76-0
7-15 LB⅝ 3400 gd 18000 clm cd mi 29 1:00 1:30³2:01 6 2° 1 2 2½ 6⁸¾ 2:02⁴ 21.50 (L.DuMont) LrnLrrne,LncrMnbr,TypnTm 74-0
7- 4 YR 7000 gd 15000 clm mi 30¹1:01⁴1:31²2:06² 7 7 4° 3° 6⁵¼ 6¹⁷ 2:09 16.90 (C.Abbatiello) StdyTwstr,BrtChance,FlyRvl 57-0

3-1 **3** 21000 White

J. D.'S KELLY ch m, 4, by Robert E. Adios—Linda's Delight by Harry's Delight
James Doherty, Burt Sivin & Steve Ronay, N.J.
Trainer-Ja. Doherty
Lat(1)1:59³ 1979 25 7 7 0 13,648
Owen2:04 1978 41 6 9 6 8,900
$13,131 — 3, 2:04 Driver-JAMES DOHERTY, 9-27-40 (161) RED-WHITE-GREEN
9-21 Fox⅝ 3800sy21000 clm hcp mi 30⁴1:01³1:32³2:03 2 1 1 1 1½ 5²¾ 2:03³ *1.30 (Ja.Doherty) Slicion,TuckWilly,SndyByrd 54-0
9-14 Fox⅝ 3800 sy 21000clm hcp mi 30¹1:02²1:32²2:02² 4 3 3 3 3¹ 2¹ 2:02³ 14.00 (Ja.Doherty) CndyBand,JDsKelly,SndyByrd 70-0
9- 7 Fox⅝ 3800 ft 24000 clm cd mi 30¹1:01²1:31³2:01¹ 7 7 7 7 7⁵¼ 6⁵ 2:02¹ 5.80 (Ja.Doherty) RghtCssN,TkwayWil,BruinTm 78-0
9- 1 Fox⅝ 2700 ft 79nw5000 cd mi 30³1:01¹1:31⁴2:01¹ 7 4° 3 3 3¹ 4⁴¼ 2:02 *2.00 (Ja.Doherty) MountnJester,RmyN,ClmbLk 78-0
8-24 Fox⅝ 3000 ft 79nw6000 cd mi 29⁴1:00²1:30¹2:00¹ 8 4 4 4 4¹ 4¹¼ 2:01 4.10 (Ja.Doherty) FrntrKngt,MghtyEdn,RomyN 70-0
8-10 ScD⅝ 2500 gd nw5000 cd mi 30⁴1:03¹1:34²2:04⁴ 4 3 3 3° 3¹½ 1¹ 2:04⁴ 6.00 (J.Adamsky) JDsKlly,BrtsAntq,JcnthdhVlntrJck
8- 4 Lat¹ 1600 ft nw1200 cd mi 30 1:02⁴1:33¹2:03² 4x 8 8 7 6⁶ 6⁶½ 2:04³ 2.20 (T.Tharps) MiniForsure,PrinceKabbe,Carot

---

5-1 **4** 15000 Green

ROMANOV HANOVER b h, 9, by Dancer Hanover—Ribbon Hanover by Torpid
Ray & Eva LaBonte, Palmer, Mass.
Trainer-C. Petro
M(1)1:59³ 1979 26 7 2 4 32,706
LB(⅝)2:02² 1978 22 1 2 3 4,311
$48,481 — 5, 2:00⁴ (⅝) Driver-CATELLO MANZI, 6-27-50 (155) WHITE-BLUE
9- 8 LB⅝ 4000 ft 17500 clm cd mi 29³1:00¹1:32²2:02 5 6 4° 3° 3²½ 6¹⁴½ 2:04⁴ 3.20 (C.Petro) BrolgaBoy,HiSykes,WinsmChf 67-0
9- 1 LB⅝ 4000 ft 17500 clm cd mi 29¹1:00²1:30²2:01² 6 7 8 8 8⁵ 4⁴ 2:02¹ 8.80 (C.Petro) Urok,J.M.Cal,NandinaWard 72-0
8-18 Fox⅝ 3500 sy 79w5000 cd mi 29¹1:02³1:33 2:05 5 4 4 5° 6⁸½ 5¹³¾ 2:07⁴ 4.20 (G.Kamal) MntKO,MrcBhn,GodOfWelth 60-0
8-11 Fox⅝ 5000sy20000 clm hcp mi 30 1:02²1:34¹2:04² 6 6 4° 3° 6³¼ 6²⁰ 2:08² 4.00 (Jo.Hogan) CindyBand,Brazil,ChrlieShar 60-0
8- 3 M¹ 9500 ft 20000 clm mi 29¹ :59¹1:30²1:59¹ 1 4 3° 2° 1¹½ 5³¼ 1:59⁴ 6.50 (C.Petro) EmpBtrc,FrmsJim,EstLAmbr 75-0
7-30 M¹ 10200 ft 17500 clm mi 29⁴ :57⁴1:28 1:58¹ 5 8 8 8°°6³½ 4⁴¼ 1:59 4.00 (C.Petro) SpdRouser,TakeLeave,Pursue 80-0
7-23 M¹ 10200 ft 17500 clm mi 30⁴ :59²1:30 1:59³ 4 6 6 4° 4¹¾ 1¹½ 1:59³ 7.20 (C.Petro) RomanovHn,BGPrde,Tognotti 77-0

6-1 **5** 17500 Black

BRET CONQUERED b g, 4, by Bret Hanover—No No Hill by Hi Hill
Mark Lancaster, N.H., Bruce & Louis Weinstein, Mass.
Trainer-M. Lancaster
M(1)1:58⁴ 1979 25 2 2 1 18,407
GrR(⅝)2:04¹ 1978 15 4 3 0 7,500
$7,572 — 3, T-1:58² (1) Driver-MARK LANCASTER, 9-23-48 (150) BLUE-GOLD
9-21 LB⅝ 3200 sy 17500 clm cd mi 29 1:02¹1:32⁴2:04³ 8 1 1 1 1½ 6⁷ 2:06 6.90 (M.Lancaster) JollyPtRvnh,RglJck,MintoDon 67-0
9-16 LB⅝ 4000 ft 21000 clm cd mi 28¹ :59³1:30¹2:01¹ 5 1 2 3 3¹¾ 7³½ 2:01⁴ 5.80 (M.Lancaster) HiSyks,NndinaWrd,MstrRcky 70-0
9- 9 LB⅝ 4000 ft 21000 clm cd mi 29³1:01 1:30⁴2:01² 5 7 7° 8° 8⁷¼ 7⁶¾ 2:02⁴ 5.60 (M.Lancaster) InHmWy,JhnQArab,SudThndr 64-0
8-19 LB⅝ 4400 ft 24000 clm cd mi 29³ :59³1:29²2:01 5 5 5 2° 2¹¼ 6⁶¼ 2:02¹ 3.00 (M.Lancaster) TontoLb,RnkyDnk,PrtOrleans 79-0
8-11 LB⅝ 4400 sy 24000 clm cd mi 30²1:03 1:33³2:04 3 2 2 2° 2nk 4⁶ 2:05¹ *1.30 (M.Lancaster) TontoLbl,Container,Trckertoo 62-1
8- 1 M¹ 9500 ft 25000 clm mi 29³ :59³1:29²1:59¹ 1 2 2 3 2¹¼ 2hd 1:59¹ 8.10 (M.Lancaster) TmlyOrbt,BrtConq.,DsrtStp 82-0
7-25 M¹ 9500 ft 25000 clm mi 29 :58²1:28⁴1:59 3 7 6°ix6°4³ 7⁵¼ 2:00 4.70 (M.Lancaster) DsrtStp,FlyDrmN,Wintrgrdn 80-0

4-1 **6** 15000 Yellow

BEV'S FLYING BOY b g, 5, by Flying Bret—Starlight Way by Star's Pride
Gloria George, Robert Dalpiaz & Lillian Bein, N.J.
Trainer-H. Williams
M(1)2:00 1979 28 2 1 4 22,000
LB(⅝)2:00² 1978 27 8 3 6 22,835
$37,826 — 3, 2:00¹(⅝) Driver-HAROLD WILLIAMS, 4-2-20 (190) BLUE-WHITE
9-21 LB⅝ 3200 sy 15000 clm cd mi 29 1:02¹1:32⁴2:04³ 2xx8 8 8 8²⁰½x8xdis 3.70 (H.Kelly) JollyPtRvnh,RglJck,MintoDon 67-0
9-14 Fhld 3600 ft 15000 clm cd mi 31¹1:03 1:34¹2:04³ 1x 4 4 4 4¹¹¼4¹⁴¾ 2:07³ *1.90 (H.Kelly) HymttN,PrnWlcm,SmartRtrn 75-0
9- 6 Fhld 3600 gd15000 clm cd mi 29³1:01¹1:33 2:04² 3 4 4° 4° 6⁶ 7³½ 2:05 *2.50 (H.Williams) Skuttlebug,JrsyPat,BrnHope 75-0
8-29 Fhld 3600 ft 15000 clm cd mi 29⁴1:00¹1:30³2:02² 5 7 7 6° 6⁵ 3¹¾ 2:02⁴ 7.50 (H.Kelly) AlfonsoN,DckChmp,BevFlBoy 85-0
8-20 Fhld 3600 ft 15000 clm cd mi 31³1:03 1:33³2:03¹ 7 8 8 8° 8⁸½ 8⁸¾ 2:05 11.20 (H.Williams) MrWnstn,FstKght,HymttusN 80-0
8-14 Fhld ft Qua mi 31³1:02²1:34¹2:05⁴ 5 6 6 3°°1½ 1¾ 2:05⁴ N.B. (H.Williams) BevFBoy,WbheLmbr,Fourflsh 70-0
8- 6 Fhld 4000 ft 15000 clm cd mi 30 1:00⁴1:31³2:01² 4 2°xx8x8 8dis 8dis 8.40 (H.Williams) RstcZphyr,AftEgr,BeausFnle 80-0

7-2 **7** 15000 Pink

VALLI A b g, 8, by Highland Laird—Miami Maid by Red Travis (F)
Middle May Farms, Inc., Cutchogue, N.Y.
Trainer-P. Ingrassia, Jr.
MR2:03¹ 1979 15 2 4 2 7,349
MR2:02 1978 20 2 0 1 4,015
$22,068 — 7, 2:02 Driver-PAUL INGRASSIA, JR., 12-24-41 (140) RED-TAN
9- 2 MR 2800 ft B3-C1 hcp mi 30²1:02⁴1:34 2:03⁴ 1 2 2 2° 3²¼ 4⁵½ 2:04⁴ 2.60 (J.RiccoJr) BonJohn,BtlrWvrly,AprilHigh 72-0
8-26 MR★ 2800 ft B3-C1 hcp mi 30³1:02³1:33²2:04¹ 1 1 1 1 1½ 2½ 2:04¹ *1.20 (J.RiccoJr) PnsvStar,ValliA,BnniesJohn 77-0
8-19 MR★ 2200 ft C1 mi 29³1:01 1:31⁴2:03¹ 5 1° 1 1 1¹ 2¹¼ 2:03² *1.50 (J.RiccoJr) Trix,Mir,ValliA,MikeSuccess 71-0
8-11 MR 3300 gd 15000 clm mi 31²1:04¹1:33 2:04³ 6 1 2 1 1¹ 1nk 2:04³ 3.90 (J.RiccoJr) ValliA,SlickBullet,SprtsSpcl 57-0
8- 4 MR 3300 ft 15000 clm mi 30¹1:00⁴1:31⁴2:03 4 1° 1 1 1¹ 2¾ 2:03¹ 3.20 (J.RiccoJr) SprtsSpcl,ValliA,DonLopez 75-0
7-29 MR★ 3300ft15000clm hcp mi 29⁴1:00³1:31¹2:01⁴ 1 2 2 2° 2nk 2nk 2:01⁴ *1.90 (J.RiccoJr) SundownHn,ValliA,SlickBullet 72-0
7-23 MR 2800 ft 12500 clm mi 28⁴ :59 1:29⁴2:00¹ 8 7° 6° 7° 7⁶¾ 3¹⁰ 2:02¹ 16.90 (J.RiccoJr) ShrmPrncss,LCourier,ValliA 73-0

10-1 **8** 17500 Black-Yellow

HOLT LOBELL b h, 4, by Adios Vic—High Rock by Tar Heel
Emanuel & Albert I. Berman & Howard Edward Davis, Smyrna, Del.
Trainer-E. Davis
LB(⅝)2:02⁴ 1979 23 1 4 5 7,314
LB(⅝)2:02² 1978 22 2 2 3 4,602
$6,963 — 3, 2:02² (⅝) Driver-EDDIE DAVIS, 11-17-43 (167) RED-WHITE
9-22 LB⅝ 3200 gd 17500 clm cd mi 29³1:00 1:31²2:01 2 3 4° 5° 5⁶¾ 7¹⁶ 2:04¹ 8.40 (E.Davis) JodyGrttnN,VllyJrry,CrtnyHn 61-0
9-14 LB⅝ 4000 gd 79nw9000 cd mi 32 1:03⁴1:32⁴2:03 4 4 4 4 4⁵¾ 6⁶½ 2:04¹ 7.80 (E.Davis) RbbBTm FthMchl,CmdnAdmrl 68-0
9- 7 LB⅝ 4000 ft 79nw9000 cd mi 30¹1:01 1:31²2:00⁴ 6 3° 4 6 6⁴¾ 7¹² 2:03¹ 10.60 (E.Davis) Gamrec,RobbBTm,CmdAdmrl 74-0
8-30 LB⅝ 3000 ft 79nw6000 cd mi 30¹1:01¹1:31⁴2:02⁴ 5 2 2 2 3¹¼ 1hd 2:02⁴ 5.30 (E.Davis) HoltLbll,GldnArwy,JoelGeor 78-0
8-18 LB⅝ 3000 sy 79nw6000 cd mi 30 1:03²1:33²2:04 7 7 7 7 7⁶ 3⁵½ 2:05 6.90 (E.Davis) VlntLeader,JoeNick,HoltLbell 64-0
8-10 LB⅝ 3000 ft 79nw6000 cd mi 29³1:01²1:31¹2:02 2 4 4 2° 2hd 2¾ 2:02¹ 8.30 (E.Davis) SpkdBoots,HoltLbl,ACsBrucie 75-0
7-26 Brd⅝ 3000 ft nw2500 L5 cd mi 29⁴1:01³1:31⁴2:02⁴ 4 1 1 1 1¹ 3³ 2:03² 3.30 (E.Davis) SwiftDick,KennySntr,HoltLb 82-0

TRACKMAN: 3—7—6

(4) **PACE—1 MILE**
Warming-Up Saddle Cloth GREEN

PURSE $5,500

EXACTA WAGERING THIS RACE

FLEMINGTON ELKS CLUB

WINNERS IN EXCESS OF $15,000 IN 1979 NOT PREFERRED.

ASK FOR HORSE BY PROGRAM NUMBER

5-1 **1** Red

JOLLY JUDGE b c, 3, by Jolly Roger—Dolly's Ace by Meadow Ace
Clinton & Connie Ruble & Joy M. Wertheim, West Chester, Pa.
Trainer-J. Wertheim
LB(⅝)2:03¹ 1979 22 2 5 5 23,328
$1,724 — 2, 2:04 (⅝) Driver-MARVIN MAKER, 1-17-47 (120) RED-WHITE-BLACK
LB(⅝)2:04 1978 5 1 1 0 1,724

9- 8 LB⅝ 5500 ft 79w12500 cd mi 30³1:01¹1:31³2:02 4 6 7° 8° 78½ 79 2:03⁴ 8.70 (M.Maker) Ralute,CmdnChrstain,KungFu 64-0
9- 1 LB⅝ 5500 ft 79w12500 cd mi 28⁴ :59 1:30¹2:01¹ 4 6° 6° 8° 83½ 57 2:02³ 4.50 (E.Davis) KeystonePnt,Ralute,Nanfort 72-0
8-25 LB⅝ 7000 ft 3yr Inv mi 29²1:01³1:30³1:59² 3 4 5° 4° 52¾ 614¼ 2:02¹ 26.90 (M.Lancaster) MdwButler,SilentOpera,Visor 77-0
8-18 Fhld 14160 ft 3yr Stk mi 29²1:01²1:31⁴2:01¹ 5 7 3° 2° 31 32½ 2:01³ 4.40 (M.Maker) DrmyIsle,KittysCicero,JllyJdg 65-0
8-11 LB⅝ 4500 sy 79nw12500 cd mi 30³1:01³1:32²2:03¹ 4 3 4° 3° 2½ 1½ 2:03¹ 5.80 (M.Maker) JllyJdge,EDBret,CmdnAntnio 62-1
8- 4 Fhld 13960 ft 3yr Stk mi 29⁴1:01¹1:31³2:01³ 1 1 1 1 1x½x2x5½ 2:02³ 5.70 (J.Scorsone) TdlwsHtTddy,JllyJdg,OnTpsB 85-0
7-29 LB⅝ 4500 gd 79nw10000 cd mi 30¹1:02 1:32¹2:01³ 1 3 4 5 51¾ 41¼ 2:01⁴ 9.50 (J.Scorsone) DrmyIsle,KanHan,FrdmBret 69-0

3-1 **2** Blue

RED FEVER ch h, 4, by High Ideal—Peggy Lee Hanover by Lehigh Hanover
Neil P. & Deborah Glickman, Cheltenham, Pa.
Trainer-D. Cote
LB(⅝)2:02¹ 1979 25 1 9 1 19,310
$38,967 — 3, 2:00¹ (⅝) Driver-DEL COTE, 12-12-36 (192) WHITE-RED
LB(⅝)2:00¹ 1978 30 3 5 9 31,343

9-23 LB⅝ 5500 ft 79w15000 cd mi 29²1:00¹1:29³1:59⁴ 8 2° 1 3 32½ 46¾ 2:01¹ 21.20 (D.Cote) DennisHn,CoverUp,CmdChrtn 58-0
9-16 LB⅝ 5500 ft 79w12500 cd mi 29⁴1:01²1:32 2:00⁴ 2 2 2 3 31¼ 21¼ 2:01 8.00 (D.Cote) YngSwartz,RedFever,VicksJ 68-0
9- 8 LB⅝ 4500 ft 79nw12500 cd mi 29¹1:01 1:31⁴2:02¹ 4 1 1 1 11 1nk 2:02¹ 6.10 (D.Cote) RedFever,BillieRn,RockyGrdn 65-0
9- 1 LB⅝ 4500 ft 79nw12500 cd mi 29¹1:01³1:31¹2:00³ 3 5 5 5 65¼ 68¾ 2:02² 3.80 (D.Cote) HppyGoBye,BayPns,AftCrprl 72-0
8-25 LB⅝ 4500 ft 79nw12500 cd mi 28⁴ :58⁴1:28⁴2:00¹ 6 7 8° 7 74½ 64¼ 2:01 7.20 (D.Cote) JstAFella,NickJoe,HppyGBye 75-0
8-17 LB⅝ 4000 ft 79nw10000 cd mi 29⁴1:00¹1:30¹2:01 3 1 1 1 11 2nk 2:01 *1.60 (D.Cote) NavyLobell,RedFever,Bolton 64-0
8-11 LB⅝ 5500 sy 79w12500 cd mi 31 1:01³1:32²2:02³ 8 3 3 3° 32¼ 65 2:03³ 6.90 (D.Cote) MrryWrry,EdMiss,MaybeHigh 62-1

8-1 **3** White

CAMDEN ANTONIO br g, 4, by Harold J.—Camden Adieu by Adios Boy
Charles S. & Forrest L. Bartlett, Camden, N.C
Trainer-H. S. Myers
RcR2:01¹ 1979 22 4 4 4 18,364
$9,373 — 3, 2:03¹ (⅝) Driver-ROBERT MYERS, 5-11-44 (185) WINE-SILVER
Lau(⅝)2:03¹ 1978 27 5 5 4 9,250

9-22 LB⅝ 5500 gd 79w15000 cd mi 29³1:01²1:31 2:01 2ix6 5 5 5dis 5dis 2:06⁴ 3.20 (R.Myers) GdbyAlmhrst,ByPnes,Tchnclr 60-0
9-16 LB⅝ 4500 ft 79nw12500 cd mi 29¹1:00 1:30 2:01² 4 6 6° 2°°2 12¾ 2:01² 3.00 (R.Myers) CmdnAntn,FrKck,MnrtMnsht 70-0
9- 9 LB⅝ 4500 ft 79nw12500 cd mi 29⁴1:01²1:31 2:01² 6 1 2° 2 21 81½ 2:01³ 4.50 (R.Myers) SpkdBoots,KeyKaola,HHFhld 67-0
9- 1 LB⅝ 4300 ft 79nw12500 cd mi 31 1:03 1:32⁴2:02¹ 7 7 7 7 75¼ 53¼ 2:02⁴ 13.60 (R.Myers) SprtyBrn,HHFrhld,SpkdBts 72-0
8-26 LB⅝ 4500 ft 79nw12500 cd mi 29²1:01¹1:30⁴2:00¹ 3 2 3 2 21¼ 22½ 2:00³ 6.30 (R.Myers) DblJudy,CmdAntn,HHFrhld 73-0
8-19 LB⅝ 4500 ft 79nw12500 cd mi 29⁴1:01 1:30³2:01¹ 8 7 7 7 63¼ 32¼ 2:01³ 10.20 (R.Myers) Ralute,AftnCrprl,CmdAntonio 77-0
8-11 LB⅝ 4500 sy 79nw12500 cd mi 30³1:01³1:32²2:03¹ 2 2 3 4 52½ 31¾ 2:03³ 3.00 (R.Myers) JllyJdge,EDBret,CmdnAntnio 62-1

8-1 **4** Green

E D BRET b h, 5, by Bret Hanover—March Mist by Dale Frost
Dennis Lane, River Edge, N.J.
Trainer-J. Smith, Jr.
M(1)1:58² 1979 23 3 2 3 17,140
$5,232 — 4, 2:02⁴ (⅝) Driver-JACK SMITH, JR., 9-28-46 (175) MAROON-GOLD
PcD(⅝)2:02⁴ 1978 11 4 1 1 5,232

9-23 LB⅝ 5500 ft 79w15000 cd mi 29²1:00¹1:29³1:59⁴ 7 8 8 7° 79 68 2:01² 19.80 (J.SmithJr) DennisHn CoverUp,CmdChrtn 58-0
9-14 LB⅝ 4500 gd 79nw12500 cd mi 31⁴1:02⁴1:32³2:02⁴ 8 1° 1 1 11 1ns 2:02⁴ 36.50 (J.SmithJr) EDBret,MrkFrrstr,SnLrdElgy 70-0
9- 7 LB⅝ 4500 ft 79nw12500 cd mi 30 1:00³1:31¹2:01² 8 8 8 8 85½ 52¼ 2:01⁴ 45.50 (J.SmithJr) SunLElegy,RegILight,NickJoe 74-0
9- 1 LB⅝ 4500 ft 79nw12500 cd mi 29¹1:01³1:31¹2:00³ 6 7 7 7 54¾ 43½ 2:01¹ 11.00 (J.SmithJr) HppyGoBye,BayPns,AftCrprl 72-0
8-25 LB⅝ 4500 ft 79nw12500 cd mi 28⁴ :58⁴1:28⁴2:00¹ 1 5 5 6° 64 53¾ 2:01 3.00 (J.SmithJr) JstAFella.NickJoe.HppyGBye 75-0
8-18 LB⅝ 5500 sy 79w12500 cd mi 30³1:02²1:32³2:03³ 5 7 7° 6° 6¾ 32¼ 2:04 3.10 (C.Fitzpatrick) RmpnDan,LwnBrmin,EDBret 64-0
8-11 LB⅝ 4500 sy 79nw12500 cd mi 30³1:01³1:32²2:03¹ 5 5 5 5° 41¾ 2½ 2:03¹ *2.70 (C.Fitzpatrick) JllyJdge,EDBret,CmdnAntnio 62-1

6-1 **5** Black

MOVE FEET MOVE b h, 4, by Bret Hanover—La Fair by Amortizor
Jerome & Judith S. Taylor & Isaac E. Shmukler, Phila., Pa.
Trainer-R. Stiles, Jr.
Brd(⅝)1:59⁴ 1979 29 3 8 3 30,633
$30,287 — 3, 1:59 (⅝) Driver-R. (Bob) STILES, JR., 6-28-33 (175) BROWN-WHITE-GOLD
Brd(⅝)1:59 1978 22 3 4 6 22,367

9-22 LB⅝ 5500 sy 79w15000 cd mi 30¹1:01 1:31⁴2:01¹ 7 7 6 7 64¼ 711¾ 2:03³ 17.50 (R.StilesJr) Skr Wltz.ThkmDrm FalsfeLbl 60-0
9-15 LB⅝ 5500 ft 79w12500 cd mi 30¹1:00²1:32¹2:02 5 7 7° 5°°75¼ 76½ 2:03¹ 3.30 (R.StilesJr) HiFiMax RobbieRD MrPcckts 61-0
9- 7 Brd⅝ 6500 ft w10000 cd mi 29 :58³1:28²1:59⁴ 1 5 6 7 64¾ 2½ 1:59⁴ *1.20 (R.StilesJr) VctrVic,MoveFMv,HppyJMiss 78-0
9- 2 Brd⅝ 6500 ft w10000 cd mi 30¹1:00²1:31³2:01¹ 3 1 1 1 11½ 34 2:02 3.30 (R.StilesJr) WinStyle,MatMadra.MvFtMv 80-0
8-26 Brd⅝ 6500 ft w10000 cd mi 30¹1:00³1:30 1:59⁴ 3 4 3 2° 31¼ 31¾ 2:00¹ 2.20 (R.StilesJr) PppyFulla.ChfLys,MvFeetMv 78-0
8-18 Brd⅝ 7000 sy w10000 cd mi 29² :59 1:30²2:02² 6 3° 2° 2 21 2hd 2:02² *.50 (D.Dancer) TopalaHn,MoveFeetMove.Sep 66-0
8-11 Brd⅝ 6500 sy w10000 cd mi 31⁴1:04 1:33³2:04 2 2° 4 5 43 21 2:04¹ 2.50 (R.StilesJr) ChiefLyss,MoveFMv,StrkKing 66-0

4-1 **6** Yellow

SHOWDOWN SUGAR b g, 7, by Sugar Tree—Jay Sister by Easy Adios
Ozark Stable, Pa. & Discovery Stable, N.Y., N.Y.
Trainer-J. Shafer
LB(⅝)1:59¹ 1979 21 3 3 4 17,491
$34,657 — 6, 2:01 (⅝) Driver-JAMES SHAFER, 4-18-21 (140) DK. BLUE-RED-WHITE
LB(⅝)2:01 1978 19 2 8 4 20,496

9-23 LB⅝ 4800 ft 25000 clm cd mi 30⁴1:01¹1:31 2:00² 1 3 3° 2° 21½ 32½ 2:00⁴ 3.50 (J.Shafer) EgmntAir Chucky,ShdwdnSgr 56-0
9- 9 LB⅝ 6000ft30000 clm hcp mi 29 1:00²1:30 2:00² 7 4° 5° 7 76½ 68¾ 2:02¹ 24.50 (J.Shafer) BusPass,CoverUp.ShutOut 63-0
9- 2 LB⅝ 6000 ft30000 clm hcp mi 28² :59¹1:29¹1:59² 1 4 6 7 73½ 74½ 2:00¹ 6.90 (J.Shafer) RmpnDan,RppOak,YngSwrtz 76-0
8-25 LB⅝ 4400 ft 20000 clm cd mi 29 :59¹1:29 1:59¹ 2 4 4 4° 32 13 1:59¹ *2.80 (J.Shafer) ShwdnSgr,BNAndy,Trickertoo 77-0
8-17 LB⅝ 4400 ft 20000 clm cd mi 28² :59⁴1:30²2:00³ 8 8 8 8 54 43 2:01¹ 23.70 (J.Shafer) HHBelle,SeafldCnt,HnstExprs 64-0
8-10 LB⅝ 4400 ft 20000 clm cd mi 29¹1:01²1:30⁴2:01¹ 1 4 5° 4° 42½ 3½ 2:01¹ 18.40 (J.Shafer) SeafldCnt.BrnsMnrn ShowSgr 75-0
7-30 LB⅝ ft T-P Qua (h-d) mi 30⁴1:03 1:35¹2:05⁴ 4 2 2 3 35½ 36½ 2:07 N.B. (R.Gandolfi) TrnqlLbll,PydyJ.,ShwdnSgr 79-0

7-2 **7** Pink

RALUTE b g, 5, by Regal Yankee—Elaine Salute by Young Salute (F)
Joseph V. & Lorraine C. Muscara, Huntingdon Valley, Pa.
Trainer-J. Muscara
LB(⅝)2:00³ 1979 32 4 5 2 17,805
$7,272 — 4, 2:02 (⅝) Driver-CATELLO MANZI, 6-27-50 (155) WHITE-BLUE
LB(⅝)2:02 1978 14 3 1 2 5,366

9-22 LB⅝ 5500 gd 79w15000 cd mi 29³1:01²1:31 2:01 3 i3 4 4° 48 49½ 2:02⁴ 3.20 (C.Manzi) GdbyAlmhrst,ByPnes,Tchnclr 60-0
9-15 LB⅝ 5500 ft 79w12500 cd mi 29 :59 1:30¹2:01⁴ 7 3° 4° 4° 42¼ 62¾ 2:02² 13.40 (C.Manzi) KeyPoint,MataMdra,ChrlKngt 63-0
9- 8 LB⅝ 5500 ft 79w12500 cd mi 30³1:01¹1:31³2:02 7 1 1 1 12¼ 12½ 2:02 9.00 (C.Manzi) Ralute,CmdnChrstain,KungFu 64-0
9- 1 LB⅝ 5500 ft 79w12500 cd mi 28⁴ :59 1:30¹2:01¹ 1 4 4 5° 52¼ 2ns 2:01¹ 8.90 (S.Belote) KeystonePnt.Ralute,Nanfort 72-0
8-25 LB⅝ 5500 ft 79w12500 cd mi 29³ :59³1:30 2:00¹ 3 5 5° 4° 64 511 2:02² 5.20 (S.Belote) Sunro,FrstNBest,HleindEdwn 77-0
8-19 LB⅝ 4500 ft 79nw12500 cd mi 29⁴1:01 1:30³2:01¹ 4 4 4 4° 42 1½ 2:01¹ 5.30 (T.Wing) Ralute AftnCrprl,CmdAntonio 77-0
8-11 LB⅝ 4500 sy 79nw12500 cd mi 30³1:01³1:32²2:03¹ 6 6 6 7° 63¼ 54½ 2:04 10.80 (S.Belote) JllyJdge,EDBret,CmdnAntnio 62-1

10-1 **8** Black-Yellow

TRAFFIC FURY b h, 4, by Race Time—Tarport Martha by O'Brien Hanover
K. Ungerman, Ont., J. & L. Costello, Pa. & L. Bantle, N.Y.
Trainer-M. Harding
PPk(⅝)1:59¹ 1979 28 4 4 2 31,725
$17,219 — 3, 1:59² Driver-MIKE HARDING, 5-20-46 (188) WHITE-GOLD-BLACK
YR1:59² 1978 24 1 3 1 13,074

9-22 LB⅝ 21499 gd Stk mi 28² :57⁴1:27¹1:56² 1 4 5 7 720¼7dis 2:03⁴ 72.30 (M.Harding) Abrcrmb,ArmSplrg.SmryJdg 61-0
9-15 LB⅝ 5500 ft 79w12500 cd mi 30¹1:00²1:32¹2:02 2 4 8 8 85¾ 810 2:04 21.70 (M.Harding) HiFiMax RobbieRD,MrPcckts 61-0
9-11 LB⅝ ft Qua mi 30²1:01³1:33¹2:04 6 3° 3 3° 31½ 54¾ 2:05 N.B. (M Harding) RsIndLrd RoddyL,YnkTransit 73-0
8-11 Mea⅝ 7500 sy Inv hcp mi 30 1:01³1:31⁴2:01¹ 5 1° 1 4ex6dis 6dis 2:10 26.90 (M.Harding) FrtzTCat,JWTssmn,ArmTpn 63-0
8- 6 Nfld 100000 ft 4yr Stk mi 28³ :59²1:29 1:58¹ 6 7 7 7 69¾ 711½ 2:00² 66.20 (D.IrvineJr) RwdyYnk.PrnRpdN.ChipFrst 72-0
7-27 Lau⅝ 20000 ft 4yr Stk mi 28 :57³1:27³1:56³ 7 7 6 6 612½617½ 2:00 54.40 (M.Harding) ChipFrst,RwdyYnk.StrpMner 80-0
7-20 Stga 20000 ft 4yr Stk mi 28³ :59³1:29⁴1:58¹ 5 4 4 4° 4° 512½ 2:00³ 12.20 (J.P.Morel) RwdyYnk,JnglJvr,StripMiner 66-0

TRACKMAN: 2—7—6

(5) PACE—1 MILE

Warming-Up Saddle Cloth
BLACK

PURSE $3,800

ASK FOR HORSE BY PROGRAM NUMBER

EXACTA WAGERING THIS RACE

FISCHER AND PORTER E.R.A.A.

NON-WINNERS OF $12,000 IN 1979. Also Eligible: Non-Winners Of $17,500 in 1979 That Are Non-Winners Of A Race In Last 5 Starts.

4-1
1 Red

CAMDEN CHRISTIAN b h, 4, by Best Of All—Camden Pauline by Santios
Elwyn P. Leary, Camden, N.C.
Trainer-H. S. Myers
Lau(⅝)1:59² 1979 25 2 3 5 16,234
$24,424 — 3, 2:00¹ (⅝) Driver-ROBERT MYERS, 5-11-44 (185) WINE-SILVER
Lau(⅝)2:00¹ 1978 24 9 5 2 22,329

9-23 LB⅝ 5500 ft 79w15000 cd mi 29²1:00¹1:29³1:59⁴ 1 4 4 4° 43 36½ 2:01 11.70 (R.Myers) DennisHn,CoverUp,CmdChrtn 58-0
9-16 LB⅝ 4500 ft 79w12500 cd mi 29² :59³1:30¹2:00⁴ 2 1° 3 3 3½ 73¾ 2:01³ 8.20 (R.Myers) HHFrhld,ThndrBrt,TmlyTitle 68-0
9- 8 LB⅝ 5500 ft 79w12500 cd mi 30³1:01¹1:31²2:02 2 4 4 4° 43½ 22½ 2:02² 3.10 (R.Myers) Ralute,CmdnChrstain,KungFu 64-0
9- 1 LB⅝ 5500 ft 79w12500 cd mi 29 :59¹1:29⁴1:59² 7 1 3 4 63¼ 77 2:00⁴ 33.20 (R.Myers) VctrVic,NickawmpsLry,Sunro 70-0
8-26 LB⅝ 5500 ft 79w12500 cd mi 29¹ :59³1:29³2:00³ 6 8 8 6° 73½ 54 2:01² 9.50 (R.Myers) AdmLbll,KeysPnt,VicQuinton 76-0
8-19 LB⅝ 5500 ft 79w12500 cd mi 28⁴ :58⁴1:29¹1:59⁴ 2 4 5 6 83¾ 56¾ 2:01¹ 3.70 (R.Myers) HIFIMax,VicQuintn,KystnPnt 77-0
8-12 LB⅝ 5500 sy 79w12500 cd mi 31¹1:01²1:32¹2:01⁴ 5 6 5° 4° 42½ 34½ 2:02³ 6.30 (R.Myers) HppyHen,HIFIMax,CmdnChris 56-1

5-1
2 Blue

VALIENT LEADER b c, 3, by Columbia George—Tampa Hanover by Gamecock
Victor T. Sobolewski, Sewell, N.J.
Trainer-N. Colanero
LB(⅝)2:00⁴ 1979 16 3 3 1 9,505
$31,719 — 2, 2:00³ (⅝) Driver-CATELLO MANZI, 6-27-50 (155) WHITE-BLUE
Brd(⅝)2:00³ 1978 14 3 2 2 31,719

9-21 LB⅝ 3100 sy 79nw9000 cd mi 29⁴1:01³1:32²2:02 2 1 1 1 1½ 1¾ 2:02 *1.00 (J.Scorsone) VlntLdr,RdySetGo,BillieRoan 65-0
9-12 LB⅝ 4000 ft 79nw9000 cd mi 28⁴1:01¹1:30⁴2:00⁴ 8 3° 4 3° 22½ 2ns 2:00⁴ 3.40 (J.Scorsone) AftCrpr,VlntLdr,TheGrtAndy 64-0
9- 7 LB⅝ 4000 ft 79nw9000 cd mi 29 1:00³1:30 2:00¹ 2 4 4° 3° 32 33¾ 2:01 3.10 (J.Scorsone) EvrgBSu,LdyPrenur,ValntLdr 74-0
9- 1 LB⅝ 4000 ft 79nw9000 cd mi 29⁴1:00³1:30⁴2:00¹ 3 4 4° 2°°2nd 23 2:00⁴ *1.20 (J.Scorsone) RegalLight,VlntLdr,PLPge 74-0
8-26 LB⅝ 3000 ft 79nw6000 cd mi 30 1:00⁴1:31²2:00⁴ 2 2 1 1 1½ 1¾ 2:00⁴ *1.00 (J.Scorsone) VlntLdr,DwyrLbll,ChrtrGPen 76-0
8-18 LB⅝ 3000 sy 79nw6000 cd mi 30 1:03²1:33²2:04 3 3 2° 2° 1½ 1¾ 2:04 *1.00 (J.Scorsone) VlntLeader,JoeNick,HoltLbell 64-0
8- 9 LB⅝ ft T-P Qua mi 29¹ :58⁴1:30²2:00¹ 5 2 1 1 1¼ 2nk 2:00¹ N.B. (J.Scorsone) SignHere,VlntLder,FirstNBst 80-0

10-1
3 White

ELSIE BUTLER br m, 6, by Beau Butler—Rita's Dream by Queen Knight
Elwood Kane, Meade, Kansas
Trainer-J. Dennis, Sr.
1979 3 0 0 0 585
$164,125 — 5, 1:57⁴ (⅝) Driver J. D. DENNIS, SR., 7-5-30 (170) RED-BLUE-WHITE
Lau(⅝)1:57¹ 1978 30 9 6 3 50,600

9-23 LB⅝ 4500 ft 79nw15000 cd mi 29 :59³1:30¹2:00³ 8 7 7 6° 56 55½ 2:01³ 21.80 (J.DennisSr) SunLElgy,RbbeRD,Persudabl 58-0
9-16 LB⅝ 4500 ft 79nw12500 cd mi 29¹1:00 1:30 2:01² 8 7° 4° 4° 44½ 44¾ 2:02² 10.70 (J.DennisSr) CmdnAntn,FrKck,MnrtMnsht 70-0
9- 8 Lau⅝ 5500 ft 79w7500 cd mi 31 1:01²1:31 2:01² 3 4 4 5 53 76½ 2:02³ 3.40 (Ra.Andersen) AftFlcn,PplrLgt,AllgashBoy 73-0
9- 1 Brd⅝ ft Official Workout mi 30⁴1:03¹1:34³2:05² 2:05² (J.DennisSr)
8- 5-78 Lau⅝ 10000 ft Inv mi 30 1:01²1:30⁴2:00³ 4 5 5 5 55 54½ 2:01² 3.60 (J.Stafford) ThrsaLbll,TnyWmpm,HntrChf
7-29-78 Lau⅝ 10000 ft Inv mi 29³1:00¹1:29²1:58³ 4 3 4 5 32½ 21½ 1:58⁴ 10.30 (J.Stafford) HntrChf,ElsieBtlr,ArmbroOzark
7-22-78 Lau⅝ 10000 ft Inv mi 29⁴1:00¹1:29¹1:58² 3 3 3 2° 63½ 64¾ 1:59² 6.90 (J.Stafford) ArmbOzark,ThrsaLbll,HntrChf

---

6-1
4 Green

ROBBIE B. TIME br g, 4, by Tar Heel—Scoot Time by Good Time
Robert T. & Susan K. Unice, Westfield, N.J.
Trainer-J. Smith, Jr.
LB(⅝)1:59³ 1979 18 3 3 3 10,229
$13,137 — 3, 2:01 (⅝) Driver-JACK SMITH, JR., 9-28-46 (175) MAROON-GOLD
Brd(⅝)2:01 1978 31 4 2 3 11,548

9-22 LB⅝ 21499 gd Stk mi 28² :57⁴1:27¹1:56² 4 7 7 6 610½618 2:00 37.50 (J.SmithJr) Abrcrmb,ArmSplrg,SmryJdg 61-0
9-14 LB⅝ 4000 gd 79nw9000 cd mi 32 1:03⁴1:32⁴2:03 2 1 1 1 1nk 1½ 2:03 *1.40 (J.SmithJr) RbbBTm,FthMchl,CmdnAdmrl 68-0
9- 7 LB⅝ 4000 ft 79nw9000 cd mi 30¹1:01 1:31¹2:00⁴ 1 2 3° 2° 2hd 22½ 2:01¹ *1.90 (J.SmithJr) Gamrec,RobbBTm,CmdAdmrl 74-0
8-30 LB⅝ 4000 ft 79nw9000 cd mi 29²1:00¹1:30³2:00¹ 6 7 7° 7° 67 36¾ 2:01³ 6.00 (J.SmithJr) ArmbRvn,MstroCln,RobBTm 78-0
8-23 LB⅝ ft Qua mi 29⁴1:01 1:31²2:02 6 1 1 1 110 111½ 2:02 N.B. (J.SmithJr) RobbBTm,SirWlmB,NtlvTmbr 75-0
8-19 LB⅝ 4000 ft 79nw9000 cd mi 29⁴ :59²1:29³2:00 7 8 8 7 7dis 8dis 5.70 (C.Fitzpatrick) Naja,SpikedBts,MaestroColln 79-0
8- 9 LB⅝ 3000 ft 79nw6000 cd mi 29⁴1:01 1:29⁴2.00² 3 5 3° 2° 2hd 2¾ 2.00³ *1.30 (C.Fitzpatrick) Pirongia,RobBTm,EvrgRobb 76-0

7-2
5 Black

MAESTRO COLIN br g, 8, by Sun Lord—Better Dream by Tilly's Boy
Sidney Goldstein & Bernard Goldstein, Wyncote, Pa.
Trainer-Ho. Kelley
Brd(⅝)2:00³ 1979 21 2 4 4 12,339
$76,642 — 6, 1:59² (⅝) Driver-DONALD DANCER, 10-1-55 (125) BLUE-GOLD
Brd(⅝)1:59³ 1978 30 6 4 4 27,458

9-23 LB⅝ 3800 ft 79nw12000 cd mi 29¹ :59³1:30¹2:01² 3 2 3 3 3¹ 42½ 2:01⁴ 5.10 (D.Dancer) FrstNBst,HelndEdwn,VcEdtn 61-0
9-14 LB⅝ 4000 sy 79nw9000 cd mi 29⁴1:00³1:31¹2:02³ 8 6 5° 3° 33½ 67¾ 2:04¹ 18.60 (R.McCarthy) DwyerLb,FullaCaptn,METime 70-0
9- 7 LB⅝ 4000 ft 79nw9000 cd mi 29 1:00³1:30 2:00¹ 7 8 8° 8 85½ 710 2:02¹ 21.00 (R.McCarthy) EvrgBSu,LdyPrenur,ValntLdr 74-0
8-30 LB⅝ 4000 ft 79nw9000 cd mi 29²1:00¹1:30³2:00¹ 3 5 5° 5° 35½ 26¾ 2:01³ *2.00 (D.Dancer) ArmbRvn,MstroCln,RobBTm 78-0
8-19 LB⅝ 4000 ft 79nw9000 cd mi 29⁴ :59²1:29³2:00 1 1 2 4 65½ 3⁷ 2:01² 2.30 (R.McCarthy) Naja,SpikedBts,MaestroColln 79-0
8-12 LB⅝ 4000 sy 79nw10000 cd mi 30³1:02¹1:33²2:03² 8 7 7 7 73½ 77¼ 2:04⁴ 6.70 (R.McCarthy) TrampsHn,DblJudy,JstAFella 56-1
8- 5 Brd⅝ 7000 ft w10000 cd mi 29³1:00¹1:29¹1:59 3 5 5 6 63¾ 65½ 2:00 23.10 (D.Dancer) SwftHopfl,LrdEddie,BstJffry 86-0

3-1
6 Yellow

TIMELY TITLE b h, 5, by Bret Hanover—Worthy Eleda by Worthy Boy
Timely Title Stable, Wilmington, Del.
Trainer-R. Anderson
Brd(⅝)1:59⁴ 1979 15 5 1 2 10,385
$42,130 — 3, 1:58² (⅝) Driver-EDDIE DAVIS, 11-17-43 (167) RED-WHITE
M(1)1:59¹ 1978 6 1 0 1 5,225

9-23 LB⅝ 3800 ft 79nw12000 cd mi 29¹ :59³1:30¹2:01² 4 6 x7 7 76½ 74½ 2:02¹ *1.10 (S.Belote) FrstNBst,HelndEdwn,VcEdtn 61-0
9-16 LB⅝ 4500 ft 79nw12500 cd mi 29² :59³1:30¹2:00⁴ 1 2 2 2hd 31½ 2:01 *1.20 (D.Dancer) HHFrhld,ThndrBrt,TmlyTitle 68-0
9- 7 Brd⅝ 5000 ft nw6001 L5 cd mi 29 :59 1:29 1:59² 7 8 6° 4° 75½ 75½ 2:00² *1.30 (J.Holloway) ByeBKtty,FftyGrd,GldcrkBob 78-0
9- 2 Brd⅝ 4500 ft nw5500 L5 cd mi 30¹1:01 1:31¹2:00⁴ 5 7° 4° 1° 2½ 12½ 2:00⁴ *1.00 (D.Dancer) TmlyTitle,GldcrkBob,Clpango 80-0
8-26 Brd⅝ 3500 ft nw3000 L5 cd mi 29³ :59²1:29²1:59⁴ 5 3 2° 1 13 1¾ 1:59⁴ *1.90 (R.Hayter) TimelyTitle,MrJM,BoldRun 78-0
8-18 Brd⅝ 5000 sy nw5000 L5 cd mi 29⁴1:01³1:32³2:02⁴ 3x 8 8 8 86¾ 811¾ 2:05¹ 2.70 (R.Hayter) RDTwo,DctrJhnG,ByByMermd 66-0
8-10 Brd⅝ 4000gdnw3000 L5 cd mi 30 1:00²1:31 2:02³ 6 7 6 6° 64 1nk 2:02³ *1.50 (R.Hayter) TmlyTitle,PplrLgt,RandyHill 78-0

8-1
7 Pink

MERCHANT BLUE CHIP br c, 3, by Most Happy Fella—Mermaid Hanover by Tar Heel
James Doherty, Burt Sivin & Steve Ronay, N.J.
Trainer-D. Queen
Fox(⅝)2:01² 1979 25 5 7 3 11,925
$636 — Driver-JAMES DOHERTY, 9-27-40 (155) RED-WHITE-GREEN
1978 5 0 0 2 636

9-23 LB⅝ 3800 ft 79nw12000 cd mi 29¹ :59³1:30¹2:01² 1 4 4 4 52¾ 64½ 2:02¹ 5.40 (D.Queen) FrstNBst,HelndEdwn,VcEdtn 61-0
9-16 LB⅝ 4500 ft 79nw12500 cd mi 29² :59³1:30¹2:00⁴ 7 5° 6 6 53 63¾ 2:01³ 25.50 (D.Queen) HHFrhld,ThndrBrt,TmlyTitle 68-0
9- 9 Fox⅝ 4000 ft 79w5000 cd mi 29³1:01⁴1:31³2:01² 2 3 2 2 31½ 12 2:01² 2.60 (Ja.Doherty) MercBChip,Savant,BrnPedro 60-0
9- 2 Fox⅝ 3500 ft 79w5000 cd mi 30¹1:00¹1:29³2:00¹ 4 3 3 2 21 31¾ 2:00³ *1.50 (Ja.Doherty) GodOfWlth,MlsEld,MerBChp 80-0
8-25 Fox⅝ 2700 ft 79w5000 cd mi 30 1:00¹1:30¹2:01 7 4° 2° 3° 31 34½ 2:01⁴ *1.30 (Ja.Doherty) MlsElda,ClmbLk,MercBChip 80-0
8-19 Fox⅝ 3600 sy22500 clm cd mi 30¹1:01¹1:32⁴2:03² 3 2° 1 1 11 11¾ 2:03² 2.60 (Ja.Doherty) MrchBChip,MtylPeg,NrdgGirl 63-0
8-12 Sycs¹ 6050 ft 3yr Ec cd mi 29¹ :58²1:28⁴1:59 7 3° 1 1 2 23 36 2:00¹ 6.10 (J.Bailey) TruGln,GlannyByrd,MerBlChip

---

8-1
8 Black-Yellow

TRAMPAS HANOVER b h, 4, by Albatross—Traffic Lady by Tar Heel
Capital Hill Farms, Inc., Englishtown, N.J.
Trainer-J. Savard
LB(⅝)1:59³ 1979 9 2 1 2 6,067
$45,077 — 2, T-1:58¹ (1) Driver-JEAN SAVARD, 12-1-44 (150) RED-BLUE-WHITE
YR2:02² 1978 12 2 1 1 12,735

9-22 Fhld 4700 gd nw600ps cd mi 29¹1:00⁴1:31²2:01³ 3 5 5 5° 43½ 3½ 2:01³ 2.00 (Her.Fillon) GymeaGld,Tinglayo,TrmpsHn 70-0
9-15 Fhld 4700 ft nw600ps cd mi 30⁴1:02¹1:32³2:02¹ 5 1 2 2 22 21¼ 2:02³ 3.90 (Her.Fillon) MissCabert,TrmpsHn,BeauT 74-0
9- 1 Fhld 4700 ft nw600ps cd mi 30 1:01 1:30⁴2:01² 6 7 7° 6° 67 34½ 2:02¹ *2.00 (Her.Fillon) AndyBBye,PtrckDrm,TrmpHn 80-0
8-26 LB⅝ 4500 ft 79nw12500 cd mi 29²1:01¹1:30⁴2:00¹ 7 7 6° 7° 74½ 66½ 2:01² 6.50 (J.Savard) DblJudy,CmdAntn,HHFrhld 73-0
8-12 LB⅝ 4000 sy 79nw10000 cd mi 30³1:02¹1:33²2:03² 1 3 2° 2° 2ns 11 2:03² 3.30 (J.Savard) TrampsHn,DblJudy,JstAFella 56-1
8- 5 LB⅝ 3000 ft 79nw6000 cd mi 29³1:00¹1:30 1:59³ 5 2° 1 1 13 17¾ 1:59³ 4.60 (J.Savard) TrmpsHn,StdyShre,PprBChp 83-0
7-28 LB⅝ 3300 ft 79nw6000 cd mi 31²1:04¹1:34¹2:03³ 5 5 5 5 52½ 43¾ 2:04² 7.00 (J.Savard) DwyerLbl,PiperBlChp,MsMlr, 78-0

TRACKMAN: 6—5—1

(6) **PACE—1 MILE**
Warming-Up Saddle Cloth
BLUE

PURSE $5,500

EXACTA WAGERING THIS RACE

B'NAI B'RITH — UPPER DUBLIN LOGE

WINNERS IN EXCESS OF $15,000 IN 1979 NOT PREFERRED.

ASK FOR HORSE BY PROGRAM NUMBER

8-1 **1** Red
MEADOW BUTLER b c, 3, by Adios Butler—Meadow Kack by Sampson Hanover
C. C. Amento & Robert M. D'Intino, Philadelphia, Pa.
$2,600 — 2, 2:014 (⅝) Driver-JOE GREENE, 7-3-36 (169) WHITE-GREEN-BLACK
Trainer-Ho. Kelley
Brd(⅝)1:584 1979 13 5 2 1 24,249
LB(⅝)2:014 1978 8 3 0 0 2,600
9-23 LB⅝ 5500 ft 79w15000 cd mi 292 :5941:2911:584 5 5 5° 6° 58½ 511¾ 2:011 3.10 (J.Greene) YnkBmbr.SothNrwlk.VicQntn 56-0
9-16 LB⅝ 7000 ft 3yr Inv mi 30 1:0121:3042:00 4 1 1 1 1nd 22½ 2:002 2.20 (J.Greene) WnngStyl,MdwBltr,BrkngPnt 680-
9- 3 Fhld 70000 ft 3yr C Stk mi 29 :5731:27 1:554 1 6 x8 8 8dis 8dis 17.80 (J.Greene) HotHttr,TjnaTaxi,MplLStrk 80-0
8-25 LB⅝ 7000 ft 3yr Inv mi 2921:0131:3031:592 4 1° 1 1 11 12 1:592 *2.00 (J.Greene) MdwButler,SilentOpera,Visor 77-0
8-18 RR 15000 sy Inv mi 292 :5941:30 2:013 5 6 6° 8x 817 824 2:062 7.00 (J.Larente) OilStrike,FuryAlma,RebelBret 60-0
8- 5 Brd⅝ 6500 ft w10000 cl mi 283 :5941:30 1:584 4 1 1 1 12 12 1:584 *.80 (R.Hayter) MdwBtlr.StrkKng.ComPrfrmr 86-0
7-28 Nfld 14300 ft 3yr C Stk mi 274 :5821:2821:592 3 3 3 2° 2½ 41½ 1:593 2.60 (R.Hayter) BrnyBBtlr,AndyHdw,ElcMax 73-0

3-1 **2** Blue
GOODBYE ALMAHURST b h, 6, by Shadow Wave—Vitamin Hanover by Tar Heel
B. Yellin, R. Yorio, M. McCaffery, W. Dempsey, N.Y. & Pa
$44,888 — 4, 2:02 (⅝) Driver-MARK LANCASTER, 9-23-48 (166) BLUE-GOLD
Trainer-B. Yellin
M(1)1:574 1979 18 5 4 3 52,150
RR2:031 1978 26 3 3 2 18,041
9-22 LB⅝ 5500 gd 79w15000 cd mi 2931:0121:31 2:01 6 i4 2° 1 16 18 2:01 *1.80 (M.Lancaster) GdbyAlmhrst,ByPnes,Tchnclr 60-0
9-15 LB⅝ 5500 ft 79w12500 cd mi 29 :59 1:3012:014 1 4 3 3 31½ 42½ 2:021 3.30 (J.Scorsone) KeyPoint,MataMdra,ChrlKngt 63-0
9-11 LB⅝ ft Qua mi 3021:0131:3312:04 5 6 6 6° 65 43½ 2:043 N.B. (J.Scorsone) RslndLrd RoddyL,YnkTransit 73-0
6-23 M1 16000 ft 40000 clm mi 284 :59 1:2841:574 1 3 3 4° 33 1¾ 1:574 *2.20 (R.Samson) GdbyeAlm,BenChancey,Boone 78-0
6-16 M1 16000 ft 40000 clm mi 293 :5921:2841:574 1 4 4 4° 32½ 34 1:583 *1.40 (S.Goudreau) KrstlsBllt,KeyMars,GdbyAlm 82-0
6- 9 M1 16000 ft 40000 clm mi 29 :57 1:2641:562 7 8 8 8 57 24 1:571 19.70 (R.Samson) FghtTheFoe,GdbyeAlm.Boone 71-0
6- 1 M1 16000 ft 40000 clm mi 291 :5811:2731:573 2 6 6 7° 57 53½ 1:581 3.60 (T.Wing) NvleLdr,StndRmOnly,StgaStn 71-0

6-1 **3** White
KANSAS HANOVER br c, 3, by Albatross—Kaycee Hanover by Tar Heel
Emanuel Berman & Albert I. Berman, Pottstown, Pa.
$3,016 — 2, 2:02 (⅝) Driver-EDDIE DAVIS, 11-17-43 (167) RED-WHITE
Trainer-E. Davis
LB(⅝)1:594 1979 17 7 2 1 16,210
LB(⅝)2:02 1978 8 2 3 2 3,016
9-22 LB⅝ 4500gd 79nw15000 cd mi 29 :5941:31 1:594 2 4 4 1° 15 110½ 1:594 *2.20 (E.Davis) KnsHn,CmndPrfrmr.HighDnA 60-0
9-15 LB⅝ 5500ft3yr79 w12500cd mi 3011:0011:2922:00 3 2° 1 2 4x1¾6101¾ 2:021 4.30 (E.Davis) EvrgBkySu.Gamrec,Drmy Isle 65-0
9- 8 Fhld 6000 ft 79w12000 cd mi 3011:0011:31 2:011 3 1°ix7 be pulled up dnf 3.50 (E.Davis) OverStrng,StrnFcs.EmbChck 70-0
9- 2 LB⅝ 7000 ft 3yr Inv mi 28 :5911:2811:59 3 3° 3 2° 21½ 44½ 1:594 4.90 (E.Davis) SlntOpra,BbyDmpl.RcyPrdgy 76-0
8-25 Fhld 4700 ft nw600ps cd mi 2941:0011:31 2:01 7 1 1 1 13 11½ 2:01 1.90 (E.Davis) KnssHn,GymeaGld.PtrckDrm 80-0
8-16 LB⅝ 4500 sy 79nw12500 cd mi 3121:0241:3222:03 2 2 1 1 11½ 21½P5 2:031 *1.80 (E.Davis) DblJdy+FrstNBest+JstAFella 64-0
8-12 LB⅝ 4500 sy 79nw12500 cd mi 2941:0041:3222:031 7 1° 2 3 41½ 3½ 2:031 7.60 (E.Davis) Nanfort,HHFreehld.KansasHn 56-1

7-2 **4** Green
DENNIS HANOVER b g, 3, by Steady Star—Darling Almahurst by Bret Hanover
Barr M. Stable, Ottawa, Ont., Canada
$9,985 — 2, 2:023 Driver-JAMES MILLER, 9-13-45 (155) BLUE-GOLD
Trainer-S. Forbes
LB(⅝)1:594 1979 19 5 4 3 26,769
Stga2:023 1978 15 2 0 0 9,985
9-23 LB⅝ 5500 ft 79w15000 cd mi 2921:0011:2931:594 5 1 2 1 1nd 13¾ 1:594 *1.30 (J.Miller) DennisHn CoverUp,CmdChrtn 58-0
9-16 LB⅝ 7000 ft 3yr Inv mi 30 1:0121:3042:00 3 6 6 6° 63½ 53½ 2:003 19.80 (J.Miller) WnngStyl,MdwBltr,BrkngPnt 680-
9- 9 LB⅝ 7000 ft 3yr Inv mi 2911:0031:2921:591 5 6 6° 5° 43 42½ 1:593 14.70 (J.Miller) WinnStyle,YnkBmb,SkrtWltz 68-0
9- 2 Brd⅝ 6500 ft w10000 cd mi 2841:0021:3042:004 6 6 6 5° 52¾ 1ns 2:004 3.80 (J.Miller) DennisHn,+MrLonly,+JessSam 80-0
8-26 Brd⅝ 6500 ft w10000 cd mi 3011:01 1:3021:591 5 6 6 5° 65 68 2:004 10.80 (J.Miller) DchStrttn RacTWin MatMadr 78-0
8-14 RR 11000 ft C1 cd mi 2931:0041:3122:011 1 2 3 4° 22½ 3¾ 2:012 6.90 (F.Popfinger) SultanHn,RuddHall.DnnsHan 72-0
8- 7 RR 11000 ft C1 cd mi 2941:01 1:3042:002 4 7 7° 6° 65½ 65½ 2:012 *2.70 (Her.Fillon) JJsDmno,RudHall,Mch!sCndy 72-0

6-1 **5** Black
DREAMY ISLE b g, 3, by Isle Of Wight—Dreamy Hobby Horse by Race Time
Frank A. Perry, William M. Camp, Jr. & Daniel J. Smith, N.J.
$2,673 — 2, 2:063 (⅝) Qua Driver-DAN SMITH, 12-28-48 (170) MAROON-GOLD
Trainer-D. Smith
Fhld2:011 1979 15 4 8 1 28,580
Q-LB(⅝)2:063 1978 4 0 1 2 2,673
9-15 LB⅝ 5500ft3yr79 w12500cd mi 3011:0011:2922:00 1 1 3 4 53 35¾ 2:011 2.50 (D.Smith) EvrgBkySu.Gamrec,Drmy Isle 65-0
9- 9 LB⅝ 7000 ft 3yr Inv mi 2911:0031:2921:591 4 2 5 6 65½ 58 2:004 4.20 (D.Smith) WinnStyle,YnkBmb,SkrtWltz 63-0
8-25 LB⅝ 7000 ft 3yr Inv mi 2921:0131:3031:592 2 i3 3° 2° 21 46 2:003 2.10 (D.Smith) MdwButler SilentOpera,Visor 77-0
8-18 Fhld 14160 ft 3yr Stk mi 2921:0121:3142:011 1 2 1 1 11 12½ 2:011 *.40 (D.Smith) DrmyIsle,KittysCicero,JllyJdg 65-0
8- 4 Fhld 14160 ft 3yr Stk mi 293 :5911:2932:001 7 7° 5° 4° 2hd 2¾ 2:002 N.B. (D.Smith) JMNibble DrmyIsle Gortdarrg 85-0
7-29 LB⅝ 4500 gd 79nw10000 cd mi 3011:02 1:3212:013 7 6 5° 4° 41¾ 11½ 2:013 *1.30 (D.Smith) DrmyIsle.KanHan FrdmBret 63-0
7-22 LB⅝ 7500 ft 3yr Inv mi 2941:0021:2931:59 5 5 5° 2° 2½ 2¾ 1:591 3.60 (D.Smith) EvrgrBck,DrmyIsle,HppyAbb 77-0

5-1 **6** Yellow
‡SOUTH NORWALK b h, 4, by Laverne Hanover—Supple Yankee by Adios Don
James A. Marshall, Washington, D.C.
$45,416 — 3, 1:58 (⅝) Driver-W. (Windy) DONAWAY, 12-20-46 (155) PURPLE-GOLD
Trainer-W. Donaway
M(1)1:583 1979 21 3 3 5 27,838
Lau(⅝)1:583 1978 33 6 4 7 44,285
9-23 LB⅝‡ 5500 ft 79w15000 cd mi 292 :5941:2911:584 4 4 4 3 34 25¾ 2:00 10.60 (W.Donaway) YnkBmbr.SothNrwlk VicQntn 56-0
9-15 LB⅝‡ 5500 ft 79w12500 cd mi 3011:0021:3212:02 7 8 8 7° 65 4nk 2:02 14.30 (W.Donaway) HiFiMax.RobbieRD.MrPockts 61-0
9- 8 Brd⅝‡ 7000 ft w10000 cd mi 284 :5941:2841:59 7 7 7 7 76¾ 68¾ 2:004 12.20 (W.Donaway) LordEddie.PppyFulla ChfLyss 70-0
9- 2 Brd⅝‡ 7000 ft w10000 cd mi 3011:0111:31 2:003 3 4 5 6 52¾ 51¼ 2:004 6.30 (W.Donaway) TarKeel,BestJeffrey,Lismore 80-0
8-26 Brd⅝‡ 6500 ft w10000 cd mi 3011:01 1:3021:591 4 5 5 6 54½ 53½ 1:594 1.50 (W.Donaway) DchStrttn RacTWin MatMadr 78-0
8-18 OD‡ 3450 ft 4-5yr Stk mi 2941:0221:3332:022 1 1 1 1 1ns 1hd 2:022 *.70 (W.Donaway) SoNorlk MndvGdFri,HrvaRnb 70-0
8-11 Lau⅝‡ 9000 sy 4-5yr Stk mi 2921:0021:3022:00 4 1 2 3 32 31 2:001 3.70 (W.Donaway) THFred,ManGFri,SouthNrwlk 70-0

4-1 **7** Pink
SKIRT WALTZ b f, 3, by Adios Vic—Queenly Blue Chip by Bye Bye Byrd
U. C. Steele, Bloomsburg, Pa.
$00 — Driver-MARVIN MAKER, 1-17-47 (120) RED-WHITE-BLACK
Trainer-R. Roadarmel
M(1)1:594 1979 19 5 3 1 30,997
1978 0 0 0 0
9-22 LB⅝ 5500 sy 79w15000 cd mi 3011:01 1:3142:011 5 4° 4 2° 11½ 13½ 2:011 *1.70 (M.Maker) SkrtWltz,ThlmDrm,FalsfeLbl 60-0
9-16 LB⅝ 7000 ft 3yr Inv mi 30 1:0121:3042:00 2 5 3° 2° 2hd 63¾ 2:004 9.30 (M.Maker) WnngStyl,MdwBltr,BrkngPnt 680-
9- 9 LB⅝ 7000 ft 3yr Inv mi 2911:0031:2921:591 3 5 2° 1° 2ns 32¼ 1:593 11.40 (M.Maker) WinnStyle,YnkBmb.SkrtWltz 68-0
9- 2 LB⅝ 7000 ft 3yr Inv mi 28 :5911:2811:59 7 7 7 6° 55 56 2:001 9.10 (M.Maker) SlntOpra,BbyDmpl.RcyPrdgy 76-0
8-25 LB⅝ 7000 ft 3yr Inv mi 2921:0131:3031:592 1 x6 6 6 64½ 511 2:013 3.00 (M.Maker) MdwButler,SilentOpera Visor 77-0
8-18 LB⅝ 7000 sy 3yr Inv mi 31 1:0241:3132:011 5 2°°1 1 11½ 11½ 2:011 5.10 (M.Maker) SkrtWltz,HappyAbbe,SlntOpr 64-0
8-10 LB⅝ 2200 ft 79nw4000 cd mi 3011:0021:31 2:00 4 1° 1 1 11½ 13 2:00 *.90 (M.Maker) SkrtWltz.OptclIllusn PaydayJ 75-0

8-1 **8** Black-Yellow
MR POCKETS b g, 6, by Lehigh Hanover—Miss Barbie by Tar Boy
Ronald L. Ruggles, Fort Lee, N.J.
$72,242 — 4, 1:58 (1) Driver-STEVE CASANOVA, 10-9-46 (135) BLACK-YELLOW-GREEN
Trainer-S. Casanova
M(1)1:583 1979 24 6 3 8 35,164
M(1)1:584 1978 25 5 3 1 23,973
9-22 LB⅝ 5500 gd 79w15000 cd mi 2941:0111:3142:013 1 6 7° 6° 74 85¾ 2:024 *3.10 (S.Casanova) HpGoBye,CylnPrnc,YngSwrtz 60-0
9-15 LB⅝ 5500 ft 79w12500 cd mi 3011:0021:3212:02 1 6 5° 4° 42½ 3nd 2:02 5.20 (S.Casanova) HiFiMax,RobbieRD,MrPockts 61-0
9- 8 Brd⅝ 4500 ft nw4001 L5 cd mi 2841:0031:2932:002 3 5 3 1 13 33 2:01 3.70 (S.Casanova) AbbesFancy,AdHoc MrPockts 70-0
8-25 Brd⅝ 5000sy nw6000 L5 cd mi 2921:0021:3042:003 6 8 8° 8° 87¼ 76½ 2:014 4.30 (S.Casanova) AdHoc.Cipango,Staveley 76-0
8-19 Brd⅝ 7000 ft w10000 cd mi 292 :5911:2921:59 7 8 8 8 77 69 2:004 17.20 (S.Casanova) LrdEddie DchssStrttn,TrKeel 78-0
8-12 Brd⅝ 4000 sy nw4000 L5 cd mi 3011:0131:3212:032 3 6 7 6° 63 1½ 2:032 *.70 (S.Casanova) MrPckts,ByeByeKtty HerbieC 58-0
8- 4 Brd⅝ 4000 ftnw4000 L5 cd mi 2921:0021:2942:001 6 6° 6° 5° 52½ 1¾ 2:001 3.10 (S.Casanova) MrPckts,MataMdra,TarKeel 84-0

TRACKMAN: 2—4—7

(7)

PACE—1 MILE

Warming-Up Saddle Cloth
RED

PURSE $4,500

ASK FOR HORSE BY PROGRAM NUMBER

TRIFECTA WAGERING THIS RACE

TASTY BAKING COMPANY — M.B.A.

NON-WINNERS OF $15,000 IN 1979. Also Eligible: Non-Winners Of $30,000 In 1979 That Are Non-Winners Of A Race In Last 5 Starts.

3-1 **1** Red

SUNDERCHIEF
br g, 6, by Georgacks Victor—Stereo Hanover by Dancer Hanover
Otto J. Sunder, Philadelphia, Pa.
Trainer-M. Sunder
LB(⅝)1:58² 1979 28 4 2 6 24,430
$69,786 — 5, 1:58⁴ (⅝) Driver-MARK LANCASTER, 9-23-48 (150) BLUE-GOLD LB(⅝)1:58⁴ 1978 33 10 3 4 52,825

9-23 LB⅝ 4500 ft 79nw15000 cd mi 29 :59³1:30¹2:00³ 1x 8 8 8 8⁹¼ 6¹¹¼ 2:02⁴ *1.10 (J.Scorsone) SunLElgy,RbbeRD,Persudabl 58-0
9- 9 LB⅝ 5500 ft 79w12500 cd mi 29³1:00 1:29⁴1:59³ 3 2° 1 1 1ns 3²½ 2:00 *2.00 (J.Scorsone) NickaLry,DelroyN,Sunderchf 67-0
9- 2 LB⅝ 6000 ft40000 clm hcp mi 28² :59¹1:29¹1:59² 7 5° 3° 2° 3¹½ 4²½ 1:59⁴ *2.20 (J.Scorsone) RmpnDan,RppOak,YngSwrtz 76-0
8-25 VD¾ 6000 ft Inv hcp mi 29¹1:00³1:29 1:58² 3 4 5 5 5⁷½ 5⁹½ 2:00¹ 10.30 (J.Scorsone) BonCFrnt,MtrxHn,MlsNBrnd 68-0
8-19 LB⅝ 6000 ft 40000 clm hcp mi 29⁴1:00²1:30 2:00¹ 8 3° 2 2° 2hd 3nk 2:00¹ 5.40 (J.Scorsone) HghOnHy,HppyHenry,Sndrchf 77-0
8-11 LB⅝ 8000 sy Pref mi 29⁴1:00¹1:30²2:00 7 3°°xx8 8 8¹⁷ 8dis 2:05³ 15.70 (J.Scorsone) BrtRchrd,KlipMnbr,MrOvrnte 62-1
8- 5 LB⅝ 5500 ft 79w10000 cd mi 30¹1:00³1:30²1:59³ 3 2° 1 1 1¹½ 1¹½ 1:59³ 2.60 (J.Scorsone) Sunderchf,DelroyN,StwStar 83-0

7-2 **2** Blue

MARK FORRESTER
b h, 6, by Super Wave—Lyn Forrester by Gamecock
Forrester Farms & S. Warrington, Clayton & Townsend, Del.
Trainer-S. Warrington
LB(⅝)2:01⁴ 1979 6 4 1 0 8,895
$132,196 — 5, 1:58³ (⅝) Driver-STEVE WARRINGTON, 12-25-51 (160) GREY-RED-WHITE LB(⅝)1:58³ 1978 31 7 6 5 51,690

9-21 LB⅝ 3800 sy 79nw12000 cd mi 29³1:03 1:33 2:03² 5 1 1 1 1½ 1¹ 2:03² 2.80 (S.Warrington) MrkFrrstr,DwyrLb,FtthMchl 67-0
9-14 LB⅝ 4500 gd 79nw12500 cd mi 31⁴1:02⁴1:32³2:02⁴ 4 6 6° 4° 2¹ 2ns 2:02⁴ 4.00 (S.Warrington) EDBret,MrkFrrstr,SnLrdElgy 70-0
9- 5 LB⅝ 4000 sy 79nw9000 cd mi 30⁴1:04²1:35¹2:04³ 3 1 1 1 1¹½ 1½ 2:04³ *2.50 (S.Warrington) MrkFrrstr,DwyrLbll,CkieClovr 75-0
8-12 LB⅝ 4000 sy 79nw10000 cd mi 30³1:02¹1:33²2:03² 3 2 1 1 1ns 4²½ 2:04 2.10 (S.Warrington) TrampsHn,DblJudy,JstAFella 56-1
7-27 LB⅝ 3800 ft 79nw8000 cd mi 30¹1:02²1:33¹2:03 5 1 1 1 1¹½ 1¹½ 2:03 *.90 (S.Warrington) MarkForst,PrunoHn,MerickLb 76-0
7-20 LB⅝ 3300 ft 79nw6000 cd mi 30⁴1:03¹1:32⁴2:01⁴ 8 1 1 1 1hd 1½ 2:01⁴ *2.40 (S.Warrington) MarkFrrstr,Illusion,PrnoHan 76-0
7-12 LB⅝ ft T-P Qua mi 30⁴1:02²1:32²2:02² 3 2 2 3 3¹½ 2²½ 2:02⁴ N.B. (S.Warrington) PetFxndr,MrkFrrstr,NndnWrd 80-0

10-1 **3** White

HIGH DON A.
b g, 7, by Caroldon Lehigh—Mon Patri by Chamfer (F)
Earl Reisenweaver & Ronald DiLeo, Telford, Pa.
Trainer-R. Reisenweaver
LB(⅝)2:01² 1979 20 6 2 3 14,057
$0,500 — None In USA Driver-ROY REISENWEAVER, 10-27-37 (175) GREEN-WHITE None In USA 1978 25 6 8 3 5,724

9-22 LB⅝ 4500gd 79nw15000 cd mi 29 :59⁴1:31 1:59⁴ 1 2 3 3° 4⁶½ 3¹²½ 2:02¹ 7.30(R.Reisenweaver) KnsHn,CmndPrfrmr,HighDnA 60-0
9-15 LB⅝ 3600 ft 15000 clm cd mi 30²1:01²1:30⁴2:01² 5 2° 1 2 2¹½ 1nk 2:01² 11.00(R.Reisenweaver) HghDonA,MgtySmth,JdyGrtN 65-0
9- 9 LB⅝ 3600 ft 15000 clm cd mi 29⁴1:01³1:32 2:03¹ 4 2 2° 2° 2hd 1² 2:03¹ 10.50(R.Reisenweaver) HgDonA,SlnBBye,FrkyRoma 68-0
9- 1 Brd⅝ 5000 ft 15000 clm hcp mi 30 :59³1:29⁴2:01 4 3° 3° 6° 7⁴½ 6⁵½ 2:02 21.20(R.Reisenweaver) ViknqAlm,VllyJrry,EdQForwd 80-0
8-26 Brd⅝ 5500 ft 17500 clm hcp mi 29³1:00²1:31³2:01³ 5 4 4 6 8 7⁴½ 6³ 2:02¹ 14.80(R.Reisenweaver) LitAlbie,JessSam,VikingAlmh 78-0
8-19 Brd⅝ 5000 ft 17500 clm hcp mi 28 :59²1:29¹2:00³ 5 4 4 4° 4²½ 6⁶ 2:01⁴ 14.70(R.Reisenweaver) LttlAlbie,VkngAlma,Epitome 78-0
8-11 Brd⅝ 4000sy17500clm hcp mi 29 1:01¹1:32 2:03 8 4° 3° 3° 3³½ 4⁵½ 2:04 18.50(R.Reisenweaver) EdQFrwd,Epitome,LittleAlbie 66-0

8-1 **4** Green

SPIKED BOOTS
b h, 6, by Overtrick—Spiked Heels by Tar Heel
Charles R. McCormick, Dayton, Ohio
Trainer-S. King, Jr.
LB(⅝)2:01² 1979 12 4 4 1 12,182
$2,518 — 3, 2:01⁴ (1) Driver-SAM BELOTE, 6-13-52 (170) GREEN-GRAY-RED Q-Mea(⅝)2:05⁴ 1978 0 0 0 0

9-16 LB⅝ 4500 ft 79nw12500 cd mi 29² :59³1:30¹2:00⁴ 3 4 4 4° 4¹½ 4²½ 2:01¹ 5.00 (S.Belote) HHFrhld,ThndrBrt,TrnlyTtle 66-0
9- 9 LB⅝ 4500 ft 79nw12500 cd mi 29⁴1:01²1:31 2:01² 7 7 7° 7° 7⁶ 1nk 2:01² 12.80 (S.KingJr) SpkdBoots,KeyKaola,HHFhld 67-0
9- 1 LB⅝ 4500 ft 79nw12500 cd mi 31 1:03 1:32⁴2:02¹ 5 5 4° 4° 3²½ 3²½ 2:02³ 2.60 (S.Belote) SprtyBrn,HHFrhld,SpkdBts 72-0
8-25 LB⅝ 4000 ft 79nw9000 cd mi 30¹1:02¹1:32 2:02 3 3 3 2° 2nk 1³½ 2:02 4.00 (S.Belote) SpkdBts,RglLght,HnstExprss 77-0
8-19 LB⅝ 4000 ft 79nw9000 cd mi 29⁴ :59²1:29³2:00 6 7 6 6 5⁴½ 2⁴½ 2:00⁴ 8.30 (S.Belote) Naja,SpikedBts,MaestroColln 79-0
8-10 LB⅝ 3000 ft 79nw6000 cd mi 29³1:01²1:31²2:02 3 6 6° 3°°4¹½ 1² 2:02 3.70 (S.Belote) SpkdBoots,HoltLbl,ACsBrucie 75-0
8- 2 LB⅝ 3300 sy 79nw6000 cd mi 29 1:00³1:30¹2:01⁴ 3 5 6° 6° 7⁷½ 6²½ 2:02² 8.30 (C.EndicottJr) RossiCollins,BigReturn,Avrum 75-0

8-1 **5** Black

WIDOW'S SUPER
b h, 4, by Super Wave—Keystone Widow by Good Time
Fermer & Frank Perry & Lorimer Midgett, N.C.
Trainer-J. Manning
LB(⅝)2:00 1979 19 7 1 0 21,000
$30,095 — 2, 2:00³ (⅝) Driver-ROBERT MYERS, 5-11-44 (185) WINE-SILVER Q-LB(⅝)2:03³ 1978 10 0 3 0 10,380

9-22 LB⅝ 5500 sy 79w15000 cd mi 30¹1:01 1:31⁴2:01¹ 2 5 5° 5° 8⁶½ 8¹⁶½ 2:04² 5.60 (R.Myers) SkrtWltz,ThlmDrm,FalsfeLbl 60-0
9-15 LB⅝ 5500 ft 79w12500 cd mi 30¹1:00²1:32¹2:02 6 3 4 6 5³½ 6¹½ 2:02¹ 3.80 (E.Davis) HiFiMax,RobbieRD,MrPockts 61-0
9- 1 LB⅝ 5500 ft 79w12500 cd mi 29 :59¹1:29⁴1:59² 8 2° 2 2 3¹½ 8⁹½ 2:01¹ 6.30 (E.Davis) VctrVic,NickawmpsLry,Sunro 70-0
8-24 YR 12000 ft B2 cd mi 29²1:00³1:31³2:01¹ 4 8 8 8° 8⁹½ 8⁷½ 2:02⁴ 12.20 (T.Wing) TrckLease,NvrWrng,OBSmykn 72-0
8-18 Fhld 7500 ft Pref mi 30³1:01¹1:31¹2:01¹ 2xx7 7 7 7⁶½ 6⁵½ 2:02² 9.60 (E.Davis) PACarlos,JaneDnne,PnnState 65-0
8-11 Fhld 6500 ft 79w10000 cd mi 30¹1:01¹1:32³2:02 6 1 1 1 1¹ 1¹ 2:02 5.80 (E.Davis) WdwSpr,Tngalayo,ChndBoots 70-0
8- 5 LB⅝ 5500 ft 79w10000 cd mi 30¹1:00³1:30²1:59³ 7 8 7 7 6⁴½ 6⁵ 2:00³ 24.10 (C.Fitzpatrick) Sunderchf,DelroyN,StwStar 83-0

4-1 **6** Yellow

SUN LORD'S ELEGY
b h, 4, by Sun Lord—Dottie Wave by Shadow Wave
George E. & Irene Doane, Goshen, N.Y.
Trainer-Ho. Kelley
LB(⅝)2:00³ 1979 13 4 2 3 14,950
$82,530 — 3, 1:57⁴ (⅝) Driver-DONALD DANCER, 10-1-55 (125) BLUE-GOLD Brd(⅝)1:57⁴ 1978 28 4 5 2 55,126

9-23 LB⅝ 4500 ft 79nw15000 cd mi 29 :59³1:30¹2:00³ 6 5 5° 3° 3²½ 1²½ 2:00³ 2.70 (D.Dancer) SunLElgy,RbbeRD,Persudabl 58-0
9-14 LB⅝ 4500 gd 79nw12500 cd mi 31⁴1:02⁴1:32³2:02⁴ 1 3 3 5 5²½ 3¹ 2:03 *1.10 (R.McCarthy) EDBret,MrkFrrstr,SnLrdElgy 70-0
9- 7 LB⅝ 4500 ft 79nw12500 cd mi 30 1:00³1:31¹2:01² 2 3 5 5 5²½ 1nk 2:01² 2.00 (R.McCarthy) SunLElegy,ReglLight,NickJoe 74-0
8-30 Stga 26386 ft 4yr Stk mi 29⁴1:00¹1:30 1:58³ 4 6 5° 6° 6 6⁵½ 1:59³ 8.70 (R.McCarthy) Nickylou,JSSkip,MlsEBrnda 71-0
8-24 LB⅝ 4000 ft 79nw9000 cd mi 30⁴1:02 1:31⁴2:01¹ 1 3 1 1 1¹½ 1³½ 2:01¹ *1.10 (R.McCarthy) SnLrdElgy,Gamrec,TGrtAndy 73-0
8-16 LD⅝ 3000 ft 79nw6000 cd mi 30 1:01¹1:30⁴2:01 2 5 3° 1 1¹½ 1²½ 2:01 2.00 (R.McCarthy) SnLrdElgy,Crmnl,BrnsMnslon 65-0
8- 4 Brd⅝ 5000 ftnw6000 L5 cd mi 29 1:01³1:32⁴2:02 2 4 4 5 5³½ 2¹½ 2:02¹ 3.50 (D.Richards) ByeBMrmd,SunLElgy,Sep 84-0

5-1 **7** Pink

STOWE STAR
b h, 7, by Dancer Hanover—Puddles by Tar Heel
Emanuel & Albert Berman, Pottstown, Pa.
Trainer-E. Davis
LB(⅝)1:59 1979 21 6 2 3 28,875
$63,382 — 6, 1:59 (⅝) Driver-EDDIE DAVIS, 11-17-43 (167) RED-WHITE Brd(⅝)1:59 1978 33 5 3 8 31,800

9-22 LB⅝ 5500 sy 79w15000 cd mi 30¹1:01 1:31⁴2:01¹ 3 3 3 4 3²½ 4⁷ 2:02³ 9.20 (E.Davis) SkrtWltz,ThlmDrm,FalsfeLbl 60-0
9-18 LB⅝ ft Qua mi 28⁴1:00³1:30²2:01⁴ 5 2 2 2 3⁴½ 3³½ 2:02² N.B. (J.Wyatt) RumGold,CycPrnc,StoweStar 73-0
8-19 LB⅝ 5500 ft 79w12500 cd mi 28⁴ :58⁴1:29¹1:59⁴ 8 1 1 1 2¹½ 8⁹½ 2:01³ 12.30 (E.Davis) HiFiMax,VicQuintn,KystnPnt 77-0
8-12 LB⅝ 5500 sy 79w12500 cd mi 31 1:01²1:33 2:03¹ 8 1 2 2 2¹½ 4³½ 2:03⁴ 5.80 (E.Davis) MariaJ,CyclonePrnc,DelroyN 56-1
8- 5 LB⅝ 5500 ft 79w10000 cd mi 30¹1:00³1:30²1:59³ 8 1 2 2 2¹½ 3¹½ 1:59⁴ 28.20 (E.Davis) Sunderchf,DelroyN,StwStar 83-0
7-28 LB⅝ 6000 ft 79w10000 cd mi 29⁴ :59¹1:28²1:57⁴ 1 2 1 1 1¹½ 4⁶½ 1:59 *.70 (E.Davis) FalsfeLb,ThelmDr,ShdyAlrRd 77-0
7-22 LB⅝ 6000 ft 79w10000 cd mi 30²1:01 1:30 1:59⁴ 3 1 1 1 1 1½ 1¹½ 1:59⁴ 2.60 (E.Davis) StoweStr,ManMnsht,FlsfLbll 78-0

6-1 **8** Black-Yellow

PERSUADABLE
b h, 7, by Tarport Count—Persuasion by Knight Dream
Stephanie Coney, Tom Perkins & Murray Kenney, Maine
Trainer-D. Queen
M(1)1:57¹ 1979 14 2 2 4 19,960
$176,811 — 6, 1:57² (⅝) Driver-JAMES DOHERTY, 9-27-40 (161) RED-WHITE-GREEN NE(⅝)1:57² 1978 28 5 1 4 41,490

9-23 LB⅝ 4500 ft 79nw15000 cd mi 29 :59³1:30¹2:00³ 2 3 3° 1 1¹½ 3³½ 2:01¹ 9.60 (D.Queen) SunLElgy,RbbeRD,Persudabl 58-0
9-16 LB⅝ 5500 ft 79w12500 cd mi 29¹ :59³1:29³1:59⁴ 8 8 6° 6° 8⁶½ 8⁸½ 2:01³ 49.70 (D.Queen) NckwmpLry,KCThr,StpltnPlc 68-0
9- 9 Fox⅝ 8000 ft Inv hcp mi 30 1:00¹1:30 1:59² 3 1° 2 4 4² 5⁹½ 2:01² 6.60 (H.MacInnis) FrtnMoy,Cheviot,RipplngChf 60-0
8-31 St. Johns 20000 ft Stk mi 28⁴ :59⁴1:29³2:00⁴ 7 7 5 4° 4⁴½ 3³½ 2:01³ 2.40 (Ja.Doherty) KCThree,PowerBaron,Persuadable
8-26 Fox⅝ 8000 ft Inv hcp mi 28⁴ :58³1:27⁴1:57³ 4 3 6 6 6³ 4⁴½ 1:58² 1.80 (Ja.Doherty) Cheviot,RippChief,CEHooker 78-0
8-12 Fox⅝ 8000 sy Inv hcp mi 30¹1:01 1:32¹2:02 5 2 1 1 1¹ 2² 2:02² *1.40 (Ja.Doherty) FrncyStar,Prsuadable,BttyJoC 50-0
8- 1 M¹ 12000 ft nw8000 mi 29² :58¹1:28 1:57¹ 1 6 6 7° 6³½ 1hd 1:57¹ 14.70 (Ja.Doherty) Persuadable,ApSkl,Delty 82-0

TRACKMAN: 1—2—6

(8) PACE—1 MILE

Warming-Up Saddle Cloth
BROWN

PURSE $9,000

ASK FOR HORSE BY PROGRAM NUMBER

10th Race Advanced Trifecta Windows Now Open

EXACTA WAGERING THIS RACE

B'NAI B'RITH — NEW GENERATION CHAPTER

PREFERRED

10-1 **1** Red

BRETS RICHARD

br h, 4, by Meadow Skipper—Hail To Bret by Bret Hanover
Glen Terrace Racing Stables, Brooklyn, N.Y.
$22,469 — 3, 1:58 (1) Driver-MARK LANCASTER, 9-23-48 (150) BLUE-GOLD
Trainer-K. Primer
M(1)1:56² 1979 29 3 5 4 48,935
M(1)1:58 1978 15 2 2 2 12,020

9-22 LB⅝ 9000 sy Pref mi 30³1:02¹1:32¹2:01¹ 4 3 3 4 43½ 41½ 2:01² 4.20 (M.Lancaster) MrOvrnite,NickLeroy,FlshLbll 60-0
9-15 LB⅝ 10000 ft Pref mi 29¹1:01 1:31²2:00¹ 3 4 5 7 74 86 2:01² 6.00 (M.Lancaster) BestaFella,MrWight,FlshLbll 63-0
9- 8 YR 17000 ft A2-A3 hcp mi 28⁴ :59 1:29⁴2:00 7 8 8 8 8x158dis 31.50 (Jo.Kopas) FightTFoe,DblGene,KrryGold 65-0
9- 1 LB⅝ 8000 ft Pref mi 30¹1:01³1:31 1:59² 1 4 4° 2° 2nk 3½ 1:59² *1.80 (T.Wing) FlashLbll,JstaTnkr,BrtRchrd 70-0
8-26 LB⅝ 12000 ft Inv mi 28⁴ :58¹1:27⁴1:57² 3 2 1 1 1¾ 41 1:57³ 3.30 (T.Wing) BlazDave,NblPrnc,JstaTnkr 74-0
8-19 LB⅝ 12000 ft Inv mi 29² :59⁴1:29 1:57⁴ 3 4 2° 3° 2nd 56½ 1:59 6.90 (T.Wing) ChpprFrst,MrWght,MlvnStrk 74-0
8-11 LB⅝ 8000 sy Pref mi 29⁴1:00¹1:30²2:00 5 7 6 5° 43½ 13 2:00 6.50 (M.Lancaster) BrtRchrd,KlipMnbr,MrOvrnte 62-1

4-1 **2** Blue

MR. OVERNITE

b h, 9, by Overtrick—Roxburgh Carmen by Goose Bay
J. M. S. Stable, Watchung, N.J.
$361,617 — 5, 1:57¹ (⅝) (P) Driver-JAMES LARENTE, JR., 2-10-60 (120) BLUE-GOLD
Trainer-J. Larente
LB(⅝)1:58³ 1979 22 6 2 2 37,615
LB(⅝)1:59² 1978 26 4 2 5 40,486

9-22 LB⅝ 9000 sy Pref mi 30³1:02¹1:32¹2:01¹ 5 1 2 3 31½ 1¾ 2:01¹ 5.40 (J.Larente) MrOvrnite,NickLeroy,FlshLbll 60-0
9-15 Fhld 7500 ft Pref mi 29²1:00⁴1:30 2:00⁴ 3 4 2° 2° 44½ 66¾ 2:02¹ 2.80 (H.Kelly) JaneDunne,OverStrength,LGT 74-0
9- 8 LB⅝ 10000 ft Pref mi 28³ :58¹1:28²1:58³ 1 2 4 3° 43 68½ 2:00¹ 5.00 (J.LarenteJr) RightOver,JstaTinkr,RdnyLbll 65-0
9- 1 LB⅝ 8000 ft Pref mi 30¹1:01³1:31 1:59² 6 1 2 3 31½ 41 1:59³ 8.50 (J.Larente) FlashLbll,JstaTnkr,BrtRchrd 70-0
8-25 LB⅝ 8000 ft Pref mi 29¹1:00²1:29³1:58³ 6 2 2 2 2hd 12¼ 1:58³ 8.40 (J.LarenteJr) MrOvernite,RghtOver,FailLbll 77-0
8-18 LB⅝ 8000 sy Pref mi 29⁴ :59³1:29²1:59³ 2 1 2 3 31½ 53½ 2:00¹ 5.00 (J.LarenteJr) JstaTinker,MariaJ,DxtrAlba 64-0
8-11 LB⅝ 8000 sy Pref mi 29⁴1:00¹1:30²2:00 3 5 4 6 65 33 2:00³ 3.90 (J.LarenteJr) BrtRchrd,KlipMnbr,MrOvrnte 62-1

3-1 **3** White

FORTUNE MOY

b m, 7, by Most Happy Fella—Poplar Lebel by Bye Bye Byrd
Fortune Valley Farms, Inc., Kingston, N.Y.
$150,994 — 5, 1:56³(1) Driver-JAMES DOHERTY, 9-27-40 (161) RED-WHITE-GREEN
Trainer-D. Queen
M(1)1:56⁴ 1979 24 10 2 3 84,270
M(1)1:58² 1978 17 3 1 3 22,925

9-23 Fox⅝ 8000 ft Inv hcp mi 29⁴1:01³1:31¹1:59² 4 1 1 1 11½ 11½ 1:59² *.70 (Ja.Doherty) FrtnMoy,MilesESteve,Cheviot 54-0
9- 9 Fox⅝ 8000 ft Inv hcp mi 30 1:00¹1:30 1:59² 5 5 5 2° 21 1nk 1:59² *1.30 (Ja.Doherty) FrtnMoy,Cheviot,RippingChf 60-0
8-19 Fox⅝ 8000 sy Inv hcp mi 29⁴1:01²1:32⁴2:01³ 5 2° 1 1 11 12½ 2:01³ *.70 (Ja.Doherty) FrtuneMoy,FncyStar,RipChief 63-0
8- 5 Fox⅝ 8000 ft Inv hcp mi 30³1:00⁴1:30 1:58 5 5 5 4 41½ 34¼ 1:58⁴ *.50 (Ja.Doherty) RipChief,FancyStar,FrtnMoy 85-0
7-22 Fox⅝ 20000 ft Inv hcp mi 28¹ :59¹1:27⁴1:57¹ 6 7 6 4° 41¾ 22 1:57³ 3.80 (Ja.Doherty) RmblnWillie,FrtnMoy,CEHkr 85-0
7-15 Fox⅝ 8000 gd Inv hcp mi 29² :59³1:29⁴1:58³ 5 6 6 6° 62¼ 11½ 1:58³ 2.90 (Ja.Doherty) FrtnMoy,MilesEStede,RipChf 75-0
7- 8 Fox⅝ 8000 ft Inv hcp mi 29¹1:00⁴1:29 1:58³ 6 6 6 6° 63¼ 3nd 1:58³ 1.50 (Ja.Doherty) RipChief,MilesEStde,FrtnMoy 85-0

7-2 **4** Green

JUSTA TINKER

b h, 5, by Adios Butler—Resurrexi by Knight Dream
Chas. J. Fitzpatrick, N.C. & Paige West, Salisbury, Md.
$65,755 — 4, 1:59² (1) Driver-CHAS. FITZPATRICK, 6-13-26 (160) GREEN-WHITE-RED
Trainer-C. Fitzpatrick
M(1)1:56⁴ 1979 21 4 3 7 39,125
M(1)1:59² 1978 17 5 1 3 45,320

9-23 LB⅝ 12000 ft Inv mi 28² :59²1:29 1:58³ 2 4 5 7 54½ 74¾ 1:59³ 4.90 (C.Fitzpatrick) TexasTea,BstaFlla,TheBattlr 58-0
9-16 LB⅝ 25000 ft FA Inv mi 29² :59²1:28²1:57 5 6 6° 6° 64¾ 35¼ 1:58 24.30 (C.Fitzpatrick) DirectSctr,NevelLdr,JstaTnkr 67-0
9- 8 LB⅝ 10000 ft Pref mi 28³ :58¹1:28²1:58³ 4 4 2° 1 12½ 22 1:59 *.90 (C.Fitzpatrick) RightOver,JstaTinkr,RdnyLbll 65-0
9- 1 LB⅝ 8000 ft Pref mi 30¹1:01³1:31 1:59² 5 6 6° 4° 41¾ 2nk 1:59² 2.20 (C.Fitzpatrick) FlashLbll,JstaTnkr,BrtRchrd 70-0
8-26 LB⅝ 12000 ft Inv mi 28⁴ :58¹1:27⁴1:57² 5 6 6 6 63¼ 3hd 1:57² 8.20 (C.Fitzpatrick) BlazDave,NblPrnc,JstaTnkr 74-0
8-18 LB⅝ 8000 sy Pref mi 29⁴ :59³1:29²1:59³ 6 6 6 6° 63¾ 11 1:59³ 3.20 (C.Fitzpatrick) JstaTinker,MariaJ,DxtrAlba 64-0
8-12 Brd⅝ 7500 sy w10000 cd mi 29 :59¹1:28⁴1:59³ 2 4 2 2 21¼ 1½ 1:59³ 1.70 (C.Fitzpatrick) JustaTnkr,SwiftHpful,Saigon 58-0

5-1 **5** Black

FLASH LOBELL

b h, 6, by Adios Vic—Freight Line by Tar Heel
Crystal Brook Farm, Inc., Colts Neck, N.J.
$119,104 — 4, 1:56⁴ (1) Driver-JOE GREENE, 7-3-36 (169) WHITE-GREEN-BLACK
Trainer-C. LeCause
M(1)1:57⁴ 1979 15 6 3 3 45,370
Q-M(1)1:58² 1978 5 0 0 0 2,410

9-22 LB⅝ 9000 sy Pref mi 30³1:02¹1:32¹2:01¹ 1 2 1 1 11½ 3¾ 2:01² *1.50 (C.LeCause) MrOvrnite,NickLeroy,FlshLbll 60-0
9-15 LB⅝ 10000 ft Pref mi 29¹1:01 1:31²2:00¹ 2 2 2 3 31¼ 32 2:00³ 4.20 (C.LeCause) BestaFella,MrWight,FlshLbll 63-0
9- 8 Fhld 10000 ft Inv mi 28⁴1:00 1:29²1:58² 6 7 5° 5° 67½ 56¾ 1:59⁴ 6.80 (C.LeCause) AlsknStrk,NoHitter,MrWight 70-0
9- 1 LB⅝ 8000 ft Pref mi 30¹1:01³1:31 1:59² 2 2 1 1 1nk 1nk 1:59² 2.60 (C.LeCause) FlashLbll,JstaTnkr,BrtRchrd 70-0
8-25 Fhld 8500 ft Pref Inv mi 29³1:00⁴1:31¹1:59² 5 1 1 1 11 12 1:59² *.90 (C.LeCause) FlashLb,FWlronhd,JaneDnne 80-0
8-18 Fhld 9500 gd Inv mi 28² :58²1:29 1:59 5 7 6 6° 64½ 34½ 1:59⁴ 4.90 (C.LeCause) MaximusHn,NevelLdr FlashLb 65-0
8-11 Fhld 10000 ft Inv mi 29⁴ :59⁴1:29³2:00 3 2° 3 3 22 1¾ 2:00 3.90 (C.LeCause) FlshLbll,MxmsHan,FWlrnhd 70-0

6-1 **6** Yellow

SCOTT'S CHANCE

b h, 4, by Adios Butler—Laura Scott by Scotland
Kellori Stables, Lititz, Pa.
$2,394 — 2, 2:04 (⅝) Driver-DONALD DANCER, 10-1-55 (125) BLUE-GOLD
Trainer-F. Schreiber
Brd(⅝)1:58⁴ 1979 23 10 3 7 38,969
DD(⅝)2:05 1978 1 1 0 0 550

9-15 LB⅝ 10000 ft Pref mi 29¹1:01 1:31²2:00¹ 1 3 3 5 52¼ 42½ 2:00³ 8.90 (R.Myers) BestaFella,MrWight,FlshLbll 63-0
9- 8 Brd⅝ 10000 ft Inv mi 28³ :59²1:28³1:58⁴ 1 2 1 2 2hd 1¾ 1:58⁴ 3.00 (D.Dancer) ScttChnce,SwftHpfl,KCThree 70-0
8-26 Brd⅝ 7000 ft w10000 cd mi 29¹1:00 1:28²1:58² 5 1 1 1 1ns 23 1:59 *2.20 (R.Hayter) KCThree,ScttChnc,BstJeffrey 78-0
8-19 Brd⅝ 7500 ft w10000 cd mi 28⁴ :59⁴1:29 1:58² 5 1 1 1 11¼ 21 1:58³ 5.80 (R.Hayter) Saigon,ScttsChnc,BstJeffrey 78-0
8-11 Brd⅝ 7000 sy w10000 cd mi 29⁴1:00²1:30 2:01 1 2 1 1 11 11½ 2:01 4.30 (R.Hayter) ScottChnc,DchssStrt,TarKeel 66-0
8- 5 Brd⅝ 7000 ft w10000 cd mi 29³1:00¹1:29³1:59 4 1 2 3 31¼ 43 1:59³ 10.60 (R.Hayter) SwftHopfl,LrdEddie,BstJffry 86-0
7-22 Brd⅝ 7000 ft w10000 cd mi 29¹ 59⁴1:29²1:59⁴ 5 2 1 1 12 31¾ 2:00¹ 3.70 (R.Hayter) PACarlos,BstJffry,ScttsChnc 80-0

10-1 **7** Pink

NICKAWAMPUS LEROY

b g, 8, by Harold J.—Sue Quinton by Meadow Ace
Willie J. Lewis, Onley, Va.
$387,755 — 4, 1:57² (⅝) Driver-JAMES RATHBONE, 8-8-50 (180) WHITE-GOLD-GREEN
Trainer-J. Rathbone
LB(⅝)1:58⁴ 1979 31 4 8 7 43,255
LB(⅝)2:00¹ 1978 23 1 2 5 26,895

9-22 LB⅝ 9000 sy Pref mi 30³1:02¹1:32¹2:01¹ 3 5 4° 2° 21½ 2¾ 2:01² 6.40 (J.Rathbone) MrOvrnite,NickLeroy,FlshLbll 60-0
9-16 LB⅝ 5500 ft 79w12500 cd mi 29¹ :59³1:29³1:59⁴ 1 2 4 4° 42½ 1hd 1:59⁴ 3.10 (J.Rathbone) NckwmpLry,KCThr,StpltnPk 68-0
9- 9 LB⅝ 5500 ft 79w12500 cd mi 29³1:00 1:29⁴1:59³ 2 1 2 3 31½ 12 1:59³ 2.20 (J.Rathbone) NickaLry,DelroyN,Sunderchf 67-0
9- 1 LB⅝ 5500 ft 79w12500 cd mi 29 :59¹1:29⁴1:59² 6 3 1° 1 11¼ 22½ 1:59⁴ *2.70 (J.Rathbone) VctrVic,NickawmpsLry,Sunro 70-0
8-25 LB⅝ 8000 ft Pref mi 29¹1:00²1:29³1:58³ 4 5 6 5° 55½ 45¾ 1:59⁴ 4.40 (J.Rathbone) MrOvernite,RghtOver,FailLbll 77-0
8-19 LB⅝ 5500 ft 79w12500 cd mi 29 1:00 1:29²1:58⁴ 1 3 2° 1 12 13½ 1:58⁴ 3.80 (J.Rathbone) NckwmpsLry,CvrUp AdmrHLb 74-0
8-12 LB⅝ 5500 sy 79w12500 cd mi 31 1:01²1:33 2:03¹ 1 5 6 6 7x3¾x5x6¼ 2:04² 8.90 (J.Rathbone) MariaJ,CyclonePrnc,DelroyN 56-1

6-1 **8** Black-Yellow

NOBLE PRINCE

b h, 7, by Noble Victory—Prudence Special by Something Special
Peter T. Recigno, Jr., Willow Grove, Pa.
$32,675 — 6, T-1:55² (1) Driver-ALAN MYER, 6-9-26 (185) GREEN-WHITE-GOLD
Trainer-A. Myer
M(1)1:55⁴ 1979 24 6 5 3 55,420
LB(⅝)2:00² 1978 28 7 4 5 32,675

9-23 LB⅝ 12000 ft Inv mi 28² :59²1:29 1:58³ 1 3 3 5 43½ 63¾ 1:59² 7.50 (A.Myer) TexasTea,BstaFlla,TheBattlr 58-0
9-16 LB⅝ 25000 ft FA Inv mi 29² :59²1:28²1:57 3 4 5 5 53½ 55½ 1:58 20.10 (A.Myer) DirectSctr,NevelLdr,JstaTnkr 67-0
9- 9 LB⅝ 25000 ft FA Inv mi 28¹ :58¹1:27⁴1:57¹ 7 6 6 8 78½ 78 1:58⁴ 19.80 (A.Myer) DirSctr,MlvnStrk,NvlLeader 64-0
9- 2 LB⅝ 12000 ft Inv mi 27⁴ :58²1:26⁴1:56² 6 6 6 6 66½ 68 1:58 4.10 (A.Myer) NvleLdr,MlvnStrk,SmmryJdg 76-0
8-26 LB⅝ 12000 ft Inv mi 28⁴ :58¹1:27⁴1:57² 2 4 4 4° 42 2ns 1:57² *1.60 (A.Myer) BlazDave,NblPrnc,JstaTnkr 74-0
8- 4 M¹ 50000 ft FA mi 28² :55⁴1:24³1:53 6 6 7 7 86¾ 810½ 1:55 39.30 (A.Myer) Abercromie,TrySctch,LeBRge 79-0
7-29 LB⅝ 12000 sy Inv mi 29⁴1:01⁴1:31⁴1:59⁴ 1 2 2 2 21¾ 35½ 2:00⁴ *1.30 (A.Myer) GoldiesVic,MlvnStrk,NblPrnc 69-0

TRACKMAN: 3—4—2

(9) PACE—1 MILE

Warming-Up Saddle Cloth
ORANGE

PURSE $5,500

10th Race Advanced Trifecta Windows Now Open
EXACTA WAGERING THIS RACE

WINNERS IN EXCESS OF $15,000 IN 1979 NOT PREFERRED.

ASK FOR HORSE BY PROGRAM NUMBER

5-1 **1** Red — **VICTOR VIC** b h, 4, by Adios Vic—Naomis Best by Bengazi Hanover
Elwood Kane, Meade, Kans. — Trainer-J. Dennis, Sr.
M(1)1:59 1979 33 6 7 0 39,375
$33,069 — 3, 2:00 (⅝) Driver-J. D. DENNIS, SR., 7-5-30 (178) RED-BLUE-WHITE — Brd(⅝)2:00 1978 29 6 6 7 28,768
9-23 LB⅝ 5500 ft 79w15000 cd mi 29² :59⁴1:29¹1:58⁴ 1 3 3° 5° 6⁹½ 6²²½ 2:03² 5.90 (J.DennisSr) YnkBmbr,SothNrwlk,VicQntn 56-0
9-16 LB⅝ 5500 ft 79w12500 cd mi 29¹ :59³1:29³1:59⁴ 3 4 7 7 6⁵ 5⁵¼ 2:00⁴ 3.90 (J.DennisSr) NckwmpLry,KCThr,StpltnPlc 63-0
9- 7 Brd⅝ 6500 ft w10000 cd mi 29 :58³1:28²1:59⁴ 6 8 8 8 7⁴½ 1½ 1:59⁴ 1.80 (J.DennisSr) VctrVic,MoveFMv,HppyJMiss 78-0
9- 1 LB⅝ 5500 ft 79w12500 cd mi 29 :59¹1:29⁴1:59² 3 6 7° 7° 4²¼ 1²½ 1:59² 4.90 (M.Schwartz) VctrVic,NickawmpsLry,Sunro 70-0
8-26 LB⅝ 5500 ft 79w12500 cd mi 29¹ :59³1:29³2:00³ 2 6 5° 3°°i5²½ 6⁷ 2:02 3.70 (M.Schwartz) AdmLbll,KeysPnt,VicQuinton 76-0
8-18 PcD⅝ 5000 sy Inv hcp mi 35⁴1:09 1:39³2:11 5 4 2• 4° 4³ 4⁷ 2:12² *1.40 (S.Beegle) HesaTgrToo,Cobber,QckTmpr 60-0
8-11 PcD⅝ 5000 sl Inv mi 32²1:03²1:34 2:06⁴ 2 2 2 2 2⁶ 2²¼dh 2:07¹ *1.30 (S.Beegle) ScatJack,VctrVicdhEmperVan 63-0

8-1 **2** Blue — **ROBBIE R. D.** b h, 6, by Harold J.—Bachelor's Reward by Bachelor Hanover
Romuld Deinarowicz, Sewell, N.J. — Trainer-M. Roane
Brd(⅝)2:01 1979 22 3 5 3 15,460
$97,559 — 4, 1:58³ (⅝) Driver-ROBERT MYERS, 5-11-44 (185) WINE-SILVER — Brd(⅝)1:59¹ 1978 13 3 3 2 26,294
9-23 LB⅝ 4500 ft 79nw15000 cd mi 29 :59³1:30¹2:00³ 4 4 4° 2° 2¹¼ 2¹½ 2:00⁴ 7.20 (R.Myers) SunLElgy RbbeRD Persudabl 58-0
9-15 LB⅝ 5500 ft 79w12500 cd mi 30¹1:00²1:32¹2:02 4 2° 2 3 3¹½ 2nd 2:02 8.10 (R.Myers) HiFiMax,RobbieRD,MrPockts 61-0
9- 7 Brd⅝ 5000 ft nw6001 L5 cd mi 29 :59 1:29 1:59² 5 7 8 7° 6⁴¼ 5⁴½ 2:00¹ 10.50 (P.Battis) ByeBKtty,FftyGrd,GldcrkBob 78-0
8-29 Brd⅝ 4000 ftnw4000 L5 cd mi 29² :59³1:29¹1:59³ 6 1 2 2 2¹½ 2² 2:00 *2.00 (H.Frazier) DctrJhnG.,RbbieRD,SunBnny 80-0
8-19 Brd⅝ 3000ft nw3000 L5 cd mi 29⁴1:00⁴1:30²2:01 3 4 6 6 3¹ 1²½ 2:01 2.90 (P.Battis) RbbieRD,HerbieC,SlpyRevival 78-0
8-12 Brd⅝ 3000 sy nw2500 L5 cd mi 29¹1:00²1:30⁴2:02² 2 4 4 4° 4³¼ 2½ 2:02² 4.20 (P.Battis) Mgtylmprs,RobRD,SlpyRvival 58-0
8- 3 Brd⅝ 2000sy nw2000 L5 cd mi 29⁴1:01 1:31 2:02¹ 5 1 2 2° 2hd 1⁴½ 2:02¹ *.60 (R.Hayter) RobbieRD,PplrLght,HarryLee 80-0

10-1 **3** White — **YOUNG MR. POCKETS** b g, 4, by Lehigh Hanover—Miss Barbie by Tar Boy
M T Pockets Stables, Fort Lee, N.J. — Trainer-S. Casanova
Brd(⅝)1:59³ 1979 27 7 2 0 25,914
$4,290 — 3, 2:03³ (⅝) Driver-STEVE CASANOVA, 10-9-46 (135) BLACK-YELLOW-GREEN — Lau(⅝)2:03³ 1978 12 1 2 1 4,290
9-23 LB⅝ 5500 ft 79w15000 cd mi 30 1:00¹1:30¹1:59³ 1 2 3 3 2²½ 6⁶¼ 2:00⁴ 17.10 (S.Casanova) Stpl'nPlace,KCThree,RipRuss 58-0
9-15 LB⅝ 5000 ft 30000 clm cd mi 29²1:00²1:30²2:00³ 6 1 1 1 1¹½ 1² 2:00³ 4.00 (S.Casanova) YngMPckts,BndRhy,HgOnHy 61-0
9- 6 Brd⅝ 3500 ftnw3000 L5 cd mi 29²1:00¹1:30²2:01 5 2° 1 1 1²½ 1¹ 2:01 *.90 (S.Casanova) YngMrPckt,LstSip,HghHTny 80-0
8-29 Brd⅝ 2300synw1501 L5 cd mi 31 1:02 1:32³2:02² 3 1 1 1 1²¼ 1⁴½ 2:02² *1.40 (S.Casanova) YngMPckts,TstTms,OMnFrw 80-0
8-21 Brd⅝ 2300ft nw1000 L5 cd mi 29³1:00⁴1:31²2:02 4 1 1 1 1² 2hd 2:02 *.80 (S.Casanova) Nwll,YngMrPckts,TstngTms 74-0
8- 4 Brd⅝ 2300 ftnw1500 L5 cd mi 29³1:00 1:29²2:00² 3 6 2° 2° 2¹ 4³ 2:01 *1.30 (S.Casanova) OMntFrwd,InvrtBoy,Pharmac 84-0
7-27 Brd⅝ 2500 ft nw2000 L5 cd mi 29¹1:01²1:31³2:01³ 7 8 7 4° 4⁸½ 5¹⁰½ 2:03⁴ *.50 (S.Casanova) MstHFrst,MstHThlm,KeySnz 80-0

4-1 **4** Green — **H H FREEHOLD** b h, 4, by Isle Of Wight—Fair Sandy by Hodgen
Ralph S. Weaver, Allentown, Pa. — Trainer-J. Smith, Jr.
LB(⅝)2:00¹ 1979 21 3 4 5 19,850
$32,774 — 3, 1:59 (1) Driver JACK SMITH, JR., 9-28-46 (175) MAROON-GOLD — M(1)1:59 1978 25 6 6 3 32,609
9-22 LB⅝ 5500 gd 79w15000 cd mi 29⁴1:01¹1:31⁴2:01³ 5 5 5° 4° 5³ 4³½ 2:02¹ 3.80 (J.SmithJr) HpGoBye,CylnPrnc,YngSwrtz 60-0
9-16 LB⅝ 4500 ft 79nw12500 cd mi 29² :59³1:30¹2:00⁴ 5 6 5 5° 6³½ 1½ 2:00⁴ 4.20 (J.SmithJr) HHFrhld,ThndrBrt,TmlyTitle 68-0
9- 9 LB⅝ 4500 ft 79nw12500 cd mi 29⁴1:01²1:31 2:01² 8 8 8 8 8⁷½ 3½ 2:01² 10.50 (J.SmithJr) SpkdBoots,KeyKaola,HHFhld 67-0
9- 1 LB⅝ 4500 ft 79nw12500 cd mi 31 1:03 1:32⁴2:02¹ 4 4 2° 2° 1² 2²¼ 2:02³ 5.70 (J.SmithJr) SprtyBrn,HHFrhld,SpkdBts 72-0
8-26 LB⅝ 4500 ft 79nw12500 cd mi 29²1:01¹1:30⁴2:00¹ 6 6 4° 5° 5²½ 3⁴¼ 2:01 11.10 (J.SmithJr) DblJudy,CmdAntn,HHFrhld 73-0
8-18 LB⅝ 4500 sy 79nw12500 cd mi 31²1:02⁴1:32²2:03 4 6 7• 8° 8⁵¼ 6⁴½ 2:03⁴ 2.30 (W.Cameron) DblJdy†FrstNBest†JstAFella 64-0
8-12 LB⅝ 4500 sy 79nw12500 cd mi 29⁴1:00⁴1:32²2:03¹ 1 6 6 6 6³ 2ns 2:03¹ *2.00 (J.Larente) Nanfort,HHFreehld,KansasHn 56-1

8-1 **5** Black — **MAXIMUS HANOVER** b h, 5, by Albatross—Matara by Tar Heel
Bard W. & Ellen Ludwig, Pottstown, Pa. — Trainer-E. Davis
Fhld1:59 1979 29 7 9 2 50,655
$54,549 — 4, 2:00³ (⅝) Driver EDDIE DAVIS, 11-17-43 (167) RED-WHITE — LB(⅝)2:00³ 1978 30 4 3 8 24,321
9-23 LB⅝ 5500 ft 79w15000 cd mi 29² :59⁴1:29¹1:58⁴ 6 6 6 4 4⁵½ 4⁸½ 2:00² 5.10 (E.Davis) YnkBmbr SothNrwlk VicQntn 56-0
9-16 LB⅝ 5500 ft 79w12500 cd mi 29¹ :59³1:29³1:59⁴ 7 7 3° 2° 2¹½ 6⁷½ 2:01¹ 12.00 (J.Wyatt) NckwmpLry,KCThr,StpltnPlc 63-0
9- 8 Fhld 10000 ft Inv mi 28⁴1:00 1:29²1:58² 1 2 2 2 2³ 4⁴½ 1:59¹ 3.80 (E.Davis) AlsknStrk,NoHitter,MrWight 70-0
9- 1 LB⅝ 8000 ft Pref mi 30¹1:01³1:31 1:59² 3 3 3 5 5²½ 5²½ 1:59⁴ 10.50 (E.Davis) FlashLbll,JstaTnkr,BrtRchrd 70-0
8-26 LB⅝ 12000 ft Inv mi 28⁴ :58¹1:27⁴1:57² 6 1° 2 3 3² 6¹¹½ 1:59³ 3.70 (E.Davis) BlazDave,NblPrnc,JstaTnkr 74-0
8-18 Fhld 9500 gd Inv mi 28² :58²1:29 1:59 1 3 1° 1 1¹½ 1¹½ 1:59 2.20 (E.Davis) MaximusHn,NevelLdr FlashLb 65-0
8-11 Fhld 10000 ft Inv mi 29⁴ :59⁴1:29³2:00 5 5 5 5 3³½ 2² 2:00¹ 2.90 (E.Davis) FlshLbll,MxmsHan,FWlrnhd 70-0

7-2 **6** Yellow — **CYCLONE PRINCE** br h, 5, by Columbia George—Suzette Hanover by Dancer Hanover
Cyclone Racing Stable, Que., L. Pietronuto, J. Demas, B. Yellin — Trainer-B. Yellin
M(1)1:56 1979 19 3 3 0 19,145
$27,728 — 4, 2:01³ Driver-SAM BELOTE, 6-13-52 (170) GREEN-GRAY-RED — YR2:01³ 1978 28 1 9 3 19,372
9-22 LB⅝ 5500 gd 79w15000 cd mi 29⁴1:01¹1:31⁴2:01³ 2 3 3 3 3¹½ 2ns 2:01³ 7.90 (S.Belote) HpGoBye,CylnPrnc,YngSwrtz 60-0
9-18 LB⅝ ft Qua (h-d) mi 28⁴1:00³1:30³2:01⁴ 2 3 3 3 2⁴ 2¹½ 2:02 N.B. (B.Bronfman) RumGold,CycPrnc,StoweStar 73-0
8-19 LB⅝ 5500 ft 79nw12500 cd mi 28⁴ :58⁴1:29¹1:59⁴ 1 2 3 4 5²½ 6⁹¼ 2:01³ *2.40 (M.Lancaster) HiFiMax,VicQuintn,KystnPnt 77-0
8-12 LB⅝ 5500 sy 79nw12500 cd mi 31 1:01²1:33 2:03¹ 4 7 7° 7° 6³ 2²½ 2:03³ *3.00 (M.Lancaster) MariaJ,CyclonePrnc,DelroyN 56-1
8- 3 M¹ 9500 ft nw5500 cd mi 28² :57⁴1:27¹1:56 7 2 2 2 1²½ 1⁴ 1:56 9.50 (Jo.Campbell) CyclonePrnc,Pub,FlyFMnstrl 75-0
7-30 M¹ 9000 ft nw5000 cd mi 29⁴ :58⁴1:29 1:58¹ 7 7 7 5 4⁴½ 4⁵½ 1:59¹ 5.00 (Jo.Campbell) TopalaHn,FlFMnstrl,NsvChrs 80-0
7-20 M¹ 10000 ft 22500 clm mi 29⁴ :59¹1:28⁴1:58² 1 3 3 5 6⁴½ 6⁸ 2:00 9.00 (L.Williams) RmpnDan,SkysDpkmt,HiSykes 77-0

3-1 **7** Pink — **THELMAS DREAM** b m, 4, by Most Happy Fella—Brets Dream by Bret Hanover
Charter Oak Stable, Mary Rounick, Pa. & Eric Roberts, N.Y. — Trainer-J. Larente
Sycs(1)1:57⁴ 1979 20 2 7 3 33,756
$22,729 — 3, 2:02 (⅝) (P) Driver-JAMES LARENTE, JR., 2-10-60 (120) BLUE-GOLD — LB(⅝)2:02 1978 14 3 7 2 22,729
9-22 LB⅝ 5500 sy 79w15000 cd mi 30¹1:01 1:31⁴2:01¹ 8 8 8 8° 7⁴½ 2³½ 2:01⁴ 5.20 (J.Larente) SkrWltz,ThlmDrm FalsfeLbl 60-0
9-16 LB⅝ 5500 ft 79w12500 cd mi 29 1:00²1:29²1:59⁴ 6 8 7 6 5¹½ 4²½ 2:00¹ 5.20 (J.LarenteJr) DblJudy,DelroyN,DchesStrttn 65-0
9- 9 LB⅝ 5500 ft 79w12500 cd mi 29³1:00 1:29⁴1:59³ 8 4° 4° 2° 2ns 4²½ 2:00¹ 10.70 (J.LarenteJr) NickaLry,DelroyN,Sunderchf 67-0
8-30 Stga 27386 ft 4yr F Stk mi 29⁴1:00¹1:30 1:58³ 2 4 4 4° 4 5²½ 1:59 7.10 (J.Larente) Nickylou,JSSkppr,MilesEBrenda
8-18 Sycs¹ 10000synw25000 Lc mi 31 1:01¹1:34²2:03⁴ 6 4 5° 5° 5⁶½ 5⁷½ 2:05¹ 6.30 (J.Larente) MilesESteve,YnkCrsn,ShrpBChip
8-12 Sycs¹ 17175 ft 4yr F Stk mi 29 :58⁴1:28²1:57⁴ 1 3 3° 2° 2nd 1½ 1:57⁴ 3.00 (J.LarenteJr) ThelmasDrm,DorisLdy,HppyBChip
8- 5 LB⅝ 5500 ft 79w10000 cd mi 30³1:02²1:31 2:00⁴ 5 7° 6° 6° 6i5½ 2hd 2:00⁴ 3.40 (J.LarenteJr) MriaJ.,ThlmDrm,HppyGoBye 81-0

6-1 **8** Black-Yellow — **VIC QUINTON** b h, 5, by Adios Vic—Peach Quinton by Harold J.
Clarence W. & Melvin L. Lewis, Accomac, Va. — Trainer-J. Rathbone
M(1)1:57 1979 27 5 3 5 31,100
$26,841 — 4, 1:57¹ (1) Driver-JAMES RATHBONE, 8-8-50 (180) WHITE-GOLD-GREEN — M(1)1:57¹ 1978 23 6 5 2 26,491
9-23 LB⅝ 5500 ft 79w15000 cd mi 29² :59⁴1:29¹1:58⁴ 3 2 2 2 2²½ 3⁸½ 2:00² 6.60 (J.Rathbone) YnkBmbr SothNrwlk VicQntn 56-0
9-15 LB⅝ 5500 ft 79w12500 cd mi 30¹1:00²1:32¹2:02 8 5° 3° 2° 2½ 5nk 2:02 12.00 (J.Rathbone) HiFiMax,RobbieRD,MrPockts 61-0
9- 8 LB⅝ 5500 ft 79w12500 cd mi 30 :59⁴1:30 2:00³ 6 6 6° 6° 6⁴½ 4⁴½ 2:01² 5.30 (J.Rathbone) HppyGBye,HiFiMax,SprtyBrn 65-0
9- 2 LB⅝ 5500 ft 79w12500 cd mi 29¹ :59⁴1:29³2:00 2 2 3 3 3¹½ 3²½ 2:00² 10.40 (J.Rathbone) DblJudy,AdmrlLbll,VicQntn 76-0
8-26 LB⅝ 5500 ft 79w12500 cd mi 29¹ :59³1:29³2:00³ 4 1 1 1 1²½ 3²½ 2:01 *2.00 (J.Rathbone) AdmLbll,KeysPnt,VicQuinton 76-0
8-19 LB⅝ 5500 ft 79w12500 cd mi 28⁴ :58⁴1:29¹1:59⁴ 5 7 6° 5° 4¹½ 2⁴½ 2:00³ 2.50 (J.Rathbone) HiFiMax,VicQuintn,KystnPnt 77-0
8-11 LB⅝ 8000 sy Pref mi 29⁴1:00¹1:30²2:00 6 1° 2 4 5³½ 7⁹ 2:01⁴ 25.20 (J.Rathbone) BrtRchrd,KlipMnbr,MrOvrnte 62-1

TRACKMAN: 7—6—4

(10)

PACE—1 MILE

Warming-Up Saddle Cloth BLUE & WHITE

PURSE $4,200

ASK FOR HORSE BY PROGRAM NUMBER

TRIFECTA WAGERING THIS RACE

CLAIMING ALLOWANCE
Five-Year-Olds & Older To Be Claimed For $20,000, Four-Year-Olds To Be Claimed For $24,000, Three-Year-Olds To Be Claimed For $28,000. (Fillies & Mares Allowed 20%)

3-1 — **1** — 20000 Red

JOE ALLEN N b g, 8, by Lordship—Fallacina by Fallacy
M. Rubach & D. Van Deventer, West New York & Newark, N.J.
Trainer-D. Van Deventer
M(1)2:011 1979 25 1 6 5 28,589
$40,755 — 7, 2:004 (1) Driver-TOM VAN DEVENTER, 6-4-47 (170) MAROON-WHITE-BLACK
Sacr(1)2:004 1978 33 2 7 9 27,947

9-22 LB⅝ 4200 sy 20000 clm cd mi 3031:0121:3122:022 3 4 4 4 43 33½ 2:03 5.50(T.VanDeventer) Staveley,CrnlStrkr,JoeAllnN 60-0
9- 2 LB⅝ 5000 ft 25000 clm cd mi 282 :5811:2821:593 5 6 6 7 75½ 56¼ 2:004 4.00(T.VanDeventer) BusPass,EmpBtrce,ShutOut 76-0
8-25 LB⅝ 5000 ft 25000 clm cd mi 293 :5921:2942:011 5 6 7 8 84 21½ 2:012 7.00(T.VanDeventer) KeyPrvelt,JoeAllnN,MidPerk 75-0
8-18 LB⅝ 5000 sy 25000 clm cd mi 3031:02 1:3142:022 1 3 1 3 32 31¾ 2:024 *2.00 (C.Manzi) EvrgrnMrc,MidPerk,JoeAllnN 64-0
8-12 LB⅝ 5000 sy 25000 clm cd mi 3111:0241:3432:044 6 7° 4° 2° 41¾ 87¾ 2:062 3.60 (R.DeSantis) Dunsinane,SsndSct,SinglLife 56-1
8- 4 M1 12000 ft 25000 clm mi 293 :59 1:2841:58 9 1° 2 3 42½ 3nk 1:58 27.60 (M.Gagliardi) ArmRym,ThrLbl,JoeAllnN. 79-0
7-26 M1 14400 ft 25000 clm mi 283 :5721:2721:574 4ix3 2 3 39 510½dh1:594 8.60 (S.Goudreau) FrstyPnn,Nerissa,LehighStne 79-0

4-1 — **2** — 24000 Blue

LEISA MAY b m, 7, by Sir Painter—Palace Affair by Shadow Wave
M. T. Pockets Stable & Double R. Triple M. Stable, N.J.
Trainer-S. Casanova
Brd(⅝)2:00 1979 22 4 1 3 17,656
$65,887 — 5, 1:582 (1) Driver-STEVE CASANOVA, 10-9-46 (135) BLACK-YELLOW-GREEN
HP(⅝)2:001 1978 32 5 1 4 24,102

9-15 LB⅝ 4400 ft 24000 clm cd mi 292 :5911:2932:002 5 6 6°7°xx7xdisx8xdis 5.50 (S.Casanova) Lavanto, SingleLife, RivalBoy 65-0
9- 3 Brd⅝ 4000 ft nw4000 L5 cd mi 2931:0121:3222:004 6 6 4° 4° 55½ 78½ 2:022 3.80 (S.Casanova) FiftyGrnd,MstHFrst,SagwBay 80-0
8-25 Brd⅝ 6000 sy F-M cd mi 2921:00 1:2942:00 1 2 2 2 21½ 32½ 2:002 *1.50 (S.Casanova) AbbsFncy,HpyJMss,LeisaMy 76-0
8-21 Brd⅝ 2500ft nw2500 L5 cd mi 2811:0021:3032:001 2 2 1 1 11½ 13½ 2:001 *.90 (S.Casanova) LesiaMy,KajamJms,LucchHn 74-0
8-12 Brd⅝ 4000 sy nw4000 L5 cd mi 3011:0031:3032:023 5 4 2° 2° 22 35½ 2:033 *.70 (S.Casanova) DctJhnG,SntasHlpr,LeisaMay 58-0
8- 4 Brd⅝ 5000ft24000 clm hcp mi 293 :5921:2922:002 7 2° 1 1 11½ 2hd dh2:002 3.00 (S.Casanova) CraNvlle,HghDonA,dhLsaMay 84-0
7-28 Brd⅝ 7000 ft F-M Opn mi 2941:0041:30 1:583 3 5 7 8 64½ 68½ 2:001 20.90 (S.Casanova) ThrsLbl WinnStyle.SlpyRvvl 82-0

5-2 — **3** — 20000 White

CORNELL STREAKER b g, 5, by C. K. Adios—Warrior Miss by Meadow War
David & Herman Darmofal, Scranton, Pa.
Trainer-E. Davis
LB(⅝)2:004 1979 28 7 2 3 29,888
$11,850 — 4, 2:021 (1) Driver-EDDIE DAVIS, 11-17-43 (167) RED-WHITE
M(1)2:021 1978 14 2 1 4 11,850

9-22 LB⅝ 4200 sy 20000 clm cd mi 3031:0121:3122:022 1 2 2 3 21½ 2hd 2:022 2.90 (E.Davis) Staveley,CrnlStrkr.JoeAllnN 60-0
8-31 LB⅝ 3400 ft12500z clm cd mi 2911:0031:3112:004 8 2 2 1 11¾ 16¾ 2:004 8.80 (M.Lancaster) CrnllStrkr,ElMgnfA,DstDrum 72-0
8-24 LB⅝ 3400 ft 12500 clm cd mi 2831:0111:3142:034 5 2 1 1 16 11½ 2:034 *2.30 (M.Lancaster) CrnllStrkr,ElMgnfcA,FrnkAn 72-0
8-16 LB⅝ 3600 ft 15000 clm cd mi 3031:01 1:32 2:024 2 1 1 1 2½ 41¾ 2:031 *1.80 (J.Scorsone) LmsLrrn,TyrlnDrm,BllyBaker 68-0
8- 9 LB⅝ 3400 ft 12500 clm cd mi 29 1:0111:3132:014 2 1 1 1 11½ 11½ 2:014 *.80 (J.Scorsone) CrnStrkr,EgypTrs,GameYank 76-0
7-26 LB⅝ 3000 gd 10000 clm cd mi 2931:0121:3212:03 7 1 1 1 12 14 2:03 3.70 (J.Scorsone) CrnllStrkr,ShrBlck,RylScptr 76-0
7-15 LB⅝ 3400 gd 12500 clm cd mi 29 1:00 1:3032:01 8 1 2 4 52¾ 58¾ 2:024 3.80 (J.Scorsone) LrnLrrne,LncrMnbr,TypnTm 74-0

6-1 — **4** — 20000 Green

JOEL GEORGE b g, 5, by Columbia George—Jovial Wick by Gene Abbe
Ronald S. Worth, Freehold, N.J.
Trainer-R. Worth
LB(⅝)2:03 1979 23 1 1 2 7,645
$52,019 — 4, 1:591 (1) Driver-JAMES DOHERTY, 9-27-40 (155) RED-WHITE-GREEN
Sacr(1)1:591 1978 27 3 3 5 21,268

9-22 LB⅝ 4200 sy 20000 clm cd mi 3031:0121:3122:022 6 6 6x 7 615½615½ 2:052 12.30 (M.Maker) Staveley,CrnlStrkr,JoeAllnN 60-0
9-12 LB⅝ 4000 ft 79nw9000 cd mi 2841:0111:3042:004 2 1 1 2 33 45¾ 2:02 6.90 (M.Lancaster) AftCrpr,VlntLdr,TheGrtAndy 64-0
9- 5 LB⅝ 3000 sy 79nw6000 cd mi 2921:0011:3212:03 4 1° 1 1 11½ 1nk 2:03 2.50 (M.Maker) JoelGeorge HndYnk,TyrlnDrm 75-0
8-30 LB⅝ 3000 ft 79nw6000 cd mi 3011:0111:3142:024 7i 5 5 5 54 32½ 2:031 10.50 (C.Manzi) HoltLbll,GldnArwy,JoelGeor 78-0
8-23 LB⅝ 3000 ft 79nw6000 cd mi 2941:0121:31 2:01 4 6 6 7 74½ 84 2:014 18.60 (C.Manzi) ArmRvn,FlyFlyMnstrl,SubOz 71-0
8-16 LB⅝ ft Qua mi 3141:0321:3512:063 3 1 1 1 13 110½ 2:063 N.B. (C.Manzi) JoelGeo,ArmbUte,DrZweig 67-0
6-12 M1 11400 ft 20000 clm mi 29 :5831:29 1:59 7 8 7 7 86¾ 86 2:001 9.90 (C.Manzi) SunTrDean,EvilDuke,EddLnda 66-0

6-1 — **5** — 20000 Black

JESTER J br h, 6, by Harold J.—Frosty Leaf by Dale Frost
Don Friedman & Allen Karr, Brooklyn & Crangeburg, N.Y.
Trainer-J. Bernstein
M(1)2:012 1979 21 2 2 1 11,076
$48,068 — 4, 2:004 (⅝) Driver-JAMES BERNSTEIN, 11-10-46 (138) BLACK-RED-WHITE
RR2:03 1978 29 3 2 6 27,450

9-23 LB⅝ 4200 ft 20000 clm cd mi 2921:01 1:3032:003 6 7 6 4 44½ 43½ 2:011 30.60 (J.Bernstein) SingleLife, Riptorn, HotPipes 60-0
9-15 LB⅝ 4400 ft 20000 clm cd mi 292 :5911:2932:002 2 4 4 4° 52¾ 43¾ 2:011 17.60 (J.Bernstein) Lavanto, SingleLife, RivalBoy 65-0
9- 9 MR★ 2200 ft C1-C2 hcp mi 2911:00 1:32 2:033 4 6 4 1° 13 14 2:033 *1.60 (J.RiccoJr) JesterJ,FrmlExpr,FlyFSmmy 63-0
8-31 MR 2200 ft C1 mi 2921:0011:3212:034 3 4 3° 1° 12½ 2¾ 2:04 4.30 (J.RiccoJr) Vlntlny,JstrJ.,Supplement 67-0
8-26 MR★ 2800 ft B3-C1 hcp mi 3031:0231:3322:041 3 4 4 7 75 72 2:043 9.60 (R.Camper) PnsvStar,ValliA,BonnieJohn 77-0
8-19 MR★ 2200 ft C1 mi 2931:01 1:3142:031 2 4 4° 4° 52½ 52¾ 2:034 5.30 (R.Camper) TrixMir,ValliA,MikeSuccess 71-0
8-12 MR★ 2800 sy B3-C1 hcp mi 3221:0411:3542:074 2 4 5 5° 57 211 2:10 4.90 (R.Camper) BonnieJhn,JstrJ.,LeadFree 53-0

8-1 — **6** — 20000 Yellow

NANDINA WARD ro g, 5, by Frosty Dream—Wise Betty by Wise Hanover
Del Cote & Henry Faragalli, Jr., N.J. & Pa.
Trainer-D. Cote
LB(⅝)1:594 1979 23 4 3 5 18,665
$21,797 — 3, 2:00 (⅝) Driver-DEL COTE, 12-12-36 (165) WHITE-RED
LB(⅝)2:014 1978 22 3 3 2 9,849

9-23 LB⅝ 3800 ft 17500 clm cd mi 284 :5941:30 1:594 6 6° 8 6° 63¾ 58¾ 2:013 8.30 (D.Cote) PaulaClip,SddnThndr,BrnBrat 61-0
9-16 LB⅝ 4000 ft 17500 clm cd mi 291 :5931:3012:011 4 6 8 8 76 22½ 2:013 9.40 (D.Cote) HiSyks.NndinaWrd,MstrRcky 70-0
9- 8 LB⅝ 4000 ft 17500 clm cd mi 2931:0011:3222:02 3 4x 7 7 714¼7dis 2:083 4.10 (D.Cote) BrolgaBoy,HiSykes.WinsmChf 67-0
9- 1 LB⅝ 4000 ft 17500 clm cd mi 2911:0021:3022:012 3 6 7° 7 73½ 34 2:021 7.20 (D.Cote) Urok,J.M.Cal,NandinaWard 72-0
8-26 LB⅝ 4400 ft 20000 clm cd mi 30 1:0041:3012:011 2 4 4° 4° 32¾ 76 2:022 7.10 (D.Cote) Lavanto RinkyDink.RivalBoy 76-0
8-18 LB⅝ 4000 sy 17500 clm cd mi 2921:0131:3112:024 4 1° 1 1 1hd 2¾ 2:03 4.90 (D.Cote) BrnsBrt,NndnaWrd,EgmtAlr 64-0
8- 9 LB⅝ 4000 ft 17500 clm cd mi 2931:00 1:30 2:013 7 6 6° 6°°65¾ 34½ 2:022 40.80 (D.Cote) JMCal,EgmontAir,NndnaWrd 74-0

8-1 — **7** — 20000 Pink

FULLA CAPTAIN br g, 5, by Fulla Napoleon—Lady Diamond by Captain Eddie
Emanuel Greenbaum, Wenonah, N.J.
Trainer-M. Schwartz
LB(⅝)2:011 1979 18 2 1 3 8,085
$37,326 — 4, 2:00 (1) Driver-MARK SCHWARTZ, 2-10-53 (155) BLUE-WHITE-GOLD
M(1)2:00 1978 21 1 6 1 21,770

9-25 LB⅝ 3100 ft 79nw9000 cd mi 2941:0221:3242:022 7 7 7 7 77 65¼ 2:032 5.30 (M.Schwartz) KeynteHn StTPrt.ChrtrGPny 64-0
9-14 LB⅝ 4000 sy 79nw9000 cd mi 2941:0031:3112:023 4 7 7° 5° 55½ 23¾ 2:032 4.30 (M.Schwartz) DwyerLb.FullaCaptn,METime 70-0
9- 6 LB⅝ 3000 ft 79nw6000 cd mi 2931:0021:3022:011 6 7 5° 4 42½ 15 2:011 5.50 (M.Schwartz) FllaCptn.BrwdReese.PrunoHn 78-0
8-31 LB⅝ 3000 ft 79nw6000 cd mi 3031:0231:3212:021 8 7 7 6 63¼ 42¼ 2:023 44.10 (W.Hamming) WorAChnc,AED,ShiawayPch 70-0
8-24 LB⅝ 3000 ft 79nw6000 cd mi 2921:0041:3012:003 6 8 8 7° 812 58½ 2:021 6.80 (M.Schwartz) BrnMsn,BrwdRs.WrthAChnc 73-0
8-16 LB⅝ 3000 ft 79nw6000 cd mi 30 1:0111:3042:01 1 3 4 3° 3ix3 7disP6 2:074 5.70 (M.Schwartz) SnLrdElgy,Crmnl BrnsMnslon 65-0
8-10 LB⅝ 3000 ft 79nw6000 cd mi 2931:0121:3112:02 6 7 8° 6°°73¼ 41¼ 2:021 7.60 (M.Schwartz) SpkdBoots,HoltLbl,ACsBrucie 75-0

No. 6—MIGHTY SMOOTH—Scratched

TRACKMAN: 3—1—2

HOLD ALL TICKETS UNTIL RESULT IS DECLARED OFFICIAL

The First Race

This involves animals entered to be claimed for prices ranging between $10,000 and $15,000. We eliminate Salems Misty (unimpressive qualifier); James Myron (youngster paced bravely on sloppy track last time, but off-track form will not help us tonight, and his September 12 effort was unpromising); Nevele Prize (no energy).

Wimbleton	1:01:1 (11)	2:05:1 (7) = 18
The Very Best	1:00:3 (14)	2:03:4 (14) = 28
Beanda	:59:2 (20)	2:02:3 (20) = 40
Travis Lobell	1:01 (12)	2:03:3 (15) = 27
Ozzie Bluegrass	:59:2 (20)	2:03:3 (15) = 35

Wimbleton spent the first three quarters on the outside, earning 15 points, plus 2 for post position, totaling 35.

The Very Best gets 2 for the stretch gain, 15 for the extra-hard work on the outside, 5 as a beaten favorite, and 5 for Marvin Maker, ending with 55.

Beanda raced in the slop last time. We rate his race of September 13, when the track was slightly off but the times were representative for this class of animal. The gelding gets 5 for roughing it, 1 for post position and a final 46.

Travis Lobell's local race of September 14 earns 1 for the stretch gain, 10 for the outside effort and 5 for Donald Dancer, who subs for Walter Laudien, less 3 for the poor post. The final figure is 40.

Ozzie Bluegrass raced behind Beanda on September 13 and will not earn enough credits to compensate for this outside post.

The Very Best deserved to be the even-money favorite but only beat Beanda (3.20 to 1) by a mere neck, paying $4. James Myron (20 to 1) was third and Travis Lobell (6 to 1) fourth.

The Second Race

Two-year-olds are eligible for this, but only three-and four-year-olds have turned up. The last fast-track outing of Trojan Lobell was at Liberty Bell's sister raceway, Brandywine. The gelding produced figures on that occasion which no other horse in this field has come close to matching. Having already raced on this oval. Trojan should be ready tonight. To rate other horses would be a waste of effort.

And so it went. Trojan Lobell led from wire to wire, paying a nifty $5.80. For some reason beyond my comprehension, the favorite at 1.70 to 1 was Georgia Tech, who finished a distant last.

Incidentally, Brandywine times are equivalent to Liberty Bell times. The USTA tabulation printed in raceway programs rates the two tracks at identical speed.

The Third Race

Eric Time and Rossi Collins have been away too long. J. D.'s Kelly is a newcomer. Romanov Hanover is another absentee. Bret Conquered showed no particular sting on September 16. Bev's Flying Boy is a breaker. Valli A has not been here before. Holt Lobell has not shown the speed needed to race from post 8. An unplayable race. We have eliminated the entire field!

Favored as the least unattractive of a dubious lot, J. D.'s Kelly, the Massachusetts shipper, led all the way, beat Bret Conquered by two lengths and paid $4.60.

The Fourth Race

This is for pacers that have won at least $15,000 this year but have not been included on the Liberty Bell racing secretary's preferred list of the best horses on the grounds.

Eliminations: Jolly Judge (away too long); Traffic Fury (not from this post after those last two performances).

Red Fever	1:00:1 (14)	2:01:1 (18) = 32
Camden Antonio	1:00 (15)	2:01:2 (17) = 32
E D Bret	1:00:1 (14)	2:01:2 (17) = 31
Move Feet Move	1:00:2 (13)	2:03:1 (8) = 21
Showdown Sugar	1:01:1 (9)	2:00:4 (20) = 29
Ralute	1:01:2 (8)	2:02:4 (10) = 18

Red Fever picks up 5 for being parked and 2 for the improved post position. The final rating is 39.

Camden Antonio was so badly interfered with during the first quarter-mile on September 22 that he never got back into the race. We use his September 16 outing, in which he loses 5 for the rise in class, but gains it right back for the good stretch gain, plus 15 for roughing it—a rating of 47.

E D Bret gets 1 point for the little gain in the stretch and 5 for being parked plus 2 for the better post: 39.

We use Move Feet Move's September 15 race on a dry track, which was in essentially the same class as tonight's. He gets 15 for struggling gamely on the outside plus 2 for post position. A final rating of 38.

Showdown Sugar steps up in class, which costs him 5. His outer post subtracts 2 more. But he gets 10 for roughing it and 5 for Jim Shafer. Final rating is 37.

Ralute was in the same September 22 scrimmage as Camden Antonio, suffering interference during the first quarter. However, he recovered and finished the mile in one piece. I finally decided to rate him off that race rather than his vastly superior effort of September 15, reasoning that his mediocre figures of September 22 might be due more to the rigors of his three previous races than to the interference he encountered. At any rate, he gets 10 for the interference and the parked-out symbol, minus 2 for post position, plus 5 for Cat Manzi, ending with 31. If we had rated the previous race, it would have added to a 52, making him the selection.

He finished fourth at 8 to 1, and our selection, Camden Antonio (4 to 1), finished sixth. The winner was Showdown Sugar, the favorite, who paid $6.60. E D Bret (8 to 1) was second. Showdown Sugar would have been the choice of most handicapping procedures that ignore half-mile time, concentrating on final time and suitable modifications thereof. After playing around with all the handicapping examples in this book, and experimenting for a few nights at the local raceway, the reader will achieve independent conclusions as to the merits of pace handicapping.

The Fifth Race

This is for pacers that either have not won $12,000 this year or have won less than $17,500 without winning a race in their last five starts. The contention seems to be among the horses with the three inside post positions, although, as we shall see, a really sharp operator might find reason to rate Merchant Blue Chip.

Camden Christian	1:00:1 (17)	2:01 (19) = 36
Valient Leader	1:01:1 (12)	2:00:4 (20) = 32
Elsie Butler	:59:3 (20)	2:01:3 (16) = 36

Camden Christian drops in class, earning 5, and gets 5 more for roughing it. The rating is 46.

Valient Leader's last race was in slop, but his effort of September 1∠ earns 3 for stretch gain, 10 for roughing it and 2 for post position, less 5 for the switch from a 10-point driver to a 5-point one. Final rating is 42.

Elsie Butler gets 1 for a stretch gain, 5 for parking out and 2 for post position: 44.

The top-rated Camden Christian went off at a whopping 13 to 1 and lost by half a length to the 12 to 1 Merchant Blue Chip. The place price was a pleasant $10.60. Valient Leader was the even-money favorite and finished third, with Elsie Butler sixth at 5 to 1. A supercareful handicapper might have noticed that Merchant Blue Chip was to be driven by its regular pilot and part owner, the highly capable Jim Doherty, who customarily wins 15 percent of his starts, and would earn the animal an extra 5 points. Such a handicapper might well have decided that the three-year-old colt's romp along the fence on September 23 was the trainer's final exercise of the animal before returning it to the hard-knocking Doherty. On that theory, the previous, more vigorous effort would have been the one to rate, and it would have made Merchant Blue Chip an equal choice with Camden Christian. I acknowledge without embarrassment that none of this occurred to me until the race was over. As they say, hindsight always provides 20/20 vision.

The Sixth Race

Dreamy Isle and South Norwalk do not figure here, and Mr Pockets is scratched.

Meadow Butler	:59:4 (20)	2:01:1 (13)	= 33
Goodbye Almahurst	1:01:2 (12)	2:01 (14)	= 26
Kansas Hanover	:59:4 (20)	1:59:4 (20)	= 40
Dennis Hanover	1:00:1 (18)	1:59:4 (20)	= 38
Skirt Waltz	1:01:2 (12)	2:00:4 (15)	= 27

Meadow Butler gets 10 for the effort on the outside, plus 1 for post position—a total of 44.

Goodbye Almahurst recovered from early interference plus a quarter-mile of pacing outside without cover and scored a smashing victory, which gets him 2 points for the stretch gain, 10 for the interference and parked-out symbol, and 5 for Mark Lancaster. His rating is 43.

Kansas Hanover moves up from non-winners fo $15,000 to winners thereof, losing 5, but gets it back for the stretch gain, plus 5 for roughing it, 1 for post position and 5 for Eddie Davis. Final: 51.

Dennis Hanover seems to have been on the fence all the way but had no picnic, shuffling back and forth between the lead and second place but finally drawing off in the stretch. Gets 4 for the stretch gain: a total of 42.

Skirt Waltz raced in the slop last time, but did nicely the time before in an invitational race against members of her own age group. She gets 5 for dropping somewhat in class, 10 for roughing it and 5 for Marvin Maker, less 1 for post position. Rating is 46.

Goodbye Almahurst again paced with great power, winning as 3 to 2 favorite over Dennis Hanover (6 to 1). Kansas Hanover was third at 3.70 to 1, with Meadow Butler fourth at 2.80 to 1.

The Seventh Race

The reader may be able to share the recognition that this race, like occasional others, requires no paper work. A brief glance shows that nothing in the field can match Sun Lord's Elegy in terms of half-mile and final times, plus credit for gaining in the stretch, roughing it and having a 5-point driver. Sunderchief's basic figures for his effort of September 9 are slightly superior to those of the other horse, but he loses 5 points for switching from his regular driver, Joe Scorsone, the only 10-point driver with whom we deal on this program. Do the figures for yourself and you'll see that the first impression is accurate. Sun Lord's Elegy won and paid $5.

The Eighth Race

Here again, the winner is evident to anyone who simply checks the figures. Fortune Moy's winning time of 1:59:2 at Foxboro is the equal of a flat 1:59 at Liberty Bell (as shown by the USTA comparative speed tabulation published in the program). The only animal in the field that might come close is Justa Tinker, whose last effort was anything but energetic. Fortune Moy won, paying $3.40. Justa Tinker was second, a 2.80 to 1 second favorite. It may be argued with complete logic that handicappers should not take chances on shippers from other tracks. The argument applies with most force to horses of the lower ranks. But at the preferred level and above, animals ship quite well, reproducing their recent form despite the excitements of travel and the uncertainties of new surroundings.

The Ninth Race

Here's another conditioned affair for winners of $15,000 who are not on the local preferred list. Thelmas Dream is scratched. Young Mr. Pockets and Maximus Hanover seem off form. After an undemanding qualifier on September 18, Cyclone Prince raced against the fence on September 22. Whether he is ready to exert himself or not, we have no recent figures to go on; although that powerful win in 1:56 at The Meadowlands on August 3 identifies him as at least potentially the best in this field. Vic Quinton also raced along the wood last out, finishing close enough to justify use of his previous race.

Victor Vic	:59:4 (19)	2:03:2 (12) = 31
Robbie R. D.	:59:3 (20)	2:00:4 (20) = 40
H H Freehold	1:01:1 (12)	2:02:1 (13) = 25
Vic Quinton	1:00:2 (16)	2:02 (14) = 30

Victor Vic adds 10 for roughing it, for a total of 41. Robbie R. D. drops 5 for the class boost, but picks up 10 for roughing it and 1 for post position. Final rating is 46.

H H Freehold gets 10 for the half-mile of outside exertion, for a final 35. And Vic Quinton's performance of September 15 costs 5 for class but supplies 1 for the stretch gain and 15 for the three quarters on the outside. Final rating is 41, not enough of an edge to justify support in post position 8.

The betting favorite at 2.10 to 1 was Maximus Hanover, who finished sixth. Robbie R. D. was fourth at 3.90 to 1. Cyclone Prince, the second favorite, won, paying $7. Vic Quinton, at 14.70 to 1, finished second, paying $9.60 to place.

The Tenth Race

Only two contenders in this field of claimers. We can eliminate Joe Allen N for lack of punch, Leisa May because of the probable aftereffects of her September 15 ordeal, Joel George for poor form, Jester J likewise and Fulla Captain also. We use Cornell Streaker's fast-track effort of August 31.

Cornell Streaker	1:00:3 (16)	2:00:4 (20) = 36
Nandina Ward	:59:4 (20)	2:01:3 (16) = 36

Cornell Streaker loses 5 for the rise in class, but recovers it for the gain in the stretch, adds 3 for post position and 5 for Eddie Davis, ending with 44.

Nandina Ward loses 5 for moving up in class, but gets 10 for roughing it on the outside. Final is 41.

The favored Cornell Streaker won it, paying $4.20. Second was Nandina Ward, who went off at an astonishing 13 to 1 and paid $7.20 to place. Joe Allen N was third.

We found nine races playable, but might have been well advised to skip the ninth race, in which we probably should have been too frightened of Cyclone Prince to bet against him, although not willing to bet on him. In any event, we did not do badly. Our winners were The Very Best ($4), Trojan Lobell ($5.80), Sun Lord's Elegy ($5), Fortune Moy ($3.40) and Cornell Streaker ($4.20). We also were in the way of a couple of nice place prices.

17

THE MEADOWLANDS

July 25, 1979

A NICE 80 DEGREES and a fast track. A typical crowd of almost 16,000 will wager more than $1.8 million.

The list of leading drivers includes some of the continent's very best. Furthermore, tonight's program is distinguished by the presence of several immortals, attracted by a rich series of Grand Circuit races for high-class two-year-olds. Aside from those all-time greats, whose races on this program are handicappable without recourse to our rating procedure, we shall have occasion to recognize the special powers of John Campbell and Shelly Goudreau, who win 20 percent of their starts and are entitled to 10 extra points in the handicapping. The following have been winning at least 15 percent during the 266 days of this meeting, and get 5 points for their horses: Carmen Alessi, Mark Lancaster, Cat Manzi and Jack Parker, Jr. As happens at any raceway, the leading dash winners here have not all been maintaining high averages. For example, Jim Doherty, one of North America's leaders in victories and purse earnings throughout 1979, has won only 12.5 percent of his starts at this meeting.

Here is a reasonably accurate table of post-position values:

Post:	1	2	3	4	5	6	7	8	9	10
Rating:	7	6	6	6	6	5	4	4	3	3

1979 OFFICIAL PROGRAM /$1

THE MEADOWLANDS
East Rutherford, N.J.

(1) PACE—1 MILE

Warming-Up Saddle Cloth
RED

PURSE $8,000

1st Half of Daily Double

CLAIMING PRICE $15,000
(Four-Year-Old Stallions & Geldings Granted 25% Allowance)

ASK FOR HORSE BY PROGRAM NUMBER

9-2 | **1** | 18750 Red

HALS STAR — b g. 4, by Hal Brooks—Marcellus Gal by Marcellus — Trainer-C. Alessi
Roy D. Markham, Chicago, Ill. — BmlP(5/8)2:072 1979 6 1 1 0 1,752
$00 — Driver-CARMEN ALESSI, 5-26-38 (138) GOLD-WHITE-BLUE — 1978 0 0 0 0
7- 7 M1 ft Qua mi 29 1:004 1:323 2:003 7 2 2 2° 1nk 35 2:013 N.B. (C.Alessi) GeminiBoyA,LveGem,HalsStr 71-0
5-12 M1 ft T-P Qua mi 301 1:013 1:32 2:013 4 2 2 2 3½ 3¼ 2:022 N.B. (C.Alessi) Goyo,JesseSam,HalsStar 56-0
4-21 BmlP5/8 3200 ft nw2 cd mi 321 1:034 1:353 2:063 2x 9 9 9 9dis 9dis 2.10 (W.Temple) TrtwdParade,ScootrKey,HldOnHrry
4-13 BmlP5/8 4400 ft nw3 cd mi 311 1:023 1:322 2:032 7 5° 2° 2° 34 48½ 2:051 *2.80 (W.Temple) BlackSarah,KaysCanny,ColonelClay
3-30 BmlP5/8 3200 gd nw2 cd mi 314 1:04 1:361 2:093 6x 7° 2° 1 2xnk 925 2:143 *.90 (W.Temple) MntnKngdm,FlyJrry,BaronsPalace
3-16 BmlP5/8 2800 ft nw2 cd mi 322 1:06 1:374 2:09 2 x7x 7 7 7dis 7dis *.60 (W.Temple) Swoop,MajorPeak,CoffeeSkipper

---

5-1 | **2** | 15000 Blue

BARON PARKER — b g. 5, by Baron Hanover—Pandora Parker by Parker Byrd — St.-R. Samson—Tr.-V. Staker
David Silverman & Larry Pollock Stables, Que. — M(1)2:014 1979 25 1 7 2 24,955
$44,938 — 3, T-1:583 (1) Driver-ROBERT SAMSON, 10-7-49 (140) WHITE-BLACK — NE(5/8)1:593 1978 23 4 6 1 11,824
7-17 M1 8500 sy 17500 clm mi 302 1:004 1:312 2:014 8 10 9° 7° 66 76 2:03 37.00 (R.Samson) GryWrthy,NvlGoose,ShyBksht 78-2
7-10 M1 8500 ft 17500 clm mi 302 :592 1:294 1:594 6 7 8 9 54¾ 77 2:011 12.30 (R.Samson) DsrtStp,NvleGoose,JhnQArab 68-0
7- 3 M1 8500 ft 17500 clm mi 283 :582 1:293 1:584 10 10 8° 8° 97¾ 96½ 2:00 37.20 (R.Samson) FrostyPenn,PropWash,Eisiam 75-0
6-20 M1 8500 ft 17500 clm mi 291 1:00 1:303 2:00 8 10 9 8 57 54½ 2:004 20.30 (R.Samson) CrdnlChfA,TomHeel,LtnKngt 75-0
6- 7 M1 8500 ft 17500 clm mi 301 1:01 1:322 2:012 3 4 4 6 42¼ 2nk 2:012 10.90 (R.Samson) WknGlnfrn,BrnPrkr,GdBtrBst 71-0
5-30 M1 9500 ft 17500 clm mi 281 :582 1:30 1:593 5 2 2 5 66 57¼ 2:01 4.50 (R.Samson) GnrlMjr,SouthHost,PropWash 71-0

7-2 | **3** | 15000 White

ARMBRO OCTANE — b g, 8, by Adios Vic—Armbro Electra by Rodney — Trainer-R. Chick
Leisure Stable, Inc., Hazlet, N.J. — M(1)2:004 1979 12 1 1 1 8,929
$143,510 — 7, 1:564 (1) Driver-JAMES DOHERTY, 9-27-40 (161) RED-WHITE-GREEN — M(1)1:564 1978 25 8 4 0 63,030
7- 4 M1 8500 sl 17500 clm mi 292 1:00 1:304 2:001 10 10 9 9 76½ 65 2:011 7.50 (Ja.Doherty) Wkakno,SkyDplmt,GdBttrBst 57-
6-21 M1 9500 ft 20000 clm mi 304 1:001 1:302 2:003 1 3 3 2° 2¾ 3½ 2:004 *1.30 (Ja.Doherty) BangrLb,LocalSctt,ArmOctne 71-0
6-13 M1 8500 ft 17500 clm mi 281 :584 1:302 1:592 9 10 10 9° 5¾ 22 1:594 4.30 (Ja.Doherty) DesertStp,ArmOctne,KeyPnzr 69-0
6- 4 M1 9600 ft 15000z clm mi 284 1:002 1:304 2:001 7 8 7°i9° 86¼ 87½ 2:013 *2.10 (T.Wing) Lavanto,Phew,SamNover 64-0
5-29 M1 11400 sl 20000 clm mi 293 1:002 1:30 2:012 4 6° 4° 3°x814 820 2:052 3.80 (T.Morgan) ArionLb,TarBoyAds,FrskRma 61-
5-21 M1 9600 ft 15000 clm cd mi 292 1:004 1:312 2:004 4 6 6 6° 54¼ 13 2:004 *3.50 (T.Wing) ArmOctne,Lavnto,MstrWnstn 66-0

3-1 | **4** | 15000 Green

LOPEZ CHARGE — b g, 6, by Lopez Hanover—Fleck by First Charge — St.-C. Manzi—Tr.-P. Fortin
College Point Stable & Double C Stable, N.Y. — M(1)1:594 1979 22 2 0 2 14,000
$5,645 — 5, 2:023 (5/8) Driver-CATELLO MANZI, 6-27-50 (164) WHITE-BLUE — LB(5/8)2:023 1978 16 3 3 2 5,580
7-17 M1 8500 sy 17500 clm mi 302 1:004 1:312 2:014 4 3 4 6 55 42¾ 2:022 3.70 (C.Manzi) GryWrthy,NvlGoose,ShyBksht 78-2
7-10 M1 8000 ft 15000 clm mi 30 :59 1:30 1:594 2 1 1 1 12½ 12½ 1:594 *2.00 (C.Manzi) LpzChrge,KeyAtlas,MirClrnce 68-0
7- 3 M1 8500 ft 17500 clm mi 283 :582 1:293 1:584 8 1 2 2 21¾ 63 1:592 20.30 (C.Manzi) FrostyPenn,PropWash,Eisiam 75-0
6-20 M1 8500 ft 17500 clm mi 293 :584 1:291 1:594 1 3 4 2° 41½ 54½ 2:003 4.70 (C.Manzi) GdBttrBst,PrpWsh,WknGlnfn 75-0
6- 7 M1 8500 ft 17500 clm mi 301 1:01 1:322 2:012 7 6 6 5° 53¾ 42¾ 2:02 8.70 (C.Manzi) WknGlnfrn,BrnPrkr,GdBtrBst 71-0
5-30 M1 8000 ft 15000 clm cd mi 291 :593 1:30 2:001 2 2 3 3 31½ 3¾ 2:001 *1.50 (C.Manzi) JCnBmpkn,FrwrdYnk,LpzChrg 71-0

15-1 | **5** | 15000 Black

MT EATON FASHION — b g, 7, by Fashion Tip—Knightime Gale by Reeds Knight — Trainer-N. McClurg
Norman R. McClurg, Toledo, Ohio — M(1)1:583 1979 17 2 0 0 11,860
$29,902 — 6, 2:01 (1) Driver-MICKEY McNICHOL, 9-12-48 (164) BLUE-WHITE-BLACK — M(1)2:01 1978 19 1 1 2 11,420
7-23 M1 8000 ft 15000 clm mi 30 :592 1:294 1:591 1 4 5 5 56 65½ 2:001 47.90 (D.Johnson) JCnBmpkn,GdBttrBst,NchkTr 77-0
7-10 M1 ft T-P Qua mi 293 1:004 1:313 2:012 4 6 6 5° 66¼ 47¼ 2:024 N.B. (D.Johnson) ArmTex,HHBelle,YndRhytGB 78-0
7- 7 M1 ft Qua mi 303 1:014 1:322 2:012 3 5 4° 4° 45¼ 512¾ 2:04 N.B. (D.Johnson) MrkGrrsn,KntrKtie,ThBlzrdA 71-0
7- 3 M1 8000 ft 15000 clm mi 292 :592 1:301 2:002 10x10 10 10 1010½ 1020 2:042 10.80 (Jo.Campbell) NchakoTr,DckChmp,BvsFlyBy 75-0
6-19 M1 8000 ft 15000 clm mi 29 :573 1:28 1:59 10x10 10 10 10dis 10dis 6.60 (L.Williams) GryWrthy,CrcleKim,GmmyHll 73-0
6- 5 M1 8500 gd 17500 clm mi 302 1:002 1:304 1:593 10 10 10 10 106¼ 78 2:011 7.20 (D.Johnson) BigOzzie,DesertStp,BstBzzre 71-1

8-1 | **6** | 15000 Yellow

NICELY NEIL — b g, 5, by Tarport Neil—Jerboa by Rudagar — Trainer-H. Camden
Howard Camden & Frank Collazo, Jr. & Sr., N.J. — Q-M(1)2:033 1979 6 0 1 0 2,538
$1,169 — 2, 2:093 Driver-JOHN CAMPBELL, 4-8-55 (156) WHITE-MAROON — 1978 2 0 0 1 374
7-17 M1 9000 sy 12500 clm mi 29 :592 1:31 2:012 5 6° 7° 5° 32¼ 2ns 2:012 11.40 (Jo.Campbell) MgtyMjr,NclyNeil,DwnsRoad 78-1
7-10 M1 ft Qua mi 304 1:001 1:303 2:003 4 2 3 2° 31½ 48½ 2:021 N.B. (F.CollazoJr) LoveGem,SteveRyan,Puissant 78-0
7- 3 M1 ft Qua mi 294 1:024 1:34 2:033 5x 6 6 5° 41 12½ 2:033 N.B. (F.CollazoJr) NclyNeil,TinasLee,GminiBoyA 74-0
6-27 M1 9600 ft 15000 clm cd mi 29 :58 1:28 1:591 2 2° 3 3° 9¾ 924½ 2:04 9.50 (J.KingJr) Waikakano,MtyMjr,PrncLrnN 67-0
6-11 M1 9600 gd 15000 clm mi 29 1:00 1:31 2:021 9 9 9 8 76¼ 810½ 2:041 20.90 (H.Camden) MtyTom,PrncLrnN,AdvncCpy 59-2
6- 5 M1 ft Qua (h-d) mi 293 :593 1:294 2:001 4 6 6 6 42¾ 21½ 2:002 N.B. (F.CollazoJr) FllRspct,NclyNeil,HckrySprte 77-0

30-1 | **7** | 15000 Pink

PROJECTS REDDY — b g, 8, by Project Apollo—Redish Brown by Widower Creed — Trainer-A. Boccio
Double EE Stables, Hackensack, N.J. — PPk(5/8)2:01 1979 18 2 3 0 6,600
$34,100 — 7, 2:00 (5/8) Driver-AL BOCCIO, 11-29-39 (210) BROWN-GOLD — Mea(5/8)2:00 1978 31 5 4 4 12,475
7-18 M1 10800 gd nw5000 cd mi 303 1:003 1:303 2:00 10 9 9 7 85 89¼ 2:014 84.70 (A.Boccio) OsbShwOff,RdyStGo,CrytslRm 69-1
6-20 M1 8000 ft 15000 clm mi 31 1:01 1:32 2:012 8 9 8 8 87½ 87½ 2:024 66.60 (A.Boccio) TaroHn,FathersImge,FlyDeal 75-0
5-28 M1 10200 ft 17500 clm mi 294 :591 1:30 2:003 8 2° 1x10x1022 10dis 40.10 (A.Boccio) InitialBrgd,EddLnda,SprBuck 74-0
5-22 M1 10800 ft nw5000 cd mi 291 :584 1:293 2:00 9 7 8 9 107½ 96¼ 2:011 53.40 (A.Boccio) DeesKgtdhGldTwnkl,FlyDrmN 67-0
5-15 M1 11400 ft 20000 clm mi 284 :583 1:284 1:591 5 3° 2° 9 1012 914 2:02 49.20 (A.Boccio) EbonyRck,FrstMrk,FlyFlyStr 67-0
5- 8 M1 7500 ft 17500z clm mi 29 :573 1:27 1:591 4 1 2 6 88½ 84½ 2:00 16.20 (B.D.Wallace) FrskyRoma,Critical,RwlngsSt 74-0

20-1 | **8** | 15000 Gray

LAST BUY — br g, 9, by Forward—Wee Doll by U Scott — Trainer-E. Cobb
Gabriel Mastrobuoni, Teresa Van Laar & G. C. O. Stables, N.Y. — Q-M(1)2:014 1979 10 0 0 0 560
$18,066 — 8, 2:032 Driver-EDDIE COBB, 3-1-20 (184) BLUE-WHITE — Fhld2:032 1978 22 2 2 3 6,205
7-10 M1 8000 ft 15000 clm mi 30 :59 1:30 1:594 4 6 7 9 99 710 2:014 12.50 (E.Cobb) LpzChrge,KeyAtlas,MirClrnce 68-0
7- 3 M1 8000 ft 15000 clm mi 292 1:011 1:322 2:01 5 8 8 8 88½ 78 2:023 23.70 (E.Cobb) PrncRbltn,JCnBmpkn,KeyPnzr 75-0
6-26 M1 ft Qua mi 31 1:004 1:311 2:014 2 1 1 1 12 1¾ 2:014 N.B. (E.Cobb) LastBuy,AngryWve,StdyStrkr 78-0
6- 6 M1 8000 ft 15000 clm cd mi 291 :591 1:291 2:004 2 5 2° 5° 912 914 2:033 13.30 (T.Wing) MikeDdly,GryWrthy,RblClrita 69-0
5-30 M1 8000 ft 15000 clm cd mi 291 :593 1:30 2:001 9 10 10 9° 105¼ 87¾ 2:014 64.80 (E.Cobb) JCnBmpkn,FrwrdYnk,LpzChrg 71-0
5-24 M1 8500 sy 17500 clm mi 294 1:00 1:31 1:591 7 8 8 7 810½ 89 2:01 30.00 (E.Cobb) SokysDplomt,ArmTex,Critical 63-0

8-1 | **9** | 15000 Purple

ROBBIE COLLINS — b g, 5, by Lieutenant Gray—Shy Adios by Adios — Trainer-A. Armando
Fred Wernli, Little Falls, N.J. & Charles Tomeo, N.Y. — M(1)2:002 1979 14 2 3 1 18,462
$35,379 — 4, 1:591 (1) Driver-MARK LANCASTER, 9-23-48 (166) BLUE-GOLD — M(1)1:591 1978 22 5 3 1 29,186
7-17 M1 8500 ft 17500 clm mi 29 :581 1:283 1:591 10 10 10 10 76¼ 64¼ 2:00 21.40 (J.ParkerJr) KeyPanzer,JhnQArab,Parling 78-0
7- 3 M1 8500 ft 17500 clm mi 283 :582 1:293 1:584 3 7 5° 4° 75¾ 76 2:00 5.30 (D.Johnson) FrostyPenn,PropWash,Eisiam 75-0
6-19 M1 9600 ft 15000 clm mi 292 1:002 1:304 2:004 9 9 8° 6° 44¼ 13½ 2:004 3.70 (D.Johnson) RbbieClln,RmnvHn,StppnHnry 73-0
6- 4 M1 9600 ft 15000 clm mi 30 :593 1:303 2:004 9 8° 6° 3° 21 43¼ 2:013 3.60 (G.Wright) OverServe,TkeLeave,KeyPanzr 64-0
5-28 M1 9600 ft 15000 clm mi 293 :584 1:284 2:004 3 7 6 4 52¼ 32¼ 2:012 3.80 (D.Johnson) PoseidonA,Phew,RobbieCllns 74-0
5-22 M1 ft Qua mi 303 1:014 1:313 2:001 4 5 5 4° 36 35½ 2:011 N.B. (D.Johnson) PhlThBll,HpyPlyby,RbbieCllns 66-0

10-1 | **10** | 18750 Blue-Red

STEADY SHORE — b g, 4, by Steady Star—Shore Lot by Adios Boy — St.-L. Williams—Tr.-F. Vidler
Stanley Kaufman, Howard Beach, N.Y. — 1979 7 0 0 2 1,661
$5,735 — 3, 2:032 (5/8) Driver-LEW WILLIAMS, 3-1-47 (140) BLUE-GOLD-WHITE — Lau(5/8)2:032 1978 18 4 6 3 5,314
7-20 M1 9000 ft nw5000 cd mi 293 :58 1:281 1:592 6 8 7 5 33½ 51¾ 1:594 13.70 (L.Williams) Hakatoa,KoalaBrvado,SfldCnt 77-0
7- 7 LB5/8 3800 ft 15000 clm mi 302 1:021 1:322 2:03 2 4 5 7 84½ 31 2:031 9.00 (M.Maker) DosteDrum,Shvnde,StdyShre 65-0
7- 1 LB5/8 4500 ft 17500 clm mi 29 :593 1:302 2:011 1 4 4 3° 35½ 68¼ 2:024 14.30 (M.Maker) ChrlieKgt,Jollifictn,CrltnChf 73-0
6-24 Brd5/8 3500 ft nw2500 cd mi 293 1:02 1:313 2:023 3 3 4 4 42¼ 43 2:031 7.40 (W.Ross) AdHoc,ButlerBaron,Evinrudy 64-0
6-16 Brd5/8 3500 ft nw2500 cd mi 293 1:021 1:322 2:022 6 6 6 6 75¾ 52¾ 2:03 6.40 (W.Ross) HerbieC,EmbChck,WgtSprme 80-0
6- 7 Brd5/8 2500 ft nw1500 cd mi 311 1:022 1:324 2:031 9 9 9 8 75 32½ 2:033 41.00 (W.Ross) JillRock,ShwnTmhwk,StdyShr 78-0

SELECTIONS: 4—3—1

C—DENOTES CONVENTIONAL SULKY

② PACE—1 MILE
Warming-Up Saddle Cloth
BLUE

PURSE $11,400

2nd Half of Daily Double
Exacta Wagering This Race

NON-WINNERS OF $5,500 IN LAST 7 STARTS. WINNERS OF A
RACE IN LAST 4 STARTS INELIGIBLE.
NEW JERSEY OWNED OR BRED

ASK FOR HORSE BY PROGRAM NUMBER

10-1

1 — Red

RUSTY DOMINO
b h, 5, by Lyss Hanover—Marisa Domino by Tag Me
Anthony Domino, Tinton Falls, N.J.
Driver-HAROLD KELLY, 5-3-35   (165)   BLUE-GOLD-WHITE
$1,620 — 4, 2:08⁴

Trainer-A. Domino
Fhld2:05² 1979 25 4 5 2 12,698
Fhld2:08⁴ 1978 4 1 1 0   1,620

7-18 M¹	108CO gd nw5000 cd mi 30	31:0031:3032:0	0	9	8	8	9	95¹	79¹	2:014	9.70	(J.ParkerJr)	OsbShwOff,RdyStGo,CrytsIRm 69-1
7-11 M¹	10800 ft nw5C00 cd mi 30²	:5941:3021:593	10	13	10	10	74²	74²	2:003	10.70	(J.ParkerJr)	RealTrsr,ArrvasBd,TpThBttlN 72-0
7- 2 M¹	9000 ft nw5000 cd mi 28²	:5741:2831:583	7	9	8°	6°	33	34¹	1:59³	10.90	(J.ParkerJr)	ClsToYou,SndFIght,RstyDmno 70-0
6-25 M¹	9000 ft nw5000 cd mi 29¹	:5911:2911:594	9	10	10	x9	84¹	55	2:004	29.20	(J.KingJr)	NtveMss,IntnseFIla,ClsToYou 69-0
6-15 M¹	10000 ft nw5500 cd mi 28³	:5741:2811:58	2	3	2	32¹	52¹	2:002	6.40	(S.Goudreau)	PrfctAngle,ScttNpIn,GeoMrvl 80-0
6- 8 M¹	9000 ft nw5500 cd mi 30	21:0011:31 2:00¹	4	1	1	1	1ʰᵈ	56	2:01²	9.80	(Jo.Campbell)	MariaJ,GnghsKhn,DrmIngBtlr 75-0

12-1

2 — Blue

CANOE
b h, 10, by Arrivederci Byrd—Kyak by Greentree Adios
Laura E. DiMambro, Englishtown, N.J.
Driver-JAMES DOHERTY, 9-27-40   (161)   RED-WHITE-GREEN
$149,101 — 8, 1:58² (1)

Trainer-J. DiMambro
M(1)1:591 1979 25 3 3 0 15,264
MR1:59³ 1978 33 4 2 4 21,111

7-18 M¹	10800 gd nw5000 cd mi 30	31:0031:3032:0	2	5	5	6	63¹	67²	2:013	4.20	(Ja.Doherty)	OsbShwOff,RdyStGo,CrytsIRm 69-1
7- 6 M¹	9000 ft nw5000 cd mi 29	31:00 1:2941:583	7	8°	7°	8°°9¹2¹9²0¹	2:023	9.60	(R.Blum)	KeenasVc,AbITsman,GaelcRm 68-0
6-28 M¹	10000 ft nw5500 cd mi 30	:5921:2932:00	6	7	7°	7°	63¹	61¹	2:001	10.90	(R.Blum)	ArmRhytm,GaelcRum,QkTmpr 68-0
6-21 M¹	10000 ft nw5500 cd mi 30	:5841:2741:593	8	7	7	75¹	65¹	2:003	10.20	(C.Manzi)	FutureLbll,KeyPoint,NiftyVic 71-0
6-13 M¹	9000 ft nw5000 cd mi 29	:5941:3042:00	2	3	3	5	43¹	52	2:002	9.50	(J.KingJr)	RedRoger,MiniShotA,KungFu 69-0
6- 7 M¹	16800 ft 30000 clm mi 29³	:5841:2821:574	10	10	10	10	10⁹¹10¹7¹	2:011	52.70	(H.Kelly)	GrssInd,DaveyJck,BerniesSpcl 71-0

3-1

3 — White

BIG GEORGE (J)
br h, 5, by Henry—Bohunk by Eustace Hanover
Anne T. Stevenson, Wilmington, Del.
Driver-PRESTON BURRIS, JR., 9-20-32   (165)   WHITE-BLUE-GOLD
$48,625 — 3, 2:00³ (1)

Trainer-P. Burris, Jr.
LB(⅝)2:00⁴ 1979 18 1 3 5 16,545
RR2:02³ 1978 24 3 4 7 28,540

7-16 M¹	9000 ft nw5000 cd mi 29	2:5311:2741:572	5	7	7	6	57	45¹	1:58²	9.50	(P.BurrisJr)	InnrCrcle,AdmrILb,TriosDsgn 74-0
7- 9 M¹	11000 ft nw7000 cd mi 28	3:5821:2741:583	1	3	3°	63¹	53¹	1:59	4.00	(P.BurrisJr)	DmanteHn,GaySchnll,TpalaHn 71-0
6-17 LB⁵	5000 ft nw12500 cd mi 29	31:0031:2931:582	1	3	4	42¹	41¹	1:58³	6.10	(P.BurrisJr)	QckBrry,HHFreehld,ThndrBrt 75-0
6-10 LB⁵	6500 ft w15001 cd mi 29²	:5921:3021:593	4	6	6°	5²	26	2:004	*1.90	(P.BurrisJr)	AdmrILb,BigGeo,RippingOak 69-0
6- 3 LB⁵	6500 sy w15001 cd mi 29¹	:5911:2931:594	6	8	4°	62¹	53¹	2:002	10.20	(P.BurrisJr)	Americus,VictorVic,HHFrhld 62-0
5-27 LB⁵	6500 ft w15001 cd mi 29³	:5841:2821:573	5	5	4°	43¹	35¹	1:592	5.40	(P.BurrisJr)	ArmTurk,ThndrBret,BigGeo 65-0

9-2

4 — Green

GEORGANA ARDEN
b m, 4, by Columbia George—Mim Arden by Thorpe Hanover
Jaisan Inc. & Ted Wing Stable, Inc., Secaucus & Paramus
Driver-TED WING, 7-30-48   (144)   GREEN-WHITE-RED
$22,491 — 3, 2:01⁴ (⅝)

St.-T. Wing—Tr.-C. Guidetti
Q-LB(⅝)2:02² 1979 14 1 0 3 14,630
LB(⅝)2:01⁴ 1978 22 8 5 2 22,491

7-19 LB⁵	ft Qua mi 30	11:0131:33 2:02²	5	3	3	1°	12¹	1⁹	2:022	N.B.	(T.Wing)	GeoArdn,RumGld,AdlbrtsSon 78-0
5- 4 M¹	12000 ft 30000 clm mi 28	41:0021:3011:584	10	5	3°	2°°	44	71⁰¹	2:004	17.40	(T.Wing)	ArmTwny,EvsWtch,ShyBksht 59-0
4-19 M¹	8C00 ft nw5500 cd mi 30	31:0031:3022:002	5	6	7°	7°	54¹	33¹	2:01	*.80	(T.Wing)	CycInPrnce,HHBelle,GeoArdn 55-0
4-13 M¹	12000 ft 30000 clm mi 30	1:3012:002	2	5	6	7	75¹	53¹	2:004	3.30	(T.Wing)	BwtchDndy,SkyPgss,GeoArdn 44-0
4- 6 M¹	13000 ft 35000 clm mi 29	41:0041:32 2:003	8	9	8°	6°	63	73¹	2:012	9.70	(T.Wing)	ArmTwny,StngtCnt,ClssTchN 39-2
3-30 M¹	ft 40000 clm mi 29⁴	1:0021:3112:001	1	1	1¹	75¹	59¹	1:591	4.20	(T.Wing)	RealTrsr,TnysWmpm,LrdLbN 61-0

6-1

5 — Black

MERLIN BYRD
b g, 8, by Express Byrd—Merlyn Joy by Cliff Alto
Eagle Three Stable, Inc., Fort Lee, N.J.
Driver-CATELLO MANZI, 6-27-50   (164)   WHITE-BLUE
$35,117 — 7, 2:00³

Trainer-M. Santa Maria
M(1)1:592 1979 20 1 1 3 10,770
RR2:003 1978 32 6 4 5 21,960

7-18 M¹	10800 gd nw5000 cd mi 30	31:0031:3032:00	7	1	2	3°	91¹²	2:022	7.60	(C.Manzi)	OsbShwOff,RdyStGo,CrytsIRm 69-1
7-10 M¹	9000 ft nw5000 cd mi 29	3:5831:28 1:581	7	1	4	5	77	89²	2:001	5.10	(C.Manzi)	Persuadable,RedFvr,DrJacoby 68-0
7- 3 M¹	ft Qua mi 29¹	1:32¹2:01	1	5	3	5	4	35¹	2:014	N.B.	(C.Manzi)	BhmsHrn,Dromicia,MrInByrd 74-0
6-28 M¹	16800 ft 30000 clm mi 28³	:57 1:2641:562	3	2°	3	7	91⁹	911³	2:03¹	56.20	(C.Manzi)	SlvrWarr,FlySprks,EgtFrAce 68-0
6-15 M¹	18000 ft 35000 clm mi 28²	:5831:2941:591	3	6	7	8	97	97¹	2:004	26.00	(Ja.Doherty)	GrssInd,StrtchBret,JwllsDrm 80-0
6- 8 M¹	15000 ft 40000 clm mi 28⁴	:5831:2731:574	5	5	4	43¹	64¹	1:583	24.90	(Ja.Doherty)	JMSam,FrostyZip,CortIndHn 73-0

4-1

6 — Yellow

PEANUT GALLERY
br h, 4, by Meadow Skipper—Drama Girl by Lehigh Hanover
Richard E. & Patricia Bonvie, Englishtown, N.J.
Driver-MICKEY McNICHOL, 9-12-48   (164)   BLUE-WHITE-BLACK
$21,930 — 3, 1:58² (1)

Trainer-M. McNichol
M(1)1:593 1979 19 1 3 2 14,690
M(1)1:582 1978 15 3 2 3 21,930

7-12 M¹	13000 ft nw8000 cd mi 29	:5831:2741:582	1x10	10	10	10ᵈⁱˢ10ᵈⁱˢ	43.40	(M.McNichol)	AprilBay,MssCabert,NoHitter 75-0
6-26 M¹	14000 ft nw8500 cd mi 29	:5741:2711:564	9	10	10	10¹⁰¹10¹⁴¹	1:593	66.50	(M.McNichol)	ArmTyson,GaelcRm,FrFury 65-0
6-13 M¹	13000 ft nw8500 cd mi 29²	1:0011:3111:594	4	6	1°	1	1¹x	77¹	2:011	13.20	(M.McNichol)	DillonLb,HappyKit,PACarlos 70-0
5-30 M¹	11000 ft nw6750 cd mi 29⁴	1:0141:3312:01	1	4	3°	2°	43¹	33¹	2:014	6.40	(M.McNichol)	SssfrsJW,StrkeKing,PntGllry 71-0
5-24 M¹	10000 sy nw6250 cd mi 29	:5911:29 1:59	2	5	6	6	52²	2¹	1:591	4.20	(M.McNichol)	Bolton,PeanutGllry,KeyPrvelt 63-0
5-17 M¹	13000 ft nw8000 cd mi 28³	:5831:2831:574	6	8	9	10	87¹	87¹	1:593	33.50	(M.McNichol)	MrchntMar,SkipChck,AdmBrt 71-0

6-1

7 — Pink

READY SET GO
b h, 4, by Race Time—Mona Lobell by Solicitor
Profit & Pleasure Stables, Elizabeth, N.J.
Driver-TOM LUCHENTO, 2-25-46   (195)   GREEN-WHITE
$16,596 — 3, 1:58⁴ (1)

St.-T. Luchento—Tr.-N. Luchento
1979 18 0 2 1   7,935
M(1)1:584 1978 19 3 2 2 16,431

7-18 M¹	10800 gd nw5000 cd mi 30	31:0031:3032:00	5	3	1°	1°	1²	23	2:01	6.10	(T.Luchento)	OsbShwOff,RdyStGo,CrytsIRm 69-1
7-10 M¹	11400 ft 20000 clm mi 29¹	:5911:2911:584	9	3°	2	3	34	78	2:002	41.00	(T.Luchento)	StrClssc,EmprssBea,DeesKgt 68-0
6-29 M¹	9000 ft nw5000 cd mi 30²	:5921:2922:002	9	9	10	9	99¹	88	2:02	16.50	(T.Luchento)	MurWrry,EstLynAmbr,DrJcby 67-0
6-20 M¹	9000 ft nw5000 cd mi 29	:5941:2841:593	9	9	9	88	63¹	2:001	13.80	(T.Luchento)	WarrenJhn,QnCllns,QckTmper 75-0
6-12 M¹	9000 ft nw5000 cd mi 30	:5841:3011:592	5	6	6	522	42	2:004	12.10	(Ri.Quartier)	TrnrPlyby,BeaMagee,KeyPrvlt 66-0
6- 5 M¹	10800 gd nw5000 cd mi 30	11:0021:31 2:00²	7	6	6	63¹	53¹	2:01	6.00	(T.Luchento)	RghtOn,EDBret,MstHppyGrm 71-1

30-1

8 — Gray

DREXEL MAJESTY
br h, 6, by Gamecock—Miss Lightning by Grandaughters Boy
Domenico Putorti, Mickleton, N.J.
Driver-JACK PARKER, JR., 7-19-55   (153)   RED-BLUE-WHITE
$16,305 — 4, 2:01⁴ (⅝)

Trainer-D. Putorti
Brd(⅝)2:02³ 1979 18 8 1 0   3,224
1978 17 0 3 1   8,424

7-18 M¹	10800 gd nw5000 cd mi 30	31:0031:3032:00	3	6	7	8°	74¹	47	2:012	43.50	(M.McNichol)	OsbShwOff,RdyStGo,CrytsIRm 69-1
7- 9 M¹	9000 ft nw5000 cd mi 30	:5941:30 1:593	9	9	6	7°°98¹	911¹	2:013	75.40	(M.McNichol)	ELynAmbr,GrnAstro,GeoMrvl 71-0
6-29 M¹	9000 ft nw5000 cd mi 30²	:5921:2922:002	6	7	7	8	88¹	98¹	2:02	44.80	(T.Wing)	MurWrry,EstLynAmbr,DrJcby 67-0
6-19 M¹	9000 ft nw5000 cd mi 28²	:5831:2841:59	3	9	6°	7°	79	77¹	810	2:01	56.70	(S.Torre)	Kistime,Idaten,BaronsBrat 73-0
6-13 M¹	14000 ft nw9000 cd mi 28⁴	:5811:2741:57	9	10	10	10¹²10¹⁷¹	2:002	62.30	(S.Torre)	Inspcrtion,JHBaron,StphnSctt 71-0
5-30 Brd⁵	4000 ft nw5000 cd mi 29³	1:01 1:3122:023	5	6	6	5°	54	1ʰᵈ	2:023	6.10	(K.Hankins)	DrxlMjsty,HghHpTny,BlckMgc 76-0

20-1

9 — Purple

CORGEN RECHARGE
b c, 3, by Fulla Napoleon—Dancing Step by Newport Chief
Anthony Genovese, Union City, N.J.
Driver-DON SIDER, 11-13-48   (153)   RED-GRAY-BLACK
$00 —

Trainer-D. Sider
1979 9 0 1 0   2,606
1978 0 0 0 0

7-14 M¹	ft Qua mi 28¹	:5731:2711:57	1	5	5	4	41²¹3²0¹	2:01	N.B.	(D.Sider)	SanMario,Viper,CrgenRechrg 80-0
7- 9 MR	1200 ft nw1 cd mi 31	31:02 1:3312:04³	7	5	6	52¹	52¹	2:052	13.10	(J.Gilmour)	HnyJoPrdse,MllNcksPrd,KshClpr
7- 2 MR	1200 ft nw1 cd mi 30	21:0121:3332:03⁴	1	1	1	27	41⁹	2:073	2.70	(J.Gilmour)	AmzngGigi,MllNcksPrd,BshBshBt
6-26 MR	ft Qua mi 32	11:0431:3542:081	2	1	1	1¹¹	21¹	2:082	N.B.	(L.Gilmour)	EricWy,CrgnRchrg,NnnckGld 62-0
5- 1 M¹	8400 ft nw1 cd mi 30	21:01 1:3232:013	5	8	8°	°°96¹	91⁶¹	2:05	45.50	(L.Gilmour)	ShutEye,PiratesCove,CcroKte 60-0
4-24 M¹	8400 ft nw1 cd mi 29	:59 1:2932:00¹	4	4	5	64¹	75	2:013	10.30	(L.Gilmour)	Jystick,JamacaBoy,BhmsHeron 59-0

8-1

10 — Blue-Red

CORTLAND HANOVER
br h, 7, by Tar Heel—Court Intrigue by Duane Hanover
Gerald & Faith Pullen, New Egypt, N.J.
Driver-LES PULLEN, 12-8-31   (184)   BROWN-GOLD
$66,475 — 4, 1:57³ (⅝)

Trainer-G. Pullen
Fhld2:02² 1979 27 3 3 4 16,311
Brd(⅝)2:01¹ 1978 19 3 3 0   7,530

7-11 M¹	10800 ft nw5000 cd mi 30²	:5941:3021:593	2	4	2°	2°	2³¹	52¹	2:00²	4.90	(L.Pullen)	RealTrsr,ArrvasBd,TpThBttlN 72-0
6-29 M¹	18000 ft 35000 clm mi 29⁴	:59 1:2811:574	9	9	9	87¹	88	1:59²	102.30	(L.Pullen)	ArmTawny,SssfrsRm,SentrCV 67-0
6-22 M¹	18000 gd 35000 clm mi 29⁴	1:0031:3021:593	2	4	4	5°	77¹	61²	2:02	22.20	(G.Pullen)	TotalFrgt,ArmTwny,JwllsDrm 71-1
6-16 M¹	16000 ft 40000 clm mi 29³	:5921:2841:57	2	5	6	76¹	88¹	1:592	17.10	(L.Pullen)	KrstIsBllt,KeyMars,GoBHppy 80-0
6- 8 M¹	15000 ft 40000 clm mi 28⁴	:5831:2731:574	7	10	10	86	33¹	1:582	43.90	(L.Pullen)	JMSam,FrostyZip,CortIndHn 73-0
6- 2 Fhld	6000 ft w10001 cd mi 29¹	:5941:2932:00¹	8	8	3°	4³	32¹	2:013	10.30	(H.Kelly)	BeGoodTm,VegasStr,FnlDcsn 75-0

SELECTIONS: 3-6-4

C—DENOTES CONVENTIONAL SULKY

(3)

PACE—1 MILE

Warming-Up Saddle Cloth
WHITE

PURSE $8,000

Exacta Wagering This Race

CLAIMING PRICE $15,000
(Three-Year-Old Fillies Granted 60% Allowance)
(Four-Year-Old Mares Granted 40% Allowance)

ASK FOR HORSE BY PROGRAM NUMBER

15-1 | **1** | 15000 | Red

MY DIRECT KNIGHT b h, 7, by Sampson Direct—Anita Knight by Knight Dream — Trainer-T. DiCicco
Bellmont Stable, Valley Stream, N.Y. — 1979 12 0 0 2 3,675
$90,456 — 6, 1:58⁴ (1) Driver-JACK PARKER, JR., 7-19-55 (153) RED-BLUE-WHITE — Hol(1)1:58⁴ 1978 48 8 11 7 44,289
7-16 M¹ 9000 ft nw5000 cd mi 29 1:00²1:30²1:59² 7 8 5° 4° 8⁸¾10¹⁰¼ 2:01² 35.50 (J.ParkerJr) MnkniAce,MnStOut,GrnAstro 74-0
7- 1 PcD⅝ 3200 ft w4001 cd mi 29³1:00⁴1:30¹2:01⁴ 6 1 1 1 2¹ 7⁶¼ 2:03 13.70 (T.DiCicco) Cobber,JerseySampson,Strato 71-0
6-23 M¹ ft Qua mi 30 1:01 1:31¹2:00 3 3 3 2 2⁵ 4¹⁷ 2:03² N.B. (M.Lancaster) FrstyPenn,RyansHpe,I'mBack 76-0
6-20 M¹ 8500 ft 17500 clm mi 29³ :58⁴1:29¹1:59⁴ 5 2° 2 5 9⁹¼ 9¹⁷¼ 2:03¹ 16.60 (M.Lancaster) GdBttrBst,PrpWsh,WknGlnfn 75-0
6-12 M¹ ft T-P Qua mi 29³1:01¹1:32³2:02 5 1 2 3 2¹½ 4¼ 2:02 N.B. (M.Lancaster) AllenHn,HiLeRgrd,PrncRbltn 66-0
3-20 M¹ 10000 ft 25000 clm mi 29¹ :59³1:30⁴2:00³ 4 2° 2 4 9⁹ 9²¹½ 2:04⁴ 13.00 (R.Kuebler) JniesTm,Vanavara,UnitasHn 52-0

9-2 | **2** | 21000 | Blue

BRADLEYS DOLL br m, 4, by J R Skipper—Poplar Lady by Poplar Dell — Trainer-W. Robinson
David, Patricia & Paul Goodrow & Eddy Gotfryd, Ont. — GrR(⅝)2:01² 1979 23 4 6 4 15,044
$11,336 — 3, 2:07² (⅝) Driver-RAY REMMEN, 5-28-47 (185) WHITE-GREEN-GOLD — Moh(⅝)2:07² 1978 23 2 6 3 11,336
7-18 M¹ 9500 gd 20000 clm mi 30¹ :59⁴1:30²1:59¹ 7 8 8 9° 9⁷¼10¹⁵ 2:02¹ 7.50 (Jo.Campbell) DsrtStp,DelHrbrt,PaulasClppr 69-1
7-11 M¹ 9500 ft 20000 clm mi 30 1:00 1:30 1:59¹ 2 4 5 4 6²½ 5⁷ 2:00³ *2.80 (S.Goudreau) JmboDllr,PlcidByrd,TmlyOrbt 72-0
7- 2 GrR⅝ 4500ft23000 clm hcp mi 29³1:00³1:30²2:01¹ 4 6 6 4° 3²½ 2³½ 2:02 *1.25 (M.Corbett) LynLomac,BrdysDll,TrryPrkr 72-0
6-25 GrR⅝ 4900ft28000 clm hcp mi 30 1:00²1:30²2:00² 5 6 6 6 6⁴ 4⁴¼ 2:01¹ 3.75 (W.Hicks) WnstnAlm,ValiantIdes,StwrtsBlz
6-18 GrR⅝ 4900ft28000 clm hcp mi 30 1:01³1:32 2:02 9 5 5 6° 7⁴½ 3² 2:02² 4.90 (M.Corbett) DrnGdRse,AnnesRip,BrdysDll 70-0
6- 8 GrR⅝ 4300 ft 18000 clm mi 29³1:01¹1:30⁴2:01² 2 5 4° 1 1ns 1hd 2:01² *3.05 (M.Corbett) BrdysDll,ElklsBeautiful,TrryPrkr

---

5-1 | **3** | 15000 | White

FRILLAWAY RED (J) b g, 7, by Buckeye Champ—Frillaway by Santo Eden — St.-A. Abbatiello—Tr.-J. Hudak
Remsen Mill Acres, Neptune, N.J. — M(1)2:01⁴ 1979 18 3 1 2 19,248
$68,055 — 6, 2:01 (1) Driver-BEN WEBSTER, 11-8-39 (138) RED-WHITE-BLACK — M(1)2:01 1978 13 5 1 0 21,390
7-17 M¹ 9000 sy 12500 clm mi 29 :59²1:31 2:01² 6 7 6 6°°4⁴ 4²¼ 2:01⁴ 6.50 (B.Webster) MgtyMjr,NclyNeil,DwnsRoad 78-1
7- 3 M¹ 9000 ft 12500 clm mi 29 :58⁴1:30 1:59⁴ 7 9 9° 4°°2¹½ 4⁶½ 2:01 3.50 (B.Webster) StarN,Sugarlne,ForeseesDrm 75-0
6-19 M¹ 9000 ft 12500 clm mi 30²1:00¹1:30 2:01 2 4 4 4 3²¼ 4⁵ 2:02 2.80 (C.Manzi) DownsRd,AeneasLb,NrdnsStr 73-0
5-28 M¹ 9000 gd 12500 clm mi 30⁴1:02³1:32³2:03² 10 10 7° 7° 8⁴½ 8⁴½ 2:04¹ 13.70 (H.Kelly) FranklyScarlet,Amitai,StarN 71-2
5-21 M¹ 9600 ft 15000 clm cd mi 29²1:00⁴1:31²2:00⁴ 7 7 7 7° 6⁶½ 6⁶½ 2:02 3.90 (C.Manzi) ArmOctne,Lavnto,MstrWnstn 66-0
5-14 M¹ 9800 gd 15000 clm mi 30 1:00³1:32²2:02¹ 8 9 10 8°°3²½ 4⁴½ 2:03 3.60 (B.Webster) CrnllStrkr,Lavanto,ScndGsser 56-1

12-1 | **4** | 24000 | Green

NATIVE PLEASURE b f, 3, by Adios Vic—Spring Sue by Hunting Song — St.-W. Popfinger—Tr.-W. Jacobs
George Christopher & Wm. Popfinger, Fla. — PPk(⅝)2:02³ 1979 14 2 1 1 6,095
$55 — 2, 2:04² (1) Driver-W. (Bill) POPFINGER, 10-9-36 (196) GREEN-WHITE — Lex(1)2:04² 1978 8 1 0 0 55
7-17 M¹ 8500 ft 17500 clm mi 29 :58¹1:28³1:59¹ 1 5 5 4 8⁷¼10⁹ 2:01 54.90 (B.Nickells) KeyPanzer,JhnQArab,Parling 78-0
7-10 M¹ 8000 ft 15000 clm mi 29³ :59²1:29³1:59² 4 6 6 10 10⁹¼10¹⁴ 2:02¹ 53.10 (B.Nickells) Parling,CllMeKsh,KeyPanzer 68-0
6-26 M¹ 8500 ft 17500 clm mi 28⁴ :58²1:28¹1:59¹ 4 8 9 9 9¹³¾8¹² 2:01³ 64.10 (J.Brown) AnnRedstr,TkeLve,GryWrthy 65-0
6-14 M¹ 24110 ft 3yr F Ec mi 29⁴1:01²1:31⁴2:01 2 5 5 5 5¹¹¾5¹⁴¼ 2:03⁴ 19.90 (W.Popfinger) ShrryAlm,BbyDmplng,RcyPrd 70-0
6- 4 M¹ 9000 ft nw5000 cd mi 29¹ :59 1:28³1:58² 3 7 6 6 6⁹ 5¹³¼ 2:01 8.60 (W.Popfinger) MrMH,FlashLobell,GentleTag 64-0
5-28 M¹ 9000 sy nw5000 cd mi 30⁴1:00⁴1:32³2:03 1 4 4 6° 4³½ 2² 2:03² 13.20 (Ja.Doherty) MplLfRbbie,NtvPlsre,Nokoro 68-2

3-1 | **5** | 15000 | Black

PARLING b g, 11, by Laureldale—Dainty Alice by Great Parrish — Trainer-C. Alessi
Carmen Alessi, Bolingbrook, Ill. — M(1)1:59² 1979 4 1 0 1 5,395
$64,879 — 10, 2:00⁴ (1⅛) Driver-CARMEN ALESSI, 5-26-38 (138) GOLD-WHITE-BLUE — Arl(1⅛)2:00⁴ 1978 15 3 4 2 16,699
7-17 M¹ 8500 ft 17500 clm mi 29 :58¹1:28³1:59¹ 9 9 9 9° 5⁵ 3¹¼ 1:59² 6.70 (C.Alessi) KeyPanzer,JhnQArab,Parling 78-0
7-10 M¹ 8000 ft 15000 clm mi 29³ :59²1:29³1:59² 3 4 5 3° 2¹½ 1½ 1:59² 8.60 (C.Alessi) Parling,CllMeKsh,KeyPanzer 68-0
6-23 M¹ ft Qua mi 30⁴1:02¹1:32³2:02³ 6 1 1 1 1¹ 2¹ 2:02⁴ N.B. (C.Alessi) MstrArnie,Parling,NickeliAds 76-0
6-13 Spk⅝ 8150 ft 20000 clm mi 29⁴1:00⁴1:31²2:01⁴ 7 8 8 9° 9¹⁰ 9⁸½ 2:03³ 13.60 (W.Crone) PpprShkr,AwayBret,FlyStraight
6- 2 May 7500 ft 18000 clm mi 30¹1:01 1:32¹2:03 5 5 5° 6° 4¹½ 5³½ 2:03³ 13.60 (W.Crone) StrFarmer,BeansTonite,PrsnOrgn
12-19 May 7200 ft 15000 clm hcp mi 30²1:02 1:33²2:05² 3 2 2° 3 5⁴½ 7¹⁴ 2:08¹ *1.50 (C.Alessi) TheLastWrd,HghlndFeud,Garrick

---

8-1 | **6** | 15000 | Yellow

YENDA RHYTHM GB b h, 10, by Direct Rhythm—Yenda Eden by Morris Eden — St.-R. Samson—Tr.-V. Staker
David Silverman, St. Laurent, Que. — M(1)2:01³ 1979 10 1 2 1 9,890
$87,327 — 9, 1:59 (1) Driver-ROBERT SAMSON, 10-7-49 (140) WHITE-BLACK — M(1)1:59 1978 33 11 3 4 68,796
7-10 M¹ ft T-P Qua mi 29³1:00⁴1:31³2:01² 8 4 4 4 3⁴½ 3⁶ 2:02³ N.B. (B.Nickells) ArmTex,HHBelle,YndRhytGB 78-0
5-29 M¹ 8000 sy 15000 clm mi 29⁴1:00²1:31³2:02³ 2 3 3 3° 6⁴½ 8¹¹ 2:04⁴ 2.50 (R.Samson) MajorHn,DosteDrum,RglShne 61-
5-24 M¹ 8000 sy 15000 clm mi 28³ :57³1:28¹1:58³ 4 5° 4° 3 5⁶½ 7¹¹½ 2:00⁴ *1.60 (R.Samson) MtEtnFshn,ArmStlla,FrnkAnn 63-0
5-16 M¹ 8000 ft 15000 clm mi 28⁴1:00³1:31 2:01³ 6 7 7 7° 5³½ 1¹½ 2:01³ 4.10 (R.Samson) YndaRhyGB,Skttlbug,FlyDeal 70-0
5- 8 M¹ 7000 ft 15000 clm mi 29¹ :59³1:30¹2:00⁴ 2 3 4 5 3² 3¹½ 2:01¹ 3.50 (R.Samson) CapHousr,PrpWsh,YndRhyGB 74-0
4-26 M¹ 7000 sy 15000 clm mi 30² :59⁴1:30¹2:03¹ 3 4 4 2 2¹½ 2³ 2:03⁴ *2.50 (R.Samson) CrdnlChfA,YndRhGB,JCnBmp 59-

---

15-1 | **7** | 15000 | Pink

REGAL JACK blk g, 7, by Regal Scott—Cilla Black by Express Direct — St.-T. Foster—Tr.-S. Dorfman
Sandra L. Brill, Oceanside, N.Y. — 1979 3 0 0 0 400
$1,723 — None At Mile Driver-RENE POULIN, 7-18-51 (155) BROWN-GOLD-WHITE — Last Raced In 1977
7-10 M¹ 8000 ft 15000 clm mi 30 :59 1:30 1:59⁴ 7 2 3 5 4⁵½ 5⁸½ 2:01³ 31.50 (R.Poulin) LpzChrge,KeyAtlas,MirClrnce 68-0
6-22 M¹ 9000 ft nw5000 cd mi 29³ :58²1:28⁴1:58² 6 8 8 6° 6⁴½ 9¹³½ 2:01¹ 37.40 (R.Poulin) EDBret,BartsJeff,MrrysWrry 71-0
6-13 M¹ 12000 ft 25000 clm mi 29³ :57⁴1:28 1:58³ 8 9 9 9 8⁸½ 7¹⁹½ 2:02³ 34.30 (R.Poulin) BbbyGrrsn,Rwhllion,FlyBlckie 69-0
6- 5 M¹ ft Qua mi 31 1:00³1:30⁴2:01² 1 1 3 3 3² 2¹½ 2:01³ N.B. (R.Poulin) MplLnNlry,RglJack,Imabaron 77-0

5-2 | **8** | 15000 | Gray

TREV COUNSEL b h, 5, by Timely Counsel—Missy by Warpath — Trainer-N. Aronica
Nicholas Aronica, Richard DeHart, Bloomingdale & Wayne, N.J. — M(1)2:00³ 1979 22 2 3 3 21,665
$34,062 — 3, 2:02 Driver-JAMES DOHERTY, 9-27-40 (161) RED-WHITE-GREEN — RP(⅝)2:04¹ 1978 42 3 5 6 10,436
7-18 M¹ 12000 gd 22500 clm mi 29² :59³1:28¹1:59 9 i8 8 7 7⁹ 7¹³ 2:01³ 30.70 (Ja.Doherty) LehighStne,Nerissa,FrstyPnn 69-1
7-11 M¹ 12000 ft 22500 clm mi 30²1:00²1:30³1:59⁴ x2 9 9°10 10⁷½ 8⁵¼ 2:00⁴ 12.20 (Ja.Doherty) RwlngsStrt,Nerissa,Flghtlne 72-0
7- 3 M¹ 10000 ft 22500 clm mi 30 1:00 1:30¹1:58³ 8 2 3 4 3³½ 3³¼ 1:59¹ 25.40 (Ja.Doherty) RmpinDan,NtveMss,TrevCnsl 75-0
6-22 M¹ 10000 gd 22500 clm mi 30 1:00¹1:30²2:00⁴ 1 7 7 4° 2¹½ 3¹½ 2:01¹ 15.90 (G.Wright) TmlyOrbt,DsrtStep,TrvCounsl 71-1
6-15 M¹ 9500 ft 20000 clm mi 29¹ :57¹1:27²1:56³ 7 10 9 8 8¹⁰½6¹⁵ 1:59³ 14.40 (Ja.Doherty) SlvrWrrior,SeminoleChf,JayZ 80-0
6- 8 M¹ 9500 ft 20000 clm mi 29 :58³1:28¹1:58² 4 3ix4 5 3⁵ 2¹¹ 2:00³ 5.30 (Ja.Doherty) SilverWarr,TrevCnsl,LtColJoe 73-0

12-1 | **9** | 15000 | Purple

MIGHTY TOMMIE b g, 8, by Mighty Medium—Miss Laconia by Calumet Forever — St.-J. Kelley, Jr.—Tr.-M. Kelley
Joan Deluca & Mitchell Kelley, Edison, N.J. — M(1)2:02¹ 1979 20 2 3 3 9,710
$53,017 — 5, 2:02 (⅝) Driver-MITCHELL KELLEY, 7-15-55 (173) RED-BLACK-WHITE — Fhld2:04 1978 36 4 5 8 15,260
7- 9 M¹ 9600 ft 15000 clm mi 29³1:00³1:31 2:02¹ 4 7 1 9° 9⁵½ 9³½ 2:02⁴ 9.00 (J.KelleyJr) TodaroHnvr,Overturn,Phew 71-0
6-27 M¹ 10200 ft 17500 clm mi 29³ :59⁴1:30 2:00² 2 3 4 6 10⁵½10¹¹½ 2:02⁴ 11.30 (M.Kelley) EvilDuke,LatinKgt,RylThmas 67-0
6-11 M¹ 9600 gd 15000 clm mi 29 1:00 1:31 2:02¹ 5 7 6° 6° 5³½ 1⁵½ 2:02¹ 10.90 (M.Kelley) MtyTom,PrncLrnN,AdvncCpy 59-2
6- 2 Fhld 3800 ft 15000 clm mi 29⁴1:01¹1:31³2:01⁴ 7 7 7 6 5¹⁰½3⁸½ 2:03² 9.70 (J.KelleyJr) AftnEagr,BeaMagee,MtyTom 75-0
5-28 Fhld 3800 ft 15000 clm mi 31¹1:03¹1:34⁴2:04⁴ 1 2 3 4 2¹ 2nk 2:04⁴ 2.40 (M.Kelley) SmsMjsty,MtyTom,MssStrkr 70-0
5-22 Fhld 3800 ft 15000 clm mi 29⁴1:01²1:32³2:03³ 4 1° 1 1 1¹½ 3¹½ 2:04 4.30 (M.Kelley) SmsMjsty,BluFlmA,MtyTom 72-0

SELECTIONS: 8—5—2

No. 9—LORD LOBELL N—Scratched

New Betting Machine Demonstrations Tonight

DEMONSTRATIONS OF THE NEW TIM 300 BETTING MACHINES, WHICH WILL BE HERE FOR THE THOROUGHBRED MEET STARTING SEPTEMBER 4, WILL BE GIVEN NIGHTLY FROM 7 UNTIL 11 IN THE GRANDSTAND, CLUBHOUSE AND PEGASUS. THE BETTING MACHINES OF THE FUTURE ARE HERE NOW. MAKE A FREE SAMPLE BET TONIGHT. ASK AT THE INFORMATION BOOTH FOR THE LOCATION ON YOUR FLOOR.

④ PACE–1 MILE
Warming-Up Saddle Cloth
GREEN

PURSE $15,000

ASK FOR HORSE BY PROGRAM NUMBER

Trifecta Wagering This Race
N.J.R.C. Rule 29:53(i) mandates an Exacta where field is less than 9 at wagering time.
WOODROW WILSON QUALIFYING HEAT
EARLY CLOSING EVENT No. 2—(1st Div.)—TWO-YEAR-OLDS
(1st 4 in the official order of finish qualify for the $862,750
Woodrow Wilson Final Wednesday, August 1).

10-1 / 1 / Red
EASY COME EASY GO
b c, 2, by Meadow Skipper—Lady Emily by Hillsota
Leon & Lorraine R. Machiz, Great Neck, N.Y.
St.–W. Haughton—Tr.–A. Thomas
Lex(1)2:03¹ 1979 6 2 0 2 3,424
$00 —
Driver–W. (Bill) HAUGHTON, 11-2-23 (154) WHITE-GREEN-GOLD

7-14 Lat¹	22000 ft 2yr Stk mi 29 :59 1:29¹1:58³	9	7	7	5° 43½ 5¹	2:00	4.00 (W.Haughton)	CbbrAlm,FlshAlm,EncoreUnPrise
6-27 Lex¹	15105 ft 2yr Stk mi 28⁴ :574¹2731:57²	4	5	5	3° 3¹³ 31¹½	1:59³	12.30 (W.Haughton)	Whamo,TrsrReef,EasyCmeEasyGo
6-20 Lex¹	900 ft nw500 cd mi 30⁴1:02 1:3332:03¹	4	3	3	2° 2¹⅛ 11½	2:03¹	1.70 (W.Haughton)	EsyComeEsyGo.MartinSenour.Why
6-15 Lex¹	100 ft 2yr mi 32 1:02²1:3332:05	2	1	2	1° 1ⁿᵈ 11½	2:06	N.B. (W.Haughton)	EsyCmEsyGo.TrbaHn.RklssAbandon
6- 7 Lex¹	100 ft 2yr mi 32¹1:02⁴1:3332:03	3	6	6° 5 61¹½69		N.B. (W.Haughton)	TrsrReef,LdyCroupier,JhnnyOrange

---

3-1 / 2 / Blue
TREASURE REEF
b c, 2, by Silent Majority—Reef Miss by Tar Mite
J. Louis Levesque & Irving Liverman, Que.
Trainer–Gl. Garnsey
Lex(1)2:02² 1979 7 2 3 1 11,384
$00 —
Driver–GLEN GARNSEY, 1-1-33 (170) DARK BLUE-LIGHT BLUE

7-14 VD⅝	16100 ft 2yr Stk mi 28² :59 1:28⁴1:57³	4	1	1	1¹ 31½ 23	1:58¹	2.80 (Gl.Garnsey)	Niatross,TrsreReef,JDsBuck 90-0
7- 8 BB⅝	23100 ft 2yr Stk mi 29 2:02¹:304²:01⁴	9	1	1	1ⁿᵈ 3²	2:02¹	10.55 (S.Waller)	DoradoHn.AllTheWy,TrsrReef 76-0
6-27 Lex¹	15105 ft 2yr Stk mi 28⁴ :574¹2731:57²	6	3	2	2⁵ 25	1:58²	8.80 (S.Waller)	Whamo,TrsureReef,EsyCmEsyGo
6-22 Lex¹	1300 ft nw2 cd mi 29¹1:004²:304²:01³	4	3	4	3²½ 2½	2:01³	3.70 (W.Smythe)	OrnateHill,TreasureReef.SimiO
6-16 Lex¹	800 ft nw1 cd mi 2921:00³1:314²:02²	5	4	2° 1	1² 1ⁿᵏ	2:02²	°.70 (Gl.Garnsey)	TreasureReef,SlyBird,SlntPrincess

---

9-2 / 3 / White
MAPLE FRITZ
b c, 2, by Breadwinner—Miss Step N. by False Step
Bernard Isaacs, Shaker Heights, Ohio
Trainer–G. Cameron
Brd(⅞)2:00² 1979 10 3 3 1 15,903
$00 —
Driver–GARY CAMERON, 4-8-44 (157) BLUE-WHITE-GREEN

7-18 M¹	12500 gd 2yr mi 302¹:0021:31 1:59³	4	1	1	1½ 1½	1:59⁴	4.20 (G.Cameron)	TylerB,Fndment½, MidasAlm 69-1
7- 9 ScD⅝	13400 gd 2yr mi 30¹:021:331²:02³	6	4	1	1² 11¹	2:02³	°.30 (G.Cameron)	MpleFrtz,Smo OLite,LbtsSgrFt
7- 2 ScD⅝	1600 ft 2yr Mdn cd mi 28⁴1:00 1:342:02¹	1	1	1	1¹ 14	2:02¹	°.50 (C.Wall)	MpleFrtz,Bl bbles DoneDidit
6-25 Nfld	12700 ft 2yr mi 30 1:01²1:314²:03¹	3	3	2° 2° 32	35½	2:04¹	°.60 (G.Cameron)	StdyCloud,StdyRich,MpleFrtz 96-0
6-19 Det¹	14499 ft 2yr mi 30 1:001¹:30 1:59⁴	9	9	9	9 55½ 86½	2:01	5.70 (C.Cameron)	M ,MrJimBob,Brdgewater

---

8-1 / 4 / Green
BULLION
b c, 2, by Meadow Skipper—Sterlings Glamour by Overtrick
Bullion Stables, Long Valley, N.J.
St.– opas—Tr.–Jo. Kopas
GrR 1979 9 3 1 1 3,555
$00 —
Driver–JACK KOPAS, 10-16-28 (185) GREEN-WHITE

7-17 GrR⅝	31900 ft 2yr Stk mi 28⁴ :591¹:283¹:58²	4	9	8	7° 77½ 71¹	2:00³	e6.85 (B.Davies)	DoradoHnvr,Tyrant,Alberton 72-0
7- 9 GrR⅝	2000 ft 2-3yr Mdn cd mi 31¹¹:022²:022	1	2	1	1 12½ 14	2:02	°.40 (Ja.Kopas)	Bullion.RylDncrN,HighIndFre 72-0
6-26 BR	35750 ft 2yr Stk mi 30 1:02²1:31 2:01⁴	6	8	9	8ix725 7dis	2:07⁴	4.20 (Ja.Kopas)	MidasAlm,CutAcrss,GllntAlm 75-0
6-20 M¹	10000 ft 2yr mi 303¹:003¹:302¹:01	8	7	7° 4°°43½ 54		2:01⁴	6.60 (Jo.Kopas)	HpyCllns,BrtsRgn,PrdncCllns 75-0
6-12 M¹	20611 ft 2yr C Ec mi 29 1:002¹:302¹:59²	12	11	10	10 10¹²½91³½	2:02	e24.30 (Jo.Kopas)	Whamo,MapleFritz,FiskHan 66-0

15-1 / 5 / Black
ALBUQUERQUE N
b c, 2, by Adover Rainbow—Lady Lopez by Lopez Hanover
Green, White & Red Stable, Rexdale, Ont.
Trainer–J. Stadelman
M(1)1:59² 1979 7 3 0 1 7,365
$00 —
Driver–JOHN STADELMAN, 1-8-44 (148) TURQUOISE-WHITE-GOLD

7-18 M¹	10000 gd 2yr mi 30 :59 1:29¹1:59²	5	2	3	2 1¹ 1²	1:59²	9.70 (J.Stadelman)	AlbqrqueN,SurfrSctt,AvnLrry 69-1
7-11 M¹	10000 ft 2yr mi 29⁴ :59²1:30¹1:59¹	5	4	5	4° 33 35	2:00¹	36.90 (J.Stadelman)	TylerB,BurtPloma,AlbqrqueN 72-0
7- 4 M¹	12500 sl 2yr mi 30¹1:001¹:303²:00⁴	5	6	5	8° 84½ 99½	2:02³	50.50 (J.Stadelman)	GeneHn,BarnumLb,StneRacer 57-
6-20 Brd⅝	2000 ft 2yr mi 29²1:003¹:311²:03¹	8	5	4° 4° 42¾ 64¹		2:04	4.80 (J.Stadelman)	GoforeSeven,Jobim,MrTempo 78-0
6-13 Brd⅝	2000 ft 2yr C-G mi 29⁴1:041¹:32 2:03²	5	7	6	4° 43½ 1ⁿᵏ	2:03²	21.50 (J.Stadelman)	AlbuqrqueN,GoforeSvn,Jobim 72-0

15-1 / 6 / Yellow
SLY BEAU
b c, 2, by Sly Attorney—Coral by Bret Hanover
S. M. Tarasco, A. S. Latessa & A. L. Linden, Ohio
Trainer–G. Latessa
Nfld2:08⁴ 1979 8 2 4 1 9,296
$00 —
Driver–JOHN CAMPBELL, 4-8-55 (156) WHITE-MAROON

7-19 BR	20000 ft 2yr Stk mi 294¹:002¹:312²:02¹	6	2° 2	2 21	2²	2:02¹	5.40 (R.Plano)	DmndSprklr,SlyBeau,HueKsh 77-0
7-12 Nfld	1500 ft 2yr nw1 cd mi 31⁴1:05 1:3522:05¹	8	1	1	2 21½ 22	2:05³	°.30 (R.Plano)	Uplift,SlyBeau,KnightRage 81-0
7- 1 MR	11341 gd 2yr Stk mi 281¹:01 1:314²:03⁴	5	1	1	1¹½ 21⅛	2:04¹	20.00 (R.Plano)	Mstrmind,SlyBeau,ArmVital 65-0
6-18 Nfld	3000 ft 2yr Opn mi 31¹¹:04 1:3442:04³	2	1	1	2 2½ 2²½	2:05⁴	2.70 (R.Plano)	Albarado,SlyBeau,BravoButlr 56-0
6-11 Nfld	2000 ft 2yr Opn mi 313¹:032²1:35¹2:07²	5ix8	8	78½ 76½		2:08⁴	4.60 (R.Plano)	RylChnc,WrriorAlm,StrkgHeir 64-0

10-1 / 7 / Pink
HAPPY COLLINS
br c, 2, by Most Happy Fella—Cindys Tar Heel by Tar Heel
Max Buran & Abe Farber, Merrick & White Plains, N.Y.
Trainer–E. Harner
M(1)2:01 1979 9 5 2 0 21,947
$00 —
Driver–ELDON HARNER, 7-20-33 (165) MAROON-GOLD

7-17 M¹	10000 sy 2yr C mi 30² :594¹:30 2:01	9¹	5	4	4 4dis	2:11¹	4.50 (E.Harner)	GeneHanover,Hive,Maxcelsior 78-1
7-11 M¹	12500 ft 2yr mi 2931¹:004¹:59⁴	9	3	3	6° 84½ 751	2:00⁴	6.70 (E.Harner)	MidasAlm,Searights,BrtsRgn 72-0
6-30 MR	11891 sy 2yr Stk mi 30 1:02 1:324²:03²	4	1° 1	1 11½ 2ⁿˢ	2:03²	°.60 (E.Harner)	TrstyTghGuy,HpyCllns,TylerB 62-0
6-20 M¹	10000 ft 2yr mi 3031¹:003¹:302²:01	3	2	1	1¹ 11½	2:01	°.10 (E.Harner)	HpyCllns,BrtsRgn,PrdncCllns 75-0
6-12 MR	18600 ft 2yr Ec mi 291¹:003¹:314²:02³	3	1° 1	1 12½ 12½		2:02³	e°.40 (E.Harner)	HppyCllns,CosmoGeo,Knickers 55-0

6-1 / 8 / Gray
ENCORE UN PRISE
b c, 2, by Strike Out—Uniquity by True Duane
Beejay Stable Reg'd., Beamsville, Ont.
St.–W. Haughton—Tr.–A. Thomas
Lex(1)2:01 1979 8 3 1 3 5,589
$00 —
Driver–PETER HAUGHTON, 9-22-54 (155) WHITE-GREEN-GOLD

7-14 Lat¹	22000 ft 2yr Stk mi 29 :59 1:29¹1:58³	5	3° 3	4° 32 33½	1:59¹	24.00 (C.Jenkins)	CbbrAlm,FlshAlm,EncoreUnPrise
6-27 Lex¹	15105 ft 2yr Stk mi 28⁴ :591¹:293¹:59¹	6	4	5	57 310½	2:01¹	12.10 (C.Jenkins)	StrmDmage,CbbrAlm,EncrUnPrse
5-19 Det¹	14499 ft 2yr mi 30 1:001¹:30 1:59³	6	4° 1	1 87½ 916½	2:03	°2.30 (W.Haughton)	MajsticLb,MrJimBob,Bridgewater
6-13 Lex¹	1100 sy nw2 cd mi 32 1:043¹:374²:08⁴	3	1	1	13 15	2:08⁴	°.80 (W.Haughton)	EncoreUnPrise.ShipRace,Fussy
6- 6 Lex¹	1000 ft nw2 cd mi 30³1:013¹:3212:01	6	1	1	1¹½ 11½	2:01	3.50 (C.Jenkins)	EncoreUnPrise,LakeWales,ElginHn

---

4-1 / 9 / Purple
TYLER B
b c, 2, by Most Happy Fella—Tarport Cheer by Tar Heel
Tyler B Stable, Meadow Lands, Pa
St.–Del. Miller—Tr.–A. J. Choquette
M(1)1:59¹ 1979 9 4 1 2 18,325
$00 —
Driver–DEL MILLER, 7-5-13 (154) GOLD-BROWN

7-18 M¹	12500 gd 2yr mi 302¹:0021:31 1:59³	1	4	4	2° 2¹ 1ⁿᵏ	1:59³	7.00 (W.Herman)	TylerB,Fndment1st,MidasAlm 69-1
7-11 M¹	10000 ft 2yr mi 29⁴ :59²1:30¹1:59¹	1	4	1° 1 1¹ 1¹	1:59¹	°1.40 (W.Herman)	TylerB,BurtPloma,AlbqrqueN 72-0
6-30 MR	11891 sy 2yr Stk mi 30 1:02 1:324²:03²	3	3	2° 2° 44½ 34¹	2:04¹	3.70 (Del.Miller)	TrstyTghGuy,HpyCllns,TylerB 62-0
6-19 Det¹	14499 ft 2yr mi 30 1:001¹:30 1:59³	7	7	7	7° 44½ 66½	2:00⁴	6.70 (Del.Miller)	MajestcLb,MrJimBob,Bridgewater
6-12 M¹	20611 ft 2yr C Ec mi 29² :591¹:291¹:59⁴	2	4	5	6° 54½ 43	2:00²	e°12.20 (Del.Miller)	BrtsReign,SpdyArlnr,GeneHn 66-0

15-1 / 10 / Blue-Red
SANS STRIKE
ch c, 2, by Strike Out—Briarwood Loraine by Battle Front
Stanley, Agnes & Sophie Kaufman, N.Y. & Fla.
Trainer–W. Ross
M(1)2:02 1979 7 3 0 2 8,446
$00 —
Driver–LEW WILLIAMS, 3-1-47 (140) BLUE-GOLD-WHITE

7-14 VD⅝	16450 ft 2yr mi 27¹ :57 1:27 1:57¹	9	7	5° 2° 53 85½	1:58¹	37.90 (J.Bailey)	Whamo,MckaleeStrk,JiffyBoy 90-0
7- 4 M¹	1000 gd 2yr C mi 304¹:0221:33 2:024	8	4	5	2° 12 13½	2:02⁴	9.60 (L.Williams)	SansStrk,WldBSkpr,SkprBob 57-
6-27 M¹	12500 ft 2yr mi 30 :583¹:284¹:594	7	2	2	2½ 12 13½	2:00¹	36.20 (L.Williams)	BarnumLb,MrJmBb,SansStrk 67-0
6-13 M¹	10000 ft 2yr mi 293¹:01 1:314²:02	4	4	3° 3¹½ 1ⁿᵈ	2:02	4.60 (W.Ross)	SansStrike.FWRocky,Charmax 69-0
6- 6 Brd⅝	15750 ft 2yr C-G Ec mi 31¹1:012¹:321²:01³	4	5	4	2° 2½ 49½	2:03³	9.50 (W.Ross)	CoolWind,AlbaTme,MdwNorm 74-0

99-1 / 11 / Light Blue
APPLE SUNDAY
b c, 2, by Romano Hanover—Miss Noble Adios by Noble Adios
Bud Foley, Hillside, N.J.
Trainer–J. Reese
Q-Fhld2:11 1979 2 0 0 0
$00 —
Driver–RHEO FILION, 9-11-45 (173) RED-GOLD-WHITE

7-19 Brd⅝	2500 ft 2yr nw2 cd mi 314¹:022¹:324²:06²	4	4	2° 5 77½ 817	2:07¹	75.10 (P.Battis)	GttaGoNw,StngtCadence,KeyPryr
7-11 Brd⅝	2500 ft 2yr mi 29 1:004¹:322²:024	5	5° 3° 6 710 7dis	2:08³	63.80 (F.Melia)	TotemHn,GoforeSvn,ThatCat 84-0
6-30 M¹	ft Qua mi 313¹:012¹:313²:014	4	2	3	4 51035dis	2:07¹	N.B. (F.Melia)	BreakingPnt,ArmUlstr,Ararat 72-
6-26 M¹	ft Qua mi 30 1:011¹:32 2:02	1	7	6	5 315 5dis	2:11¹	N.B. (F.Melia)	LadinoHn,SandToy,HMSJolly 78-0
6-19 M¹	ft Qua mi 302¹:013¹:322²:014	1	3	4	4 513 7dis	2:09	N.B. (J.Reese)	DonBbCllns,IrnDle,AdlbrtsQn 73-0

SELECTIONS: 2–9–3

No. 11—APPLE SUNDAY—Scores From 2nd Tier
No. 1 EASY COME EASY GO & No. 8 ENCORE UN PRISE SAME STABLE BUT SEPARATE BETTING INTERESTS.

(5) TROT—1 MILE

Warming-Up Saddle Cloth
BLACK

PURSE $15,000

ASK FOR HORSE BY PROGRAM NUMBER

Exacta Wagering This Race

FORD MOTOR CO. E.S.P. SPECIAL

NON-WINNERS OF $11,000 IN LAST 7 STARTS.

4-1 — 1 — Red

TIC COLLINS
blk h, 6, by Torrence Hanover—Tickled by Stars Pride — St.-Del. Insko—Tr.-C. Connor, Jr.
Vanwey Farms, Highland Mills, N.Y. — 1979 17 0 3 6 18,741
$199,329 — 4, 2:01 (1) Driver-CHARLES CONNOR, JR., 7-18-55 (166) PURPLE-GOLD PPk(⅝)2:01⁴ 1978 24 6 3 2 33,610
7-12 M¹ 15000 ft nw10000 cd mi 30²1:00⁴1:31²2:01 6 7 8 7° 7⁴ 3½ 2:01 22.20 (C.ConnorJr) Pindar,BlueGrssPrd,TicCllins 75-0
7- 7 M¹ ft Qua mi 30²1:00¹1:31¹2:01⁴ 5 3° 1 1 2hd 2¾ 2:02² N.B. (C.ConnorJr) ToryKip,TicCllns,SportsPage 71-0
5-23 RR 15000 sy B2 mi 31¹1:03²1:35³2:05³ 5 7 6° 4° 3³ 3²½ 2:06 1.60 (Del.Insko) Savvy,ShiawayChmp,TicCllns 62-0
5-16 RR 15000 ft B2 mi 31¹1:02 1:33 2:04 6 6 6° 4° 3½ 2½ 2:04¹ 6.50 (Del.Insko) StrpntJt,TicCllns,ScttyGrad 70-0
5- 9 RR 13000 ft B2 mi 29⁴1:01¹1:31²2:02² 3 3 3° 2° 2½ 4½ 2:02³ 3.70 (Del.Insko) KeyHllmrk,CntOfCmlt,StrptJt 68-0
4-28 MR 6500 gd Opn mi 30 1:02²1:34⁴2:06⁴ 7 7 7° 4° 4²½ 3⁵ 2:07⁴ 4.50 (J.Gilmour) Giacomo,BroDesire,TicCollins 52-0

3-1 — 2 — Blue

KEYSTONE JUDEEN
b m, 5, by Harlan Dean—Miss Judy Ann by Stars Pride — Trainer-S. Guy
Muriel & Geneva Knill, Woodbine, Md. — Lau(⅝)1:59¹ 1979 20 6 2 4 15,817
$5,306 — 4, 2:04³ Driver-STEPHEN GUY, 10-28-51 (145) GOLD-GREEN RcR2:04³ 1978 12 6 2 1 5,306
7-16 Lau⅝ 3000 ft Lc cd mi 29¹ :59³1:29¹1:59¹ 4 1 1 1 1⁸ 1¹³½ 1:59¹ .70 (S.Guy) KeyJdeen,FulvioHn,GtpstBea 87-0
7- 9 Lau⅝ 3000 ft Lc cd mi 29³ :59⁴1:31⁴2:03¹ 2 1 2 2 2¹ 1²½ 2:03¹ 1.60 (S.Guy) KeyJudeen,GtpstBea,HpyRdg 80-0
6-29 Lau⅝ 6000 ft Pref hcp mi 28⁴ :59⁴1:30 2:00 3 4 4 5 4⁸ 4⁸½ 2:01³ 16.50 (R.Werkheiser) RdrWind,BckysPrze,ChrlsHwk 77-0
6-22 Lau⅝ 6000 ft Pref mi 28⁴1:00¹1:31¹2:02² 8 7 7 7 5⁶½ 3³½ 2:03¹ 25.00 (R.Werkheiser) RdrWnd,CrlslsCndy,KeyJdeen 75-0
6-15 RcR 7000 ft Pref hcp mi 30¹1:01³1:32¹2:04¹ 6 6 7x 7 7dis 7dis 16.00 (R.Werkheiser) RdrWind,HTsDvd,CrlslsCindy 75-0
6- 8 RcR 7000 ft Pref mi 30 1:02³1:33¹2:03⁴ 5ix7 7 7 7²⁰ 7disP6P5 8.90 (R.Werkheiser) CrlslsCndy,RdrWnd,CgrSlnjn 80-0

9-2 — 3 — White

TAKE A HOLD
b h, 4, by Speedster—Lindys Lady by Worthy Boy — St.-R. Samson—Tr.-V. Staker
Clancy Farms, Dollard Des Ormeaux, Que. — Q-M(1)2:03³ 1979 13 1 1 3 11,650
$9,018 — 3, 2:07 Driver-ROBERT SAMSON, 10-7-49 (140) WHITE-BLACK Que2:07 1978 18 2 0 2 3,436
7-12 M¹ 15000 ft nw10000 cd mi 30²1:00⁴1:31²2:01 4x 9 9 9 9⁷ 7⁴½ 2:02 4.00 (R.Samson) Pindar,BlueGrssPrd,TicCllins 75-0
7- 3 M¹ 16000 ft nw13500 cd mi 28⁴ :59¹1:29 1:58⁴ 8 9 8 8 7⁸½ 5⁴½ 1:59³ 16.80 (R.Samson) ArniesDrt,PeerGynt,TwnEscrt 75-0
6-19 M¹ 10000 ft nw6000 cd mi 30 1:00²1:31²2:02 2 6 6 7° 7⁶½ 3½ 2:02 °2.70 (Jo.Campbell) EricG,BestRecord,TakeAHold 73-0
6- 4 M¹ 10000 ft nw6000 cd mi 29⁴ :59¹1:29³2:00³ 1 4 5 3° 3⁴ 5² 2:01 °1.00 (R.Samson) ArniesDrt,HzorTByrd,JcksnS 64-0
5-28 M¹ 10000 gd nw6000 cd mi 29⁴1:01 1:31³2:03² 9 9 8° 7° 4⁴½ 3ns 2:03² 6.40 (R.Samson) SatinCrwn,KeyTryst,TkeAHld 71-2
5-21 M¹ 11000 ft nw6500 cd mi 30²1:00 1:30²2:01 6 8 6° 6° 4³ 2³ 2:01³ 7.30 (R.Samson) MplLfSctr,TkeAHld,KeyTryst 66-0

12-1 — 4 — Green

TUFFARIN A
b g, 9, by Tuft—Romarin by U Scott — Trainer-J. Foley
Jean Paul & Gilles Gauthier, L. Dudinsky, Mont-Fort Farm, Que. — BB(⅝)2:01⁴ 1979 19 5 2 4 20,773
$46,029 — 8, 2:07 (⅝) Driver-SERGE GRISE, 6-29-44 (165) ORANGE-WHITE BB(⅝)2:07 1978 16 2 5 2 11,281
7-18 M¹ 13000 gd nw8000 cd mi 29¹1:00²1:32¹2:02 2 5 3 3 4² 3² 2:02¹ 5.50 (Jo.Campbell) EricG,GlncoeNotice,TuffarinA 69-1
6-25 M¹ 14000 ft 25000 clm hcp mi 30¹ :59³1:31 2:01 7 8 8 7 7x⁸ 7¹⁶ 2:04¹ 6.70 (S.Grise) ArborBachlr,Alzan,WynDrnly 69-0
6-17 BB⅝ 6500 ft w4001 cd mi 29³1:00⁴1:30²2:01 2 5 5 4° 3³ 4²½ 2:01³ e2.30 (J.P.Gauthier) FirbrdThndr,Haygood,ShiawyChmp
6- 9 BB⅝ 3600 ft 18000 clm hcp mi 29³1:00³1:31¹2:01⁴ 6 3 4 6 4³ 1nk 2:01⁴ 4.50 (J.P.Gauthier) TuffrinA,NblEndeavour,TPLndsy
6- 4 BB⅝ ft Qua mi 30¹1:02⁴1:33⁴2:05³ 3 2 2 2 2³ 2³ 2:06¹ N.B. (S.Grise) PluckyDean,TuffarinA,Haskah
4-22 BB⅝ 4200 ft 25000 clm hcp mi 30²1:01³1:32 2:04 8 8 8 i7° 7⁴ 8⁵½ 2:05 *1.55 (J.P.Gauthier) RynDeSleil,ThMssnry,JnkyrdDog

9-2 — 5 — Black

BUTTONWOOD ODIN
b h, 5, by Speedy Streak—Tarport Terri by Kimberly Kid — Trainer-E. Gilman
J. Richard Colby, Newburyport, Mass. — NE(⅝)2:02² 1979 5 3 2 0 9,125
$21,812 — 4, 2:02² (⅝) Driver-ED GILMAN, 5-10-39 (175) WHITE-GREEN NE(⅝)2:02² 1978 18 8 5 1 19,777
7-17 M¹ 18000 sy nw15000 cd mi 32²1:01⁴1:32³2:02¹ 3 3 5 7 3¹½ 2¹½ 2:02² 10.70 (A.Day) ThDstmn,BttnwdOdin,PrGynt 78-2
7- 9 NE⅝ 3000 ft Pref hcp mi 29²1:01²1:31²2:02² 6 4 4 3° 2hd 1¹½ 2:02² *1.00 (E.Gilman) BttnwdOdin,MrNashua,KllyDunlae
6-25 NE⅝ 2500 ft w2001 cd mi 30³1:02³1:33 2:04¹ 5 5 5 2° 2hd 1³ 2:04¹ *.50 (E.Gilman) BttnwdOdin,DstyDeal,DrcyH 60-0
6-18 NE⅝ 2500 sy w2001 cd mi 31⁴1:04²1:35³2:06⁴ 3ix6 6 5 5⁵ 2hdP1 2:06⁴ °.50 (E.Gilman) BttnwdOdin,FrnchWntr,DrcyH 60-0
6-11 NE⅝ 2500 ft w2001 cd mi 29²1:01¹1:31 2:03 4 3° 3 3 3²½ 2½ 2:03 2.80 (E.Gilman) DrcyH,BttnwdOdin,MrNashua 78-0
6- 2 NE⅝ ft Qua mi 31⁴1:04¹1:36 2:07² 7 1 1 1 1¹ 1¹ 2:07² N.B. (E.Gilman) BttnwdOdin,SpnkyBtty,NsyHoot

12-1 — 6 — Yellow

GLENCOE NOTICE
b g, 5, by Formal Notice—Quick Newport by Newport Dream — Trainer-W. Norris
Walter Norris, London, Ont., Morris Feldman, Montreal, Que. — Q-M(1)2:01⁴ 1979 23 2 4 3 21,951
$49,092 — 4, 2:02³ (1) Driver-WALTER NORRIS 7-6-43 (150) BEIGE-BROWN M(1)2:02³ 1978 26 7 3 5 33,310
7-18 M¹ 13000 gd nw8000 cd mi 29¹1:00²1:32¹2:02 1 2 2 2 1¹ 2nk 2:02 4.50 (Ja.Doherty) EricG,GlncoeNotice,TuffarinA 69-1
7- 5 M¹ 15000 ft nw10000 cd mi 29¹1:00¹1:30 2:00 8 9° 9° 7° 6⁷ 5⁵½ 2:01 7.90 (Jo.Campbell) KyTryst,BrllntYnk,ArmThmsn 64-0
6-28 M¹ 14000 ft nw8500 cd mi 30¹1:00¹1:31 2:01³ 2 3 5 5 4⁴½ 5² 2:02 6.70 (Ja.Doherty) CncrgeStphniesClt,BlGrssPrd 68-0
6-21 M¹ 13000 ft nw8000 cd mi 30 :59⁴1:30¹2:00⁴ 3 4 5 7 5⁵½ 5⁴½ 2:01³ 5.50 (W.Norris) HighARsng,BlGrssPrd,NglCrg 71-0
6-16 M¹ ft T-P Qua mi 30²1:00 1:30¹2:01⁴ 3 4 3 3 3²½ 1hd 2:01⁴ N.B. (Ja.Doherty) GlncoeNtc,TrDawDk,PwrDeal 82-0
6-10 BB⅝ 6250 ft nw750ps cd mi 29³1:00⁴1:31²2:03 9 2° 1 2 2nk 8¹¹ 2:05¹ 7.75 (W.Norris) Haygd,IdealAngus,LvOfAbsnc 80-0

10-1 — 7 — Pink

CHARLAUS HAWK
br h, 5, by Carlisle—Coryza by Newport Dream — Trainer-W. Marsh
Chas. F. Sauers, Forest Hill, Md. — Brd(⅝)2:02 1979 18 5 2 4 22,850
$32,494 — 4, 2:03¹ (⅝) Driver-WAYDE MARSH, 2-12-38 (200) DK. BLUE-LT. BLUE-GOLD Brd(⅝)2:03¹ 1978 13 2 3 2 10,665
7-14 Brd⅝ 5000 ft nw8000 cd mi 28⁴1:00³1:30⁴2:02 2 1 1 1 1³ 1² 2:02 *.80 (W.Marsh) ChrlsHwk,CgrStrlnjn,GibsnLb 76-0
6-29 Lau⅝ 6000 ft Pref hcp mi 28⁴ :59⁴1:30 2:00 6 3° 3 3 3³ 3⁴½ 2:01 6.10 (W.Marsh) RdrWind,BckysPrz,ChrlsHwk 77-0
6-22 Brd⅝ 8000 ft Pref mi 30¹1:02²1:32¹2:01² 2 1 1 1 1⁵ 4² 2:01⁴ 11.40 (W.Marsh) SpeedyDve,ElSilcar,BckysPrz 76-0
6-15 Brd⅝ 8000 ft Pref mi 29¹1:00⁴1:30²2:01¹ 6 2 2 2 2x¹½5¹³½ 2:04 18.70 (W.Marsh) BuckysPrize,Pindar,Sabalist 80-0
6- 1 RcR 9000 ft 4-5yr Stk mi 30³1:01³1:32⁴2:03 1 1 1 1 1¹⁰ 1¹¹½ 2:03 N.B. (W.Marsh) ChrlsHwk,JbileesJoy,ChrlsCrscnt
5-25 Brd⅝ 10000 gd Inv hcp mi 29⁴1:00⁴1:32 2:02¹ 4 2 4 4° 3¹ 3¹½ 2:02³ 47.20 (W.Marsh) YnkBndt,BdfrdSprt,ChrlsHwk 70-0

12-1 — 8 — Gray

LITTLE SCUDDER
ch h, 4, by Florlis—Emilie Frost by Frost Ridge — Trainer-R. Gurfein
Henry Street Stable & Judy Adler, N.J. & R. Gurfein, N.Y. — Stga2:05² 1979 20 6 2 4 18,460
$4,499 — 3, 2:07 (1) Driver-JACK PARKER, JR., 7-19-55 (153) RED-BLUE-WHITE Lat(1)2:07 1978 8 1 2 1 3,996
7-12 M¹ 15000 ft nw10000 cd mi 30²1:00⁴1:31²2:01 3 4 4 4° 3¹½ 4½ 2:01 11.40 (J.ParkerJr) Pindar,BlueGrssPrd,TicCllins 75-0
6-23 MR 6000 ft Opn mi 30²1:02 1:31²2:03¹ 1 2 3 3 3³ 3²½ 2:03³ 3.10 (R.Donofrio) GerardVee,Elebon,LttlScuddr 63-0
6-19 MR 3300 ft B3-C1 hcp mi 30³1:01²1:32³2:05 6 6 6° 5°°3x¹x6P7 2:06¹ °1.10 (R.Donofrio) MadDoc,UplnSmoke,JetAngel 68-0
6-11 MR 2700 gd C1-C2 hcp mi 30³1:01³1:34¹2:06¹ 8 7 6 2°°1² 1³½ 2:06¹ °1.10 (R.Donofrio) LttlScddr,JetAngl,SSArrdnde 52-0
6- 4 MR 2000 ft C2 mi 29⁴1:03²1:34²2:06¹ 2 4 3° 1 1²½ 1⁵½ 2:06¹ °.80 (R.Donofrio) LttlScddr,SctrMgoo,StdrdRgl 67-0
5-26 MR gd Qua mi 32²1:04³1:36³2:08 2 1 1 1 1⁸ 1¹⁸ 2:08 N.B. (R.Donofrio) LittlScudder,HiBi,FlmngSpd 58-0

8-1 — 9 — Purple

HIGH AND RISING
b g, 6, by Add Hanover—Bold Girl by Demon Rum — Trainer-S. Richardson
Stanton Richardson, Ocean City, Md. — M(1)2:00⁴ 1979 8 1 0 1 8,630
$5,405 — 5, 2:07² Driver-JAMES DOHERTY, 9-27-40 (161) RED-WHITE-GREEN RcR2:07² 1978 9 4 0 2 4,015
7- 5 M¹ 15000 ft nw10000 cd mi 29¹1:00¹1:30 2:00 3 7 7 6°x9¹² 9²¹ 2:04¹ 2.90 (Ja.Doherty) KyTryst,BrllntYnk,ArmThmsn 64-0
6-21 M¹ 13000 ft nw8000 cd mi 30 :59⁴1:30¹2:00⁴ 1 6 4° 2° 2½ 1ns 2:00⁴ 4.40 (Ja.Doherty) HighARsng,BlGrssPrd,NglCrg 71-0
6-13 M¹ 12000 ft nw7500 cd mi 30¹1:01 1:31³2:02² 6 7 7 6°°4³x 4²½ 2:02⁴ 4.90 (Ja.Doherty) PAScrplrn,MrtLtlJhn,KyTryst 69-0
6- 1 RcR 5000 ft w4001 cd mi 30²1:02²1:33¹2:03³ 1 5 5 7 7⁴ 6² 2:04 4.80 (S.Richardson) KeyJudeen,CrlslsCndy,CrlslsPaul
5-25 RcR 5000 ft w4001 cd mi 30²1:02³1:33⁴2:04 3 5 5 4°°4² 3¹½ 2:04² 10.50 (P.Myer) CrlslCndy,RdrWind,HghAndRsng
5-18 RcR 5000 sy w4001 cd mi 32 1:06¹1:39¹2:11³ 5 8 8 7 7⁶ 6³½ 2:12² 11.10 (S.Richardson) BalHD,RdrWind,KeysJudeen 60-0

30-1 — 10 — Blue-Red

TWO TWENTY DREAM
b c, 3, by Dream Of Glory—Prudy Hanover by Stars Pride — Trainer-Den. Filion
Patricia A. & Vernon G. Gochneaur, Aurora, Ohio — Mea(⅝)2:05⁴ 1979 11 2 1 1 8,775
$15,586 — 2, 2:10³ (⅝) Driver-RHEO FILION, 9-11-45 (170) RED-GOLD-WHITE RP(⅝)2:10³ 1978 11 1 3 4 15,586
7-14 Brd⅝ 5000 ft nw8000 cd mi 28⁴1:00³1:30⁴2:02 8 8 8 8 6⁶½ 7⁸½ 2:03⁴ 58.00 (Den.Filion) ChrlsHwk,CgrStrlnjn,GbsnLb 76-0
7- 6 Brd⅝ 5500 ft nw7000 cd mi 30⁴1:00⁴1:32²2:02⁴ 5 6 6 5 4³ 3⁷ 2:04¹ 36.50 (A.Dagenais) ArmSolar,ArmTed,TwTwDrm 76-0
7- 1 Brd⅝ 5500 ft w7501 cd mi 30⁴1:02 1:32⁴2:03 5 6 7 7 7⁶½ 6⁶ 2:04¹ 34.50 (Den.Filion) ScttyGradte,GbsnLb,Sabalist 74-0
6-20 M¹ 16000 ft nw13500 cd mi 30¹1:00⁴1:30³2:00² 5 6° 7 7 7¹² 7²⁴ 2:05¹ 43.60 (Den.Filion) SatinCrwn,ImaLula,MdwDmjo 75-0
6-12 M¹ ft Qua mi 30⁴1:02 1:32³2:02 3 3 3 3 3⁵½ 3¹⁴½ 2:04⁴ N.B. (Den.Filion) BstRcrd,BkrTStr,TwoTwDrm 66-0
5-31 Nfld 15700 sy 3yr Stk mi 31³1:03¹1:35³2:08 8 6° 5 4° 6⁶ 8¹²½ 2:10² 8.90 (R.Wood) JnCltwn,HiLifeTad,LbtsPlFce 66-0

SELECTIONS: 2—1—3

C—DENOTES CONVENTIONAL SULKY

(6) PACE—1 MILE

Warming-Up Saddle Cloth
YELLOW

PURSE $15,000

ASK FOR HORSE BY PROGRAM NUMBER

Exacta Wagering This Race

WOODROW WILSON QUALIFYING HEAT

EARLY CLOSING EVENT No. 2—(2nd Div.)—TWO-YEAR-OLDS
(1st 4 in the official order of finish qualify for the $862,750 Woodrow Wilson Final Wednesday, August 1).

10-1 — 1 — Red

GENE HANOVER b c, 2, by Albatross—Gigi Barmin by Greentree Adios — St.-S. Dancer—Tr.-J. Hafford
Mr. & Mrs. Dancer, Rose Hild Breeding Farm, Dawson & Grant, Jr. — M(1)2:004 1979 8 4 1 2 19,932
$00 — Driver-STANLEY DANCER, 7-25-27 (159) BLUE-GOLD

7-17 M1 10000 sy 2yr C mi 302 :5941:30 2:01 8 1 1 1 130 131 2:01 2.30 (S.Dancer) GeneHanover,Hive,Maxcelsior 78-1
7-11 M1 12500 ft 2yr mi 2931:0331:3941:594 4x 9 8 7 53½ 65 2:004 *2.10 (S.Dancer) MidasAlm,Searights,BrtsRgn 72-0
7- 4 M1 12500 sl 2yr mi 3011:0011:3032:004 4 1 1 4 51½ 1nk 2:004 4.90 (S.Dancer) GeneHn,BarnumLb,StneRacer 57-
6-22 LB⅝ 15815 sy 2yr Stk mi 2941:00 1:3021:593 1 2 1 1 1½ 35½ 2:003 *.60 (S.Dancer) DearStar,JDsBuck,GeneHanvr 63-0
6-12 M1 20611 ft 2yr C Ec mi 292 :5911:2911:594 6 5 1 1 11 31½ 2:00 e*1.20 (S.Dancer) BrtsReign,SpdyArlnr,GeneHn 66-0
6- 6 Brd⅝ 16050 ft 2yr C-G Ec mi 2941:0021:30 1:594 8 7 6 5 53¾ 26¼ 2:011 e3.10 (S.Dancer) Whamo,GeneHanover,TylerB 74-0

6-1 — 2 — Blue

DENALI b c, 2, by Most Happy Fella—Slip Away by Meadow Pace — Trainer-D Ackerman
Richard S. Staley, Beverly Hills, Calif. — Det(1)1:593 1979 7 3 2 0 8,249
$00 Driver-DOUG ACKERMAN, 10-26-27 (175) BLUE-GRAY

7-12 Det1 5800 ft nw2 cd mi 283 :5911:2731:57 10 7 7 7° 68 26 1:581 *1.10 (D.Ackerman) ImaDew,Denali,TVSonsplendor
7- 2 Det1 4400 ft nw2 cd mi 291 :5931:30 1:593 2 4 3° 1 11 15 1:593 *1.00 (D.Ackerman) Denali,ShiawayCarole,PGJoey
6-19 Det1 14499 ft 2yr Stk mi 30 1:0011:30 1:593 8 8 8 8 98 56½ 2:004 11.10 (D.Ackerman) MajesticLb,MrJimBob,Bridgewater
6-12 Det1 7500 ft 2yr C mi 2941:0211:3212:02 1 5 5 6° 73 1hd 2:02 6.20 (D.Ackerman) Denali,Bridgewater,Twoanapiece
6- 5 Det1 1000 ft 2yr C mi 2921:0111:3312:022 7 5 5 4 4x3 27 2:034 N.B. (D.Ackerman) Bridgewater,Denali,Chenango
5-28 Det1 500 ft 2yr C mi 3141:0231:3342:05 1 6 2° 2 22 16 2:05 N.B. (D.Ackerman) Denali,GeeJet,MyFiddleSticks

---

12-1 — 3 — White

CORINTUS b c, 2, by Armbro Nesbit—Corinne Sterling by Adios Butler — St.-W. Haughton—Tr.-A. Thomas
Richard Herman, Fla. & Walter Tworkowski, N.Y. — RcR2:053 1979 9 2 3 0 16,320
$00 — Driver-PETER HAUGHTON, 9-22-54 (155) WHITE-GREEN-GOLD

7-14 VD¾ 16400 ft 2yr Stk m 271 :57 1:27 1:571 1 3 9 9 64½ 53¼ 1:574 e31.70 (P.Haughton) Whamo,MckaleeStrk,JffyBoy 90-0
7- 8 BB⅝ 23100 ft 2yr Stk mi 29 1:0241:3042:014 7 3 2° 2° 2hd 43¼ 2:022 e1.75 (W.Haughton) DoradoHn,AllThWy,TrsrReef 76-0
7- 2 Stga 27310 ft 2yr Stk mi 2941:0041:3112:011 4 2 2 3 3 23 2:014 11.60 (P.Haughton) StrmDmge,Corintus,FiskHn 85-0
6-22 LB⅝ 15815 sy 2yr Stk mi 2941:00 1:3021:593 10 6 6 6° 66½ 613 2:021 e7.60 (J.Greene) DearStar,JDsBuck,GeneHn 63-0
6-15 RcR 13050 ft 2yr Stk mi 3131:0231:3412:053 7 2° 1° 1 11 11¼ 2:053 *1.40 (W.Haughton) Corintus,BeauStr,RdgwdExpr 75-0
6- 5 LB⅝ 300 ft 2yr mi 3131:03 1:3312:03 2 1 1 2 2hd 2¾ 2:031 N.B. (W.Haughton) JffyBoy,Corintus,SonnySilver 76-0

40-1 — 4 — Green

F W ROCKY b c, 2, by Bogart Hanover—Sweet Lips by Santo Eden — Trainer-T. DeVitas
Rock N Knoll Farm, Stewartsville, N.J. — 1979 9 0 2 0 6,130
$00 — Driver-JOHN CAMPBELL, 4-8-55 (156) WHITE-MAROON

7-18 M1 10000 gd 2yr mi 30 :59 1:2911:592 3 5 5 5 34½ 59¼ 2:011 3.40 (J.KingJr) AlbqrqueN,SurfrSctt,AvnLrry 69-1
7-11 M1 10000 ft 2yr mi 2941:0021:3112:003 3 6 5° 4° 21½ 2ns 2:003 3.30 (Jo.Campbell) ElginHn,FWRocky,RickysHeel 72-0
7- 4 M1 10000 gd 2yr mi 3041:0331:3442:052 8 8° 6° 7° 74½ 52¼ 2:054 7.30 (Jo.Campbell) HpyJffry,TrsTchst,CrtlndTpht 57-
6-20 M1 10000 ft 2yr mi 3031:0031:3032:01 6 8 5° 5° 65¾ 716½ 2:031 21.20 (W.Bresnahan) HpyCllns,BrtsRgn,PrdncCllns 75-0
6-13 M1 10000 ft 2yr mi 2931:01 1:3142:02 2 7 7 8° 63½ 2hd 2:02 22.00 (Jo.Campbell) SansStrike,FWRocky,Charmax 69-0
6- 6 M1 10000 ft 2yr mi 3011:00 1:31 2:012 4 8 9 9 77¼ 69 2:031 41.40 (W.Bresnahan) MrJmBb,KrzrsYms,TThlThvg 69-0

5-2 — 5 — Black

NIATROSS b c, 2, by Albatross—Niagara Dream by Bye Bye Byrd — Trainer-C Galbraith
Niagara Acres, N.Y. & Clint Galbraith, Orlando, Fla. — VD(¾)1:573 1979 4 4 0 0 10,175
$00 — Driver-CLINT GALBRAITH, 7-22-37 (150) PURPLE-WHITE

7-14 VD¾ 16100 ft 2yr Stk mi 282 :59 1:2841:573 10 3 1 1 1½ 13 1:573 *1.20 (C.Galbraith) Niatross,TrsrReef,JDsBuck 90-0
7- 9 VD¾ 2000 ft nw2000 cd mi 283 :5921:3011:592 4 2 2 2° 1hd 12 1:592 *.70 (C.Galbraith) Niatross,MrRaySctt,YnkAirlnr 76-0
7- 2 VD¾ 2000 sy nw2000 cd mi 3121:0331:35 2:071 5 1 2 1 1½ 11 2:071 *1.50 (C.Galbraith) Niatross,BlltVanPce,YnkArlnr 65-4
6-22 VD¾ 250 ft 2yr mi 29 1:0111:3122:023 1 1 1 2 21½ 13 2:023 N.B. (D.Galbraith) Niatross,MarloHn,LisaFinest 70-0
6-13 VD¾ ft Qua mi 3041:0211:3312:041 2 1 1 1 14 113 2:041 N.B. (C.Galbraith) Niatross,Callijero,SssyTower 63-0
6- 5 VD¾ ft Qua mi 2831:0121:3212:021 2 3 1° 1 11½ 13 2:021 N.B. (C.Galbraith) Niatrss,RveilleByrd,ByeBCapt 81-0

2-1 — 6 — Yellow

WHAMO br c, 2, by Flying Bret—Mannart Royal Ann by Race Time — Trainer-C. Clark
Flying Bret Inc., New York, N.Y. — VD(¾)1:571 1979 6 6 0 0 34,833
$00 — Driver-CHARLES CLARK, 7-26-24 (165) GRAY-BLUE-GOLD

7-14 VD¾ 16400 ft 2yr Stk mi 271 :57 1:27 1:571 6 2° 1 1 11½ 11 1:571 *.20 (C.Clark) Whamo,MckaleeStrk,JiffyBoy 90-0
6-27 Lex1 15105 ft 2yr Stk mi 284 :5741:2731:572 2 1 1 1 15 15 1:572 *.10 (C.Clark) Whamo,TreasrReef,EsyCmeEsyGo
6-12 M1 20611 ft 2yr C Ec mi 29 1:0021:3021:592 4 1 1 1 11½ 12 1:592 *.40 (C.Clark) Whamo,MapleFritz,FiskHan 66-0
6- 6 Brd⅝ 16050 ft 2yr C-G Ec mi 2941:0021:30 1:594 4 2 1 1 1nk 16¼ 1:594 *.60 (C.Clark) Whamo,GeneHanover,TylerB 74-0
5-16 Lex1 900 ft nw2 cd mi 2941:0131:3141:594 8 1° 1 1 110 116 1:594 *.20 (C.Clark) Whamo,QueensChrm,WnningBlnkr
5-10 Lex1 600 ft nw1 cd mi 30 1:0131:3122:00 2 1 1 1 14 12½ 2:00 *.20 (C.Clark) Whamo,FrdmTm,MartinSenour

---

15-1 — 7 — Pink

SURFER SCOTT b c, 2, by Brets Star—Surfer Girl by Race Time — St.-W. Haughton—Tr.-A. Thomas
Joseph Caico, Charles Glovsky, Edward & Rodney Andrews, Mass. — Brd(⅝)2:04 1979 4 2 1 0 3,473
$00 — Driver-W. (Bill) HAUGHTON, 11-2-23 (154) WHITE-GREEN-GOLD

7-18 M1 10000 gd 2yr mi 30 :59 1:2911:592 2 1 2 1 21 22 1:594 *1.90 (P.Haughton) AlbqrqueN,SurfrSctt,AvnLrry 69-1
7- 5 M1 13463 ft 2yr NJSS mi 2931:00 1:3112:004 4 7 7 9 67¾ 53¼ 2:012 *2.00 (W.Haughton) DbleDevil,Didit,KreizrsYamis 64-0
6-27 Brd⅝ 300 ft 2yr C-G mi 3021:02 1:3312:04 6 1 2 1 11½ 113½ 2:04 N.B. (W.Haughton) SrfrSctt,CaptScky,MstFklFlla 65-0
6-20 Brd⅝ 300 ft 2yr C-G mi 3141:0431:36 2:054 5 1 1 1 11½ 18 2:054 N.B. (W.Haughton) SurferSctt,TrlyGndlfo,VAStr 72-0

10-1 — 8 — Gray

FUNDAMENTALIST b c, 2, by Albatross—Timely Blue Chip by Bret Hanover — Trainer-G. Riegle
George Segal, Highland Park, Ill. — ScD(⅝)2:014 1979 5 1 3 0 3,225
$00 — Driver-GENE RIEGLE, 6-3-28 (185) CHARTREUSE-RED

7-18 M1 12500 gd 2yr mi 3021:0021:31 1:593 5 3 3 5 53¼ 2nk 1:593 35.30 (G.Riegle) TylerB,Fndmentlst,MidasAlm 69-1
7- 3 Mea⅝ 15215 ft 2yr Stk mi 3021:0131:3112:00 8 8 6° 5° 44 613½ 2:023 4.40 (G.Riegle) DearStr,JDsBuck,DallasSpur 71-0
6-26 ScD⅝ 100 ft 2yr C-G mi 3041:0311:3222:014 3 1 1 1 16 111½ 2:014 N.B. (A.Riegle) Fundamntlst,SafetySkpr,Stevatar
6-19 ScD⅝ 100 ft 2yr C-G mi 3011:0131:33 2:033 2 4 4 1° 2hd 22½ 2:04 N.B. (A.Riegle) SmpsnDLte,Fndamntlst,IrnstnFlla
6-12 ScD⅝ 100 ft 2yr C-G mi 3141:0421:37 2:051 4 2 3 3 2½ 22¾ 2:064 N.B. (G.Riegle) DshgAlm,Fundamntlst,MstlyMlvin

---

8-1 — 9 — Purple

ALBERTON b c, 2, by Armbro Omaha—Alice Wejover by Overtrick — St.-Ja. Kopas—Tr.-Jo. Kopas
Estate Of J. Elgin Armstrong, Brampton, Ont. — FlmD2:01 1979 8 4 2 1 24,436
$00 — Driver-JACK KOPAS, 10-16-28 (185) GREEN-WHITE

7-17 GrR⅝ 31900 ft 2yr Stk mi 284 :5911:2831:582 12 5 4 5 44½ 32¾ 1:59 e6.85 (Ja.Kopas) DoradoHnvr,Tyrant,Alberton 72-0
7- 8 FlmD 17514 ft 2yr C Stk mi 2931:0041:3132:01 4 2 1 1 11 11 2:01 *.55 (Ja.Kopas) Alberton,BchtreeCnt,BeauJm 78-0
7- 2 GrR⅝ 21066 ft 2yr Stk mi 2921:0141:3212:01 x5 9 9 9° 76¾ 69 2:024 e4.40 (R.Waples) Tyrant,DoradoHn,AllTheWay 72-0
6-23 BB⅝ 18433 ft 2yr Stk mi 2921:0031:3122:002 1 2 2 2° 2¾ 21½ 2:003 e2.10 (Ja.Kopas) Tyrant,Alberton,RdleafSrprs 56-0
6-16 Sud 19852 ft 2yr C Stk mi 3031:0411:3532:043 3 2 2 2 22½ 21 2:044 *.50 (Ja.Kopas) ScttsWndr,Albrton,CrlwdDar 79-0
6- 3 Moh⅝ 2400 ft nw2 cd mi 3041:05 1:3542:043 1 1 1 1 11½ 13 2:043 1.55 (Ja.Kopas) Alberton,SlkyShkr,RsnForRno 79-0

15-1 — 10 — Blue-Red

J Ds BUCK b c, 2, by Adios Vic—J D Betty by Harold J — Trainer-J. Miller
Barr-M Stable, Ottawa, Ont. — 1979 5 0 3 2 9,799
$00 — Driver-JIM MILLER, 9-13-45 (160) BLUE-GOLD

7-14 VD¾ 16100 ft 2yr Stk mi 282 :59 1:2841:573 8 9° 4° 4° 43¼ 35¾ 1:584 9.70 (J.Miller) Niatross,TrsreReef,JDsBuck 90-0
7- 3 Mea⅝ 15215 ft 2yr Stk mi 3021:0131:3112:00 2 2 2 2 21½ 24¼ 2:004 e10.60 (J.Miller) DearStr,JDsBuck,DallasSpur 71-0
6-22 LB⅝ 15815 sy 2yr Stk mi 2941:00 1:3021:593 2 1 2 3 32 24¼ 2:003 e22.70 (J.Miller) DearStar,JDsBuck,GeneHn 63-0
5-30 Brd⅝ 300 ft 2yr mi 3031:0231:33 2:041 3 3 3 4 44 36 2:052 N.B. (J.Miller) GreyHorse,KawarthaTrzan,JDsBck
5-18 Brd⅝ 300 ft 2yr mi 3041:0221:3242:041 7 1° 1 1 1½ 2hd 2:041 N.B. (S.Forbes) TotemHn,JDsBuck,SansStrike 63-0

SELECTIONS: 6—5—2

No. 3 CORINTUS & No. 7 SURFER SCOTT—Same Stable But Separate Betting Interests.

C—DENOTES CONVENTIONAL SULKY

(7) PACE—1 MILE

Warming-Up Saddle Cloth
PINK

PURSE $15,000

Exacta Wagering This Race

WOODROW WILSON QUALIFYING HEAT

EARLY CLOSING EVENT No. 2—(3rd Div.)—TWO-YEAR-OLDS
(1st 4 in the official order of finish qualify for the $862,750 Woodrow Wilson Final Wednesday, August 1).

ASK FOR HORSE BY PROGRAM NUMBER

10-1 — 1 — Red

ALBA TIME — b c, 2, by Albatross—Lydia Time by Good Time — Barr-M Stable, Ottawa, Ont. — Trainer-J. Miller — LB(⅝)2:033 1979 6 2 2 0 13,262
$00 — Driver-JIM MILLER, 9-13-45 (160) BLUE-GOLD

7-14 VD¾ 16400 ft 2yr Stk mi 271 :57 1:27 1:571 3 5 3 5 42½ 63¾ 1:58 64.40 (J.Miller) Whamo,MckaleeStrk,JiffyBoy 90-0
7- 3 Mea⅝ 14915 ft 2yr Stk mi 3011:02 1:3112:014 5 1 2 2° 32½ 46¼ 2:03 2.20 (J.Miller) Ebony,AdlbrtsBrze,MorganHn 71-0
6-22 LB⅝ 15815 sy 2yr Stk mi 2941:0231:3322:033 6 4° 3 3 31¼ 11¼ 2:033 e1.50 (J.Miller) AlbaTime,JiffyBoy,FiskHn 67-0
6- 6 Brd⅝ 15750 ft 2yr C-G Ec mi 3111:0121:3212:013 1 1 2 3 31 x21¼ 2:014 2.40 (J.Miller) CoolWind,AlbaTm,MdwNorm 74-0
5-26 Brd⅝ 300 ft 2yr mi 3041:0121:3212:013 5 3° 1 2 22 23 2:021 N.B. (J.Miller) GeneHanover,AlbaTime,Jobim 60-0
5-18 Brd⅝ 300 ft 2yr mi 3121:0421:3422:052 5 5 5 1 11½ 14¾ 2:052 N.B. (J.Miller) AlbaTime,Jobim,HolyWater 63-0

9-2 — 2 — Blue

STONE RACER — b c, 2, by Race Time—Ricci Reenie First by Tar Heel — Twiggy Stables, Inc., Great Neck, N.Y. — Trainer-R. Bencal — RR2:034 1979 5 2 2 1 6,375
$00 — Driver-JOE MARSH, JR., 6-20-34 (125) GRAY-BLUE-RED

7-18 RR 7000 ft 2yr C-G cd mi 31 1:0341:3422:034 5 1 1 1 12½ 12¼ 2:034 1.40 (J.MarshJr) StnRcr,PppaCpello,HrbrsAuRevoir
7- 4 M1 12500 sl 2yr mi 3011:0011:3032:004 1 2 3 7 62½ 31½ 2:01 14.00 (J.MarshJr) GeneHn,BarnumLb,StneRacer 57-
6-27 M1 1000 ft 2yr C mi 2941:01 1:32 2:014 3 1 2 3 21¾ 21½ 2:02 N.B. (J.MarshJr) KeyWinner,StneRcr,DustyFlla 70-0
6-20 YR 1500 ft 2yr mi 3131:03 1:35 2:054 2 1 3 2° 2nk 11½ 2:054 N.B. (J.MarshJr) StnRcr,PppaCpllo,DnllsRmeo 76-0
6-13 YR 1500 ft 2yr mi 3241:0531:3722:09 3 3 3 4 43 2nk 2:09 N.B. (J.MarshJr) PppaCpello,StnRacer,Marrek 67-0

10-1 — 3 — White

ARMBRO VIENNA — b c, 2, by Adios Vic—Armbro Roma by Most Happy Fella — Serge A. Savard, St. Bruno D'Movle, Que. — St.-Ja. Kopas—Tr.-Jo. Kopas — GrR(⅝)2:012 1979 9 5 0 0 5,685
$00 — Driver-JACK KOPAS, 10-16-28 (185) GREEN-WHITE

7-17 GrR⅝ 31900 ft 2yr Stk mi 284 :5911:2831:582 5 10 9 8 87¾ 69¾ 2:002 e6.85 (T.Strauss) DoradoHnvr,Tyrant,Alberton 72-0
7-12 GrR⅝ 2000 ft 2-3yr Mdn cd mi 3041:0141:3142:012 7 2° 1 1 12 18¾ 2:012 *.35 (Ja.Kopas) ArmVienna,DvysStr,FracoStr 32-0
7- 2 GrR⅝ 21066 ft 2yr Stk mi 2921:0141:3212:01 3 3 3 4 43¾ 46½ 2:021 e4.40 (Ja.Kopas) Tyrant,DoradoHn,AllTheWay 72-0
6-23 BB⅝ 18533 ft 2yr Stk mi 2911:0041:3021:594 2 4 4x 8x 9dis 9dis 2:083 e31.50 (Ja.Kopas) DoradoHn,AlThWay,InvsblDc 56-0
6-12 M1 20611 ft 2yr C Ec mi 292 :5911:2911:594 5 1 2 2° 910½1019¼ 2:033 e1.60 (Jo.Kopas) BrtsReign,SpdyArlnr,GeneHn 66-0
6- 5 YR 1500 sy 2yr mi 3141:0421:3512:062 4 6 6° 1 14½ 16½ 2:062 N.B. (R.Rash) ArmbroVienna,Bullion,Rijan

---

4-1 — 4 — Green

BURT PALOMA — b c, 2, by Armbro Nesbit—Brettina Paloma by Bret Hanover — William Farber, West Bloomfield, Mich. — Trainer-D. Elliott — 1979 5 0 2 0 4,098
$00 — Driver-JOHN CAMPBELL, 4-8-55 (156) WHITE-MAROON

7-18 M1 12500 gd 2yr mi 3021:0021:31 1:593 6 5 5 4° 41¾ 4¼ 1:593 8.00 (Jo.Campbell) TylerB,Fndmentlst,MidasAlm 69-1
7-11 M1 10000 ft 2yr mi 294 :5921:3031:591 4 6 4° 2° 21 2½ 1:591 2.80 (Jo.Campbell) TylerB,BurtPloma,AlbqrqueN 72-0
7- 2 LB⅝ 2200 ft 2yr nw1 cd mi 3011:0211:3212:031 5 3 3 2° 1hd 21 2:032 56.10 (D.Elliott) Didit,BurtPaloma,JMGary 71-0
6-25 LB⅝ 300 ft 2yr mi 32 1:0431:3622:07 4xx6 6 6 58¾ 49¼ 2:084 N.B. (D.Elliott) DrzzlMst,JDsBnda,SwmpwtrSue
6-18 LB⅝ 300 ft 2yr mi 294 :5941:2932:014 1 6 6 7 718¾421¼ 2:06 N.B. (D.Elliott) ByeBAlba,PpprsQn,FlwngStr 82-0

6-1 — 5 — Black

SILENT TORCH — b c, 2, by Silent Majority—Torchie Cam by Meadow Chuck — Hubert Horst Riedel, Fort Lauderdale, Fla. — St.-W. Haughton—Tr.-A. Thomas — M(1)2:014 1979 8 3 0 0 800
$00 — Driver-PETER HAUGHTON, 9-22-54 (155) WHITE-GREEN-GOLD

7-17 M1 10000 sy 2yr C mi 302 :5941:30 2:01 7ax3x 5 x5 dnf 11.40 (P.Haughton) GeneHanover,Hive,Maxcelsior 78-1
7-11 M1 1000 ft 2yr C mi 3031:0111:3112:014 3 4 1 1 12½ 12½ 2:014 N.B. (W.Haughton) SlntTrch,WldBSkpr,RealRwrd 78-0
7- 4 Brd⅝ 2500 gd 2yr mi 2931:0421:3612:062 2 6 5 5°ix712¾7dis 2:151 11.20 (R.Dudley) GofreSvn,Jobim,LrdAlbatrss 60-0
6-27 Brd⅝ 2000 ft 2yr mi 3021:02 1:3232:042 8 3° 1 1 11½ 63 2:05 *1.70 (R.Dudley) LrdAlbatross,Jobim,MrTempo 74-0
6-20 Brd⅝ 2000 ft 2yr mi 2921:0031:3112:031 5 2 2x 8 712¼719¾ 2:071 1.80 (R.Dudley) GoforeSeven,Jobim,MrTempo 78-0
6- 8 Brd⅝ 300 ft 2yr mi 3121:0311:3332:041 4 2 2 1 13 13 2:041 N.B. (R.Dudley) SlntTrch,MfllaRnbw,JthroHlly 75-0

10-1 — 6 — Yellow

ELGIN HANOVER — b c, 2, by Steady Star—Ella Skipper by Meadow Skipper — C & K Stables, Somers, N.Y. — St.-W. Popfinger—Tr.-W. Jacobs — M(1)2:003 1979 5 2 1 1 5,499
$00 — Driver-W. (Bill) POPFINGER, 10-9-36 (196) GREEN-WHITE

7-11 M1 10000 ft 2yr mi 2941:0021:3112:003 2 3 1° 1 11½ 1ns 2:003 *1.20 (W.Popfinger) ElginHn,FWRocky,RickysHeel 72-0
6-29 Lex1 900 sy nw1 cd mi 3331:0611:3842:09 4 1 2 2° 24 21¾ 2:092 *1.10 (W.Jacobs) TeddyHnvr,ElginHnvr,TarbaHnvr
6-22 Lex1 1300 ft nw2 cd mi 2911:0021:3042:013 7 7 8 8° 65 44 2:022 3.90 (W.Jacobs) OrnateHill,TreasureReef,SimiQ
6-16 Lex1 ft Qua mi 3111:0041:3212:023 6 2 1° 1 15 112 2:023 N.B. (W.Jacobs) ElginHnvr,EbeSStory,IkeL
6- 6 Lex1 1000 ft nw2 cd mi 3031:0131:3212:01 3 4 4i 3 35½ 310½ 2:03 9.40 (W.Popfinger) EncoreUnPrise,LkeWales,ElginHn
5-30 Lex1 100 ft 2yr cd ml 3241:0511:3612:053 2 3 3 2° 2¾ 1hd 2:053 N.B. (W.Popfinger) ElginHn,Dalliance,EsyComeEsyGo

---

15-1 — 7 — Pink

RATHMORE (J) — b c, 2, by Jolly Rodger—J M Dorthy by Adios Ronnie — Howard Camden, Frank Collazo, Jr. & Sr., N.J. — Trainer H. Camden — 1979 7 0 2 2 4,585
$00 — Driver-SHELLY GOUDREAU, 5-27-48 (162) RED-GOLD

7-12 M1 10000 ft 2yr mi 3021:0311:3042:011 3 7 7 6 45½ 2hd 2:011 8.30 (Jo.Campbell) SpdyArlnr,Rathmre,QltyBlChp 75-0
7- 5 M1 13463 ft 2yr NJSS mi 2931:00 1:3112:004 10 8 8 8°°78¼ 65¾ 2:02 54.10 (Jo.Campbell) DbleDevil,Didit,KreizrsYamis 64-0
6-21 M1 13465 ft 2yr NJSS mi 3031:0021:3022:014 2 4 6 6 64¾ 3¾ 2:02 N.B. (S.Goudreau) HghRum,AurCougar,Rathmre 75-0
6-16 M1 1000 ft 2yr NJSS mi 3231:0341:3422:034 2 4 5 5 57 56½ 2:05 N.B. (Jo.Campbell) Terrorst,LesterH,RmnEmpror 82-0
6- 9 M1 1000 ft 2yr NJSS mi 3111:0111:32 2:014 3 6 6 7 66 511½ 2:04 N.B. (H.Camden) Terrorst,AuroraCougar,Synek 73-0
5-29 Fhld 1000 ft 2yr NJSS mi 3111:03 1:3342:053 2 3 3 3 33 22 2:06 N.B. (H.Camden) JuliasCeasar,Rathmore,Synek 70-0

8-1 — 8 — Gray

BRETS REIGN — b c, 2, by Bret Hanover—Queens Idyl by Good Time — Lakeville Stable, Lake Success, N.Y. — Trainer-L. Meittinis — M(1)1:594 1979 10 2 2 1 15,430
$00 — Driver-HERVE FILION, 2-1-40 (163) RED-BLUE-WHITE

7-18 M1 12500 gd 2yr mi 3021:0021:31 1:593 10 9 8 7 75¾ 78½ 2:011 21.60 (P.Haughton) TylerB,Fndmentlst,MidasAlm 69-1
7-11 M1 12500 ft 2yr mi 2931:0031:3041:594 7 6 7 9 74¾ 31¼ 2:00 16.90 (B.Webster) MidasAlm,Searights,BrtsRgn 72-0
7- 4 M1 12500 sl 2yr mi 3011:0011:3032:004 2 4 4 1 1hd 88¼ 2:022 4.40 (B.Webster) GeneHn,BarnumLb,StneRacer 57-
6-27 M1 12500 ft 2yr mi 30 :5831:2841:594 9 8 8 7° 67½ 611¼ 2:02 4.10 (Her.Filion) BarnumLb,MrJmBb,SansStrk 67-0
6-20 M1 10000 ft 2yr mi 3031:0031:3032:01 9 6 2° 2° 21 21¼ 2:011 2.20 (Her.Filion) HpyCllns,BrtsRgn,PrdncCllns 75-0
6-12 M1 20611 ft 2yr C Ec mi 292 :5911:2911:594 11 6 7 5 33 1hd 1:594 16.00 (Her.Filion) BrtsReign,SpdyArlnr,GeneHn 66-0

3-1 — 9 — Purple

JIFFY BOY — b c, 2, by Steady Star—Lacy Hanover by Meadow Ace — Edward & Lydia Ajmo, Miami Lakes, Fla. — St.-W. Haughton—Tr.-A. Thomas — LB(⅝)2:024 1979 6 2 2 1 6,296
$00 — Driver-W. (Bill) HAUGHTON, 11-2-23 (154) WHITE-GREEN-GOLD

7-14 VD¾ 16400 ft 2yr Stk mi 271 :57 1:27 1:571 5 9 8° 8 86 31 1:572 e31.70 (Gl.Garnsey) Whamo,MckaleeStrk,JffyBoy 90-0
7- 2 Stga 27310 ft 2yr Stk mi 2941:0041:3112:011 3x 6 6 6 6 67 2:023 2.90 (W.Haughton) StrmDamage,Corintus,FiskHn 85-0
6-22 LB⅝ 15815 sy 2yr Stk mi 2941:0231:3322:033 2 2 4° 4° 21¼ 21¼ 2:034 e2.20 (DougMiller) AlbaTime,JiffyBoy,FiskHn 67-0
6-12 LB⅝ 300 ft 2yr mi 3041:02 1:33 2:024 4 1 1 1 14 113¾ 2:024 N.B. (DougMiller) JiffyBoy,Didit,PeppersQueen 65-0
6- 5 LB⅝ 300 ft 2yr mi 3131:03 1:3312:03 3 4 4 1° 1hd 1¾ 2:03 N.B. (DougMiller) JiffyBoy,Corintus,SonnySilver 76-0
5-28 LB⅝ 300 ft 2yr mi 3111:0421:3432:043 6 5 4° 4° 33 21¾ 2:05 N.B. (DougMiller) JDsMmory,JffyBoy,VkngBrat 71-0

20-1 — 10 — Blue-Red

WILD BILLS SKIPPER — blk c, 2, by Meadow Skipper—Ata Whitney by Shadow Wave — William J. Perretti, Hackensack, N.J. — Trainer-G. Berkner — 1979 7 0 4 0 734
$00 — Driver-BEN WEBSTER, 11-8-39 (138) RED-WHITE-BLACK

7-18 M1 10000 gd 2yr mi 30 :59 1:2911:592 1 3 1° 3° 610 722¼ 2:034 2.70 (Jo.Campbell) AlbqrqueN,SurfrSctt,AvnLrry 69-1
7-11 M1 1000 ft 2yr C mi 3031:0111:3112:014 5 1° 2 2 22½ 22½ 2:021 N.B. (Jo.Campbell) SilntTrch,WldBllSkpr,RlRwrd 78-0
7- 4 M1 1000 gd 2yr C mi 3041:0221:33 2:024 6 1 2 3 33 23¼ 2:032 N.B. (Jo.Campbell) SansStrk,WldBSkpr,SkprBob 57-
6-27 M1 1000 ft 2yr C mi 2941:01 1:32 2:014 2 4 6 7 66 59¾ 2:034 N.B. (Jo.Campbell) KeyWinner,StneRcr,DustyFlla 70-0
6-22 MR 1200 sy 2yr cd mi 31 1:0221:3512:074 2 2 3 4 32 514 2:103 5.80 (G.Berkner) CrmOfFrgt,CstlGrdn,Knickers 58-0
6-15 MR 250 ft 2yr mi 3311:0631:3812:092 4 2 2 3° 31 2hd 2:092 N.B. (G.Berkner) GrcieKsh,WldBSkpr,BddySwft 70-0

SELECTIONS: 9—4—2

No. 5 SILENT TORCH & No. 9 JIFFY BOY—Same Stable But Separate Betting Interests.

C—DENOTES CONVENTIONAL SULKY

(8) TROT—1 MILE

Warming-Up Saddle Cloth
GRAY

PURSE $18,000

Exacta Wagering This Race

NON-WINNERS OF $16,000 IN LAST 7 STARTS. ALSO ELIGIBLE: NON-WINNERS OF 4 PARI-MUTUEL RACES LIFETIME.

ASK FOR HORSE BY PROGRAM NUMBER

6-1 **1** Red

CASUAL POWER(J) b h, 4, by Regal Pick—Casual Hanover by Caleb — Trainer-A. Cooper
Arnold & Irene Dworkis, Sebastian & Antoinette Messineo, N.J — M(1)1:594 1979 16 2 1 3 28,190
$61,603 — 3, 2:044 Driver-LLOYD GILMOUR, 10-3-45 (157) RED-GRAY — Fhld2:044 1978 17 5 5 2 40,923
7-17 M1 18000 sy nw15000 cd mi 3221:0141:3232:021 6 5° 2° 1° 21½ 811¼ 2:042 7.00 (L.Gilmour) ThDstmn,BttnwdOdin,PrGynt 78-2
7-10 M1 20000 ft Opn mi 29 :59 1:2921:581 4 8 8 8 96½ 911 2:002 69.10 (L.Gilmour) Dblmnt,CrwnsStr,LndysBjngl 68-0
7- 3 M1 20000 ft nw20000 cd mi 292 :5931:2941:582 10 7° 6° 5° 98½ 916 2:013 96.00 (L.Gilmour) CrwnsStr,CldCmfort,Amalulu 75-0
6-19 M1 20000 ft nw20000 cd mi 2941:00 1:3011:591 5 x9 9 9 9dis 9dis 15.90 (L.Gilmour) CrownsStar,Amalulu,IdleLove 73-0
6-12 M1 20000 ft nw20000 cd mi 29 :5911:30 2:002 1 4 4 4 42¼ 31¾ 2:003 4.50 (Del.Miller) MjrPmp,YnkBandit,CsualPwr 66-0
6- 4 M1 35000 ft Inv mi 283 :59 1:3021:592 8 10 9 9 9x129dis 36.30 (L.Gilmour) LndyBjngls,Amalulu,CrwnStr 64-0

8-1 **2** Blue

IMA LULAC b m, 6, by Hickory Pride—Noccalula by Spectator — St.-J. O'Brien—Tr.-R. Burrows
Duncan A. MacDonald, Sydney, N.S. — Q-M(1)2:02 1979 9 0 2 0 15,500
$520,921 — 4, 1:571 (1) Driver-JOE O'BRIEN, 6-25-17 (144) GOLD-WHITE — Hol(1)1:582 1978 21 7 3 2 107,250
6-26 M1(c) 20000ft nw20000 cd mi 2841:0011:2931:592 6 1 1 3 x99½ 919¼ 2:032 10.10 (J.O'Brien) CrwnsStr,IdleLove,YnkBandit 65-0
6-20 M1(c) 16000ft nw13500 cd mi 3011:0041:3032:002 8 1 1 1 11½ 2½ 2:002 *1.20 (J.O'Brien) SatinCrwn,ImaLula,MdwDmjo 75-0
6-11 M1(c) 35000 gd Inv mi 284 :5931:2941:591 7 8 8 9x10211023 2:034 34.20 (J.O'Brien) KeyPioneer,ThDstmn,CrwnStr 59-2
6- 4 M1(c) 35000 ft Inv mi 283 :59 1:3021:592 6 1 1 1 21½ 73½ 2:00 11.20 (J.O'Brien) LndyBjngls,Amalulu,CrwnStr 64-0
5-28 M1(c) 30000 sy Inv hcp mi 3121:0221:3312:022 2 1 1 1 1¾ 21½ 2:023 7.50 (J.O'Brien) Calvert,ImaLula,Amalulu 68-2
5-21 M1(c) 30000ftOpn-Inv hcp mi 283 :5731:2821:583 8 8 8 8 74¾ 65½ 1:593 19.20 (J.O'Brien) LndyBjngls,ThDstmn,CrwnStr 66-0

7-2 **3** White

RAIDER WINDSWEPT br g, 7, by Smokey Windswept—Lullabeck by The Intruder — Trainer-S. Guy
James & John Swart, Jr., Va. & Meredith Capper, Md. — Lau(⅝)2:00 1979 10 4 3 1 17,780
$49,217 — 5, 2:011 (⅝) Driver-STEPHEN GUY, 10-28-51 (145) GOLD-GREEN — Brd(⅝)2:03 1978 13 3 3 1 10,595
7-13 Brd⅝ 6500 ft 79w5001 cd mi 2831:0031:3022:011 6 3 3 2° 2nk 1hd 2:011 3.30 (S.Guy) RdrWind,ElSilcar,BckysPrze 84-0
7- 6 Brd⅝ 6500 ft 79w5001 cd mi 2841:0021:3012:011 1 5 2 2° 31 31½ 2:012 *1.00 (S.Guy) ElSilcar,BckysPrze,RdrWind 76-0
6-29 Lau⅝ 6000 ft Pref hcp mi 284 :5941:30 2:00 5 1° 1 1 11 12¼ 2:00 2.90 (S.Guy) RdrWind,BckysPrz,ChrlsHwk 77-0
6-22 Lau⅝ 6000 ft Pref mi 2841:0011:3112:022 1 5 4° 1° 11 1nk 2:022 2.50 (S.Guy) RdrWind,CrlslCndy,KeyJudeen 75-0
6-15 RcR 7000 ft Pref mi 3011:0131:3212:041 5 2° 2 1 11 1¾ 2:041 3.10 (S.Guy) RdrWind,HTsDavid,CrlslCndy 75-0
6- 8 RcR 7000 ft Pref mi 30 1:0231:3312:034 4 3 2° 2° 21 21½ 2:04 5.90 (S.Guy) CrlslCndy,RdrWind,CgrSlnjun 80-0

6-1 **4** Green

SATIN CROWN b h, 4, by Speedy Crown—Satiny Hanover by Florlis — Trainer-D. Sider
HIJJI Inc. & Cheryl Ann Racing Stable, Lawrence & Brooklyn, N.Y. — M(1)2:00 1979 11 3 3 0 29,250
$480 — Driver-DON SIDER, 11-13-48 (153) RED-GRAY-BLACK — Last Raced in 1977
7-17 M1 18000 sy nw15000 cd mi 3221:0141:3232:021 4 1 3 5 75½ 67¾ 2:034 4.20 (D.Sider) ThDstmn,BttnwdOdin,PrGynt 78-2
7-11 M1 11000 ft nw6500 cd mi 3021:0011:3022:00 7 2 1° 1 1hd 11½ 2:00 *1.10 (D.Sider) SatinCrown,EricG,TownFriar 72-0
7- 3 M1 16000 ft nw13500 cd mi 284 :5911:29 1:584 7 7x10x10 10dis10dis 2.30 (D.Sider) ArniesDrt,PeerGynt,TwnEscrt 75-0
6-26 M1 20000 ft nw20000 cd mi 2841:0011:2931:592 5 8 9 8° 55½ 54¼ 2:001 19.60 (D.Sider) CrwnsStr,IdleLove,YnkBandit 65-0
6-20 M1 16000 ft nw13500 cd mi 3011:0041:3032:002 3 2 2 3 21½ 1½ 2:002 3.50 (D.Sider) SatinCrwn,ImaLula,MdwDmjo 75-0
6- 7 M1 16000 ft nw11500 cd mi 30 1:0021:3132:003 4 7° 6° 4° 21½ 2½ 2:003 6.70 (D.Sider) MplLfSctr,StnCrwn,MdwDmj 71-0

9-2 **5** Black

BUCKYS PRIZE br g, 5, by Carlisle—Buckys Gal by B F Coaltown — Trainer-M. Galentine
Edgar B. & Mariana P. Baylis, Chesapeake City, Md. — Brd(⅝)2:011 1979 16 5 4 4 28,450
$83,126 — 4, 2:013 (⅝) Driver-KEN McNUTT, 10-15-33 (157) GREEN-BLACK-WHITE — Brd(⅝)2:013 1978 34 10 6 7 47,825
7-13 Brd⅝ 6500 ft 79w5001 cd mi 2831:0031:3022:011 5 4° 4 4° 41¾ 3hd 2:011 2.00 (R.Hayter) RdrWind,ElSilcar,BckysPrze 84-0
7- 6 Brd⅝ 6500 ft 79w5001 cd mi 2841:0021:3012:011 3 2 3 3 21 2nk 2:011 2.90 (W.Ross) ElSilcar,BckysPrze,RdrWind 76-0
6-29 Lau⅝ 6000 ft Pref hcp mi 284 :5941:30 2:00 4 2 2 2° 21 22¼ 2:002 *1.30 (V.White) RdrWind,BckysPrz,ChrlsHwk 77-0
6-22 Brd⅝ 8000 ft Pref mi 3011:0221:3212:012 1 2 2 3 21 31¾ 2:014 3.50 (R.Hayter) SpdyDove,ElSilcar,BuckysPrz 76-0
6-15 Brd⅝ 8000 ft Pref mi 2911:0041:3022:011 1 3 4 4 42¾ 1hd 2:011 3.00 (R.Hayter) BuckysPrize,Pindar,Sabalist 80-0
6- 8 Brd⅝ 10000 ft Pref-Inv hcp mi 3021:0141:31 2:011 1 3 3 3 32½ 32½ 2:013 5.50 (W.Ross) BdfrdSpirit,ElSilcar,BckysPrz 80-0

10-1 **6** Yellow

RASMERRY b m, 4, by Speedster—Tosca Worthy by Worthy Boy — Trainer-S. Noble III
Wilton Acres, Wilmington, Ohio — ScD(⅝)2:022 1979 9 4 2 0 16,170
$7,102 — 3, 2:032 (⅝) Driver-SAM NOBLE III, 12-15-53 (140) RED-WHITE — ScD(⅝)2:032 1978 15 4 1 3 7,102
7-17 M1 18000 sy nw15000 cd mi 3221:0141:3232:021 9 9 9 8° 64 47 2:033 6.20 (S.NobleIII) ThDstmn,BttnwdOdin,PrGynt 78-2
7- 5 ScD⅝ 6000 ft Pref hcp mi 31 1:0141:3222:024 4 4 2° 2° 2nk 11¼ 2:024 *.40 (S.NobleIII) Rasmerry,FatPat,FloridaLady
6-21 ScD⅝ 6000 ft Pref mi 3111:0311:32 2:022 2 3 3 3 3¾ 12 2:022 *.90 (S.NobleIII) Rasmerry,ArniesFrtne,GlchrstCnty
6-13 ScD⅝ 10000 ft nw20000 cd mi 30 1:0021:3022:002 3 5 5 3°°23 22½ 2:004 4.30 (S.NobleIII) CamiAlm,Rasmerry,Abaron
6- 7 ScD⅝ 6000 sy Pref mi 31 1:0511:3532:07 3 5 5 6° 58¾ 11¼ 2:07 *2.10 (S.NobleIII) Rasmerry,VivianF,FatPat
5-31 ScD⅝ 3500 sy Opn mi 3041:0311:3432:052 5 6° 2° 2° 1hd 11½ 2:052 *1.20 (S.NobleIII) Rasmerry,LogansPride,UncleErnie

20-1 **7** Pink

KEYSTONE TRYST b h, 4, by Hickory Pride—Keystone Truly by B F Coaltown — St.-M. Lancaster—Tr.-J. W. Lancaster
Mark & J. Wm. Lancaster, N.H. & Frank Woodberry, Mass. — M(1)2:00 1979 16 1 1 4 17,009
$8,065 — 3, T-2:044 (1) Driver-MARK LANCASTER, 9-23-48 (165) BLUE-GOLD — Brd(⅝)2:053 1978 12 3 1 1 4,869
7-17 M1 18000 sy nw15000 cd mi 3221:0141:3232:021 7 2° 1 3 99½ 920 2:061 23.50 (M.Lancaster) ThDstmn,BttnwdOdin,PrGynt 78-2
7- 5 M1 15000 ft nw10000 cd mi 2911:0011:30 2:00 2 2 3 3 31¾ 1¾ 2:00 9.00 (M.Lancaster) KyTryst,BrllntYnk,ArmThmsn 64-0
6-28 M1 14000 ft nw8500 cd mi 3011:0011:31 2:013 6 7° 4° 4°°33½ 62½ 2:02 21.00 (M.Lancaster) Cncrge,StphniesClt,BlGrssPrd 68-0
6-21 M1 13000 ft nw8000 cd mi 30 :5941:3012:004 5 5 6 6° 44¼ 44¼ 2:013 6.40 (M.Lancaster) HighARsng,BlGrssPrd,NglCrg 71-0
6-13 M1 12000 ft nw7500 cd mi 3011:01 1:3132:022 3 5 4° 4°°22¼ 32¼ 2:024 2.20 (M.Lancaster) PAScrplrn,MrtLtlJhn,KyTryst 69-0
5-28 M1 10000 gd nw6000 cd mi 2941:01 1:3132:032 1 3 2° 1° 12 2ns 2:032 2.80 (M.Lancaster) SatinCrwn,KeyTryst,TkeAHld 71-2

15-1 **8** Gray

OVERLAND HANOVER b h, 5, by Ayres—Our Speed by Speedster — Trainer-L. LeBlanc
Jean C. Galvis & Leonard LeBlanc, Mass. — M(1)2:011 1979 10 5 0 1 14,810
$16,164 — 4, 2:042 (⅝) Driver-JAMES DOHERTY, 9-27-40 (161) RED-WHITE-GREEN — NE(⅝)2:042 1978 10 6 0 0 4,890
7-17 M1 18000 sy nw15000 cd mi 3221:0141:3232:021 1 4 6 4° 42 57¼ 2:033 7.20 (Ja.Doherty) ThDstmn,BttnwdOdin,PrGynt 78-2
7- 3 M1 20000 ft nw20000 cd mi 292 :5931:2941:582 5 6 8 9 87 87 1:594 37.70 (Ja.Doherty) CrwnsStr,CldCmfort,Amalulu 75-0
6-12 M1 20000 ft nw20000 cd mi 29 :5911:30 2:002 8 8 6° 6° 5be3¼43½ 2:01 22.60 (J.O'Brien) MjrPmp,YnkBandit,CsualPwr 66-0
6- 4 NE⅝ 2000 sy w2001 cd mi 3121:0431:3532:071 4 6 3° 2° 1ns 12 2:071 *.40 (Jo.Hogan) OvrlandHn,DcsBrthdy,DarcyH 63-0
5-22 M1 13000 ft nw8000 cd mi 302 :5941:3032:011 4 4 3° 2° 1hd 1nk 2:011 3.60 (Ja.Doherty) OvrlndHn,SatinCrwn,Sabalist 67-0
5-15 M1 13000 ft nw8000 cd mi 291 :5941:2922:004 6 6° 5 5° 34 33 2:012 9.60 (Ja.Doherty) AutmnScn,CltwnGB,OvrlndHn 67-0

4-1 **9** Purple

EL SILCAR b m, 5, by Carlisle—Jemmyranda by Jenko Hanover — Trainer-R. Gosman
Gladys & Seaford Leager, Jr., Galena, Md. — Brd(⅝)2:011 1979 7 2 3 1 14,035
$64,868 — 4, 2:011 (⅝) Driver-BEN WEBSTER, 11-8-39 (138) RED-WHITE-BLACK — Lau(⅝)2:011 1978 18 8 4 2 36,126
7-13 Brd⅝ 6500 ft 79w5001 cd mi 2831:0031:3022:011 4 2° 2 3 31¼ 2hd 2:011 *1.80 (H.Frazier) RdrWind,ElSilcar,BckysPrze 84-0
7- 6 Brd⅝ 6500 ft 79w5001 cd mi 2841:0021:3012:011 4 1° 1 1 11 1nk 2:011 1.70 (H.Frazier) ElSilcar,BckysPrze,RdrWind 76-0
6-22 Brd⅝ 8000 ft Pref mi 3011:0221:3212:012 6 6 5 4° 42 2hd 2:012 3.20 (H.Frazier) SpdyDove,ElSilcar,BckysPrze 76-0
6-15 Brd⅝ 8000 ft Pref mi 2911:0041:3022:011 5x 6 6 6 623 6dis *.90 (H.Frazier) BuckysPrize,Pindar,Sabalist 80-0
6- 8 Brd⅝ 10000 ft Pref-Inv hcp mi 3021:0141:31 2:011 3 2 2 1 11¼ 21 2:012 *1.60 (H.Frazier) BdfrdSprit,ElSilcar,BckysPrz 80-0
6- 1 Brd⅝ 8000 ft Pref mi 2921:0011:3022:011 4 1 3 3 31 12 2:011 5.00 (H.Frazier) ElSilcar,BckysPrz,KnwdHmpt 77-0

12-1 **10** Blue-Red

PEER GYNT ch g, 5, by Noble Gesture—Bustle by Florlis — Trainer-J. Foley
J. P. & Gabrielle Gauthier, Mont-Fort Farm, Pauline Quimte, Que. — Q-BB(⅝)2:042 1979 16 8 2 1 34,160
$10,367 — 3, 2:071 (⅝) Driver-SERGE GRISE, 6-29-44 (165) ORANGE-WHITE — Moh(⅝)2:071 1978 21 3 3 0 6,363
7-17 M1 18000 sy nw15000 cd mi 3221:0141:3232:021 2x 8 7° 6° 53 36¾ 2:033 7.00 (J.P.Gauthier) ThDstmn,BttnwdOdin,PrGynt 78-2
7-12 M1 15000 ft nw10000 cd mi 3021:0041:3122:01 5 6 6° 5° 53 51¾ 2:012 *1.30 (S.Grise) Pindar,BlueGrssPrd,TicCllins 75-0
7- 3 M1 16000 ft nw13500 cd mi 284 :5911:29 1:584 3 6 6 5° 45¾ 21¾ 1:591 34.40 (S.Grise) ArniesDrt,PeerGynt,TwnEscrt 75-0
6-26 M1 20000 ft nw20000 cd mi 2841:0011:2931:592 7 9 8° 9° 88¾ 813½ 2:02 34.10 (J.P.Gauthier) CrwnsStr,IdleLove,YnkBandit 65-0
6-18 BB⅝ 10000 ft Inv hcp mi 3031:0131:3232:024 1 5 4° 3° 2¾ 21 2:03 13.80 (J.P.Gauthier) MiniModel,PeerGynt,RBJet 76-0
6-11 BB⅝ 6500 ft w4001 cd mi 3041:0311:3432:051 7 5 4° 2° 21 1½ 2:051 e3.60 (J.P.Gauthier) PeerGynt,FrbrdThndr,DctrFbian

SELECTIONS: 3—9—5

C—DENOTES CONVENTIONAL SULKY

(9)

PACE—1 MILE

Warming-Up Saddle Cloth
PURPLE

PURSE $9,500

10th RACE TRIFECTA WINDOWS NOW OPEN

CLAIMING PRICE $20,000
(Three-Year-Old Colts & Geldings Granted 50% Allowance)
(Four-Year-Old Stallions & Geldings Granted 25% Allowance)

ASK FOR HORSE BY PROGRAM NUMBER

9-2 **1** — 30000 — Red

JOYSTICK
br g, 3, by Lindys Joy Boy—Gun Tag Forbes by Cimarrons Forbes
Heghoush & John Shegerian, Hillsdale, N.J.
$00 — Driver-MIKE GAGLIARDI, 8-25-48 (189) MAROON-BLACK-WHITE
St.-M. Gagliardi—Tr.-A. Modiano
M(1)2:001 1979 11 1 2 2 13,912
1978 0 0 0 0

7-17 M1 11400 ft nw2 cd mi 2821:0031:31 2:003 10 9 8 6 48 38 2:021 19.90 (M.Gagliardi) GeeJay,FritzMelwoe,Joystick 78-0
7-10 M1 11400 ft nw2 cd mi 2941:00 1:3021:594 10 10 8° 6°°5½ 48 2:012 28.80 (M.Gagliardi) FWBstr,EvrgrnSndy,JMHssel 68-0
6-26 M1 11400 ft nw2 cd mi 3011:0041:2941:593 10x 9 9 9 913 9dis 2:05 2.00 (M.Gagliardi) HHBttle,KngBmbr,JMHussel 65-0
6-19 M1 11400 ft nw2 cd mi 29 :59 1:2912:00 6 1 1 1 1nk 43½ 2:003 *2.00 (M.Gagliardi) ArmUwin,StrOfWght,TwllaLb 73-0
6-12 M1 11400 ft nw2 cd mi 30 1:0031:3031:594 4 4 4 x9 10dis10dis 2.60 (M.Gagliardi) Savage,FrmnsMagic,TristnLb 66-0
6- 5 M1 14760 gd 3yr NJSS mi 282 :5741:2841:593 4 6 6 6° 41½ 21 1:594 16.70 (M.Gagliardi) PassItOn,Joystick,BlueEagle 71-1

10-1 **2** — 20000 — Blue

TIMES SQUARE N
b g, 8, by Fallacy—Red Square by Forward
Mrs. Noel S. & Mitchell Kelley & Mars Stable, N.Y.
$16,918 — 7, 2:001 (1) Driver-MITCHELL KELLEY, 7-15-55 (173) RED-BLACK-WHITE
St.-J. Kelley, Jr.—Tr.-M. Kelley
YR2:032 1979 13 1 0 1 6,865
M(1)2:001 1978 16 1 1 2 9,640

7-18 M1 9500 gd 20000 clm mi 301 :5941:3021:591 9 10 9° 8 86¼ 87 2:003 48.60 (M.Gagliardi) DsrtStp,DelHrbrt,PaulasClppr 69-1
7-11 M1 9500 ft 20000 clm mi 30 1:00 1:30 1:591 3 5 7 6 5x2¼77 2:003 10.70 (M.Lancaster) JmboDllr,PlcidByrd,TmlyOrbt 72-0
7- 3 M1 8500 ft 17500 clm mi 283 :5821:2931:584 1 5 3° 3° 43 52¾ 1:592 12.10 (M.Kelley) FrostyPenn,PropWash,Eisiam 75-0
6-22 M1 9000 ft nw5000 cd mi 291 :59 1:2731:571 7 8 8° 9° 99¾ 912½ 1:593 31.30 (M.Kelley) BllsAdvc,DrmlngBtlr,JdgFrst 71-0
6-13 M1 10000 ft nw6000 cd mi 292 :5911:2931:592 4 7 8 10 95 94¼ 2:001 39.50 (M.Kelley) StdyStrkr,GrrsnLpz,EgtFrAce 69-0
6- 7 M1 11000 ft nw6500 cd mi 301 :5921:29 1:584 2 5 6 4° 88½ 98½ 2:002 16.80 (M.Kelley) Visite,ZoomsBoy,JerrysPrince 71-0

4-1 **3** — 20000 — White

EIGHTY FOUR ACE
br h, 7, by Tar Heel—Arlene Dares by Meadow Gene
Miriam & Milton Prince, Livingston, N.J.
$78,090 — 6, 1:58 (1) Driver-JIM KING, JR., 2-16-52 (143) RED-GREEN-WHITE
Trainer-E. Looney
M(1)2:014 1979 23 1 1 5 20,726
M(1)1:58 1978 24 5 1 3 22,381

7-20 M1 14400 ft 25000 clm mi 2941:0011:2931:582 6 6 8 8° 84½ 87¼ 1:594 6.60 (J.KingJr) HghScreN,BndRhyt,JwllsDrm 77-0
7-12 M1 14400 ft 25000 clm mi 283 :5821:29 1:583 10 8° 7° 6° 52½ 31 1:584 11.30 (J.KingJr) Tacoma,EvrgrnMrc,EghtFrAce 75-0
7- 5 M1 14400 ft 25000 clm mi 281 :5721:2741:572 8 9 9 9 79½ 69½ 1:591 3.50 (J.KingJr) StphnDirN,BndRhyt,BNAndy 64-0
6-28 M1 16800 ft 30000 clm mi 283 :57 1:2641:562 5 7 7° 4 45¾ 39½ 1:581 13.60 (J.KingJr) SlvrWarr,FlySprks,EgtFrAce 68-0
6-19 M1 10000 ft nw6000 cd mi 29 :5831:2841:581 2 3 3 3° 22 42¾ 1:584 4.40 (J.KingJr) PepeDncr,HppyHnry,SprtyBrn 73-0
6-13 M1 10000 ft nw6000 cd mi 292 :5911:2931:592 1 1 2 3 41¾ 31¼ 1:593 5.10 (J.KingJr) StdyStrkr,GrrsnLpz,EgtFrAce 69-0

12-1 **4** — 30000 — Green

FLIGHTLINE
b c, 3, by Airliner—Armbro Oteca by Tar Heel
H. Hernandez, K. Ross, N.J., D. Laudien, Del. & L. Mutschler, Pa.
$00 — Driver-WALTER LAUDIEN, 12-9-45 (155) BLACK-GOLD
St.-W. Laudien—Tr.-C. Hauser
LB(⅝)2:02 1979 15 2 2 4 8,058
1978 0 0 0 0

7-18 M1 12000 gd 22500 clm mi 292 :5931:2811:59 3 i5 4° 4 69 819½ 2:024 5.30 (J.ParkerJr) LehighStne,Nerissa,FrstyPnn 69-1
7-11 M1 12000 ft 22500 clm mi 3021:0021:3031:594 8 1° 2 3 32¼ 31½ 2:00 17.10 (J.ParkerJr) RwlngsStrt,Nerissa,Flghtlne 72-0
7- 4 M1 12000 sl 22500 clm mi 292 :5921:30 2:002 3 3 6 6 31½ 41 2:003 5.60 (W.Laudien) ThorLb,MplLnNelray,Nerissa 57-
6-27 M1 12000 ft 22500 clm mi 294 :5941:2931:593 2 6 7 7 54 31½ 2:00 23.70 (W.Laudien) BndRhthm,MplLNlry,Flghtlne 67-0
6-18 LB⅝ 2400 ft nw2 cd mi 2941:01 1:3142:02 2 3 3 1° 11½ 1½ 2:02 5.00 (W.Laudien) Flghtline,MdngtRogr,RustyEd 73-0
6-11 LB⅝ 2400 ft nw4000 cd mi 3021:0131:3412:05 3 2° 2 1° 11 21½ 2:051 *1.30 (W.Laudien) MabdoGuy,Flghtlne,FiberGlss 64-1

15-1 **5** — 20000 — Black

DEES KNIGHT
br g, 7, by Miracle Knight—Jana Dee by Jean Laird
Helene Feldman & Deborah Evilsizor, Livingston & Freehold, N.J.
$32,352 — 6, 2:01 (⅝) Driver-DEBBIE EVILSIZOR, 2-19-47 (130) WHITE-PURPLE-GREEN
Trainer-C. W. Evilsizor
M(1)2:00 1979 16 1 2 3 10,428
ScD(⅝)2:01 1978 33 5 6 4 11,814

7-18 M1 9500 gd 20000 clm mi 301 :5941:3021:591 8 9 10 10 108¾ 99½ 2:01 31.10 (D.Evilsizor) DsrtStp,DelHrbrt,PaulasClppr 69-1
7-10 M1 11400 ft 20000 clm mi 293 :5911:2911:584 4 8 9 9 87½ 35½ 1:594 19.70 (D.Evilsizor) StrClssc,EmprssBea,DeesKgt 68-0
7- 3 M1 11400 ft 20000 clm mi 284 :5721:2721:573 1 7 9 10 77¼ 87 1:59 *2.20 (S.Goudreau) HghScrN,RwlngsSt,DctrVoss 75-0
6-25 M1 10000 ft 22500 clm mi 2931:00 1:2941:592 3x10 10 10 108½1014be 2:021 *2.60 (B.Nickells) RompnDan,Nokoro,GoodValue 69-0
6-18 M1 10000 ft 22500 clm mi 283 :5921:2911:59 6 7 8 7 76 2nk 1:59 10.90 (S.Goudreau) ELVon,DeesKngt,BndRhythm 76-0
6- 7 M1 14400 ft 25000 clm mi 2941:00 1:2911:583 1 5 7 9 65¾ 66¾ 2:00 7.10 (S.Goudreau) MdwBilly,EbonyRock,Goren 71-0

8-1 **6** — 20000 — Yellow

FIELD BYRD
b g, 9, by Arrivederci Byrd—Meadow Joanna by Adios Butler
Larry Pollock Stables & David Silverman, Que.
$153,127 — 6, 1:563 (1) Driver-ROBERT SAMSON, 10-7-49 (140) WHITE-BLACK
St.-R. Samson—Tr.-V. Staker
M(1)2:002 1979 22 2 2 3 23,900
M(1)1:571 1978 28 4 3 4 37,863

7-18 M1 9500 gd 20000 clm mi 301 :5941:3021:591 1 5 5° 5° 63½ 75 2:001 *2.10 (R.Samson) DsrtStp,DelHrbrt,PaulasClppr 69-1
7- 7 M1 12000 ft 25000 clm mi 293 :5741:2731:581 3 8 9 9 97¼ 75½ 1:591 4.40 (R.Samson) LclSctt,Vancouver,FlyBlackie 71-0
6-26 M1 12000 ft 25000 clm mi 29 :5831:2731:573 4 7 6° 5 45½ 35½ 1:583 *2.80 (R.Samson) LionBrwn,BigBoyBrt,FldByrd 65-0
6-15 M1 12000 ft 25000 clm mi 30 :59 1:2911:583 10 8 8 7° 65½ 44 1:592 31.80 (R.Samson) MdwBlly,LionBrwn,GoodChris 82-0
6- 8 M1 12000 ft 25000 clm mi 29 :5811:28 1:582 9 10 9° 7°°66 58 2:00 8.70 (R.Samson) StretchBret,Scolbay,Eisiam 73-0
5-29 M1 13000 sl 25000 opt clm mi 292 :5931:31 2:003 5 8 8 7 46 43½ 2:011 17.90 (R.Samson) MrJW,GreatSport,TitanAlma 61-

---

3-1 **7** — 20000 — Pink

JAMBO DOLLAR
b h, 7, by Overcall—Mardela Hanover by Knight Dream
Frank Vacchiano, Ridley Park, Pa.
$82,355 — 5, 1:591 (1) Driver-JACK PARKER, JR., 7-19-55 (153) RED-BLUE-WHITE
Trainer-J. Parker, Sr.
M(1)1:591 1979 21 2 2 1 18,905
Hol(1)1:594 1978 30 2 4 4 18,900

7-17 M1 10000 sy 22500 clm mi 3031:00 1:30 2:002 5 10 10 7 84½ 89¼ 2:021 *2.00 (J.ParkerJr) WarrenJhn,ELVon,DnldsSngN 78-1
7-11 M1 9500 ft 20000 clm mi 30 1:00 1:30 1:591 4 6 4° 5° 31 15 1:591 3.00 (J.ParkerJr) JmboDllr,PlcidByrd,TmlyOrbt 72-0
6-30 M1 12000 ft 25000 clm mi 30 1:00 1:2821:584 9 10 9 9 96½ 86¾ 2:001 16.60 (J.ParkerSr) RylHoof,DulaneyHn,Oversight 68-0
6-19 M1 12000 ft 25000 clm mi 291 :5821:28 1:584 8 8 7° 7°°65¾ 78½ 2:002 5.30 (J.ParkerJr) BrtsSctchC,BNAndy,LordLbN 73-0
5-22 M1 12000 ft 25000 clm mi 292 :5921:2921:59 8 9 9 9° 84½ 2¾ 1:591 4.90 (Jo.Campbell) GrsslndJmboDllr,ThrstyAndy 67-0
5-17 M1 9500 ft 20000 clm mi 2941:0031:3121:593 6 7 7 5°°12 15 1:593 3.40 (J.ParkerJr) JmboDollar,Russlow,ArionLb 71-0

8-1 **8** — 20000 — Gray

TIME STREAM
br h, 8, by Gallant Armbro—Alright Honey by Right Time
Donkel Stable, Robert Kramer, Gary Lewis & Timothy Norton, Calif.
$68,832 — 7, 1:584 (1) Driver-SHELLY GOUDREAU, 5-27-48 (162) RED-GOLD
Trainer-S. Goudreau
Sacr(1)2:012 1979 12 2 1 0 5,615
Hol(1)1:584 1978 37 6 5 4 31,898

7-18 M1 9500 gd 20000 clm mi 301 :5941:3021:591 2 2 1 1 1ns 64 2:00 6.80 (S.Goudreau) DsrtStp,DelHrbrt,PaulasClppr 69-1
7-10 M1 12000 ft 25000 clm mi 282 :5541:26 1:572 8 2° 2° 4° 99 816½ 2:003 19.70 (Jo.Campbell) ClsscTchN,NtvMss,DulanyHn 68-0
7- 3 M1 12000 ft 25000 clm mi 274 :57 1:2721:572 6 2° 1 2 43 811½ 1:593 13.90 (S.Goudreau) ShutOut,Scolbay,LionBrown 75-0
6-26 M1 ft (h-d) Qua mi 31 1:0041:3122:013 4 1 1 1 11 31½ 2:014 N.B. (M.Budway) DelHrbrt,MrGrgryN,TmStrm 78-0
6- 1 Sacr1 3400ft18000 clm hcp mi 2921:01 1:3032:001 3 1° 1 2 34 66 2:012 4.20 (D.Ratchford) CootaFrost,RajahN,DukeWoollen
5-25 Sacr1 3400ft18000 clm hcp mi 2911:0021:3222:021 3 1° 1 1 1hd 21½ 2:022 6.00 (S.Bayless) DkeWoollen,TmeStream,CootaFrst

---

6-1 **9** — 25000 — Purple

GRAY WORTHY
b g, 4, by Lieutenant Gray—Queens Girl by Worthy Boy
Wayne Robert Prim, Carthage, N.C.
$9,328 — 3, 2:041 Driver-JOHN CAMPBELL, 4-8-55 (156) WHITE-MAROON
Trainer-Do. Garbarino
M(1)1:59 1979 16 3 1 3 18,380
MR2:041 1978 21 3 4 6 7,407

7-17 M1 8500 sy 17500 clm mi 3021:0041:3122:014 10 8° 7° 4° 43½ 1¾ 2:014 6.00 (Jo.Campbell) GryWrthy,NvlGoose,ShyBksht 78-2
7- 3 M1 8500 ft 17500 clm mi 283 :5821:2931:584 4 8 7° 6° 65 42½ 1:591 *2.30 (Jo.Campbell) FrostyPenn,PropWash,Eisiam 75-0
6-26 M1 8500 ft 17500 clm mi 284 :5821:2811:591 7 7 7 6° 56½ 32 1:593 *2.00 (Jo.Campbell) AnnRedstr,TkeLve,GryWrthy 65-0
6-19 M1 8000 ft 15000 clm mi 29 :5731:28 1:59 4 4 4 4 31½ 11 1:59 3.20 (J.ParkerJr) GryWrthy,CrcleKim,GmmyHll 73-0
6- 6 M1 8000 ft 15000 clm cd mi 291 :5911:2912:004 5 7 6° 8° 66½ 2ns 2:004 4.40 (Jo.Campbell) MikeDdly,GryWrthy,RblClrita 69-0
5-29 M1 8500 sl 17500 clm mi 3031:0211:3222:03 6 6 7 6 65½ 67½ 2:043 5.10 (C.Manzi) WkinGlnfrn,BstBzzr,RwlngSt 61-

---

20-1 **10** — 20000 — Blue-Red

STREAKER N
b h, 8, by Bachelor Hanover—Disturb by Johnny Globe
The Pauper Stable & Len Kompinski, Lancaster, N.Y.
$51,491 — 6, 2:03 Driver-LLOYD GILMOUR, 10-3-45 (157) RED-GRAY
St.-P. Laframboise—Tr.-N. Morford
Btva2:073 1979 26 1 4 8 10,898
Btva2:05 1978 38 5 6 7 20,650

7-20 M1 10000 ft 22500 clm mi 294 :5911:2841:582 7 9 8 9 87 710 2:002 61.90 (A.MacRae) RmpnDan,SkysDplmt,HiSykes 77-0
7-14 M1 12000 ft 25000 clm mi 302 :5841:28 1:58 9 9 9 9 97½ 910¼ 2:00 54.10 (P.Laframboise) BgBdNck,Dn'tLngr,AndyPndy 75-0
7- 7 M1 ft T-P Qua mi 32 1:0231:3212:02 7 7 5° 2 23 22¾ 2:023 N.B. (P.Laframboise) TadsPride,StrkrN,Publisher 71-0
6-30 BR 4000 sl nw10000 cd mi 3131:04 1:3432:044 8 7 8 7 64½ 54½ 2:054 13.40 (P.Laframboise) NpNFght,SprWhz,AzucrVrn 68-0
6-23 BR 5000 ft 25000 clm hcp mi 3041:0221:33 2:032 8 8 8 2 819¾823¼ 2:08 15.30 (G.Guindon) MrcryAlm,RaysDghtr,OrvlLad 63-0
6-16 BR 5000 ft 25000 clm hcp mi 3231:0331:3342:033 7 6 6 7 63½ 44 2:042 7.50 (F.Haslip) KiwlDivide,OrrvilleLd,CalKght 82-0

SELECTIONS: 7—3—1

C—DENOTES CONVENTIONAL SULKY

(10) PACE—1 MILE

Warming-Up Saddle Cloth
BLUE-RED

PURSE $9,500

ASK FOR HORSE BY PROGRAM NUMBER

Trifecta Wagering This Race

N.J.R.C. Rule 29:53(i) mandates an Exacta where field is less than 9 at wagering time.

CLAIMING PRICE $20,000
(Four-Year-Old Mares Granted 40% Allowance)
(Four-Year-Old Stallions & Geldings Granted 25% Allowance)
(Mares, Five Years & Older Granted 20% Allowance)

20-1 — 1 — 25000 — Red

NOKORO

br g, 4, by Regal Yankee—Reva Rose by Nephew Hal
John Kalmar, Jericho, N.Y.
$16,092 — 3, 1:593 (1) Driver-TOM LUCHENTO, 2-25-46 (195) GREEN-WHITE
St.-T. Luchento—Tr.-N. Luchento
M(1)2:001 1979 28 3 2 6 17,299
Hol(1)1:593 1978 27 3 7 6 16,092

7-20 M1	10000 ft 22500 clm mi 294 :5911:2841:582	9 10 10 10 108¼ 810¼	2:002	62.20	(T.Luchento)	RmpnDan,SkysDplmt,HiSykes 77-0
7-13 M1	10000 ft 22500 clm mi 282 :5741:28 1:58	8 9 9 9°105¾107	1:592	43.10	(T.Luchento)	SkysDplmt,RmpnDan,ShldonO 83-0
7- 3 M1	10000 ft 22500 clm mi 30 1:00 1:3011:583	2 4 4 6 55½ 54¾	1:593	6.70	(T.Luchento)	RmpinDan,NtveMss,TrevCnsl 75-0
6-25 M1	10000 ft 22500 clm mi 2931:00 1:2941:592	9 4 6 5 32½ 23	2:00	39.70	(T.Luchento)	RompnDan,Nokoro,GoodValue 69-0
6-16 M1	12000 ft 25000 clm mi 30 :59 1:2911:583	9 10 10 10 108½ 87¼	2:001	54.20	(T.Luchento)	MdwBlly,LionBrwn,GoodChris 82-0
6- 8 M1	12000 ft nw7500 cd mi 291 :5841:2921:584	10 4° 3° 4°109½ 921	2:03	34.80	(T.Luchento)	DimanteHn,PerfctRich,Sunro 73-0

8-1 — 2 — 20000 — Blue

FLYING DREAM N

br h, 12, by Lumber Dream—Flying Jill by Flying Song
Nikki Lynn Stable, Joe Brody, Bernard & Howard Mann, N.J.
$297,119 — 9, 1:583 (⅝) Driver-CARL LeCAUSE, 1-4-41 (203) BLUE-BROWN-BEIGE
St.-C. LeCause—Tr.-K. Armer
M(1)1:594 1979 15 1 1 3 14,234
M(1)1:593 1978 29 3 5 6 39,946

7-17 M1	12000 sy 20000 clm mi 3021:0131:3142:01	2 3 7 8°°98 912¾	2:033	7.50	(C.LeCause)	HpyRdgr,EmprssBea,JsseSm 78-2
7-10 M1	11400 ft 20000 clm mi 293 :5911:2911:584	6 9 8 7 55½ 55¾	2:00	11.20	(C.LeCause)	StrClssc,EmprssBea,DeesKgt 68-0
7- 4 M1	12000 sl 22500 clm mi 292 :5921:30 2:002	2 4 5° 5° 62¾ 64¾	2:011	6.10	(C.LeCause)	ThorLb,MplLnNelray,Nerissa 57-
6-27 M1	12000 ft 22500 clm mi 294 :5941:2931:593	1 5 5 5°°64¾ 43½	2:001	2.90	(C.LeCause)	BndRhthm,MplLNlry,Flghtlne 67-0
6-21 M1	14400 ft 25000 clm mi 2941:0011:3032:00	9 10 7° 5° 32½ 22½	2:002	21.30	(C.LeCause)	Ovrsight,FlyDrmN,BigBdNck 71-0
6-14 M1	14400 ft 25000 clm mi 29 :5731:2731:591	4 7 6 6 55¾ 31½	1:592	10.70	(C.LeCause)	Goren,BusPass,FlyingDreamN 70-0

4-1 — 3 — 25000 — White

BRET CONQUERED

b g, 4, by Bret Hanover—No No Hill by Hi Hill
Mark Lancaster, N.H., Bruce & Louis Weinstein, Mass.
$7,572 — 3, T-1:582 (1) Driver-MARK LANCASTER, 9-23-48 (166) BLUE-GOLD
St.-M. Lancaster—Tr.-J. W. Lancaster
M(1)1:584 1979 18 2 1 1 15,480
GrR(⅝)2:041 1978 15 4 3 0 7,500

7-17 M1	10000 sy 22500 clm mi 3031:00 1:30 2:002	8 5° 7° 2° 11¼ 42	2:004	17.90	(M.Lancaster)	WarrenJhn,ELVon,DnldsSngN 78-1
7- 5 M1	9500 ft 20000 clm mi 282 :5911:2941:592	8 8 8 7° 64¾ 42½	1:594	5.30	(M.Lancaster)	SunTarDean,Critical,DelHrbrt 64-0
6-23 M1	12000 ft 25000 clm mi 283 :5941:30 1:593	9 5 5° 5° 53¾x916	2:024	16.40	(M.Lancaster)	FrmstdJm,AndyPndy,HiSykes 78-0
6-11 M1	10000 gd 22500 clm mi 293 :5931:3042:003	10 7° 6° 5°°21 2nk	2:003	6.30	(M.Lancaster)	Russlow,BrtCnquerd,NtveMss 59-2
6- 2 M1	12000 ft 25000 clm mi 2921:0021:3021:594	3 2 4 4 43½ix97½	2:011	13.90	(M.Lancaster)	BstrAlm,BNAndy,KssoffAndy 63-0
5-26 M1	13000 ft 25000 clm mi 293 :5841:2921:59	4 4 2° 2° 21 55¼	2:00	10.90	(M.Lancaster)	HpyTch,JrryPrnc,ThrstyAndy 57-0

12-1 — 4 — 24000 — Green

H H BELLE

ch m, 5, by Raritan—Yankee Kate by Yankee Chief
R. Yorio, B. Yellin, J. Rosenberg, P. Novey & R. Falus, N.Y. & N.J.
$22,615 — 4, 2:034 (⅝) Driver-LEW WILLIAMS, 3-1-47 (140) BLUE-GOLD-WHITE
Trainer-B. Yellin
Q-M(1)2:052 1979 12 0 2 2 8,345
WR(⅝)2:034 1978 33 9 6 3 13,258

7-17 M1	10000 sy 22500 clm mi 3031:00 1:30 2:002	3 1 1 3 73½ 74½	2:011	22.70	(L.Williams)	WarrenJhn,ELVon,DnldsSngN 78-1
7-10 M1	ft T-P Qua mi 2931:0041:3132:012	7 2 2 2 22 23	2:02	N.B.	(M.Lancaster)	ArmTex,HHBelle,YndaRhyGB 78-0
6-11 M1	10000 gd 22500 clm mi 293 :5931:3042:003	5 1 3 2 98½ 914	2:032	4.20	(R.Samson)	Russlow,BrtCnquerd,NtveMss 59-2
6- 2 M1	12000 ft 25000 clm mi 302 :5941:30 1:592	6 4 4 6 65½ 45	2:002	6.80	(R.Samson)	ClsscTchN,HpyTch,EmprsBea 63-0
5-26 M1	13000 ft 25000 clm mi 291 :5821:29 1:59	6 5 7 7 64½ 33½	1:593	10.90	(R.Samson)	DeejyPnn,PcngDonut,HHBelle 57-0
5-21 M1	10000 ft nw6250 cd mi 284 :5831:2821:574	9 9 9 9 86½ 67¼	1:591	15.00	(R.Samson)	JHBrn,TitanAlm,MnnStndOut 66-0

5-1 — 5 — 20000 — Black

DEL HERBERT

ro h, 9, by Dean Herbert—Diane Herbert by Governor Herbert
Wm. Ellerington, Brian Peifer & Greg Wright, Ont.
$118,167 — 6, 2:023 (⅝) Driver-GREG WRIGHT, 1-26-46 (183) BLUE-WHITE
St.-G. Wright—Tr.-D. Johnson
M(1)2:01 1979 14 2 4 2 21,730
WR(⅝)2:031 1978 38 6 7 4 16,927

7-18 M1	9500 gd 20000 clm mi 301 :5941:3021:591	10 1 2 3 31½ 21½	1:592	8.20	(G.Wright)	DsrtStp,DelHrbrt,PaulasClppr 69-1
7- 5 M1	9500 ft 20000 clm mi 282 :5911:2941:592	6 2 2 3 32 32	1:594	3.60	(D.Johnson)	SunTarDean,Critical,DelHrbrt 64-0
6-26 M1	ft Qua mi 31 1:0041:3122:013	2 2 2 2 21 11½	2:013	N.B.	(D.Johnson)	DelHrbrt,MrGrgryN,TmStrm 78-0
5- 5 M1	10000 ft 25000 clm mi 292 :5841:2911:59	5 2 3 4 31½ 21	1:591	4.10	(G.Wright)	SprtCoat,DelHrbrt,BarklyLdy 61-0
4-20 M1	10000 sy 25000 clm mi 3031:0031:3032:01	4 3 4° 3° 22 11¾	2:01	6.00	(G.Wright)	DelHerbert,BigBoyBret,TinaJ 54-2
4-21 M1	10000 gd 25000 clm mi 2931:0031:3142:013	7 1 2 3 31½ 5½	2:014	3.90	(G.Wright)	TinaJ,DtchHllLrd,BrtsSctchC 51-1

8-1 — 6 — 25000 — Yellow

WINTERGARDEN

b h, 4, by Speedy Scot—Soprano by Stars Pride
Jetliner Stable, Montreal, Que.
$18,863 — 3, 2:014 (⅝) Driver-JAMES DOHERTY, 9-27-40 (161) RED-WHITE-GREEN
St.-Ja. Doherty—Tr.-W. Koch
BB(⅝)2:05 1979 23 1 5 2 16,836
BB(⅝)2:014 1978 21 4 4 3 14,522

7-18 M1	9500 gd 20000 clm mi 301 :5941:3021:591	3 4° 3° 2° 2ns 53¼	1:594	10.20	(Ja.Doherty)	DsrtStp,DelHrbrt,PaulasClppr 69-1
7- 7 M1	12000 ft 25000 clm mi 293 :5741:2731:581	5 9 8 8° 85¾ 64¼	1:59	19.50	(Ja.Doherty)	LclSctt,Vancouver,FlyBlackie 71-0
6-28 M1	10000 ft nw5500 cd mi 294 :5941:2941:594	8 9 10 10 94½ 64½	2:003	25.30	(Ja.Doherty)	WldwdGeo,CrwnBay,CounslrR 68-0
6-23 M1	ft Qua mi 30 1:0021:3122:003	1 6 6 6 59½ 56¼	2:014	N.B.	(Ja.Doherty)	Pursue,RebccasPrd,DrJacoby 76-0
6-13 BB⅝	5000 ft 30000 clm hcp mi 3021:02 1:33 2:022	5 6 6 4° 42 52¾	2:033	4.15	(R.Gendron)	KeyGoliath,IbexAngus,Cousin 70-0
6- 6 BB⅝	5000 ft 30000 clm hcp mi 2921:02 1:3112:011	3 5 5 6 54¼ 4¾	2:012	22.25	(G.Gendron)	KeyGoliath,SnzzyDrum,Prphtstwn

---

9-2 — 7 — 20000 — Pink

MAPLE LANES NELRAY (J)

br g, 5, by Airliner—Valley Pearl by Hi Los Forbes
David Elliott (Lessee), Bordentown, N.J.
$62,653 — 4, 1:593 (1) Qua Driver-JOHN CAMPBELL, 4-8-55 (156) WHITE-MAROON
Trainer-D. Elliott
Q-M(1)2:012 1979 7 0 5 0 12,350
Q-Det(1)1:593 1978 20 3 0 2 10,823

7-20 M1	9500 ft 20000 clm mi 30 1:00 1:2941:591	6 7 6 5° 53 64¾	2:001	*1.50	(Jo.Campbell)	EsyAndy,BaronsBrat,JdgeFrst 77-0
7- 4 M1	21000 sl 22500 clm mi 292 :5921:30 2:002	9 8° 7° 7° 2½ 2¾	2:003	4.30	(Jo.Campbell)	ThorLb,MplLnNelray,Nerissa 57-
6-27 M1	12000 ft 22500 clm mi 294 :5941:2931:593	8 1 1 1 11 21¼	1:594	3.80	(Jo.Campbell)	BndRhthm,MplLNlry,Flghtlne 67-0
6-19 M1	11400 ft 20000 clm mi 29 :5831:2831:592	1 3 1° 1 12½ 2hd	1:592	*1.20	(Jo.Campbell)	ShldnO,MplLnNlry,ShneDale 73-0
6- 9 M1	ft Qua mi 3031:01 1:3142:012	8 6° 5° 4° 41½ 31¼	2:013	N.B.	(Jo.Campbell)	PrncsNndna,RebPrd,MpLNlry 73-0
6- 5 M1	ft Qua mi 31 1:0031:3042:012	2 2 1 1 12 11½	2:012	N.B.	(Jo.Campbell)	MpleLnsNlry,RglJack,Imabrn 77-0

15-1 — 8 — 20000 — Gray

SEMINOLE CHIEF

b g, 6, by Race Time—Fingos Queen by Calumet Fingo
David Bellucci, Jr. & Sr., Loomis & Los Altos Hills, Calif.
$37,903 — 5, 1:56 (1) Driver-CATELLO MANZI, 6-27-50 (164) WHITE-BLUE
Trainer-L. Bond
1979 17 0 1 2 6,155
M(1)1:56 1978 27 6 1 5 30,705

7-17 M1	10000 sy 22500 clm mi 3031:00 1:30 2:002	7 2° 5°x1010dis10dis		9.10	(B.Webster)	WarrenJhn,ELVon,DnldsSngN 78-1
6-30 M1	12000 ft 25000 clm mi 30 1:00 1:2821:584	7 3°x10x1010disx10dis		11.30	(G.Wright)	RylHoof,DulaneyHn,Oversight 68-0
6-23 M1	14000 ft 30000 clm mi 292 :5931:3031:592	4 1° 3 4 65 84¾	2:002	17.20	(A.Craig)	Grsslnd,Don'tLngr,ClsscTchN 78-0
6-15 M1	9500 ft 20000 clm mi 291 :5711:2721:563	8 2° 2i 2 22 25½	1:573	13.30	(S.Goudreau)	SlvrWrrior,SeminoleChf,JayZ 80-0
6- 8 M1	9500 ft 20000 clm mi 29 :5831:2831:582	1 2i 2 2 23 412½	2:004	15.90	(A.Craig)	SilverWarr,TrevCnsl,LtColJoe 73-0
5-30 M1	10000 ft 20000 clm mi 284 :59 1:2841:583	7 1 1 2 33 56¾	2:00	5.80	(A.Craig)	RylThms,BckyTnnr,BvsFlyBoy 71-0

12-1 — 9 — 28000 — Purple

TINA J

br m, 4, by Harold J—Princess McKlyo by Walter McKlyo
Albert Mukdsi, Flint, Mich., Art Sherman, Bellmore, N.Y.
$6,904 — 3, 2:03 Driver-RAY REMMEN, 5-28-47 (185) WHITE-GREEN-GOLD
St.-R. Remmen—Tr.-L. Remmen
M(1)2:012 1979 19 3 5 3 26,155
RcR2:03 1978 17 5 2 3 6,904

7-18 M1	9500 gd 20000 clm mi 301 :5941:3021:591	6 3 4 4 42½ 43¼	1:594	17.90	(R.Remmen)	DsrtStp,DelHrbrt,PaulasClppr 69-1
7- 5 M1	9500 ft 20000 clm mi 282 :5911:2941:592	1 4 4 4° 42¾ 53	2:00	*2.10	(R.Remmen)	SunTarDean,Critical,DelHrbrt 64-0
6-28 M1	9500 ft 20000 clm mi 294 :5911:2911:582	2 4 4 4° 33 26	1:593	7.70	(R.Remmen)	LocalScott,TinaJ,Critical 68-0
6-15 M1	9500 ft 20000 clm mi 291 :5711:2721:563	4 5 5 5° 36 412¾	1:591	8.70	(R.Remmen)	SlvrWrrior,SeminoleChf,JayZ 80-0
6- 4 M1	10000 ft 22500 clm mi 30 1:0031:3011:592	5 7 8° 6° 77 56½	2:003	5.70	(R.Remmen)	FrmstdJim,CyclnPrnc,Russlw 64-0
5-28 M1	10000 sy 22500 clm mi 3011:00 1:3022:022	6 1 2 2 31½ 61½	2:023	4.90	(R.Remmen)	HlndEdwn,SgrVAbb,JhnQArab 68-2

3-1 — 10 — 20000 — Blue-Red

DESERT STEP

blk g, 11, by Hi Los Forbes—Newport Lady by Newport Chief
Joseph F. Fanelli, Wayne, Pa.
$44,402 — 10, 2:003 (1) Driver-JACK PARKER, JR., 7-19-55 (153) RED-BLUE-WHITE
Trainer-J. Parker, Jr.
M(1)1:591 1979 14 4 2 3 24,195
M(1)2:003 1978 24 10 2 0 28,619

7-18 M1	9500 gd 20000 clm mi 301 :5941:3021:591	5 7 7° 7° 52¾ 11½	1:591	2.50	(J.ParkerJr)	DsrtStp,DelHrbrt,PaulasClppr 69-1
7-10 M1	8500 ft 17500 clm mi 302 :5921:2941:594	4 6 6 3° 21 14½	1:594	*1.20	(J.ParkerJr)	DsrtStp,NvleGoose,JhnQArab 68-0
6-29 M1	10000 ft 22500 clm mi 294 :59 1:29 1:584	7 1 1° 3 32½ 54½	1:593	*2.40	(J.ParkerJr)	ThrstyAndy,BigOzzie,ArionLb 67-0
6-22 M1	10000 gd 22500 clm mi 30 1:0011:3022:004	9 1° 3 5 74 21¼	2:01	*2.70	(J.ParkerJr)	TmlyOrbt,DsrtStep,TrvCounsl 71-1
6-13 M1	8500 ft 17500 clm mi 281 :5841:3021:592	8 9 9 6°°42¾ 12	1:592	*2.40	(J.ParkerJr)	DesertStp,ArmOctne,KeyPnzr 69-0
6- 5 M1	8500 gd 17500 clm mi 3021:0021:3041:593	5 6 6 6° 43½ 2½	1:593	5.50	(J.ParkerJr)	BigOzzie,DesertStp,BstBzzre 71-1

SELECTIONS: 10—3—7

No. 7 BUSTER ALMAHURST—Scratched

The First Race

An $8,000 purse for $15,000 claimers. This is the big time. Eliminations: Hals Star (no recent competition); Baron Parker (sloppy strip last out, nothing the time before); Armbro Octane (absentee); Mt Eaton Fashion (dull); Nicely Neil (liked the slop but has shown absolutely nothing when playing for keeps on a dry track during past two years); Projects Reddy (no energy); Last Buy (nothing here); Robbie Collins (ditto); Steady Shore (under cover all the way last time and still lost position in the stretch).

We have only one contender, Lopez Charge, who paced without much distinction in the slop last time but led all the way against this kind of field and won with some authority on July 10.

The favored Lopez Charge paid $6.60, topping Steady Shore by a neck. Armbro Octane finished fourth as 2.80 to 1 second favorite and Nicely Neil (4.70 to 1) was dead last.

The Second Race

This is for pacers that have not won $5,500 in their last seven starts and have also failed to win one race in their last four attempts. Canoe and Peanut Gallery are scratched. We can eliminate Rusty Domino, Merlin Byrd and Corgen Recharge for showing no energy in their latest. Georgana Arden goes as an absentee with a slow qualifier at Liberty Bell. Big George did little last time out, but the times of the race were so superior that it might be sensible to give him a rating off his performance of July 9. The track was a bit slow for Ready Set Go last time, so we use his effort of July 10. We also use Drexel Majesty's next-to-last.

Big George	:58:2 (20)	1:59 (20) = 40
Ready Set Go	:59:1 (16)	2:00:2 (13) = 29
Drexel Majesty	:59:4 (13)	2:01:4 (6) = 19
Cortland Hanover	:59:4 (13)	2:00:1 (14) = 27

No need to go on. As you can tell in a minute with pencil and paper, Big George gets the highest rating here.

He deserved it, paying $4.20 and beating 11 to 1 Rusty Domino by a neck. Georgana Arden was the crowd's second choice at 2.50 to 1 and finished third.

The Third Race

Here again there is no need to become too elaborate. Parling has by far the best basic figures and then gets extra credit for moving down in class, gaining in the stretch, roughing it, improving his post position and hauling Carmen Alessi. Nothing else is close.

But something else won. Trev Counsel, coming sharply down in class beat the 34 to 1 Native Pleasure by a neck, paying $7.60. Parling, favored at even money, was hung up outside Regal Jack for a full half-mile and faded from second to fourth.

The Fourth Race

Comes now some glamour—a prep race for the $862,750 Woodrow Wilson Pace. The first four finishers among these two-year-olds will be eligible to the big event. Just look at the names of the drivers. Reference to the USTA table of comparative track speeds indicates that Treasure Reef's recent second at Vernon Downs was the equivalent of a 1:57:4 mile at The Meadowlands. On the other hand, the youngster seems to spend most of his time racing alongside the rail. In this kind of field as in any other, it is best to look for some extra vigor. Tyler B shows that quality. His last race was over a rather slow strip but his previous was in fast going. His obvious liking for this track is of some importance. Delvin Miller will help in the bike (to put it mildly). Tyler B certainly seems to meet the handicapping standards that we have been propounding in this book.

And the price was right. Tyler B overcame early interference, roughed it for half a mile (including a quarter-mile outside of two horses), and drew off to beat Sans Strike by a length and three-quarters. He paid $10.20. The favored Treasure Reef was in the lead at the three-quarters pole but faded (1.10 to 1). Sans Strike paced an extremely big race at 17.40 to 1, justifying another look at the past-performance record. His latest race at Vernon Downs was every bit as fast as Treasure Reef's, in company that had traveled much faster. Furthermore, he had roughed it with great bravery for half a mile. By the way, Billy Haughton finished third with Easy Come Easy Go at 19.20 to 1.

The Fifth Race

This is for trotters. Keystone Judeen is scratched. Concentrating on horses with local form, we find that the best time belongs by a considerable margin to Take a Hold, who left from the outside on July 3, trailed a :59:3 half and gained five lengths in the stretch to finish in 1:59:3 against somewhat tougher company than he faces tonight. No other entrant matches these figures. Readers may observe that Take a Hold broke in his last start, but does not seem to be a chronic breaker, which justifies using his next-to-last. Although he did next to nothing in the early stages of that race, his brisk finish comes under the heading of exertion, signifying good form.

Take a Hold spent half a mile on the outside before seizing the lead in the stretch and holding off the fast-closing Little Scudder to win by half a length. The winner paid $10. Little Scudder went off at almost 16 to 1. Buttonwood Odin was favored at 9 to 5 but finished fifth.

The Sixth Race

Here is another qualifying heat for the glamorous Woodrow Wilson Pace, but with less to go on than we had in Tyler B's heat. The two shippers from Vernon Downs, Niatross and Whamo, seem to have all the speed. Whamo's mile of July 14 was the equivalent of a Meadowlands trip in 1:56:4. Furthermore, he has already demonstrated that he races well after travel, whereas Niatross has raced only at Vernon Downs, and not quite so rapidly. Let us pick the logical Whamo.

Niatross won in 1:56:2, defeating Denali (11 to 1) by three-quarters of a length. Whamo went off at 3 to 5 and finished third after leading into the stretch. Niatross went on to unanimous acclaim as North America's "Horse of the Year."

The Seventh Race

Yet another qualifying heat for the Woodrow Wilson. Notice that Burt Paloma was a close second to the fine Tyler B on the fast strip of July 11. Jiffy Boy paced swiftly in his last at Vernon Downs but has been unable to win away from Liberty Bell. He will not be helped by the outside post, either.

Burt Paloma closed fast to win by a neck from Armbro Vienna (24 to 1). He paid $5.80. Jiffy Boy went off at 1.90 to 1 but finished sixth after racing on the outside for three quarters.

The Eighth Race

I consider this trot essentially unplayable. The relatively few horses with measurable recent fast-track form on the local oval are not so hot. Raider Windswept, Buckys Prize and El Silcar, the Brandywine shippers, may be better than any of them, but the class of the race is not high enough to encourage play on shippers.

For the record, El Silcar won it, paying $8. Ima Lula was next (5.50 to 1) and Buckys Prize (4.90 to 1) was third. Raider Windswept turned up seventh at 4 to 1.

The Ninth Race

These are entered to be claimed for prices of $20,000 to $30,000. Many of the starters paced on sloppy or good strips in their latest engagements, and we shall be reaching back into their records for more representative performances. As the reader may have noticed, we have no prejudice against past performances on good tracks when the times are close to those recorded on fast tracks.

We can eliminate Joystick (no energy); Dees Knight (ditto); Field Byrd (ditto); and Streaker N (ditto). No need to rate Times Square N and Flightline, whose times seem hopelessly inferior at the outset.

But before we begin the actual rating of contenders, we can scarcely fail to notice the :55:4 half-mile to which Time Stream was pacing in second position on the outside on July 10. That astonishing figure is much better than any other in this field; and the three parked-out symbols, plus the drop in class, guarantee that no other contender will approach this horse's final rating. If you are the least uncertain about this, by all means go through the full rating process. Remember that Shelly Goudreau is a 20 percent driver, as is John Campbell, who drove Time Stream on July 10 and drives the contending Gray Worthy tonight.

I should point out that I am fully aware that Time Stream lost by more than 16 lengths on July 10, and that it is best to eliminate horses beaten by more than eight. However, exceptions are easily made for horses that pace three-quarters of a mile on the outside, some of it while pressing a half-mile pace of :55:4.

Time Stream went a quarter of a mile on the outside, but in front, fell briefly behind the favored Eighty Four Ace in the stretch but came again to win by three-quarters of a length, paying a remarkable $26.60 and $11.60 for the place. Jambo Dollar (3.90 to 1) was third and Gray Worthy (6.10 to 1) was fourth.

The Tenth Race

More claimers, priced from $20,000 to $28,000. Eliminate Nokoro (no zip); Flying Dream N (ditto); H H Belle (same); Del Herbert (scratched); Seminole Chief (breaker); and Tina J (no punch).

Bret Conquered	:59:1 (20)	1:59:4 (17)	= 37
Wintergarden	:59:4 (17)	1:59:4 (17)	= 34
Maple Lanes Nelray	1:00 (16)	2:00:1 (15)	= 31
Desert Step	:59:4 (17)	1:59:1 (20)	= 37

Bret Conquered is up in claiming price over the July 5 race, but not actually up in class enough to worry about. Gets 2 for the stretch gain, 5 for parking out, 2 for post position and 5 for Mark Lancaster. Final rating: 51.

We can use Wintergarden's latest race, the times in which were representative, even though the track was labeled "good." No deduction for class, but 15 for roughing it, less 1 for the post. Final: 48.

Maple Lanes Nelray adds 5 for roughing it and 10 for Campbell, less 1 for post. Final is 45.

Desert Step beat Wintergarden in that July 28 race, which we use for rating purposes. The old gelding gets 5 for the stretch gain, 10 for roughing it and 5 for Parker, less 3 for post position. Final: 54.

Is Desert Step's 3-point margin enough to justify supporting the old fellow when he leaves from the extreme outside? Go back to page 216 and you'll see that he deserves to be the favorite.

He came on like a wild horse from seventh at the three-quarter pole to a length and a half in front at the wire, paying $5.60. Flying Dream N (12 to 1) was second and Wintergarden (4.60 to 1) was third. Bret Conquered was forced into a break by interference and ended seventh at 4.70 to 1.

We found eight playable races and nailed the following winners: Lopez Charge ($6.60), Big George ($4.20), Tyler B ($10.20), Take a Hold ($10), Burt Paloma ($5.80), Time Stream ($26.60), and Desert Step ($5.60).

18 ROOSEVELT RACEWAY

August 13, 1979

THE TEMPERATURE IS 74 and the half-mile strip is fast. The only driver whose horses will get an extra 10 points from us tonight is Carmine Abbatiello, a national leader who usually wins 20 percent of his starts. Those who get 5 points as winners of 15 percent of their races are John Chapman, Rejean Daigneault, Donald Dancer, Norman Dauplaise, Herve Filion (whose batting average has decreased in recent seasons), Lucien Fontaine, John Kopas, James Marohn, Joe Marsh, Jr., and Bill Popfinger.

Readers who want to use the post-position values normal for half-mile raceways (see page 216), will suffer no harm. The following is only slightly different but reflects recent happenings at Roosevelt:

Post:	1	2	3	4	5	6	7	8
Rating:	8	6	6	6	6	4	3	3

The First Race

This is a trot for animals of no great speed. We should eliminate Rare (winless in 14); Speedy Marsha (much traveled but little raced, and probably needs work); Superpatriot (a returnee who seems uncomfortable on a half-mile strip); Speedster Waverly (winless in 19); Limit Up (a breaker who returns from a slow qualifier); and Be Free (too little for the outside post).

The contenders are Herbars Harmony and Sharp Honey. Herve Filion is not here, but Rejean Daigneault will drive this horse, earning the extra

WHERE IT ALL BEGAN, WHERE IT IS TODAY

ROOSEVELT RACEWAY

OFFICIAL PROGRAM AND PAST PERFORMANCES • MONDAY, AUGUST 13, 1979

FRIDAY

UNE DE MAI TROT

PURSE $35,000

SATURDAY

CHALLENGE CUP TROT

INVITATIONAL — PURSE $50,000

MORN. LINE

1 TROT
ONE MILE
WARM-UP
SADDLE CLOTH— BLUE
CLASS C-2

$2 DAILY DOUBLE—1st Half

"Mickey Felice's Steak House"

PURSE $10,000

BLUE — **1** — Morn. Line 3

HERBARS HARMONY
br h, 4, by Speedy Crown, Myola by Mediterranean (Tr.-M. Lavallee) (St.-Her. Filion)
Capital Hill Farms, Inc., Englishtown, N.J. RR 2:05:2 1979 24 2 6 2 31,180.
($15,174) 3, 2:05:2 (½) HERVE FILION (163) Red-Blue-White PcD(½) 2:05:2 1978 17 3 5 2 12,864.
8-6 RR gd C-2 10000 m 30 1:01:1 1:33:1 2:05:2 8 6 6 6° 5/5½ 1/ⁿᵏ 2:05:2 9.10(HrFln)H'Hrmny,HTsDvd,S'Honey 78
7-23 RR ft C-2 10000 m 30:4 1:02 1:32:4 2:04:1 7 6 5° 3° x4/10 6/14 2:07 *1.70(HrFln)SngA'DncMn,RgnaRse,Rare 78
7-10 YR ft C-2 9000 m 30:4 1:02:2 1:34 2:05:2 8 8 5° 4° 5/1½ 4/2 2:05:4 7.60(HrFln)Nlhni,SpdstrWvrly,RedC'Jet 72
7-3 YR ft C-2 9000 m 31:2 1:02:3 1:33:2 2:04:3 3 2 2° 2° 2/1 3/2¼ 2:05 *2.20(GFln)Nlhni,RedC'Jet,HrbrsHrmny 76
6-26 YR ft C-2 9000 m 31:1 1:03:4 1:34:3 2:05:3 5 5 4 3° 2/¼ 2/1¼ 2:06 *1.60(HrFln)CircleKall,H'Hrmny,R'C'Jet 63
6-19 YR ft C-2 9000 m 30:3 1:02:2 1:35 2:06 7 5° 4° 2° 2/½ 2/ⁿᵏ 2:06 8.90(HrFln)F'lssScot,H'Hrmny,LmitUp 71
6-12 YR ft C-2 9000 m 30:4 1:01:2 1:33:4 2:05:3 3 6 6° 5° 4/7 4/2¾ 2:06:1 5.40(GFllion)BeFree,Nelahini,Rare 64
5-22 RR ft C-1 11000 m 30:3 1:02 1:33:3 2:04:3 1 1 2 4 5/1½ 6/5¾ 2:05:4 8.40(HrFln)FrtunaKash,M'Mouth,V'San 64

RED — **2** — Morn. Line 5

RARE
b m, 4, by Porterhouse, Bar Lady by Barlow Hanover (Tr.-J. Cruise)
Joan Cruise, Westbury, N.Y. (qua)RR 2:08:4 1979 14 0 2 4 12,750.
($7,120) 3, 2:09:2 JIMMY CRUISE (193) Green-Red Hilliard 2:09:2 1978 19 5 4 4 7,070.
7-30 RR ft C-2 10000 m 30:4 1:02:2 1:34:1 2:05:1 8 7 7 7° 6/6½ 7/6 2:06:2 16.90(ECrus)SsquiSnstn,HTsDvd,BeFree 78
7-23 RR ft C-2 10000 m 30:4 1:02 1:32:4 2:04:1 4 5 6 7° 6/12 3/9½ 2:06 7.10(ECrus)SngA'DncMn,RgnaRse,Rare 78
7-3 YR ft C-2 9000 m 31:2 1:02:3 1:33:2 2:04:3 7 7 7 7 5/7½ 5/4 2:05:2 23.00(ECrus)Nlhni,RedC'Jet,HrbrsHrmny 76
6-26 YR ft C-2 9000 m 31:1 1:03:4 1:34:3 2:05:3 7 7 6 6 5/7½ 5/5½pl4 2:06:3 16.10(ECruse)CrcleKall,H'Hrmny,R'C'Jet 63
6-12 YR ft C-2 9000 m 30:4 1:01:2 1:33:4 2:05:3 1 3 4 4 3/5 3/1½ 2:05:4 4.90(ECruise)BeFree,Nelahini,Rare 64
6-5 YR sy C-2 9000 m 32:1 1:05:3 1:37:1 2:08:2 2 3 2° 2°2x/2 x7x/4¾ 2:09:2 4.00(ECrus)WhtPlains,BeFree,Nelahini 65
5-21 RR ft C-2 10000 m 30:3 1:03:3 1:34:4 2:06:1 4 7 8 7 7/10 5/6¼ 2:07:2 3.60(JCrus)HrlmGrgia,BeFree,K'Nrway 64
5-7 RR ft C-2 9000 m 30:3 1:03:3 1:35:1 2:07:1 7 7 8° 6°°x8/9 7/20 2:11:1 11.20(ECrus)WhtePlns,HrlmGrga,JstRon 58

YELLOW — **3** — Morn. Line 6

SPEEDY MARSHA
b m, 6, by Speedy Streak, Marsha Harvester by Florican (Tr.-J. Faraldo)
Annroc Stables, Huntington, New York 1979 3 0 0 0 250.
($161,768) 4, 2:04 JOE FARALDO (170) White-Green-Black YR 2:04:2 1978 19 2 2 2 15,390.
7-14 MR ft B-3/C-1 2800 m 29:2 1:01 1:31:4 2:03:1 5 4° 4° 3° 3/4½ 6/7½ 2:04:3 12.10(Frldo)NghtRmblr,EsyKsh,JetAngl 75
* 7-6 YR ft qua m 30:3 1:02 1:33:3 2:05:2 2 4 3° 4 4/5½ 4/7½ 2:06:4 N.B.(JFrldo)Nobiliary,CprsMills,L'Gesture
5-25 RcR ft Cd 5000 m 30:2 1:02:3 1:33:4 2:04 6 7° 6° 7 6/9½ 6/14 2:06:4 31.40(TTall)CrlslsCndy,R'Wndswpt,H'A'Rsng
5-18 RcR sy Cd 5000 m 32 1:06:1 1:39:1 2:11:3 1 4 4 5 4/1½ 5/3 2:12:1 5.40(TTall)BalHD,RdrWndswept,K'Judeen
* 5-11 RcR ft tp qua m 31:4 1:04:3 1:36:1 2:08:2 1 1 1 1 1/2 2/1 2:08:3 N.B.(TTall)DkeOfDvr,SpdyMrsha,B'VicBye
* 12-15 YR ft tp qua m 32 1:03:3 1:35:1 2:07 2 x7 6 5 5/17 5/25 2:12 N.B.(JFara)StrpntJett,JstCruisin,W'ATam
* 12-5 RR gd qua m 32:1 1:04:1 1:36 2:07:4 3 5 4 5° 5/4 6/4¾ 2:08:4 N.B.(JFara)SwtLollipop,JfrsnPmp,K'Empre
11-7 RR ft C-1 9500 m 30:2 1:01:2 1:32:3 2:04:1 2 3 3° 8 8/11 8/16 2:07:2 8.90(Frldo)ECOakie,K'stnS'ndr,Vilnese 56

BLACK — **4** — Morn. Line 4

SUPERPATRIOT (NY)
b h, 4, by Songcan, Myra by Diller Hanover (Tr.-L. Battaglia) (St.-N. Dauplaise)
L-Bar Farms Corp., Goshen, N.Y. LB(½) 2:02:4 1979 3 1 0 0 1,900.
($74,652) 2, 2:10:2 NORMAN DAUPLAISE (166) Brown-Gold-White (qua)YR 2:04:4 1978 14 0 3 0 27,300.
7-27 LB(½) ft Cd 3800 m 29:2 :59 1:30:2 2:02:4 2 1 3 3 3/1½ 1/1½ 2:02:4 16.60(RPoulin)S'patriot,DougAgain,L'Pride
6-27 M(1) ft Cd 11000 m 30:1 1:00:4 1:32 2:02:3 8 4 6 5° 5/3½ 7/7¾ 2:04:1 57.20(RPoulin)ArmThmsn,VtryFlag,TwnFrar
6-19 M(1) ft Cd 10000 m 30:2 1:00:2 1:31:2 2:02 3 7 8 6 9/8 10/7 2:03:2 53.30(RPoulin)EricG,BestRcrd,TakeAHold
* 6-5 M(1) ft tp qua m 29:4 59:4 1:30 1:59:4 4 3 3 3 3/6 4/14 2:02:3 N.B.(RPoulin)ToRiJhnny,EricG,TownFriar
* 2-17 RR ft tp qua m 31:4 1:04:3 1:36:4 2:09 1 2 2 2° 1/ⁿᵏ 2/5 2:10 N.B.(GRegn)HpyHA,S'patriot,EchoB'Phil 7
* 1-23 RR ft qua m 31:1 1:03:2 1:35 2:08 2 1 1 4 5/6 5/12 2:10:2 N.B.(GRegn)JfrsnPmp,Rscmn,JrryCrdN 35
10-16 RR ft C-2 9500 m 30:4 1:02:2 1:33:3 2:06:1 8 7 7 7 7/8 7/6¼ 2:07:2 14.20(CAbb)S'Crlsle,HrbrsH'ny,C'Empre 47
10-3 YR ft C-1 8000 m 30:3 1:01:3 1:33:3 2:05:3 8 6° 5x°7 7/24 7/ᵈⁱˢ 4.80(HrFln)JustRon,JrryCrdN,Nelahini 54

WHITE — **5** — Morn. Line 6

SPEEDSTER WAVERLY
b g, 5, by Speedster, Waverly Hostess by Florlis (Tr.-M. Santa Maria)
Eagle Three Stable, S. Price, Fort Lee, N.J. 1979 19 0 3 1 11,660.
($33,728) 4, 2:04:4 (½) MERRIT DOKEY (140) White-Red-Blue Spk(½) 2:04:4 1978 32 5 4 6 27,215.
8-6 RR gd C-2 10000 m 30 1:01:1 1:33:1 2:05:2 3 3 3 3 4/3½ 5/3¼ 2:06 4.20(MDoky)H'Hrmny,HTsDvd,S'Honey 78
7-23 RR ft C-2 10000 m 30:4 1:02 1:32:4 2:04:1 8 7 7° 5° 5/11 5/11 2:06:2 9.00(Doky)SngA'DnceMn,RgnaRse,Rare 78
7-10 YR ft C-2 9000 m 30:4 1:02:2 1:34 2:05:2 7 4 3° 1° 1/ʰᵈ 2/1¼ 2:05:4 33.90(Doky)Nlhni,SpdstrWvrly,RedC'Jet 72
7-3 YR ft C-2 9000 m 31:2 1:02:3 1:33:2 2:04:3 6 6 6° 6°°6/8¾ 6/7 2:06 19.90(S'Mria)Nlhni,RdC'Jet,HrbrsHrmny 76
6-19 YR ft C-2 9000 m 30:3 1:02:2 1:35 2:06 2 4 5 6 6/3½ 7/3 2:06:3 3.50(S'Mria)F'lssSct,H'Hrmny,LimitUp 71
6-12 YR ft C-2 9000 m 30:4 1:01:2 1:33:4 2:05:3 7 8 8 6 5/10 5/5¼ 2:06:4 9.50(S'Mria)BeFree,Nelahini,Rare 64
6-5 YR sy C-2 9000 m 32:1 1:05:3 1:37:1 2:08:2 8 8 6° 6° 6/5¼ 4/3¼ 2:09 19.60(S'Mria)WhtPlns,BeFree,Nelahini 65
5-14 RR sy C-2 10000 m 30 1:02 1:33:2 2:05:4 8 8 8 7 6/4¾ 3x/ⁿᵏpl4 2:05:4 16.60(S'Mra)F'rlssSct,HTsDvid,Nelahini 58

PURPLE — **6** — Morn. Line 5

SHARP HONEY (NY)
b m, 4, by Sharpshooter, Miel by Blaze Hanover (Tr.-L. Meittinis)
T. Milici, P. Valentino, R. Aubry, L. Klein, N.Y. PPk(½) 2:05 1979 20 5 4 3 25,754.
($00.00) HEIKKI KORPI (130) Black-Orange-White (qua)PPk(½) 2:08:1 1978 0 0 0 0
8-6 RR gd C-2 10000 m 30 1:01:1 1:33:1 2:05:2 5 5 5 4° 3/3½ 3/½ 2:05:3 11.90(LFont)H'Hrmny,HTsDvd,S'Honey 78
7-30 RR ft C-2 10000 m 30:4 1:02:2 1:34:1 2:05:1 6 5 5 5° 5/4½ 5/5 2:06:1 8.00(HrFln)SsquiSnstn,HTsDvd,BeFree 78
* 7-20 RR ft qua m 31:2 1:03 1:35:1 2:06:1 1 2 2 2 3/2 2/1¼ 2:06:2 N.B.(LFont)OnToGlory,S'Honey,Tigger 81
7-5 Lau(½) ft Cd 3400 m 30:1 1:01:2 1:31:3 2:04:1 7 9 6° 5° 9/10 9/7¾ 2:05:4 8.00(WRbrts)HTsDvid,HerrAyres,CindyH
6-29 OD ft Cd 1000 m 31 1:03:2 1:35:4 2:07 1 3 3 3° 2/ⁿᵏ 2/1 2:07:1 *.70(ALong)QuadWhite,S'Hony,CmdnSpndr
6-23 MR ft 4yr Stk 16322 m 30:4 1:02:3 1:34:1 2:04:1 3 7 6 7 6/3¾ 6/10 2:06:1 N.B.(GGlmr)FrtunaKsh,B'Swllw,T'Escrt 63
* 6-20 OD ft qua m 34 1:05:4 1:37:4 2:10 6 2° 1 1 1/½ 1/3¼ 2:10 N.B.(JLare)ShrpHoney,DffyFirst,M'Nubby
6-5 RcR ft Cd 3700 m 30:4 1:02:3 1:34:3 2:05:2 3 5 5° 3°°1/½ 1/3¾ 2:05:2 *1.50(WRbrts)ShrpHny,EppiesChrtr,CindyH

ORANGE — **7** — Morn. Line 8

LIMIT UP
br c, 3, by Speedy Crown, Excella by His Excellency (Tr.-H. McIntosh)
D. Auciello, G. Grippo, R. Friedman, N.Y. MR 2:07 1979 11 1 2 1 9.058.
($180) HUGH McINTOSH (190) Turquoise-Gold-White 1978 3 0 0 1 180.
* 7-31 RR ft tp qua m 30 1:01 1:31:3 2:03:2 2 3 2 2 2/4 3/4 2:04:1 N.B.(HMcIntsh)JDsWdly,SmkyPte,L'Up 80
7-28 RR ft 3yr Opn 175225 m 31:1 1:03 1:32:3 2:02:2 x2 x8 8 8 8/ᵈⁱˢ 8/ᵈⁱˢ 15.10(Wbstr)ChiolaHn,C'Cristy,LegndHn 82
7-14 LB(½) ft 3yr Stk19470m 29 1:00:3 1:31:1 2:01:4 4 1x°9 8° 8/8¾ 8/15 2:04:4 13.60(McIntsh)GatorBwl,TmmyCrwn,AtArms
7-7 PcD(½) ft 3yrStk 18870m 29:3 1:01:3 1:31:1 2:01:1 2 1 1° 2 2/1¼ 2/3¾ 2:02 12.10(McIntsh)GatorBwl,LmtUp,TmmyCrwn
6-26 YR ft C-2 9000 m 31:1 1:03:4 1:34:3 2:05:3 1 4 3° 2 3x/1½x4x/4pl5 2:06:2 2.90(McIntsh)CrclKall,H'Hrmny,R'C'Jet 63
6-19 YR ft C-2 9000 m 30:3 1:02:2 1:35 2:06 5 3 1 1 1/½ 3/½ 2:06 5.20(M'Intsh)F'lssSct,H'Hrmny,LmitUp 71
* 6-15 YR ft tp qua m 30 1:01:3 1:33:1 2:03:1 3 5 5 5 5/13 3/15 2:06:1 N.B.(HMcIntsh)M'W'side,S'Moon,L'Up 76
6-8 Brd(½) ft 3yr ec 16400 m 30:2 1:01:4 1:33 2:02:1 8 3 2 3 4/2½ 5/4 2:03 56.40(HMcIntsh)ChiolaHn,Courtly,LgendHn

---

GREEN — **8** — Morn. Line 12

BE FREE
b g, 11, by Tuft, Free Land by Light Brigade (Tr.-Wa. Warrington)
S. Warrington, C. Scorda, S. Sadles, P.&I. Kasofsky, N.Y. YR 2:05:3 1979 20 4 3 6 24,752.
($21,527) STEVEN WARRINGTON (160) Grey-Red-White 1978 14 0 3 2 3,307.
8-6 RR gd C-2 10000 m 30 1:01:1 1:33:1 2:05:2 1 x7x 7 7 7/15 7/10 2:07:2 4.10(SWrgtn)H'Hrmny,HTsDvd,S'Honey 78
7-30 RR ft C-2 10000 m 30:4 1:02:2 1:34:1 2:05:1 1 2 3 3° 4/3½ 3/3 2:05:4 5.20(SW'gtn)SsquiSnstn,HTsDvd,BeFree 78
7-11 YR ft C-1 10000 m 30:2 1:02:1 1:34:3 2:05 7 x8x 8 8 8/ᵈⁱˢ 8/ᵈⁱˢ 22.70(SW'gtn)A'broTudr,W'Plns,VtrySan 74
7-4 YR gd C-1 10000 m 32 1:04:2 1:36:1 2:08:1 3 2° 2° 4° 4/8¼ 4/3¾ 2:09 4.60(SWrgtn)SuddnSng,W'Plains,C'Kall 57
6-12 YR ft C-2 9000 m 30:4 1:01:2 1:33:4 2:05:3 5 2° 2 1° 1/2 1/1¼ 2:05:3 *2.70(SW'gtn)BeFree,Nelahini,Rare 64
6-5 YR sy C-2 9000 m 32:1 1:05:3 1:37:1 2:08:2 4 2 3 3 3/2½ 2/½ 2:08:2 2.40(SW'gtn)WhtPlns,BeFree,Nelahini 65
5-21 RR ft C-2 10000 m 30:3 1:03:3 1:34:4 2:06:1 6 3 3 5 5/4 2/2½ 2:06:3 6.50(SW'gtn)HrlmGrgia,BeFree,K'Nrwy 64
5-8 RR ft C-1 10000 m 29:4 1:02:1 1:33:2 2:04 4 5 6 7 6/9½ 5/7¾ 2:05:2 14.80(SW'gtn)S'Chmp,S'Shbra,FlrdaLdy 64

SCRATCHED—DING DONG DANDY (8), lame. A.E.—BE FREE—races in P.P. of scratched horse.

2 PACE — DAILY DOUBLE—2nd Half

ONE MILE

"Whiskey Wagon Bar of Centereach"

WARM-UP SADDLE CLOTH—RED

CLAIMING ALLOWANCE — **PURSE $9,000**

5-yr.-olds & up $22,000; 4-yr.-olds $27,000; 3-yr.-olds $33,000; 3 to 6-yr. fillies & mares add $4,400.

BLUE — **1** — $26,400

PROVOCATION (NY) blk m, 5, by Good Time Boy, Provoke by Torpid (Tr.-A. Crescenzo)
A. & L. Crescenzo & J. DiMaggio, Commack, N.Y. RR 2:03:3 1979 24 5 3 1 30,875.
($40,445) 4, 2:03:1 REJEAN DAIGNEAULT (140) Red-Blue RR 2:03:1 1978 15 2 3 1 14,025.
8-3 RR ft clm alw 22000 m 30:2 1:01:1 1:31:2 2:02:1 7 7 7 7 4/5½ 2/2¼ 2:02:3 19.70(RDgnlt)SmmyHnvr,Prvctn,N'Drct 78
7-23 RR ft clm alw 22000 m 29:4 1:01:2 1:30:4 2:02:1 6 6 6° 6° 6/4¾ 5/3½ 2:02:4 11.00(HrFln)KldreTmmy,KvnSctt,Ultimo 78
7-13 YR ft clm alw 22000 m 29:1 1:00:4 1:32:3 2:02:1 1 3 4 6 5/4¼ 5/4¼ 2:03 8.10(GFln)F'Mrn'g,S'brdL't,Pericoloso 82
7-6 YR ft clm alw 22000 m 29:1 59:2 1:30:1 2:01:2 1 3 3° 6 6/8 7/11 2:03:3 3.60(GFln)BnDixie,BrnrdJmes,G'Crcle 71
6-28 YR ft clm alw 22000 m 29:2 1:01:3 1:32:2 2:02:2 8 8 5° 4°°4/7½ 4/10 2:04:2 13.20(HrFln)AttaWmba B'Buty MrAloof 66
6-18 YR ft clm alw 22000 m 30 1:01:1 1:32:2 2:05 5 7 7 6° 5/1½ 1/1½ 2:05 3.20(HrFln)Prvction,StdyJosie,GntlJimA 69
6-8 YR ft clm alw 22000 m 29:3 1:00:4 1:32 2:03 4 6 6° 6° 5/3¼ 4/1½ 2:03:2 6.00(JMrhn)ARJet,D'Apprch,D'Charger 69
5-29 RR ft clm alw 18000Z m 31:2 1:02:4 1:33:2 2:03:3 1 1 1 1 1/1½ 1/1¼ 2:03:3 *1.30(Dplse)Prvocation,JPAmmo,T'CshN 62

RED — **2** — $22,000

FANTASTIC BUTLER ch h, 5, by Adios Butler, Josedale Cindy Hal by Josedale Lucky Hal (Tr.-L. Battaglia)(St.-N. Dauplaise)
Y. Glaser, Atlantic Beach, N.Y. YR 2:00:4 1979 16 3 2 1 21,380.
($53,733) 3, 2:01:4 NORMAN DAUPLAISE (166) Brown-Gold-White YR 2:03 1978 21 1 2 3 13,885.
8-1 RR ft clm alw 22000 m 29:3 1:00:2 1:31 2:02 6 1 1 1 1/3 1/1½ 2:02 *1.90(Dpls)F'stcBtlr,FllChrg,CptnsReef 80
7-21 RR ft clm 27000 m 29:4 1:00:3 1:30:4 2:00:4 4 5 5 4°°3/1 5/4 2:01:3 2.90(Dplse)LordsScrt,J'Chancy,Terandy 76
7-12 YR ft clm alw 22000 m 29:2 1:00:3 1:32:2 2:02 7 5 5° 2°°1/hd 1/½ 2:02 8.20(Dplse)FntstcBtlr,Relntlss,SprsAll 80
7-4 YR gd clm 27000 m 29:4 1:02 1:33:1 2:04:2 1 2 2 3 2/1 2/1½ 2:04:3 3.40(NDpls)CallT'Arms,F'Btlr,CntryFrd 57
6-23 YR ft clm alw 33000 m 29:1 59:3 1:30:2 2:00:3 7 7 8° 8 8/11 7/8¾ 2:02:2 48.10(Dplse)LkyBrsh,SkppnSm,O'G'Mine 77
6-2 RR ft clm alw 33000 m 30 1:01:1 1:31:2 2:01:1 2 2 2 2 2/2 4/3½ 2:01:4 6.70(NDpls)LkyBrsh,TriosDesign CnslrR 60
5-23 RR sy clm 33000 m 30:3 1:03 1:33:4 2:03:4 8 8 8 8° 7/6½ 8/7 2:05:1 23.30(Dplse)JJsRingo,C'Angus,C'Dcision 62
5-11 RR ft clm alw 33000 m 28:4 59:4 1:30:2 2:00:1 4 5 6 7 4/4 4/2½ 2:00:3 37.80(NDpls)GdT'Ryle,Nadala,O'G'Mine 59

YELLOW — **3** — $22,000

ARRUNDI b g, 6, by Hondo Hanover, Kurrundi by Mighty Warrior (Tr.-J. Miritello)
Bull-Mar Stable, Albertson, N.Y. YR 2:02 1979 19 3 5 1 16,444.
($9,038) N.R. CARMINE ABBATIELLO (145) Gold-Red N.R. 1978 21 8 2 2 6,347.
8-2 RR ft clm alw 27000 m 29:2 1:01:1 1:32:3 2:02 8 3° 3° 4° 7/10 8/20 2:06 38.30(FPop)Advntrer,T'Cree,SrprsR'thm 80
7-24 RR ft clm alw 27000 m 30:1 1:01:3 1:32 2:02 5 6 6° 5° 4/3 2/3¾ 2:02:4 5.30(Insko)A'John,Arndi,B'Jms-Ad'rdh 80
7-17 RR ft clm alw 27000 m 30:1 1:02 1:33 2:03:1 8 8 5° 5° 5/2 4/3½ 2:03:4 22.70(DInsko)F'Fella,S'Rhythm,B'Duane 80
7-5 YR ft clm alw 22000 m 29:1 1:00 1:31 2:02 1 1 1 1 1/1½ 1/2¼ 2:02 *3.10(DInsko)Arundi,MvngStdy A'Shbra 61
6-26 YR ft clm alw 22000 m 30 1:00 1:31:3 2:03 4 4 4 6 4/5 4/4½ 2:03:4 4.70(Insko)Trndy,NppysBoy,TmprdKen 63
6-15 YR ft clm alw 18000 m 28:3 59:1 1:30:4 2:02 7 3 3 2° 2/½ 2/½ 2:02:1 6.80(DInsko)KldreTmy,Arundi,H'H'Lyss 82
6-8 YR ft clm alw 22000 m 29:3 1:00:4 1:32 2:03 7 4 5 5 6/5½ 7/3½ 2:03:4 6.00(Insko)ARJet,D'Apprch,D'Charger 69
5-30 RR ft clm alw 18000 m 30:1 1:01:4 1:31:4 2:02:4 1 3 3° 2° 2/2 1/1¾ 2:02:4 13.60(Insko)Arrundi,BionicButy,Savitar 66

BLACK — **4** — $22,000

ROCKET ALLEY blk g, 5, by Adios Harry, Vanity Van by Matador (Tr.-R. Rapetti)
Stephen Perdoch, Bronx, N.Y. YR 2:02:1 1979 21 2 2 4 15,280.
($35,857) 3, 2:01:1 (1) REAL CORMIER (140) Blue-Orange RcR 2:02:3 1978 33 5 3 10,771.
* 8-3 RR ft qua m 30:1 1:01 1:32:1 2:02:2 3 1 1 1 2/hd 5/4½ 2:03:1 N.B.(RCrmr)RamOJ,TimT'Ad's,C'Dcisn 82
7-30 RR ft clm alw 22000 m 29:3 59:3 1:31 2:01 1 x3x pulled up DNF 9.30(JMrhn)SailorJo,Hapuka,BionicButy 78
* 7-24 RR ft qua m 30 1:03 1:33 2:02:4 1 2 2 2 3/1¼ 3/2½ 2:03:1 N.B.(JMrhn)AftnGallnt,Padrino,R'Alley 81
7-16 RR ft clm alw 22000 m 30:3 1:01 1:31:3 2:03 6 3 3 3 3/1¼ 7/3 2:03:3 17.60(JMrhn)Tppr,BrnrdJames,GmeGale 78
7-9 YR ft C-3 Cd 8000 m 29:2 1:00 1:31:1 2:01:3 3 2° 2° 3 6/7¾ 7/15 2:04:3 2.60(RDg't)JhnRQntn,AzlaSpnr,GmeRlr 71
6-27 YR ft C-3 Cd 8000 m 30 1:01 1:31:1 2:01:2 4 x7 6° 8 8/20 8/22 2:05:4 *1.40(Mrhn)K'NwTm,TrumnHn,M'W'sde 66
6-15 YR ft clm alw 22000 m 29:1 58:4 1:30:1 2:02:1 2 1 2 1 1/1 1/½ 2:02:1 5.10(JMrhn)RocktAlly,Terandy,QckGlncr 82
6-5 YR sy clm alw 15000 m 29:3 1:00:2 1:31:1 2:02:2 5 3° 1 1 1/6 1/7 2:02:2 3.20(JMrhn)RcktAlley,Wnnafrda,B'Lad 65

WHITE — **5** — $22,000

NICKELI ADIOS b g, 5, by Caliburn, Dolls Point by Oban (Tr.-K. McNutt)
Elias Fotinos, Union, N.J. Brd(½) 2:02:4 1979 20 4 4 4 12,884.
($2,775) N.R. KENNETH McNUTT (157) Green-White-Black 1978 11 0 1 1 437.
8-3 RR ft clm alw 22000 m 30:2 1:01:1 1:31:2 2:02:1 6 3 4 4° 5/6 4/4¾ 2:03:1 7.50(KMcNtt)SmmyHnvr,Prvctn,N'Drct 78
7-12 M(1) ft clm 25000 m 28:3 58:2 1:29 1:58:3 8 1° 3 5 8/4¾ 10/8½ 2:00:1 17.90(KM'Ntt)Tacoma,E'grnMarc,E'F'Ace
* 7-7 M(1) ft qua m 28:4 :59 1:30 1:59:4 5 3 3 4 4/2¾ 5/1½ 2:00 N.B.(KM'Ntt)AdmBrdN,YnkPaul,ArdriEgl
* 6-23 M(1) ft qua m 30:4 1:02:1 1:32:3 2:02:3 4 2 3 4 4/4¾ 3/9½ 2:04:2 N.B.(KM'Ntt)MstrArnie,Parlig NckliAd's
6-21 M(1) ft clm 25000 m 29:4 1:00:1 1:30:3 2:00 10 4° 2 4 10/8 10/20 2:04:1 63.80(KM'Ntt)Ovrsght,FlyDrmN,BigBdNck
6-14 M(1) ft clm 30000 m 28:3 :59 1:28:3 1:58:2 1 3 3 3 3/2 4/6½ 1:59:3 40.20(KM'Ntt)TotalFrght,AllAtOnce,FstJet
6-7 M(1) ft clm 30000 m 29:3 58:4 1:28:2 1:57:4 2 x4 3° 6° 6/6½ 8/13 2:00:2 25.00(KM'Ntt)Grsslnd,DavyJck,BerniesSpcl
5-31 M(1) ft clm 30000 m 30 59:4 1:29:2 1:58 6 3 4 3 3/4 5/6 1:59:1 11.20(KM'Ntt)Grsslnd,AllAtOnce,E'FrAce

---

PURPLE — **6** — $22,000

KEVEN SCOTT b g, 8, by Brooks Hanover, B Scott by Chief Wisco (Tr.-F. Mule)
Margaret & Charles Fernandes, Jr. Massapequa, N.Y. RR 2:00:4 1979 27 2 3 7 28,315.
($145,692) 7, 2:02:3 JOE MARSH, JR. (125) Grey-Blue-Red RR 2:02:3 1978 36 6 4 7 43,405.
8-3 RR ft clm alw 22000 m 29:3 1:01:2 1:31:2 2:01:4 6 7 8 7° 5/10 4/6½ 2:03 4.90(MrshJr)F'Mrn'g,FerDke,GooseStp 78
7-23 RR ft clm alw 22000 m 29:4 1:01:2 1:30:4 2:02:1 2 3 5 5 5/3½ 2/nk 2:02:1 *2.00(MrshJr)KldreTmy,KvnSctt,Ultimo 78
7-12 YR ft clm alw 22000 m 30:1 1:02 1:32:3 2:03:1 7 7 5° 4° 4/1 5/1¾ 2:03:3 12.70(MrshJr)Ambridge,BrtHart MsEdna 80
7-3 YR ft clm alw 22000 m 29:4 1:01:1 1:32:3 2:02:4 5 6 8 6°°4/2¼ 4/4¾ 2:03:4 *1.40(M'hJr)MssEdna,MJrDlIN,NpysBoy 76
6-25 YR ft clm alw 27000 m 29:3 1:00:1 1:30:2 2:01 6 6 7 6° 5/3½ 6/6¼ 2:02:2 14.30(M'hJr)CllT'Arms,DrnN'Tm,S'Stvn 68
6-14 YR ft clm alw 27000 m 29:2 1:00:4 1:30:3 2:00:3 1 2 3 6° 5/4½ 5/3¾ 2:01:2 *1.40(CAbb)DrnN'Tm,GdODde,BstOfGld 72
6-5 YR gd clm alw 27000 m 30:1 1:01:3 1:32:1 2:03:1 7 7 7 7° 6/3¾ 4/3¾ 2:04 8.20(MrshJr)D'T'lne,SthrnSnp,BstO'Gld 65
5-28 RR sy clm alw 27000 m 30:3 1:02:1 1:33:1 2:03:3 4 5 5° 4° 4/2 2/½ 2:03:3 3.10(MrshJr)GdODude,KvnSct,BstOfGld 60

ORANGE — **7** — $31,400

SKIPPER SUE b m, 4, by Sir Carlton, Hasta Luego by Steady Beau (Tr.-M. Smorra) (St.-J. Chapman)
Lawrence Kadish, N.Y., N.Y. YR 2:01:3 1979 14 4 1 1 19,225.
($3,315) 3, 2:03:4 (½) JOHN CHAPMAN (157) Green-White QCD(½) 2:03:4 1978 26 16 2 0 3,315.
8-1 RR ft clm alw 22000 m 29:3 1:00:2 1:31 2:02 2 2ex 5 8 8/dis 8/dis 2.30(Chap)F'tstcBtlr,FllChrg,CptnsReef 80
7-21 RR ft C-2 Cd 10000 m 29:4 1:01:2 1:32:1 2:02:3 6 7 6° 5° 5/2¾ 6/2¾ 2:03:1 4.10(Chap)Cnsprcy,H'Andra,CndyA'hrst 76
7-10 YR ft clm alw 22000 m 30 1:00:1 1:30:4 2:01:3 2 1 1 1 1/4 1/5 2:01:3 *1.70(Chap)SkprSue,CrlnaScout,MlvnsIdl 72
7-3 YR ft clm alw 22000 m 29:2 1:01:1 1:31:2 2:02 3 3 3 1° 1/2 1/nk 2:02 2.70(JChap)SkprSue,KldreTmy BrtHrt 76
6-22 YR ft clm alw 18000 m 29:1 1:01:3 1:33 2:03:3 1 1 1 1 1/1½ 1/4½ 2:03:3 *1.10(JChap)SkipprSue,Oswald,OurStaci 69
6-13 YR ft clm alw 18000 m 29:4 1:00 1:32:3 2:02:4 5ix accident DNF 4.60(JChap)TmToCall,TrprtEric,T'CshN 67
6-4 YR ft clm alw 18000 m 29:3 1:00:4 1:32 2:03:3 4 6 5° 4° 4/4½ 5/4 2:04:2 *1.40(Chap)HnknHnry,BrctAd's,Nalabor 62
5-24 RR ft clm alw 18000 m 29:3 1:00:4 1:31:4 2:02:2 4 1 2 2 3/1 2/½ 2:02:2 3.70(PatJr)SwiftAndy,SkpprSue,S'Dean 62

GREEN — **8** — $22,000

BEN REED b g, 5, by Reeds Knight, Katie Chuck by Meadow Chuck (Tr.-R. Vitrano)
M. Keshin, M. Jaffe, J. Vitrano, M. Macchio, N.Y. RR 2:04 1979 20 1 2 1 11,760.
($69,309) 4, 2:01:3 ROBERT VITRANO (150) Green-White-Gold YR 2:01:3 1978 40 8 8 7 57,995.
* 8-7 RR ft qua m 31 1:02:2 1:32:1 2:02 6 7 7 6 6/8 5/11 2:04:1 N.B.(Vtrno)CrwnsFl't,ArionLbl,WenJay 71
* 7-27 RR ft tp qua m 31:2 1:02 1:33 2:03:4 4 1 1 3 4/3½ 6/12 2:06:1 N.B.(Vtrno)ScttsAce S'BluChp,PtrPrkr 81
7-6 YR ft clm alw 22000 m 28:3 :59 1:29:4 2:00:3 8 8 7° 8 8/17 8/24 2:05:2 29.40(Vtrno)CoolWve,T'prtAce,G'Mastr 71
6-28 YR ft clm alw 22000 m 30:1 1:02 1:32:2 2:03:3 7 4 5 4 5/2 5/2½ 2:04 19.40(Vtrno)G'JimA,CptnVideo B'Knght 66
6-18 YR ft clm alw 22000 m 29:3 59:3 1:30:1 2:01:2 2 4 4 4 4/1¼ 3/2½ 2:01:4 11.20(Vtrno)SayNoMre,BnDxie,BnReed 69
6-11 YR gd C-3 Cd 8000 m 31:1 1:02:2 1:34 2:06:1 3 6 5° 6° 6/4¾ 6/3 2:06:4 18.90(RVtrno)PrviteEye,T'GrtHrb,V'Max 58
5-28 RR sy C-3 Cd 9000 m 30:1 1:02:2 1:33:2 2:03:4 6 7 8 8° 6/4¾ 7/10 2:05:4 16.20(Vtrno)TmlyThrp,MgcCrpt,FullChrg 60
5-21 RR ft C-3 Cd 9000 m 28:4 58:4 1:29:4 2:00:2 3 5 5 3°°2/2 4/6 2:01:3 13.80(Vtrno)RcktDlln,SpnakrN,TrumnHn 64

MORN. LINE

3 PACE $3.00 BIG TRIPLE

ONE MILE

WARM-UP SADDLE CLOTH—YELLOW

"Kay Jordon's Cabaret of Deer Park"

CLAIMING ALLOWANCE **PURSE $9,000**

5-yr.-olds & up $22,000; 4-yr.-olds $27,000; 3-yr.-olds $33,000; 3 to 6-yr. fillies & mares add $4,400.

BLUE — 4 — **1** — $22,000

BRET HART

b h, 8, by Bret Hanover, Cindys Knight by Knight Dream (Tr.-A. Alkes)
Allan & Morris Alkes, Westbury, N. Y. RR 2:02:4 1979 19 2 4 2 22,210.
($199,563) 5, 2:00:2 (1) ALLAN ALKES (160) Blue-Red-White YR 2:02 1978 31 1 5 5 29,205.

7-31 RR ft clm 27000 m 31:2 1:02:4 1:33:2 2:02:2 5 5 2° 2° 3/2¼ 6/9 2:04:1 44.20(AAlks)J'boChncy,S'Exprs,L'rsNbl 80
7-21 RR ft clm 27000 m 29:4 1:00:3 1:30:4 2:00:4 5 6 6 6 6/7¼ 6/11 2:03 14.50(Alkes)LrdsScrt,J'Chancy,Terandy 76
7-12 YR ft clm alw 22000Z m 30:1 1:02 1:32:3 2:03:1 5 6 3° 2° 2/¾ 2/1¼ 2:03:2 4.20(Insko)Ambridge,BrtHart,MssEdna 80
7-3 YR ft clm alw 22000 m 29:2 1:01:1 1:31:2 2:02 7 7 7 5° 4/3½ 3/nk 2:02 7.40(DInsko)SkprSue,KldreTmy,BrtHrt 76
6-22 YR ft clm alw 22000 m 29:3 1:00:4 1:31:4 2:02:4 3 6 6° 5° 3/2¾ 2/¾ 2:03 *1.70(Insko)FarmrLbll,BretHrt,TrprtAce 69
6-12 YR ft clm alw 27000 m 29:1 1:00:3 1:31 2:01:1 4 5 5 5 5/6 4/5¾ 2:02:2 8.80(ELoh)FntstcFella,G'Vikar,TKWilly 64
6-2 RR ft clm alw 27000 m 31 1:02:1 1:32:3 2:02:3 4 5 6 5 4/3½ 3/1 2:02:4 11.50(DInsko)G'fulVikr,ClncyLbll,BretHrt 60
5-26 RR ft clm 27000 m 29:2 1:00:1 1:31:1 2:01:3 6 7 7° 7° 7/8¼ 4/4¼ 2:02:2 31.30(Insko)S'Spann,C'Success,F'F'Rcky 56

RED — 5 — **2** — $22,000

GLENTOHI N

b g, 10, by Keep Away, Worthy Scott by Worthy Monarch (Tr.-J. Tremblay) (St.-R. Daigneault)
S. Mike, R. Daigneault Westbury, N.Y. YR 2:02:3 1979 19 10 1 2 42,100.
($52,956) 9, 2:03:2 REJEAN DAIGNEAULT (140) Red-Blue Chrlottetwn 2:03:2 1978 29 7 4 8 16,297.

* 8-7 RR ft qua m 31 1:02:2 1:32:1 2:02 2 4 5 5 5/7 4/7¾ 2:03:3 N B.(RDgnlt)CrwnsFl't,ArionLbl,WnJay 71
6-19 YR ft clm alw 27000 m 30:4 1:01:4 1:32:3 2:02:1 3 3 3° 3° 3/3½ 5/5 2:03:1 3.10(RDgnlt)CntKf,S'CreedA,K'stnMrgr 71
6-9 YR ft clm alw 27000 m 29:2 1:00:1 1:30:4 2:01:3 4 3 5 5 6/3½ 5/2¾ 2:02:1 2.60(RDgnlt)B'Dandy,E'Rain LtlChrgrA 70
5-30 RR ft clm alw 33000 m 29:3 1:01:1 1:31:2 2:00:3 8 4 4° 3° 3/2 4/6½ 2:01:4 12.80(RDgnlt)ClIT'Arms,SprBeetle,C'Vic 66
* 5-26 RR ft qua m 30:3 1:02:3 1:33:4 2:04:4 1 2 2 2 1/½ 1/1 2:04:4 N.B.(RDg't)GlnthiN,SlyChnc,DmndChrgr 64
5-19 RR ft clm alw 33000 m 29:3 59:2 1:30:1 2:00:3 1 2 3 3 3x/1¼ 8/20 2:04:3 1.90(RDg'lt)B'Grard,LoisMaine,N'Arrvl 58
5-12 Fhld sy Cd 6500 m 29:3 1:00:1 1:30:1 2:02:2 1x 3 3 3° 3/5 4/4½ 2:03:1 *1.50(RDgnlt)BitOFun,ChndsB'ts,F'bllFrwrd
5-4 RR ft clm alw 33000 m 29:3 :59 1:29:4 2:01 2 1 2 1 3/1 3/2¼ 2:01:2 3.10(RDgnlt)SgtPhlN,Nadala,GlentohiN 61

YELLOW — 5 — **3** — $22,000

NANDINA DIRECT

br h, 5, by Sly Yankee, Dark Doll by Thorpe Hanover (Tr.-P. Carbone) (St.-H. Carbone)
Ray & Dom Carotenuto, Bronx, N.Y. YR 2:02:4 1979 25 3 2 4 24,160.
($30,130) 4, 2:01 CARMINE ABBATIELLO (145) Gold-Red RR 2:01 1978 24 5 1 2 28,025.

8-3 RR ft clm alw 22000 m 30:2 1:01:1 1:31:2 2:02:1 2 5 6 6° 8/8½ 3/3¼ 2:02:4 10.60(Marohn)SmmyHn,Prvocatn,N'Drct 78
7-23 RR ft C-3 Cd 9000 m 29:3 1:01 1:32 2:01:3 4 5 5° 4x° acc. DNF 7.50(Doky)Marbyrd,S'sdeHn,MrPrfntne 78
7-11 YR ft C-3 Cd 8000 m 30:3 1:02:1 1:31:2 2:01:1 5 5 7° 8°°5/7¼ 4/6½ 2:02:2 12.40(JMrhn)C'wdVic R'noHvn CrtnlyR't 74
6-27 MR ft B-3/C-1 3100 m 30:1 1:01:4 1:32:3 2:02:3 4 6 x7 7 7/dis 7/dis 15.10(CG'nco)J'Dnne,BttrB'Ksh,PppyJck 68
6-20 YR ft C-2 Cd 9000 m 29:2 1:00:4 1:31:3 2:01:1 7 8 8 8 8/8¼ 8/8¼ 2:02:4 68.00(JMrhn)Nghtwrk,PhilT'Till,FllaBGd 76
6-12 YR ft C-2 Cd 9000 m 29:1 1:01:1 1:31:1 2:02:1 6 7 7 7° 7/7½ 5/7½ 2:03:3 23 80(JMrhn)B'RbrtD,RdngtnHll ElteTip 64
6-4 YR ft C-2 Cd 9000 m 30:3 1:02:1 1:33:4 2:03:3 6 6 6° 6°°4/2½ 5/4¾ 2:04:3 17.50(JMrhn)T'lyThrp,B'uMnde,F'F'Brd 62
5-22 RR ft C-1 11000 m 29:4 1:01:3 1:33 2:02:2 3 5 8 8°°8/7½ 8/7¾ 2:04 19.40(JMrhn)ZgyT'Pianist,SwtLou,P'Bco 64

BLACK — 6 — **4** — $22,000

JOHNNY MOD

br g, 7, by Morris Eden, Ar La Mode by Plebe (Tr.-K. Thomas)
Keith Burns & Noel Morris, Australia (qua)RR 2:01:4 1979 10 1 0 1 2,828.
($9,893) N.R. JOHN CAMPBELL (156) White-Maroon N.R. 1978 22 6 5 3 7,292.

8-3 RR ft clm alw 22000 m 30:2 1:01:1 1:31:2 2:02:1 1 1 2 2 2/4 5/6 2:03:2 2.80(KThmas)SmmyHnvr,Prvctn,N'Drct 78
7-24 RR ft clm alw 27000 m 29:1 1:00:2 1:30:2 2:00:2 8 8 7° 8° 8/11 8/13 2:03 39 80(KThms)VsslsGem,SsieCool,Hmwrk 80
* 7-17 RR ft tp qua m 30:1 1:01:3 1:31:4 2:03 2 1 1 1 1/nk 2/½ 2:03 N B.(KThms)BasilCourt,J'Mod,B'Prvlge 79
7-6 M(1) ft Cd 9000 m 29:1 59:2 1:30:1 1:59 2 3 5 7 10/9 10/17 2:02:2 36 50(KThms)MjrStorm,MtyClimb,CrwnBay
6-25 M(1) ft Cd 9000 m 28:3 58:2 1:29:2 1:58:1 6 1° 4 5 8/9 10/22 2:02:3 27.60(KThms)RgliLght,HpyAbbe,BndMusic
6-18 M(1) ft Cd 9000 m 29 59:1 1:30:2 1:59:4 3 6 6 6 4/5¾ 4/5¼ 2:01 17.70(KThms)Sunro,Trentonian,BsyT'Bbe
6-6 M(1) ft Cd 9000 m 30:1 59:2 1:30 1:59:4 2 3 2 2 8/8¼ 8/11 2:02 5.90(KThms)DvdsBychk,GaySchnll,RedRgr
* 5-29 RR ft qua m 30 1:00:3 1:31 2:01:4 3 1 1 1 1/8 1/7 2:01:4 N.B.(KThms)JhnnyMod,FireKngA,SntrPrd

---

WHITE — 3 — **5** — $22,000

WINNAFREDA

b m, 8, by Out To Win, Gold Mecca by Mecca Chief (Tr.-G. Phalen)
Virginia Young, Milford, Del. RR 2:02:3 1979 21 8 6 2 37,410.
($54,884) 6, 2:01:4 GEORGE PHALEN (135) Blue-White RR 2:03 1978 35 2 5 5 27,150.

8-2 RR ft clm alw 18000 m 31:2 1:02:2 1:32:3 2:02:3 1 1 1 1 1/3 1/3½ 2:02:3 3.60(GPhln)Wnfrda,GdbyRbie,T'prtAce 80
7-25 RR ft clm alw 15000Z m 30:1 1:01:4 1:32:2 2:03:3 2 3 3° 1 1/3½ 1/2 2:03:3 2.30(RCrmr)Wnfreda,SwnDxtr,Juliec'r 80
7-12 YR ft clm alw 15000 m 30 1:01:3 1:31:3 2:02:4 1 3 2° 1 2/½ 2/nk 2:02:4 2.80(Crmr)SntrPrde,Wnfrda,BrtsRchie 80
7-2 YR ft clm alw 15000 m 29:3 1:01:1 1:32 2:02:4 3 5 5° 4° 3/5 4/4¾ 2:03:4 4 40(Crmr)ReuterN,K'Always VicToria 72
6-21 YR ft clm alw 15000 m 29:4 1:00:4 1:32:2 2:03 4 5 5° 3° 2/½ 3/½ 2:03 3.50(Crmr)L'Enzym,ShaW'Wlle,W'frda 65
6-12 YR ft clm alw 15000 m 30 1:02 1:32:3 2:03:3 1 4 5° 4° 3/3¼ 2/4½ 2:04:2 *1.10(Crmr)FllaNick,Wnfrda,Ad'sChims 64
6-5 YR sy clm alw 15000 m 29:3 1:00:2 1:31:2 2:02:2 3 5 6 5 3/7½ 2/7 2:03:4 *1.20(RCrmr)RcktAlley,Winnafrda B'Lad 65
5-22 RR ft clm alw 18000 m 29:2 1:01:2 1:32:3 2:03 5 6 6° 4° 3/2¾ 5/2¼ 2:03:2 4.50(HnFln)ClpprKid,AtaNorton,Savitar 64

PURPLE — 12 — **6** — $22,000

SOUTHERN SNIP

b g, 9, by James Scott, Southern Pride by Southern Van (Tr.-L. Derrico)
NeptuneStblsInc Wenger Derrico,Summer,Krieger YR 2:03:3 1979 26 1 6 2 22,170.
($22,248) N.R. MERRIT DOKEY (140) White-Red-Blue (qua)RR 2:05:1 1978 13 0 3 1 6,067.

7-30 RR ft clm alw 22000 m 29:2 59:4 1:31:2 2:02 2 3 4 7 4/7½ 3/11 2:04:1 19.00(MDky)A'Sahbra,SgrV'Abbe,S'Snip 78
7-20 RR ft clm alw 22000 m 29:2 1:02:4 1:32:4 2:04:1 1 x3x be pulled up DNF 7.70(Doky)MvngStdy,BigUrge,SailorJoe 79
7-12 YR ft clm alw 22000 m 29:2 1:00:3 1:32:2 2:02 4 3° 3° 3° 6/7½ 7/8 2:03:3 11.10(Doky)FntstcBtlr,Relntlss,SprseAll 80
7-3 YR ft clm alw 22000 m 29:2 1:01:1 1:31:2 2:02 1 1 1 2 3/2¼ 5/2¼ 2:02:2 4.60(MDokv)SkprSue KldreTmy,BrtHrt 76
6-25 YR ft clm alw 27000 m 29:3 1:00:1 1:30:2 2:01 7 7 6° 8 8/12 8/17 2:04:2 87.80(Font)ClIT'Arms,DrnN'Tme,S'Stvn 68
* 6-19 YR ft qua m 30 1:02:1 1:32 2:03 7 7 7 7° 7/12 6/9¾ 2:05 N.B.(Doky)Tremor,Mrdck,ImgeOfLaura 68
6-14 YR ft clm alw 27000 m 30 1:01:2 1:33:1 2:03:3 8 8 8° 8 8/11 8/17 2:07 14.00(CAbb)MtnJan,JohnRegl,SpdyStvn 72
6-5 YR gd clm alw 27000 m 30:1 1:01:3 1:32:1 2:03:1 6 1 3 3 2/1½ 2/1¼ 2:03:2 11.50(CAbb)D'T'lne,SthrnSnp,BstO'Gld 65

ORANGE — 8 — **7** — $22,000

FULL CHARGE (NY)

br g, 5, by Byegone, Darlyn Dear by Dartmouth (Tr.-J. Mojica)
Joseph & Steven Vavrica, Bronx, N.Y. YR 2:04:3 1979 22 2 2 2 17,120.
($19 003) 4, 2:01:3 JAMES MAROHN (115) Purple-White MR 2:01:3 1978 31 5 5 1 11,950.

8-1 RR ft clm alw 22000 m 29:3 1:00:2 1:31 2:02 8 7 3 2 2/3 2/1½ 2:02:1 39.90(PatJr)F'stcBtlr,FllChrg,CptnsReef 80
7-23 RR ft clm alw 22000 m 29:4 1:01:2 1:30:4 2:02:1 5 5 4° 4° 4/3½ 4/2½ 2:02:3 14.40(PatJr)KldreTmmy,KvnSctt,Ultimo 78
7-11 YR ft C-3 Cd 8000 m 30:3 1:02:1 1:31:2 2:01:1 7 7 6 5 6/7¾ 5/7½ 2:02:3 79.30(PatJr)C'wdVic,RmnoHvn,CrtnlyR't 74
7-2 YR ft C-3 Cd 8000 m 29 59:2 1:30 2:00:3 6 6 6 5° 8 8/14 8/20 2:04:3 31.20(Doky)GFella BCrk,HTrvlr-GRulr4h 72
6-25 YR ft C-3 Cd 8000 m 29:4 1:00:1 1:31:2 2:02:4 1 3 2° 2° 2/3 7/4¾ 2:03:4 6.40(MDky)MrtyD'Ray,B'Bret M'Trndo 68
6-12 YR ft C-3 Cd 8000 m 29 1:00 1:32:2 2:03 2ex4be pulled up DNF 8 60(MDky)FlaBGd,GlnbysFla,GmeRulr 64
6-5 YR sy C-3 Cd 8000 m 29:3 1:00:3 1:32:1 2:02:3 5 7 7 6°°4/2½ 4/2½ 2:03 16.90(PatJr)PalmCrt,FllaBGd,HhniesBst 65
5-28 RR sy C-3 Cd 9000 m 30:1 1:02:2 1:33:2 2:03:4 4 5 5° 3° 2/1 3/6½ 2:05 4.90(MDky)TmlyThrp,MgcCrpt,FullChrg 60

GREEN — 8 — **8** — $26,400

CAPTAINS REEF

b m, 5, by Captain Courageous, Keystone Pearl by Bye Bye Byrd (Tr.-M. Lavallee) (St.-Her. Filion)
Capital Hill Farms, Inc., Englishtown, N.J. RR 2:00:3 1979 23 7 4 3 42,780.
($62 380) 3, 1:59:2 (⅝) HERVE FILION (163) Red-Blue-White RR 2:02 1978 28 3 4 4 26,840.

8-1 RR ft clm alw 22000 m 29:3 1:00:2 1:31 2:02 3 4 4 3° 3/5 3/1¾ 2:02:2 2.80(HrFln)F'stcBtlr,FllChrg,CptnsReef 80
7-14 LB(⅝) ft clm 24000 m 29 58:4 1:28:2 1:59:4 1x 8 8 8 8/dis 8/dis 11 90(JM'GvrnIII)SamsMjsty,VicksJ,RvlBoy
7-8 LB(⅝) ft clm 24000 m 28:4 58:2 1:29:1 1:59:4 2 5 5 5 5/3¼ 5/7¾ 2:01:2 *1.80(HrFln)ChrlKngt SmMjsty,Container
6-24 LB(⅝) ft clm 30000 m 31 1:02:4 1:33:4 2:03 1 4 6 7 7/4 7/6½ 2:04:2 *1.60(HrFln)RippOak RinkyDink,MidPrk
6-14 M(1) ft clm 36000 m 28:3 :59 1:28:3 1:58:2 10 10 10 9 9/10 9/15 2:01:2 5.90(HrFln)TotalFrgt AllAtOnce FstJet
5-22 RR ft clm alw 27000 m 29:2 59:3 1:30 2:00:3 1 3 4 4 4/3½ 1/ns 2:00:3 *1.80(HrFln)C'Reef,SprBeetle,D'Cntstr 64
5-12 RR sy clm alw 27000 m 30:4 1:02:4 1:34:3 2:06 8 8 8 7 6/3¼ 3/1 2:06:1 15.70(HrFln)PayT'Prc,AshlyLbl,CptnsRf 60
4-20 YR ft clm alw 27000 m 30 1:01:1 1:31:2 2:02:4 3 5 4° 3° 2/1 1/1¼ 2:02:4 *2.00(HrFln)CptnsReef,V'Vickie,L'Brush 52

4 PACE

ONE MILE

WARM-UP SADDLE CLOTH—BLACK

$2.00 EXACTA

"Deborah Hospital Rose Weiss Chapter"

CLASS C-3—THREE-YEAR-OLDS **PURSE $9,000**

BLUE **1**

KEYSTONE SUAVE (NY) b g, 3, by Most Happy Fella, Keystone Squaw by Adios (Tr.-M. Lavallee) (St.-Her. Filion)
Capital Hill Farms, Inc., Englishtown, N.J. Fhld 2:01 1979 11 2 2 1 12,705.
($2,070) 2, 2:07:1 HERVE FILION (163) Red-Blue-White Stga 2:07:1 1978 8 2 0 0 2,070.
8-6 RR ft C-3 Cd 9000 m 31 1:02:2 1:32 2:03:4 2 3 3 4 3/6 3/1½pl2 2:04 3.40(HrFln)SwpsHn,K'Suave,H'Travllr 78
7-23 RR ft C-3 Cd 11250 m 29 1:00 1:31 2:01:2 2 4 5 5 5/5½ 3/5½ 2:02:2 3.10(HrFln)R'Flla,FourF'Brd,K'tnSuave 78
7-16 RR ft C-3 Cd 9000 m 30:1 1:02:1 1:33:1 2:03:2 1 2 3 6° 5/4¼ 4/2¼ 2:03:4 *1.30(HrFln)HstlrsBoy,SpnakrN,H'Trvlr 78
7-3 YR ft C-2 Cd 9000 m 30 1:01:1 1:31:3 2:01:4 5 6 6 7 8/4¼ 6/5 2:02:4 16.10(GFln)Blsphme,ByeNKsh BoysWay 76
6-20 YR ft C-2 Cd 9000 m 29:2 1:00:4 1:31:3 2:01:1 2 4 6 7°°7/6¼ 7/5¼ 2:02:1 8.10(GFln)Nghtwrk,PhlTheTill,FllaBGd 76
6-2 Fhld ft Cd 4800 m 29:1 1:00:2 1:31:2 2:01 5 2 2 2 3/2 1/1½ 2:01 4.90(HrFln)K'stnSuave,MerickLbl,VanEsts
5-27 LB(⅝) ft Cd 5500 m 29:4 1:02 1:30:4 2:01:3 5 7 6° 6° 7/6½ 7/10 2:03:3 *1.30(HrFln)NavyLbl,LckyKid,RaceyProdigy
5-12 RR sy 3yr Cd 7500 m 31:1 1:03:1 1:34:4 2:06 8 8 7° 6° 6/6½ 5/4 2:06:4 16.00(HrFln)FltFlla,M'H'Nevle,HzrTrvlr 60

RED **2**

FLY FLY TIMMY (NY) b c, 3, by Fly Fly Byrd, Adorada by Lieut Mike (Tr.-E. Palmieri)
Paul Mahoney & Joseph Krug, N.J. YR 2:02:2 1979 16 2 2 2 11,310.
($6,816) 2, 2:00:2 (1) REJEAN DAIGNEAULT (140) Red-Blue Syr(1) 2:00:2 1978 9 3 1 2 6,816.
8-6 RR ft C-3 Cd 9000 m 31 1:02:2 1:32 2:03:4 1 1 1 2ix 4/6½ 5/5½pl4 2:05 *1.90(RDgnlt)SwpsHn,K'Suave,H'Travllr 78
7-23 RR ft C-3 Cd 9000 m 29:1 1:00:4 1:31:3 2:01:2 5 6 6° 6° 6/5 7/5½ 2:02:2 4.50(RDgnlt)AdmrlBret Parsly,SunShld 78
7-16 RR ft C-2 Cd 10000 m 30:4 1:02:1 1:32:3 2:02:1 8 8 7° 8° 8/7¼ 8/11 2:04:2 22.50(HrFln)JJsDmino,A'Blazer,G'Fella 78
7-10 YR ft C-2 Cd 9000 m 29:4 1:00:4 1:31 2:00:3 1 2 2 2 2/2 4/1½ 2:00:4 3.80(RDg't)PncTme,AlphaLbl,ClnlLBar 72
7-2 YR ft C-3 Cd 8000 m 29:2 1:00:3 1:31:4 2:02:2 3 5 2° 1 1/nk 1/1 2:02:2 8.50(RDgnlt)F'F'Timmy,J'RQntn,T'Frst 72
6-25 YR ft C-2 Cd 9000 m 29:4 1:01:1 1:31:4 2:01:4 3 5 7 8 8/6¾ 8/4½ 2:02:3 11.70(LFont)HhnsBst,Blsphme,KatDncr 68
6-13 Stga ft Cd 1600 m 31 1:03:2 1:34:2 2:04:3 6 4 4° 3°°2 1/¾ 2:04:3 *.80(GFrshy)F'F'Tmy,BJConor,LstyNassau
6-5 Stga gd Cd 1800 m 31:1 1:01:3 1:32:2 2:03:2 2 3 2° 2° 2 2/½ 2:03:2 *1.70(GFrshy)AtaSteve,F'F'Tmy,RedThorn

---

YELLOW **3**

SWAPS HANOVER b c, 3, by Meadow Skipper, Sweetsie Hanover by Dancer Hanover (Tr.-S. Levy) (St.-G. Sholty)
John Confort, Jr., Manhasset, N.Y. M(1) 1:59:3 1979 12 3 1 0 14,765.
($1,365) 2, 2:07:1 (⅝) SANFORD LEVY (160) Brown-White-Gold ScD(⅝) 2:07:1 1978 10 1 1 0 1,365.
8-6 RR ft C-3 Cd 9000 m 31 1:02:2 1:32 2:03:4 5 2 2 3ix 2/3 2/nkpl1 2:03:4 9.80(SLevy)SwpsHn,K'Suave,H'Travllr 78
7-30 RR ft C-3 Cd 9000 m 30 1:01:2 1:31 2:02 4 6 4° 3° 4/4½ 8/5½ 2:03 14.00(SLvy)SunShld,JMNible,Afrethght 78
* 7-24 RR ft qua m 30 1:03 1:33 2:02:4 5 5 7 6 6/4¾ 5/5½ 2:04 N.B.(Levy)AftnGllnt,Pdrind,RocketAlly 81
6-21 M(1) ft Cd 10000 m 29:4 :59 1:29:2 1:59 8 8 8 7 8/6¼ 8/10 2:01 46.00(Levy)SwftHpeful,ZoomsBoy,MrgnoHn
6-11 M(1) gd Cd 10000 m 29:3 59:4 1:31:4 1:59:4 4 7 9 5°°5/4¾ 7/6½ 2:01:1 31.00(SLevy)DrctSctr,FullRspct,KeyTryon
5-31 M(1) ft Cd 10000 m 30 59:2 1:29:2 1:59:3 6 7 7° 6° 7/6½ 7/6½ 2:00:4 12.10(SLevy)WldAHrry,MrngoHn,ScttNpln
5-24 M(1) sy Cd 10000 m 29:4 59:1 1:29:4 1:59 9 4° 3° 2° 2/1½ 8/7 2:00:2 13.10(SLevy)AndyClns,WldAHrry,PnsnGal
5-17 M(1) ft Cd 10000 m 29:2 59:3 1:29:1 1:58:4 8 9 9 8 7/5¾ 6/3½ 1:59:2 15.00(SLevy)IronDale,KeyTryon,WildAHarry

---

BLACK **4**

SPINNAKER N b c, 3, by Drummer Boy, Amy Hanover by Alfred Hanover (Tr.-K. Dawson)
Valley Farms, Ringtown, Pa RR 2:03:2 1979 24 2 4 4 22,760.
($12,293) 2, 2:03 DONALD DANCER (130) Blue-Gold RR 2:03 1978 17 4 3 5 12,293
8-6 RR ft C-3 Cd 9000 m 31 1:02:2 1:32 2:03:4 3 x7 7° 6° 7/18 7/18pl6 2:08:1 3.80(DDncr)SwpsHn,K'Suave,H'Travllr 78
7-23 RR ft C-3 Cd 9000 m 29:1 1:00:4 1:31:3 2:01:2 3 5 5° 4° 4/3 5/3¾ 2:02:1 3.90(DDncr)AdmrlBrt,Parsley,SunShld 78
7-16 RR ft C-3 Cd 9000 m 30:1 1:02:1 1:33:1 2:03:2 4 5 6° 3° 4/1½ 2/¾ 2:03:3 6.30(LFont)HstlrsBoy,SpnakrN,H'Trvlr 78
7-11 YR ft C-2 Cd 9000 m 29:4 1:00 1:30:3 2:00:4 2 5 4° 3° 6/5½ 6/7 2:02:1 7.10(DDncr)PlmC'rt.Encnto,LbrtyA'hrst 74
7-4 YR gd C-2 Cd 9000 m 30:2 1:01:4 1:32:3 2:04 7 7 7x 7 7/16 7/23 2:08:3 44.20(DDncr)R'Hall,JRsBoy-M'Cambrodh 57
6-25 YR ft C-2 Cd 9000 m 29:4 1:01:1 1:31:4 2:01:4 8 4 5 5 5/3½ 5/1½ 2:02:1 58.60(HrFln)HhnsBst,Blsphme,KatDncr 68
6-18 YR ft C-2 Cd 9000 m 29:3 1:01:1 1:32 2:02:2 7 4 3° 3° 4/5¾ 8/8¾ 2:04:1 31.50(HrFln)Colossal,H'Hangman,L'Scrt 69
5-28 RR sy C-3 Cd 9000 m 30:2 1:02:2 1:33 2:03:2 3 4 4° 4° 2/2 1/2 2:03:2 4.30(DDncr)SpnkrN,SnysdeHn,M'DlRay 60

WHITE **5**

J Ks BEST br c, 3, by Best Of All, Solar Dance by Airliner (Tr.-J. Paton)
Michael Deutsch, Bernadette Matura, Conn YR 2:01:2 1979 20 3 7 2 24,815.
($3,120) DAVID DUNCKLEY (150) Brown-White (qua)RcR 2:08 1978 10 0 2 0 3,120.
8-6 RR ft C-3 Cd 9000 m 31 1:02:2 1:32 2:03:4 4 5 6 7 6/13 6/7½pl5 2:05:1 4.90(Dnckly)SwpsHn,K'Suave,H'Travllr 78
7-23 RR ft C-2 Cd 10000 m 29:3 1:01 1:31:1 2:01 3 5 5° 8 8/13 7/14 2:03:4 13.60(Dnckly)SultanHn,Oxygn,LbrtyA'hst 78
7-16 RR ft C-2 Cd 10000 m 30:4 1:02:1 1:32:3 2:02:1 4 5 6° 6° 6/4½ 5/4½ 2:03 6.30(Dnckly)JJsDmino,A'Blazer,G'Flla 78
7-6 YR ft 3yr Cd 7500 m 30 1:01:1 1:31:2 2:01:2 4 1 1 1 1/1½ 1/½ 2:01:2 2.90(Dnckly)JKsBst.DnnysFirst,CJBret 71
6-29 YR ft 3yr Cd 7500 m 29:1 59:2 1:31 2:00:3 3 1 1 2 3/2½ 3/3½ 2:01:2 *1.40(DDnkly)JJsDomino,CJBret,JKsBest 69
6-22 YR ft 3yr Cd 7500 m 29:4 59:4 1:31:2 2:02 1 2 2 4 4/1½ 3/¾ 2:02:1 *1.00(Dnckly)PwrSrve,M'H'Nvle,JKsBst 69
6-14 YR ft 3yr Cd 7500 m 30:2 1:00:2 1:31:1 2:01:1 4 5 4° 4° 3/2½ 2/2½ 2:01:4 *1.50(Dnckly)C'Tony,JKsBest,JJsDmino 72
6-2 RR ft 3yr Cd 8000 m 29:3 1:00:1 1:30:3 2:02:2 4 5 5° 4° 4/1½ 4/1½ 2:02:3 2.60(Dnckly)SunShield,CJBrt,P'AndyD 60

PURPLE **6**

MEADOW CAMBRO (NY) b c, 3, by Fulla Napoleon, Meadow Bonda by Adios (Tr.-Jo. Kopas)
Yves Lauzon, Lauzon Stables, Inc., Can. RR 2:02 1979 14 2 2 0 15,685.
($18 595) 2, 2:04:4 JOHN KOPAS (185) Green-White YR 2:04:4 1978 13 2 2 2 18,595.
8-6 RR ft C-2 Cd 10000 m 29:3 1:00:4 1:31:2 2:02 2 4 4° 3° 2/½ 5/4 2:02:4 4.50(JoKps)S'Ace AlphaLbll,LbrtyA'hst 78
7-30 RR ft C-2 Cd 10000 m 30 1:01 1:30:1 2:01:3 8 7 7 7 8/5½ 5/3½ 2:02:1 52.40(JoKps)BoysWay,KatDancr,VghnHn 78
7-23 RR ft C-2 Cd 10000 m 29:3 1:01 1:31:1 2:01 4 6 7 5° 5/6 5/6½ 2:02:1 6.10(JoKps)SultanHn Oxygn,LbrtyA'hst 78
7-11 YR ft C-2 Cd 9000 m 30:1 1:01:3 1:31:1 2:01:2 5 3 3° 2° 2/1 2/2½ 2:01:4 9.70(JoKps)ThmsvwBlz,M'Cmbro,A'Blzr 74
7-4 YR gd C-2 Cd 9000 m 30:2 1:01:4 1:32:3 2:04 3 2 1 1 1/nk 2/nkdh 2:04 10.70(JoKps)R'Hall,JRsBoy-M'Cambrodh 57
6-26 YR ft C-2 Cd 9000 m 29:1 59:3 1:30:1 1:59:4 8 8 8 6 5/8 4/11 2:02 44.50(JoKps)F'A'hrst,H'Hngmn,BdTAce 63
6-18 YR ft C-3 Cd 8000 m 29:2 1:00:1 1:31 2:02:1 6 6 6° 5° 2/nk 1/1½ 2:02:1 7.10(JoKps)M'Cmbro,BuckoHn,M'D'Ray 69
6-11 YR gd C-2 Cd 9000 m 30:4 1:02 1:32:2 2:03:4 7 8 6° 6° 8/15 8/18 2:07:2 63.60(JoKps)T'Lease,FuryA'hrst,K'Mrgr 58

ORANGE **7**

THANK GOODNESS br c, 3, by Armbro Nesbit, Tarport Karen by Thorpe Hanover (Tr.-A. Nelson) (St.-D. Insko)
Helen Buck, Far Hills, N.J. RR 2:01 1979 11 1 1 2 7,694.
($6,011) 2, 2:00:4 (1, CHARLES CONNOR, JR. (150) Purple-Gold Lex(1) 2:00:4 1978 11 5 1 2 6,011.
8-6 RR ft C-2 Cd 10000 m 30:2 1:00:1 1:30:1 2:02 1 1 1 1 2/hd 7/10 2:04 3.10(Insko)Oxygen,Colossal,GlnbysFella 78
7-30 RR ft C-2 Cd 10000 m 30 1:00:1 1:31:4 2:02:2 1 4x 7 7 7/13 7/16 2:05:3 2.60(Insko)LbrtyA'hst,A'Blazer,G'Fella 78
7-21 RR ft 3yr Cd 8000 m 30 1:01:1 1:30:4 2:01 1 1 1 1 1/3½ 1/3 2:01 *1.70(Insko)T'Gdnss,DlRbllious,P'AndyD 76
7-12 YR ft 3yr Cd 7500 m 30:1 1:01:4 1:32 2:01:3 4 5 4° 2° 2/hd 2/hd 2:01:3 7.10(Insko)DblEntry.T'Gdness,TdrB'Chp 80
7-5 YR ft 3yr Cd 7500 m 29:3 1:00:2 1:30:3 2:01:4 2 3 3° 2° 3/1 7/5½ 2:02:4 3.00(Insko)HstlrsBoy,Scaucus,P'AndyD 61
6-28 YR ft 3yr Cd 7500 m 29:1 1:00:4 1:30:4 2:03 6 2 3 3 4/1½ 6/¾ 2:03:1 7.20(Insko)S'Ace LbrtyA'hrst UnEsp'r 66
6-15 YR ft 3yr Cd 7500 m 30 59:4 1:30 2:00:1 5 5 5 5° 4/8 5/11 2:02:2 3.00(DInsko)S'Fella,PwrSrve,M'H'Nevle 32
6-8 YR ft 3yr Cd 7500 m 30:1 1:01:4 1:32:2 2:02 8 8 8° 6° 7/13 4/4 2:02:4 22.20(DInsko)F'BigOnes,Colosal,H'tlrsBoy 69

GREEN **8**

CLOVERLEAF TONY b g, 3, by Sampson Direct, Deemed Worthy by Worthy Boy (Tr.-P. Valvanis) (St.-L. Fontaine)
L. Fontaine & R. Kiviat, Bedford, N.Y. YR 2:01:1 1979 12 4 0 1 10,755.
($00.00) LUCIEN FONTAINE (154) Green-White-Red 1978 0 0 0 0
8-6 RR ft C-3 Cd 9000 m 31 1:02:2 1:32 2:03:4 7 6 4° 1° 1/3 1/nkpl7 2:03:4 6.40(LFont)SwpsHn,K'Suave,H'Travller 78
7-23 RR ft C-3 Cd 9000 m 29:1 1:00:4 1:31:3 2:01:2 2 4 3° 2° 3/2 4/3¾ 2:02:1 *2.50(LFont)AdmrlBrt,Parsley,SunShld 78
7-16 RR ft C-2 Cd 10000 m 30:4 1:02:1 1:32:3 2:02:1 7 7 8 7 7/6½ 7/8¼ 2:03:4 27.60(LFont)JJsDmino,A'Blazer,G'Fella 78
7-9 YR ft C-2 Cd 9000 m 29:3 1:00:3 1:30:3 2:00:4 6 6 6x 8 8/18 8/21 2:05 3.30(LFont)N'BHrtg,FllaBGd,PhlT'Till 71
6-28 YR ft 3yr Cd 7500 m 29:1 1:00:4 1:30:4 2:03 8 8° 6° 6° 6/3¾ 4/¼ 2:03 3.60(LFont)S'Ace,LbrtyA'hrst,UnEsp'r 66
6-21 YR ft 3yr Cd 7000 m 30:1 1:01:2 1:32:1 2:02:4 3 3 1 1 1/¾ 1/1 2:02:4 *.40(Font)ClvrlfTony,WrrnMS,L'Timmy 65
6-14 YR ft 3yr Cd 7500 m 30:2 1:00:2 1:31:1 2:01:1 1 1 1 1 1/2 1/2½ 2:01:1 4.90(LFont)C'Tony,JKsBest,JJsDomino 72
5-31 RR ft 3yr Cd 8000 m 30 1:01:1 1:32:4 2:02:4 4 7 7° 6°°7/7 7/4½pl6 2:03:4 4.00(Font)EARbrts,HyprAd's,HstlrsBoy 66

SCRATCHED—AFORETHOUGHT (6), sick. A.E.—MEADOW CAMBRO—races in P.P. of scratched horse.

⑤ PACE

ONE MILE

WARM-UP SADDLE CLOTH— WHITE

CLASS C-3

FOUR & FIVE-YEAR-OLDS—HORSES & GELDINGS.

$2.00 EXACTA

PURSE $9,000

BLUE 1 (3)

BEAU MONDE
b h, 5, by Nevele Bigshot, Shadydale Mini by American Adios
Norman & Sandra Brill, Samuel Behar, N.Y. (Tr.-T. Foster)
($71,769) 4, 2:00:4   HERVE FILION (163)   Red-Blue-White

										1979 17 0 4 1 11,710.
										YR 2:00:4 1978 18 6 3 4 50,070
8-6 RR	ft C-3 Cd 9000 m 30:2 1:01:3 1:32	2:03:1	7	8	7	6°	6/3½	2/½		2:03:1	14.20 (HrFln) Snysde Hn, B'Mnde, Mgc Crpt 78
7-30 RR	ft C-3 Cd 9000 m 29:2	59:2 1:30:2 2:01:1	1	4	4	6	8/9½	7/7½		2:02:3	2.80 (HrFln) Gme Rulr, S'sde Hn, Mgc Crpt 78
7-16 RR	ft C-3 Cd 9000 m 29	1:00 1:31:1 2:01:2	1	5	5°	5°	3/4¼	2/3½		2:02	*1.60 (HrFln) T'prd Ken, Beau Mnde, B'Crk 78
7-10 YR	ft C-2 Cd 9000 m 29:4 1:00:4 1:31	2:00:3	7	7	8	8	6/8	5/6½		2:01:4	20.10 (HrFln) Pnc Tme, Alpha Lbl, Cln lLBar 72
7-3 YR	ft C-2 Cd 9000 m 30	1:01:1 1:31:3 2:01:4	8	8	8	8*	7/4½	8/7½		35.40	(Dplse) Blsphme, Bye NKsh, BoysWay 76
6-20 YR	ft C-3 Cd 9000 m 29:2 1:00:4 1:31:3 2:01:1	6	6	5*	5*	6/5½	6/4½			2:02:1	2.80 (Font) Nghtwrk, Phi The Till, Fila BGd 76
6-13 YR	ft C-2 Cd 9000 m 30:1 1:01:3 1:32	2:02:1	2	3	2°	2°	2/½	2/1		2:02:2	2.40 (Font) Hppy HA, Beau Mnde, T'Donut 67
6-4 YR	ft C-2 Cd 9000 m 30:3 1:01:1 1:33:4 2:03:3	1	2	2	3	3/1½	2/1			2:03:3	3.40 (NDpls) Tmly Thrp, B'uMnde, F'F'Brd 62

RED 2 (4)

TRUMAN HANOVER
br h, 4, by Tar Heel, Truly Hanover by Adios
Walter Bodie, Flushing, New York (Tr.-J. Paton)
($27,750) 3, 2:00:2   JOE MARSH, JR. (125)   Grey-Blue-Red

										RR 2:02 1979 15 1 3 5 16,550.
										MR 2:00:2 1978 27 6 3 5 26,820
8-6 RR	ft C-2 Cd 10000 m 30:2 1:00:3 1:31:4 2:02:2	3	4	4	7	7/3½	7/3			2:03	18.30 (MrshJr) Kat Dncr, K'Nw Tm, VivaMx 78
7-23 RR	ft C-2 Cd 10000 m 29:1 1:00	1:30:1 2:00:4	3	4	6	6	6/7¼	7/7		2:02:1	11.90 (MrshJr) Cdrwd Vic, Stud Stll, JRs Boy 78
7-16 RR	ft C-3 Cd 9000 m 29:4 1:01:2 1:32	2:02	5	1	1	1	1/½	1/1½		2:02	3.00 (MrshJr) Trmn Hn, F'F'Brd, T'Grt Hrb 78
7-4 YR	gd C-3 Cd 8000 m 30	1:01:1 1:34:4 2:05:1	6	1	3	4	3/1	3/1½		2:05:2	4.10 (M'hJr) Rnees Flla, K'N'Tm, Trmn Hn 57
6-27 YR	ft C-3 Cd 8000 m 30	1:01 1:31:1 2:01:2	3	1	1	1	1/½	2/1		2:01:2	9.40 (M'shJr) K'N'Tm, Trumn Hn, M'W'sde 66
6-18 YR	ft C-3 Cd 8000 m 29	1:01 1:32 2:01:4	3	4	4°	7	7/12	7/18		2:05:2	4.70 (ELoh) Slr Systm, MJMahone, SACrst 69
6-4 YR	ft C-3 Cd 8000 m 30:2 1:02:3 1:33:2 2:03:3	5	3	3	3x/2	7/15			2:06:3	2.20 (M'shJr) G'Islnd, Brdlys Crk, Knwd Str 62
5-28 RR	sy C-3 Cd 9000 m 30:4 1:01:4 1:34:2 2:04:2	2	3	2*	2°	1/1½	4/2½		2:04:3	*1.40 (M'hJr) Rght Agn, Trmn Hn, Hhnes Bdi 60

YELLOW 3 (4)

BILL DERROR
b h, 4, by Flying Bret, Bantie Beau by Steady Beau
Flying Bret, Inc., Deer Park, N.Y. (Tr.-B. DeFonce)
($8,595) 3, 2:04:4   CARMINE ABBATIELLO (145)   Gold-Red

										RR 2:04:1 1979 9 2 2 1 12,800.
										Fhld 2:04:4 1978 9 1 2 1 8,595.
7-30 VD(⅝)	ft Cd 3500 m 28:2 1:01 1:28:4 1:58:2	3	2	3	3°	4/2½	4/8½		2:00	4.70 (CClrk) Cdr Strke, Chnc Tmchi, Smth Tnky
7-23 VD(⅝)	ft Cd 3500 m 28:1 :58	1:27 1:57:3	3	2	2	3/6	3/9		1:59:2	13.90 (CClrk) Artillery, Over Chnge, Bill Derror
* 7-17 VD(⅝)	ft qua m 31:1 1:03:2 1:34:1 2:04:1	4	1	2	2	1/5	1/15		N.B. (CClrk) Bill Derror, Swt Cnnamon, JJByrd
* 7-10 VD(⅝)	ft qua m 29:3 1:00:1 1:29:3 2:00:2	5	2	2	2	2/2	2/		2:00:3	N.B. (CClrk) Artillery, Bill Drror, Bntn Brwnie
3-6 RR	sy C-2 Cd 9000 m 31:1 1:02:2 1:33	2:03:3	4	3	5°	5°	5x/2½	8/u1½		13.70 (JRchsn) Chrls Hn, M'Trndo, Stdy Lde 48
2-26 RR	gd C-2 Cd 8000 m 31:1 1:02:4 1:33:4 2:05:2	5	1° 2	1°	1	1/½			2:05:2	3.80 (JRchsn) Bll Dror, S'full Str, Rckt Dilln 35
2-6 RR	ft C-3 Cd 7500 m 30	1:01:3 1:32:2 2:02:3	6	1° 3	3	4/4	7/12		2:05	16.60 (JRchsn) Pppa G, Mdw Artst, Cln lLBar 32
1-30 RR	ft C-3 Cd 7500 m 30:2 1:01:1 1:32:4 2:03:3	6	2	4	5	5/3½	4/4½		2:04:3	7.80 (JRchsn) The Pckr, Cln lLBar, VivaMx 32

BLACK 4 (8)

BUD T ACE ⓃⓎ
ro g, 5, by Paul T Ace, The Lady by Jamie
Joan Cruise, Westbury, N.Y. (Tr.-J. Cruise)
($77,565) 4, 2:01:4   EARL CRUISE (193)   Green-Red-White

										RR 2:03:4 1979 23 3 4 2 23,362.
										YR 2:01:4 1978 36 5 6 8 48,815.
8-6 RR	ft C-3 Cd 9000 m 29:4 1:00:2 1:31:3 2:03:2	4	5	5	7	8/4	5/1½		2:03:3	11.00 (ECrus) T'Frost, M'H'Nvle, Azlia Spinr 78
7-23 RR	ft C-3 Cd 11250 m 29	1:00 1:31	2:01:2	6	7	7/7½	5/7		2:02:4	7.10 (ECrus) R'Flla, FourF'Byrd, K'Suave 78
7-16 RR	ft C-3 Cd 10000 m 30	1:00:3 1:31:1 2:01:4	5	6	6°	7°	8/5½	6/6½		2:03:1	14.50 (ECrus) Fila BGd, Bye B'Man, Encanto 78
7-4 YR	gd C-2 Cd 9000 m 30:2 1:01:4 1:32:3 2:04	4	6	6°	6/7½	6/7½			2:06:1	5.40 (ECrus) R'Hall, JRs Boy-M'Cambro^dh 57
6-26 YR	ft C-2 Cd 9000 m 29:1	59:3 1:30:7 1:59:4	3	4°	4°	4/7½	3/11		2:02	7.00 (ECrus) F'A'hrst, H'Hngmn, Bd TAce 63
5-28 RR	sy C-2 Cd 10000 m 30	1:01:2 1:32:2 2:02	4	6*	5°	6/6½	5/4½		2:02:4	3.00 (ECrus) M'Bnne, Fury A'st-M'Ldde^dh 60
5-21 RR	ft C-2 Cd 10000 m 30	1:02:1 1:33:1 2:03:1	5	6°	6	5/4½	2/hd		2:03:1	3.80 (ECrus) T'T'Adios, Bd TAce, M'Bnnie 64
5-14 RR	sy C-3 Cd 9000 m 29:4 1:01:4 1:32:1 2:04:2	5	7	6°	6	6/4½	4/4½		2:04:2	6.50 (ECrus) T'Blaze, FourF'Byrd, K'Dancr 58

WHITE 5 (10)

SHOW N GOOD
ch h, 4, by Good Show, Success Ella by Greentree Adios
Ettore Annunziata, Mahopac, N.Y. (Tr.-D. Dunckley)
($8,654) 3, 2:01:4 (⅝)   DAVID DUNCKLEY (150)   Brown-White

										YR 2:03:2 1979 19 2 2 0 17,418.
										GrR(⅝) 2:01:4 1978 28 3 6 1 7,963.
8-6 RR	ft C-3 Cd 9000 m 29:1 1:30:4 2:02:1	7	7	7°	6°	6/5½	5/4		2:03	10.10 (Dnckly) F'Nck, Brnz HnA, MrPrfntne 78
7-23 RR	ft C-3 Cd 9000 m 3 1:01:3 1:32:1 2:02:4	2	4	5	4	4/3½	4/½		2:03	3.70 (Dnckly) C'Right, M'Tornado, S'Endvr 78
7-16 RR	ft C-3 Cd 10000 m 30:1 1:00:4 1:31	2:01	7	7	7°	8	8/10	8/9½		2:02:4	53.50 (Dnckly) Cln lLBr, JRs Boy, Mdw Artst 78
7-4 YR	gd C-2 Cd 9000 m 30:3 1:02:1 1:33	2:04:1	6	7	7	6/6½	4/5		2:05:2	43.20 (Crmr) H'Hngmn, T'Blu Chip, Kt Dncr 72
* 6-29 YR	gd qua m 30:2 1:02:1 1:33:3 2:04:3	6	6	6	6/4½	4/4½			2:05:2	N.B. (Dnckly) Fst Strke, Trckn Sm, KdyNck 68
5-1 RR	ft C-1 10000 m 30:1 1:01:2 1:32	2:01:3	2	4	2*	3°	4/2	7/4½		2:02:3	23.40 (HnFln) Set Point, Dsh O'Brn, Pysn Bco 61
4-24 RR	ft C-1 10000 m 30:1 1:01:4 1:29:4 2:01	2	4	4	4	4/5	4/4			2 01:4	16.80 (HnFln) Tby Tar, Sntr Fred, Mdw Artst 54
4-17 RR	ft C-1 Cd 9000 m 30:3 1:01:4 1:32:3 2:03:2	2	3	5	7	7/4½	7/5½		2:04:2	5.70 (HnFln) Kgt N'Armr, Cln lLBr, M'Artst 48

PURPLE 6 (5)

GOOSE ISLAND
b h, 5, by Columbia George, Cass Hanover by Dean Hanover
DKesslcr, R&STarlowe, MSpielberg, SWiener, N.Y. (Tr.-E. Berry) (St.-J. Drolet)
($60,399) 4, 2:00:3   LUCIEN FONTAINE (154)   Green-White-Red

										RR 2:01:1 1979 21 3 1 2 19,640.
										YR 2:00:3 1978 35 6 3 3 39,505.
8-3 RR	ft clm alw 27000 m 28:4 1:00:1 1:30:3 2:01:2	4	3	1	2°	1/hd	6/5		2:02:2	*2.60 (LFont) C'Angus, Thndr Lbl, Oscr Mnr 78
7-25 RR	ft clm alw 22000 m 30	1:00:1 1:30:3 2:02	5	1	1	1	1/5	1/5		2:02	*2.40 (Font) Gsel slnd, Cntry Frd, Adlde Ldy 80
7-16 RR	ft clm alw 22000 m 29:3	59:3 1:30:3 2:02	8	3° 2	5	6/5½	7/7½		2:02:2	19.90 (Font) Ashly Lbl, GdChrs, Kystn Mrgr 78
7-7 YR	ft clm 27000 m 28:4	59:1 1:31:2 2:02:2	7	1	1	2	4/3½	4/9½		2:04:2	13.20 (M'shJr) Spncr CrdA, Thndr Lbl, F'Flla 74
6-27 YR	ft C-2 9000 m 29:2	59:4 1:30:4 2:01:1	4	1	2	4	7/9½	8/14		2:04	26.10 (RDgnlt) Trck Lease, S'Stull, S'Systm 66
6-19 YR	ft C-3 9000 m 29:1 1:01:3 1:31	2:01:1	8	8	8°	8/9½	8/10			2:03:1	21.50 (CAbb) Rdngtnn Hll, Bars Rbrt D, S'Stul 71
6-12 YR	ft C-2 9000 m 29:1 1:01:1 1:31:2 2:02:1	1	1	1	7/5½	7/12			2:04:3	*1.40 (CAbb) B'Rbrt D, Rdngtn Hll, Elte Tip 64
6-4 YR	ft C-3 Cd 8000 m 30:2 1:01:1 1:33:4 2:03:3	1	2	3	1	1/n*			2:03:3	*.80 (CAbb) G'Islnd, Brdlys Crk, Knwd Str 62

ORANGE 7 (8)

TIMELY FROST ⓃⓎ
b h, 4, by Most Happy Fella, Syndicette by Shadow Wave
Syvanus King, Jr., lessee, New Holland, Penna. (Tr.-S. King)
($15,501) 3, 2:01:4   SYL KING, JR. (180)   Green-White-Black

										RR 2:03:2 1979 9 1 1 3 10,055.
										RR 2:01:4 1978 17 1 2 2 12,190.
8-6 RR	ft C-3 Cd 9000 m 29:4 1:00:2 1:31:3 2:03:2	5	6	7	8°	7/3	1/hd		2:03:2	38.40 (KngJr) T'Frost, M'H'Nvle, Azlia Spinr 78
7-23 RR	ft C-3 Cd 11250 m 29	1:00	1:31	2:01:2	7	7	6°	6°	6/6	7/7½		2:02:4	26.50 (SKngJr) R'Flla, FourF'Brd, K'Suave 78
7-16 RR	ft C-3 Cd 9000 m 30	1:00:1 1:30:2 2:02:4	3	5	7° 6°	6/6	7/7¼			2:04:1	18.60 (SKng Jr) MrAAA'Tmly Frst, R'Fella 78
7-9 YR	ft C-3 Cd 8000 m 29:2 1:00	1:31:1 2:01:3	8	8°	7° 5/7½	5/13			2:04:1	31.60 (SKngJr) Jhn RQntn, A'Spnnr, Gme Rlr 71
7-2 YR	ft C-3 Cd 8000 m 29:2 1:00 1:30:3 1:31:4 2:02:4	6	7	7°	5°	4/1	3/2½		2:03:2	36.30 (SKngJr) F'F'Timmy, J'RQntn, T'Frst 72
6-18 YR	ft C-3 Cd 8000 m 30	1:01 1:32 2:01:4	3	3	3°	4/4½	4/7			2:03:1	11.30 (KingJr) Solr Systm, MJMhne, SACrst 69
6-7 LB(½)	ft C-3 Cd 4500 m 29:3	59:2 1:30:1 2:02:4	8	5°	4	6°	6/2½	3/2½		2:01	28.30 (SKngJr) Tonto Lbl, GdChrs, B'luMnd 69
6-1 LB(½)	ft C-3 Cd 4500 m 30	1:02:4 1:33:2 2:02:3	6	7	8°	6°	6/6½	3/2		2:03	15.60 (SKngJr) Dart Gun, Satrn A'hst, T'Frost

---

GREEN 8 (8)

MARBYRD
b h, 4, by Bye Bye Byrd, Adios Martha by Adios
Khartoum Sales, Inc., Brooklyn, N.Y. (Tr.-M. Loewe) (St.-W. Popfinger)
($17,421) 3, 1:59:2 (1)   WILLIAM POPFINGER (186)   Green-White

										RR 2:01:3 1979 6 2 0 0 5,990.
										M(1) 1:59:2 1978 17 3 1 2 17,016.
7-23 RR	ft C-3 Cd 9000 m 29:3 1:01	1:32	2:01:3	1	2	2	3	4/1½	1/hd		2:01:3	11.50 (WPop) Mrbyrd, S'sde Hn, MrPrfntne 78
7-16 RR	ft C-3 Cd 9000 m 29:4 1:00	1:30:2 2:02:4	6	7	5° 6/7½	8/6½			2:04:1	14.10 (WPop) MrAAA, Tmly Frst, Rnees Flla 78
7-3 YR	ft C-3 Cd 8000 m 30	1:01:1 1:32:2 2:02:4	7	1	1	2	2/1½	7/6½		2:04	4.30 (FPop) Encnto, M'Artist, Crtnly Rght 76
6-25 YR	ft C-3 Cd 9000 m 30:1 1:01:1 1:31:4 2:01:4	7	6°	4°	4°	4/3	7/3½		2:02	14.70 (WPop) Hhns Bst, Blsphme, Kat Dncr 68
6-15 Lex(1)	ft Opn 3000 m 30:2	58:4 1:28:4 1:58:3	2	2	2	2	2/3½	4/8½		2:00:1	5.60 (JBrwn) Ltle Mjority, S'Sphire, A'Kisco
6-9 Lex(1)	ft C-2 Opn Cam 33	1:02:1 1:33 2:03:1	3	1	1	1/hd	1/½			2:03:1	4.20 (JBrwn) Mrbyrd, Shrp Bret, Brdys Blllt
* 6-2 Lex(1)	ft qua m 30:4 1:02:1 1:34:2 2:05:1	1	1	2	2/2	1/8½				2:05:1	N.B. (JBrwn) Mrbyrd, Grge Way, H'cmng Guse
10-24 RR	ft C-3 Cd 9500 m 30:1 1:01:1 1:31:2 2:02:1	3	6	5° 5/4½	8/10			2:04:1	2.80 (WPop) Bud Hn, Yonkers, Grnd Gainer 43

6 PACE

ONE MILE

WARM-UP SADDLE CLOTH—PURPLE

CLASS C-3

FOUR & FIVE-YEAR-OLDS—HORSES & GELDINGS.

$3.00 BIG TRIPLE

PURSE $9,000

BLUE **1**

BRAVO BRET b h, 4, by Bret Hanover, Shoo Shoo Byrd by Poplar Byrd (Tr.-S. King, Jr.)
Sylvanus King, Jr. (Lessee) New Holland, Pa. Fhld 2:05:3 1979 20 1 3 3 13,624.
($6,502) 3, 2:04:1 (⅝) SYL KING, JR. (180) Green-White-Black LB(⅝) 2:04:1 1978 18 2 5 4 6,502.
7-30 RR ft C-3 Cd 9000 m 29:4 1:02 1:32:3 2:02 5 6 5° 4° 4/5½ 6/6 2:03:1 30.20(SKingJr)K'N'Tme,B'HnA,MrP'tne 78
7-23 RR ft C-3 Cd 9000 m 29:3 1:01 1:32 2:01:3 7 7 7° 7ix 6/dis 6/dis 43.10(SKingJr)Mrbrd,S'sdeHn,MrPrfntne 78
7-10 YR ft C-3 Cd 8000 m 29:3 1:01:1 1:32:1 2:02:1 3 4 4° 5° 6/3½ 5/5 2:03:1 19.90(SKingJr)M'Artist,M'DlRy,M'Trndo 72
7-3 YR ft C-3 Cd 8000 m 29 1:01:1 1:32 2:02:4 4 6 7 7° 6/4 5/5¼dh 2:03:4 8.60(SKngJr)E'cnto,M'Artst,CrtnlyRght 76
6-25 YR ft C-3 Cd 8000 m 29:4 1:00:1 1:31:2 2:02:4 3 4 4° 3°°3/3½ 2/3 2:03:2 11.40(KngJr)MrtyD'Ray,B'Bret,M'Trndo 68
° 6-19 YR ft qua m 29:4 1:01:2 1:32:3 2:02:4 4 3 3 4 4/7 3/5½ 2:03:4 N.B.(SKngJr)TmmyNZ,J'Chncy,BrvoBrt 68
5-14 RR sy C-3 Cd 9000 m 29:4 1:00:2 1:31:2 2:03 7 7 7 4°°4/2½ 2/1¾ 2:03:2 20.60(KngJr)P'Duane,BrvoBrt,TrumnHn 58
5-7 RR ft C-3 Cd 8000 m 29 1:00 1:30 2:00:3 2 4 4° 4° 3/3½ 3/5½ 2:01:3 11.30(KngJr)Stckngtwn,PhlT'Till,B'Bret 58

RED **2**

BRONZE HANOVER A b g, 5, by Trainer Hanover, Bronze Cheval by Lawn Raider (Tr.-R. Bencal)
A. Eilenberg, Jasons Stable, N.Y. BM(1) 2:01:1 1979 20 3 3 2 19,144.
($9,952) N.R. REJEAN DAIGNEAULT (140) Red-Blue N.R. 1978 22 6 3 2 4,688.
8-6 RR ft C-3 Cd 9000 m 29:1 1:00:2 1:30:4 2:02:1 5 5 2° 2° 2/2 2/1½ 2:02:2 *1.30(CAbb)F'Nick,BrnzHnA,MrPrfntne 78
7-30 RR ft C-3 Cd 9000 m 29:4 1:02 1:32:3 2:02 6 1 1 1 1/½ 2/½ 2:02:1 *1.90(CAbb)K'N'Tme,BrnzHnA,MrP'tne 78
7-16 RR ft C-2 Cd 10000 m 30 1:00:3 1:31:1 2:01:4 7 7 8 8 7/4½ 7/7½ 2:03:1 22.90(CAbb)FllaBGd,ByeB'Man,Encanto 78
7-4 YR gd C-2 Cd 9000 m 30:2 1:01:4 1:32:3 2:04 5 1 2 3 3/1½ 4/1½ 2:04:1 8.80(CAbb)R'Hall,JRsBoy-M'Cambrodh 57
6-26 YR ft C-2 Cd 9000 m 29:1 59:3 1:30:1 1:59:4 4 5 5 5° 6/8½ 6/12 2:02:1 4.50(JMrhn)F'A'hrst,H'Hngmn,BdTAce 63
6-13 M(1) ft Cd 10000 m 29:2 59:1 1:29:3 1:59:2 10 10 10 9°°10/5½ 10/8½ 2:01 30.80(CMnzi)StdyStrkr,GrrsnLpz,E'FourAce
6-5 YR sy C-2 Cd 9000 m 29:1 1:00 1:32 2:03:1 5 6 6 8 8/3½ 4/1½ 2:03:2 6.40(JMrhn)PhilT'Till,N'wrk,Blspheme 65
5-28 RR sy C-2 Cd 10000 m 32:2 1:02:2 1:33 2:03:1 1 2 3 4 3/1½ 3/2 2:03:3 4.00(JMrhn)StdyLdr,Blsphme,BrnzHnA 60

YELLOW **3**

THE GREAT HERB (NY) b h, 4, by Tempered Yankee, Adios Fanny by Parading Adios (Tr.-E. Brisson)
Lewis Bennett, Bayside, N.Y. PPk(⅝) 2:01:4 1979 18 1 2 2 8,582.
($9,081) 3, 2:03 E. (ANDRE) BRISSON (155) Grey-Blue-Red YR 2:03 1978 19 1 2 1 9,081.
8-6 RR ft C-3 Cd 9000 m 29:1 1:00:2 1:30:4 2:02:1 2 3 5 5 4/4 4/2½ 2:02:4 18.60(EBrssn)F'Nck,BrnzHnA,MrPrfntne 78
7-23 RR ft C-3 Cd 11250 m 29 1:00 1:31 2:01:2 3 5 4° 4° 4/4½ 6/7½ 2:02:4 19.80(EBrissn)R'Flla,FourF'Brd,K'Suave 78
7-16 RR ft C-3 Cd 9000 m 29:4 1:01:2 1:32 2:02 4 4 3° 3° 2/½ 3/5½ 2:03 8.50(LFont)TrmnHn,F'F'Brd,T'GrtHerb 78
7-9 YR ft C-3 Cd 8000 m 28:3 1:00:4 1:31:2 2:01:2 2 4 2° 2° 2/ns 2/3½ 2:02:1 16.50(LFont)SpnT'Btle,T'G'Hrb,S'sdeHn 71
7-2 YR ft C-3 Cd 8000 m 29:2 1:00:3 1:31:4 2:02:2 8 6 4° 3° 2/nk 5/3½ 2:03 65.40(LFont)F'F'Timmy,J'RQntn,T'Frost 72
6-20 YR ft C-3 Cd 8000 m 30:2 1:01 1:32 2:02:2 1 4 4 6 7/2½ 7/2½ 2:02:4 11.90(LFont)A'Spinnr,J'RQntn,S'T'Bttle 76
6-11 YR gd C-3 Cd 8000 m 31:1 1:02:2 1:34 2:06:1 1 2 3 3° 3/2 2/½ 2:06:1 7.90(LFont)PrivteEye,T'GrtHrb,V'Max 58
6-4 YR ft C-3 Cd 8000 m 29:4 1:00:3 1:31:1 2:03 6 7 6 7 7/3½ 7/8½ 2:04:3 37.90(JChap)ElteTip,S'sideHn,GlnbysFlla 62

BLACK **4**

HOME BASE br h, 4, by Direct Home, Ohios Lady by Ohio Time (Tr.-B. W. Norris)
D. R. Junk, Washington C. H., Ohio RR 2:01:4 1979 22 3 1 2 19,580.
($11,997) 3, 2:01:2 (⅝) REAL CORMIER (140) Blue-Orange ScD(⅝) 2:01:2 1978 18 3 3 0 6,089.
° 8-3 RR ft qua m 30:4 1:01:3 1:31:4 2:02 3 4 3° 4° 4/6½ 3/7½ 2:03:2 N.B.(Crmr)SntrPrd,NblPrdN,HmeBase 82
7-30 RR ft C-3 Cd 9000 m 29:2 59:2 1:30:2 2:01:1 7 1° 1 2 7/9½ 8/12 2:03:3 22.00(MrshJr)GmeRlr,S'sdeHn,MgcCrpt 78
7-11 YR ft C-2 Cd 9000 m 30:1 1:01:3 1:31:1 2:01:2 8 8 7° 7° 8/8 8/7 2:02:4 82.00(Crmr)ThmsvwBlz,M'Cmbro,A'Blzr 74
7-3 YR ft C-2 Cd 9000 m 30 1:01:1 1:31:3 2:01:4 2 4 3° 2° 3/1½ 4/4½ 2:02:4 11.60(Crmr)Blsphme,ByeNKsh,BoysWay 76
6-5 YR sy C-2 Cd 9000 m 29:1 1:00 1:32 2:03:1 6 5 5° 4°°3/½ 8/3½ 2:03:4 19.00(Crmr)PhilT'Till,N'wrk,Blaspheme 65
5-28 RR sy C-2 Cd 10000 m 32:2 1:02:2 1:33 2:03:1 4 3 2° 3° 6/8 8/12 2:05:3 7.20(RCr'r)StdyLdr,Blaspheme,BrnzHnA 60
5-15 RR ft C-1 11000 m 28:4 58:3 1:29:1 1:59:1 6 8 8° 8 8/17 7/21 2:03:2 42.40(RCrmr)H'dnHn,TmprdBrd,R'T'Klln 62
5-8 RR ft C-1 10000 m 29 1:00:1 1:30:1 2:00:2 5 6 6° 5° 5/3½ 3/5dh 2:01:2 20.40(Crmr)C'LBr,P'prd,WMnstr-HBsedh 64

WHITE **5**

BASIL COURT b g, 4, by Golcourt, Elezia by Nephew Hal (Tr.-M. Santa Maria)
Giannone,TimbercroftStable,Castellano,Stern,Gordon,N.Y (qua)RR 2:03 1979 8 1 0 1 1,465.
($00.00) JOE MARSH, JR. (125) Grey-Blue-Red 1978 1 0 0 0
7-30 RR ft C-3 Cd 9000 m 29:4 1:02 1:32:3 2:02 1 3 4 5 6/7½ 7/6½ 2:03:1 5.00(M'hJr)K'N'Tme,BrnzHnA,MrP'tne 78
7-23 RR ft C-3 Cd 9000 m 29:3 1:01 1:32 2:01:3 2 3 4 6 5/6½ 5/7½ 2:03 2.80(M'shJr)Mrbrd,S'sdeHn,MrPrfntne 78
* 7-17 RR ft tp qua m 30:1 1:01:3 1:31:4 2:03 4 4 4 4° 3/1½ 1/½ 2:03 N.B.(MrshJr)BasilCourt,J'Mod,B'Prvlge 79
3-10 Pukekohe(NewZealand) approx. 1⅜ m 3:38:2 finished 9th; (L.Purdon) ChillyDream, BillyBrydon, TayBridge
2-24 Wellington(NewZealand) approx. 1¾ m 3:10 finished 7th; (L.Purdon) Chinta, ScottishAffair, GipsyWay
2-21 Wellington(NewZealand) approx. 1⅞ m 2:38:3 finished 7th; (L.Purdon) AlecPeterson, DeepHanover, HighviewMin
2-14 Manawatu(NewZealand) approx. 1¾ m 3:32 finished 7th; (L.Purdon) SlyChick, Toronui, RussellJames
2-12 Manawatu(NewZealand).. approx. 1⅝ m 2:37:4 finished 3rd; (L.Purdon) TempestBelle, Candillo, BasilCourt

---

PURPLE **6**

KILDARE TIMMY b h, 5, by Albatross, Lavish Hanover by Adios (Tr.-R. Connor)
Jarob Stable Corp., Beechurst, N.Y. YR 2:02 1979 26 4 2 4 28,700.
($10,014) 3, 2:03:1 JAMES MAROHN (115) Purple-White 1978 5 0 0 0 680.
7-30 RR ft C-3 Cd 9000 m 29:1 59:1 1:30 2:01:3 6 8 8 8 7/4½ 4/2½ 2:02 6.10(RDg'lt)CrtnlyRght,GdChrs,A'Spnnr 78
7-23 RR ft clm alw 22000 m 29:4 1:01:2 1:30:4 2:02:1 3 1 1 1 1/2 1/nk 2:02:1 3.00(Crmr)KldreTmmyl,KvnSctt,Ultimo 78
7-13 YR ft clm alw 22000 m 28:4 1:00:2 1:31 2:01:2 1 2 2° 1 1/nk 5/4 2:02:1 2.00(Crmr)Terandy,HHLeslie,MrAloof 82
7-3 YR ft clm alw 22000 m 29:2 1:01:1 1:31:2 2:02 4 4 5 4° 2/2 2/nk 2:02 3.50(RCrmr)SkprSue,KldreTmy,BrtHrt 76
6-26 YR ft clm alw 22000 m 29:3 59:4 1:31:3 2:03:3 8 3°°7 7 7/3 7/3 2:04:1 27.30(RCrmr)CntryFred,Rlntlss,RcktDlln 63
6-15 YR ft clm alw 18000 m 28:3 59:1 1:30:4 2:02 4 1° 1 1 1/½ 1/½ 2:02 8.10(RCrmr)KldreTmy,Arundi,H'H'Lyss 82
6-6 YR ft clm alw 18000 m 30:2 1:00:4 1:32:1 2:03:1 8 i7 7 7°°5/3½ 5/4½ 2:04:1 38.20(RCrmr)Dayvndr,H'H'Lyss,Whiskey 69
5-30 RR ft clm alw 18000 m 30:1 1:01:4 1:31:4 2:02:4 4 4 4° 4° 3/3½ 4/2 2:03:1 3.00(RCrmr)Arrundi,BionicButy,Savitar 66

ORANGE **7**

GOOSE STEP br g, 5, by Battleground, Smart Stepper by Attorney (Tr.-A. Alkes)
A. Alkes, Otto Sunder, M. & B. Alkes, N.Y. RR 2:02:2 1979 24 6 2 6 38,380.
($49,246) 4, 2:02:4 ALLAN ALKES (160) Blue-Red-White RR 2:02:4 1978 32 6 5 3 39,005.
8-3 RR ft clm alw 22000 m 29:3 1:01:2 1:31:2 2:01:4 1 2 2 3 3/3½ 3/5 2:02:4 7.80(AAlks)FrstMrn'g,FerDke,GseStep 78
7-24 RR ft clm alw 27000 m 30:1 1:01:3 1:32 2:02 1 1 1 1 3/2 8/8 2:03:3 8.00(AAlks)A'John,Arndi,B'Jms-Ad'rdh 80
7-17 RR ft clm alw 27000 m 30:1 1:02 1:33 2:03:1 7 1 1 1 1/½ 6/4 2:04 9.70(AAlkes)F'Fella,S'Rhythm,B'Duane 80
7-6 YR ft clm alw 40000 m 29:2 1:00:1 1:31:3 2:00:2 8 3° 2° 4° 7/17 7/dis 34.80(Alkes)ErthLite,GdT'Ryle,RoyRwrd 71
6-20 YR ft clm alw 40000 m 29:1 1:00:1 1:31:1 2:00:3 6 2° 3 5 7/6½ 7/15 2:03:3 18.10(AAlkes)ErthLite,GdTmeRayle,Rgncy 76
6-2 RR ft clm alw 40000 m 28:4 59:2 1:30:2 2:02 1 1 1 1 1/nk 3/2 2:02:2 10.50(AAlkes)StrlngClay,GdT'Ryle,GseStp 60
5-26 RR ft clm 40000 m 29:4 1:01 1:31:1 2:02 5 1 1 1 1/1 5/4½ 2:03 11.80(Alkes)ErthLite,AdovrLbl,B'Paloma 56
5-15 RR ft C-1 11000 m 28:4 58:3 1:29:1 1:59:1 8 4° 2° 4 6/14 8/23 2:03:4 27.80(Alkes)H'dnHn,TmprdBrd,R'T'Klln 62

GREEN **8**

MARTY DEL RAY (NY) b g, 4, by Romeo Hanover, Modest Miss by Good Time (Tr.-A. Nelson) (St.-D. Insko)
M. & C. Robinson, S. & H. Silverman, F. Wallace YR 2:02:4 1979 21 1 4 4 19,560.
($43,575) 3, 2:02:4 CARMINE ABBATIELLO (145) Gold-Red YR 2:02:4 1978 16 1 3 3 35,810
8-6 RR ft C-3 Cd 9000 m 29:4 1:00:2 1:31:3 2:03:2 2 1 1 1 1/½ 4/1 2:03:3 7.00(DInsko)T'Frst,M'H'Nvle,AzliaSpinr 78
7-30 RR ft C-3 Cd 9000 m 29:4 1:02 1:32:3 2:02 8 7 8 8° 8/8 8/6½ 2:03:2 20.00(Insko)K'NwTme,BrnzHnA,MrP'tne 78
7-16 RR ft C-3 Cd 9000 m 29:4 1:00 1:30:2 2:02:4 6 2° 3 4 5/7 4/2½ 2:03:1 8.80(Insko)MrAAA,TmlyFrst,RneesFlla 78
7-10 YR ft C-3 Cd 8000 m 29:3 1:01:1 1:32:1 2:02:1 4 2 2 3 2/1 2/½ 2:02:2 2.90(Insko)M'Artist,M'DlRay,M'Trnado 72
7-3 YR ft C-3 Cd 8000 m 29 59:1 1:30 2:01 3 2 4 5° 4/1½ 5/2 2:01:2 2.50(DInsko)VivaMax,CdrwdVic,MrAAA 76
6-25 YR ft C-3 Cd 8000 m 29:4 1:00:1 1:31:2 2:02:4 2 1 1 1 1/3 1/3 2:02:4 4.00(Insko)MrtyD'Ray,BrvoBrt,M'Trndo 68
6-18 YR ft C-3 Cd 8000 m 29:2 1:00:1 1:31 2:02:1 8 7 7° 7 5/2 3/4½ 2:03:1 11.20(Insko)M'Cmbro,BuckoHn,M'D'Ray 69
6-5 YR sy C-3 Cd 8000 m 29:3 1:00:3 1:32:1 2:02:3 1 3 3 5° 5/2½ 5/3 2:03:1 *1.90(CAbb)PalmCrt,FllaBGd,HhniesBst 65

MORN. LINE

7 PACE

ONE MILE

WARM-UP SADDLE CLOTH—ORANGE

CLASS C-2—THREE-YEAR-OLDS **PURSE $10,000**

BLUE **1** — 5

FAYGIE

br g, 3, by Best Of All, Bountiful Bird by Bye Bye Byrd (Tr.-J. Giorgianni)
J. M. Giorgianni, M. Joseph & Gary S. Safier, N.J. MR 2:01:2 1979 22 5 5 3 27,654
($2,200) 2, 2:05:2 (1) JAMES GIORGIANNI (150) Orange-Black-White M(1) 2:05:2 1978 7 1 0 1 2,200

7-31 RR ft C-1 Cd 11000 m 29:1 59:4 1:29:4 2:00:2 3 2 2 3 3/1 7/3¼ 2:01 17.20(G'giani)RdngtnHll,DnsHn,JJsDmno 8
7-24 RR ft C-1 Cd 11000 m 29:2 1:01 1:30:4 2:01:1 8 8 8 8 7/5¾ 6/4¼ 2:02 32.80(Grgiani)T'prdBrd,PncTm,IRSTme 8
7-17 RR ft C-1 Cd 11000 m 30:4 1:01:3 1:31:2 2:01:1 4 2 2 3 3/1 3/1¼ 2:01:2 14.30(Giorgnni)D'Stks,MchlsCndy,Faygie 8
7-7 LB(⅝) ft Inv 7500 m 29:3 59:1 1:28:3 1:58:1 6 6 5° 4° 4/1¼ 7/3¾ 1:59 42.40(JGrgnni)Americus,D'Isle,FrdmBret
7-1 Gosh gd 3yr Stk 17900 m 29:2 1:00:4 1:31:4 2:01 2 1 1 1 1/1½ 3/4½ 2:02 N.B.(JGrgnni)MststYnk,KeySioux,Faygie
6-24 LB(⅝) ft Cd 6500 m 29 59:4 1:30:4 2:00:1 2 4 4 2° 2/1 5/2½ 2:00:3 5.60(JGrgnni)Americus,CrysRum,AukByrd
6-10 MR A ft 3yr ec 12800 m 29:1 59:4 1:31:1 2:01:2 2 1 1 1 1/1 2/¼ 2:01:3 5.40(Grginni)K'Sioux,Faygie,BnnaStrnd 7
6-3 MR Aft ft 3yr ec 4500 m 29:3 1:00:3 1:31:3 2:00:4 2 2 2 3 3°/½ 2/1½ 2:01 2.50(JG'nni)K'eSioux,Faygie,BanaStrnd 7

RED **2** — 3

J M NIBBLE

b c, 3, by Adios Ronnie, Meadow Frances by Meadow Rice (Tr.-M. Lavallee) (St.-Her. Filion)
Capital Hill Farms, Inc., Englishtown, N.J. Fhld 2:00:1 1979 16 4 2 1 23,444
($00.00) HERVE FILION ((153) Red-Blue-White 1978 0 0 0 0

8-4 Fhld ft 3yr Stk 14160 m 29:3 59:1 1:29:3 2:00:1 4 6 7° 5 4/1¼ 1/¾ 2:00:1 N.B.(HrFln)JMNbble,DrmyIsle,Gortdarrig
7-30 RR ft C-3 Cd 9000 m 30 1:01:2 1:31 2:02 8 1 1 2 2/2 2/1 2:02:1 10.60(HrFln)SunShld,JMNible,Afrethght
7-19 M(1) ft Cd 12000 m 29:1 57:3 1:28:3 1:58 2 4 4 6 6/3¼ 4/1¼ 1:58:1 37.20(HrFln)RealTreasure,MelHn,DxtrAlb
7-11 YR ft C-3 Cd 8000 m 30:3 1:02:1 1:31:2 2:01:1 8 8 8 7 7/9¾ 6/10 2:03:1 41.30(GFln)C'wdVic,RmnoHvn,CrtnlyR't 7
7-3 YR ft C-3 Cd 8000 m 29 59:1 1:30 2:01 6 8 8 8° 6/4¼ 6/3 2:01:3 34.50(GFln)VivaMax,CedrwdVic,MrAAA 7
6-25 M(1) ft Cd 10000 m 29:1 59:2 1:30:4 2:00 8 i9 7 6° 7/4¼ 7/8 2:01:3 92.20(DnFln)KngNik,FullRespct,TaurusChip
6-19 M(1) ft 3yr Stk 14360 m 31 59:4 1:29 1:58:1 2 1 3 5° 6/8 7/20 2:02:1 N.B.(HrFln)MrryIsle,DrmyIsle,SassfrsJW
6-5 M(1) gd 3yr Stk 14760 m 29 58:3 1:30:1 2:00:4 1 3 3 2° 1/2 1/1 2:00:4 9.10(HrFln)JMNbble,JllyJdge,FurmnsMgc

---

YELLOW **3** — 5

KEYSTONE SIOUX

b c, 3, by Bye Bye Byrd, Sampsons Maid by Sampson Hanover (Tr.-L. Meittinis)
Woodstock Stud, David Kessler, N.Y. MR 2:00:4 1979 20 5 1 2 28,955
($987) 2, 2:04 JOHN CHAPMAN (157) Green-White Stga 2:04 1978 5 1 1 2 987

7-31 RR ft C-1 Cd 11000 m 29:3 1:01:2 1:31 2:00:1 1 4 6 7 7/7½ 6/4½ 2:01 15.50(Crmr)KgtNArmr,FllaBGd,M'Candy 8
7-24 RR ft C-1 Cd 11000 m 29 1:00:4 1:32:1 2:00:4 3 4 5 5 4/5 4/7 2:02:1 9.70(HrFln)AlsknStrk,D'Hrbrt,DnnisHn 8
7-17 RR ft C-1 Cd 11000 m 30:4 1:01:3 1:31:2 2:01:1 5 5 6° 7° 6/5½ 6/4½ 2:02 4.20(HrFln)DbleStks,MchlsCndy,Faygie 8
7-10 YR ft C-1 Cd 10000 m 29 1:01:1 1:30:3 2:00:4 4 5 5° 4° 2/3 3/2½ 2:01:1 2.70(HrFln)CBChck,DblStks,K'stnSoux 7
7-2 Gosh gd Stk 17900 m 29:2 1:00:4 1:31:4 2:01 1 2 2 2 2/1½ 2/2¾ 2:01:3 N.B.(Chap)MstestYnke,KystnSioux,Faygie
6-25 YR ft C-1 Cd 10000 m 29:3 1:01:1 1:30:4 2:00:3 x6 8 8° 7°°8/9½ 7/13 2:03:1 11.60(HrFln)Preprd,PlyT'Gme,CBChuck 6
6-19 YR ft C-1 Cd 10000 m 29:4 1:01 1:30:3 2:01 7 7 8° 5°°3/3 8/5½ 2:02 4.40(HrFln)KshMine,MrcleChris,St'twn 7
6-10 MR A ft 3yr ec 12800 m 29:1 59:4 1:31:1 2:01:2 3 2 3 3 2/1 1/¼ 2:01:2 *.40(HrFln)K'Sioux,Faygie,BannaStrnd 7

BLACK **4** — 6

ADMIRAL BRET

b c, 3, by Bret Hanover, Fleet Donut by Good Time (Tr.-A. Nelson) (St.-D. Insko)
Renaissance Stable, Curtis Claymont, N.Y. RR 2:01:2 1979 17 2 3 1 20,50
($2,226) 2, 2:05:4 (⅝) CHARLES CONNOR, JR. (150) Purple-Gold Mdws(⅝) 2:05:4 1978 14 3 0 1 2,22

7-23 RR ft C-3 Cd 9000 m 29:1 1:00:4 1:31:3 2:01:2 4 1 1 1 1/2 1/2½ 2:01:2 5.00(Insko)AdmrlBret,Parsley,SunShld 7
7-16 RR ft C-2 Cd 10000 m 30:4 1:02:1 1:32:3 2:02:1 5 6 5 5 5x/3¾ 6/4½ 2:03 12.60(Insko)JJsDmino,A'Blazer,G'Fella 7
7-10 YR ft C-2 Cd 9000 m 29:4 1:00:4 1:31 2:00:3 8 8 7° 7° 8/9 6/8½ 2:02:1 17.70(Insko)PnceTme,AlphaLbl,ClnlLBar 7
6-14 M(1) ft Cd 16000 m 29:1 58:3 1:28:4 1:58:1 7 9 9 8° 8/6 7/9 2:00 10.80(CnnrJr)LttleToRi,MrMH,ThelmsDrn
6-5 M(1) gd Cd 15000 m 29:2 59:2 1:28:4 1:58:2 5 2 3 2 2/3 4/3¾ 1:59:1 6.30(CnnrJr)GrtSport,SportsmanN,Zoome
5-25 M(1) ft Opn 25000 m 28:3 58:2 1:28:3 1:57:2 4 5 5 7 6/4 5/3 1:58 15.50e(CnnrJr)HpyMtrng,AntnusHn,NvlLd
5-17 M(1) ft Cd 13000 m 28:3 58:3 1:28:3 1:57:4 1 4 2° 1 1/2 3/1½ 1:58 8.90(CnnrJr)MrchntMar,SkpChck,AdmrlB
5-1 M(1) ft Cd 8000 m 28:2 1:00:2 1:31:1 1:59 5 8 6° 4° 2/1¾ 2/2 1:59:2 17.80(CnnrJr)DllsCourt,AdmrlBrt,KntT'Gr

---

WHITE **5** — 4

AARONS BLAZER

ch c, 3, by Adios Elmer, Brendas Honey Time by Rhythm Time (Tr.-H. Folk) (St.-C. Foos, Jr.)
Courtney Foos, Jr., Phoenixville, Pa. Skvle Dns 2:02:2 1979 14 9 3 1 15,76
($6,219) 2, 2:05:2 COURTNEY FOOS, JR. (174) Blue-White-Black Skvle Dns 2:05:2 1978 13 8 2 1 6,21

7-30 RR ft C-2 Cd 10000 m 30 1:00:1 1:31:4 2:02:2 2 5 3 5 5/4 2/1 2:02:3 *2.10(FoosJr)LbrtyA'hst,A'Blazr,G'Fella 7
7-16 RR ft C-2 Cd 10000 m 30:4 1:02:1 1:32:3 2:02:1 3 3 2° 2° 2/½ 2/¼ 2:02:1 2.70(FoosJr)JJsDmino,A'Blazer,G'Fella
7-11 YR ft C-2 Cd 9000 m 30:1 1:01:3 1:31:2 2:01:2 6 6 5° 5° 5/3½ 3/2¾ 2:02 7.90(FoosJr)Th'svwBlz,M'Cmbro,A'Blzr
6-27 SkvleDns ft Stk 3816 m 30:4 1:04 1:35:1 2:05:1 2 1° 1 1 1/3 1/3¼ 2:05:1 *.20(DRomo)A'Blzr,FlyngHnry,H'CityChm
6-20 SkvleDns ft Stk 3016 m 30:2 1:01 1:32 2:03:1 2 1° 2° 2° 2/hd 4/3¾ 2:04 *.25(DRomo)SqreThms,H'C'Chmp,B'AirM
6-13 SaintJohn gd Stk 3645m 32:2 1:05 1:36 2:06:2 1 1 1 1 1/1½ 1/3¾ 2:06:2 N.B.(DRomo)A'Blzr,KlkrrnBrwr,SpclRwrd
6-6 SkvleDns ft Stk 3770 m 30:1 1:01:4 1:33:3 2:04:1 6 3° 1 1 1/1½ 1/2¼ 2:04:1 *.30(DRomo)A'Blzr,KlkrrnBrwr,MstrStar
6-2 SkvleDns ft Inv 4000 m 29:3 1:00:2 1:31:1 2:01:2 4 4 4 2° 1x/2 2/6¾ 2:02:4 *.80(DRomo)Kaweco,A'Blazer,PowrBaron

---

PURPLE **6** — 8

COLOSSAL

br c, 3, by Columbia George, Glenda Rum by Demon Rum (Tr.-M. DeBowskie) (St.-V. Dancer)
National Hill Farm & Marc Brummel, Trenton, N.J. YR 2:02:2 1979 22 4 5 3 20,86
($00.00) DONALD DANCER (130) Blue-Gold 1978 0 0 0 0

8-6 RR ft C-2 Cd 10000 m 30:2 1:00:1 1:30:1 2:02 3 4 5 4° 3/½ 2/½ 2:02 8.80(DDncr)Oxygn,Colossal,GlnbysFella
7-24 RR ft C-1 Cd 11000 m 29:2 1:01 1:30:4 2:01:1 4 6 7° 7° 6/5½ 7/4½ 2:02 14.70(DDncr)T'prdBrd,PencTm,IRSTme
7-17 RR ft C-1 Cd 11000 m 30:4 1:01:3 1:31:2 2:01:1 7 7 5 6 5/3½ 4/1¾ 2:01:3 30.80(DDncr)DblStks,MchlsCndy,Faygie
7-9 YR ft C-1 Cd 10000 m 29:2 1:01 1:31:2 2:00:3 4 5 6 5 5/5 3/5¾ 2:01:4 39.00(DDncr)FltFlla,SmpleFlla,Colossal
6-18 YR ft C-2 Cd 9000 m 29:3 1:01:1 1:32 2:02:2 5 1 1 1 1/½ 1/nk 2:02:2 2.70(DDncr)Colossal,H'Hngman,L'Scrt
6-8 YR ft 3yr Cd 7500 m 30:1 1:01:4 1:32:2 2:02 4 2 3 3 2/2 2/hd 2:02 6.90(DDncr)F'BigOnes,Colossal,H'lrsBoy
5-31 RR ft 3yr Cd 8000 m 30 1:01:1 1:32:4 2:02:4 x5 8 i8 9° 8/7½ 4/4 2:03:3 11.50(DD'cr)EARbrts,HyprAd's,HstlrsBoy
5-24 RR ft 3yr Cd 8000 m 29:2 59:4 1:30:2 2:01:4 4 2 5 6° 5/6 4/6 2:03 5.70(DDncr)EARbrts,JKsBest,UnEspoir

---

ORANGE **7** — 5

SUN SHIELD

b c, 3, by Columbia George, Selka Diamond by Meadow Ace (Tr.-J. Cruise)
A. Stevenson, R. Stump, Indiana RR 2:02 1979 13 4 1 2 18,17
($00.00) JIMMY CRUISE (193) Green-Red 1978 0 0 0 0

8-6 RR ft C-2 Cd 10000 m 29:3 1:00:4 1:31:2 2:02 5 7 7 8° 8/5¾ 6/4 2:02:4 5.50(ECrus)S'Ace,AlphaLbll,LbrtyA'hst
7-30 RR ft C-3 Cd 9000 m 30 1:01:2 1:31 2:02 5 7 8° 6° 7/5¼ 1/1 2:02 *1.10(ECrus)SunShld,JMNible,Afrethght
7-23 RR ft C-3 Cd 9000 m 29:1 1:00:4 1:31:3 2:01:2 6 7 8° 8° 8/5¾ 3/2¾ 2:02 3.20(ECrus)AdmrlBret,Parsley,SunShld
7-16 RR ft C-3 Cd 9000 m 30:1 1:02:1 1:33:1 2:03:2 5 7 7 7 6/6 5/2½ 2:03:4 2.70(ECruse)HstlrsBoy,SpnakrN,H'Trvlr
6-21 M(1) ft Cd 10000 m 29:4 :59 1:29:2 1:59 1 4 4 4° 5/4 6/5 2:00 2.60(JCrus)SwftHpful,ZoomsBoy,Mrngol
6-14 M(1) ft Cd 10000 m 29:2 1:00 1:29:4 1:59:4 5 6 4°°2°°1/nk 5/2½ 2:00:1 2.50(JCrus)PiratesCove,Afrthght,Mrngol
6-2 RR ft 3yr Cd 8000 m 29:3 1:00:1 1:30:3 2:02:2 7 7 7° 6°°5/2 1/nk 2:02:2 4.40(JCrus)SunShield,CJBret,P'AndyD
5-26 RR ft 3yr Cd 8000 m 30:2 1:02 1:32 2:03:2 7 8 8 8 7/6½ 3/1¼ 2:03:3 13.60(JCrus)BckoHn,PrncAndyD,SunShld

---

GREEN **8** — 10

GLENBYS FELLA (NY)

b c, 3, by Most Happy Fella, Keystone Julia by Bye Bye Byrd (Tr.-C. Carr) (St.-L. Brogl)
Glenby Farms, M. Sternberg & B. Villani, N.Y. YR 2:00:3 1979 21 4 4 6 26,8
($1,427) 2, 2:05 CARMINE ABBATIELLO (145) Gold-Red Fhld 2:05 1978 7 1 1 2 1,42

8-6 RR ft C-2 Cd 10000 m 30:2 1:00:1 1:30:1 2:02 2 3 2° 2° 1/hd 3/1¾ 2:02:2 3.10(CAbb)Oxygn,Colossal,GlnbysFella
7-30 RR ft C-2 Cd 10000 m 30 1:00:1 1:31:4 2:02:2 5 1 2 2 2/1 3/2 2:02:4 20.80(DDncr)LbrtyA'hst,A'Blazr,G'Fella
7-16 RR ft C-2 Cd 10000 m 30:4 1:02:1 1:32:3 2:02:1 6 2 3 3 3/1¼ 3/2 2:02:3 23.40(DDncr)JJsDmino,A'Blazer,G'Fella
7-9 YR ft C-2 Cd 9000 m 29:3 1:00:3 1:30:3 2:00:4 8 8 7i° 6° 6/8¾ 6/10 2:02:4 24.50(DDncr)N'HHrtg,FllaBGd,PhlT'Till
7-2 YR ft C-3 Cd 8000 m 29 59:2 1:30 2:00:3 1 3 3 2° 2/nk 1/nk 2:00:3 3.40(DDncr)GFlla,BCrk,HTrvlr-GRulrdh
6-20 YR ft C-3 Cd 8000 m 30:2 1:01 1:32 2:02:2 4 2 2 3 3/1 5/¾ 2:02:3 2.00(DDncr)A'Spinnr,J'RQntn,S'T'Bttle
6-12 YR ft C-3 Cd 8000 m 29 1:00 1:32:2 2:03 1 2 2 3 3/1 2/½ 2:03 2.60(DDncr)FlaBGd,GlnbysFla,GmeRulr
6-4 YR ft C-3 Cd 8000 m 29:4 1:00:3 1:31:1 2:03 5 6 5° 5° 5/2 3/2¼ 2:03:2 3.00(DDncr)ElteTip,S'sideHn,GlnbysFlla

8 PACE

ONE MILE

$2.00 EXACTA

WARM-UP SADDLE CLOTH—GREEN

CLASS C-2 FOUR & FIVE-YEAR-OLDS—HORSES & GELDINGS.

PURSE $10,000

BLUE **1**

RENEES FELLA (NY)

b g, 5, by Most Happy Fella, Renee Wick by Gene Abbe (Tr-J. Pagano)
Joseph Pagano, Elmont, N.Y. RR 2:01:2 1979 25 3 2 2 25,245.
($69,170) 4, 2:00:1 (1) CARMINE ABBATIELLO (145) Gold-Red M(1) 2:00:1 1978 29 5 4 1 33,065.

7-30 RR ft C-2 Cd 10000 m 30 1:01 1:30:1 2:01:3 6 6 6° 6° 6/3½ 6/3¼ 2:02:1 3.20(CAbb)BoysWay,KatDancr,VghnHn 78
7-23 RR ft C-3 Cd 11250 m 29 1:00 1:31 2:01:2 4 2 1 1 1/2 1/5 2:01:2 *2.20(CAbb)R'Flla,FourF'Brd,K'tnSuave 78
7-16 RR ft C-3 Cd 9000 m 29:4 1:00 1:30:2 2:02:4 7 7 6 7 7/7¾ 3/1¾ 2:03:1 11.70(CAbb)MrAAA,TmlyFrst,RneesFlla 78
7-4 YR gd C-3 Cd 8000 m 30 1:01:3 1:34:4 2:05:1 1 2 5 7 4/1½ 1/nk 2:05:1 3.40(CAbb)RneesFlla,K'NwTm,TrmnHn 57
6-25 YR ft C-3 Cd 8000 m 29:4 1:00:1 1:31:2 2:02:4 5 5 6 5° 6/4½ 6/3¼ 2:03:2 6.70(JDups)MrtyD'Ray,B'Bret,M'Trndo 68
6-11 YR gd C-3 Cd 8000 m 30:2 1:02 1:33:1 2:05 8 8 8 8°°6/7½ 4/5¾ 2:06:1 29.30(JDupis)S'System,GdK'Don,G'Jerry 58
6-4 YR ft C-3 Cd 8000 m 30:4 1:02:3 1:33:2 2:02:3 6 1 1 2 3/5½ 4/8½dh 2:04:1 4.90(JDpuis)B'RbrtD,SlrSystm,K'N'Tme 62
5-28 RR sy C-3 Cd 9000 m 29:4 1:01:4 1:34:2 2:04:2 5 1 3 3 5/2¾ 4/3¾ 2:05 9.90(Dups)RghtAgn,TrmnHn,HhniesBst 60

RED **2**

KAWARTHA NEW TIME

b h, 5, by Good Time, Betty Hanover by Dancer Hanover (Tr.-K. Dawson)
Valley Farms, Ringtown, Pa. YR 2:01:2 1979 19 2 2 2 18,660.
($137,897) 4, 1:57:2 (⅝) DONALD DANCER (130) Blue-Gold Brd(⅝) 1:57:2 1978 47 7 9 8 96,499.

8-6 RR ft C-2 Cd 10000 m 30:2 1:00:3 1:31:4 2:02:2 1 3 3° 3° 2/½ 2/ns 2:02:2 2.30(DDncr)KatDncr,K'NwTm,VivaMax 78
7-30 RR ft C-3 Cd 9000 m 29:4 1:02 1:32:3 2:02 4 5 3° 2° 2/½ 1/½ 2:02 3.40(DD'cr)K'N'Tme,BrnzHnA,MrP'tne 78
7-16 RR ft C-3 Cd 9000 m 29 1:00 1:31:1 2:01:2 8 3° 2 4 5/7½ 8/10 2:03:2 11.20(DDncr)T'prdKen,BeauMnde,B'Crk 78
7-4 YR gd C-3 Cd 8000 m 30 1:01:3 1:34:4 2:05:1 4 5 4° 3°°2/hd 2/nk 2:05:1 *2.50(DD'cr)RneesFlla,K'NwTm,TrmnHn 57
6-27 YR ft C-3 Cd 8000 m 30 1:01 1:31:2 2:01:2 2 3 4 3° 2/½ 1/½ 2:01:2 9.10(GFln)K'NwTm,TrumnHn,M'W'sde 66
6-4 YR ft C-3 Cd 8000 m 30:4 1:02:3 1:33:2 2:02:3 1 2 3 5 5/6½ 3/7½ 2:04:1 2.00(HrFln)B'RbrtD,SlrSystm,K'N'Time 62
5-28 RR sy C-2 Cd 10000 m 30 1:01:2 1:32:2 2:02 7 2 2 4 4/4½ 7/6¾ 2:03:2 12.00(HrFln)M'Bnne,FuryA'st-M'Lddedh 60
5-21 RR ft C-2 Cd 10000 m 30 1:02:2 1:33:1 2:03:1 1 2 2 4 4/2½ 4/½ 2:03:2 6.80(DDncr)T'T'Adios,BudTAce,M'Bnnie 64

YELLOW **3**

FULLA NICK (NY)

b g, 5, by Fulla Napoleon, Miss Marshall by Gold Worthy (Tr.-J. Bressler) (St.-P. Appel)
P. Appel, T. Misiak, Sterling Ridge Stable, N.Y. RR 2:02:1 1979 13 3 1 2 17,080.
($39,993) 4, 2:02:1 PAUL APPEL (165) Black-White RR 2:02:1 1978 27 3 7 4 33,575.

8-6 RR ft C-3 Cd 9000 m 29:1 1:00:2 1:30:4 2:02:1 4 1 1 1 1/2 1/1½ 2:02:1 3.20(Appel)F'Nick,BrnzHnA,MrPrfntne 78
7-30 RR ft C-3 Cd 9000 m 29:1 59:1 1:30 2:01:3 5 2° 1° 1° 3/1½ 6/4¼ 2:02:2 21.90(Appl)CrtnlyRght,GdChrs,AzlaSpnnr 78
7-16 RR ft C-3 Cd 9000 m 29:4 1:01:2 1:32 2:02 6 x6x 6 6 6x/17 6/dis 11.60(PAppl)TrmnHn,F'F'Brd,T'GrtHerb 78
7-9 YR ft clm alw 27000Z m 29:4 1:01:1 1:31:1 2:01:1 5 5 3° 3 4/6 5/10 2:03:1 3.80(CAbb)WthyTar,S'N'Mre,Y'shrsWo 71
6-29 YR ft clm al 22000Z m 29:3 1:01 1:32:1 2:02:3 6 2 3 4 3/2 2/½ 2:02:4 5.20(PAppl)Ad'sRunE,FllaNck,G'Mastr 69
6-20 YR ft clm alw 18000 m 29:2 1:01:3 1:33 2:02:1 4 5 5° 3°°1/ns 1/2 2:02:1 3.90(Appel)FllaNck,HHLslie,Pericoloso 76
6-12 YR ft clm alw 15000 m 30 1:02 1:32:3 2:03:3 3 1 1 1 1/3 1/4½ 2:03:3 5.00(Appl)FllaNick,Wnfrda,Ad'sChmes 64
* 6-5 YR ft qua m 30:3 1:02:1 1:32:3 2:03:3 6 6 6° 6° 5/4½ 4/3¾ 2:04:2 N.B.(PAppl)TrffcFury,BkrooTm,RipLse 73

BLACK **4**

SPIN THE BOTTLE

b h, 4, by Meadow Skipper, Pucker Up by Henry T Adios (Tr.-R. Connor)
CPlusStable,L.Gartenburg,W.Jacobowitz,N.Y. YR 2:01:2 1979 11 1 0 2 9,110.
($23,781) 3, 2:00:4 (⅝) JAMES MAROHN (115) Purple-White BB(⅝) 2:00:4 1978 23 4 9 3 19,745.

8-6 RR ft C-2 Cd 10000 m 30:3 1:03:1 1:34 2:03:4 2 4 3° 3° 3/2 3/3½ 2:04:2 3.40(JMrhn)SlrSystm,S'town,S'T'Bottle 78
7-23 RR ft C-2 Cd 10000 m 29:2 1:00:2 1:31:2 2:01:4 8 8 8 7°°6/4 5/3 2:02:2 16.30(JMrhn)BoysWy,T'prdKen,VivaMx 78
7-16 RR ft C-2 Cd 10000 m 30 1:00:3 1:31:1 2:01:4 2 x5 4° 6° 6/3¾ 4/5½ 2:03 *2.30(M'shJr)FllaBGd,ByeB'Man,Encnto 78
7-9 YR ft C-3 Cd 8000 m 28:3 1:00:4 1:31:2 2:01:2 6 6 5° 5° 5/1½ 1/3¾ 2:01:2 10.20(MrshJr)SpnT'Btl,T'G'Hrb,S'sdeHn 71
7-2 YR ft C-3 Cd 8000 m 29 59:2 1:30 2:00:3 7 7 7° 6° 4/6½ 5/9 2:02:2 3.80(RDgnlt)GFlla,BCrk,HTrvlr-GRulrdh 72
6-20 YR ft C-3 Cd 8000 m 30:2 1:01 1:32 2:02:2 2 5 5° 4° 5/1½ 3/½ 2:02:3 *1.60(RDgnlt)A'Spinnr,J'RQntn,S'T'Btle 76
6-5 YR sy C-2 Cd 9000 m 29:1 1:00 1:32 2:03:1 8 8 8 7°°7/2¾ 5/1½ 2:03:2 39.80(RDgnlt)PhilT'Till,N'wrk,Blspheme 65
5-28 RR sy C-2 Cd 10000 m 30 1:00:3 1:31:3 2:02 8 7 7° 5°°5/4½ 8/6 2:03:1 22.70(RDgnlt)CrgsKid,KatDncr,Nghtwork 60

WHITE **5**

TEMPERED KEN (NY)

b g, 4, by Tempered Yankee, Carolina Gal by Airliner (Tr.-J. Darish) (St.-M. Lawhon)
Carolina Manor Farm, Timmonsville, S.C. RR 2:01:2 1979 17 2 3 3 18,470.
($10,775) 3, 2:06:4 (1) JOHN DARISH (176) Gray-Red-White M(1) 2:06:4 1978 15 1 2 0 10,775.

8-6 RR ft C-2 Cd 10000 m 30:2 1:00:3 1:31:4 2:02:2 2 2 1 1 1/½ 4/1½ 2:02:3 3.70(Darish)KatDncr,K'NwTm,VivaMax 78
7-23 RR ft C-2 Cd 10000 m 29:2 1:00:2 1:31:2 2:01:4 6 2 2 3 4/1¾ 2/1 2:02 10.40(JDrsh)BoysWay,T'prdKen,VivaMx 78
7-16 RR ft C-3 Cd 9000 m 29 1:00 1:31:1 2:01:2 2 6 6° 2°°2/½ 1/3½ 2:01:2 8.90(JDsh)T'prdKn,BeauMnde,B'Creek 78
7-5 YR ft clm alw 22000 m 29:2 :59 1:31 2:02 1 2 3 4 3/1½ 3/1 2:02:1 7.00(JDrsh)AshleyLbll,Relentlss,T'Ken 61
6-26 YR ft clm alw 22000 m 30 1:00 1:31:3 2:03 7 8 7° 7/5½ 3/3¾ 2:03:4 17.40(JDrsh)Trndy,NppysBoy,TmprdKen 63
6-15 YR ft clm alw 18000 m 29:2 59:4 1:31:1 2:01:1 4 6 6° 2° 2/1½ 2/2½ 2:01:3 4.30(JDrsh)Relentless,T'Ken,S'Torch 82
6-7 YR ft clm alw 15000 m 30:1 1:01:2 1:31:4 2:03:1 7 7 7° 7°°4/1 1/1 2:03:1 18.60(Drsh)T'Ken,R'Mjr,O'S'Dst-P'Prkidh 67
5-29 RR ft clm alw 15000 m 30:1 1:02:4 1:33:2 2:04:2 7 8 8 6 7/8½ 6/2½ 2:04:4 44.70(JDrsh)GldnTrck,RmlsMjr-E'Stardh 62

PURPLE **6**

BELIER DOST (NY)

b g, 5, by Most Happy Fella, Quebec Mir by Adios Mir (Tr.-M. Lavallee) (St.-Her. Filion)
The Quinto Barn, Morganville, N.J. YR 2:01 1979 19 3 0 1 19,700.
($65,725) 4, 2:00:1 (⅝) HERVE FILION (163) Red-Blue-White LB(⅝) 2:00:1 1978 33 2 4 5 31,322.

7-31 RR ft C-1 Cd 11000 m 29:3 1:01:2 1:31 2:00:1 2 5 8 8 8/11 8/12 2:02:3 18.30(HrFln)KgtNArmr,FllaBGd,M'Candy 80
7-24 RR ft C-1 Cd 11000 m 28:3 1:00:3 1:31:2 2:01:4 6 6 6 5 5/2½ 6/3 2:02:2 15.10(HrFln)KshMine,FllaBGd,K'NArmor 80
7-17 RR ft C-1 11000 m 27:3 58:1 1:29:2 1:59:4 3 1° 1 2 4/6 7/14 2:02:3 13.30(Crmr)FstStrk,Scniclsl,KngtNArmr 80
7-9 YR ft C-1 Cd 10000 m 29:2 1:01 1:31:2 2:00:3 5 1 2 2 4/3½ 4/5¾ 2:01:4 56.10(RCrmr)FltFlla,SmpleFlla,Colossal 71
6-28 YR ft B-3 11000 m 28:3 59:2 1:31 2:01:2 7 7 7 7 7/7½ 7/7pl6 2:02:4 70.00(MDky)RblBrt,EricLyss,T'Invstmnt 66
6-21 YR ft B-3 11000 m 29 58:3 1:28:1 1:59:1 1 2 3 3 4/8 7/12 2:01:3 16.20(Doky)A'Rmblr,TmlssTitle,THFrrst 65
6-14 YR ft B-3 11000 m 30:1 1:00:2 1:30:4 2:01:1 8 8 8 8 8/6½ 7/7½ 2:02:3 43.50(MDky)R'T'Killn,TmlssTitle,C'Boots 72
6-4 YR ft C-1 Cd 10000 m 29:2 1:00:4 1:30:4 2:01 1 1 1 1 1/1 1/1¼ 2:01 5.00(JMrhn)Bel'rDst,T'T'Ad's,Z'T'Pnist 62

ORANGE **7**

TIM TOM ADIOS

blk h, 5, by Thomas Adios, Little One by Jack Of Hearts (Tr.-J. Tremblay) (St.-R. Daigneault)
Michael Cavallo, Washington, Township, N.J. RR 2:01:1 1979 22 2 3 3 21,220.
($67,860) 3, 2:00 (⅝) REJEAN DAIGNEAULT (140) Red-Blue NE(⅝) 2:00:1 1978 41 8 10 2 40,124.

* 8-3 RR ft qua m 30:1 1:01 1:32:1 2:02:2 1 5 3° 2° 1/hd 2/½ 2:02:2 N.B.(RDg'lt)RamOJ,T'T'Adios,C'ndDcsn 82
7-30 RR ft C-2 Cd 10000 m 29:3 1:00:1 1:30:4 2:00:3 8 8 8° 8 7/8 7/9¾ 2:02:3 11.80(RDgnlt)MrAAA,L'Scrt,Stckngtwn 78
7-17 RR ft C-1 11000 m 29 1:00:4 1:30:4 2:00:2 3 6 6° 6° 7/5¾ 7/7½ 2:01:4 2.40(RDg't)T'Blze,T'prdBrd,NstyHHrtg 80
7-10 YR ft C-1 Cd 10000 m 29 1:01:1 1:30:3 2:00:4 7 8 8 8 8/13 8/8½ 2:02:2 11.00(RDgnlt)CBChck,DbleStks,K'Sioux 72
7-3 YR ft C-1 Cd 10000 m 30:4 1:01:2 1:31:2 2:00:4 8 8 8° 8° 8/6¾ 8/5½ 2:01:4 11.30(RDgnlt)TrckLse,IRSTm-PlyT'Gmdh 76
6-27 YR ft C-1 10000 m 30:1 1:00:3 1:32:2 2:02:2 5 6 6 4° 4/2½ 2/ns 2:02:2 *1.10(RDgnlt)B'Clre,T'T'Ad's,LtaRmnce 66
6-20 YR ft C-1 10000 m 29:3 1:00:2 1:29:4 2:00 2 4 4° 4° 3/5½ 3/3 2:00:3 *1.70(RDgnlt)M'J'Brt'r,IRSTm,T'T'Ad's 76
6-13 YR ft C-1 Cd 10000 m 30:1 1:02:2 1:32:3 2:02:2 8 5 4° 6° 5/3½ 5/4 2:03:1 12.00(RD'nlt)C'agusKd,MrclChrs,T'vwBlz 67

GREEN **8**

STOCKINGTOWN

ch h, 5, by Don Baker, Agnellas Queen by New Discovery (Tr.-J. Rathbone)
Donald Hunt. Woodstown, N.J. RR 2:00:3 1979 20 2 4 4 25,630.
($25,606) 4, 2:02:3 (⅝) REAL CORMIER (140) Blue-Orange LB(⅝) 2:02:3 1978 36 5 5 2 14,031.

8-6 RR ft C-2 Cd 10000 m 30:3 1:03:1 1:34 2:03:4 3 1 1 1 1/1 2/¼ 2:03:4 *2.30(JRthbn)SlrSystm,S'twn,S'T'Bottle 78
7-30 RR ft C-2 Cd 10000 m 29:3 1:00:1 1:30:4 2:00:3 1 1 1 1 1/1 3/1½ 2:00:4 3.70(Rthbne)MrAAA,L'Scrt,Stckngtwn 78
7-17 RR ft C-1 11000 m 29 1:00:4 1:30:4 2:00:2 7 2° 5 5 5/3½ 6/6 2:01:3 20.80(Crmr)T'Blze,TmprdBrd,NstyHHrtg 80
7-3 YR ft C-1 Cd 10000 m 30:4 1:01:2 1:31:2 2:00:4 2 4 4° 4° 4/2½ 5/3¾ 2:01:3 15.10(Rthbn)TrckLse,IRSTm-PlyT'Gmdh 76
6-26 YR ft C-1 Cd 10000 m 29:3 1:00 1:30:4 2:00 1 3 2° 2° 4/3 6/8½ 2:01:3 4.30(JRthbn)TmlyThrp,Scniclsl,CrgsKid 63
6-19 YR ft C-1 Cd 10000 m 29:4 1:01 1:30:3 2:01 3 1° 2 2 2/2 3/1½ 2:01:1 6.70(Rthbn)KshMine,MrcleChris,St'twn 71
6-12 YR ft C-1 Cd 10000 m 29:4 1:01:1 1:31:2 2:01 2 4 4° 4° 4/2 5/4¾ 2:02 6.40(JRthbn)SrpcoHn,B'B'Btlr,Scniclsl 64
5-29 RR ft C-1 11000 m 29:4 1:00:3 1:30:4 2:00:4 7 1 1 1 1/1½ 3/2 2:01:1 7.00(Rthbne)T'Title,SwtLou,Stckngtwn 62

9 PACE — ONE MILE

WARM-UP SADDLE CLOTH—GREY

CLASS C-2

FOUR & FIVE-YEAR-OLDS—HORSES & GELDINGS.

$2.00 EXACTA

PURSE $10,000

BLUE **1**

HAHNIES BEST b h, 5, by Best Of All, Hahnie by Bullet Hanover (Tr.-R. Robinet)
Rudolphe Robinet, Westbury, N.Y. RR 2:01:1 1979 22 3 2 5 23,690.
($46,255) 4, 2:01:4 MERRIT DOKEY (140) White-Red-Blue YR 2:01:4 1978 20 2 3 2 20,155
8-6 RR ft C-2 Cd 10000 m 30:2 1:00:3 1:31:4 2:02:2 7 8 8 8° 8/4½ 8/4¼ 2:03:1 33.40(MDky)KatDncr,K'NwTm,VivaMax 78
7-30 RR ft C-2 Cd 10000 m 29:3 1:00:1 1:30:4 2:00:3 4 5 7 6 6/4 5/4¼ 2:01:2 25.90(MDky)MrAAA,LrdsScrt,Stckngtwn 78
7-17 RR ft C-1 11000 m 29 1:00:4 1:30:4 2:00:2 4 7 7° 8° 8/7¾ 8/9¼ 2:02:1 24.30(Insko)T'Blze,TmprdBrd,NstyHHrtg 80
7-10 YR ft C-1 Cd 10000 m 29 1:01:1 1:30:3 2:00:4 8 2 2 3 6/6¾ 7/5¾ 2:02 31.90(MDky)CBChck,DblStks,K'stnSioux 72
7-2 YR ft C-1 Cd 10000 m 30:1 1:00:4 1:32:1 2:02 3 1 2 3 3/1 3/1½ 2:02:1 20.60(MDoky)W'Monstr,M'Candy,H'Best 72
6-25 YR ft C-2 Cd 9000 m 29:4 1:01:1 1:31:4 2:01:4 2 1 1 1 1/hd 1/nk 2:01:4 *1.90(RDgnlt)HhnsBst,Blsphme,KatDncr 68
6-18 YR ft C-3 Cd 8000 m 29:2 1:01:2 1:33 2:03:4 4 2 1 1 1/2 1/3¾ 2:03:4 *1.80(RDg't)HhnsBst,S'sdeHn,MklsTrndo 69
6-5 YR sy C-3 Cd 8000 m 29:3 1:00:3 1:32:1 2:02:3 3 5 5° 4° 3/1½ 3/1½ 2:02:4 2.30(Steal)PalmCrt,FllaBGd,HhniesBst 65

RED **2**

MONEY ORDER br h, 4, by Entrepreneur, Miss Volstadt by Volstadt (Tr.-R. Rash)
Longwood Stable, New York, N.Y. YR 2:02:2 1979 23 2 3 1 24,355.
($35,235) 3, 2:01 RUSSELL RASH (175) Red-Black-Silver YR 2:01 1978 25 8 3 2 35,235
7-31 RR ft C-1 Cd 11000 m 30:3 1:02 1:32:2 2:02:2 6 5 5 6 5/4½ 4/1½ 2:02:4 15.30(RRsh)KshMine,ScnicIsle,PrfctRch 80
7-24 RR ft C-1 Cd 11000 m 28:3 1:00:3 1:31:2 2:01:4 5 1 1 1 1/½ 7/3½ 2:02:2 5.10(RRsh)KshMine,FllaBGd,K'NArmor 80
7-17 RR ft C-1 11000 m 29 1:00:4 1:30:4 2:00:2 8 8 8 7 6/5½ 5/4¾ 2:01:2 18.60(Rash)T'Blze,TmprdBrd,NstyHHrtg 80
7-9 YR ft C-1 Cd 10000 m 29:2 1:01 1:31:2 2:00:3 2 3 4 4° 2/3½ 5/6¾ 2:02 5.70(Rash)FleetFlla,SmpleFlla,Colossal 71
6-28 YR ft B-3 11000 m 29:2 1:00 1:30:2 2:00:4 6 6 5 8 8/4½ 7/4 2:01:3 20.80(RRsh)T'Title,R'Mckalee,T'BluChp 66
6-21 YR ft B-3 11000 m 28:2 :58 1:28:3 1:59 5 6 5° 4° 4/2½ 6/7 2:00:2 9.80(RRash)D'O'Brn,SwtJmbre,C'Boots 65
6-14 YR ft B-3 11000 m 30:1 1:00:2 1:30:4 2:01:1 3 4 2° 2° 1/½ 4/1½ 2:01:2 3.60(RRsh)R'T'Killean,TmlssTitle,C'B'ts 72
6-7 YR ft B-3 11000 m 29:1 59:3 1:30:3 2:00 7 7 7 7° 6/5¼ 5/6 2:01:1 25.20(RRash)ShwyCub,TmlssTtl,R'T'Klln 67

YELLOW 4 **3**

ENCANTO b g, 4, by Nansemond, Dazzling Time by Good Time (Tr.-T. Lail
Thomas Lail, Thomas Tame, Leo Morse, N.J. YR 2:02:4 1979 20 3 4 2 26,170
($39,867) 3, 2:01:2 HERVE FILION (163) Red-Blue-White RR 2:01:2 1978 28 6 0 3 31,575
8-6 RR ft C-2 Cd 10000 m 30:2 1:00:3 1:31:4 2:02:2 8 1 2 5 4/2 6/2¼ 2:02:4 36.40(HrFln)KatDncr,K'NwTm,VivaMax 78
7-30 RR ft C-2 Cd 10000 m 29:3 1:00:1 1:30:4 2:00:3 7 3° 3° 7° 8/10 8/20 2:04:3 17.90(HrFln)MrAAA,LrdsScrt,Stckngtwn 78
7-16 RR ft C-2 Cd 10000 m 30 1:00:3 1:31:2 2:01:4 4 3 5 5 4/2½ 3/3¼ 2:02:2 5.20(HrFln)T'Blze,ByeB'Man,Encanto 78
7-11 YR ft C-2 Cd 9000 m 29:4 1:00 1:30:3 2:00:4 1 3 5 4 3/1½ 2/¾ 2:01 5.00(GFln)PlmC'rt,Encanto,LbrtyA'hrst 74
7-3 YR ft C-3 Cd 8000 m 29 1:01:1 1:32 2:02:4 1 3 3° 1° 1/1½ 1/¾ 2:02:4 *.90(Doky)Encnto,MdwArtst,CrtnlyRght 76
6-25 YR ft C-3 Cd 8000 m 29:2 1:00:2 1:31 2:01:2 3 5 5° 4°°2/2 2/hd 2:01:2 *1.60(MrshJr)MgcCrpt,Encnto,BrdlysCrk 68
6-18 YR ft C-3 Cd 8000 m 29:2 1:01:2 1:33 2:03:4 7 7 7 6/4¾ 6/4¾ 2:04:4 10.30(HrFln)HhnsBst,S'sdeHn,MklsTrndo 69
6-5 YR sy C-2 Cd 9000 m 29:1 1:00 1:32 2:03:1 7 7 7° 5° 5/2 6/1¾ 2:03:3 37.60(MrshJr)PhilT'Till,N'wrk,Blspheme 65

BLACK 3 **4**

RAM O J (NY) b h, 4, by Kat Byrd, Luan Mar by Greentree Adios (Tr.-J. Vance
Paul & Margaret Vance & Fashion Farms, Inc., N.Y. (qua)RR 2:02:2 1979 0 0 0 0
($62,128) 3, 2:00 FRANK POPFINGER (160) Blue-Gold YR 2:00 1978 19 3 3 1 44,729
* 8-3 RR ft qua m 30:1 1:01 1:32:1 2:02:2 6 7 7° 4° 3/1 1/½ 2:02:2 N.B.(FPop)RamOJ,T'T'Adios,CmndDcsn 8
* 5-8 RR ft qua m 31 1:02 1:32:4 2:04:3 3 4 2° 1 1/½ 1/hd 2:04:3 N.B.(RDgnlt)RamOJ,Atawayne,PrsnHall 6
10-10 RR ft C-1 Cd 10500 m 29:3 59:2 1:29:4 2:00:2 3 3 3° 3° 4/5 6/10 2:02:2 5.40(Font)PrtLbl,SwtJmbree,BttrTrth 5
10-2 YR ft C-1 Cd 8000 m 29:2 1:00:1 1:30 2:00:1 5 2 2° 2° 3/1½ 4/6 2:01:2 2.80(Font)H'TheHeel,T'Invstmnt,P'Lbll 5
9-25 YR ft C-1 Cd 8000 m 30:2 1:00:1 1:31 2:02 4 7 6° 1°°2/hd 2/¾ 2:02:1 2.90(LFont)SACrest,RamOJ,S'Jmbree 6
9-16 YR ft 3yr Inv 15000 m 29 58:3 1:29:3 2:00 3 6 6 5 5/6½ 4/6½ 2:01:1 17.80(Font)P'Walnut,B'OfPwr,S'Jdgmnt 6
9-9 VD(½) ft 3yr Stk 25200 m 27:2 57:1 1:26:3 1:57 10 8 9 9 8/6½ 10/12 1:59:2 22.30(Vance)HpyEscrt,A'broTigr,Z'T'Pianis
* 9-2 YR ft qua m 30:2 1:01:1 1:32:2 2:02:3 4 6 5° 1° 1/¾ 2/3 2:03:1 N.B.(Vance)GzllsBoy,RamOJ,OldG'Mine 7

WHITE 8 **5**

SPECIAL EVENT blk h, 5, by Special Dream, Miss Mildred Belle by Gugelhupf (Tr.-J. Cruise
James Conway, Jr., Jimmy Cruise, Westbury, N.Y. RR 2:01:1 1979 20 2 6 3 29,40(
($43,954) 4, 1:59:1 (1) EARL CRUISE (193) Green-Red-White Sac(1) 1:59:1 1978 38 4 4 5 18,748
8-6 RR ft C-2 Cd 10000 m 30:3 1:03:1 1:34 2:03:4 5 6 8 7 5/3 5/5¾ 2:05 11.90(ECrus)SlrSystm,S'town,S'T'Bottle 7
7-30 RR ft C-2 Cd 10000 m 30 1:01 1:30:1 2:01:3 5 5 5 5 5/3½ 4/2¼ 2:02 12.70(ECrus)BoysWay,KatDancr,VghnHn 7
7-17 RR ft C-1 11000 m 27:3 58:1 1:29:2 1:59:4 2 4 5 5 7/9½ 6/12 2:02:1 12.50(ECrus)FstStrk,ScnicIsl,KgtNArmr 8
7-10 YR ft C-1 Cd 10000 m 29 1:01:1 1:30:3 2:00:4 6 7 6 7 7/8¾ 6/4¼ 2:01:3 43.90(ECrus)CBChck,DblStks,K'stnSioux 7
6-18 YR ft C-1 Cd 10000 m 29:2 1:01:4 1:31:1 2:00:3 3 4 6 6 5/9¾ 5/11 2:02:4 22.70(ECrus)RdMckle,Preprd,MchlsCndy 6
6-11 YR gd C-1 Cd 10000 m 30 1:00:4 1:31:4 2:02:4 2 4 5 5 4/4 5/¾ 2:03 8.50(ECrus)KshMine,P'T'Game,M'Cndy 5
5-29 RR ft C-1 11000 m 29:2 1:00:4 1:30:2 2:00:2 6 6 6 6 5/3½ 4/3 2:01 15.50(ECrus)RceT'Killn,KshMine,B'Way 6
5-21 RR ft C-2 Cd 10000 m 29:2 1:00:2 1:31:1 2:01:1 2 4 4° 4° 4/1½ 1/1¾ 2:01:1 3.90(ECrus)SpclEvnt,TrznB'Chp,R'Chnc 6

PURPLE 8 **6**

GAME RULER ro h, 4, by Chris Time, Royal Colette by Gene Abbe (Tr.-L. Battaglia) (St.-N. Dauplaise
Dave Hamburger, Saddle Rock Stable, N.Y. RR 2:01:1 1979 26 4 3 7 29,79
($16,168) 3, 2:04:1 NORMAN DAUPLAISE (166) Brown-Gold-White Nfld 2:04:1 1978 20 3 3 4 6,32
8-6 RR ft C-2 Cd 10000 m 29:3 1:00:4 1:31:2 2:02 3 5 5 7 7/5¼ 8/8¼ 2:03:3 9.50(Dplse)S'Ace,AlphaLbll,LbrtyA'hst 7
7-30 RR ft C-3 Cd 9000 m 29:2 59:2 1:30:2 2:01:1 4 3 3 3° 2/2 1/¾ 2:01:1 6.00(Dplse)GmeRulr,S'sdeHn,MgcCrpt 7
7-16 RR ft C-3 Cd 9000 m 29:4 1:00 1:30:2 2:02:4 1 2 2 2 2/5 5/2¾ 2:03:2 5.10(Dolse)MrAAA,TmlyFrst,RneesFlla 7
7-9 RR ft C-3 Cd 8000 m 29:2 1:00 1:31:1 2:01:3 5 6 6° 4°°3/4 3/2 2:02 5.90(Dpls)JhnRQntn,AzlaSpnnr,GmeRlr 7
7-2 YR ft C-3 Cd 8000 m 29 59:2 1:30 2:00:3 5 5 6 5 6/6½ 3/5½dh 2:01:3 10.80(Dplse)GFlla,B'Crk,HTrvlr-GRulrdh 7
6-25 YR ft C-3 Cd 8000 m 29:2 1:00:2 1:31 2:01:2 6 7 7 7 6/6½ 6/4 2:02:1 10.70(NDpls)MgcCrpt,Encnto,BrdlysCrk 6
6-12 YR ft C-3 Cd 8000 m 29 1:00 1:32:2 2:03 7 6 5° 4° 4/1½ 3/2 2:03:2 43.90(NDpls)FlaBGd,GlnbysFla,GmeRulr
6-4 YR ft C-3 Cd 8000 m 30:4 1:02:3 1:33:2 2:02:3 5 6 4 6° 6/7¾ 4/8¼dh 2:04:1 12.10(NDpls)B'RbrtD,SlrSystm,K'N'Time 6

ORANGE 10 **7**

COURAGEOUS KID b h, 5, by Entrepreneur, Air Belle by Airliner (Tr.-J. Darish) (St.-M. Lawho
Carolina Manor Farm, Timmonsville, S.C. RR 2:02 1979 17 2 3 1 21,32
($67,170) 3, 2:02:1 JOHN DARISH (176) Gray-Red-White RR 2:02:4 1978 22 4 4 2 33,91
8-6 RR ft C-2 Cd 10000 m 30:3 1:03:1 1:34 2:03:4 4 5 6 5 4/2 4/5¼ 2:04:4 9.50(JDrsh)SlrSystm,S'town,S'T'Bottle
7-24 RR ft C-1 Cd 11000 m 29:2 1:01 1:30:4 2:01:1 3 5 5° 5° 8/6½ 8/7¾ 2:02:4 13.60(JDarish)T'prdBrd,PencTm,IRSTm
7-17 RR ft C-1 11000 m 27:3 58:1 1:29:2 1:59:4 6 6 6° 4° 3/5 4/8¼ 2:01:2 9.10(JDash)FstStrk,ScnicIsl,KgtNArmr
7-3 YR ft C-1 Cd 10000 m 30:4 1:01:2 1:31:1 2:00:4 7 7 7 7 6/4¾ 7/5¼ 2:01:4 34.40(JDrsh)TrckLse,IRSTm-PlyT'Gmdh
6-26 YR ft C-1 Cd 10000 m 29:3 1:00 1:30:4 2:00 2 4 5 5 5/3 3/4¼ 2:00:4 15.60(Darish)TmlyThrp,ScnicIsl,CrgsKid
6-19 YR ft C-1 Cd 10000 m 29:4 1:01 1:30:3 2:01 2 4 4° 3° 4/3½ 7/5¼ 2:02 7.40(JDrsh)KshMine,MrcleChris,St'twn
6-13 YR ft C-1 Cd 10000 m 30:1 1:02:2 1:32:3 2:02:2 6 3 3 3° 2/hd 1/¾ 2:02:2 44.90(JDrsh)C'agusKd,MrclChrs,T'vwBlz
6-5 YR gd C-1 Cd 10000 m 30 1:01:2 1:32:2 2:02:2 8 8 7° 7° 7/9 7/9 2:04:1 46.50(JDrsh)DshO'Brn,T'Blaze,BoysWay

GREEN 5 **8**

THE PACKER b g, 4, by Adios Cleo, Miss Loutown by Sisters Son (Tr.-M. Smorra) (St.-J. Chapma
Edward Klein, Southfield, Mich. RR 2:03:1 1979 21 3 2 3 29,07
($10,474) 3, 2:00:2 (1) JOHN CHAPMAN (157) Green-White Det(1) 2:00:2 1978 12 8 2 0 10,47
7-31 RR ft C-1 Cd 11000 m 29:3 1:01:2 1:31 2:00:1 3 3 4 5 4/4½ 5/4½ 2:01 5.50(Chap)KgtNArmor,FllaBGd,M'Cndy
7-24 RR ft C-1 Cd 11000 m 28:3 1:00:3 1:31:2 2:01:4 8 8 8 6 8/5¾ 5/3 2:02:2 41.20(MTlsn)KshMine,FllaBGd,K'NArmr
7-11 YR ft C-1 Cd 10000 m 28:3 59:1 1:29:3 1:59:3 6 6 6° 6° 6/5½ 5/5 2:00:3 22.50(Chap)P'T'Gme,KgtNArmr,D'Hrbrt
7-5 YR ft B-3 11000 m 28:4 59:4 1:30:4 2:00:4 2 3 4 5 5/2½ 5/3¾ 2:01:3 8.10(Chap)TwnsndHn,Ttn,A'st,PysnBco
6-26 Det(1) ft Cd 7500 m 29:4 59:2 1:29:2 1:59:4 3 4 4 2° 2/1 4/4 2:00:3 2.20(TTay)ShiwyPppn,GrlOM'Drms,R'Ch
5-30 RR ft B-3 13000 m 30 1:01:4 1:32:1 2:01:3 6 6 7° 4°°5/2½ 8/5½ 2:02:3 14.80(JChap)IdealRich,JRPower,OurHap
5-23 RR sy B-3 13000 m 29:3 1:01 1:30:1 2:00 3 2 2 3 3/4 3/6¾ 2:01:2 8.10(Chap)H'dwnHn,M'H'Diane,T'Packr
5-16 RR ft B-3 13000 m 29:1 58:2 1:29:1 2:00:1 3 5 5 4 3/3 2/¾ 2:00:2 6.90(JChap)CRsDrm,ThePackr,BillyVon

PACE

ONE MILE

$3.00 BIG TRIPLE

10

WARM-UP SADDLE CLOTH—BROWN

CLASS C-3
THREE, FOUR & FIVE-YEAR-OLDS—COLTS, HORSES & GELDINGS.

PURSE $9,000

MORN. LINE

3 BLUE **1** **ARION LOBELL** b g, 4, by Adios Vic, Adiana Hanover by Tar Heel (Tr.-M. DeBowskie) (St.-V. Dancer)
Norman & Judy Kay, National Hill Fms., S. Brummel, N.Y. M(1) 2:00 1979 14 2 2 3 20,585.
($30,672) 3, 1:59:2 (1) DONALD DANCER (130) Blue-Gold M(1) 1:59:2 1978 21 4 1 2 27,361.
* 8-7 RR ft qua m 31 1:02:2 1:32:1 2:02 1 2 2 2 2/2½ 2/5 2:03 N.B.(DDncr)CrwnsFlght,ArionLbl,W'Jay 71
6-29 M(1) ft clm 22500Z m 29:4 :59 1:29 1:58:4 6 2 4 7 6/6¼ 3/2¾ 1:59:2 4.20(CMnzi)ThrstyAndy,BigOzzie,ArionLbl
6-21 M(1) ft clm 25000 m 29:4 1:00:1 1:30:3 2:00 7 2 4 7 5/5 6/6¼ 2:01:1 3.90(CMnzi)Ovrsight,FlyDrmN,BigB'Nick
6-13 M(1) ft clm 22500 m 29:4 1:00:3 1:30:2 2:00 4 2 3 3 2/2½ 1/1¼ 2:00 *2.70(CMnzi)ArionLbl,EvrgrnMrc,GrgsPrde
6-5 M(1) gd clm 20000 m 28:4 57:1 1:27:4 1:59:4 1 3 4 6 7/4¾ 2/¾ 2:00 *1.90(CMnzi)TarB'Ad,ArionLbl,BckeyePrde
5-29 M(1) sl clm 20000 m 29:3 1:00:2 1:30 2:01:2 8 2 3 4 3/1¾ 1/3¼ 2:01:2 27.60(CMnzi)ArionLbl,TarB'Ads,FrskRma
5-23 M(1) sy clm 22500 m 29:3 59:3 1:30 1:59:1 8 1 5 6 5/4¾ 4/9¾ 2:01:1 13.30(JoCmpbl)EbnyRck,TrvCnsl,HlndEdwn
5-17 M(1) ft clm 20000 m 29:4 1:00:3 1:31:2 1:59:3 8 1 1 1 2/2 3/6½ 2:00:4 19.10(CMnzi)JmboDollar,Russlow,ArionLbl

4 RED **2** **AZALIA SPINNER** br g, 4, by Henry T Adios, Mini Song by Victory Song (Tr.-T. Foster)
Norman Brill, Oceansde, N.Y. YR 2:02:2 1979 28 4 2 5 28,725.
($44,431) 3, 2:00:2 (1) JAMES MAROHN (115) Purple-White Det(1) 2:00:2 1978 44 13 11 6 30,561.
8-6 RR ft C-3 Cd 9000 m 29:4 1:00:2 1:31:3 2:03:2 1 2 3° 2° 2/¾ 3/½ 2:03:2 4.90(JMrhn)T'Frst,M'H'Nvle,AzliaSpinr 78
7-30 RR ft C-3 Cd 9000 m 29:1 59:1 1:30 2:01:3 3 6 6° 4°° 2/1½ 3/1¾ 2:02 9.80(JMrhn)CrtnlyRght,GdChrs,A'Spnnr 78
7-16 RR ft C-3 Cd 9000 m 29:4 1:00 1:30:2 2:02:4 2 4 4° 3° 3/5½ 7/4¾ 2:03:3 1.80(Mrhn)MrAAA,TmlyFrst,RneesFlla 78
7-9 YR ft C-3 Cd 8000 m 29:2 1:00 1:31:1 2:01:3 4 5 5° 2 2/1½ 2/nk 2:01:3 3.10(JMrhn)JhnRQntn,AzlaSpnr,GmeRlr 71
7-2 YR ft C-3 Cd 8000 m 29:2 1:00:3 1:31:4 2:02:2 7 3° 5 6 6/4 6/3¼ 2:03 13.20(Crmr)F'F'Timmy,J'RQntn,T'Frost 72
6-20 YR ft C-3 Cd 8000 m 30:2 1:01 1:32 2:02:2 5 6 6 5° 4/1 1/½ 2:02:2 18.40(JMrhn)A'Spinnr,J'RQntn,S'T'Bttle 76
6-12 YR ft C-3 Cd 8000 m 29 1:00 1:32:2 2:03 3 5 3° 2° 2/½ 4/2 2:03:2 13.70(JMrhn)FlaBGd,GlnbysFla,GmeRulr 64
6-4 YR ft C-3 Cd 8000 m 29:4 1:00:3 1:31:1 2:03 8 1° 3 3 4/1 5/4¾ 2:04 31.20(NDpls)EliteTip,S'sdeHn,GlnbysFlla 62

4 YELLOW **3** **SPRINGFIELD ENDEAVOUR** b g, 5, by Jack Chance, Gabrielle by Chandelier (Tr.-P. Carbone) (St.-H. Carbone)
Hard Six Enterprises, Inc., N.Y. (qua)RR 2:03 1979 8 0 2 1 1,682.
($00.00) CARMINE ABBATIELLO (145) Gold-Red 1978 0 0 0 0
8-6 RR ft C-3 Cd 9000 m 29:4 1:00:2 1:31:3 2:03:2 3 4 4° 5° 4/1¾ 7/3¾ 2:04 3.90(HrFln)T'Frost,M'H'Nvle,AzliaSpinr 70
7-23 RR ft C-3 Cd 9000 m 29:3 1:01:3 1:32:1 2:02:4 3 1 1 1 1/1½ 3/½ 2:02:4 *1.50(JMrhn)C'Right,M'Tornado,S'Endvr 78
* 7-17 RR ft qua m 30.1 1.01 1:32 2:03 2 5 4° 1 1/3 1/3 2:03 N.B.(JMrhn)S'fldEndvr,B'Byrd,FllaChse 79
3-21 Methven(NewZealand) approx. 1⅝ m 3:42:3 finished 5th; (RCameron) AngeloDundee, WayneMartial, StopThe
2-24 Timaru(NewZealand) approx. 1⅝ m 3:29 finished 2nd; (MDeFilippi) Frost Gilda, SprngfieldEndeavour, OssieMilne
2-13 Methven(NewZealand) approx. 1⅝ m 3:31:3 finished 7th; (RCameron) Hesitate, JohnnyRue, GypsyAveril
2-6 Oamaru(NewZealand) approx. 1⅝ m 3:34 finished 2nd; (RCameron) WinningWay, SpringfieldEndeavour, Sarabelle
1-5 Waikouaiti(NewZealand) approx. 1⅝ m 3:35:1 finished 9th; (RCameron) CharlieBriar, CatherineOfAragon, SmartAveril

5 BLACK **4** **JOHN R QUINTON** br h, 5, by Brown Star, Margaret Quinton by Meadow Ace (Tr.-L. Meittinis)
Lou Meittinis, David & Adrienne Sobol, N.Y. YR 2:01:3 1979 9 1 2 0 8,800.
($75,133) 4, 2:01:3 HERVE FILION (163) Red-Blue-White RR 2:01:3 1978 43 9 3 6 56,350.
8-6 RR ft C-2 Cd 10000 m 29:3 1:00:4 1:31:2 2:02 7 2° 1 2 3/1 7/7¼ 2:03:2 19.70(HrFln)S'Ace,AlphaLbll,LbrtyA'hst 78
7-23 RR ft C-2 Cd 10000 m 29:2 1:00:2 1:31:2 2:01:4 2 3 4 5 7/4½ 6/3¼ 2:02:2 4.80(HrFln)BoysWay,T'prdKen,VivaMx 78
7-16 RR ft C-2 Cd 10000 m 30:1 1:00:4 1:31 2:01 8 8 8 7 6/7 7/8½ 2:02:3 21.80(HrFln)ClnlLBar,JRsBoy,MdwArtst 78
7-9 YR ft C-3 Cd 8000 m 29:2 1:00 1:31:1 2:01:3 7 4 4° 1 1/1½ 1/nk 2:01:3 *2.20(CAbb)JhnRQtn,AzlaSpnnr,GmeRlr 71
7-2 YR ft C-3 Cd 8000 m 29:2 1:00:3 1:31:4 2:02:2 5 1° 1 2 3/1 2/1 2:02:3 *1.30(CAbb)F'F'Timmy,J'RQntn,T'Frost 72
6-20 YR ft C-3 Cd 8000 m 30:2 1:01 1:32 2:02:2 7 1° 1 1 1/½ 2/½ 2:02:2 7.50(M'shJr)A'Spinnr,J'RQntn,S'T'Btle 76
6-12 YR ft C-2 Cd 9000 m 29:1 1:01:1 1:31:1 2:02:1 3 4 4° 5° 6/7¼ 6/7¾ 2:03:4 9.20(LFnt)B'RbrtD,RdngtnHll,EliteTip 64
6-4 YR ft C-2 Cd 9000 m 30:3 1:02:1 1:33:4 2:03:3 8 8 8° 8° 8/8½ 8/11 2:05:4 30.50(LFont)TmlyThrp,B'uMnde,F'F'Brd 62

WHITE **5** **S A CREST** b h, 4, by Columbia George, Bye Bye Mollie by Bye Bye Byrd (Tr.-A. Mann) (St.-F. Popfinger)
Anna & Sam Schulsinger, Brooklyn, N.Y. YR 2:03:1 1979 14 2 0 1 12,440.
($45,972) 3, 2:00:1 FRANK POPFINGER (160) Blue-Gold YR 2:00:1 1978 28 5 5 2 36,820.
8-6 RR ft C-3 Cd 9000 m 29:4 1:00:2 1:31:3 2:03:2 7 7 6° 4°°3/1½ 6/1½ 2:03:3 6.20(FPop)T'Frost,M'H'Nvle,AzliaSpinr 78
7-30 RR ft C-3 Cd 9000 m 29:4 1:02 1:32:3 2:02 2x 8 7° 6° 5/6½ 4/3¾ 2:02:3 5.60(FPop)K'NwTme,BrnzHnA,MrP'tne 78
7-16 RR ft C-3 Cd 9000 m 29 1:00 1:31:1 2:01:2 6 2 3° 3° 4/6½ 7/10 2:03:2 20.50(FPop)T'prdKn,BeauMnde,B'Creek 78
7-4 YR gd C-3 Cd 8000 m 30 1:01:3 1:34:4 2:05:1 2 3 1 1 1/hd 4/1¾ 2:05:3 4.60(FPop)RneesFlla,K'NwTm,TrmnHn 57
6-26 YR ft C-3 Cd 8000 m 30:2 1:00:1 1:31:2 2:03:1 2 3 3 3 3/1 1/nk 2:03:1 *1.40(FPop)SACrst,BuckoHn,CedrwdVic 63
6-18 YR ft C-3 Cd 8000 m 29 1:01 1:32 2:01.4 7 7 7 6 3/4½ 3/4 2:02:3 7.50(FPop)SolrSystm,MJMhne,SACrest 69
6-4 YR ft C-3 Cd 8000 m 29:4 1:00:3 1:31:1 2:03 1 3x 8° 8 8/13 8/18 2:06:3 *1.90(FPop)EliteTip,S'sideHn,GlnbysFlla 62
5-28 RR sy C-3 Cd 9000 m 29:4 1:01:4 1:34:2 2:04:2 6 7 7 8°°7/3¾ 5/3¾ 2:05:1 24.50(FPop)RghtAgn,TrmnHn,HhniesBst 60

PURPLE **6** **ELITE TIP** b h, 5, by Fashion Tip, Armbro Fiesta by Sampson Hanover (Tr.-M. Santa Maria)
K&MStable,AGiannone,FiveStarStable,Westbury,NY RR 2:02:3 1979 27 5 0 5 32,155.
($49,296) 4, 1:58:4 (1) JOE MARSH, JR. (125) Grey-Blue-Red M(1) 1:58:4 1978 27 6 5 3 32,766.
8-6 RR ft C-3 Cd 9000 m 29:1 1:00:2 1:30:4 2:02:1 8 8 8 8 8/7¼ 8/6½ 2:03:2 12.40(Doky)F'Nick,BrnzeHnA,MrPrfntne 78
7-30 RR ft C-3 Cd 9000 m 29:2 59:2 1:30:2 2:01:1 2 5 5° 4° 4/3¾ 4/1½ 2:01:2 2.90(Dokey)GmeRulr,S'sideHn,MgcCrpt 78
7-16 RR ft C-3 Cd 9000 m 29 1:00 1:31:1 2:01:2 5 8 8° 7° 6/7¼ 5/7¼ 2:02:4 4.40(MDky)T'prdKen,BeauMnde,B'Crk 78
7-9 YR ft C-2 Cd 9000 m 29:3 1:00:3 1:30:3 2:00:4 7 7 8 7 7/9¾ 5/10 2:02:4 28.00(MDoky)N'HHrtg,FllaBGd,PhlT'Till 71
6-19 YR ft C-2 Cd 9000 m 29:4 1:01:3 1:31 2:01:1 7 7 7 7 6/5¾ 4/2¾ 2:01:4 43.00(NDpls)RdngtnHll,BarsRbrtD,S'Stul 71
6-12 YR ft C-2 Cd 9000 m 29:1 1:01:1 1:31:1 2:02:1 2 2 2 3 3/3½ 3/3 2:02:4 5.00(MDky)B'RbrtD,RdngtnHall,ElteTp 64
6-4 YR ft C-3 Cd 8000 m 29:4 1:00:3 1:31:1 2:03 4 5 4° 4° 3/1 1/2 2:03 5.20(MrshJr)ElteTp,S'sdeHn,GlnbysFlla 62
5-28 RR sy C-3 Cd 9000 m 29:4 1:01:4 1:34:2 2:04:2 7 8 8° 5°°6/3¾ 6/4¾ 2:05:2 26.40(Doky)RghtAgn,TrmnHn,HhniesBst 60

ORANGE **7** **MONAS WHITESIDE** b h, 4, by Henry T Adios, Mona Rush by Rush Hour (Tr.-A. Nelson) (St.-D. Insko)
Four And One Stables, Morrison, Ill. RR 2:05:4 1979 12 1 1 3 9,720.
($24,210) 3, 2:02:4 CHARLES CONNOR, JR. (150) Purple-Gold RR 2:02:4 1978 20 5 6 0 24,210.
8-6 RR ft C-3 Cd 9000 m 29:1 1:00:2 1:30:4 2:02:1 6 6 4° 4° 5/4¼ 7/5 2:03:1 24.60(Insko)F'Nick,BrnzeHnA,MrPrfntne 78
7-16 RR ft C-3 Cd 9000 m 29 1:00 1:31:1 2:01:2 3 4 4 6 7/7¾ 4/7 2:02:4 7.40(Insko)T'prdKen,BeauMnde,B'Crk 78
7-4 YR gd C-3 Cd 8000 m 30 1:01:3 1:34:4 2:05:1 5 7 7 5°°5/3½ 6/9¾ 2:07:1 12.40(CnnrJr)RneesFlla,K'N'Tm,TrmnHn 57
6-27 YR ft C-3 Cd 8000 m 30 1:01 1:31:1 2:01:2 5 4 5 5 5/5¼ 3/2¾ 2:02 2.20(Insko)K'NwTm,TrumnHn,M'W'sde 66
6-20 YR ft C-3 Cd 8000 m 30:2 1:01 1:32 2:02:2 6 7 7 7° 6/2½ 6/2¼ 2:02:4 4.30(Insko)A'Spinnr,J'RQntn,S'T'Btle 76
* 6-15 YR ft tp qua m 30 1:01:2 1:33:1 2:03:1 5 2 2 1 1/10 1/12 2:03:1 N.B.(Insko)M'Whtesde,S'Moon,LimitUp 76
2-26 RR gd C-3 Cd 8000 m 30:3 1:00:4 1:32:3 2:03:4 5 8 7° 6°°7/8½ 7/7¾ 2:05:2 4.50(CnrJr)GseStep,ShwNGd,LkadatVn 35
2-10 RR ft C-3 7000 m 30:4 1:03 1:34:3 2:05:4 7 7 7 7 5/6½ 1/hd 2:05:4 6.40(Insko)M'Whiteside,N'Drct,H'Best 13

GREEN **8** **MIKLOUS TORNADO** b g, 5, by Hobo Ruble, Heritage Tiricia by Every Time (Tr.-P. Valvanis) (St.-L. Fontaine)
Dana Stable & Lucien Fontaine, N.Y. YR 2:02 1979 25 2 3 6 25,050.
($90,575) 4, 1:59:1 (1) LUCIEN FONTAINE (154) Green-White-Red M(1) 1:59:1 1978 36 9 3 6 66,190.
7-30 RR ft C-3 Cd 9000 m 29:1 59:1 1:30 2:01:3 4 7 7 7° 6/3¼ 5/3¾ 2:02:2 5.40(Font)CrtnlyRght,GdChrs,AzlaSpnr 78
7-23 RR ft C-3 Cd 9000 m 29:3 1:01:3 1:32:1 2:02:4 1 2 2 2 3/1¼ 2/ns 2:02:4 4.60(LFont)C'Right,M'Tornado,S'Endvr 78
7-10 YR ft C-3 Cd 8000 m 29:3 1:01:1 1:32:1 2:02:1 2 3 3° 2° 4/1¾ 3/3¾ 2:03 8.70(LFont)M'Artist,M'DlRay,M'Trndo 72
7-3 YR ft C-3 Cd 8000 m 29 59:1 1:30 2:01 4 6 6 7 8/7 7/7¾ 2:02:3 6.70(LFont)VivaMax,CdrwdVic,MrAAA 76
6-25 YR ft C-3 Cd 8000 m 29:4 1:00:1 1:31:2 2:02:4 4 2 3 4 4/4½ 3/3 2:03:2 *2.50(Font)MrtyD'Ray,BrvoBrt,M'Trndo 68
6-18 YR ft C-3 Cd 8000 m 29:2 1:01:2 1:33 2:03:4 6 1 3 3 4/2¾ 3/3¾ 2:04:3 12.80(Font)HhnsBst,S'sdeHn,MklsTrndo 69
6-5 YR sy C-2 Cd 9000 m 30:1 1:01:3 1:32:1 2:02:2 8 1° 3 5 5/9 8/11 2:04:3 39.50(LFont)NstyHHrtg,KatDncr,HpyHA 65
5-28 RR sy C-2 Cd 10000 m 31:3 1:03 1:33:3 2:03:4 3 3 5 6 7/7 7/6 2:05 16.90(LFont)M'Candy,NoB'Deal,F'F'Brd 60

5 points. The computation is not necessary. Herbars Harmony won from the extreme outside last week, beating Sharp Honey among others. Tonight Sharp Honey, who had a pronounced advantage in post position last time, is at a disadvantage in that respect. Also, the mare hauled Lucien Fontaine last time but is without that considerable asset tonight.

We get off to a good start. Herbars Harmony tops it from wire to wire, paying $5.20. Limit Up (17.40 to 1) arrives next, followed by Rare (6.80 to 1) and Sharp Honey (7 to 1).

The Second Race

Here is a claimer for $22,000 older male stock, with younger ones and females carrying price tags ranging to $31,400. We can eliminate Rocket Alley (a breaker coming off a slow qualifier); Skipper Sue (who had a traumatic experience last time and is not up to that outer post); and Ben Reed (a terrible qualifying performance). Note that we use the next-to-last performances of the first three contenders on the list.

Provocation	1:01:2 (14)	2:02:4 (14)	= 28
Fantastic Butler	1:00:3 (20)	2:01:3 (20)	= 40
Arrundi	1:01:3 (15)	2:02:4 (14)	= 29
Nickeli Adios	1:01:1 (17)	2:03:1 (12)	= 29
Keven Scott	1:01:2 (16)	2:03 (13)	= 29

Provocation loses 5 for the slight rise in class, recovers 2 for the stretch gain, plus 10 for roughing it, 4 for post and 5 for Daigneault. Final is 44.

Fantastic Butler gets 5 for the reduction in class, 10 for pacing so wide at the three-quarter mark and 5 for Norman Dauplaise. Final is 60.

Arrundi earns 5 for dropping in class, 10 for roughing it and 10 for Abbatiello for a final rating of 54.

Nickeli Adios gets 1 for the stretch gain, 5 for the parked-out symbol and 2 for post position. Final: 37.

Keven Scott gets 4 for gaining in the stretch, 5 for roughing it and 5 for Joe Marsh, Jr. Final: 43.

Fantastic Butler got to the front at once and remained there, paying $5. Nickeli Adios (9.90 to 1) was second and Arrundi (2.60 to 1) third.

The Third Race

Conditions are the same as in the previous race, but Captains Reef is the only entrant with a price higher than $22,000. I doubt that I need to do formal ratings here. Neither will the reader who has learned to begin the handicapping process by running the eye down the column that displays the individual horses' final times, and then inspects other features of the past-performance lines that include the fastest final times. In this case, Nandina Direct stands out rather conspicuously. Those who do the actual ratings for practice will find that Captains Reef is our second choice.

The race ended that way, with Nandina Direct pulling away in the stretch and paying $5.60. Captains Reef, with Norman Dauplaise, went off at 11.40 to 1, came rapidly at the end and paid $10 for the place. Glentohi N (7.50 to 1) finished third.

The Fourth Race

Six of these three-year-olds were knocked around in an extremely rough race exactly a week ago. Meadow Cambro is the only contender whose latest race is a proper basis for rating. Thank Goodness, who showed nothing out of the inside post last time, is no contender out of post 7. Neither is Keystone Suave, who seems to have clung to the inside rail in both his latest starts.

Fly Fly Timmy	1:00:4 (20)	2:02:2 (19) − 39
Swaps Hanover	1:01:2 (17)	2:03 (16) = 33
Spinnaker N	1:00:4 (20)	2:02:1 (20) = 40
J Ks Best	1:01 (19)	2:03:4 (12) = 31
Meadow Cambro	1:00:4 (20)	2:02:4 (17) = 37
Cloverleaf Tony	1:00:4 (20)	2:02:1 (20) = 40

Fly Fly Timmy adds 10 for racing outside and 5 for Daigneault for a final rating of 44.

Swaps Hanover gets 10 for the half-mile outside. The final rating is 43.

Spinnaker N gets 10 for roughing it and 5 for Donald Dancer. Final: 55.

J Ks Best deserves 5 for the reduction in class and 5 for roughing it. Final: 41.

Meadow Cambro gets 5 for dropping class and 10 for roughing it, less 2 for the post position, plus 5 for John Kopas. Final: 55.

Cloverleaf Tony adds 10 for roughing it, less 3 for the outside post, plus 5 as a beaten favorite and 5 for Lucien Fontaine. Final: 57.

Cloverleaf Tony lacks the 3-point edge recommended for outside horses on page 216. On the other hand, the odds are quite liberal. Let us agree that, for purposes of this book, the race is passed. In real life, racegoers would consider the recent vigor of Cloverleaf Tony and his driver and might play them. Or might play both them and the Meadow Cambro–John Kopas team.

Cloverleaf Tony rushed to the lead and won by four, paying $9.80 as second choice in the wagering. The favored Meadow Cambro (2.20 to 1) suffered interference halfway and finished last. J Ks Best (20 to 1) was second, with Swaps Hanover third at 4.40 to 1.

The Fifth Race

We can eliminate Beau Monde (0 for 17); Truman Hanover (who showed so little in the higher class); Bill Derror (a shipper); Bud T Ace (not much zip lately); and the two outside horses. Marbyrd's last race was a win, to be sure, and in fast time for this field, to be sure, and he also has Bill Popfinger. But he raced under cover all the way, and will be unable to do that tonight.

It seems to me that Goose Island has an edge over the others. If anything, he is moving down rather than up in class. Fontaine is driving in superb form and should be able to take the Goose to the front at the start.

Marbyrd roughed it for half a mile and won in a fine drive, paying $56. Readers who rate him among the contenders will find no way of handicapping him as the winner. Bud T Ace (5.70 to 1) was second and Bill Derror (5.30 to 1) was third. Goose Island was fourth at 5.10 to 1, beating the favored Truman Hanover (2.10 to 1).

The Sixth Race

Bronze Hanover A is by far the likeliest member of this field. Kildare Timmy paced a faster mile off a faster half-mile time. But even if given a rating because of the dubious stretch gain after racing on the fence, Kildare will not match the points earned by the other as a beaten favorite who roughed it for half a mile.

The gelding was everybody's choice and led all the way, paying $3.40. Kildare Timmy was second choice at 3.80 to 1 and ended fifth. Bravo Bret (19.60 to 1) was second, with Basil Court (5.70 to 1) third.

The Seventh Race

We can toss out Faygie, who has spent each of his local races on the fence. Keystone Sioux has been equally unimpressive. Sun Shield is in a tough spot near the outside.

J M Nibble	1:01:2 (14)	2:02:1 (16) = 30
Admiral Bret	1:00:4 (17)	2:01:2 (20) = 37
Aarons Blazer	1:00:1 (20)	2:02:3 (14) = 34
Colossal	1:00:1 (20)	2:02 (17) = 37
Glenbys Fella	1:00:1 (20)	2:02:2 (15) = 35

We regard J M Nibble as a contender because of the alacrity with which he got from the extreme outside to the early lead in his last local outing on July 30. He now loses 5 for the rise in class, but picks up 1 for the stretch gain and 5 for that early exertion, which at a half-mile track is a sign of energy as dependable as a parked-out symbol. He also adds 3 for the better post and 5 for Dauplaise, who drives tonight. Final: 39.

Admiral Bret is accepted as a contender because he gained half a length in the stretch after braving it out in front all the way. He drops 5 for the class boost, but regains 1 for the stretch gain. Final: 33.

Aarons Blazer is another marginal contender, but did gain three in the stretch, for which he gets 3 points, plus 5 as beaten favorite. In some circumstances, we might have regarded this one's latest race not as ratable but only as a reason to rate the previous one. But the previous one would have produced a lower rating because of the slow half-mile time. Final rating: 42.

Colossal gets 5 for roughing it, less 2 for the post, plus 5 for Dancer. Final is 45.

Glenbys Fella picks up 10 for roughing it, less 3 for the post, plus 10 for Abbatiello. Final: 52.

A nice handicapping margin for the outside horse. He justified it by getting to the front at once and drawing away to win by six lengths. He paid an astounding $32.20 (and $13.60 to place). Faygie (9 to 1) was second and Admiral Bret (6.20 to 1) third. Aarons Blazer was favored at 2.80 to 1 but broke stride and finished last.

The Eighth Race

Among the likely contenders, the three inside horses have the best basic figures. But only Renees Fella has Abbatiello or a 4-point credit for post position.

Kawartha New Time, who will turn out to be your second choice in the handicap ratings, won it and paid $5 as the crowd favorite. Renees Fella, second choice at 3.30 to 1 was fourth. Tim Tom Adios (12 to 1) was second and Tempered Ken (9 to 1) third.

The Ninth Race

This race demonstrates a handicapping principle stated on page 266. A horse whose last race was a qualifier is a good pick if its performance in the qualifier was superior to the recent performances of the animals it is about to face. Ram O J stands out clearly. If raceway audiences had not been conditioned to avoid horses moving into pari-mutuel competition from qualifiers, Ram O J would have been a short-priced favorite instead of second choice.

He defeated the favored Money Order (1.70 to 1) by a neck, paying $6.

The Tenth Race

Once burned, twice shy. This time the crowd noticed that one of the starters, Arion Lobell, had paced a faster mile in its qualifying race of August 7 than had any other member of this field in its own last race, except Miklous Tornado, who is in the outside post. They sent Arion as a 2.70 to 1 favorite and he repaid them with an impressive victory, paying $7.40 while defeating S A Crest (4.60 to 1) and John R Quinton (5.20 to 1) in that order.

To fortify the crowd's decision, one might consider that Arion Lobell's better performances at The Meadowlands brought him to the wire in times superior to those of which his rivals are capable—even after allowing for the New Jersey strip's extra two seconds of speed.

On the other hand, the record offers no clear evidence that Arion Lobell is comfortable on the tight turns of a half-mile track. Neither does it tell us whether the gelding was sucked along to a 2:03 finish in its qualifier, as the past-performance line implies.

I would have eliminated Arion Lobell as a probable loser and would have been wrong. But the governing principle is right more often than wrong. Rate the contenders yourself. I would not include Miklous Tornado, by the way. He roughed it a bit, but not with the vigor needed for the outside post. I believe our selection would be S A Crest. See for yourself.

Another good evening at the races. We were able to play eight races. Our winners were Herbars Harmony ($5.20), Fantastic Butler ($5), Nandina Direct ($5.60), Bronze Hanover A ($3.40), Glenbys Fella ($32.20) and Ram O J ($6).

19 RULES AND REGULATIONS OF THE UNITED STATES TROTTING ASSOCIATION

RULE 1.
Mandate

Section 1. The following Rules and Regulations, having been duly enacted, are hereby declared to be the official Rules and Regulations of The United States Trotting Association which shall apply to and govern the Registration of Standard Bred Horses and the conduct of all racing by Members and upon Member Tracks. All rules and regulations and/or modifications or amendments thereto adopted by the Board of Directors shall become effective on May 1st following the Annual Meeting at which they were adopted.

All published conditions and programs of Member Tracks shall state that said races shall be conducted under and governed by the Rules and Regulations of The United States Trotting Association, with only such exceptions stated as are specifically authorized and permitted.

§ 2. In the event there is a conflict between the rules of The United States Trotting Association and the rules or conditions promulgated by any of its members, the rules of The United States Trotting Association shall govern.

§ 3. In the event U.S.T.A. denies membership to an individual or defers a decision beyond thirty (30) days pending further investigation to determine if he meets the requirements of the By-Laws relative to membership; and in the event a State Racing Commission determines that such person fully meets its requirements and licenses such person to participate at meetings under the jurisdiction of such Commission, U.S.T.A. will issue an eligibility certificate and/or a driver's license limited to such meetings and keep performance records on such person and his horses while racing at such meetings in the same manner and for the same fee as for members.

RULE 2.
Authorities and Terms

Section 1. The term "President" or "Executive Vice-President" in these Rules refers to the President or Executive Vice-President of The United States Trotting Association. "Board of Review" refers to the Board comprised of the Directors from the Association District where the matter originated. The term "Association" when used in these rules refers to The United States Trotting Association.

RULE 3.
Violations

Section 1. Any Member of this Association violating any of its Rules or Regulations, shall be liable upon conviction, to a fine not exceeding One Thousand Dollars ($1,000.00) or suspension, or both, or expulsion from the Association, unless otherwise limited in the rules.

The conviction of any Corporate Member of this Association of a violation of any of its rules or regulations may also subject the Officers of the said corporation to a penalty not exceeding that which is hereinabove provided.

§ 2. Any attempt to violate any of the Rules and Regulations of this Association falling short of actual accomplishment, shall constitute an offense, and, upon conviction, shall be punishable as hereinabove provided.

RULE 4.
Definitions

Section 1. **Added Money Early Closing Event.**—An event closing in the same year in which it is to be contested in which all entrance and declaration fees received are added to the purse.

§ 2. **Age, How Reckoned.**—The age of a horse shall be reckoned from the first day of January of the year of foaling, except that for foals born in November and December of any year in which case the age shall be reckoned from January 1 of the succeeding year effective November 1, 1970 and thereafter. **Provided further that for foals foaled after December 31, 1980, the exception for foals of November and December shall not apply.**

§ 3. **Appeal.**—A request for the Board of Review to investigate, consider, and review any decisions or rulings of Judges or officials of a meeting. The appeal may deal with placings, penalties, interpretations of the rules or other questions dealing with conduct of races.

§ 4. **Claiming Race.**—One in which any horse starting therein may be claimed for a designated amount in conformance with the rules.

§ 5. **Classified Race.**—A race regardless of the eligibility of horses, entries being selected on the basis of ability or performance.

§ 6. **Conditioned Race.**—An overnight event to which eligibility is determined according to specified qualifications. Such qualifications may be based upon, among other things:

(a) Horses' money winnings in a specified number of previous races or during a specified previous time.

(b) A horse's finishing position in a specified number of previous races or during a specified period of time.

(c) Age.

(d) Sex.

(e) Number of starts during a specified period of time.

(f) Special qualifications for foreign horses that do not have a representative number of starts in the United States or Canada.

(g) Or any one or more combinations of the qualifications herein listed.

(h) Use or records or time bars as a condition is prohibited.

§ 7. **Dash.**—A race decided in a single trial. Dashes may be given in a series of two or three governed by one entry fee for the series, in which event a horse must start in all dashes. Positions may be drawn for each dash. The number of premiums awarded shall not exceed the number of starters in the dash.

§ 8. **Declaration.**—A declaration is the naming of a particular horse to a particular race as a starter.

§ 9. **Declarations.**—Declarations shall be taken not more than three days in advance for all races except those for which qualifying dashes are provided.

§ 10. **Disqualification.**—It shall be construed to mean that the person disqualified is debarred from acting as an official or from starting or driving a horse in a race, or in the case of a disqualified horse, it shall not be allowed to start.

§ 11. **Early Closing Race.**—A race for a definite amount to which entries close at least six weeks preceding the race. The entrance fee may be on the installment plan or otherwise, and all payments are forfeits.

No payments on 2-year-olds in early closing events are permissible prior to February 15th of the year in which the horse is a 2-year-old.

§ 12. **Elimination Heats.**—Heats of a race split according to Rule 13, Sections 2 and 3, to qualify the contestants for a final heat.

§ 13. **Entry.**—Two or more horses starting in a race when owned or trained by the same person, or trained in the same stable or by the same management.

§ 14. **Expulsion.**—Whenever the penalty of expulsion is prescribed in these rules, it shall be construed to mean unconditional exclusion and disqualification from any participation, either directly or indirectly, in the privileges and uses of the course and grounds of a member.

§ 15. **Extended Pari-Mutuel Meetings.**—An extended pari-mutuel meeting is a meeting or meetings, at which no agricultural fair is in progress with an annual total of more than ten days duration with pari-mutuel wagering.

§ 16. **Futurity.**—A stake in which the dam of the competing animal is nominated either when in foal or during the year of foaling.

§ 17. **Green Horse.**—One that has never trotted or paced in a race or against time.

§ 18. **Guaranteed Stake.**—Same as a stake, with a guarantee by the party opening it that the sum shall not be less than the amount named.

§ 19. **Handicap.**—A race in which performance, sex or distance allowance is made. Post positions for a handicap may be assigned by the Racing Secretary. Post positions in a handicap claiming race may be determined by claiming price.

§ 20. **Heat.**—A single trial in a race two in three, or three heat plan.

§ 21. **In Harness.**—When a race is made to go "in harness" it shall be construed to mean that the performance shall be to a sulky **as defined in Section 38 of this rule.**

§ 22. **Late Closing Race.**—A race for a fixed amount to which entries close less than six weeks and more than three days before the race is to be contested.

§ 23. **Length of Race and Number of Heats.**—Races or dashes shall be given at a stated distance in units not shorter than a sixteenth of a mile. The length of a race and the number of heats shall be stated in the conditions. If no distance or number of heats are specified all races shall be a single mile dash except at fairs and meetings of a duration of 10 days or less, where the race will be conducted in two dashes at one mile distance.

§ 24. **Maiden.**—A stallion, mare or gelding that has never won a heat or race at the gait at which it is entered to start and for which a purse is offered. Races or purse money awarded to a horse after the "official sign" has been posted shall not be considered winning performance or affect status as a maiden.

§ 25. **Match Race.**—A race which has been arranged and the conditions thereof agreed upon between the contestants.

§ 26. **Matinee Race.**—A race with no entrance fee and where the premiums, if any, are other than money.

§ 27. **Nomination.**—The naming of a horse or in the event of a futurity, the naming of foal in utero to a certain race or series of races, eligibility of which is conditioned on the payment of a fee at the time of naming and the payment of subsequent sustaining fees and/or starting fees.

§ 28. **Overnight Event.**—A race for which **declarations** close not more than three days (omitting Sundays) or less **than one day** before such race is to be contested. In the absence of conditions or notice to the contrary, all entries in overnight events must close not later than 12:00 noon the day preceding the race.

§ 29. **Protest.**—An objection, properly sworn to, charging that a horse is ineligible to a race, alleging improper entry or declaration, or citing any act of an owner, driver, or official prohibited by the rules, and which, if true, should exclude the horse or driver from the race.

§ 30. **Record.**—The fastest time made by a horse in a heat or dash which he won. A Standard Record is a record of 2:20 or faster for two-year-olds and 2:15 or faster for all other ages.

§ 31. **Stake.**—A race which will be contested in a year subsequent to its closing in which the money given by the track conducting the same is added to the money contributed by the nominators, all of which except deductions for the cost of promotion, breeders or nominators awards belongs to the winner or winners. In any event, except as provided in Rule 11, Section 7, all of the money contributed in nominating, sustaining, and starting payments must be paid to the winner or winners.

§ 32. **Two in Three.**—In a two in three race a horse must win two heats to be entitled to first money.

§ 33. **Two-Year Olds.**—No two-year-old shall be permitted to start in a dash or heat exceeding one mile in distance and no two-year-old shall be permitted to race in more than two heats or dashes in any single day. Starting any two-year-old in violation of this rule shall subject the member track to a fine of not less than $25.00 and the winnings of such two-year-old shall be declared unlawful. Provided, however, that for any two-year-old events where nominations for same have closed prior to January 1, 1971, the provisions of the 1970 version of Rule 4, Section 33 shall govern.

§ 34. **Walk Over.**—When only horses in the same interest start, it constitutes a walk over. In a "stake race" a "walk over" is entitled to all the stake money and forfeits. To claim the purse the entry must start and go once over the course.

§ 35. **Winner.**—The horse whose nose reaches the wire first. If there is a dead heat for first, both horses shall be considered winners. Where two horses are tied in the summary, the winner of the longer dash or heat shall be entitled to the trophy. Where the dashes or heats are of the same distance and the horses are tied in the summary, the winner of the faster dash or heat shall be entitled to the trophy. Where the dashes or heats are of the same distance and the horses are tied in the summary and the time, both horses shall be considered winners.

§ 36. **Wire.**—The wire is a real or imaginary line from the center of the judges' stand to a point immediately across, and at right angles to the track.

§ 37. **Contract Track.**—A pari-mutuel track, not a member of this Association, which receives data and services pursuant to Article VII, Section 7 (c) of the Association's By-Laws.

§ 38. **Sulky Defined.**—**For the purpose of these rules a sulky shall be defined as a dual-shaft, dual-wheel racing vehicle. The use of any sulky in competition at any member race track shall be subject to the approval of the Judges, and where the general condition, over-all construction, or a particular structural feature of a sulky is determined by the Judges to be dangerous or unsafe, they shall not approve its use in competition.**

RULE 5.
Track Members

Section 1. Whenever races are conducted each member track shall display its certificate of membership in this Association for the current year and specified dates. Horses racing after January 1, 1940, upon due notice (at least 45 days wherever possible) to members on tracks which are not in contract or which are not in membership with The United States Trotting Association or the Canadian Trotting Association, or racing on tracks in membership with the Association on dates that have not been sanctioned by the Association shall from the date of the first such race be ineligible to race in anything but a free-for-all, and he is barred from classified and claiming and conditioned races and no eligibility certificate will be issued on that horse in the future. In the event of a bona fide sale of the horse to an innocent party or upon satisfactory proof that the owner of such horse was deceived as to the absence of contract with such track, the non-membership of such track or failure to be sanctioned for such dates, the penalty

hereinbefore provided may be limited in the discretion of the Board of Review. Such horse may be restored to eligibility and may be admitted to classified, claiming and conditioned races and may receive USTA eligibility certificate upon the payment of the sum of $10 per start with a maximum of $50 for any one meeting to cover the cost of establishing and verifying the racing performances of that horse on such non-member or non-contract track.

§ 2. **Location of Judges' Stand.**—The Judges' stand shall be so located and constructed as to afford to the officials an unobstructed view of the entire track and no obstruction shall be permitted upon the track, or the centerfield which shall obscure the officials' vision of any portion of the track during the race. Any violation of this section shall subject the member to a fine not exceeding $500 and immediate suspension from membership by the President or Executive Vice-President, subject to appeal.

§ 3. **Hippodroming Ban.**—All races conducted by Member tracks shall be bona fide contests with the winner receiving the largest share of the purse and the balance of the purse distribution made according to the order of finish. No hippodroming or other arrangement for equal distribution of the purse money among the contestants is permitted. Violation of this rule will subject the track member, officials in charge, and the owners and drivers to fine, suspension, or expulsion.

§ 4. **Default in Payment of Purses.**—Any member that defaults in the payment of a premium that has been raced for, shall stand suspended, together with its officers.

§ 5. **Time to File Claims for Unpaid purses.**—Unless claims for unpaid premiums shall be filed with this Association within sixty days after the date the race is contested the Association may release any performance bond that had been required.

§ 6. If at a meeting of a member a race is contested which has been promoted by another party or parties, and the promoters thereof default in the payment of the amount raced for, the same liability shall attach to the members as if the race had been offered by the member.

§ 7. **Dishonored Checks.**—Any member who shall pay any purse, or charges due The United States Trotting Association, or a refund of entrance fees by draft, check, order or other paper, which upon presentation is protested, payment refused, or otherwise dishonored, shall by order of the Executive Vice-President be subjected to a fine not exceeding the amount of said draft, check or order and shall be suspended from membership until the dishonored amount and fine are paid to the Executive Vice-President.

§ 8. **Minimum Advertised Purse or Schedule of Purses.**—When any member track advertises minimum purses or purses for a class and conducts any race for that class for less than said advertised minimum or class purse, such track member shall be fined by the Executive Vice-President the difference between the advertised minimum or advertised purse and the lesser purse for which such race was conducted unless there is a contract with a horsemen's association concerning purse distributions.

§ 9. **Removal of Horses From the Grounds.**—No horse shall be ordered off the grounds without at least 72 hours notice (excluding Sunday) to the person in charge of the horse.

§ 10. **Driver Awards.**—Except as herein stated, no member track in the United States shall advertise to pay or pay any awards other than to the Owners, Nominators, or Breeders of money winning horses. Awards may be made to drivers of horses breaking or equaling track or world records, or to leading drivers at meetings.

§ 11. **Paddock Rules.**—Every extended pari-mutuel track shall:

(1) Provide a paddock or receiving barn.

(2) The paddock or receiving barn must be completely enclosed with a man-tight fence and all openings through said fence shall be policed so as to exclude unauthorized personnel therefrom.

(3) Horses must be in the paddock at the time prescribed by the Presiding Judge, but in any event at least one hour prior to post time of the race in which the horse is to compete. Except for warm-up trips, no horse shall leave the paddock until called to the post.

(4) Persons entitled to admission to the paddock:

(a) Owners of horses competing on the date of the race.

(b) Trainers of horses competing on the date of the race.

(c) Drivers of horses competing on the date of the race.

(d) Grooms and caretakers of horses competing on the date of the race.

(e) Officials whose duties require their presence in the paddock or receiving barn.

(5) No driver, trainer, groom, or caretaker, once admitted to the paddock or receiving barn, shall leave the same other than to warm up said horse until such race, or races, for which he was admitted is contested.

(6) No person except an owner, who has another horse racing in a later race, or an official, shall return to the paddock until all races of that program shall have been completed.

(7) No more than two members of a registered stable, other than the driver, shall be entitled to admission to the paddock on any one racing day.

(8) During racing hours each track shall provide the services of a blacksmith within the paddock.

(9) During racing hours each track shall provide suitable extra equipment as may be necessary for the conduct of racing without unnecessary delay.

(10) Each track shall see that the provisions of this rule are rigidly enforced and a fine not to exceed $500.00 for each violation of this rule may be imposed.

§ 12. **Photo Finish, Head Numbers—Starting Gate.**—At all member tracks where pari-mutuel wagering is allowed, a photo finish, head numbers, and starting gate must be used. At all extended pari-mutuel meetings, the member must provide for a back-up starting gate as well. Whenever the Judges use a photo to determine the order of finish, it shall be posted for public inspection. Photo finish equipment shall not be acceptable unless a spinner or target is used therewith.

§ 13. **Payment of Dues.**—If a member fails to pay the dues prescribed by the By-Laws of the Association within thirty (30) days of notice of the amount due, the member together with its officers and directors may be suspended from membership in the Association.

§ 14. **Driver Insurance.**—Each member conducting an extended pari-mutuel meeting shall prepare and prominently display, in the Race Secretary's office, a statement giving the name of the company with which they carry driver insurance.

§ 15. **Supervision of Meeting.**—Although members have the obligation of general supervision of their meeting, interference with the proper performance of duties of any official is hereby prohibited.

§ 16. **Breath Analyzer Requirements.—** **(a) For Extended Pari-Mutuel Tracks.** Every extended pari-mutuel track shall be equipped with a breath analyzer device and all Drivers, Judges, Starters, drivers of the starting gate and Marshals shall be required to submit to a breath analyzer test at each racing program in which they participate. In the case of drivers, if the results of such test show a reading of more than .05 percent of alcohol in the blood, such driver shall not be permitted to drive and an investigation will be started to determine if there has been a violation of Rule 17, Section 7 (c). In the case of Judges, Starters, **drivers of the starting gate** and Marshals, if the result of a breath analyzer test results in a reading of more than .05 percent of alcohol in the blood, that individual shall be relieved of his duties for that program and a report shall be made to the respective State Racing Commissions and the U.S.T.A. for appropriate action.

(b) For Other Than Extended Pari-Mutuel Meetings. Drivers, Judges, Starters, **drivers of the starting gate** and Marshals shall submit to a breath analyzer test when requested by the Presiding Judge or an authorized agent of this Association. The results of the test will be governed by the provisions of the preceding paragraph.

§ 17. **The personal use of any illegal drug, medicant, stimulant, depressant, narcotic or hypnotic is prohibited. At all member tracks any individual may be required to submit to a urine and/or blood sample relative to the detection of the above.**

§ 18. **Quarter Pole Markers.—**At all member tracks the quarter-mile pole, half-mile pole and three-quarter-mile pole shall be clearly marked.

RULE 6.
Race Officials

Section 2. **Officials Required.—**In every race over the track of a member, the Manager shall appoint or authorize the appointment of three men familiar with the rules to act as Judges, one of whom shall be designated as Presiding Judge, who shall be in charge of the stand. He shall also appoint a licensed Starter, three Timers, and a competent person to act as Clerk of the Course.

At all matinees there shall be at least one licensed official in the Judges' stand.

§ 2. No license shall be granted to any person not in membership with this Association.

§ 3. Any member track permitting an unlicensed person to officiate when a license is required shall be fined not exceeding $100 for each day such unlicensed person officiates. Any person officiating without being licensed as required by these rules or acting as an official at any meeting not in membership with this Association, or the Canadian Trotting Association, shall be fined not exceeding $100 for each day he acts as such an official; PROVIDED HOWEVER, that nothing herein contained shall prevent any person from officiating at a contract track.

§ 4. **Officials at Extended Meetings.—**No presiding Judge, **Associate Judge,** Starter or Race Secretary shall be qualified to serve as such at an extended pari-mutuel harness race meeting or a grand circuit meeting without a license valid for pari-mutuel meetings or grand circuit meetings. A Barrier Judge, Patrol Judge, Clerk of Course, **Identifier** or Paddock Judge who serves at an extended pari-mutuel meeting or at pari-mutuel meetings totaling more than ten days during a race season must have a license valid for pari-mutuel meetings. Starters, Presiding Judges and Race Secretaries holding pari-mutuel licenses are authorized to officiate at all meetings, and Associate Judges holding pari-mutuel licenses are authorized to serve as Presiding Judges at pari-mutuel meetings of ten days or less and at non pari-mutuel meetings. No person shall serve as an Associate Judge at any pari-mutuel meeting in the United States unless he is a member of the USTA. The Executive Vice-President may permit an exchange of license in the various capacities above, upon proper application. The fee for each such license shall be **$10.00** for all categories with the exception of the Patrol Judge and Clerk of the Course which shall be **$5.00, which fees shall be in addition to the fees for** active membership in this Association. The applicant for such license must satisfy the Executive Vice-President that he possesses the necessary qualifications, both mental and physical, to perform the duties required. Elements to be considered among others shall be character, reputation, temperament, experience, and knowledge of the rules and of the duties of a racing official. No official acting as Judge at a pari-mutuel meeting shall serve as a Race Secretary or Clerk of the Course at such meeting. No licensed official shall be qualified to act as such at any pari-mutuel meeting where he is the owner or otherwise interested in the ownership of any horse participating at such meeting. Any refusal to grant this license to a person who had been so licensed in the past may be reviewed by the Board of Appeals as provided in Article IX of the By-Laws.

§ 5. **Disqualification to Act as Official.**— A person under suspension, expulsion, or other disqualification, or who has any interest in or any bet on a race or has an interest in any of the horses engaged therein, is disqualified from acting in any official capacity in that race. In the event of such disqualification the management shall be notified by the disqualified person and shall appoint a substitute. Any person who violates this restriction shall be fined, suspended or expelled.

§ 6. **Suspension or Revocation of Official's License.**—An official may be fined, suspended, or his license may be revoked or denied at any time by the President or Executive Vice-President for incompetence, failure to follow or enforce the rules, or any conduct detrimental to the sport including drinking within 4 hours prior to the time he starts work as an official. Such license may be reinstated by the President or Executive Vice-President in his discretion upon such terms as he may prescribe. Any revocation or suspension of license hereunder may be reviewed by the Board of Appeals as provided in Article IX of the By-Laws.

§ 7. **Ban on Owning or Dealing in Horses.** —No employee of any pari-mutuel track whose duties include the classification of horses shall directly or indirectly be the owner of any horse racing at such meeting, nor shall he participate financially directly or indirectly in the purchase or sale of any horse racing at such meeting. Any person violating this rule shall be suspended by the Executive Vice-President.

§ 8. **Judges' Stand Occupants.**—None but the Judges, the Clerk of the Course, the Secretary, Starter and Timers, Official Announcer, and Officers, Officials, and Directors of this Association, and the State Racing Commission having jurisdiction shall be allowed in the Judges' stand during a race. Any association violating this rule shall be fined not to exceed $100.

§ 9. **Improper Acts by an Official.**—If any person acting as Judge or an official shall be guilty of using insulting language to an owner, driver, or other person, or be guilty of other improper conduct, he shall be fined not exceeding $500, or be expelled.

§ 10. **Presiding Judge.**—No person shall act as Presiding Judge where purses are raced for unless he is a member of and holds a license for the current year from this Association.

A Presiding Judge's license shall be issued by the Executive Vice-President upon payment of an annual fee of **$10.00, which fee shall be in addition to the fee for active membership in this Association,** when the applicant therefor has established that his character and reputation, knowledge of the rules, harness horse experience, temperament and qualifications to perform the duties required are satisfactory. However, a license limited to one public race meeting not exceeding five days in duration may be issued for $5.00 but no Judge shall receive more than one such limited license a year.

(a) The Presiding Judge shall have supervision over:

1) Associate Judges
2) Patrol Judges
3) Paddock Judge
4) Finish Wire Judge
5) Clerk of Course
6) Timers
7) **Identifier**

(b) Shall examine the official track license issued by the Association and if the license is not produced shall make public announcement that the meeting shall not proceed.

(c) Notify owners and drivers of penalties imposed.

(d) Report in writing to the Executive Vice-President violations of the rules by a member, its officers or race officials giving detailed information.

(e) Make such other reports as required by the Executive Vice President.

(f) Sign each sheet of the judges' book verifying the correctness of the information contained therein.

(g) Be responsible for the maintenance of the records of the meeting and the forwarding thereof to The United States Trotting Association except in cases of a contract track in which the contract provides otherwise.

Services of the Presiding Judge shall be paid for by the track employing him and he shall not act as a Starter, announcer or an officer at any meeting at which he officiates as Presiding Judge.

Failure of the Presiding Judge to see that the rules of the Association and the rules of any Racing Commission are complied with may be grounds for revocation and may be grounds for denial of a license for the subsequent year.

§ 11. The Judges shall have authority while presiding to:

(a) Inflict fines and penalties, as prescribed by these rules.

(b) Determine all questions of fact relating to the race.

(c) Decide any differences between parties to the race, or any contingent matter which shall arise, such as are not otherwise provided for in these rules.

(d) Declare pools and bets "off" in case of fraud, no appeal to be allowed from their decision in that respect. All pools and bets follow the decision of the Judges. Such a decision in respect to pools and bets shall be made at the conclusion of the race upon the observations of the judges and upon such facts as an immediate investigation shall develop. A reversal or change of decision after the official placing at the conclusion of the heat or dash shall not affect the distribution of betting pools made upon such official placing. When pools and bets are declared off for fraud, the guilty parties shall be fined, suspended or expelled.

(e) Control the horses, drivers, and assistants and punish by a fine not exceeding $100.00 or by suspension or expulsion, any such person who shall fail to obey their orders or the rules. In no case shall there be any compromise or change on the part of the Judges or members of punishment prescribed in the rules, but the same shall be strictly enforced. Members shall not remove or modify any fine imposed by the Judge of a race, review any order of suspension, expulsion, or interfere with the Judges performing their duties.

(f) Examine under oath all parties connected with a race as to any wrong or complaint. Any person required to appear before the Judges for a hearing or examination who shall fail to appear after due notice in writing shall be penalized as provided in (e) above.

(g) Consider complaints of foul from the patrols, owners, or drivers in the race and no others.

§ 12. It shall be the duty of the Judges to:

(a) Exclude from the race any horse that in their opinion is improperly equipped, dangerous, or unfit to race which shall include sick, weak, and extremely lame horses. No horse shall race with a tube in its throat. No horse may race unless he has unimpaired vision in one eye and no horse infected with equine infectious anemia, or a carrier thereof, shall race.

(b) Investigate any apparent or possible interference, or other violation of Rule 18, Section 1, whether or not complaint has been made by the driver.

(c) Investigate any act of cruelty seen by them or reported to them, by any member towards a race horse during a meeting at which they officiate. If the Judges find that such an act has been committed, they shall suspend or fine the offending member not to exceed $500.00, and submit a written report within ten days, of their findings and action, to the Executive Vice-President. The Executive Vice-President shall have all the authority conferred upon the Judges by this section, and in addition may order an investigation and hearing and impose a penalty for any act of cruelty or neglect of a horse committed by any member whether on or off the premises of any racetrack.

(d) Immediately thereafter or on the day of the race conduct an investigation of any accidents to determine the cause thereof, and the judges shall completely fill out an accident report and mail to the Association Office.

(e) Observe closely performance of the drivers and the horses to ascertain if there are any violations of Rule 18; particularly, interference, helping, or inconsistent racing, and exhaust all means possible to safeguard the contestants and the public.

(f) Grant a hearing at a designated time before a penalty may be imposed upon any party. All three Judges should be present if possible, and at least the Presiding Judge and one Associate Judge must be present at all Judges' hearings. The Judges may inflict the penalties prescribed by these rules. **It shall be the duty of the Judges to notify the party of a hearing as soon as possible, but in any event, where there is an alleged driving violation, said notice shall be furnished no later than 12:00 noon the day following the race.**

In the event the Judges believe that a person has committed a rule violation and has left the grounds and they are unable to contact him, and hold a hearing thereon, they may make an investigation and send a detailed written report to the Executive Vice-President of this Association. The Executive Vice-President may impose a penalty not to exceed 10 days without a hearing based upon the report of the Judges. No penalty in excess of 10 days shall be imposed before a hearing is granted.

It shall be the duty of the Judges to submit in writing, a complete list of all witnesses questioned by them at any hearing, which list of witnesses, along with the testimony of such witnesses, shall be forwarded to the Executive Vice-President along with the reports required in Rule 6, Section 10.

The testimony of all witnesses questioned by the Judges shall be recorded by one of the following methods: written, signed statements, tape recorders or court reporter's transcript. At all extended pari-mutuel tracks Judges shall use tape recorders to record their hearings.

No decision shall be made by the Judges in such cases until all of the witnesses called by the Judges and the person so required to appear before the Judges have given their testimony. Any person charged with a rule violation shall be given at least until 12:00 noon of the following day to prepare his defense if he so requests.

All penalty notices will carry the exact reason why the penalty has been imposed together with the wording of the rule violated.

All penalties imposed on any driver will be recorded on the reverse side of his driver's license by the Presiding Judge.

(g) It shall be the duty of the Judges to declare a dash or heat of a race no contest in the event the track is thrown into darkness during the progress of a race by failure of electricity.

§ 13. It shall be the procedure of the Judges to:

(a) Be in the stand fifteen minutes before the first race and remain in the stand for ten minutes after the last race, and at all times when the horses are upon the track.

(b) Observe the preliminary warming up of horses and scoring, noting behavior of horses, lameness, equipment, conduct of the drivers, changes in odds at pari-mutuel meetings, and any unusual incidents pertaining to horses or drivers participating in races.

(c) Have the bell rung or give other notice, at least ten minutes before the race or heat. Any driver failing to obey this summons may be punished by a fine not exceeding $100.00 and his horse may be ruled out by the Judges and considered drawn.

(d) Designate one of their members to lock the pari-mutuel machines immediately upon the horses reaching the official starting point. The Presiding Judge shall designate the post time for each race and the horses will be called at such time as to preclude excessive delay after the completion of two scores.

(e) Be in communication with the Patrol Judges, by use of patrol phones, from the time the Starter picks up the horses until the finish of the race. Any violation or near violation of the rules shall be reported by the Patrol Judge witnessing the incident and a written record made of same. At least one Judge shall observe the drivers throughout the stretch specifically noting changing course, interference, improper use of whips, breaks, and failure to contest the race to the finish.

(f) Post the objection sign, or inquiry sign, on the odds board in the case of a complaint or possible rule violation, and immediately notify the announcer of the objection and the horse or horses involved. As soon as the Judges have made a decision, the objection sign shall be removed, the correct placing displayed, and the "Official" sign flashed. In all instances the Judges shall post the order of finish and the "Official" sign as soon as they have made their decision. In addition the Judges shall cause the "Inquiry" sign to be posted whenever there has been an accident during the course of the race.

(g) Display the photo sign if the order of finish among the contending horses is less than half-length or a contending horse is on a break at the finish. After the photo has been examined and a decision made, a copy or copies shall be made, checked by the Presiding Judge, and posted for public inspection.

§ 14. **Patrol Judges.**—At the discretion of the Judges, patrol may be appointed by the member, but such patrols shall be approved by the Presiding Judge and work under his direction. At extended pari-mutuel meetings and at other meetings conducting one or more races with a purse value of $5,000 or over, at least two (2) Patrol Judges shall be employed. It shall be their duty to phone or repair to the Judges' stand and report all fouls and improper conduct. The result of a heat or dash shall not be announced until sufficient time has elapsed to receive the reports of the patrols. Where there is a Patrol car, only one Patrol Judge shall be required.

§ 15. **Emergency Appointment of Official.** —If any licensed official is absent or incapacitated, the member or director, or officer of the association, may appoint a substitute at such meeting, or until another licensed official can be procured. If such official acts for more than three days, he shall apply for a license in that capacity. Notice of any temporary appointment shall be wired immediately to the main office of this Association. This power may only be used in case of unavoidable emergencies. Any Director of this Association, in an emergency, may exercise any or all of the functions of any official or licensee.

§ 16. **Starter.**—No person shall be permitted to start horses on a track in membership with this Association unless he holds a Starter's license for the current year. Upon sufficient information as to good character, knowledge of these rules and ability to do the work, a license to start horses may be issued by the Executive Vice-President upon payment of an annual fee of **$10.00, which fee shall be in addition to the fee for active membership in this Association.** However, a license limited to start horses in matinee races, or at one public race meeting not exceeding five days in duration may be issued to members upon payment of annual fee of $5.00, but no starter shall receive more than one such license in any one year.

§ 17. The Starter shall be in the stand or starting gate fifteen minutes before the first race. The Starter, prior to starting any race at a meeting, shall examine the official track license issued by this Association and in the event the same is not produced, shall make public announcement that the meeting shall not proceed. He shall have control over the horses and authority to assess fines and/or suspend drivers for any violation of the rules from the formation of the parade until the word "go" is given. He may assist in placing the horses when requested by the Judges to do so. He shall notify the Judges and the drivers of penalties imposed by him. He shall report violations of the rules by a member or its officers, giving detailed information. His services shall be paid for by the member employing him. An Assistant Starter may be employed when an association deems it necessary. At all meetings at which the premiums do not exceed three thousand dollars, the Starter may also act as an Associate Judge.

§ 18. **Clerk of Course.**—The Clerk of the Course shall:

(a) At request of Judges assist in drawing positions.

(b) Keep the Judges' Book provided by the U.S.T.A. and record therein:

(1) All horses entered and their eligibility certificate numbers.

(2) Names of owners and drivers and drivers' license numbers.

(3) The charted lines at non-fair pari-mutuel meetings. At fairs, the position of the horses at the finish. At all race meetings, the money won by the horse at that track.

(4) Note drawn or ruled out horses.

(5) Record time in minutes, seconds and fifths of seconds.

(6) Check eligibility certificates before the race and after the race shall enter all information provided for thereon, including the horse's position in the race if it was charted.

(7) Verifying the correctness of the Judges' Book including race time, placing and money winnings, reasons for disqualifications, if any, and see that the book is properly signed.

(8) Forward Judges' book, charts and marked programs from all meetings the day following each racing day.

(9) Notify owners and drivers of penalties assessed by the officials.

(c) Upon request may assist Judges in placing horses.

(d) After the race, return the eligibility certificate to owner of the horse or his representative when requested.

Failure to comply with any part of this rule and make the above listed entries legible, clear and accurate, may subject either the Clerk or the Member, or both, to a fine of not to exceed $50.00 for each violation.

§ 19. **Timers.**—At each race there shall be three Timers in the Judges' or Timers' stand except when an electric timing device approved by the Executive Vice-President of the Association, is used, in which event there shall be one Timer. The chief timer shall sign the Judges' Book for each race verifying the correctness of the record. All times shall be announced and recorded in fifths of seconds. An approved electronic or electric timing device must be used where horses are started from a chute.

The Timers shall be in the stand fifteen minutes before the first heat or dash is to be contested. They shall start their watches when the first horse leaves the point from which the distance of the race is measured. The time of the leading horse at the quarter, half, three-quarters, and the finish shall be taken. If odd distances are raced, the fractions shall be noted accordingly.

§ 20. **Paddock Judge.**—Under the direction and supervision of the Presiding Judge, the Paddock Judge will have complete charge of all paddock activities as outlined in Rule 5 Section 10. The Paddock Judge is responsible for:

(a) Getting the fields on the track for post parades in accordance with the schedule given to him by the Presiding Judge.

(b) Inspection of horses for changes in equipment, broken or faulty equipment, head numbers or saddle pads.

(c) Supervision of paddock gate men.

(d) Proper check in and check out of horses and drivers.

Check the identification of all horses coming into the Paddock including the tattoo number.

(e) Direction of the activities of the paddock blacksmith.

(f) The Paddock Judge will immediately notify the Presiding Judge of anything that could in any way change, delay or otherwise affect the racing program.

The Paddock Judge will report any cruelty to any horse that he observes to the Presiding Judge.

(g) The Paddock Judge shall see that only properly authorized persons are permitted in the paddock and any violation of this rule may result in a fine, suspension or expulsion.

§ 21. **Program Director.**—Each extended pari-mutuel track shall designate a Program Director.

(a) It shall be the responsibility of the Program Director to furnish the public complete and accurate past performance information as required by Rule 7, Section 2.

(b) No person shall act as a Program Director at an extended pari-mutuel meeting unless he has secured a license from this Association. A license may be granted to any person who, by reason of his knowledge, experience and industry, is capable of furnishing accurate and complete past performance information to the general public.

(c) The annual fee for such license shall be **$10.00, which fee shall be in addition to the fee for active membership in this Association.**

§ 22. **Duties of Patrol Judges.**—The Patrol Judges shall observe all activity on the race track in their area at all times during the racing program. They shall immediately report to the Presiding Judge:

(a) Any action on the track which could improperly affect the result of a race.

(b) Every violation of the racing rules.

(c) Every violation of the rules of decorum.

(d) The lameness or unfitness of any horse.

(e) Any lack of proper racing equipment.

The Patrol Judges shall, furthermore:

(a) Be in constant communication with the Judges during the course of every race and shall immediately advise the Judges of every rule violation, improper act or unusual happening which occurs at their station.

(b) Submit individual daily reports of their observations of the racing to the Presiding Judge.

(c) When directed by the Presiding Judge shall attend hearings or inquiries on violations and testify thereat under oath.

§ 23. **Licensed Charter.**—The charting of races shall be done only by a licensed charter and he shall be responsible for providing a complete and accurate chart. A license may be granted only to a person who has the knowledge, training and industry to accomplish this. The annual fee for such a license shall be **$5.00, which fee is in addition to the fee for active membership in this Association.**

§ 24. **Mandatory Charting.**—At all extended pari-mutuel meetings and Grand Circuit Meetings the charting of races is mandatory and the track shall employ a licensed Charter to fulfill the requirements of this section.

§ 25. **Identifier.**—**At all extended pari-mutuel meetings the track member shall employ an identifier licensed by this Association, whose duty it shall be to check the identification of all horses coming into the paddock, to include the tattoo number, color, and any markings. The identifier shall be under the immediate supervision of the Paddock Judge and the general supervision of the Presiding Judge. Any discrepancy detected in the tattoo number, color, or markings of a horse shall be reported immediately to the Paddock Judge, who shall in turn report same forthwith to the Presiding Judge.**

RULE 7.
Identification of Horses

Section 1. Bona Fide Owner or Lessee.—Horses not under lease must race in the name of the bona fide owner. Horses under lease must race in the name of the lessee and a copy of the lease must be recorded with this Association. Persons violating this rule may be fined, suspended or expelled.

§ 2. **Program Information.**—A printed program shall be available to the public at all meetings where purses are raced for. All programs shall furnish:

(a) Horse's name and sex.

(b) Color and age.

(c) Sire and dam.

(d) Owner's name.

(e) Driver's name and colors.

At extended pari-mutuel meetings the following additional information shall be furnished:

(f) In claiming races the price for which the horse is entered to be claimed, **less allowances for age and sex,** must be indicated.

(g) At least the last six (6) performance and accurate chart lines. (See Rule 14, Section 2, Sub-Section (d). An accurate chart line shall include: Date of race, place, size of track if other than a half-mile track, symbol for free-legged pacers, track condition, type of race, distance, the fractional times of the leading horse including race time, post position, position at one quarter, one half, three quarters, stretch with lengths behind leader, finish with lengths behind leader, individual time of the horse, closing dollar odds, name of the driver, names of the horses placed first, second and third by the Judges. The standard symbols for breaks and park-outs shall be used, where applicable.

(h) Indicate drivers racing with a provisional license.

(i) Indicate pacers that are racing without hopples.

(j) Summary of starts in purse races, earnings, and best win time for current and preceding year. A horse's best win time may be earned in either a purse or non-purse race. Whenever the best win time of a horse taken to a single shaft sulky is published it shall be designated with the symbol SS as a suffix.

(k) The name of the trainer.

(l) The consolidated line shall carry date, place, time, driver, finish, track condition and distance, if race is not at one mile.

(m) At Fair and other non-extended meetings where pari-mutuel wagering is permitted the printed program shall contain at least a current summary on each horse to include the number of starts, firsts, seconds and thirds in the current year and also the earnings and best winning time for the current year.

§ 3. **Failure to Furnish Reliable Program Information** may subject the track and/or Program Director to a fine not to exceed $500.00 and/or the track and/or the Program Director may be suspended until arrangements are made to provide reliable program information.

§ 4. **Inaccurate Information.**—Owners,

drivers, or others found guilty of providing inaccurate information on a horse's performance, or of attempting to have misleading information given on a program may be fined, suspended, or expelled.

§ 5. **Check on Identity of Horse.**—Any track official, officer of this Association, or owner, trainer, or driver of any horse declared in to race wherein the question arises may call for information concerning the identity and eligibility of any horse on the grounds of a member, and may demand an opportunity to examine such horse or his eligibility certificate with a view to establish his identity or eligibility. If the owner or party controlling such horse shall refuse to afford such information, or to allow such examination, or fail to give satisfactory identification, the horse and the said owner or party may be barred by the member, and suspended or expelled by the President or Executive Vice-President.

§ 6. **False Chart Lines.**—Any official, clerk, or person who enters a chart line on an eligibility certificate when the race has not been charted by a licensed charter may be fined, suspended, or expelled.

§ 7. **Frivolous Demand for Identication.** Any person demanding the identification of a horse without cause, or merely with the intent to embarrass a race shall be punished by a fine not exceeding $100 or by suspension, or expulsion.

§ 8. **Tattoo Requirements.**—No horse that has not been tattooed will be permitted to start at an extended pari-mutuel meeting unless the permission of the Presiding Judge is obtained and arrangements are made to have the horse tattooed. Any person refusing to allow a horse to be tattooed **by a U.S.T.A. representative** may be fined, suspended or expelled, or further applications for registrations submitted by such person may be refused.

No horse may start in any race at an extended pari-mutuel or Grand Circuit meeting unless it is fully identified. The burden of establishing the identity of a horse rests with the person or persons having charge of the horse at the meeting, and in connection therewith any person found guilty of fraud or attempted fraud or any person who aids in any way in the perpetration of a fraud, or any person who participates in any attempt at fraud shall be expelled. Provided further that the provisions of this section shall not be interpreted as relieving the Paddock Judge and/or the Identifier from any responsibilities outlined in Rule 6, Sections 20 and 25.

§ 9. **Withholding Registration or Eligibility Certificate.**—Any person withholding a registration or eligibility certificate from the owner or lessee of a horse, after proper demand has been made for the return thereof, may be suspended until such time as the certificate is returned.

RULE 8.
Racing, Farm, Corporate or Stable Name

Section 1. Racing, farm, corporate, or stable names may be used by owners or lessees if registered with this Association giving the names of all persons who are interested in the stable or will use the name. The fee for such registration is $100.00. All stockholders of a corporation formed after April 1, 1962 and racing a horse must be members of the Association. The Executive Vice-President shall be notified immediately if additional persons become interested in a registered stable or if some person listed in a registration disassociates himself from the stable. Failure to do so will place the stable in violation of Rule 12, Section 3. Two stables cannot be registered under the same name and the Executive Vice-President may reject an application for a name that is confusing to the public, unbecoming to the sport, or exceeds 25 letters. All owners and persons listed in a registered stable, whether incorporated or not, shall be liable for entry fees and penalties against the registered stable. In the event one of the owners or persons listed in a registered stable is suspended, all the horses shall be included in accordance with Rule 22, Section 6. When a stable name is not in active use for a period of three consecutive years it will be placed on the inactive list.

When a stable name is inactive for a period of 15 years it will be presumed to be abandoned and may be reissued upon proper application.

§ 2. **Signature on Transfers and Other Documents Relating to Racing, Farm, Corporate and Stable Names.**—Only the signature of the corresponding officer of a racing, farm, corporate or stable name will be recognized on transfers and other documents pertaining to such organizations. Documents bearing the signature of the stable by the corresponding officer will be considered binding upon the members thereof.

Each member of a registered farm, corporate or stable should sign a document designating the name and address of the corresponding officer thereof—for future applications only.

RULE 9.
Eligibility and Classification

Section 1. **Eligibility Certificate.**—No horse shall be permitted to start in any race at a member track unless a current U.S.T.A. or validated C.T.A. eligibility certificate at the proper gait is obtained. The party making the declaration of a horse to a race shall present the eligibility certificate at the time of declaration or the declaration may be refused. Provided however, that telegraphic or telephone declarations may be accepted so long as the party making the declaration furnishes adequate program information, but the eligibility certificate must be presented when the horse arrives at the track and before he races.

The aforementioned requirements of this Section notwithstanding, the Judges may permit a horse to start without a current eligibility certificate being presented if they are satisfied that all of the following requirements have been met:

1. The issuance of the eligibility certificate for the horse is verified.

2. The eligibility of the horse to the event is established.

3. Satisfactory arrangements are made to have the performance information for the horse recorded on the eligibility certificate following the start and prior to any subsequent start.

In the event a horse is permitted to start without an eligibility certificate for the proper gait being on file with the Race Secretary at the time of the race, the owner or trainer may receive a fine in the amount of $50.00 and the track member may be fined in the amount of $10.00. The Race Secretary, or when the meeting is held at a contract track, the Association's authorized representative, shall check each eligibility certificate and certify to the Judges as to the eligibility of all the horses.

§ 2. **Fee for Eligibility Certificate and Replacement Certificate.**—The fee for a 1978 eligibility certificate shall be $5.00, and for 1979 and thereafter, the fee shall be $10.00. In the event of the loss or destruction of an eligibility certificate, a replacement certificate may be issued to the same owner upon payment of a base fee of $10.00 plus $2.00 additional for each start made by the horse during the current year, with the maximum charge to be $30.00. The application for the replacement certificate must be accompanied by a signed statement from the owner or trainer certifying that the original certificate is lost or destroyed and listing the starts, together with all fair races, qualifying races, and matinee races made by the horse during the current year.

Applications for eligibility certificates must state the name and address of the owner, and the sex, age and breeding of the horse.

§ 3. **Issuance of Eligibility Certificate.**

(a) An eligibility certificate shall be issued only to an active member of this Association in good standing and shall not be issued to an owner or horse under penalty except as provided in Rule 1, Section 3.

(b) **Joint Ownership.**—When a horse is owned jointly by two or more parties, all owners must be members in good standing in this Association before an eligibility certificate will be issued.

(c) **Sale or Lease During Current Year.**— When a horse is sold or leased after an eligibility certificate is issued for the current year, the seller or his agent duly authorized in writing shall deliver the eligibility and current registration certificates of the horse to any licensed official of this Association. If the horse is to be leased an original executed copy of said lease shall be delivered therewith. Said official shall examine such Registration Certificate to verify that it is in proper order and that the current registered owner is the same as the current holder of the eligibility certificate and that the prospective transferees or lessees are members of this Association in good standing. If the endorsements are satisfactory said official shall endorse the eligibility certificate to the new owner and forward the Registration Certificate or the lease to the Registrar for proper transfer or recording of lease as the case may be.

Failure to forward the registration certificate or an executed copy of the lease within twenty (20) days after purchase or lease of an animal which is racing will subject the buyer or lessee to a fine not to exceed $100.00.

(d) **Leased Horses.**—Any horse on lease must race in the name of the lessee. No eligibility certificate will be issued to a horse under lease unless a copy of the lease is filed with the Association and unless both lessor and lessee are current members of this As-

sociation in good standing. Beginning with eligibility certificates issued for 1978 and thereafter the name of both the owner and lessee shall be noted on the eligibility certificates of leased horses.

(e) **Procedure Where Eligibility Certificate Is Not Endorsed.**—If the eligibility certificate is not endorsed to him, the new owner or lessee must apply for an eligibility certificate, pay the regular fee, send satisfactory information on the starts made by the horse during the current year which will include all fair races, qualifying races and matinee races.

(f) **Information Required From Horses Racing at Canadian Tracks.**—Prior to declarations, owners of horses having Canadian eligibility certificates shall furnish the Racing Secretary with a Canadian eligibility certificate completely filled out for the current year, which has a certificate of validation attached thereto. Residents of Canada under Canadian Trotting Association jurisdiction holding eligibility certificates who are members of this Association may obtain a validation certificate by filing an application with this Association. Residents of the United States and the Maritime Provinces holding Canadian eligibility certificates **for the current year** must have the horse registered in current ownership in The United States Trotting Association register before a validation certificate can be obtained by filing an application with this Association. The fee shall be the same as that for an eligibility certificate. This validation certificate may then be attached to the Canadian eligibility certificate and used at tracks in membership with this Association. **Provided, however, that where the Canadian elegibility certificate is not for the current year, a complete U.S.T.A. eligibility certificate application must be submitted along with the Canadian eligibility certificate and the fee therefor shall be $5.00 plus $2.00 per start for each start during the current year, with a maximum total charge of $25.00.**

No validation certificate will be issued in the name of the lessee unless a copy of the lease is on file with either The United States Trotting Association or the Canadian Trotting Association.

(g) **Tampering With Eligibility Certificates.**—Persons tampering with eligibility certificates may be fined, suspended or expelled and winnings after such tampering may be ordered forfeited.

(h) **Corrections On Eligibility Certificates.**

—Corrections on eligibility certificates may be made only by a representative of this Association or a licensed official who shall place on the certificate his initial and date.

(i) **Withholding Eligibility Certificates On Horses Not Tattooed.**—An eligibility certificate may be denied to any person refusing to permit his horses to be tattooed.

§ 4. **Information Required On Horses That Have Raced In A Country Other Than Canada.**—No eligibility certificate will be issued on a horse coming from a country other than Canada unless the following information, certified by the Trotting Association or governing body of that country from which the horse comes, is furnished:

(a) The number of starts during the preceding year, together with the number of firsts, seconds and thirds for each horse, and the total amount of money won during this period.

(b) The number of races in which the horse has started during the current year, together with number of firsts, seconds and thirds for each horse and the money won during this period.

(c) A detailed list of the last six starts giving the date, place, track condition, post position or handicap, if it was a handicap race, distance of the race, his position at the finish, the time of the race, the driver's name, and the first three horses in the race.

§ 5. (a) **Registration of Standard and Non-Standard Bred Horses.**—All foals of 1937 and thereafter shall be registered in current ownership either as Standard or Non-Standard. If registration is properly applied for and all fees paid, an eligibility certificate for one year may be issued and marked "registration applied for."

(b) **Horses 15 Years of Age or Older.**—No eligibility certificate shall be issued to any horse that is fifteen years of age or older to perform in any race except in a matinee.

(c) **Use of Eligibility Certificates During the Month of January.**—Authorization may be granted to use eligibility certificates from the previous year during the month of January.

(d) **Bar On Racing of Yearlings.**—No eligibility certificate will be issued on any horse under two years of age.

(e) Except as provided in paragraph (a) of this Section, no eligibility certificate will be issued on any horse not registered with this Association.

§ 6. **Racing Stables and Corporations.—Limitation on Number of Owners.**—

(a) Eligibility Certificates will be issued to a corporation only when the corporation is recorded with the Association to show the officers, directors and stockholders.

(b) No entity whether it be a partnership, a corporation or a registered stable, comprising more than ten (10) persons will be acceptable either to race or to lease horses for racing.

(c) For the purposes of determining the maximum of ten (10) persons described in (b) above, who can be involved in the ownership or lease of a horse for racing purposes, a spouse, and blood relatives of a single family limited to sons, daughters, father, mother, brothers, sisters, aunts, uncles, grandparents, nieces and nephews shall be regarded collectively as one shareholder partner or member as the case may be.

(d) Wherever there are more than five owners or more than five lessees of a horse for racing purposes the use of a stable name, registered under the provisions of Rule 8, Section 1 is mandatory.

(e) **Where a stallion three years of age or older has been syndicated for breeding purposes for $100,000.00 or more, the provisions of Subsections (b) and (c) herein notwithstanding, the President or Executive Vice-President may approve the involvement of more than ten persons either to race or lease a horse for racing purposes.**

§ 7. **Eligibility.**—For purposes of eligibility, a racing season or a racing year shall be the calendar year. In recording winnings, gross winnings will be used and odd cents will be dropped and disregarded.

§ 8. **Time Bars Prohibited.**—No time records or bars shall be used as an element of eligibility.

§ 9. **Date When Eligibility Is Determined.**—Horses must be eligible when entries close but winnings on closing date of eligibility shall not be considered.

In mixed races, trotting and pacing, a horse must be eligible to the class at the gait at which it is stated in the entry the horse will perform.

§ 10. **Conflicting Conditions.**—In the event there are conflicting published conditions and neither is withdrawn by the member, the more favorable to the nominator shall govern.

§ 11. **Standards for Overnight Events.**—The Race Secretary should prescribe standards to determine whether a horse is qualified to race in overnight events at a meeting. **Where time standards are established at a meeting for both trotters and pacers, trotters shall be given a minimum of two seconds allowance in relation to pacers.**

§ 12. **Posting of Overnight Conditions.**— Conditions for overnight events must be posted at least 18 hours before entries close at meetings other than extended pari-mutuel meetings.

At extended pari-mutuel meetings, condition books will be prepared and races may be divided or substituted races may be used only where regularly scheduled races fail to fill, except where they race less than 5 days a week. Such books containing at least three days racing program will be available to horsemen at least 24 hours prior to closing declarations on any race program contained therein.

The Race Secretary shall forward copies of each condition book and overnight sheet to the U.S.T.A. office as soon as they are available to the horsemen.

§ 13. **Types of Races to be Offered.**—In presenting a program of racing, the racing secretary shall use exclusively the following types of races:

1. Stakes and Futurities.
2. Early Closing and Late Closing Events.
3. Conditioned Races.
4. Claiming Races.
5. Preferred races limited to the fastest horses at the meeting. These may be Free-For-All Races, JFA, or Invitationals. Horses to be used in such races shall be posted in the Race Secretary's office and listed with the Presiding Judge. Horses so listed shall not be eligible for conditioned overnight races unless the conditions specifically include horses on the preferred list. Twelve such races may be conducted during a 6-day period of racing at tracks distributing more than $100,000 in overnight purses during such period and not more than 10 such races shall be conducted at other tracks during a 6-day period of racing, provided that at least two of these races are for three year olds, four year olds, or combined three and four year olds. At tracks which race less than 5 days per week, not more than ten such races may be conducted during a 6-day period. Purses offered for such races shall be at least 15% higher than the highest purse offered for a conditioned race programmed the same racing week.

No 2-year-old or 3-year-old will be eligible to be placed on the preferred or invitational list to race against older horses until it has won 7 races unless requested by the owner or authorized agent. The owner or authorized agent may withdraw such request at his discretion.

Where a meeting is in progress in December and continues in January of the subsequent year, races and earnings won at that meeting may be computed in determining whether a horse may be placed on the preferred list.

6. Classified races are permitted when authorized by the State Racing Commission.

§ 14. **Limitation on Conditions.**—Conditions shall not be written in such a way that any horse is deprived of an opportunity to race in normal preference cycle. Where the word "preferred" is used in a condition it shall not supersede date preference. Not more than three also eligible conditions shall be used in writing the conditions for any overnight event.

§ 15. **Dashes and Heats.**—Any dash or any heat shall be considered as a separate race for the purposes of conditioned racing.

§ 16. **Named Races.**—Named races are not permitted except for preferred races for the fastest horses at a meeting as set forth in Section 13 (5) above, and invitational two, three or four-year-old races with a purse at least 15% higher than the highest purse offered for a conditioned race programmed the same racing week.

§ 17. **Selection or Drawing of Horses.**— For all overnight events, starters and also eligibles shall be drawn by lot from those properly declared in, except that a Race Secretary must establish a preference system for races as provided for in Rule 14 Section 5. However, where necessary to fill a card, not more than one conditioned race per day may be divided into not more than two divisions after preference has been applied and the divisions may be selected by the Racing Secretary. For all other overnight races that are divided the division must be by lot unless the conditions provide for a division based on performance, earnings or sex.

§ 18. **Posting Requirements.**—Names of all horses at the track ready to race shall be posted by gait in the declaration room, together with all the pertinent information concerning such horse which may be required to determine eligibility of such horse to conditioned races offered at the track. There shall be a separate posting of two, three and four-year-olds.

§ 19. **Supplemental Purse Payments.**— Supplemental purse payments made by a track after the termination of a meeting will be charged and credited to the winnings of any horse at the end of the racing year in which they are distributed, and will appear on the eligibility certificate issued for the subsequent year. Such distribution shall not affect the current eligibility until placed on the next eligibility certificate by this Association.

§ 20. **Rejection of Declaration.**—

(a) The Racing Secretary may reject the declaration on any horse whose eligibility certificate was not in his possession on the date the condition book is published.

(b) The Racing Secretary may reject the declaration on any horse whose past performance indicates that he would be below the competitive level of other horses declared, provided the rejection does not result in a race being cancelled.

§ 21. **Substitute and Divided Races.**— Substitute races may be provided for each day's program and shall be so designated. Entries in races not filling shall be posted. A substitute race or a race divided into two divisions shall be used only if regularly scheduled races fail to fill.

If a regular race fills it shall be raced on the day it was offered.

Overnight events and substitutes shall not be carried to the next racing day.

§ 22. **Opportunities to Race.**—A fair and reasonable racing opportunity shall be afforded both trotters and pacers in reasonable proportion from those available and qualified to race. Claiming races may be carded to the proportion of each week's racing program as the number of claiming authorizations on file with the Racing Secretary bears to the total number of horses on the grounds which are qualified and available for racing.

§ 23. **Qualifying Races.**—A horse qualifying in a Qualifying race for which no purse is offered shall not be deprived by reason of such performance of his right to start in any conditioned race.

§ 24. **Definition of "Start."**—The definition of the word "start" in any type of condition unless specifically so stated will include only those performances in a purse race. Qualifying and matinee races are excluded.

§ 25. **Sandwiching Races.**—Not more than five races may be sandwiched.

§ 26. When it is determined that a horse is infected with, and/or is a carrier of equine infectious anemia by means of the "Gel Immuno-Diffusion" method developed by Dr.

Leroy Coggins, hereinafter known as the "Coggins Test" and conducted by an approved laboratory, such horse shall, thereafter, be prohibited from racing and/or being stabled as a track member.

(a) A negative "Coggins Test Certificate" properly identifying the horse by tattoo number issued by an approved laboratory, certifying that within the prior twelve months the horse has been tested negative shall be presented to a track member for any horse before it will be allowed entrance to, or remain upon, the grounds of a track member conducting meetings.

(b) Declarations shall not be accepted for any horse to any race unless the declarer has furnished the Race Secretary with a negative "Coggins Test" written certificate for that horse, as required by sub-section (a) above.

(c) No eligibility or validation certificate shall be issued for a horse from which a positive "Coggins Test" has been reported. If an eligibility or validation certificate is issued and it is determined thereafter that the horse for which the certificate has been issued has equine infectious anemia and/or is a carrier thereof, the certificate must be returned immediately by the holder to this Association.

§ 27. **Exhibition Races.**—Where non-betting promotional races such as celebrity races, junior driving championships, collegiate driving championships or other similar events are conducted by member tracks, such races shall be regarded as exhibitions and performances therein shall not be noted on eligibility certificates or otherwise officially credited to either horses or drivers. Any money awarded or paid on such races shall not be credited to the horses or drivers as official earnings and shall not affect the eligibility of participating horses to any subsequent event.

RULE 10.
Claiming Races

Section 1. **Who May Claim.**—An owner and/or lessee of a horse that has been declared and programmed to start in a purse race at that meeting. An authorized agent may claim for a qualified owner. Any member seeking to effect a false claim by inducing another to claim a horse for him will be subject to the penalties provided by Section 10 herein.

§ 2. Prohibitions.—

(a) No person shall claim his own horse, nor shall he claim a horse trained or driven by him.

(b) No person shall claim more than one horse in a race.

(c) No qualified owner or his agent shall claim a horse for another person.

(d) No owner shall cause his horse to be claimed directly or indirectly for his own account.

(e) No person shall offer, or enter into an agreement, to claim or not to claim, or attempt to prevent another person from claiming any horse in a claiming race.

(f) No person shall enter a horse against which there is a mortgage, bill of sale, or lien of any kind, unless the written consent of the holder thereof shall be filed with the Clerk of the Course of the Association conducting such claiming race.

(g) Any entry in a claiming race cannot declare for a subsequent race until after the claiming race has been contested.

(h) No mare known to be in foal may be declared into a claiming race.—

§ 3. Claiming Procedure.—

(a) **Owner's Credit.**—The owner must have to his credit with the track giving the race an amount equivalent to the specified claiming price plus the requisite fees for transfer of registration.

(b) **Owner's Consent.**—No declaration may be accepted unless written permission of the owner is filed with the Race Secretary at the time of declaration.

(c) **On Program.**—The basic claiming price for which each horse is entered shall be printed on the program, but all claims shall be for the adjusted price after the prescribed allowances made for sex and/or age have been added to the basic price.

(d) **Claim Box.**—All claims shall be in writing, sealed and deposited at least fifteen minutes before the time originally scheduled for the race to begin, in a locked box provided for this purpose by the Clerk of the Course.

(e) **Opening of Claim Box.**—No official shall open said box or give any information on claims filed until after the race. Immediately after the race, the claim box shall be opened and the claim, if any, examined by the Judges.

(f) **Multiple Claims on Same Horses.**— Should more than one claim be filed for the same horse, the owner shall be determined by lot by the Judges.

(g) **Delivery of Claimed Horse.**—A horse claimed shall be delivered immediately by the original owner or his trainer to the successful claimant upon authorization of the Presiding Judge. The horses' halter must accompany the horse. Altering or removing the horse's shoes will be considered a violation of this rule.

(h) **Refusal to Deliver Claimed Horse.**— Any person who refuses to deliver a horse legally claimed out of a claiming race shall be suspended together with the horse until delivery is made.

(i) **Vesting of Title to Claimed Horse.**— Every horse claimed shall race in all heats or dashes of the event in the interest and for the account of the owner who declared it in the event, but title to the claimed horse shall be vested in the successful claimant from the time the word "go" is given in the first heat or dash, and said successful claimant shall become the owner of the horse, whether it be alive or dead or sound or unsound, or injured during the race or after it, provided however that the final vesting of title to a claimed horse is subject to the conditions and provisions of Rule 10, Section 3 (n).

(j) **Affidavit by Claimant.**—The judges shall require any person making a claim for a horse to make affidavit that he is claiming said horse for his own account or as authorized agent and not for any other person. Any person making such affidavit willfully and falsely shall be subject to punishment as hereinafter provided.

(k) **Penalty for Thirty Days.**—If a horse is claimed, no right, title or interest therein shall be sold or transferred except in a claiming race for a period of 30 days following the date of claiming.

(l) **Return of Claimed Horse to Owner or Stable.**—No horse claimed out of a claiming race shall be eligible to start in any race in the name or interest of the original owner for thirty days, nor shall such horse remain in the same stable or under the care or management of the first owner or trainer, or anyone connected therewith unless reclaimed out of another claiming race.

(m) **Scratched Horse.**—The successful claimant of a horse programmed to start may, at his option, acquire ownership of a claimed horse, even through such claimed horse was scratched and did not start in the claiming race from which it was scratched. The successful claimant must exercise his option by 9:00 a.m. of the day following the claiming race to which the horse was programmed and scratched. **No horse may be** claimed from a claiming race unless the race is contested.

(n) **Blood Sample Procedure If Horse Is Claimed.**—In the event a horse is claimed a blood sample shall be taken by a licensed veterinarian, and the sample identified as being from a claimed horse shall be forwarded within 24 hours to an approved laboratory to be tested for equine infectious anemia. Pending the receipt of a negative test for equine infectious anemia the monies paid for the claimed horse shall be held by the track member. In the event of a positive test for equine infectious anemia the ownership of the claimed horse shall revert to the owner from whom the horse was claimed and the claiming monies shall be returned to the person or persons who claimed the horse. The cost of the test is to be borne by the claimant and the test may be waived by the claimant at his discretion by so indicating on the claiming slip.

§ 4. **Claiming Price.**—Subject to the conditions of Rule 10, Section 3 (n) the track shall pay the claiming price to the owner at the time the registration certificate is delivered for presentation to the successful claimant.

§ 5. **Claiming Conditions.**—Aside from claiming price, conditions and allowances in claiming races may be based only on age and sex. Whenever possible claiming races shall be written to separate horses five years old and up from young horses and to separate males from females. If sexes are mixed, males shall be given a price allowance, provided, however, that there shall be no price allowance given to a spayed mare racing in a claiming race.

Optional claiming races shall not be used unless limited to horses six years old and up.

§ 6. **Minimum Price.**—No claiming race shall be offered permitting claims for less than the minimum purse offered at that time during the same racing week.

§ 7. **Determination of Claiming Price.**—Except as provided in Section 3 (k) of this rule, and except as provided in Rule 9, Section 20, no horse owner shall be prohibited from determining the price for which his horse shall be entered.

§ 8. (a) If the Judges determine that the declaration of any horse to a claiming race is fraudulent on the part of the declarer they may void the claim and at the option of the claimant order the horse returned to the person declaring it in.

(b) If the Judges determine that any claim of a horse is fraudulent on the part of the person making the claim they may void the claim and may, at the option of the person declaring it in, return the horse to the person declaring it in.

§ 9. The current Registration Certificate of all horses entered in claiming races must be on file with the Racing Secretary together with a separate claiming authorization form signed by the registered owner or owners and indicating the minimum amount for which the horse may be entered to be claimed. To facilitate transfer of claimed horses the Presiding Judge may sign the transfer provided that he then send the Registration Certificate and claiming authorization to the Registrar for transfer.

§ 10. Any person violating any of the provisions of this rule, shall be fined, suspended, or expelled.

RULE 11.
Stakes and Futurities

Section 1. All stake and futurity sponsors or presentors, except contract tracks:

(a) Shall be members of this Association.

(b) Shall make an annual application for approval containing:

(1) Satisfactory evidence of financial responsibility.

(2) Proposed conditions.

(3) Sums to be deducted for organization or promotion.

(4) **Bond.** An agreement to file with the Association a surety bond in the amount of the fund conditioned on faithful performance of the conditions, including a guarantee that said stake or futurity will be raced as advertised in said conditions unless unanimous consent is obtained from owners of eligibles to transfer or change the date thereof, or unless prevented by an act of God or conditions beyond the control of the sponsor, segregation of funds and making all payments. In any instance where an association furnishes to the U.S.T.A. substantial evidence of financial responsibility satisfactory to the U.S.T.A., such evidence may be accepted by U.S.T.A. in lieu of a surety bond.

State Agency.—Where funds are held by a state or an authorized agency thereof, this provision will not apply.

Trust Funds.—Collections resulting from the forfeiting of any bond will be paid to the contestants according to the order of finish, or in the event the race is not contested, will be divided equally among owners of eligibles on the date the breach of conditions occurs.

(5) **Waiver of Bond.**—The requirement of a bond may be waived by the President of the Association upon written request of a sponsor who is a track member and whose financial statement shows a net worth of five times the amount of trust funds received from payments in stakes and futurities. Where this is permitted, the sponsor will furnish a certified copy of the bank deposit in lieu of the bond.

(c) **Rejection of Application.**—May appeal the rejection of an application to the Executive Committee within 20 days after the mailing of the notice of rejection by registered mail.

(d) **Receipt of Printed Conditions.**—U.S.T.A. must receive printed conditions of all stakes and futurities by closing date of said stakes and futurities. Printed conditions not received by closing date may be refused printing in the Stakes and Futurities Guide.

(e) **Conflicting Conditions.**—Stakes and Futurities conditions which conflict with U.S.T.A. rules and regulations may be refused printing in the Stakes and Futurities Guide.

(f) **List of Nominations.**—Shall mail list of nominations within (60) days after the date of closing to this Association.

(g) **Financial Statement.**—Shall furnish this Association with an annual financial statement of each stake or futurity and, within 30 days following day of race, submit to this Association a final financial statement.

(h) **Failure to Fill.**—Shall notify all nominators and this Association within 20 days if the stake or futurity does not fill.

(i) **List of Eligibles.**—Shall mail within (30) days a complete list of all horses remaining eligible, to this Association, segregated by age, sex and gait, and shall mail within 30 days following the last payment before the starting fee, a complete list of all horses remaining eligible, segregated by age, sex and gait, to the owners or agents of all eligibles and to this Association together with a list of any nominations transferred or substituted, if such is permitted by the conditions.

This list of eligibles shall also include a resume indicating the current financial status of the stake or futurity, or of each individual division thereof if there is more than one division, by listing the number of horses remaining eligible, the amount of money that has been paid in and the amount to be added. The purse shall constitute this amount plus starting fees, if any.

(j) **Nominating and Sustaining Payment Dates.**—Shall set the nominating date and the dates for all sustaining payments except the starting fee on the fifteenth day of the month, and there shall be no payments on yearlings except a nomination payment and such nomination payment shall be due not later than August 15th. Before taking any sustaining payments during the year the race is to be contested, the date and place of the race shall be stated. No stake or futurity sustaining fee on two-year-olds shall become due prior to March 15th, and for all other ages not prior to February 15th of any year. There shall be no conditions that call for payments in stakes or futurities to fall due after August 15th and before February 15 of the following year effective in the year 1974 and thereafter.

No more than one sustaining payment on two-year-olds in stakes and futurities that do not have a two-year-old division will be permitted. No more than two sustaining payments on any horse of any age in any calendar year with the exception of the starting fee will be approved.

Beginning with stakes and futurities closing in 1973 and thereafter, the date for closing of nominations of yearlings to stakes shall be May 15th and the date for closing of the nominations to futurities shall be July 15th.

(k) **Notice of Place and Date of Race.**—Shall, if possible, advertise the week and place the stake or futurity will be raced before taking nominations. Otherwise announcement of the week and place shall be made as soon as the stake or futurity is sold or awarded.

(l) **Forms.**—All nominations and entry forms lists of nominations and lists of eligibles shall be on standard 8½ x 11 paper. Such lists shall list the owners alphabetically.

(m) **Estimated Purse.**—No estimated purse shall be advertised or published in excess of the actual purse paid or distributed during the previous year, unless increased by guaranteed added money. No stake or futurity shall be raced for less than 75% of the average estimated purse.

(n) Beginning with any new Stakes and Futurities which originate after January 1, 1978 and for which nominations close after January 1, 1978, no conditions shall be written so as to permit a horse to race in more than two heats or dashes in a single day. This provision shall not apply to Stakes and Futurities in existence as of March 8, 1977.

(o) **Beginning with stakes and futurities for which nominations close after January 1, 1979, no conditions shall be written so as to provide for a filly division of a race with less added money than the colt division of a race, unless said conditions allow for a filly, properly nominated and sustained in the filly division, to start in the colt division upon proper declaration and the payment of the starting fee required for the colt division and the difference between any lower nominating and/or sustaining fees for the filly division and the higher nominating and/or sustaining fees for the colt division.**

§ 2. **Sponsor's Contribution.**—The sum contributed by a sponsor who is not a track member shall be considered forfeit and is to be included in the sum distributed in the event the stake or futurity is not raced, provided, however, that for the provisions of this paragraph the term "sum contributed" shall not include added money to be paid by a track member or other responsible party where the track member or other responsible party is someone other than the stake sponsor. In such a case, the stake sponsor shall not be held liable for the payment of the added money.

Effective with stakes and futurities opened in 1969 and thereafter, no stake or futurity shall be approved for extended pari-mutuel meetings if the added money is not at least 30 percent of the purse and for all other meetings at least 10 percent of the purse shall be added.

In the event a stake or futurity is split into divisions, the added money for each division shall be at least 20 percent of all nomination, sustaining and starting fees paid into such stake or futurity; provided, however, that in the case of a stake with a value of $20,000 or less, and conducted at a nonextended meeting, such stake may be divided and each division raced for an equal share of the total purse if the advertised conditions so provide.

If an event is not raced due to circumstances beyond the control of a non-track operating sponsor, then such stake sponsor is not required to contribute a sum as added money but need only refund such nominating, sustaining and starting fees as it has collected toward the canceled event.

§ 3. **Failure to Make Payment.**—Failure to make any payment required by the conditions constitutes an automatic withdrawal from the event.

§ 4. **Refund of Nomination Fee.**—In the event that a mare nominated to a futurity fails to have a live foal, the nominator may substitute a foal if the conditions so provide.

§ 5. **Registration of Names.**—All names of stakes and futurities, including names of specific events which are raced as part of any stake or futurity, may be registered with this Association for a fee of $25. Such registered names shall not be used to identify any other stake, futurity, early closer, late closer or overnight event. Names of farms or active horses, including stallions and brood mares, may not be registered as names for stakes and futurities without written permission of the owner or owners. Names of living persons may not be used without written permission of the person involved. Names of inactive horses, farms or persons no longer living must be approved by this Association before being registered.

§ 6. **Nominators' or Breeders' Awards.**—Beginning with stakes and futurities closing in 1973, and thereafter, no sponsor shall pay monetary awards to nominators or breeders out of stake or futurity funds.

§ 7. **Deductions Prohibited.**—No deduction, voluntary or involuntary, may be made from any purse or stake or futurity except that, if the conditions specifically so provide, reasonable deductions may be made for clerical, printing, postage and surety bond expenses specifically related to such purse, stake or futurity.

§ 8. **Money Division.**—Unless otherwise specified in the conditions of a stake or futurity, the money division shall be: 5 or more starters: 50-25-12-8-5%; 4 starters only: 50-25-15-10%; 3 starters only: 60-30-10%; 2 starters only: 65-35%.

§ 9. If the sponsor has failed to comply with the provisions of the within rules, the Executive Vice-President shall be authorized to refuse renewals of such Stakes and Futurities and/or to impose a fine not to exceed $100.00.

RULE 12.
Entries

Section 1. All entries must:

(a) Be made in writing.

(b) Be signed by the owner or his authorized agent except as provided in Rule 14, Section 1.

(c) Give name and address of both the bona fide owner and agent or registered stable name or lessee.

(d) Give name, color, sex, sire and dam of horse.

(e) Name the event or events in which the horse is to be entered.

(f) Entries in overnight events must also comply with the provisions of Rule 14, Section 1.

§ 2. **Payment of Starting Fee.**—Starting fee shall be due and payable with declaration to start and will not be refunded if horse fails to start unless horse dies between time of declaration to start and start of race. For purposes of clarification, starting fee shall be defined as the payment required with declaration to start.

§ 3. **Penalties.**—The penalty for noncompliance with any of the above requirements is a fine of not less than $5.00 nor more than $50.00 for each offense. If the facts are falsely stated for the purpose of deception, the guilty party shall be fined and/or suspended or expelled.

§ 4. **Receipt of Entries for Early Closing Events, Late Closing Events, Stakes and Futurities.**—All entries not actually received at the hour of closing shall be ineligible, except entries by letter bearing postmark not later than the following day (omitting Sunday) or entries notified by telegraph, the telegram to be actually received at the office of sending at or before the hour of closing, such telegram to state the color, sex, and name of the horse, the class to be entered; also to give the name and residence of the owner and the party making entry. Whenever an entry or payment in a stake, futurity, or early closing race becomes payable on a Sunday or a legal holiday that falls on Saturday, such payment is to be due on the following Monday and if made by mail the envelope must be postmarked on or before the following Tuesday. If a payment falls on a Monday that is a legal holiday, such payment is due on Tuesday, and if made by mail must be postmarked on or before the following Wednesday.

Postage Meter.—Where an entry is received by letter bearing the postage meter date without any postmark placed thereon by the Post Office Department, such postage meter date shall be considered to be a postmark for the purposes of this rule if the letter is actually received within seven days following the closing date of the event. Receipt subsequent to this time of an entry by letter bearing the metered postmark date shall not be a valid entry or payment to any event. The metered date, of course, must conform to the postmark date as set forth above in order to be valid.

§ 5. **Deviation from Published Conditions.**—All entries and payments not governed by published conditions shall be void and any proposed deviation from such published conditions shall be punished by a fine not to exceed $50 for each offense, and any nominator who is allowed privileges not in accordance with the published conditions of the race, or which are in conflict with these rules, shall be debarred from winning any portion of the purse, and the said nominator and the Secretary or other persons who allowed such privileges shall be deemed to have been parties to a fraud.

§ 6. **Where Ineligible Horse Races.**—A nominator is required to guarantee the identity and eligibility of his **nominations** and declarations and if given incorrectly he may be fined, suspended, or expelled, and any winnings shall be forfeited and redistributed to eligible entries. A person obtaining a purse or money through fraud or error shall surrender or pay the same to this Association, if demanded by the Executive Vice President, or he, together with the parties implicated in the wrong, and the horse or horses shall be suspended until such demand is complied with and such purse or money shall be awarded to the party justly entitled to the same. However, where any horse is ineligible as a result of the negligence of the Race Secretary, the track shall reimburse the owner for the resultant loss of winnings.

§ 7. **Transfer of Ineligible Horse.**—A horse entered in an event to which it is ineligible, may be transferred to any event to which he is eligible at the same gait.

§ 8. **Withholding Purse on Ineligible Horse.**—Members shall be warranted in withholding the premium of any horse, without a formal protest, if they shall receive information in their judgment tending to establish that the entry or declaration was fraudulent or ineligible. Premiums withheld under this rule shall be forthwith sent to The United States Trotting Association to await the result of an investigation by the member or by the District Board of Review, and if the eligibility of the horse is not established within thirty days he shall be barred from winning unless the case is appealed to the Board of Appeals.

§ 9. **Agreement to Race Under Rule.**—Every entry shall constitute an agreement that the person making it, the owner, lessee, manager, agent, nominator, driver, or other person having control of the horse, and the horse shall be subject to these Rules and Regulations, and will submit all disputes and questions arising out of such entry to the authority and the judgment of this Association, whose decision shall be final.

§ 10. **Early Closing Events and Late Closing Races.**—

(a) **Date and Place.**—The sponsor shall state the place and day the event will be raced and no change in date, program, events, or conditions can be made after the nominations have been taken without the written consent of the owners or trainer of all horses eligible at the time the conditions are changed.

(b) **File Conditions.**—An entry blank shall be filed with the Executive Vice-President.

(c) **Payments on the Fifteenth of the Month.**—All nominations and payments other than starting fees in early closing events shall be advertised to fall on the fifteenth day of the month.

(d) **List of Nominations.**—A complete list of nominations to any late closing race or early closing event shall be published within twenty (20) days after the date of closing and mailed to each nominator and the Executive Vice-President.

(e) **Procedure If Event Does Not Fill.**—If the event does not fill, each nominator and the Executive Vice-President shall be notified within ten (10) days and refund of nomination fees shall accompany the notice.

(f) **Transfer Provisions—Change of Gait.**—Unless a track submits its early closing conditions to the USTA at least 30 days prior to the first publication and has such conditions approved the following provisions will govern transfers in the event of a change of gait. If conditions published for early closing events allow transfer for change of gait, such transfer shall be to the slowest class the horse is eligible to at the adopted gait, eligibility to be determined at time of closing of entries, the race to which transfer may be made must be the one nearest the date of the event originally entered.

Two-year-olds, three-year-olds, or four-year-olds, entered in classes for their age, may only transfer to classes for same age group at the adopted gate to the race nearest the date of the event originally entered, entry fees to be adjusted.

§ 11. **Subsequent Payments—Lists of Eligibles.**—If subsequent payments are required, a complete list of those withdrawn or declared out shall be made within fifteen (15) days after the payment was due and the list mailed to each nominator and the Executive Vice-President.

§ 12. **Trust Funds.**—All fees paid in early closing events shall be segregated and held as trust funds until the event is contested.

§ 13. **Early Closing Events by New Member.**—No early closing events may be advertised or nominations taken therefor for a pari-mutuel meeting that has not had its application approved by the President, unless the track has been licensed for the preceding year. Members accepting nominations to Early Closing Races, Late Closing Races, Stakes and Futurities will give stable space to any horse nominated and eligible to such event the day before, the day of, and the day after such race.

§ 14. **Limitation on Conditions.**—Conditions of Early Closing Events or Late Closing Races that will eliminate horses nominated to an event or add horses that have not been nominated to an event by reason of the performance of such horses at an earlier meeting held the same season, are invalid. Early Closing Events and Late Closing Events shall have not more than two also eligible conditions.

§ 15. **Penalties.**—Any official or member who fails to comply with any provisions of this rule shall be fined, suspended or expelled, unless otherwise provided.

§ 16. **Excess Entry Fees.**—In Early Closing races, Late Closing races, and Overnight races requiring entry fees, all monies paid in by the nominators in excess of 85% of the advertised purse shall be added to the advertised purse and the total shall then be considered to be the minimum purse. If the race is split and raced in divisions, the provisions of Rule 13, Section 2 (b) shall apply.

RULE 13.
Entries and Starters Required Split Races

Section 1. An association must specify how many entries are required for overnight events and after the condition is fulfilled, the event must be contested except when declared off as provided in Rule 15.

In early closing events, or late closing events, if five or more horses are declared in to start, the race must be contested, except when declared off as provided in Rule 15. (Pari-mutuel meetings may require five interests to start.) Stakes and Futurities must be raced if one or more horses are declared in to start except when declared off as provided in Rule 15.

In an early closing event, if less horses, are declared in than are required to start, and all declarers are immediately so notified, the horse or horses declared in and ready to race shall be entitled to all the entrance money and any forfeits from each horse named.

§ 2. **Elimination Heats or Two Divisions.**—

(a) In any race where the number of horses declared in to start exceeds 12 on a half-mile track, 14 on a ⅝-mile track, or 16 on a larger track, **unless lesser numbers are specified in the conditions of the race,** the race, at the option of the track member conducting same, stated before positions are drawn, may be raced in elimination heats.

In the absence of conditions providing for a lesser number of starters, no more than two tiers of horses, allowing eight feet per horse, will be allowed to start in any race, and in no event shall there be allowed more than 12 starters on a half-mile track, 14 starters on a ⅝-mile track or 16 starters on a larger track.

(b) Where a race other than a stake or futurity is divided, each division must race for at least 75 percent of the advertised purse. (For splitting of stakes and futurities see Rule 11, Section 2).

Provided, however, that at non-extended meetings, in the case of added money early closing events, and early closers and late closers with a value of $20,000 or less, the race may be divided and raced in divisions and each division raced for an equal share of the total purse if the advertised conditions so provide.

§ 3. **Elimination Plans.**—(a) Whenever elimination heats are required, or specified in the published conditions such race shall be raced in the following manner unless conducted under another section of this rule. That is, the field shall be divided by lot and the first division shall race a qualifying dash for 30 per cent of the purse, the second division shall race a qualifying dash for 30 per cent of the purse and the horses so qualified shall race in the main event for 40 per cent of the purse. The winner of the main event shall be the race winner.

In the event there are more horses declared to start than can be accommodated by the two elimination dashes, then there will be added enough elimination dashes to take care of the excess. The per cent of the purse raced for each elimination dash will be determined by dividing the number of elimination dashes into 60. The main event will race for 40 per cent of the purse.

Unless the conditions provide otherwise, if there are two elimination dashes, the first four finishers in each dash qualify for the final; if three or more elimination dashes, not more than three horses will qualify for the final from each qualifying dash.

The Judges shall draw the positions in which the horses are to start in the main event, i.e., they shall draw positions to determine which of the two dash winners shall have the pole, and which the second position; which of the two horses that have been second shall start in third position; and which in fourth, etc. All elimination dashes and the concluding heat must be programmed to be raced upon the same day or night, unless special provisions for earlier elimination dashes are set forth in the conditions.

In the event there are three separate heat or dash winners and they alone come back in order to determine the race winner according to the conditions, they will take post positions according to the order of their finish in the previous heat or dash.

(b) In any race where the number of horses declared in to start exceeds 12 on a half-mile track, 14 on a ⅝-mile track or 16 on a mile track, unless other numbers are specified in the conditions, the race, at the option of the track members conducting the same, stated before positions are drawn, may be divided by lot and raced in two divisions with all heat winners from both divisions competing in a final heat to determine the race winner. Each division shall race two heats for 20% of the purse each heat. The remaining 20% of the purse shall go to the winner of the final heat.

(c) Whenever elimination heats are required, or specified in the published conditions of a stake or futurity, such race may be raced on the three heat plan, irrespective of any provisions in the conditions to the contrary. That is, the field shall be divided by lot and the first division shall race for thirty per cent of the purse, the second division shall race for thirty per cent, and the horses qualifying in the first and second divisions shall race the third heat for thirty per cent of the purse. If, after the third heat, no horse has won two heats, a fourth heat shall be raced by only the heat winners. The race winner shall receive the remaining ten per cent of the purse. The number of horses qualifying to return after each elimination heat will be the same as set out in Section 3 (a) of this rule.

§ 4. **Overnight Events.**—**In overnight events at extended pari-mutuel meetings and Grand Circuit meetings not more than eight horses shall be allowed to start on a half-mile track and not more than ten horses on larger tracks. Trailers are not permitted where the track has room to score all horses abreast, allowing eight feet per horse.**

§ 5. **Qualifying Race for Stake, Etc.**— Where qualifying races are provided in the conditions of an early closing event, stake or futurity, such qualifying race must be held not more than five days prior to contesting the main event (excluding Sunday) and omitting the day of the race.

RULE 14.
Declaration to Start and Drawing Horses

Section 1. **Declaration.**

(a) Unless otherwise specified in the conditions, the declaration time shall be as follows:

(1) Extended pari-mutuel meetings, 9:00 a.m.

(2) All other meetings, 10:00 a.m.

(b) No horse shall be permitted to start in more than one race on any one racing day except that at county fairs they may declare in so that they race no more than two single dashes in any one racing day. Races decided by more than one heat are considered a single race.

(c) **Time Used.**—In order to avoid confusion and misunderstanding, the time when declarations close will be considered to be **local time at the track where the race is being contested.**

(d) **Declaration Box.**—The management shall provide a locked box with an aperture through which declarations shall be deposited.

(e) **Responsibility for Declaration Box.**— The declaration box shall be in charge of the Presiding Judge.

(f) **Search for Declarations by Presiding Judge Before Opening Box.**—Just prior to opening of the box at extended pari-mutuel meetings where futurities, stakes, early closing or late closing events are on the program, the Presiding Judge shall check with the Race Secretary to ascertain if any declarations by mail, telegraph, or otherwise, are in the office and not deposited in the entry box, and he shall see that they are declared and drawn in the proper event. At other meetings, the Presiding Judge shall ascertain if any such declarations have been received by the Superintendent of Speed or Secretary of the Fair, and he shall see that they are properly declared and drawn.

(g) **Opening of Declaration Box.**—At the time specified the Presiding Judge shall unlock the box, assort the declarations found therein and immediately draw the positions in the presence of such owners or their representatives, as may appear.

(h) **Entry Box and Drawing of Horses.**— At all member tracks of this Association the entry box shall be opened by the Presiding Judge at the advertised time and the Presiding Judge will be responsible to see that at least one horseman or an official representative of the horsemen is present. No owner or agent for a horse with a declaration in the entry box shall be denied the privilege of being present. Under the supervision of the Presiding Judge, all entries shall be listed, the eligibility verified, preference ascertained, starters selected and post positions drawn. If it is necessary to reopen any race, public announcement shall be made at least twice and the box reopened to a definite time.

(i) **Procedure in The Event of Absence or Incapacity of Presiding Judge.**—At non-extended meetings in the event of the absence or incapacity of the Presiding Judge, the functions enumerated above may be performed by a person designated by said Judge, for whose acts and conduct said Judge shall be wholly responsible. If a substitution is made as herein provided, the name and address of the person so substituting shall be entered in the Judges' Book.

At any extended meeting in the event of the absence or incapacity of the Presiding Judge, the functions enumerated above may be performed by one or more Associate Judges who shall have been designated by the Presiding Judge, prior to the start of the meeting, in the form of a written notice to the governing Racing Commission and to the Chief Officer of the track at which the meeting is being conducted. A record shall be kept in the Judges' Book showing the name of the individual who performed such functions on each day of the meeting.

(j) **Drawing of Post Positions for Second Heat in Races of More Than One Dash or Heat at Pari-Mutuel Meetings.**—In races of a duration of more than one dash or heat at pari-mutuel meetings, the judges may draw post positions from the stand for succeeding dashes or heats.

(k) **Declarations by Mail, Telegraph or Telephone.**—Declarations by mail, telegraph, or telephone actually received and evidence of which is deposited in the box before the time specified to declare in, shall be drawn in the same manner as the others. Such drawings shall be final. Mail, telephone and telegraph declarations must state the name and address of the owner or lessee; the name, color, sex, sire and dam of the horse; the name of the driver and his colors; the date and place of last start; a current summary, including the number of starts, firsts, seconds, thirds, earnings and best winning time for the current year; and the event or events in which the horse is to be entered.

(l) **Effect of Failure to Declare on Time.**— When a member requires a horse to be declared at a stated time, failure to declare as required shall be considered a withdrawal from the event.

(m) **Drawing of Horses After Declarations.** —After declaration to start has been made no horse shall be drawn except by permission of the Judges. A fine, not to exceed $500, or suspension may be imposed for drawing a horse without permission, the penalty to apply to both the horse and the party who violates the regulation.

(n) **Procedure on Unauthorized Withdrawal Where There is No Opportunity for Hearing.**—Where the person making the declarations fails to honor it and there is no opportunity for a hearing by the Judges, this penalty may be imposed by the Executive Vice-President.

(o) **Horses Omitted Through Error.**— Such drawings shall be final unless there is conclusive evidence that a horse properly declared was omitted from the race through the error of a track or its agent or employee in which event the horse **shall** be added to the race but given the **last** post position, **provided the error is discovered prior to either scratch time or the printing of the program; however, in the case of early closers of more than $10,000 and stake and futurity races, the race shall be re-drawn. This shall not apply at extended pari-mutuel meetings in overnight events.**

§ 2. **Qualifying Races.**—At all extended pari-mutuel meetings declarations for overnight events shall be governed by the following:

(a) Within two weeks of being declared in, a horse that has not raced previously at the gait chosen must go a qualifying race under the supervision of a Judge holding a Presiding or Associate Judge's license for pari-mutuel meetings and acquire at least one charted line by a licensed charter. In order to provide complete and accurate chart information on time and beaten lengths, a standard photo-finish shall be in use.

(b) A horse that does not show a charted line for the previous season, or a charted line within its last six starts, must go a qualifying race as set forth in (a). Uncharted races contested in heats or more than one dash and consolidated according to (d) will be considered one start.

(c) A horse that has not started at a charted meeting by August 1st of a season must go a qualifying race as set forth above in (a).

(d) When a horse has raced at a charted meeting during the current season, then gone to meetings where the races are not charted, the information from the uncharted races may be summarized, including each start, and consolidated in favor of charted lines and the requirements of Section (b) would then not apply.

The consolidated line shall carry date, place, time, driver, finish, track condition and distance if race is not at one mile.

(e) The Judges may require any horse that has been on the Steward's List to go a qualifying race. If a horse has raced in individual time not meeting the qualifying standards for that class of horse, he may be required to go a qualifying race.

(f) The Judges may permit a fast horse to qualify by means of a timed workout consistent with the time of the races in which he will compete in the event adequate competition is not available for a qualifying race.

(g) To enable a horse to qualify, qualifying races should be held at least one full week prior to the opening of any meeting that opens before July 1st of a season and shall be scheduled at least twice a week. Qualifying races shall also be scheduled twice a week during the meeting.

(h) Where a race is conducted for the purpose of qualifying drivers and not horses, the race need not be charted, timed or recorded. This section is not applicable to races qualifying both drivers and horses.

(i) If a horse takes a win race record in a Qualifying race such record must be prefaced with the letter "Q" wherever it appears, except in a case where, immediately prior to or following the race, the horse taking the record has been submitted to an approved urine, saliva or blood test. It will be the responsibility of the Presiding Judge to report the test on the Judges' Sheet.

§ 3. **Coupled Entries.**—When the starters in a race include two or more horses owned or trained by the same person, or trained in the same stable or by the same management, they shall be coupled as an "entry" and a wager on one horse in the "entry" shall be a wager on all horses in the "entry." Provided, however, that when a trainer enters two or more horses in a stake, early closing, futurity, Free-For-All or other special event under bonafide separate ownerships, the said horses may, at the request of the association and with the of the Commission, be permitted to race as separate betting entries. The fact that such horses are trained by the same person shall be indicated prominently in the program. If the race is split in two or more divisions, horses in an "entry" shall be seeded insofar as possible, first by owners, then by trainers, then by stables, but the divisions in which they compete and their post positions shall be drawn by lot. The above provisions shall also apply to elimination heats.

At non-betting meetings or at fairs where there is no wagering, the person making an entry of more than one horse in the same race shall be responsible to designate the word "entry" on the declaration blank, providing that the horses qualify as an entry.

The Presiding Judge shall be responsible for coupling horses. In addition to the foregoing, horses separately owned or trained may be coupled as an entry where it is necessary to do so to protect the public interest for the purpose of pari-mutuel wagering only. However, where this is done entries may not be rejected.

§ 4. **Also Eligibles.**—Not more than two horses may be drawn as also eligibles for a race and their positions shall be drawn along with the starters in the race. In the event one or more horses are excused by the Judges, the also eligible horse or horses shall race and take the post position drawn by the horse that it replaces, except in handicap races. In handicap races the also eligible horse shall take the place of the horse that it replaces in the event that the handicap is the same. In the event the handicap is different, the also eligible horse shall take the position on the outside of horses with a similar handicap. No horse may be added to a race as an also eligible unless the horse was drawn as such at the time declarations closed. No horse may be barred from a race to which it is otherwise eligible by reason of

its preference due to the fact that it has been drawn as an also eligible. A horse moved into the race from the also eligible list cannot be drawn except by permission of the Judges, but the owner or trainer of such a horse shall be notified that the horse is to race and it shall be posted at the Race Secretary's Office. All horses on the also eligible list and not moved in to race by 9:00 A.M. on the day of the race shall be released.

§ 5. **Preference.**—Preference shall be given in all overnight events according to a horse's last previous purse race during the current year. The preference date on a horse that has drawn to race and been scratched is the date of the race from which he was scratched.

When a horse is racing for the first time in the current year, the date of the first declaration shall be considered its last race date, and preference applied accordingly, provided, however, that where an overnight race has been re-opened because it did not fill, all eligible horses declared in to the race prior to the re-opening shall receive preference over horses subsequently declared, irrespective of the actual preference dates.

This rule relating to preference is not applicable for any meeting at which an agricultural fair is in progress. All horses granted stalls and eligible must be given an opportunity to compete at these meetings.

§ 6. **Steward's List.**—(a) A horse that is unfit to race because he is dangerous, unmanageable, sick, lame, unable to show a performance to qualify for races at the meeting, or otherwise unfit to race at the meeting may be placed on a "Steward's list" by the Presiding Judge and declarations on said horse shall be refused, but the owner or trainer shall be notified in writing of such action and the reason as set forth above shall be clearly stated on the notice. When any horse is placed on the Steward's list, the Clerk of the Course shall make a note on the Eligibility Certificate of such horse, showing the date the horse was put on the Steward's list, the reason therefor and the date of removal if the horse has been removed.

(b) No Presiding Judge or other official at a nonextended meeting shall have the power to remove from the Steward's List and accept as an entry any horse which has been placed on a Steward's List and not subsequently removed therefrom for the reason that he is a dangerous or unmanageable horse. Such meetings may refuse declarations on any horse that has been placed on the Steward's List and has not been removed therefrom.

§ 7. **Driver.**—Declarations shall state who shall drive the horse and give the driver's colors. Drivers may be changed until 9:00 A.M. of the day preceding the race, after which no driver may be changed without permission of the judges and for good cause. When a nominator starts two or more horses, the Judges shall approve or disapprove the second and third drivers.

§ 8. It shall be the duty of the Presiding Judge to call a meeting of all horsemen on the grounds before the opening of an extended pari-mutuel meeting for the purpose of their electing a member and an alternate to represent them on matters relating to the withdrawal of horses due to bad track or weather conditions.

§ 9. In cases of questionable track conditions due to weather, the Presiding Judge shall call a meeting consisting of an agent of the track member, the duly elected representative of the horsemen and himself.

§ 10. Upon unanimous decision by this committee of three, that track conditions are safe for racing, no unpermitted withdrawals may be made.

§ 11. (a) Any decision other than unanimous by this committee will allow any entrant to scratch his horse or horses after posting ten per cent of the purse to be raced for. In the event sufficient withdrawals are received to cause the field to be less than six, then the track member shall have the right of postponement of an early closing event or stake and cancellation of an overnight event.

(b) Said money posted shall be forward to The United States Trotting Association and shall be retained as a fine, or refunded to the individual upon the decision of the District Board hearing the case at its next meeting as to whether the withdrawal was for good cause.

THE ABOVE PROCEDURE APPLIES ONLY TO THE WITHDRAWAL OF HORSES THAT HAVE BEEN PROPERLY DECLARED IN AND DOES NOT RELATE TO POSTPONEMENT WHICH IS COVERED ELSEWHERE.

RULE 15.
Postponement

Section 1. In case of unfavorable weather, or other unavoidable cause, members with the consent of the Judges shall postpone races in the following manner.

(a) Early Closing Races, Stakes, and Futurities. All shall be postponed to a definite hour the next fair day and good track.

(b) Any LATE CLOSING RACE, EARLY CLOSING RACE, and STAKE OR FUTURITY (except as provided in (d) and (e) below) that cannot be raced during the scheduled meeting shall be declared off and the entrance money and forfeits shall be divided equally among the nominators who have horses declared in and eligible to start.

(c) Any Late Closing Race, Early Closing Race or overnight event that has been started and remains unfinished on the last day of the scheduled meeting shall be declared ended and the full purse divided according to the summary. Any such race that has been started but postponed by rain earlier in the meeting may be declared ended and the full purse divided according to the summary.

(d) Stakes and Futurities should be raced where advertised and the meeting may be extended to accomplish this. Any stake or futurity that has been started and remains unfinished on the last day of the scheduled meeting shall be declared ended and the full purse divided according to the summary except where the track elects to extend meeting to complete the race. Horses that are scratched after a heat and before a race is declared finished do not participate in purse distributions from subsequent heats in the event the race is called off and declared finished.

(e) Unless otherwise provided in the conditions, in order to transfer stakes and futurities to another meeting unanimous consent must be obtained from the member and from all those having eligibles in the event. In the event of the impossibility of racing a scheduled stake or futurity because of the unavailability of the scheduled racing premises, an alternate site may be selected by the sponsor with the approval of two thirds of the owners of the horses remaining eligible.

(f) (1) At meetings of MORE THAN FIVE DAYS duration, overnight events may be postponed and carried over not to exceed two racing days.

(2) At meetings of a duration of FIVE DAYS OR LESS, overnight events and late closing races shall be cancelled and starting fees returned in the event of postponement, unless the track member is willing to add the postponed races to the advertised program for subsequent days of the meeting.

At the option of management any postponed races may be contested in single mile dashes. Where races are postponed under this rule, management shall have the privilege of selecting the order in which the events will be raced in any combined program.

(g) Where a race is postponed pursuant to any of the foregoing provisions, only those horses originally declared in to the postponed event shall be eligible to race. Where a race is postponed and moved to another location horses previously declared may withdraw without penalty.

RULE 16.
Starting

Section 1. With Starting Gate.—

(a) **Starter's Control.**—The Starter shall have control of the horses from the formation of the parade until he gives the word "go".

(b) **Scoring.**—After one or two preliminary warming up scores, the Starter shall notify the drivers to fasten their helmet chin straps and come to the starting gate. During or before the parade the drivers must be informed as to the number of scores permitted.

(c) The horses shall be brought to the starting gate as near one-quarter of a mile before the start as the track will permit.

(d) **Speed of Gate.**—Allowing sufficient time so that the speed of the gate can be increased gradually, the following minimum speeds will be maintained:

(1) For the first ⅛ mile, not less than 11 miles per hour.

(2) For the next ¹⁄₁₆ of a mile not less than 18 miles per hour.

(3) From that point to the starting point, the speed will be gradually increased to maximum speed.

(e) On mile tracks horses will be brought to the starting gate at the head of the stretch and the relative speeds mentioned in subsection (d) above will be maintained.

(f) **Starting Point.**—The starting point will be a point marked on the inside rail a distance of not less than 200 feet from the first turn. The Starter shall give the word "go" at the starting point.

(g) WHEN A SPEED HAS BEEN REACHED IN THE COURSE OF A START THERE SHALL BE NO DECREASE EXCEPT IN THE CASE OF A RECALL.

(h) **Recall Notice.**—In case of a recall, a light plainly visible to the driver shall be flashed and a recall sounded, but the starting gate shall proceed out of the path of the horses. At extended pari-mutuel tracks in the case of a recall, wherever possible, the starter shall leave the wings of the gate extended and gradually slow the speed of the gate to assist in stopping the field of horses. In an emergency, however, the starter shall use his discretion to close the wings of the gate.

(i) There shall be no recall after the word "go" has been given and any horse, regardless of his position or an accident, shall be deemed a starter from the time he entered into the Starter's control unless dismissed by the Starter.

(j) **Breaking Horse.**—The Starter shall endeavor to get all horses away in position and on gait but no recall shall be had for a breaking horse.

(k) **Recall—Reasons For.**—The Starter may sound a recall only for the following reasons:

(1) A horse scores ahead of the gate.

(2) There is interference.

(3) A horse has broken equipment.

(4) A horse falls before the word "go" is given.

(l) **Penalties.**—A fine not to exceed $100, or suspension from driving not to exceed 15 days, or both, may be applied to any driver, by the Starter for:

(1) Delaying the start.

(2) Failure to obey the Starter's instruction.

(3) Rushing ahead of the inside or outside wing of the gate.

(4) Coming to the starting gate out of position.

(5) Crossing over before reaching the starting point.

(6) Interference with another driver during the start.

(7) Failure to come up into position.

A hearing must be granted before any penalty is imposed.

(m) **Riding in Gate.**—No persons shall be allowed to ride in the starting gate except the Starter and his driver or operator, and a Patrol Judge, unless permission has been granted by this Association.

(n) **Loudspeaker.**—Use of a mechanical loudspeaker for any purpose other than to give instructions to drivers is prohibited. The volume shall be no higher than necessary to carry the voice of the Starter to the drivers.

The penalty for violation of this section shall be a fine of not to exceed $500.00 or suspension not to exceed thirty days after a hearing by the President or Executive Vice-President.

§ 2. **Holding Horses Before Start.**— Horses may be held on the backstretch not to exceed two minutes awaiting post time, except when delayed by an emergency.

§ 3. **Two Tiers.**—In the event there are two tiers of horses, the withdrawing of a horse that has drawn or earned a position in the front tier shall not affect the position of the horses that have drawn or earned positions in the second tier.

Whenever a horse is drawn from any tier, horses on the outside move in to fill up the vacancy. **Where a horse has drawn a post position in the second tier, the driver of such horse may elect to score out behind any horse in the first tier so long as he does not thereby interfere with another trailing horse or deprive another trailing horse of a drawn position.**

§ 4. **Starting Without Gate.**—When horses are started without a gate the Starter shall have control of the horses from the formation of the parade until he gives the word "go." He shall be located at the wire or other point of start of the race at which point as nearly as possible the word "go" shall be given. No driver shall cause unnecessary delay after the horses are called. After two preliminary warming up scores, the Starter shall notify the drivers to form in parade.

§ 5. The driver of any horse refusing or failing to follow the instructions of the Starter as to the parade or scoring ahead of the pole horse may be set down for the heat in which the offense occurs, or for such other period as the Starter shall determine, and may be fined from $10 to $100. Whenever a driver is taken down the substitute shall be permitted to score the horse once. A horse delaying the race may be started regardless of his position or gait and there shall not be a recall on account of a bad actor. If the word is not given, all the horses in the race shall immediately turn at the tap of the bell or other signal, and jog back to their parade positions for a fresh start. There shall be no recall after the starting word has been given.

§ 6. **Starters.**—The horses shall be deemed to have started when the word "go" is given by the Starter and all the horses must go the course except in case of an accident in which it is the opinion of the Judges that it is impossible to go the course.

§ 7. **Overhead Barrier.**—A member may use an overhead barrier or counting start in starting races and any driver who fails to obey the orders of the Starter or Assistant Starter operating same may be fined or ruled out of the race.

§ 8. **Unmanageable Horse.**—If in the opinion of the Judges or the Starter a horse is unmanageable or liable to cause accidents or injury to any other horse or to any driver it may be sent to the barn. When this action is taken the Starter will notify the Judges who will in turn notify the public.

§ 9. **Bad Acting Horse.**—At meetings where there is no wagering, the Starter may place a bad acting horse on the outside at his discretion. At pari-mutuel meetings such action may be taken only where there is time for the Starter to notify the Judges who will in turn notify the public prior to the sale of tickets on such race. If tickets have been sold, the bad acting horse must be scratched under the provision of Section 8 herein.

§ 10. **Snap Barrier.**—All handicaps shall be started with a snap barrier, unless a starting gate or walk-up start is used, and sprung simultaneously with the announcement of the word "go." Any driver allowing his horse to go into the barrier before the word "go" shall be fined $10 to $100.

§ 11. **Post Positions—Heat Racing.**—The horse winning a heat shall take the pole (or inside position) the succeeding heat, unless otherwise specified in the published conditions, and all others shall take their positions in the order they were placed the last heat. When two or more horses shall have made a dead heat, their positions shall be settled by lot.

§ 12. **Shield.**—The arms of all starting gates shall be provided with a screen or a shield in front of the position for each horse, and such arms shall be perpendicular to the rail.

§ 13. Every licensed starter is required to check his starting gate for malfunctions before commencing any meeting, and to practice the procedure to be followed in the event of a malfunction. Both the starter and the driver of the gate must know and practice emergency procedures, and the starter is responsible for the training in such procedures of drivers.

RULE 17.
Drivers, Trainers and Agents

Section 1. **Licensing of Drivers.**—No person shall drive a horse in any race on a track in membership with this Association without having first obtained from this Association an Active Membership including a driver's license. The proper license shall be presented to the Clerk of the Course before driving. Any person violating this rule **may be** fined $10.00 for each offense and no license shall be issued thereafter until such fines shall have been paid. In addition, thereto, the track member *may* be fined the sum of $5.00 for permitting a driver to start without a license. In the event of a driver's license being lost or destroyed, a replacement may be obtained upon payment of a fee in the sum of $1.00.

(a) Trainer Driver/Trainer License Fee.—Applicants for a trainer or driver/trainer license other than a Matinee driver license shall pay a fee in the amount of $15.00 in addition to their regular annual membership fee of $20.00 for an original license, and $10.00 for renewal licenses annually thereafter.

Provided, however, that the driver's license fee for foreign drivers, other that those residing in the Maritime Provinces of Canada, shall be $100.00 for an original license, unless the applicant is already licensed as a driver by the licensing authority of a foreign country in which he resides, in which latter case the fee shall be $15.00. The fee for a renewal of such a license shall be $10.00 annually thereafter.

2. **Contents of Application.**—The Executive Vice-President shall require the applicant to:

(a) Submit evidence of good moral character.

(b) Submit evidence of his ability to drive in a race and, if he is a new applicant, this must include the equivalent of a year's training experience.

(c) Be at least 12 years of age for an (MA) or (M) license and 16 years of age for an (F) license or a (Q) license.

(d) Be at least 16 years of age for a (P) license.

(e) Furnish completed application form.

(f) Submit satisfactory evidence of an eye examination indicating 20/40 corrected vision in both eyes; or if one eye blind, at least 20/30 corrected vision in the other eye; and, when requested submit evidence of physical and mental ability and/or submit to a physical examination.

(g) Applicants, other than for an M or MA license shall submit to a written examination at a designated time and place to determine his qualification to drive or train and

his knowledge of racing and the rules. In addition any driver who presently holds a license and wishes to obtain a license in a higher category who has not previously submitted to such written tests shall be required to take a written test before becoming eligible to obtain a license in a higher category.

§ 3. **Categories of Licenses.**—Driver and trainer licenses shall be issued in the following categories:

(a) (M) (Matinee) A license valid for matinee meetings only.

(b) (MA) (Matinee—Amateur) A license valid for matinee meetings and amateur racing at other meetings providing the licensee is an amateur at the time of the race.

(c) (F) (Fair) A license valid for fairs and all meetings with the exception of extended pari-mutuel meetings.

Drivers holding a license valid for fairs only who have driven at fairs must demonstrate an ability to drive satisfactorily before they will be granted a (Q) license valid for qualifying races.

(d) (Q) (Qualifying) A license valid for fairs and a license for qualifying and non-wagering races at extended pari-mutuel meetings with the approval of the Presiding Judge. The Presiding Judge shall make a report to this Association relating to the performance of such a driver in a qualifying race. The Horsemen's Committee may appoint an Advisory Committee of three drivers at any meeting to observe the qualifications, demeanor and general conduct of all drivers and report in regard thereto to the Presiding Judge, copy of any such report to be in writing and forwarded to the Association. Applicants for Qualifying licenses must be at least 16 years of age.

(e) (P) (Provisional) A license valid for fairs and for extended pari-mutuel meetings subject to satisfactory performance.

Drivers holding a Provisional license will not be considered for advancement to an (a) (Full) license until he or she has:

(1) Had at least one year's driving experience while holding a (P) (Provisional) license.

(2) Made 25 satisfactory starts at extended pari-mutuel or Grand Circuit meetings in the **two** calendar year period preceding the date of his application for a full license.

(3) Demonstrated professional competence, even though he has held the Provisional license for a year and has had 25 or more satisfactory starts.

(4) Received the written recommenda-

tion for an "A" license from a Presiding Judge before whom he has driven in pari-mutuel or grand circuit races.

(f) (A) (Full) A full license valid for all meetings.

(g) (V) (Probationary) A probationary license indicating that the driver has been guilty of rule violations and has been warned against repetition of such violations. When a driver with a probationary license commits more than one rule violations, or one major violation, proceedings may be started and he will be given a hearing either before the Executive Vice-President or the District Board of Review in the District where the last penalty was imposed, to determine if his license should be revoked.

Repeated rule violations shall be considered grounds for refusal to grant or grounds for revocation of any driver's license. A provisional, qualifying, or fair license may be revoked for one or more rule violations, or other indications of lack of qualifications, and the qualifications of drivers in these categories may be reviewed at any time, with written examinations if necessary, to determine if a driver is competent.

(h) (T) (Trainer) A license to enable the holder to train horses and be programmed as Trainer at all member tracks of this Association.

An applicant for a license as trainer must satisfy the Executive Vice-President that he possesses the necessary qualifications, both mental and physical, to perform the duties required. Elements to be considered, among others, shall be character, reputation, temperament, experience, knowledge of the rules of racing, and duties of a trainer in the preparation, training, entering and managing horses for racing. A trainer's license shall be either General or it may be issued valid for the horses owned wholly or in part by the trainer only. All trainers participating at tracks located in District 10 must be licensed as such.

An applicant shall be required to:

(1) Submit evidence of good moral character.

(2) Be at least 18 years of age.

(3) Furnish complete application form including photographs.

(4) Submit evidence of his ability to train and manage a racing stable which shall include at least three years experience working as a groom or second trainer, and satisfactory completion of a written examination.

(5) When requested, submit evidence of physical ability and/or to submit to a physical examination.

(6) When requested, submit three copies of his fingerprints.

§ 4. **License Requirements in District 10.** —At tracks located in District 10, it shall be the responsibility of all drivers and/or trainers who utilize persons in capacities which require them to be licensed, to be certain that such persons are so licensed. A fine not exceeding $100.00 may be imposed for violation of this rule.

§ 5. Any licensed driver who shall participate in a meeting or drive a horse at a meeting not in membership with this Association or the Canadian Trotting Association shall be fined not to exceed $100 for each such offense: PROVIDED HOWEVER, that nothing herein contained shall prevent any person from driving at a contract track or from participating in a meeting conducted at such a track.

(a) No person 60 years of age or older who has never previously held any type of driver license shall be issued a driver license valid for extended pari-mutuel meetings.

(b) **Physical Examination.**—An applicant for a driver's license 65 years of age or over may be required to submit annually, with his application for a driver's license, a report of a physical examination on forms supplied by the Association. If the Association so desires, it may designate the physician to perform such examination. However, in such event, the cost thereof shall be paid by the Association. No applicant who has previously held any type of driver's license shall be subsequently denied a driver's license solely on the basis of age.

(c) In the event any person is involved in an accident on the track, the Association may order such person to submit to a physical examination and such examination must be completed within 30 days from such request or the license may be suspended until compliance therewith.

§ 6. The license of any driver or trainer may be revoked or suspended at any time after a hearing by the President or Executive Vice-President for violation of the rules, failure to obey the instructions of any official, or for any misconduct or act detrimental to the sport. The President or Executive Vice-President may designate a proper person as a hearing officer who will conduct a hearing and furnish a transcript to the President or Executive Vice-President. The license may be reinstated by the President or

Executive Vice-President in his discretion upon application made to him and upon such terms as he may prescribe. Any suspension or revocation of license made hereunder may be reviewed as provided in Article IX of the By-Laws.

§ 7. The following shall constitute disorderly conduct and be reason for a fine, suspension, or revocation of a driver's or trainer's license:

(a) Failure to obey the Judges' orders that are expressly authorized by the rules of this Association.

(b) Failure to drive when programmed unless excused by the Judges.

(c) Drinking intoxicating beverages within four hours of the first post time of the program on which he is carded to drive.

(d) Appearing in the paddock in an unfit condition to drive.

(e) Fighting.

(f) Assaults.

(g) Offensive and profane language.

(h) Smoking on the track in silks during actual racing hours.

(i) Warming up a horse prior to racing without silks.

(j) Disturbing the peace.

(k) Refusal to take a breath analyzer test when directed by the Presiding Judge.

§ 8. Drivers must wear distinguishing colors and clean white pants, and shall not be allowed to start in a race or other public performance unless in the opinion of the Judges they are properly dressed.

No one shall drive during the time when colors are required on a race track unless he is wearing a type of protective helmet, constructed with a hard shell, and containing adequate padding and a chin strap in place.

§ 9. Any driver wearing colors who shall appear at a betting window or at a bar or in a restaurant dispensing alcoholic beverages shall be fined not to exceed $100 for each such offense.

§ 10. No driver can, without good and sufficient reasons, decline to be substituted by Judges. Any driver who refuses to be so substituted may be fined or suspended, or both, by order of the Judges.

§ 11. An amateur driver is one who has never accepted any valuable consideration by way of or in lieu of compensation for his services as a trainer or driver during the past ten years.

§ 12. Drivers holding an "A" license, or drivers with a "V" license who formerly held an "A" license, shall register their colors with this Association. Registered stables or corporations may register their racing colors with this Association. Colors so registered shall not be taken by any other person, registered stable or corporation.

Residents of foreign countries shall not be bound by this section until they have driven 25 or more starts in a given year in the United States.

The fee is **$100.00** for lifetime registration. The fee for a duplicate registration card is **$10.00** and the fee for changing a design once registered is $10.00. All disputes on rights to particular colors shall be settled by this Association.

The colors of deceased persons shall be released one year after death unless transfer is requested by the next of kin or other person previously designated by the deceased in writing. If a proper transfer is requested within the allotted period, a transfer shall be made pursuant to the request, upon the payment of the prescribed fee. The colors of drivers approved by the Driver Committee shall never be released for the use of others except next of kin or other person previously designated by the deceased in writing.

§ 13. Any person racing a horse at a meeting where registered colors are required by Section 12 hereof, using colors registered by any person or persons except himself or his employer, without special permission from the Presiding Judge, shall be fined $10.00.

RULE 18.
Racing and Track Rules

Section 1. Although a leading horse is entitled to any part of the track except after selecting his position in the home stretch, neither the driver of the first horse or any other driver in the race shall do any of the following things, which shall be considered violation of driving rules:

(a) Change either to the right or left during any part of the race when another horse is so near him that in altering his position he compels the horse behind him to shorten his stride, or causes the driver of such other horse to pull him out of his stride.

(b) Jostle, strike, hook wheels, or interfere with another horse or driver.

(c) Cross sharply in front of a horse or cross over in front of a field of horses in a reckless manner, endangering other drivers.

(d) Swerve in and out or pull up quickly.

(e) Crowd a horse or driver by "putting a wheel under him."

(f) Carry a horse out.

(g) Sit down in front of a horse or take up abruptly in front of other horses so as to cause confusion or interference among trailing horses.

(h) Let a horse pass inside needlessly or otherwise help another horse to improve his position in the race.

(i) Commit any act which shall impede the progress of another horse or cause him to break.

(j) Change course after selecting a position in the home stretch **or** swerve in **and** out, or bear in **and** out, in such **a** manner as to interfere with another horse or cause him to change course or take back.

(k) To drive in a careless or reckless manner.

(l) Whipping under the arch of the sulky, the penalty for which shall be no less than 10 days suspension.

§ 2. All complaints by drivers of any foul driving or other misconduct during the heat must be made at the termination of the heat, unless the driver is prevented from doing so by an accident or injury. Any driver desiring to enter a claim of foul or other complaint of violation of the rules, must before dismounting indicate to the judges or Barrier Judge his desire to enter such claim or complaint and forthwith upon dismounting shall proceed to the telephone or Judges' stand where and when such claim, objection, or complaint shall be immediately entered. The Judges shall not cause the official sign to be displayed until such claim, objection, or complaint shall have been entered and considered.

§ 3. If any of the above violations is committed by a person driving a horse coupled as an entry in the betting, the Judges shall set both horses back, if, in their opinion, the violation may have affected the finish of the race. Otherwise, penalties may be applied individually to the drivers of any entry.

§ 4. In case of interference, collision, or violation of any of the above restrictions, the offending horse may be placed back one or more positions in that heat or dash, and in the event such collision or interference prevents any horse from finishing the heat or dash, the offending horse may be disqualified from receiving any winnings; and the driver may be fined not to exceed the amount of the purse or stake contended for, or may be suspended or expelled. In the event a horse is set back, under the provisions hereof, he must be placed behind the horse with whom he interfered.

§ 5. (a) Every heat in a race must be contested by every horse in the race and every horse must be driven to the finish. If the Judges believe that a horse is being driven, or has been driven heretofore, with design to prevent his winning a heat or dash which he was evidently able to win, or is being raced in an inconsistent manner, or to perpetrate or to aid a fraud, they shall consider it a violation and the driver, and anyone in concert with him, to so affect the outcome of the race or races, may be fined, suspended, or expelled. The Judges may substitute a competent and reliable driver at any time. The substituted driver shall be paid at the discretion of the Judges and the fee retained from the purse money due the horse, if any.

(b) In the event a drive is unsatisfactory due to lack of effort or carelessness, and the Judges believe that there is no fraud, gross carelessness, or a deliberate inconsistent drive they may impose a penalty under this sub-section not to exceed ten days suspension, or a $100.00 fine.

§ 6. If in the opinion of the Judges a driver is for any reason unfit or incompetent to drive or refuses to comply with the directions of the Judges, or is reckless in his conduct and endangers the safety of horses or other drivers in the race, he may be removed and another driver substituted at any time after the positions have been assigned in a race, and the offending driver shall be fined, suspended or expelled. The substitute driver shall be properly compensated.

§ 7. If for any cause other than being interfered with or broken equipment, a horse fails to finish after starting in a heat, that horse shall be ruled out.

§ 8. Loud shouting or other improper conduct is forbidden in a race.

After the word "go" is given, both feet must be kept in the stirrups until after the finish of the race.

§ 9. Drivers will be allowed whips not to exceed 4 feet, 8 inches, plus a snapper not longer than eight inches.

§ 10. The use of any goading device, chain, or mechanical devices or appliances, other than the ordinary whip or crop upon any horse in any race shall constitute a violation of this rule.

§ 11. The brutal use of a whip or crop or excessive or indiscriminate use of the whip or crop shall be considered a violation and shall be punished by a fine of not to exceed $100.00 or suspension.

§ 12. No horse shall wear hopples in a

race unless he starts in the same in the first heat, and having so started, he shall continue to wear them to the finish of the race, and any person found guilty of removing or altering a horse's hopples during a race, or between races, for the purpose of fraud, shall be suspended or expelled. Any horse habitually wearing hopples shall not be permitted to start in a race without them except by the permission of the Judges. Any horse habitually racing free legged shall not be permitted to wear hopples in a race except with the permission of the Judges. No horse shall be permitted to wear a head pole protruding more than 10 inches beyond its nose.

§ 13. **Breaking.**

(a) When any horse or horses break from their gait in trotting or pacing, their drivers shall at once, where clearance exists, take such horse to the outside and pull it to its gait.

(b) The following shall be considered violations of Section 13 (a):

(1) Failure to properly attempt to pull the horse to its gait.

(2) Failure to take to the outside where clearance exists.

(3) Failure to lose ground by the break.

(c) If there has been no failure on the part of the driver in complying with 13(b),(1),(2), and (3), the horse shall not be set back unless a contending horse on his gait is lapped on the hind quarter of the breaking horse at the finish.

(d) The Judges may set any horse back one or more places if in their judgment any of the above violations have been committed.

§ 14. If in the opinion of the Judges, a driver allows his horse to break for the purpose of fraudulently losing a heat, he shall be liable to the penalties elsewhere provided from fraud and fouls.

§ 15. To assist in determining the matters contained in Sections 13 and 14, it shall be the duty of one of the Judges to call out every break made, and the clerk shall at once note the break and character of it in writing.

§ 16. The time between separate heats of a single race shall be no less than 40 minutes. No heat shall be called after sunset where the track is not lighted for night racing.

§ 17. Horses called for a race shall have the exclusive right of the course, and all other horses shall vacate the track at once, unless permitted to remain by the Judges.

§ 18. In the case of accidents, only so much time shall be allowed as the Judges may deem necessary and proper.

§ 19. A driver must be mounted in his sulky at the finish of the race or the horse must be placed as not finishing.

§ 20. It shall be the responsibility of the owner and trainer to provide every sulky used in a race with unicolored or colorless wheel discs on the inside and outside of the wheel of a type approved by the Executive Vice-President or by a Harness Racing Commission. In his discretion, the Presiding Judge may order the use of mud guards at pari-mutuel tracks.

§ 21. A trainer who trains and races a horse knowing said horse to be owned wholly or in part by a person or persons barred or otherwise disqualified from participating in racing shall be suspended from membership in this Association for a minimum of one year.

§ 22. Any violation of any sections of Rule 18 above, unless otherwise provided, may be punished by a fine or suspension, or both, or by expulsion. Provided, however, that where a penalty is to be imposed for an act of interference, said penalty shall be in days suspended.

RULE 19.
Placing and Money Distribution

Section 1. Unless otherwise provided in the conditions, all purses shall be distributed on the dash basis with the money awarded according to a horse's position in each separate dash or heat of the race.

Purse money distribution in overnight events shall be limited to five moneys.

§ 2. **Dashes.**—Except in the case of Stakes or Futurities, unless otherwise specified in the conditions, the money distribution in dashes shall be 45%, 25%, 15%, 10%, and 5%. (For distribution in Stakes and Futurities see Rule 11, Section 8.) In Early Closing Races, Late Closing Races or Added Money Events, if there are less than five (5) starters, the remaining premium shall go to the race winner unless the conditions call for a different distribution. In overnight events if there are less than five (5) starters the premium for the positions for which there are no starters may be retained by the track.

If there be any premium or premiums for which horses have started but were unable to finish, due to an accident, all unoffending horses who did not finish will share equally in such premium or premiums; provided, however, that where there are fewer unoffending horses failing to finish than there are premiums for which horses have started but have not finished, the number of premiums in excess of the number of unoffending horses not finishing shall go to the winner.

If there be any premium or premiums for which horses have started but were unable to finish and the situation is not covered by the preceding paragraph, such premium shall be paid to the winner.

§ 3. **Every Heat a Race.**—The purse shall be distributed as in dash races with nothing set aside for the race winner.

§ 4. **Placing System.**—If the placing system is specified in the conditions, the purse shall be distributed according to the standing of the horses in the summary. In order to share in the purse distribution, each horse must complete the race and compete in each heat to which he is eligible. A horse must win two heats to be declared the race winner and such horse shall stand first in the summary. In deciding the rank of the horses other than the race winner, a horse that has been placed first in one heat shall be ranked better than any other horse making a dead heat for first or any other horse that has been placed second any number of heats; a horse that has been placed second in one heat shall be ranked better than any other horse that has been placed third any number of heats, etc.; e.g., a horse finishing 3-6 would be ranked ahead of another horse finishing 4-4. A horse finishing in a dead heat would be ranked below another horse finishing in the same position and not in a dead heat. If there be any premium for which no horse has maintained a position, it shall go to the race winner, but the number of premiums awarded need not exceed the number of horses that started in the race. Unless otherwise specified in the conditions, the money shall be divided 50%, 25%, 12%, 8% and 5%.

§ 5. **Two In Three.**—In a two in three race, a horse must win two heats to win the race, and there shall be 10% set aside for the race winner. The purse shall be divided and awarded according to the finish in each of the first two or three heats, as the case may be. If the race is unfinished at the end of the third heat, all but the heat winners or horses making a dead heat for first shall be ruled out. The fourth heat, when required, shall be raced for the 10% set aside for the winner. If there be any third or fourth premiums, etc., for which no horse has maintained a specific place, the premium therefor shall go to the winner of that heat, but the number of premiums distributed need not exceed the number of horses starting in the race. In a two-year-old-race, if there are two heat winners and they have made a dead heat in the third heat, the race shall be declared finished and the colt standing best in the summary shall be awarded the 10%; if the two heat winners make a dead heat and stand the same in the summary, the 10% shall be divided equally between them.

RULE 20
Conduct of Racing

Section 1. No owner, trainer, driver, attendant of a horse, or any other person shall use improper language to an official, officer of this Association, or an officer of an Association in membership, or be guilty of any improper conduct toward such officers or judges, or persons serving under their orders, such improper language or conduct having reference to the administration of the course, or of any race thereon.

§ 2. No owner, trainer, driver, or attendant of a horse, or any other person, at any time or place shall commit an assault, or an assault and battery, upon any driver who shall drive in a race, or shall threaten to do bodily injury to any such driver or shall address to such driver language outrageously insulting.

§ 3. If any owner, trainer, or driver of a horse shall threaten or join with others in threatening not to race, or not to declare in, because of the entry of a certain horse or horses, or a particular stable, thereby compelling or trying to compel the Race Secretary or Superintendent of Speed to reject certain eligible entries it shall be immediately reported to the Executive Vice-President and the offending parties may be suspended pending a hearing before the District Board of Review.

§ 4. No owner, agent or driver who has entered a horse shall thereafter demand of the member a bonus of money or other special award or consideration as a condition for starting the horse.

§ 5. No owner, trainer or driver of a horse shall bet or cause any other person to bet on his behalf on any other horse in any race in which there shall start a horse owned, trained or driven by him, or which he in anywise represents or handles or in which he has an interest. No such person shall participate in exacta, quinella or other multiple pool wagering on a race in which such horse starts other than the daily double.

§ 6. **Failure to report fraudulent proposal.** If any person shall be approached with any offer or promise of a bribe, or a wager or with a request or suggestion for a bribe, or for any improper, corrupt or fraudulent act in relation to racing, or that any race shall be conducted otherwise than fairly and honestly, it shall be the duty of such person to report the details thereof immediately to the Presiding Judge.

§ 7. Any misconduct on the part of a member of this Association fraudulent in its nature or injurious to the character of the turf, although not specified in these rules, is forbidden. Any person or persons who, individually or in concert with one another, shall fraudulently and corruptly, by any means, affect the outcome of any race or affect a false registration, or commit any other act injurious to the sport, shall be guilty of a violation.

§ 8. If two or more persons shall combine and confederate together, in any manner, regardless of where the said persons may be located, for the purpose of violating any of the rules of this Association, and shall commit some act in furtherance of the said purpose and plan, it shall constitute a conspiracy and a violation.

§ 9. In any case where an oath is administered by the Judges, Board of Review, or Officer of this Association under the rules, or a Notary Public, or any other person legally authorized to administer oaths, if the party knowingly swears falsely or withholds information pertinent to the investigation, he shall be fined, suspended, or both, or expelled.

§ 10. **Financial Responsibility.**—Any participant who shall accumulate unpaid obligations, or default in obligations, or issue drafts or checks that are dishonored, or payment refused, or otherwise displays financial irresponsibility reflecting on the sport, may be denied membership in this Association or may be suspended on order by the Executive Vice-President.

§ 11. **Nerved horses.**—All horses that have been nerved shall be so designated on The United States Trotting Association registration certificate and the eligibility certificate and be certified by a practicing veterinarian. It is the responsibility of the owner of the horse at the time the horse is nerved to see that this information is placed on the registration certificate and the eligibility certificate. All horses that have been nerved prior to the adoption of this rule must also be certified and it will be the responsibility of the owner or the trainer of such horse to see that such information is carried on the registration certificate. No trainer or owner will be permitted to enter or start a horse that is high nerved. Low nerved horses may be permitted to start providing this information is published on the bulletin board in the Racing Secretary's Office.

Only posterior digital neurectomy (low nerving) or desensitization by injection of alcohol or other chemicals into the posterior digital nerve is permitted in horses to be raced. Only the posterior digital nerve and middle branches to the posterior (back) part of the foot may be severed or injected below the fetlock. The anterior (front) branches must be preserved so the horse has feeling at the coronary band at the front of the foot on both sides of the midline. No "high nerving" (above the fetlock, including volar or plantar neurectomy) or injection of alcohol or other chemicals into nerves above the fetlock to cause loss of sensation is permitted.

§ 12. **Spayed Mares.**—The fact that a mare has been spayed must be noted on the Registration Certificate, the Eligibility Certificate and any program when such mare races. It shall be the owner's responsibility to report the fact that the mare has been spayed to U.S.T.A. and return its papers for correction.

§ 13. No owner, trainer, driver, attendant or other person representing a horse which has previously tested positive for equine infectious anemia shall knowingly cause said horse to be declared into any race; and no owner, trainer, driver, attendant or other person shall seek to bring about the transfer of such a horse without first notifying the prospective purchaser or transferee of the fact that the horse had previously tested positive for equine infectious anemia.

§ 14. It shall be the responsibility of the trainer of a horse to furnish all pertinent information regarding the Coggins Test of the horse so that it may be entered on the eligibility certificate of the horse prior to the horse's first start in the current year, said information to be entered and certified by the Presiding Judge, State Steward, or Race Secretary.

§ 15. It shall be the responsibility of the trainer to see that each horse under his supervision is safely equipped for each race and, if it is determined by the Judges that a horse has been raced with unsafe or faulty equipment, the Judges may impose a fine, suspension or both.

§ 16. Any violation of any of the provisions of this rule shall be punishable by a fine, suspension, or both, or by expulsion.

RULE 21.
Stimulants, Drugs

Section 1. At every meeting except as stated herein where pari-mutuel wagering is permitted, the winning horse in every heat and/or race shall be subjected to a saliva test for the purpose of determining thereby the presence of any drug, stimulant, sedative, depressant, or medicine. At any meeting where there is a pre-race blood test of all horses and where the Commission requires a post-race urine test of the winner, a saliva test will not be required. In addition, the Judges at any meeting may order any other horse in any heat or race to be subjected to the saliva test or any other test for the purpose of determining thereby the presence of any drug, stimulant, sedative, depressant, or medicine. Also, the Judges may order any horse in a race to be subjected to a urine test. At all extended pari-mutuel meetings and at Grand Circuit meetings at least 25% of the horses subjected to a saliva test shall be given a urine test. Such horses to be selected by the Presiding Judge by lot. Such tests shall be made only by qualified veterinarians and by laboratories approved by the Executive Vice-President. In addition to the above, the winning horse in every heat or dash of a race at any track with a total purse in excess of $5,000.00 shall be subjected to both a saliva and a urine test. However, such urine test shall be counted in determining the 25% required above.

§ 2. The Executive Vice-President may, in his discretion, or at the request of a member, authorize or direct a saliva, urine or other test of any horse racing at any meeting, whether or not tests are being conducted at such meeting, provided that adequate preliminary arrangements can be made to obtain proper equipment, and the services of a competent and qualified veterinarian and an approved laboratory.

During the taking of the saliva and/or urine sample by the veterinarian, the owner, trainer or authorized agent may be present at all times. Unless the rules of the State Racing Commission or other governmental agency provide otherwise, samples so taken shall be placed in two containers and shall immediately be sealed and the evidence of such sealing indicated thereon by the signature of the representative of the owner or trainer. One part of the sample is to be placed in a depository under the supervision of the Presiding Judge and/or any other agency the State Racing Commission may designate to be safeguarded until such time as the report on the chemical analysis of the other portion of the split sample is received.

Should a positive report be received, an owner or trainer shall have the right to have the other portion of the split sample inserted in with a subsequent group being sent for testing or may demand that it be sent to another chemist for analysis, the cost of which will be paid by the party requesting the test.

§ 3. Whenever there is a positive test finding the presence of any drug, stimulant, sedative or depressant present, in the post-race test, the laboratory shall immediately notify the Presiding Judge who shall immediately report such findings to the Executive Vice-President of this Association.

When such positive report is received from the State Chemist by the Presiding Judge, the persons held responsible shall be notified and a thorough investigation shall be conducted by or on behalf of the Judges. Then a time shall be set by the Judges for a hearing to dispose of the matter. The time set for the hearing shall not exceed four racing days after the responsible persons were notified. The hearing may be continued, if in the opinion of the Judges, circumstances justify such action. At County Fairs and non-pari-mutuel meetings, in the event the Judges are unable to perform this action, the Executive Vice-President shall forthwith set a date for a prompt hearing to be conducted by him or some person deputized by him for the purpose of determining all matters concerning the administration of such drug, stimulant, sedative or depressant and the care and the custody of the horse from which the positive sample was obtained.

The decision of the Executive Vice-President or the person deputized by him shall be reduced to writing and shall be final unless the person or persons aggrieved thereby shall within 30 days appeal in writing to the Board of Appeals as provided in Article IX of the By-Laws.

Should the chemical analysis of saliva, urine or other sample of the post-race test taken from a horse indicate the presence of a forbidden narcotic, stimulant, depressant, or local anesthetic, it shall be considered prima facie evidence that such has been administered to the horse. The trainer and any other person or persons who may have had the care of, or been in attendance of the horse, or are suspected of causing such condition, shall be immediately stopped from participating in racing by the Judge and shall remain inactive in racing pending the outcome of a hearing. The horse alleged to have been stimulated shall not race during the investigation and hearing, however, other horses registered under the care of the inactive trainer may, with the consent of the Judge of the meeting, be released to the care of another licensed trainer, and may race.

§ 4. Any person or persons who shall administer or influence or conspire with any other person or persons to administer to any horse any drug, medicant, stimulant, depressant, narcotic or hypnotic to such horse within forty-eight hours of his race, shall be subject to penalties provided in Section 10 of this rule.

§ 5. Whenever the post-race test or tests prescribed in Section 1 hereof disclose the presence in any horse of any drug, stimulant, depressant or sedative, in any amount whatsoever, it shall be presumed that the same was administered by the person or persons having the control and/or care and/or custody of such horse with the intent thereby to affect the speed or condition of such horse and the result of the race in which it participated.

§ 6. A trainer shall be responsible at all times for the condition of all horses trained by him. No trainer shall start a horse or permit a horse in his custody to be started if he knows, or if by the exercise of reasonable care he might have known or have cause to believe, that the horse has received any drug, stimulant, sedative, depressant, medicine, or other substance that could result in a positive test. Every trainer must guard or cause to be guarded each horse trained by him in such manner and for such period of time prior to racing the horse so as to prevent any person not employed by or connected with the owner or trainer from administering any drug, stimulant, sedative, depressant, or other substance resulting in a post-race positive test.

§ 7. Any owner, trainer, driver or agent of the owner, having the care, custody and/or control of any horse who shall refuse to submit such horse to a saliva test or other tests as herein provided or ordered by the Judges shall be guilty of the violation of this rule. Any horse that refuses to submit to a pre-race blood test shall be required to submit to a post-race saliva and urine test regardless of its finish.

§ 8. All winnings of such horse in a race in which an offense was detected under any section of this rule shall be forfeited and paid over to this Association for redistribution among the remaining horses in the race entitled to same. No such forfeiture and redistribution of winnings shall affect the distribution of the pari-mutuel pools at tracks where pari-mutuel wagering is conducted, when such distribution of pools is made upon the official placing at the conclusion of the heat or dash.

§ 9. **Pre-Race Blood Test.**—Where there is a pre-race blood test which shows that there is an element present in the blood indicative of a stimulant, depressant or any unapproved medicant, the horse shall immediately be scratched from the race and an investigation conducted by the officials to determine if there was a violation of Section 4 of this rule.

§ 10. The penalty for violation of any sections of this rule, unless otherwise provided, shall be a fine of not to exceed $5,000, suspension for a fixed or indeterminate time, or both, or expulsion.

§ 11. All Veterinarians practicing on the grounds of an extended pari-mutuel meeting shall keep a log of their activities including:

(a) Name of horse.

(b) Nature of ailment.

(c) Type of treatment.

(d) Date and hour of treatment.

It shall be the responsibility of the Veterinarian to report to the Presiding Judge any internal medication given by him by injection or orally to any horse after he has been declared to start in any race.

§ 12. Any veterinarian practicing veterinary medicine on a race track where a race meeting is in progress or any other person using a needle or syringe shall use only one-time disposable type needles or syringe and a disposable needle shall not be re-used.

RULE 22.
Fines, Suspensions, and Expulsion

Section 1. **Fines—Suspension Until Paid.**
—All persons who shall have been fined under these rules shall be suspended until said fine shall have been paid in full.

Fines which have been unpaid for a period

of five years may be dropped from the records of the Treasurer of the Association, however, such action will not affect the suspension.

§ 2. **Recording and Posting Penalties.**— Written or printed notice thereof shall be delivered to the person penalized, notice shall be posted immediately at the office of the member, and notice shall be forwarded immediately to the Executive Vice-President by the Presiding Judge or Clerk of the Course. The Executive Vice-President shall transmit notice of suspension to the other members; and thereupon the offender thus punished shall suffer the same penalty and disqualification with each and every member.

§ 3. **Effect of Minor Penalty on Future Engagements.**—Where the penalty is for a driving violation and does not exceed in time a period of 5 days, the driver may complete the engagement of all horses declared in before the penalty becomes effective. Such driver may drive in Stake, Futurity, Early Closing and Feature races, during a suspension of 5 days or less but the suspension will be extended one day for each date he drives in such a race.

§ 4. **Disposition of Fines.**—All fines which are collected shall be reported and paid upon the day collected to the Executive Vice-President.

§ 5. **Effect of Suspension Penalty.**— Whenever the penalty of suspension is prescribed in these rules it shall be construed to mean an unconditional exclusion and disqualification from the time of receipt of written notice of suspension from the Member or the President, or Executive Vice-President, from any participation, either directly or indirectly, in the privileges and uses of the course and grounds of a member during the progress of a race meeting, unless otherwise specifically limited when such suspension is imposed, such as a suspension from driving. A suspension or expulsion or denial of membership of either a husband or wife may apply in each instance to both the husband and wife. The suspension becomes effective when notice is given unless otherwise specified. A person may be suspended, expelled or denied membership under this rule if it is determined that such person's spouse would be denied membership upon application, and this Association reserves the right to require such person's spouse to complete and submit an application in order to make such determination.

§ 6. **Effect of Penalty on Horse.**—No horse shall have the right to compete while owned or controlled wholly or in part by a suspended, expelled, disqualified or excluded person. An entry made by or for a person or of a horse suspended, expelled or disqualified, shall be held liable for the entrance fee thus contracted without the right to compete unless the penalty is removed. A suspended, disqualified or excluded person who shall drive, or a suspended or disqualified horse which shall perform in a race shall be fined not less than $50, nor more than $100, for each offense.

§ 7. **Fraudulent Transfer.**—The fraudulent transfer of a horse by any person or persons under suspension in order to circumvent said suspension, shall constitute a violation.

§ 8. **Indefinite Suspension.**—If no limit is fixed in an order of suspension and none is defined in the rule applicable to the case, the penalty shall be considered as limited to the season in which the order was issued.

§ 9. **Suspended Person.**—Any member wilfully allowing a suspended, disqualified or excluded person to drive in a race, or a suspended or disqualified horse to start in a race after notice from the President or Executive Vice-President, shall be together with its officers, subject to a fine not exceeding $100 for each offense, or suspension or expulsion.

§ 10. **Expelled Person.**—Any member wilfully allowing the use of its track or grounds by an expelled or unconditionally suspended man or horse, after notice from the President or Executive Vice-President, shall be, together with its officers, subject to a fine not exceeding $500 for each offense, or suspension or expulsion.

§ 11. Whenever a person is excluded from a pari-mutuel track by the track member, this Association shall be notified.

§ 12. An expelled, suspended, disqualified or excluded person cannot act as an officer of a track member. A track member shall not, after receiving notice of such penalty, employ or retain in its employ an expelled, suspended, disqualified or excluded person at or on the track during the progress of a race meeting. Any member found violating this rule shall be fined not to exceed $500.

§ 13. **Dishonored Check, Etc.**—Any person being a member of this Association who pays an entry, a fine or other claim to this Association or an entry or fine to another member of this Association by a draft, check, order or other paper, which upon presentation is protested, payment refused or otherwise dishonored, shall be by order of the Executive Vice-President, subject to a fine not exceeding the amount of said draft, check or order, and the winnings of the horse or horses declared illegal and said persons and horses suspended until the dishonored amount and fine are paid and the illegal winnings returned.

§ 14. **Penalty of Racing Commissions.**— All penalties imposed by the Racing Commissions of the various states shall be recognized and enforced by this Association upon notice from the Commission to the Executive Vice-President, except as provided in Section 15 of this Rule 22.

§ 15. **Reciprocity of Penalties.**—All persons and horses under suspension or expulsion by any State Racing Commission or by a reputable Trotting Association of a foreign country shall upon notice from such commission or association to the Executive Vice-President, be suspended or expelled by this Association. Provided, however, that, for good cause shown, the Board of Appeals may, upon consideration of the record of the proceedings had before such State Commission or foreign Association modify or so mould the penalty imposed to define the applicability thereof beyond the jurisdiction of the State Commission or foreign Association. Provided further that, whether or not a penalty has been imposed by a State Racing Commission, the District Board may make original inquiry and take original jurisdiction in any case as provided in Sections 2 and 15 of Article IV of the By-Laws.

§ 16. **Modification of Penalty.**—Any suspension imposed by Judges can be removed or modified by the Executive Vice-President upon the recommendation of the Judges and Member on whose grounds the penalty was imposed.

§ 17. An application for removal of expulsion imposed for starting a horse out of its class or under change of name, or both, shall not be docketed for a hearing by the District Board until all the unlawful winnings are returned for redistribution and a fine of $250 is paid.

RULE 23.
Protests and Appeals

Section 1. **Protests.**—Protests may be made only by an owner, manager, trainer or driver of one of the contending horses, at any time before the winnings are paid over,

and shall be reduced to writing, and sworn to, and shall contain at least one specific charge, which, if true, would prevent the horse from winning or competing in the race.

§ 2. The Judges shall in every case of protest demand that the driver, and the owner or owners, if present, shall immediately testify under oath; and in case of their refusal to do so, the horse shall not be allowed to start or continue in the race, but shall be ruled out, with a forfeit of entrance money.

§ 3. Unless the Judges find satisfactory evidence to warrant excluding the horse, they shall allow him to start or continue in the race under protest, and the premium, if any is won by that horse, shall be forthwith transmitted to the Executive Vice-President to allow the parties interested an opportunity to sustain the allegations of the protest, or to furnish information which will warrant an investigation of the matter by the District Board of Review. Where no action is taken to sustain the protest within thirty days, payment may be made as if such protest had not been filed.

§ 4. Any person found guilty of protesting a horse falsely and without cause, or merely with intent to embarrass a race, shall be punished by a fine not to exceed $100 or by suspension or expulsion.

§ 5. When a protest has been duly made or any information lodged with the Judges alleging an improper entry or any act prohibited or punishable under these rules, the same shall not be withdrawn or surrendered before the expiration of thirty days, without the approbation of the Executive Vice-President. If any member shall permit such a withdrawal of protest or information with a corrupt motive to favor any party, the executive officers so permitting it may be expelled by the District Board of Review.

§ 6. **Appeals.**—All decisions and ruling of the Judges of any race, and of the officers of Member Tracks may be appealed to the District Board of Review within ten (10) days after the notice of such decision or ruling. The appeal may be taken upon any question in the conduct of a race, interpretation of the rules, decisions relative to the outcome of a race, application of penalties, or other action affecting owners, drivers, or horses, but it must be based on a specific charge which, if true, would warrant modification or reversal of the decision. In order to take an appeal under Rule 18, a driver must have first made a complaint, claim, or objection as required in Rule 18. The District Board of Review may vacate, modify, or increase any penalty imposed by the Judges and appealed to the Board. In the event an appellant fails to appear at the hearing of his appeal without good cause the District Board may impose a fine not to exceed $100.00 or a suspension not to exceed thirty days to be effective at the first meeting at which he has horses entered for racing.

§ 7. Nothing herein contained shall affect the distribution of the pari-mutuel pools at tracks where pari-mutuel wagering is conducted, when such distribution is made upon the official placing at the conclusion of the heat or dash.

§ 8. All appeals shall be in writing and sworn to before a Notary or one of the Judges of the Meeting. At the time the appeal is filed, a deposit of $100, or an agreement to forfeit the sum of $100 in the event the Board determines the appeal is not justified, must accompany the appeal. In the event the District Board of Review feels that the appeal was justified, it will refund the money to the appellant. This procedure does not apply to protests.

§ 9. In case of appeal or protest to The United States Trotting Association, the purse money affected by the appeal or protest must be deposited with the Executive Vice-President pending the decision of the District Board of Review. Any purse or portion thereof withheld for any reason shall be forthwith sent to the Executive Vice-President together with a full statement showing the reason for such withholding.

§ 10. Any track member that fails to send the Executive Vice-President, within one week of the date on which it was filed, any protest or appeal filed with the member or its Judges, may be fined or suspended.

§ 11. The license of any Presiding Judge may be revoked for refusal to accept a protest or appeal, or for refusing to act as witness for a person seeking to swear to a protest or appeal.

§ 12. In every case where a penalty is imposed, and such penalty has been appealed to any appropriate appellate body, such appeal, if requested, shall stay such suspension until a hearing has been held and the merits of the appeal ruled upon. The stay will begin when the person appealing files in writing with the notice of appeal a request for a stay with the Presiding Judge and the State Commission, such notice to be filed within 48 hours after the posting of the decision or penalty from which the appeal is

taken. Notice shall be sworn to and shall state the grounds of the appeal. Security of $100.00 or an amount equal to the monetary fine, if any, shall be posted with the filing of the notice of appeal and the request for stay. Upon final disposition of the appeal the security posted will be first applied to the monetary penalty imposed, if any, and the balance returned to the person appealing. Failure of the appellant to pursue the appeal shall result in a forfeiture of the security posted.

RULE 24.
Time and Records

Section 1. **Timing Races.**—In every race, the time of each heat shall be accurately taken by three Timers or an approved electric timing device, in which case there shall be one Timer, and placed in the record in minutes, seconds and fifths of seconds, and upon the decision of each heat, the time thereof shall be publicly announced or posted. No unofficial timing shall be announced or admitted to the record, and when the Timers fail to act no time shall be announced or recorded for that heat.

§ 2. **Error in Reported Time.**—In any case of alleged error in the record, announcement or publication of the time made by a horse, the time so questioned shall not be changed to favor said horse or owner, except upon the sworn statement of the Judges and Timers who officiated in the race, and then only by order of the District Board of Review, or the Executive Vice-President.

§ 3. **Track Measurement Certificate.**—In order that the performances thereon may be recognized and/or published as official every track member not having done so heretofore and since January 1st, 1939, shall forthwith cause to be filed with the Executive Vice-President the certificate of a duly licensed civil engineer or land surveyor that he has subsequently to January 1st, 1939, measured the said track from wire to wire three feet out from the pole or inside hub rail thereof and certifying in linear feet the result of such measurement. Each track shall be measured and recertified in the event of any changes or relocation of the hub rail.

§ 4. **Time for Lapped on Break.**—The leading horse shall be timed and his time only shall be announced. No horse shall obtain a win race record by reason of the disqualification of another horse unless a horse is declared a winner by reason of the disqualification of a breaking horse on which he was lapped.

§ 5. **Time for Dead Heat.**—In case of a dead heat, the time shall constitute a record for the horses making the dead heat and both shall be considered winners.

§ 6. **Timing Procedure.**—The time shall be taken from the first horse leaving the point from which the distance of the race is measured until the winner reaches the wire.

§ 7. **Misrepresentation of Time—Penalty.** —(a) A fine not to exceed $500 shall be imposed upon any member of this Association on whose grounds there shall be allowed any misrepresentation of time, and time shall be deemed to have been misrepresented in any race, wherein a record of the same is not kept in writing. A fine imposed under this rule shall include the officers of the member.

(b) Any person who shall be guilty of fraudulent misrepresentation of time or the alteration of the record thereof in any public race shall be fined, suspended or expelled, and the time declared not a record.

§ 8. **Time Performances.**—Time performances are permitted subject to the following:

(a) Urine and saliva tests are required for all horses starting for a time performance. The provisions of Rule 21, with the exception of Section 4, relative to stimulants and drugs shall apply to time trial performances, and a violation of any section of that rule shall result in a disallowance of the time trial performance. In addition, further penalties may be imposed under the provisions of Rule 21, Section 10.

(b) An approved electric timer is required for all time performances. In the event of a failure of a timer during the progress of a time performance, no time trial performance record will be obtained.

(c) Time trial performances may be permitted by the Executive Vice-President immediately prior to or following a regularly scheduled meeting provided a full complement of licensed officials are in the Judges' Stand and provided a separate application is filed with the Executive Vice-President, thirty days in advance, listing the officials and the number of days requested.

(d) Time trial performances are limited for two-year-olds who go to equal or to beat 2:10 and three-year-olds and over who go to equal or beat 2:05.

(e) In any race or performance against time excessive use of the whip shall be considered a violation.

(f) Any consignor, agent or sales organization or other person may be fined or suspended for selling or advertising a horse with a time trial record without designating it as a time trial.

(g) Time trial performance records shall not be included in the performance lines in a race program.

(h) Time trial performances shall be designated by preceding the time with two capital Ts.

(i) When a horse performs against time it shall be proper to allow another horse or horses to accompany him in the performance but not to precede or to be harnessed with or in any way attached to him. Provided, however, that a mechanical device acceptable to the President or Executive Vice-President of this Association may be used. Provided, further, that a horse may not be used as a prompter for more than two time trial performances each time he is hitched, and may not be hitched more than three times in a single day, with at least forty minutes between each such use. It shall be the responsibility of the Presiding Judge to see that prompters are not abused.

(j) A break during a Time Trial is a losing effort and a losing performance shall not constitute a record.

RULE 25.
International Registration

Section 1. The Executive Vice-President may appoint export agents at various ports of shipping who shall upon examination and identification of the horse to be exported, indorse the application for export certificate. Every application for an export certificate must be accompanied by a certificate of registration in the current ownership and a fee in the sum of $35.00. The export certificate shall be issued and signed by the Executive Vice-President or Registrar of the Association and the corporate seal affixed thereto. No such certificate will be issued for the export of any horse under expulsion nor for any horse currently under suspension by this Association. The fee for a duplicate certificate shall be $10.00.

Except for foals under one year of age, no export certificate will be granted to any horse that is not tattooed.

§ 2. Any party or parties giving false information to procure an export certificate shall be deemed guilty of fraud and upon conviction thereof shall be fined or expelled and the horse in question may be expelled.

§ 3. If any horse registered with this Association is exported from the United States or Canada to any other country without making application for an export certificate, then the said horse will be stricken from the records of The United States Trotting Association.

§ 4. **Imported Horses.**—Horses imported into the United States from countries other than Canada, Australia and New Zealand may be registered with this Association, Non-Standard, providing the following requirements are complied with by the person or persons seeking such registration.

(a) Horse must be registered in the country of birth and certificate of such registration must accompany application.

(b) Complete history of breeding including sire, and 1st, 2nd and 3rd dams and chain of ownership must accompany application if not fully set forth on registration of origin.

(c) Clearance or export certificate from country of origin including markings, positive identification of horse, and veterinarian certificate, must accompany application.

(d) If horse is leased, a valid executed lease signed by all parties must accompany application. If lease is signed by agents, written authorization from their principals must be submitted.

(e) Person or persons seeking such registration must be members of this Association and a fee of $25.00 in the case of horses which have not raced previously, and $50.00 in the case of horses which have previously raced, must accompany the application.

(f) A standard U.S.T.A. application for registration must be filed, signed by the person to whose ownership the horse was cleared from the foreign registry.

RULE 26.
Registration of Horses

Section 1. In order to register a horse the owner thereof must be a member of this Association.

Any person authorized to sign a mating certificate, an application for registration or any of the required breeding or registration reports must be a member of this Association.

§ 2. **Standard Bred.**—Horses may be registered as Standard bred with any of the following qualifications:

(a) The progeny of a registered Standard horse and a registered Standard mare.

(b) A stallion sired by a registered Standard horse, provided his dam and granddam were sired by registered Standard horses and he himself has a Standard record and is the sire of three performers with Standard records from different mares.

(c) A mare whose sire is a registered Standard horse, and whose dam and granddam were sired by a registered Standard horse, provided she herself has a Standard record.

(d) A mare sired by a registered Standard horse, provided she is the dam of two performers with Standard records.

(e) A mare or horse sired by a registered Standard horse, provided its first, second and third dams are each sired by a registered Standard horse.

(f) No horse over four years of age is eligible for registration. For foals of 1976, no horse over three years of age is eligible for registration. For foals of 1977 and thereafter, no horse two years of age or older is eligible for registration.

(g) Horses registered standard with the Canadian Standardbred Horse Society or New Zealand Trotting Conference or the Australian Stud Book or Stud Books of selected European countries may be re-registered standard with this Association provided their records and/or qualifications meet the standards of this Association and are approved by the President, Executive Vice-President, or Registration Committee.

(h) The Standing Committee on Registration may register as Standard any horse which does not qualify under the above sections, if in their opinion he or she should be registered Standard.

§ 3. **Non-Standard Bred.**—Any horse may be registered as Non-Standard upon filing application showing satisfactory identification of the horse for racing purposes. This identification may be accomplished by furnishing the name, age, sex, sire, dam, color and markings and history of the previous owners. A mating certificate must accompany this application, showing the sire to be some type of a registered horse. Any owner standing a non-standard stallion for service must include the fact that it is non-standard in all advertisements of such service.

For foals of 1973 and thereafter, prior approval must be obtained from the standing committee on registration before breeding any horse not meeting the requirements for

Standard registration in Rule 26, Section 2 above except for foals of mares registered non-standard prior to November 1972.

§ 4. The breeder of a horse, for the purposes of registration, is the owner or lessee of the dam at the time of breeding, and when held under lease, bred on shares or in partnership, only such lease or partnership will be recognized for such purposes which is filed in the offices of The United States Trotting Association. The application for registration must be signed by the registered owner of the dam of the foal at the time of foaling, or by his agent, duly authorized in writing and filed with this Association. The signature of the owner of a foal or his authorized agent and the person responsible for recording of markings is required on the registration application. It shall be the responsibility of the person registering a foal to note the place of foaling on the application for registration, and that informaiton shall be recorded on the registration certificate and any eligibility certificate issued for the foal.

§ 5. **Mating Certificates.**—Mating certificates shall be signed by the registered owner or if the horse is under lease a letter must be filed with this Association signed by the owner of the horse stating to whom and for what period of time the horse is under lease. In addition to the letter signed by the registered owner a letter signed by the lessee stating that he will accept responsibility for the accuracy of the mating certificate during the period of time covered by the lease must be filed. In such event the lessee must sign the mating certificate. A mating certificate must be on file in the office of the Association before a certificate of registration will be issued.

§ 6. **Artificial Insemination.**—A foal conceived by semen which is frozen, desiccated, transported off the premises where it is produced or not implanted on the same day collected is not eligible for registration.

§ 7. **Breeding   Requirements.**—Before using a stallion at stud, the owner must register the stallion for breeding purposes with this Association, and the person responsible for maintaining the breeding records for the stallion may be required to establish his qualifications for same by successfully completing a written or oral examination.

It shall be the responsibility of stallion owners to have each stallion properly blood-typed and to furnish this Association with a blood-typing report from a recognized laboratory.

Stallion owners shall keep a stallion record showing the mare's name, sire and dam, color, markings, owner, breeding dates, and color, sex and foaling date of any foals born on the stallion owner's premises. The records shall be available for inspection by officers or authorized representatives of The United States Trotting Association, and shall be kept at least ten years or filed with The United States Trotting Association.

All persons standing a stallion at either public or private service shall file with this Association a list of all mares bred to each stallion, together with the dates of service. This list must be filed by September 1st of the year of breeding. In addition to the service report, a list of standardbred foals dropped on the farm with foaling dates and markings must be filed by August 1st. Failure to comply with this provision may subject the owner or lessee of the stallion to a fine of not less than $10.00 nor more than $50.00. Application for registration may be refused from any person not complying with this rule.

§ 8. **Names.**—

(a) Names for proposed registration shall be limited to four words **and a total of 18 spaces.**

(b) Horses may not be registered under a name of an animal previously registered and active unless fifteen years have elapsed since any such activity, except where the applicant is able to establish to the satisfaction of the Registrar that one or the other of the following circumstances has occurred:

(1) That the horse has died or had its name changed prior to becoming two years of age.

(2) that the horse has died or had its name changed before racing or being used for breeding purposes.

(c) Names of outstanding horses may not be used again, nor may they be used as a prefix or suffix unless the name is a part of the name of the sire or dam. A prefix or a suffix such as Junior, etc., is not acceptable.

(d) Use of a farm name in registration of horses is reserved for the farm that has registered that name.

(e) Names of living persons will not be used unless the written permission to use their name is filed with the application for registration.

(f) No horse shall be registered under names if spelling or pronunciation is similar to names already in use.

(g) Names of famous or notorious persons, trade names, or names claimed for advertising purposes, except names, or part of a name, of a registered breeding farm, will not be used.

(h) The United States Trotting Association reserves the right to refuse any name indicating a family or strain which may be misleading, or any name which may be misleading as to the origin or relationship or sex of an animal, or any name which might be considered offensive, vulgar or suggestive.

(i) Horses may be named by January 1st, subsequent to their foaling, without penalty.

(j) **The foregoing provisions of this Section notwithstanding, foals may be registered unnamed provided they are named prior to their use for either racing or breeding purposes.**

§ 9. **Photograph Requirements.**—At the discretion of the Registrar, photographs may be required to obtain a registration of a foal. At least four photographs are required, one from each side, one from the front, and one from the rear. All photographs must show leg markings.

§ 10. **Fees for Registration.**—(a) For foals of years prior to 1973 for which a complete application for registration is received, the registration fee shall be: for yearlings—$25.00; for two-year-olds—$50.00; for three and four-year-olds—$100.00.

(b) For foals of 1973, 1974, 1975 and 1976 for which a complete application for registration is received, the registration fee shall be: for applications received prior to October 1, of the year of foaling—$15.00; for applications received after October 1 of the year of foaling and prior to the date on which foal becomes a yearling—$20.00; for yearlings—$30.00; for two-year-olds—$55.00; for three and four-year-olds—$105.00.

(c) For foals of 1977 and thereafter, for which a complete application for registration is received, the registration fee shall be: for applications received prior to October 1st of the year of foaling, $15.00; for applications received after October 1st of the year of foaling and prior to the date on which the foal becomes a yearling, $20.00; for yearlings, $100.00 coupled with a satisfactory identification to the Registrar.

(d) Horses registered with the Canadian Standardbred Horse Society Records may be registered or re-registered with The United States Trotting Association upon presentation of the Canadian certificate and a $5.00 fee.

§ 11. **Fees for Transfer.**—**For each change in ownership if application is received within 90 days after date of sale, $5.00; 90 days to** six months, $10.00; six months to one year, $25.00; over one year, $100.00.

§ 12. **Fee for Duplicate Registratoin Certificate.**—A duplicate registration certificate shall be issued for **$10.00** upon receipt of the sworn affidavit of the current registered owner or owners that the original is lost, stolen or destroyed.

§ 13. **Fees for Tattooing.**—The fee for tatooing horses foaled prior to 1973 will be $5.00.

§ 14. **Fees for Re-registration to Change the Name.**—Fee for re-registration of a yearling prior to January 1st when it shall become two years old, which re-registration is solely for the purpose of a change of name, shall be $5.00. After a horse becomes a two-year-old the fee for change of name shall be $15.00. No change of name will be permitted once a horse has raced nor will any change of name be permitted for stallions or mares that have been used for breeding purposes.

§ 15. **Notice of Sale.**—Any party selling a registered horse shall immediately notify The United States Trotting Association, giving the full name and address of the new owner and the date of sale. No horse shall be transferred unless a registration certificate, together with a transfer signed by the registered owner, is filed with this Association.

§ 16. **Skipping Transfers.**—Any person who is a party whether acting as agent or otherwise, to skipping or omitting transfers in the chain of ownership of any horse, may be subjected to the penalties and procedures set forth in Section 17 hereof.

§ 17. **Penalty for Executing False Application for Registration or Transfer.**—The President, Executive Vice-President, Registration Committee or District Board of Review may summon persons who have executed applications for registration or transfer or alterations of registration certificates that have become subject to question, as well as any other person who may have knowledge thereof. Failure to respond to such summons may be punished by a fine, suspension or expulsion. If the investigation reveals that an application for registration or transfer contains false or misleading information, the person or persons responsible may be fined, suspended or expelled, and in addition may be barred from further registration or transfer of horses in the Association and such animal may be barred from registration. The decision of the President, Executive   Vice-President,   Registration

Committee or District Board of Review, as the case may be, shall be reduced to writing and shall be final unless the person or persons aggrieved thereby shall, within ten (10) days appeal in writing to the Board of Appeals as provided in Article IX of the By-Laws.

§ 18. **Fee for Careless Reporting of Markings.**—Any person filing an application for registration with incorrect information shall **be required to pay a fee in the amount of $10.00 for the correction of** each such incorrect application.

§ 19. **Cancellation of Incorrect Registration.**—If, upon any proceeding under the provisions of Section 16 of this Rule 26, it shall be determined that any outstanding registration is incorrect, the Executive Vice-President shall order immediate cancellation of such outstanding incorrect registration and shall forthwith forward notice of such cancellation to the owner of the horse which is incorrectly registered.

§ 20. Failure by a member to submit requested information or additional aids to identification relative to the breeding, registration and/or transfer of a horse to this Association may subject the member to suspension by the Executive Vice-President.

§ 21. When a registered horse dies or is disposed of, without the registration certificate accompanying the horse, the owner of the horse must notify this Association in writing and forward the registration certificate of the horse to this Association for proper cancellation.

§ 22. **Report On Unregistrable Foal.**—If a mare is bred in a given year and fails to produce a registrable foal, the owner of such mare shall, prior to December 31st of the succeeding year report to this Association on a form provided for that purpose the fact that the mare was bred and whether the mare was barren, foaled a dead foal, foaled a live foal which subsequently died, aborted or otherwise.

§ 23. The registration of foals produced by the ovum transplant method is prohibited.

§ 24. It shall be the responsibility of an individual seeking to register a foal which is a twin to so designate that fact on the application for registration and that information shall be noted on the foal's registration certificate by the Registrar. It shall be the responsibility of the owner of such foal to furnish such information to a prospective purchaser.

§ 25. **Parentage Verification Blood Test.**—Where a horse becomes the subject of a parentage verification blood test, the owner of the horse shall be required to bear the expense of conducting said test.

§ 26. The Board of Directors may designate a proper person as Registrar who may affix his signature on Registration Certificates and documents relating to import and export of horses.

INDEX TO RULES

Index